Fodor's 95
New England

D0823934

Fodor's Travel Publications, Inc.
New York • Toronto • London • Sydney • Auckland

Copyright © 1994
by Fodor's Travel Publications, Inc.

Fodor's New England

Editor: Andrew Collins
Contributors: Jonathon Alsop, Craig Altschul, Steven K. Amsterdam, Susan M. Bain, Marty Basch, Kathleen M. Brandes, Suki Casanave, Karen Cure, Christine Donohue, Mary H. Frakes, Echo Garrett, Candice Gianetti, Kimberly Grant, Tara Hamilton, David Laskin, Dawn Lawson, Betty Lowry, Bevin McLaughlin, Anne Merewood, William G. Scheller, Mary Ellen Schultz, Michelle Seaton, Peggi F. Simmons, Alison Stern, Nancy van Itallie, Malcolm Wilson
Creative Director: Fabrizio La Rocca
Cartographer: David Lindroth
Illustrator: Karl Tanner
Cover Photograph: David W. Hamilton/Image Bank

Design: Vignelli Associates

Special Sales

Contents

Maps

Foreword

While every care has been taken to ensure the accuracy of the information in this guide, the passage of time will always bring change, and consequently the publisher cannot accept responsibility for errors that may occur.

All prices and opening times quoted here are based on information supplied to us at press time. Hours and admission fees may change, however, and the prudent traveler will avoid inconvenience by calling ahead.

Fodor's wants to hear about your travel experiences, both pleasant and unpleasant. When a hotel or restaurant fails to live up to its billing, let us know and we will investigate the complaint and revise our entries where the facts warrant it. Send your letters to the editors of Fodor's Travel Publications, 201 E. 50th Street, New York, NY 10022.

Highlights '95 and Fodor's Choice

Highlights '95

Connecticut Connecticut has seen a surge in visitation between 1993 and 1994, thanks in part to its having increased its tourism budget nearly twofold and having run a major television campaign to promote its new toll-free **reservations and information service,** which can be reached by calling 800/CT–BOUND. The service will send you the state's huge and detailed handbook listing sights and accommodations, book you a room anywhere in the state, and tell you about upcoming events.

The esteemed local chain of gourmet farmers' markets, **Hay Day,** opened a restaurant in Westport this year, joining last year's establishment in Ridgefield. It's been a boom year for new dining ventures; among the most popular new eateries in the state are, in Westport, **Cafe Christina,** the **Meeting Street Grill,** and **Restaurant Zanghi,** which is in the new Inn at National Hall; in Torrington, the **Harvest Roasterie,** which was opened by the former chef of Litchfield's popular West Street Grill; in Woodbury, the **Good News Cafe,** which is presided over by world-renowned chef Carole Peck; in Branford the **Riviera Cafe;** and in New Haven the **Union League Cafe,** which now occupies the place of Robert Henry's.

Connecticut has recently become home to a couple of the nation's most luxurious—and expensive—small inns. Washington's **Mayflower Inn** commands as much as $475 a night and comprises 28 acres of perfectly landscaped grounds, a fitness center fit for a professional football team, and rooms containing original 18th-century paintings and antiques. Westport's **Inn at National Hall** occupies an ancient redbrick furniture store on the banks of the Saugatuck River and is jammed with the most exotic collection of objets d'art you can imagine. Room rates here also venture into the $400 range.

In 1993, the enormous **Foxwoods Casino** in Ledyard opened a couple of major hotels, added more shops, restaurants, and a health spa, and expanded its gaming space. In an effort to broaden Foxwoods's appeal to gamblers and nongamblers alike, theaters and dance halls have also been added, and golf courses are in the works. Also, a 3,000-seat bingo hall opened in June 1994.

Rhode Island In December 1993, a new $290 million **convention center** opened in Providence, with 365,000 square feet of meeting space and a 2,400-car parking garage. A 360-room **Westin Hotel,** adjacent to the center, will open in September 1994.

Across the street from the Convention Center, **WaterPlace** is the latest renovation of a U.S. city's industrial waterfront (similar restorations have been done in Boston, New York City, Baltimore, and Chattanooga). Completed in May 1994, WaterPlace is a pool of water built at the confluence of the Providence and Woonasquatucket rivers and surrounded by shops, restaurants, pedestrian bridges, and parks. From WaterPlace you can take an excursion aboard the ***Blackstone Valley Explorer,*** a 50-passenger vessel that plies another area that's been cleaned up in recent years, the Blackstone River.

The **Museum of Newport,** which opened in December 1993, traces the city's three centuries of prosperity—from its early days of trading through the Gilded Age to the present day. Housed in the original market building of the historic Brick Market, the museum uses clever exhibits and audiovisual programs to tell its story.

Massachusetts Access to Boston has improved with the opening of a new **central bus terminal** atop South Station, long the train terminus for Amtrak and the city's southern and western rail commuter lines. With its classical curved facade, South Station is the focus of Dewey Square, joining Summer Street with Atlantic Avenue. The station's first-phase renovation created a wonderfully bright, airy atrium with an indoor shopping and food gallery.

Less obvious to everyday travelers, but no less dramatic, will be the opening, to commerical traffic only, of Boston's **third harbor tunnel,** a 1.6-mile tube that will carry trucks and buses from South Boston to Logan Airport. Part of a massive $5 billion project that includes enlarging the Central Artery, the city's main north–south highway, the tunnel should noticeably lighten the traffic crunch in the Sumner and Callahan tunnels, which is particularly onerous at the morning and evening rush hours.

Once in town, don't miss a visit to the **Children's Museum,** which plans a June unveiling of its new **Waterfront Expansion Project.** Together with the neighboring Computer Museum, the Children's Museum has created a joint entry through "the wave," a 5,900-square-foot, dynamic contemporary structure that promises visitors an unusual experience. A pedestrian bridge inside the wave provides harbor and skyline views and leads to a new 6,900-square-foot "harbor education center" floating on a barge in the Fort Point Channel. An observation room, a fully equipped aquatic laboratory, and an interactive water exhibition are among the highly unusual features that emphasize the delicate balance between people and their environment and will amuse and inform children of all ages.

This year, America's oldest major lending library, the **Boston Public Library,** celebrates the centennial of its McKim Building, on Copley Square. A major face-lift has been performed on this monument to the city's intellectual vigor.

In fall 1995, the new **Shawmut Center** will replace the 67-year-old Boston Garden as the home of basketball's Celtics and hockey's Bruins—and become the venue for ice shows, concerts, and other sports and entertainment events. The center is designed to rise 10 stories above a rebuilt North Station train and "T" terminal.

Ferry service between Cape Cod and Martha's Vineyard has been greatly improved. The Steamship Authority received a $2 million grant in January 1994 to renovate the terminals in Hyannis and Vineyard Haven, and the sleek new ferryboat *Martha's Vineyard* is now in service, with improved seating, baggage racks, accessibility for people with disabilities, and cellular phones.

In Salem, a new Salem Maritime National Historic Site visitor center was completed in July 1994. The center has numerous exhibits and a three-screen movie depicting the area's colorful history. Within the site, the Derby and Central wharves have been restored, and plans are under way at Derby Wharf to build an East India merchant ship similar to those used in the late 18th century.

Vermont The **Frog Hollow State Craft Center,** based in Middlebury and with a branch at the Burlington Marketplace, is a highly regarded showcase for traditional and contemporary works by more than 250 Vermont craftspeople. The center received a 1993 grant from the National Endowment for the Arts to help fund an oral-history project documenting Vermont's folk-art past.

The **Catamount Trail,** a 280-mile cross-country ski trail that runs the length of the state, was made skiable from end to end in winter 1994. Volunteers dedicated to finishing the trail—which begins in Readsboro, on the Massachusetts border, and winds through the heart of the Green Mountains to North Troy, on the Canadian border—had begun work on the project in 1985. The trail is accessible to skiers of all abilities.

A $10 million expansion of the gondola at Killington Ski Resort is slated for the coming year, replacing the old gondola and vastly improving both speed and capacity. A new base facility and more ski trails will also be added.

New Hampshire Southern New Hampshire and northern Massachusetts became more accessible in January 1994, when Manchester Airport's new $65 million terminal opened, with new roads, taxi access, parking lots, and other improvements designed to enhance service to the more than 100 passenger flights that are handled here daily.

Sections of the 250-mile-long **New Hampshire Heritage Trail** have recently been opened, including a 75-mile stretch along the Merrimack River from the Massachusetts border through Nashua and Manchester to Concord, as well as a section in Franconia Notch. The trail may be used for walking, jogging, biking, and cross-country skiing and connects areas of historic and scenic interest. Eventually it will extend to Canada.

In Wolfeboro, a new museum on World War II opened in July. Features include an exhibit on vehicles, including jeeps and tanks, and memorabilia showing what life was like stateside from 1939 to 1945. A restaurant and theater will be added during the next few years.

Maine **Commercial train service** will again become a reality in Maine: In January 1995, Amtrak will begin service from Boston to Wells, Biddeford-Saco, Old Orchard Beach (in season), and Portland.

In December 1993, a ski train—the first to operate in Maine in over 30 years—began running from Portland to the Sunday River Ski Resort, with a stop in Auburn. The ride, aboard restored antique rail cars, takes a little over two hours.

Fodor's Choice

No two people will agree on what makes a perfect vacation, but it's fun and helpful to know what others think. We hope you'll have a chance to experience some of Fodor's Choices yourself while visiting New England. For detailed information about each entry, refer to the appropriate chapters in this guidebook.

Sights

Long Island Sound from the tip of Water Street in Stonington Village, CT

The mansions of Bellevue Avenue, Newport, RI

Bright purple cranberries floating on the flooded bogs just before the fall harvest on Cape Cod and Nantucket

The candy-color Victorian cottages of the Oak Bluffs Camp Ground on Martha's Vineyard

The nearly frozen-in-time town of Nantucket, whose cobblestone streets and antique houses evoke whaling days

The view from Appalachian Gap on Route 17, VT

Early October on the Kancamagus Highway between Lincoln and Conway, NH

Yacht-filled Camden Harbor, ME, from the summit of Mt. Battie

Taste Treats

Crème brûlée at the West Street Grill, Litchfield, CT

A breakfast of smoked bluefish at the 1661 Inn, Block Island, RI

Clam chowder at The Flume, Mashpee, MA

Portuguese kale soup at Land Ho!, Orleans, MA

Maple syrup right from the sugarhouse at Morse Farm, Montpelier, VT

A cone of Annabelle's ice cream in Portsmouth, NH

Lobster at a lobster pound on the Maine coast

Special Moments

Sunset at Napatree Point, Watch Hill, Westerly, RI

Biking through the dunes of Provincetown at sunset

Glimpsing Nantucket town from the approaching ferry

Whale-watching off Provincetown, MA, or Portsmouth, NH

Catching a rare glimpse of moose crossing a remote road in VT's Northeastern Kingdom

Skiing the first run of the day following a snowstorm at Sugarloaf/USA, ME

Attractions for Kids

Mystic Aquarium, Mystic, CT

The Children's Museum and the Computer Museum, Boston, MA

Old Sturbridge Village, Sturbridge, MA

Green Mountain Flyer excursion train, Bellows Falls, VT

Guiding your own "spaceship" during the "Gateway to Infinity" show at the Christa McAuliffe Planetarium in Concord, NH

Children's Museum of Maine, Portland, ME

Shopping

Antiques stores in Woodbury and New Preston, CT

The Peaceable Kingdom, Providence, RI

Crafts and antiques shops along Route 6A, Cape Cod, MA

Odyssey Bookstore, South Hadley, MA

Vermont Country Store, Weston, VT

League of New Hampshire Craftsmen shops in Exeter, Concord, Hanover, Lincoln, Manchester, Meredith, North Conway, Sandwich, and Wolfeboro, NH

L. L. Bean and the nearby outlet stores, Freeport, ME

Ski Resorts

Killington, VT, for learning to ski

Jay Peak, VT, for the international ambience

Mad River Glen, VT, for challenging terrain

Sugarbush, VT, for an overall great place to ski

Waterville Valley, NH, for vacation packages

Saddleback, ME, for scenic wilderness views

Museums

Yale Center for British Art, New Haven, CT

Rhode Island School of Design Museum, Providence, RI

Heritage Plantation, Sandwich, MA

Whaling Museum, Nantucket, MA

Sterling and Francine Clark Art Institute, Williamstown, MA

Shelburne Museum, Shelburne, VT

Hood Museum of Art, Dartmouth College, Hanover, NH

Currier Gallery of Art, Concord, NH

Maine Maritime Museum, Bath, ME

Country Inns and Bed-and-Breakfasts

Boulders Inn, New Preston, CT (*Very Expensive*)

The Inn at Castle Hill, Newport, RI (*Moderate–Very Expensive*)

Charlotte Inn, Edgartown, MA (*Very Expensive*)

Captain's House Inn, Chatham, MA (*Expensive–Very Expensive*)

Clark Currier Inn, Newburyport, MA (*Moderate–Expensive*)

Merrell Tavern Inn, Stockbridge, MA (*Moderate–Expensive*)

Vermont Marble Inn, Fair Haven (Rutland), VT (*Very Expensive*)

The Rabbit Hill Inn, Lower Waterford (St. Johnsbury), VT (*Moderate–Expensive*)

Snowvillage Inn, Snowville, NH (*Moderate–Expensive*)

The John Peters Inn, Blue Hill, ME (*Very Expensive*)

Norumbega, Camden, ME (*Very Expensive*)

Places to Eat

Abbott's Lobster in the Rough, Noank, CT (*Moderate–Expensive*)

Manisses, Block Island, RI (*Very Expensive*)

Chillingsworth, Brewster, MA (*Very Expensive*)

Club Car, Nantucket, MA (*Expensive–Very Expensive*)

Lambert's Cove Country Inn, West Tisbury, MA (*Expensive*)

Biba, Boston, MA (*Moderate–Expensive*)

Yankee Pedlar Inn, Holyoke, MA (*Moderate–Expensive*)

The Arlington Inn, Arlington, VT (*Expensive*)

Mary's, Bristol, VT (*Moderate–Expensive*)

The Balsams Grand Resort Hotel, Dixville Notch, NH (*Very Expensive*)

Arrows, Ogunquit, ME (*Expensive–Very Expensive*)

Le Domaine, Hancock, ME (*Expensive*)

New England

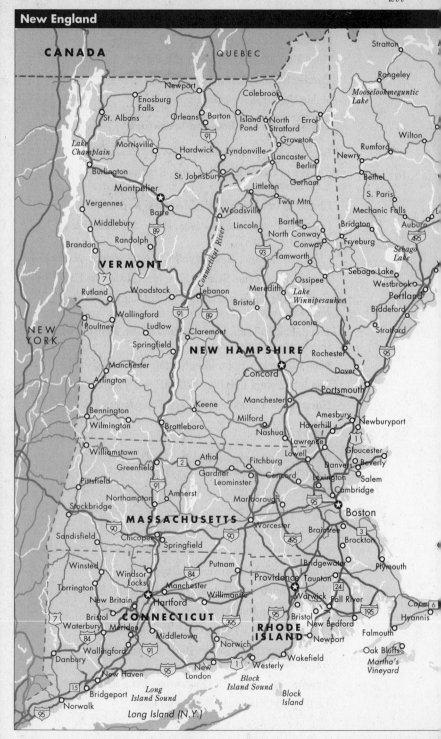

CANADA   QUEBEC

Stratton

Newport

Rongeley

Enosburg Falls

Colebrook

Mooselookmeguntic Lake

St. Albans

Orleans

Barton

Island Pond

North Stratford

Errol

Wilton

Morrisville

Hardwick

Lyndonville

Groveton

Rumford

Lake Champlain

Burlington

Lancaster

Berlin

Newry

Bethel

St. Johnsbury

Littleton

Gorham

S. Paris

Montpelier

Barre

Woodsville

Twin Mtn.

Mechanic Falls

Vergennes

Lincoln

Bartlett

Bridgton

Auburn

Middlebury

Randolph

North Conway

Conway

Fryeburg

Sebago Lake

Brandon

VERMONT

Tamworth

Sebago Lake

Westbrook

Rutland

Woodstock

Lebanon

Meredith

Ossipee

Lake Winnipesaukee

Portland

Biddeford

Wallingford

Ludlow

Bristol

Laconia

Stratford

Poultney

Claremont

NEW YORK

Springfield

NEW HAMPSHIRE

Rochester

Dover

Manchester

Concord

Portsmouth

Arlington

Keene

Manchester

Amesbury

Bennington

Milford

Haverhill

Newburyport

Wilmington

Brattleboro

Nashua

Lawrence

Gloucester

Williamstown

Lowell

Danvers

Beverly

Greenfield

Athol

Fitchburg

Lexington

Salem

Pittsfield

Gardner

Leominster

Concord

Cambridge

Northampton

Amherst

Marlborough

Boston

Stockbridge

MASSACHUSETTS

Worcester

Braintree

Sandisfield

Chicopee

Brockton

Springfield

Putnam

Bridgewater

Plymouth

Winsted

Windsor Locks

Providence

Taunton

Torrington

Manchester

Willimantic

Warwick

Fall River

Cape

Hyannis

New Britain

Hartford

Bristol

New Bedford

Bristol

Waterbury

Meriden

CONNECTICUT

RHODE ISLAND

Newport

Falmouth

Danbury

Wallingford

Middletown

Norwich

Oak Bluffs

New Haven

New London

Wakefield

Westerly

Martha's Vineyard

Bridgeport

Block Island Sound

Block Island Sound

Norwalk

Long Island Sound

Block Island

Long Island (N.Y.)

Connecticut River

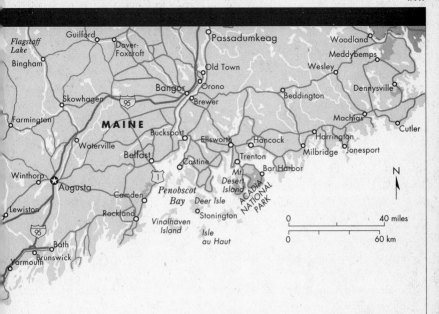

ATLANTIC OCEAN

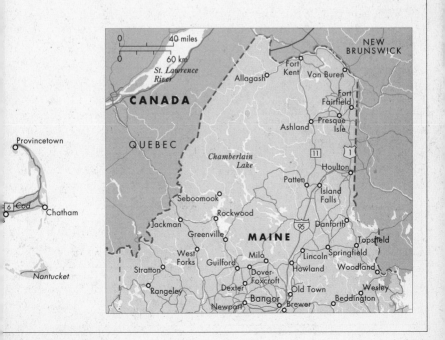

The United States

CANADA

BRITISH COLUMBIA
ALBERTA
SASKATCHEWAN
MANITOBA

Vancouver
Victoria
Seattle
Olympia
WASHINGTON
Portland
Salem
OREGON

Calgary
Regina
Winnipeg
Trans-Canada Hwy.

Columbia R.
Spokane
Great Falls
Missouri R.
MONTANA
Helena
Billings
IDAHO
Boise
Snake R.

NORTH DAKOTA
Fargo
Bismarck
SOUTH DAKOTA
Pierre
Missouri R.

Carson City
Sacramento
San Francisco
NEVADA
Fresno
CALIFORNIA
Santa Barbara
Los Angeles
San Diego

Salt Lake City
UTAH
Las Vegas
Colorado R.

WYOMING
Cheyenne
NEBRASKA
Lincoln

Denver
Colorado Springs
COLORADO
KANSAS

Flagstaff
ARIZONA
Phoenix
Tucson

Santa Fe
Albuquerque
NEW MEXICO
El Paso

OKLAHOMA
Oklahoma City
Amarillo

PACIFIC OCEAN

BAJA CALIFORNIA
SONORA
CHIHUAHUA

Dallas
TEXAS
Austin
San Antonio

Rio Grande

RUSSIA
ARCTIC OCEAN

Bering Strait
Nome
Bering Sea

ALASKA
Fairbanks
CANADA

Anchorage
Juneau

ALEUTIAN ISLANDS

PACIFIC OCEAN

MEXICO
COAHUILA
NUEVO LEON
TAMAULIPAS

0   400 miles
0   400 km

N

Honolulu
Oahu
Maui
HAWAII
Hawaii
PACIFIC OCEAN

World Time Zones

+12 +13 -9 -10 -11 -10 +11 +12

MONDAY
SUNDAY

International Date Line

-4 -3 -25

-7 -5 -4 -3:30

-9 14 15 13

4 -7

5 -8 8 9 16 17

6 10 11 18

12 -4

19 22

-5 -4 -3

20

23

21 24 -3

+11 +12 -11 -10 -9 -8 -7 -6 -5 -4 -3 -2

Numbers below vertical bands relate each zone to Greenwich Mean Time (0 hrs.).
Local times frequently differ from these general indications,
as indicated by light-face numbers on map.

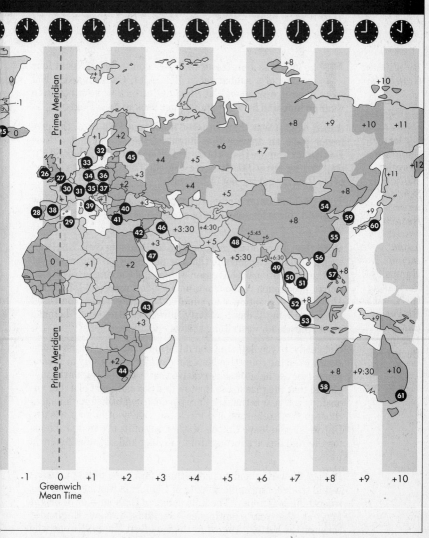

Introduction

*By William
G. Scheller*

*A
contributing
editor to*
National
Geographic
Traveler,
*William G.
Scheller
writes
frequently on
travel; his
books
include* New
Hampshire:
Portrait of
the Land and
Its People
and New
Hampshire
Backroads.

The man was a professor from Vermont who had spent four months of a sabbatical in Palo Alto, California. He had liked it well enough at first, but after a while it began to wear on him, and he was happy to get back to New England.

Asked what it was that bothered him about Palo Alto, the professor gave an answer that might strike anyone but a New Englander as more than a little odd: "Day after day," he said, "it was just so *beautiful.* It never rained. The sky never clouded over. It never got too hot or too cold."

Thus the Vermonter writes off paradise; thus the man from New England voices his suspicion of a place where it is never November.

More than a few observers, both in and outside New England, would be quick to conclude that the professor's remarks are yet another indication of the region's lingering Calvinism, of its mistrust of too much real or metaphoric good weather. Ishmael of *Moby-Dick,* a creation of an adopted New Englander, confessed to experiencing "a damp, drizzly November in my soul." Is that a model phrase for describing the way people feel here?

Not really; psychologizing about the lowering of Calvinist doomclouds over the collective New England brow is a silly academic game. Yet the habit is so pervasive that it is even regularly suggested that the reason the Boston Red Sox fall short of a championship each year is that they are predestined to disappoint us, to chasten the exuberant and mock the vanity of human wishes. But we should leave Cotton Mather out of it; the real problems for the Red Sox are inconsistent pitching and stranding men on base.

In fact, New England has something that none of its partisans would trade for an endless spate of California weather, and that something is October. The knowledge of October—or of bright May at the year's antipodes—sustains a New Englander through the hottest August or the muddiest March. No one who prefers a place where May is perpetual could understand such a thing. We are not, in these six small states, won over to Puritan gloom; we simply have a taste for hills and valleys in our weather as in our landscape. Listen again to Melville, who wrote that "truly to enjoy bodily warmth, some small part of you must be cold, for there is no quality in this world that is not what it is merely by contrast . . . If you flatter yourself that you are all over comfortable, and have been so a long time, then you cannot be said to be comfortable any more." We are comfortable up here, by Melville's lights.

Hills and valleys, sun and shadow: New England lives by variety. To the rest of America, this region is usually summed up in the visual shorthand of a white steeple rising above a village green. But lovely—and actual—as that image might be, it says nothing of the roadless spruce forest of northern Maine; the empty brick mills of Manchester, New Hampshire; the thicket of old and new suburbs surrounding Boston; or the busy streets of downtown Hartford and New Haven. And along with that white Georgian steeple, a score or more of architectural styles compete to define New England's built environment. The clean-line country saltboxes, the boxlike yet peerlessly graceful Federalist mansions of Salem and Portsmouth, and the Greek Revival farmhouses that look like democratic temples in an Arcadian wood all have one abiding virtue: their seemliness in a varied landscape. They fit the hills and valleys of New England like a land-hugging Wright house fits the prairie.

As for the diversity of its people, don't let folklore's sly country Yankees and proper Bostonians even begin to crowd New England's stage. Look at the roster of famous individuals this place has put before the world, and you'll find the names of Paul Revere and John Hancock, James Michael Curley and Marvelous Marvin Hagler, Leonard Bernstein and Martin Luther King (he studied divinity at Boston University), Julia Child and Jay Leno. The local literary reputation is one of which you will have heard; it was earned not only by the Brahmin poets Oliver Wendell Holmes and Robert Lowell, and by Ralph Waldo Emerson and Robert Frost (who made of plain New England speech one of the great poetic languages of the world), but by a French Canadian printer's son from Lowell, Massachusetts, who dreamed by the banks of the Merrimack and at tenement windows long before he went on the road: Jack Kerouac was a great New England voice and the scion of one of its most important ethnic strains.

For all this diversity, and for all our protestations that the dour echoes of Puritanism are but a part of the New England legacy, we have to admit that there is a prevailing *seriousness* here. Or perhaps *earnestness* is the word. It comes across sometimes on Town Meeting Day, when the residents of this or that obscure hamlet vote to advise the president on the proper course of action in Central America or South Africa. It comes across every day in the letters to the editor of the *Boston Globe:* Just when you think the last word has been said on a subject—or that no word need be said—someone from Cohasset or Damariscotta will check in with an epistolary rap on the knuckles. A recent letter to the *Globe* went on for three paragraphs about how we ought to wear our hats when it's cold out; another writer explained that she and her husband didn't feel comfortable about sweetening food with honey because it exploited the bees. The tradition of *right thinking* runs deep in this part of the world, and one never knows when a New Englander is going to spring out from behind a maple tree and tell you how to behave.

Fortunately, this strain of behavior is countered by the legendary Yankee independent-mindedness, which is based on the notion that while you have the right to put your two cents in, I have the right not to listen to a thing you say. Henry David Thoreau, who is something of a patron saint in some New England circles (and elsewhere), exemplified both sides of the regional character. He was never at a loss for astonishment, yet he celebrated the person who hears a "different drummer" and goes his or her own way.

"New England," the writer Bernard DeVoto stated nearly 60 years ago, "is a finished place. It is the first old civilization, the first permanent civilization in America." Do these words still apply? No doubt New England is old, in terms of civilization in North America, and if not permanent it is at least exceedingly durable. As to whether it is "finished"— well, what is ever finished until it has finished living? New England certainly hasn't, no matter how carefully it husbands its past. If there is truth and a positive meaning in DeVoto's words, it is that New England has done a better job than most places of defining the terms of its growth and the tenor of its changes. It figured out, somewhere along the way, what it wants to be. Sometimes it tries in earnest and in large measure succeeds, as in Vermont's heroic effort to maintain a rural character even as it welcomes tourism and light industry. Sometimes, as in Boston's struggle to maintain its civilized image in the face of a growing susceptibility to modern urban ills, the results are less impressive. But even New England's failings are held against a certain standard, a certain sense of the proper order of things.

Perhaps most important, New England has earned the love and loyalty of its people. A Massachusetts senator named Leverett Saltonstall once observed that "the real New England Yankee is a person who takes the midnight train home from New York." Or makes sure he is back from Palo Alto by Christmas.

1 Essential Information

Before You Go

Visitor Information

Connecticut Department of Economic Development, 865 Brook St., Rocky Hill, CT 06067, tel. 203/258–4355 or 800/282–6863.
Maine Publicity Bureau, 325-B Water St., Box 2300, Hallowell, ME 04347, tel. 207/623–0363 or 800/533–9595.
Maine Innkeepers Association, 305 Commercial St., Portland, ME 04101, tel. 207/773–7670.
Massachusetts Office of Travel and Tourism, 100 Cambridge St., Boston, MA 02202, tel. 617/727–3201 or 800/447–6277.
New Hampshire Office of Travel and Tourism Development, Box 856, Concord, NH 03302, tel. 603/271–2343 or, for a recorded message about seasonal events, 800/258–3608.
Rhode Island Department of Economic Development, Tourism Division, 7 Jackson Walkway, Providence, RI 02903, tel. 401/277–2601 or 800/556–2484.
Vermont Travel Division, 134 State St., Montpelier, VT 05602, tel. 802/828–3236 or, for a brochure, tel. 800/837–6668.
Vermont Chamber of Commerce, Department of Travel and Tourism, Box 37, Montpelier, VT 05601, tel. 802/223–3443.

Tours and Packages

Should you buy your travel arrangements to New England packaged or do it yourself? There are advantages either way. Buying packaged arrangements saves you money, particularly if you can find a program that includes exactly the features you want. You also get a pretty good idea of what your trip will cost from the outset. You have two options: fully escorted tours and independent packages. Escorted tours mean having limited free time and traveling with strangers. Escorted tours are usually via motorcoach, with a tour director in charge. Your baggage is handled, your time rigorously scheduled, and most meals planned. Escorted tours are therefore the most hassle-free way to see New England's major sights, as well as generally the least expensive. New England is a compact region, and travelers with a map and a car can cover several states in a day. So many opt to drive through the winding backroads on their own, stopping at will to shop for antiques or discount designer clothing, stay in a country inn, or tour college campuses and other attractions. Independent packages allow this kind of flexibility. They generally include airline travel and hotels, with certain options available, such as sightseeing, car rental, and excursions.

Travel agents are your best source of recommendations for both tours and packages. They will have the largest selection, and the cost to you is the same as buying direct. Whatever program you ultimately choose, be sure to find out exactly what is included: taxes, tips, transfers, meals, baggage handling, ground transportation, entertainment, excursions, sports or recreation (and rental equipment if necessary). Ask about the level of hotel used, its location, the size of its rooms, the kind of beds, and its amenities, such as pool, room service, or programs for children, if they're important to you. Find out the operator's cancellation penalties. Nearly everyone charges them, and the only way to avoid them is to buy trip-cancellation insurance. Also ask about the single supplement, a surcharge assessed to solo travelers. Some operators do not make you pay it if you agree to be matched up with a roommate of the same sex, even if one is not found by departure time. Remember that a program that has features you won't use, whether for rental sporting equipment or discounted museum admissions, may not be the most cost-wise choice for you.

Fully Escorted Tours

New England fall foliage tours are especially big. Year-round, escorted tours are usually sold in three categories: deluxe, first-class, and tourist or budget class. The most important differences are the price and the level of accommodations. Some operators specialize in one category, while others offer a range. Top operators in the deluxe category include **Maupintour** (Box 807, Lawrence, KS 66044, tel. 800/255–4266) and **Tauck Tours** (11 Wilton Rd., Westport, CT 06881, tel. 800/468–2825). In the first-class category are **Brush Hill/Gray Line** (39 Dalton Ave., Boston, MA 02199, tel. 617/236–2148), **Caravan** (401 N. Michigan Ave., Chicago, IL 60611, tel. 800/227–2862), **Collette Tours** (162 Middle St., Pawtucket, RI 02860, tel. 800/832–4656), **Domenico Tours** (751 Broadway, Bayonne, NJ 07002, tel. 800/554–8687), **Globus** (5301 S. Federal Circle, Littleton, CO 80123, tel. 303/797–2800 or 800/221–0090) and its more budget-minded sister company, **Cosmos Tourama, Mayflower Tours** (1225 Warren Ave., Downers Grove, IL 60515, tel. 708/960–3430 or 800/323–7604), **New England/Mt. Snow Vacation Tours** (Box 560, West Dover, VT 05356, tel. 800/742–7669), which has 136 programs, **Parker Tours** (218–14 Northern Blvd., Bayside, NY 11361, tel. 718/428–7800 or 800/833–9600), and **Trieloff Tours** (24301 El Toro Rd., Suite 140, Laguna Hills, CA 92653, tel. 800/248–6877 or, in CA, 800/432–7125).

Most itineraries are jam-packed with sightseeing, so you see a lot in a short amount of time (usually one place per day). To judge just how fast-paced the tour is, review the itinerary carefully. If you are in a different hotel each night, you will be getting up early each day to head out, travel to your next destination, do some sightseeing, have dinner, and go to bed, then you'll start all over again. If you want some free time, make sure it's mentioned in the tour brochure; if you want to be escorted to every meal, confirm that any tour you consider does that. Also, when comparing programs, be sure to find out if the motorcoach is air-conditioned and has a rest room on board. Make your selection based on price and stops on the itinerary.

Independent Packages

Independent packages are offered by tour operators who may also do escorted programs and by any number of other companies—from large, established firms to small, new entrepreneurs. Airline operators include **American Airlines Fly AAway Vacations** (tel. 800/321–2121), **Continental Airlines's Grand Destinations** (tel. 800/634–5555), **TWA Getaway Vacations** (tel. 800/438–2929), and **United Airlines's Vacation Planning Center** (tel. 800/328–6877). Also look into **Americantours International East** (347 5th Ave., 3rd floor, New York, NY 10016, tel. 212/683–5337 or 800/800–8942).

These programs come in a wide range of prices based on levels of luxury and options—in addition to hotel and airfare, sightseeing, car rental, transfers, admission to local attractions, and other extras, even breakfasts. Note that when pricing different packages, it sometimes pays to purchase the same arrangements separately, as when a rock-bottom promotional airfare is being offered, for example. Again, base your choice on what's available at your budget for the destinations you want to visit.

Special-Interest Travel

Special-interest programs may be fully escorted or independent. Some require a certain amount of expertise, but most are for the average traveler with an interest and are usually hosted by experts in the subject matter. When the program is escorted, it enjoys the advantages and disadvantages of all escorted programs; because your fellow travelers are apt to be passionate or knowledgeable about the subject, they can prove as enjoyable a part of your travel experience as the destination itself. The price range is wide, but the cost is usually higher—sometimes a lot higher—than for ordinary escorted tours and packages, because of the expert guiding and special activities.

UnCommon Boston Ltd. (437 Boylston St., Boston, MA 02116, tel. 617/731–5854) custom-designs individual travel programs, as will **Beckham Reception Services** (587 Washington St., Canton, MA 02021, tel. 508/771–4468 or 800/343–4323), providing you work through your travel agent.

Adventure **Battenkill Canoe, Ltd.** (Box 65, Arlington, VT 05250, tel. 802/362–2800), tours combine paddling in Vermont, Maine, and Connecticut with lodging at country inns or camping. **Trek America** (Box 470, Blairstown, NJ 07825, tel. 908/362–9198 or 800/221–0596) combines hiking, camping, and an occasional hotel.

Bicycling **Backroads** (1516 5th St., Suite L101, Berkeley, CA 94710, tel. 510/527–1555 or 800/462–2848) has a choice of inns or campsites as lodgings on their Maine and Vermont bike tours.

Fall Foliage **Parker Tours** (*see above*) and **Trieloff Tours** (*see above*) offer excursions that highlight Mother Nature's autumn palette throughout the region.

Hiking Look into **Hiking Holidays** (Box 750, Bristol, VT 05443, tel. 802/453–4816) for guided walking programs in Vermont and Massachusetts and **Hike Inn to Inn** (RR 3, Box 3115, Brandon, VT 05733, tel. 802/247–3300), whose walks travel Vermont back roads; on both programs, lodgings are in country inns.

Horseback Riding **FITS Equestrian** (685 Lateen Rd., Solvang, CA 93463, tel. 805/688–9494 or 800/666–3487) has rides through the backcountry of New Hampshire and Vermont.

Inn-Hopping **Winding Roads Tours** (249 Ball Pond Rd., New Fairfield, CT 06812, tel. 203/746–4998 or 800/240–4363) has personal—maximum eight guests per trip—tours throughout New England that include stays and meals at some of the region's most charming and historic inns.

Natural History The **National Audubon Society** (700 Broadway, New York, NY 10003, tel. 212/979–3066) has a five-day walking tour that focuses on the flora, fauna, and landscape of Vermont.

Shopping **Golden Age Festival** (5501 New Jersey Ave., Wildwood Crest, NJ 08260, tel. 800/257–8920) offers motorcoach trips for senior citizens to the Maine discount outlets and other attractions.

Skiing **Backroads** (*see above*) has several cross-country adventure tours in the gentle hills of Vermont's Northeast Kingdom for skiers of all abilities.

Whale-Watching **Oceanic Society Expeditions** (Fort Mason Center, Bldg. E, San Francisco, CA 94123, tel. 415/441–1106 or 800/326–7491) cruise the New England coastline.

Tips for British Travelers

Visitor Information Write or fax the **U.S. Travel and Tourism Administration** (Box 1EN, London W1A 1EN, tel. 071/495–4466, fax 071/409–0566) for a free USA pack.

Passports and Visas You need a valid 10-year passport to enter the United States. A visa is not necessary unless (1) you are planning to stay more than 90 days; (2) your trip is for purposes other than vacation; (3) you have at some time been refused a visa, or refused admission to the United States, or have been required to leave by the U.S. Immigration and Naturalization Service; or (4) you do not have a return or onward ticket. You will need to fill out the Visa Waiver Form, 1–94W, supplied by the airline.

To apply for a visa or for more information, call the U.S. Embassy's Visa Information Line (tel. 0891/200–290; calls cost 48p per minute or 36p per minute cheap rate). If you qualify for the visa-free travel but want a visa anyway, you must apply in writing, enclosing an SAE, to the U.S. Embassy's Visa Branch (5 Upper Grosvenor St., London W1A 2JB) or, for residents of Northern Ireland, to the U.S. Consulate General (Queen's House, Queen St., Belfast BT1 6EO). Submit a completed Nonimmigrant Visa Application (Form 156), a valid passport, a photograph, and evidence of your intended departure from the United States after a temporary visit. If you require a visa, call 0891/234–224 to schedule an interview.

Airports and Airlines Four airlines fly direct to Boston: **British Airways** (tel. 081/897–4000) and **American Airlines** (tel. 0345/789–789), departing Heathrow, and **Northwest** (tel. 0293/561–000) and **Virgin Atlantic,** (tel. 0293/747747) from Gatwick. Northwest also serves Prestwick.

Seven airlines fly direct from Heathrow to New York's JFK or Newark: **British Airways, American Airlines, Virgin Atlantic** (*see above*), **United Airlines** (tel. 081/990–9900), **Air India** (tel. 081/759–1818), **Kuwait Airways** (tel. 081/745-7772) and **El Al** (tel. 081/759-9771). **Continental** (tel. 0293/776464) flies daily from Gatwick to Newark.

Flight time is approximately seven hours on all routes.

Customs
U.S. Customs British visitors age 21 or over may import the following into the United States: 200 cigarettes or 50 cigars or 2 kilograms of tobacco; 1 U.S. liter of alcohol; gifts to a value of $100. Restricted items include meat products, seeds, plants, and fruit. Never carry illegal drugs.

U.K. Customs From countries outside the EC, such as the United States, you may import, duty-free, 200 cigarettes, 100 cigarillos, 50 cigars, or 250 grams of tobacco; 1 liter of spirits or 2 liters of fortified or sparkling wine; 2 liters of still table wine; 60 milliliters of perfume; 250 milliliters of toilet water; plus £36 worth of other goods, including gifts and souvenirs.

For further information or a copy of "A Guide for Travellers," which details standard customs procedures as well as what you may bring into the United Kingdom from abroad, contact HM Customs and Excise (New King's Beam House, 22 Upper Ground, London SE1 9PJ, tel. 071/620–1313).

Insurance Most tour operators, travel agents, and insurance agents sell specialized policies covering accident, medical expenses, personal liability, trip cancellation, and loss or theft of personal property. Some policies include coverage for delayed departure and legal expenses, winter-sports accidents, or motoring abroad. You can also purchase an annual travel-insurance policy valid for every trip you make during the year in which it's purchased (usually only trips of less than 90 days). Before you leave, make sure you will be covered if you have a preexisting medical condition or are pregnant; your insurers may not pay for routine or continuing treatment, or may require a note from your doctor certifying your fitness to travel.

The Association of British Insurers, a trade association representing 450 insurance companies, advises extra medical coverage for visitors to the United States.

For advice by phone or a free booklet, "Holiday Insurance," that sets out what to expect from a holiday-insurance policy and gives price guidelines, contact the Association of British Insurers (51 Gresham St., London EC2V 7HQ, tel. 071/600–3333; 30 Gordon St., Glasgow G1 3PU, tel. 041/226–3905; Scottish Provincial Bldg., Donegal Sq. W, Belfast BT1 6JE, tel. 0232/249176; call for other locations).

Tour Operators Tour packages to New England are available from **Americana Vacations Ltd.** (Morley House, 320 Regent St., London W1R 5AD, tel. 071/637–7853), **Jetsave** (Sussex House., London Rd., East Grinstead, W. Sussex RH19 1LD, tel. 0342/312–033), **Key to America** (15 Feltham Rd., Ashford, Middlesex, TW15 1DQ, tel. 0784/248–777), and **Transamerica Holidays** (3a Gatwick Metro Centre, Balcombe Rd., Horley RH6 9GA, tel. 0293/774–441). **Trailfinders** (42–50 Earls Court Rd., London W8 7RG, tel. 071/937–5400; 58 Deansgate, Manchester M3 2FF, tel. 061/839–3636) are best for independent travelers.

Car Rental Make the arrangements from home to avoid inconvenience, save money, and guarantee yourself a vehicle. Major firms include **Alamo** (tel. 0800/272–200), **Budget** (tel. 0800/181–181), **Europcar** (tel. 081/950–5050), and **Hertz** (tel. 081/679–1799).

In the United States, you must be 21 to rent a car; rates may be higher for those under 25. Possible extra charges may be levied for child seats, compulsory for children under 5 (about $3 per day); additional drivers (around $1.50 per day); and the all-but-compulsory Collision Damage Waiver (*see* Car Rentals, *below*). To pick up your reserved car, you will need the reservation voucher, a passport, a U.K. driver's license, and a travel insurance policy covering each driver.

When to Go

All six New England states are largely year-round destinations. While summer is a favored time all over New England, fall is balmy and idyllically colorful, and winter's snow makes for great skiing. The only times vacationers might want to stay away are during mud season in April and black-fly season in the last two weeks of May. Note that many smaller museums and attractions are open only from Memorial Day to mid-October, at other times by appointment only.

Summer is the time of outdoor music festivals (*see* Festivals and Seasonal Events, *below*). Reservations for these popular events should be made months in advance. Memorial Day is the start of the migration to the beaches and the mountains, and summer begins in earnest on July 4. Those who are driving to Cape Cod in July or August should know that Friday and Sunday are the days weekenders clog the overburdened Route 6; a better time to visit the beach areas and the islands may be after Labor Day.

Fall is the most colorful season in New England, a time when many inns and hotels are booked months in advance by foliage-viewing visitors. The first scarlet and gold colors emerge in mid-September in northern areas; "peak" color occurs at different times from year to year. Generally, it is best to visit the northern reaches in early October and then move southward as the month progresses.

All leaves are off the trees by Halloween, and hotel rates fall as the leaves do, dropping significantly until ski season begins. November and early December are hunting season in much of New England; those who venture into the woods then should wear bright orange clothing.

Winter is the time for downhill and cross-country skiing. New England's major ski resorts, having seen dark days in years when snowfall was meager, now have snowmaking equipment.

In spring, despite mud season, maple sugaring goes on in Maine, New Hampshire, and Vermont, and the fragrant scent of lilacs is never far behind.

Festivals and Seasonal Events

January　　Stowe's (VT) **Winter Carnival** heats up around midmonth; it's among the country's oldest such celebrations. Brookfield (VT) holds its **Ice Harvest Festival,** one of New England's largest. The **New England Camping and RV Show** takes place at Boston's Bayside Expo Center near the end of the month.

February　　The **Mad River Valley Winter Carnival** (VT) is a week of winter festivities including dogsled races and a masquerade ball; Burlington's **Vermont Mozart Festival** showcases the Winter Chamber Music Series. The **New England Boat Show,** the largest in the region, is held in Boston's Bayside Expo Center.

March　　This is a boon time for **maple-sugaring festivals and events:** Throughout the month and into April, the sugarhouses of Maine, New Hampshire, Massachusetts, and Vermont demonstrate procedures from maple-tree tapping to sap boiling. Many offer tastings of various grades of syrup, sugar-on-snow, traditional unsweetened doughnuts, and pickles. Also in Maine, Moosehead Lake has a renowned **Ice-Fishing Derby,** and Rangeley's **New England Sled Dog Races** attract more than 100 teams from throughout the Northeast and Canada. March 17 is traditionally a major event in Boston: Its **St. Patrick's Day Parade** is one of the nation's largest; in 1994, however, the organizer's refusal to allow the participation of gays and lesbians resulted in its cancellation.

April　　Early blooms are the draw of Bristol's (RI) **Annual Spring Bulb Display,** which takes place at Blithewolde Gardens and Arboretum, and of Nantucket's **Daffodil Festival,** which celebrates spring with a flower show, elaborate shopwindow displays, and a procession of antique cars along roadsides bursting with daffodils. You can gorge on sea grub at Boothbay Harbor's (ME) **Fishermen's Festival** the third weekend in April. Dedicated runners draw huge crowds to the **Boston Marathon,** run each year on Patriot's Day (the Monday nearest April 19).

May　　You know all those holsteins you see grazing in fields alongside Vermont's windy roads? Well, the Enosburg Falls **Vermont Dairy Festival** is just the place to celebrate the delicious fruits (or cheeses, rather) of their labor. Or, if you're a sheep fancier, stop by the **New Hampshire Sheep and Wool Festival** in New Boston, where shearing, carding, and spinning are demonstrated. Rhode Island's **May breakfasts** have been a tradition since 1867: Johnnycakes and other native dishes are served statewide at bird sanctuaries, churches, grange halls, yacht clubs, schools, and veterans posts. **Lobster Weekend** kicks off Mystic Seaport's (CT) summer of festivities with live entertainment and plenty of good food; down the coast, Bridgeport's (CT) **Barnum Festival** culminates in an enormous parade through downtown. Holyoke's (MA) **Shad Fishing Derby** is said to be the largest freshwater fishing derby in North America.

June In Vermont, you can listen to jazz at Burlington's **Discover Jazz Festival** or folk at Warren's **Ben and Jerry's One World One Heart Festival**, which is held at Sugarbush. **Jacob's Pillow Dance Festival** at Becket (MA) in the Berkshires hosts performers of various dance traditions from June through September. The spring thaw calls for a number of boating celebrations, including the *Vermont Canoe and Kayak Festival* at Waterbury State Park; the **Yale–Harvard Regatta** along New London's (CT) Thames River, the oldest intercollegiate athletic event in the country; the **Boothbay Harbor Windjammer Days**, which starts the high season for Maine's boating set; and the **Blessing of the Fleet** in Provincetown, which culminates a weekend of festivities—a quahog feed, a public dance, a crafts show, a parade. Young ones are the stars of Somerworth's (NH) **International Children's Festival**, where games, activities, and crafts keep everybody busy. **A Taste of Hartford** lets you eat your way through the capital city while listening to and watching outdoor music, dance, comedy, and magic. You can visit Providence's (RI) stately homes, some by candlelight, on one of the **Providence Preservation Society's tours.** Major crafts and antiques fairs are held in Farmington (CT) and Springfield (MA).

July **Fourth of July** parties and parades kick off throughout New England: Independence Day marks the close of Burlington's (VT) monthlong **Lake Champlain Discovery Festival.** Bristol's (RI) parade is the nation's senior Independence Day parade. Concerts, family entertainment, an art show, a parade, and fireworks are held in Bath (ME). Exeter (NH) celebrates with 18th-century Revolutionary War battle reenactments, period crafts and antiques, and a visit from George Washington himself at the American Independence Museum. And the **Mashpee Powwow** (MA) brings together Native Americans from North and South America for three days of dance contests, drumming, a fireball game, and a clambake; Native American food and crafts are sold.

Some of the better music festivals include the **Marlboro Music Festival** of classical music, held at Marlboro College (VT); Newport's (RI) **Music Festival,** which brings together celebrated musicians for a two-week schedule of morning, afternoon, and evening concerts in Newport mansions; the **Bar Harbor Festival** (ME), which hosts classical, jazz, and popular music concerts into August; and the **Tanglewood Music Festival** at Lenox (MA), which shifts into high gear with performances by the Boston Symphony Orchestra and a slew of major entertainers. Shoppers can rummage through major **antiques fairs** in Wolfeboro (NH) and Dorset (VT). Or you can simply admire the furnishings of homes during **Open House Tours** in Litchfield (CT) and Camden (ME). Boaters and the men and women who love them flock to the **Sail Festival** at New London's (CT) City Pier to watch City Pier sail races, outdoor concerts, fireworks, and the Ugliest Dog Contest. In nearby Mystic, enthusiasts can view vintage powerboats and sailboats at the **Antique and Classic Boat Rendezvous.** The **Great Schooner Race** (ME), which runs from Penobscot Bay to Rockland, features replicas and relics of the age of sail. Two of the region's most popular country fairs are held in Bangor (ME) and on Cape Cod in Barnstable (MA).

August The music festivals continue—in Newport (RI) with **Ben and Jerry's Newport Folk Festival** and **JVC's Jazz Festival** and in Essex (CT) with the **Great Connecticut Traditional Jazz Festival.** Popular arts, crafts, and antiques festivals are held at **Haystack Mountain** (VT), at the **Southern Vermont Crafts Fair** in Manchester (VT), at the **Outdoor Arts Festival** in Mystic (CT), at the **Maine Antiques Festival** in Union, and at the **Fair of the League of New Hampshire Craftsmen** at Mt. Sunapee State Park in Newbury—the nation's oldest crafts fair. Foodies should bring their appetites to Maine's **Lobster Festival** in Rockland and **Blueberry Festival** in Rangeley Lake. A few general summer fairs include the **Woodstock Fair** (CT), which has horse and ox pulls, livestock shows, Colonial crafts, puppet shows, and food; the **Hyannis Street Festival** (MA), a three-day weekend of Main Street shopping, food, and entertainment; and the **Martha's Vineyard Agricultural Fair** (MA), which includes contests, animal shows, a carnival, and evening entertainment.

September   Summer's close is met with dozens of Labor Day fairs including the **Vermont State Fair** in Rutland, with agricultural exhibits, a midway, and entertainment; the **Providence Waterfront Festival** (RI), a weekend of arts, crafts, ethnic foods, musical entertainment, and boat races; the **International Seaplane Fly-In Weekend,** which sets Moosehead Lake (ME) buzzing; and Burlington's (VT) **Champlain Valley Exposition,** which has all the features of a large county fair. Foot stomping and guitar strumming are the activities of choice at several musical events: the **Cajun & Bluegrass Music-Dance-Food Festival** at Stepping Stone Ranch in Escoheag (RI), the **National Traditional Old-Time Fiddler's Contest** in Barre (VT), the **Bluegrass Festival** in Brunswick (ME), and the **Rockport Folk Festival** in Rockport (ME). In Stratton (VT), artists and performers gather for the **Stratton Arts Festival.** One of the best and oldest **antiques shows** in New England occurs in New Haven (CT). Providence (RI) shows off its diversity during its **Annual Heritage Festival.**

Agricultural fairs not to be missed are **the Common Ground Country Fair** in Windsor (ME), an organic farmer's delight with livestock shows, ethnic food, and contra dancing; the **Deerfield Fair** (NH), one of New England's oldest, has agricultural exhibits, competitions, and entertainment; and the **Eastern States Exposition** in Springfield (MA), New England's largest agricultural show and fair. Autumn is ushered in at the **Northeast Kingdom Fall Foliage Festival** (NH), a weeklong affair hosted by the six small towns of Walden, Cabot, Plainfield, Peacham, Barnet, and Groton. Fish lovers show up in schools to attend the **Bourne Scallopfest** in Buzzards Bay (MA), where there's crafts, entertainment, and buckets of fried scallops; the **Martha's Vineyard Striped Bass and Bluefish Derby,** one of the East Coast's premier fishing contests; and the **Annual Seafood Festival** in Hampton Beach, where you can sample the seafood specialties of more than 50 local restaurants, dance to live bands, and watch fireworks explode over the ocean.

October   In Maine, the **Fryeburg Fair** features agricultural exhibits, harness racing, an iron-skillet-throwing contest, and a pig scramble. The **Nantucket Cranberry Harvest** is a three-day celebration including bog and inn tours and a crafts fair.

November   In Vermont there are two major events in this otherwise quiet month: The **EarthPeace International Film Festival** presents films dealing with environmental, human rights, and political issues for a week in Burlington, and the **Bradford Wild Game Supper** draws thousands to taste a variety of large and small game animals and birds.

December   History buffs will want to attend the **reenactment of the Boston Tea Party,** which occurs on the *Beaver II* in Boston Harbor. In Arlington (VT), the **St. Lucia Pageant** is a "Festival of Lights" that celebrates the winter solstice. Christmas celebrations are plentiful throughout New England: In **Nantucket** (RI), the first weekend of the month sees an early Christmas celebration with elaborate decorations, costumed carolers, theatrical performances, art exhibits, and a tour of historic homes. In **Newport** (RI), several Bellevue Avenue mansions open for the holidays, and there are crafts fairs, holiday concerts, and candlelight tours of Colonial homes throughout the month. At **Mystic Seaport** (CT), costumed guides escort visitors to holiday activities. Old Saybrook (CT) has a **Christmas Torchlight Parade and Muster of Ancient Fife and Drum Corps,** which ends with a carol sing at the Church Green. Historic **Strawbery Banke** (NH) has a Christmas Stroll, with carolers, through nine historic homes decorated for the season. The final day of the year is observed with festivals, entertainment, and food in many locations during **First Night Celebrations.** Some of the major cities hosting such events are Burlington (VT), Providence (RI), Boston, and, in Connecticut, Danbury, Hartford, and Stamford.

Climate   What follows are average daily maximum and minimum temperatures for some major cities in New England.

Hartford, CT

Month	Max		Month	Max		Month	Max	
Jan.	36F	2C	May	70F	21C	Sept.	74F	23C
	20	− 7		47	8		52	11
Feb.	38F	3C	June	81F	27C	Oct.	65F	18C
	20	− 7		56	13		43	6
Mar.	45F	7C	July	85F	29C	Nov.	52F	11C
	27	− 3		63	17		32	0
Apr.	59F	15C	Aug.	83F	28C	Dec.	38F	3C
	38	3		61	16		22	− 6

Boston, MA

Month	Max		Month	Max		Month	Max	
Jan.	36F	2C	May	67F	19C	Sept.	72F	22C
	20	− 7		49	9		56	13
Feb.	38F	3C	June	76F	24C	Oct.	63F	17C
	22	− 6		58	14		47	8
Mar.	43F	6C	July	81F	27C	Nov.	49F	9C
	29	− 2		63	17		36	2
Apr.	54F	12C	Aug.	79F	26C	Dec.	40F	4C
	38	3		63	17		25	− 4

Burlington, VT

Month	Max		Month	Max		Month	Max	
Jan.	29F	− 2C	May	67F	19C	Sept.	74F	23C
	11	−12		45	7		50	10
Feb.	31F	− 1C	June	77F	25C	Oct.	59F	15C
	11	−12		56	13		40	4
Mar.	40F	4C	July	83F	28C	Nov.	45F	7C
	22	− 6		59	15		31	− 1
Apr.	54F	12C	Aug.	79F	26C	Dec.	31F	− 1C
	34	1		58	14		16	− 9

Portland, ME

Month	Max		Month	Max		Month	Max	
Jan.	31F	− 1C	May	61F	16C	Sept.	68F	20C
	16	− 9		47	8		52	11
Feb.	32F	0C	June	72F	22C	Oct.	58F	14C
	16	− 9		54	15		43	6
Mar.	40F	4C	July	76F	24C	Nov.	45F	7C
	27	− 3		61	16		32	0
Apr.	50F	10C	Aug.	74F	23C	Dec.	34F	1C
	36	2		59	15		22	− 6

Information Sources   For current weather conditions and forecasts for cities in the United States and abroad, plus the local time and helpful travel tips, call the

Weather Channel Connection (tel. 900/932–8437; 95¢ per minute) from a touch-tone phone.

What to Pack

Airlines generally allow two pieces of check-in luggage and one carry-on piece per passenger. *See also* Luggage, *below.*

Clothing The principal rule on weather in New England is that there are no rules. A cold, foggy morning can and often does become a bright, 60-degree afternoon. A summer breeze can suddenly turn chilly, and rain often appears with little warning. Thus, the best advice on how to dress is to layer your clothing so that you can peel off or add garments as needed for comfort. Showers are frequent, so pack a raincoat and umbrella. Even in summer you should bring long pants, a sweater or two, and a waterproof windbreaker, for evenings are often chilly and the sea spray can make things cool on a whale-watch or deep-sea fishing trip. If you'll be walking in the woods, bring heavy boots and expect to encounter mud. Winter requires heavy clothing, gloves, a hat, warm socks, and waterproof shoes or boots.

Casual sportswear—walking shoes and jeans—will take you almost everywhere, but swimsuits and bare feet will not: Shirts and shoes are required attire at even the most casual venues. In Boston, the most cosmopolitan New England city, you may want to dress up a bit. Jacket and tie are required in better Boston restaurants, at a number of inns in the Berkshires, and in the occasional more formal dining room elsewhere.

Miscellaneous In summer, bring a hat and sunscreen. Remember also to pack insect repellent—and use it! Recent outbreaks of Lyme disease all over the East Coast make it imperative (even in urban areas) that you protect yourself from ticks from early spring through the summer.

Bring an extra pair of eyeglasses or contact lenses in your carry-on luggage. If you have a health problem that requires a prescription drug, pack enough to last the duration of the trip. Pharmacies, especially in rural areas, may be closed on Sunday. Don't pack prescription drugs in luggage that you plan to check in case your bags go astray. Pack a list of the offices that supply refunds for lost or stolen traveler's checks.

Luggage Free airline baggage allowances depend on the airline, the route,
Regulations and the class of your ticket; ask in advance. In general, on domestic flights you are entitled to check two bags—neither exceeding 62 inches, or 158 centimeters (length + width + height), or weighing more than 70 pounds (32 kilograms). A third piece may be brought aboard; its total dimensions are generally limited to less than 45 inches (114 centimeters) so it will fit easily under the seat in front of you or in the overhead compartment. In the U.S. the Federal Aviation Administration gives airlines broad latitude to limit carry-on allowances and tailor them to different aircraft and operational conditions. Charges for excess, oversize, or overweight pieces vary.

Safeguarding Before leaving home, itemize your bags' contents and their worth in
Your Luggage case they go astray. To minimize that risk, tag them inside and out with your name, address, and phone number. (If you use your home address, cover it so that potential thieves can't see it.) Put a copy of your itinerary inside each bag, so that you can easily be tracked. At check-in, make sure that the tag attached by baggage handlers bears the correct three-letter code for your destination. If your bags

do not arrive with you, or if you detect damage, immediately file a written report with the airline before you leave the airport.

Insurance In the event of loss, damage, or theft on domestic flights, airlines' liability is $1,250 per passenger, excluding the valuable items such as jewelry, cameras, and more that are listed in the fine print on your ticket. Excess-valuation insurance can be bought directly from the airline at check-in. Your homeowner's policy may fill the gap; if not, firms such as **The Travelers Companies** (1 Tower Sq., Hartford, CT 06183, tel. 203/277–0111 or 800/243–3174) and **Wallach and Company** (107 W. Federal St., Box 480, Middleburg, VA 22117, tel. 703/687–3166 or 800/237–6615) sell baggage insurance.

Getting Money from Home

Cash Machines Many automated-teller machines (ATMs) are tied to international networks such as **Cirrus** and **Plus.** You can use your bank card at ATMs to withdraw money from an account and get cash advances on a credit-card account if your card has been programmed with a personal identification number (PIN). Check in advance on limits on withdrawals and cash advances within specified periods. On cash advances you are charged interest from the day you receive the money from ATMs as well as from tellers. Transaction fees for ATM withdrawals outside your home turf may be higher than for withdrawals at home. For specific Cirrus locations in the United States and Canada, call 800/424–7787. For U.S. Plus locations, call 800/843–7587 and press the area code and first three digits of the number you're calling from (or of the calling area where you want an ATM).

Wiring Money You don't have to be a cardholder to send or receive a **MoneyGram from American Express** for up to $10,000. To send one, go to a MoneyGram agent in a retail or convenience store or American Express travel office and pay up to $1,000 with a credit card and anything over that in cash. You are allowed a free long-distance call to give the transaction code to your intended recipient, who need only present identification and the reference number to the nearest MoneyGram agent to pick up the cash. MoneyGram agents are in more than 70 countries (call 800/926–9400 for locations). Fees range from 3% to 10%, depending on the total and how you pay.

You can also use **Western Union.** To wire money, take either cash or a cashier's check to the nearest office or call and use MasterCard or Visa. Money sent from the United States or Canada will be available for pickup at agent locations in 78 countries within minutes. Once the money is in the system it can be picked up at *any* one of 22,000 locations (call 800/325–6000 for the one nearest you).

Traveling with Cameras, Camcorders, and Laptops

Film and Cameras If your camera is new or if you haven't used it for a while, shoot and develop a few test rolls of film before you leave. Store film in a cool, dry place—never in the car's glove compartment or on the shelf under the rear window.

Airport security X-rays generally aren't harmful to film with ISO below 400. To protect your film, carry it with you in a clear plastic bag and ask for a hand inspection. Such requests are honored at U.S. airports. Don't depend on a lead-lined bag to protect film in checked luggage—the airline may increase the radiation to see what's inside.

Camcorders Before your trip, put camcorders through their paces, invest in a skylight filter to protect the lens, and check all the batteries.

Videotape Videotape is not damaged by X-rays, but it may be harmed by the magnetic field of a walk-through metal detector, so ask for a hand-check. Airport security personnel may ask you to turn on the camcorder to prove that it's what it appears to be, so make sure the battery is charged.

Laptops Security X-rays do not harm hard-disk or floppy-disk storage, but you may request a hand-check, at which time you may be asked to turn on the computer to prove that it is what it appears to be. (Check your battery before departure.) Most airlines allow you to use your laptop aloft except during takeoff and landing (so as not to interfere with navigation equipment).

Traveling with Children

In New England, there's no shortage of things to do with children. Major museums have children's sections, and there are dedicated children's museums in cities large and small. Children love the road-side attractions found in many tourist areas, and miniature golf courses are easy to come by. There are beaches and boat rides, parks and planetariums, lighthouses and llama treks. Special events, such as crafts fairs and food festivals, are fun for youngsters as well. As for restaurants, you don't have to stick with fast food. Asking around will turn up family-oriented restaurants that specialize in pizza or pasta and come equipped with Trivial Pursuit cards, pull toys, fish tanks, and other families traveling with children—sure-fire entertainment for the interval between ordering and eating. Friendly's, a New England–based restaurant chain known for its legendary ice cream desserts, is particularly family-friendly: In some, you'll find crayons on the tables and a rack of children's books not far from the stack of booster seats. Like many restaurants in the region, Friendly's has a children's menu and an array of special deals for families. Chain hotels and motels also welcome children, and New England has many family-oriented resorts with lively children's programs. You'll also find family farms that accept guests and that are lots of fun for children; the Vermont Travel Division (*see* Visitor Information, *above*) publishes a directory. Rental houses and apartments abound, particularly around ski areas; off-season, these can be economical as well as comfortable touring bases. Some country inns are less enthusiastic about small fry, especially those with a quiet, romantic atmosphere and those furnished with antiques. (You won't enjoy them any more than they'll enjoy you.) So be up front about your traveling companions when you reserve. Innkeepers, concierges, and desk clerks can usually recommend baby-sitters or baby-sitting services.

The **American Lung Association** (tel. 800/458–6472) introduced the "Children's Fun Pass" in 1993; the pass costs $15 annually and gives a child free admission to more than 80 of New England's top attractions with the purchase of an adult admission. Proceeeds support the association's many programs aimed at helping children grow up smoke-free.

Publications *Family Travel Times*, published 10 times a year by **Travel With Your**
Newsletter **Children** (TWYCH, 45 W. 18th St., 7th Floor Tower, New York, NY 10011, tel. 212/206–0688; annual subscription $55), covers destinations, types of vacations, and modes of travel. TWYCH also publishes *Cruising with Children* and *Skiing with Children*.

Books *Great Vacations with Your Kids*, by Dorothy Jordan and Marjorie Cohen ($13; Penguin USA, 120 Woodbine St., Bergenfield, NJ 07621, tel. 800/253–6476), and *Traveling with Children—And Enjoying It*, by Arlene K. Butler ($11.95 plus $3 shipping per book; Globe Pequot Press, Box 833, 6 Business Park Rd., Old Saybrook, CT 06475, tel. 800/243–0495, or 800/962–0973 in CT) can help you plan your trip with children from toddlers to teens. Also available from the latter are *Recommended Family Resorts in the United States, Canada, and the Caribbean*, by Jane Wilford with Janet Tice ($12.95), and *Recommended Family Inns of America* ($12.95).

Tour Operators **Grandtravel** (6900 Wisconsin Ave., Suite 706, Chevy Chase, MD 20815, tel. 301/986–0790 or 800/247–7651) offers tours for people traveling with their grandchildren. The catalogue, as charmingly written and illustrated as a children's book, positively invites armchair traveling with lap-sitters aboard. **Rascals in Paradise** (650 5th St., Suite 505, San Francisco, CA 94107, tel. 415/978–9800 or 800/872–7225) specializes in adventurous, exotic, and fun-filled vacations for families to carefully screened resorts and hotels around the world.

Getting There
Airfares On domestic flights, children under 2 not occupying a seat travel free, and older children currently travel on the "lowest applicable" adult fare.

Baggage The adult baggage allowance applies to children paying half or more of the adult fare.

Safety Seats The Federal Aviation Administration recommends the use of safety seats aloft and details approved models in the free leaflet **"Child/Infant Safety Seats Recommended for Use in Aircraft"** (available from the FAA, APA–200, 800 Independence Ave. SW, Washington, DC 20591, tel. 202/267–3479; information hotline, tel. 800/322-7873). Airline policy varies. U.S. carriers allow FAA-approved models bearing a sticker declaring their FAA approval. Because these seats are strapped into regular passenger seats, airlines may require that a ticket be bought for an infant who would otherwise ride free.

Facilities Aloft Some airlines provide other services for children, such as children's meals and freestanding bassinets (only to those with seats at the bulkhead, where there's enough legroom). Make your request when reserving. The annual February/March issue of *Family Travel Times* details children's services on dozens of airlines ($10; *see above*). "Kids and Teens in Flight" (free from the U.S. Department of Transportation's Office of Consumer Affairs (R-25, Washington, DC 20590, tel. 202/366–2220) offers tips for children flying alone.

Hints for Travelers with Disabilities

Newer hotels and restaurants as well as those that have recently been renovated are apt to be equipped for travelers with mobility problems and sensory impairments; the passage of the Americans with Disabilities Act in 1990 should mean increasing accessibility. The official Vermont state map indicates which public recreation areas at state parks have facilities for travelers using wheelchairs. In addition, both the **Vermont Travel Division** and the **New Hampshire Office of Travel and Tourism Development** (*see* Visitor Information, *above*) publish statewide directories of accessible facilities.

Getting Around **Greyhound Lines** (tel. 800/231–2222) will carry a person with a disability and his or her companion for the price of a single fare. **Amtrak** (National Railroad Passenger Corp., 60 Massachusetts Ave. NE, Washington, DC 20002, tel. 800/872–7245, TTY 800/523–6590) advises that you request any redcap service, special seats, or wheel-chair assistance you may need when you make reservations. (Not all stations are equipped to provide these services.) All passengers with disabilities, including children, are entitled to a 15% discount on the lowest available fare. The free brochure *Access Amtrak* outlines services for the elderly and people with disabilities.

Organizations Several organizations provide travel information for people with disabilities, usually for a membership fee, and some publish news-letters and bulletins. Among them are the **Information Center for Individuals with Disabilities** (Fort Point Pl., 27–43 Wormwood St., Boston, MA 02210, tel. 617/727–5540; in MA, tel. 800/462–5015 between 11 and 4, or leave message other times; TTY 617/345–9743); **Mobility International USA** (Box 10767, Eugene, OR 97440, tel. and TTY 503/343–1284, fax 503/343–6812), the U.S. branch of an international organization based in Britain (*see below*) that has affiliates in 30 countries; **MossRehab Hospital Travel Information Service** (tel. 215/456–9603, TTY 215/456–9602); the **Travel Industry and Disabled Exchange** (TIDE, 5435 Donna Ave., Tarzana, CA 91356, tel. 818/344–3640, fax 818/344–0078); and **Travelin' Talk** (Box 3534, Clarksville, TN 37043, tel. 615/552–6670, fax 615/552–1182).

In the United Kingdom Important information sources include the **Royal Association for Disability and Rehabilitation** (RADAR, 12 City Forum, 250 City Rd., London EC1V 8AF, tel. 071/250–3222), which publishes travel information for people with disabilities in Britain, and Mobility International (228 Borough High St., London SE1 1JX, tel. 071/403–5688), an international clearinghouse of travel information for people with disabilities.

Travel Agencies and Tour Operators **Flying Wheels Travel** (143 W. Bridge St., Box 382, Owatonna, MN 55060, tel. 507/451–5005 or 800/535–6790) is a travel agency specializing in domestic and worldwide cruises, tours, and independent travel itineraries for people with mobility problems. Adventurers should contact **Wilderness Inquiry** (1313 5th St. SE, Minneapolis, MN 55414, tel. and TTY 612/379–3838), which orchestrates action-packed trips like white-water rafting, sea kayaking, and dogsledding for people with disabilities. Tours are designed to bring together people who have disabilities with those who don't.

Publications Two free publications are available from the U.S. Consumer Information Center (Pueblo, CO 81009): "New Horizons for the Air Traveler with a Disability" (include Dept. 608Y in the address), a U.S. Department of Transportation booklet describing changes resulting from the 1986 Air Carrier Access Act and the 1990 Americans with Disabilities Act, and the Airport Operators Council's *Access Travel: Airports* (Dept. 5804), which describes facilities and services for people with disabilities at more than 500 airports worldwide.

Travelin' Talk Directory (*see* Organizations, *above*) was published in 1993. This 500-page resource book ($35 check or money order with a money-back guarantee) lists names and addresses of people and organizations who offer help to travelers with disabilities. Twin Peaks Press (Box 129, Vancouver, WA 98666, tel. 206/694–2462 or 800/637–2256) publishes the *Directory of Travel Agencies for the Disabled* ($19.95), listing more than 370 agencies worldwide, and *Wheelchair Vagabond* ($14.95), a collection of personal travel tips. Add $2 per book for shipping. The Sierra Club publishes *Easy Access to National Parks* ($16 plus $3 shipping; 730 Polk St., San Francisco, CA 94109, tel. 415/776–2211). Fodor's publishes *Great American Vacations for Travelers with Disabilities*, detailing services and accessible attractions, restaurants, and hotels in New England and other U.S. destinations (available in bookstores, or call 800/533–6478).

Hints for Older Travelers

Getting Around Both **Greyhound** (tel. 800/231–2222) and **Amtrak** (tel. 800/872–7245) have special fares for older travelers.

In Hotels Notify innkeepers in advance if you want a room on the ground floor, a room with a shower, or a room with bathing facilities other than a Victorian clawfoot tub, which requires climbing in and out.

Organizations The **American Association of Retired Persons** (AARP, 601 E St. NW, Washington, DC 20049, tel. 202/434–2277) provides independent travelers who are members of the AARP (open to those age 50 or older; $8 per person or couple annually) with the Purchase Privilege Program, which offers discounts on lodging, car rentals, and sightseeing, and the AARP Motoring Plan, which furnishes domestic trip-routing information and emergency road-service aid for an annual fee of $39.95 per person or couple ($59.95 for a premium version). The AARP also arranges group tours, cruises, and apartment living through AARP Travel Experience from American Express (400 Pinnacle Way, Suite 450, Norcross, GA 30071, tel. 800/927–0111 or 800/745–4567).

Two other organizations offer discounts on lodgings, car rentals, and other travel products, along with such nontravel perks as magazines and newsletters: the **National Council of Senior Citizens** (1331 F St. NW, Washington, DC 20004, tel. 202/347–8800; membership $12 annually) and **Mature Outlook** (6001 N. Clark St., Chicago, IL 60660, tel. 800/336–6330; $9.95 annually).

Note: Mention your senior-citizen status when booking hotel reservations for reduced rates, not when checking out. At restaurants, mention it before you're seated; discounts may be limited to certain menus, days, or hours. If you are renting a car, ask about promotional rates that might improve on your senior-citizen discount.

Educational Travel The nonprofit **Elderhostel** (75 Federal St., 3rd floor, Boston, MA 02110, tel. 617/426–7788) has offered inexpensive study programs for people 60 and older since 1975. Held at more than 1,800 educational institutions, courses cover everything from marine science to Greek myths and cowboy poetry. Participants generally attend lectures in the morning and spend the afternoon sightseeing or on field trips; they live in dorms on the host campuses. Fees for programs in the United States and Canada, which usually last one week, run about $300, not including transportation.

Tour Operators The following tour operators specialize in older travelers: If you want to take your grandchildren, look into **Grandtravel** (*see* Traveling with Children, *above*); **Saga International Holidays** (222 Berkeley St., Boston, MA 02116, tel. 800/343–0273) caters to those over age 60 who like to travel in groups. **SeniorTours** (508 Irvington Road, Drexel Hill, PA 19026, tel. 215/626–1977 or 800/227–1100) arranges motorcoach tours throughout the United States and Nova Scotia, as well as Caribbean cruises.

Publications *The 50+ Traveler's Guidebook: Where to Go, Where to Stay, What to Do* by Anita Williams and Merrimac Dillon (St. Martin's Press, 175 5th Ave., New York, NY 10010; $12.95) is available in bookstores and offers many useful tips. "The Mature Traveler" (Box 50820,

Reno, NV 89513, tel. 702/786–7419; $29.95), a monthly newsletter, contains many travel deals.

Hints for Gay and Lesbian Travelers

Organizations The **International Gay Travel Association** (Box 4974, Key West, FL 33041, tel. 800/448-8550), which has 700 members, will provide you with names of travel agents and tour operators who specialize in gay travel. The **Gay & Lesbian Visitors Center of New York Inc.** (135 West 20th St., 3rd Floor, New York, NY 10011, tel. 212/463–9030 or 800/395–2315; $100 annually) mails a monthly newsletter, valuable coupons, and more to its members.

Travel Agencies and Tour Operators The dominant travel agency in the market is **Above and Beyond** (3568 Sacramento St., San Francisco, CA 94118, tel. 415/922–2683 or 800/397–2681). Tour operator **Olympus Vacations** (8424 Santa Monica Blvd. #721, West Hollywood, CA 90069; tel. 310/657–2220) offers all-gay-and-lesbian resort holidays. **Skylink Women's Travel** (746 Ashland Ave., Santa Monica, CA 90405, tel. 310/452–0506 or 800/225–5759) handles individual travel for lesbians all over the world and conducts two international and five domestic group trips annually.

Publications The premier international travel magazine for gays and lesbians is **Our World** (1104 North Nova Rd., Suite 251, Daytona Beach, FL 32117, tel. 904/441–5367; $35 for 10 issues). *Out & About* (tel. 203/789–8518 or 800/929–2268; $49 for 10 issues, full refund if you aren't satisfied) is a 16-page monthly newsletter with extensive information on resorts, hotels, and airlines that are gay-friendly.

Further Reading

New England has been home to some of America's classic authors, among them Herman Melville, Henry David Thoreau, Edith Wharton, Mark Twain, Robert Frost, and Emily Dickinson. Thoreau wrote about New England in *Cape Cod, The Maine Woods*, and his masterpiece, *Walden*. Melville's *Moby-Dick*, set on a 19th-century Nantucket whaler, captures the spirit of the whaling era. Nathaniel Hawthorne portrayed early New England life in his novels *The Scarlet Letter* and *The House of the Seven Gables* (the actual house, in Salem, Massachusetts, is open to the public for guided tours). *The Country of the Pointed Firs*, by Sarah Orne Jewett, is a collection of sketches about the Maine coast at the turn of the century.

Inside New England, by Judson Hale, the longtime editor of *Yankee* magazine, examines with humor all aspects of the six states, including small-town life, language, legends, even the weather. David Laskin's *Eastern Islands* tours many of the unbridged islands of the East Coast from Maine to Florida, including Nantucket, Martha's Vineyard, and Block Island.

Maine, A Guide Downeast, edited by Dorris A. Isaacson, and *Maine: An Explorer's Guide*, by Christina Tree and Mimi Steadman, are useful guides to sights, hotels, and restaurants throughout Maine. Among books written about the Maine islands are Philip Conkling's *Islands in Time*, Bill Caldwell's *Islands of Maine*, and Charlotte Fardelmann's *Islands Down East*. The late Kennebunk resident Kenneth Roberts set a series of historical novels, beginning with *Arundel*, in the coastal Kennebunk region during the Revolutionary War. Carolyn Chute's *The Beans of Egypt, Maine* offers a fictional glimpse of the hardships of contemporary rural life in that state.

A Guide to the Salem Witchcraft Hysteria of 1692, by David C. Brown, explores the witchcraft hysteria that swept the North Shore of Massachusetts and the Puritan culture behind it. The naturalist Henry Beston's *Outermost House* chronicles Cape Cod's seasons during a solitary year the author spent in a cabin at the ocean's edge. Practical information about the Cape and the islands is available in *Short Bike Rides on Cape Cod, Nantucket and the Vineyard*, by Edwin Mullen and Jane Griffith; *Short Nature Walks on Cape Cod and the Vineyard*, by Hugh and Heather Sadlier; *Cape Cod, Its People and Their History*, by Henry C. Kittredge (first published in 1930); and *Nantucket: The Life of an Island*, by Edwin P. Hoyt.

Vermont: An Explorers Guide, by Christina Tree and Peter Jennison, is a comprehensive guide to virtually every back road, event, attraction, town, and recreational opportunity in Vermont. Charles Morrissey's *Vermont: A History* delivers just what the title promises. Peter S. Jennison's *Roadside History of Vermont* travels the most popular highways and gives historical background on points along the way. *Without a Farmhouse Near*, by Deborah Rawson, describes the impact of change on small Vermont communities. *Real Vermonters Don't Milk Goats*, by Frank Bryan and Bill Mares, looks at the lighter side of life in the Green Mountain state.

Visitors to New Hampshire may enjoy *New Hampshire Beautiful*, by Wallace Nutting; *The White Mountains: Their Legends, Landscape, and Poetry*, by Starr King; and *The Great Stone Face and Other Tales of the White Mountains*, by Nathaniel Hawthorne. New Hampshire was also blessed with the poet Robert Frost, whose first books, *A Boy's Way* and *North of Boston*, are set here. It's commonly accepted that the Grover's Corners of Thornton Wilder's *Our Town* is the real-life Peterborough, New Hampshire.

Magnificent photographs fill the pages of *Connecticut*, by William Hubbell, with text by Roger Eddy. Sloan Wilson's novel *The Man in the Gray Flannel Suit* describes Connecticut suburban commuter life in the 1950s. A portrait of Newport, Rhode Island, in its social heyday will be found in Thornton Wilder's novel *Theophilus North*.

Finally, for a different approach to New England travel, consult Fodor's *Bed and Breakfasts and Country Inns of New England*.

Arriving and Departing

From North America by Plane

Flights are either nonstop, direct, or connecting. A **nonstop** flight requires no change of plane and makes no stops. A **direct** flight stops at least once and can involve a change of plane, although the flight number remains the same; if the first leg is late, the second waits. This is not the case with a **connecting** flight, which involves a different plane and a different flight number.

Airports and Airlines   Most major carriers serve **Logan International Airport,** in Boston, the largest airport in New England. **Bradley International Airport,** in Windsor Locks, Connecticut, north of Hartford, is convenient to southern Massachusetts and all of Connecticut. **Theodore Francis Green State Airport,** just outside Providence, Rhode Island, is another major airport. Additional New England airports served by major carriers include those in Manchester, New Hampshire; Portland and Bangor, Maine; Burlington, Vermont; and Worcester, Massachusetts. Among U.S. airlines serving the region are **American**

(tel. 800/433–7300), **Continental** (tel. 800/525–0280), **Delta** (800/221–1212), **Northwest** (tel. 800/225–2525), **TWA** (tel. 800/221–2000), **United** (tel. 800/722-5243), and **USAir** (tel 800/428–4322).

Cutting Costs The Sunday travel section of most newspapers is a good source of deals. When booking, particularly through an unfamiliar company, call the Better Business Bureau and your local or state Consumer Protection Bureau to find out whether any complaints have been registered against the company, pay with a credit card if you can, and consider trip-cancellation and default insurance.

Promotional Less expensive fares, called promotional or discount fares, are
Airfares round-trip and involve restrictions, which vary according to the route and season. You must usually buy the ticket—commonly called an APEX (advance purchase excursion) when it's for international travel—in advance (seven, 14, or 21 days are usual), although some of the major airlines have added no-frills, cheap flights to compete with new bargain airlines on certain routes.

With the major airlines the cheaper fares generally require minimum and maximum stays (for instance, over a Saturday night or at least seven and no more than 30 days). Airlines generally allow some return date changes for a $25 to $50 fee, but most low-fare tickets are nonrefundable. Only a death in the family would prompt the airline to return any of your money if you cancel a nonrefundable ticket. However, you can apply an unused nonrefundable ticket toward a new ticket, again with a small fee. The lowest fare is subject to availability, and only a small percentage of the plane's total seats will be sold at that price. Contact the U.S. Department of Transportation's Office of Consumer Affairs (I–25, Washington, DC 20590, tel. 202/366–2220) for a copy of "Fly-Rights: A Guide to Air Travel in the U.S." *The Official Frequent Flyer Guidebook* by Randy Petersen (4715-C Town Center Drive, Colorado Springs, CO 80916, tel. 719/597–8899, 800/487-8893, or 800/485–8893; $14.99, +$3 shipping and handling) yields valuable hints on getting the most for your air travel dollars.

Consolidators Consolidators or bulk-fare operators—"bucket shops"—buy blocks of seats on scheduled flights that airlines anticipate they won't be able to sell. They pay wholesale prices, add a markup, and resell the seats to travel agents or directly to the public at prices that still undercut theairline's promotional or discount fares (higher than a charter ticket but lower than an APEX ticket, and usually without the advance-purchase restriction). Moreover, some consolidators sometimes give you your money back. Carefully read the fine print detailing penalties for changes and cancellations. If you doubt the reliability of a company, call the airline once you've made your booking and confirm that you do, indeed, have a reservation on the flight.

Discount Travel clubs offer members unsold space on airplanes, cruise ships,
Travel Clubs and package tours at as much as 50% below regular prices. Membership may include a regular bulletin or access to a toll-free hotline giving details of available trips departing from three or four days to several months in the future. Most also offer 50% discounts off hotel rack rates, but double check with the hotel to make sure it isn't offering a better promotional rate independent of the club. Clubs include **Discount Travel International** (114 Forrest Ave., Suite 203, Narberth, PA 19072, tel. 215/668–7184; $45 annually, single or family), **Entertainment Travel Editions** (Box 1014 Trumbull, CT 06611, tel. 800/445–4137; $28–$48), **Great American Traveler** (Box 27965, Salt Lake City, UT 84127, tel. 800/548–2812; $29.95 annually), **Moment's Notice Discount Travel Club** (425 Madison Ave., New York,

NY 10017, tel. 212/486–0503; $45 annually, single or family), **Privilege Card** (3391 Peachtree Rd. NE, Suite 110, Atlanta, GA 30326, tel. 404/262–0222 or 800/236–9732; domestic annual membership $49.95, international, $74.95), **Travelers Advantage** (CUC Travel Service, 49 Music Sq. W, Nashville, TN 37203, tel. 800/548–1116; $49 annually, single or family), and **Worldwide Discount Travel Club** (1674 Meridian Ave., Miami Beach, FL 33139, tel. 305/534–2082; $50 annually for family, $40 single).

Publications The newsletter "Travel Smart" (40 Beechdale Road, Dobbs Ferry, NY 10522, tel. 800/327-3633; $44 a year) has a wealth of travel deals in each monthly issue.

Smoking Since February 1990, smoking has been banned on all domestic flights of less than six hours' duration; the ban also applies to domestic segments of international flights aboard U.S. and foreign carriers.

By Car

Because the six New England states form a relatively compact region with an effective network of interstate highways and other good roads linking the many cities, towns, and recreational and shopping areas that attract visitors, a car is the most convenient means of travel. Yet driving is not without its frustrations; traffic can be heavy on coastal routes and beach-access highways on weekends and in midsummer, and Newport in summer and Boston all year long are inhospitable to automobiles. Each of the states makes available, free on request, an official state map that has directories, mileage, and other useful information in addition to routings. The speed limit in much of New England is 65 miles per hour (55 in more populated areas).

Car Rentals All major car-rental companies are represented in New England, including **Alamo** (tel. 800/327-9633), **Avis** (tel. 800/331–1212, 800/879–2847 in Canada), **Budget** (tel. 800/527–0700), **Dollar** (tel. 800/800–4000), **Hertz** (tel. 800/654–3131, 800/263-0600 in Canada), and **National** (tel. 800/227–7368). In cities, unlimited-mileage rates range from $40 per day for an economy car to $50 for a large car; weekly unlimited-mileage rates range from $170 to $230. This does not include tax, which varies from state to state.

Extra Charges Picking up the car in one city and leaving it in another may entail substantial drop-off charges or one-way service fees. The cost of a collision or loss-damage waiver (*see below*) can be high, also. Some rental agencies will charge you extra if you return the car *before* the time specified on your contract; ask before making unscheduled drop-offs. Fill the tank when you turn in the vehicle to avoid being charged for refueling at what you'll swear is the most expensive pump in town.

Cutting Costs Major international companies have programs that discount their standard rates by 15%–30% if you make the reservation before departure (anywhere from 24 hours to 14 days), rent for a minimum number of days (typically three or four), and prepay the rental. More economical rentals may come as part of fly/drive or other packages, even bare-bones deals that combine only the rental and an airline ticket (*see* Tours and Packages, *above*).

Insurance and Before you rent a car, find out exactly what coverage, if any, is
Collision provided by your personal auto insurer and by the rental company.
Damage Don't assume that you are covered. If you do want insurance from
Waiver the rental company, secondary coverage may be the only type of-

fered. You may already have secondary coverage if you charge the rental to a credit card. Only Diner's Club (tel. 800/234–6377) provides primary coverage in the United States and worldwide.

In general, if you have an accident, you are responsible for the automobile. Car rental companies may offer a collision damage waiver (CDW), which ranges in cost from $4 to $14 a day. You should decline the CDW only if you are certain you are covered through your personal insurer or credit card company. In many states, laws mandate that renters be told what the CDW costs, that it's optional, and that their own auto insurance may provide the same protection.

By Train

Amtrak (tel. 800/872–7245) offers frequent daily service along its Northeast Corridor route from Washington and New York to Boston, making two stops in Connecticut (New Haven and New London) and two in Rhode Island (Westerly and Providence). Amtrak's *Montrealer* crosses Massachusetts and makes stops in New Hampshire and Vermont on its overnight run between Washington and Montréal.

The **Massachusetts Bay Transportation Authority** (tel. 617/722–5000) connects Boston with outlying areas on the north and south shores of the state. Canada's **VIA Rail** (tel. 800/361–3677) crosses Maine, providing its only rail service, en route between Montréal and Halifax, stopping at Jackman, Greenville, Brownville Junction, Mattawamkeag, Danforth, and Vanceboro.

By Bus

Greyhound Lines (tel. 800/231–2222) provides bus service to Boston and other major cities and towns in New England. **Peter Pan Bus Lines** (tel. 800/237–8747) serves Massachusetts and southern Connecticut. **Concord Trailways** (tel. 800/639–3317) connects Boston with Portland, Bangor, and coastal Maine.

Staying in New England

Shopping

Antiques, crafts, maple syrup and sugar, fresh produce, and the greatly varied offerings of the factory outlets lure shoppers to New England's outlet stores, flea markets, shopping malls, bazaars, yard sales, country stores, and farmers' markets. You'll find few trendy boutiques outside Boston, Newport, and some resort areas on the Cape, but their overstocks are sold in the many designer outlets that are commonplace in all six states. The area around New Bedford in southeastern Massachusetts is a factory outlet paradise; in Maine the outlet area runs along the coast, in Kittery, Freeport, Kennebunkport, Wells, and Ellsworth; in New Hampshire the largest outlet concentration is in North Conway.

Boston, Cape Cod, and the Berkshires harbor active artists' communities and many antiques shops, but the days of bargain prices have passed. Local newspapers and the bulletin boards of country stores carry notices of flea markets, shows, and sales that can be lots of fun—and a source of bargains as well. The **Cape Cod Antiques Dealers Association** (300 Orleans Rd., North Chatham, MA 02650, tel. 508/945–9060) publishes a directory of the area's antiques dealers and auctions. Send an SASE to the **Vermont Antiques Dealers Association** (c/o Murial McKirryher, 55 Allen St., Rutland, VT 05701) or the **Maine Antique Dealers Association** (c/o Jane Carr, 105 Mighty St., Gorham, ME 04038) for copies of their annual directories.

Opportunities abound for obtaining fresh farm produce from the source; some farms allow you to pick your own strawberries, raspberries, and blueberries, and there are maple-syrup producers who demonstrate the process to visitors. Maple syrup is available in different grades; light amber is the most refined; many Vermonters prefer grade C, the richest in flavor and the one most often used in cooking. A sugarhouse can be the most or the least expensive place to shop, depending on how tourist-oriented it is. Small grocery stores are often a good source of less-expensive syrup. The **Massachusetts Association of Roadside Stands** (Department of Agriculture, 100 Cambridge St., Boston, MA 02202, tel. 617/727–3018) prepares a list of pick-your-own fruit farms in that state. The **Massachusetts Maple Producers Association** (Box 377, Ashfield, MA 01330, tel. 413/628–3912) has a list of sugarhouses. The **New Hampshire Department of Agriculture** (Box 2042, Concord, NH 03302, tel. 603/271–3551) publishes lists of maple-syrup producers and farmers' markets in New Hampshire.

Sales Tax Connecticut sales tax is 6%; Rhode Island, 7%; Massachusetts, 5% (except clothing purchases under $150, which are not taxed); Vermont, 5%; and Maine, 6%. New Hampshire has no sales tax.

Sports and Outdoor Activities

Biking Cape Cod has miles of bike trails, some paralleling the National Seashore, most on level terrain. Other favorite areas for bicycling are the Massachusetts Berkshires and the New Hampshire lakes region. Biking in Maine is especially scenic in and around Kennebunkport, Camden, and Deer Isle; the carriage paths in Acadia National Park are ideal. Free information is available from the Maine Publicity Bureau and the Vermont Travel Division; other sources include **Maine Sport** (Rte. 1, Rockport 04856, tel. 207/236–8797 or 800/722–0826), the **Rhode Island Bicycle Coalition** (Box 4781, Rumford 02916), and **Vermont Bicycle Touring** (Box 711, Bristol 05443, tel. 802/453–4811).

Boating and In most lakeside and coastal resorts, sailboats and powerboats can
Sailing be rented at a local marina. Newport, Rhode Island, and Maine's Penobscot Bay are famous sailing areas. Lakes in New Hampshire and Vermont are splendid for all kinds of boating. The Connecticut River in the Pioneer Valley and the Housatonic River in the Berkshires are popular for canoeing.

Camping Many state parks have campgrounds. Contact the state tourist board for a complete list of campgrounds and information on facilities, reservations, and numbers of sites.

Hiking Probably the most famous trails are the 255-mile **Long Trail,** which runs north–south through the center of Vermont, and the Maine-to-Georgia **Appalachian Trail,** which runs through New England on both private and public land (contact the Appalachian Mountain Club, Box 298, Gorham, NH 03581, tel. 603/466–2725, and the White Mountains National Forest, Box 638, Laconia, NH 03247, tel. 603/528–8721). You don't have to hike it in its entirety; doing a short section at a time is also an option. You'll find good hiking in many state parks throughout the region, and New Hampshire's White Mountains are crisscrossed by trails. The **Audubon Society of New Hamp-**

shire (3 Silk Rd., Concord, NH 03301, tel. 603/224–9909) maintains marked trails for hikers.

Hunting and Fishing Maine's North Woods are loaded with moose, bear, deer, and game birds. Elsewhere, deer and small-game hunting are big in the fall. Anglers will find sport aplenty throughout the region as well—surf-casting along the shore, deep-sea fishing in the Atlantic on party and charter boats, fishing for trout in rivers, and angling for bass, landlocked salmon, and other fish in freshwater lakes. Sporting goods stores and bait-and-tackle shops are reliable sources for li-censes, necessary in fresh waters, and for leads to the nearest hot spots. Also contact Connecticut's **Department of Environmental Protection** (79 Elm St., Fisheries Division, Hartford 06106, tel. 203/566–2287); the **Maine Department of Inland Fisheries and Wildlife** (284 State St., State House Station 41, Augusta, ME 04333, tel. 207/287–2043); the **Massachusetts Division of Fisheries and Wildlife** (100 Cambridge St., Boston, MA 02202, tel. 617/727–3151); the **New Hampshire Fish and Game Department** (2 Hazen Dr., Concord, NH 03301, tel. 603/271–3421); Rhode Island's **Department of Environ-mental Management, Division of Fish and Wildlife** (4808 Tower Hill Rd., Wakefield, RI 02879, tel. 401/789–3094); or the **Vermont Fish and Wildlife Department** (103 S. Main St., Waterbury, VT 05676, tel. 802/241–3700).

Beaches

Long, wide beaches edge the New England coast from southern Maine to southern Connecticut; the most popular are on Cape Cod, Martha's Vineyard, Nantucket, and the shore areas north and south of Boston; in the Kennebunk area of Maine; on Long Island Sound in Rhode Island; and the coastal region of New Hampshire. Many are maintained by state and local governments and have lifeguards on duty; they may have picnic facilities, rest rooms, changing facilities, and concession stands. Depending on the locale, you may need a parking sticker to use the lot. The waters are at their warmest in August, though they're cold even at the height of summer along much of the Maine coast. Inland, there are small lake beaches, most notably in New Hampshire and Vermont.

National and State Parks and Forests

National and state parks offer a broad range of visitor facilities, in-cluding campgrounds, picnic grounds, hiking trails, boating, ranger programs, and more. State forests are usually somewhat less devel-oped. For more information on any of these, contact the state tour-ism offices (*see* Visitor Information, in Before You Go, *above*).

Rhode Island State Parks Fifteen state parks permit camping, including **Burlingame State Park, Charlestown Breachway, Fishermen's Memorial State Park, Arcadia State Park,** and the **Ninigret Park.**

Massachusetts National Parks **Cape Cod National Seashore,** a 40-mile stretch of the Cape between Eastham and Provincetown, is protected from development and of-fers excellent swimming, bike riding, bird-watching, and nature walks.

State Parks Some of the newest parks in Massachusetts have been created by the Urban Heritage State Park Program, which celebrates the Indus-trial Revolution of the 19th century in Lowell, Gardner, North Ad-ams, Holyoke, Lawrence, Lynn, Roxbury, and Fall River. Leaflets describing all these parks as well as other state parks and forests are available from the **Department of Environmental Management** (Division of Forests and Parks, 100 Cambridge St., Boston 02202, tel. 617/727–3159).

Vermont The 275,000-acre **Green Mountain National Forest** (231 Main St.,
National Forest Rutland, VT 05701, tel. 802/747–6700) extends south from the center of the state to the Massachusetts border. Hikers treasure the miles of hiking trails; canoeists work its white-water streams; and campers and anglers find plenty to keep them happy. Among the most popular spots are the Falls of Lana near Middlebury; Hapgood Pond between Manchester and Peru, the first section of the forest to be acquired by the federal government; Silver Lake near Middlebury; and Chittenden Brook near Rochester. There are six wilderness areas. The **Green Mountain Club** (R.R. 1, Box 650, Waterbury Center, VT 05677 tel. 802/244–7037) publishes a number of helpful maps and guides.

State Parks The 43 parks owned and maintained by the state contain numerous recreational areas that may include hiking trails, campsites, swimming, boating facilities, nature trails (some have an on-site naturalist), and fishing. The official state map details the facilities available at each. The **Department of Forests, Parks, and Recreation** (tel. 802/241–3655) provides park information.

New The **White Mountain National Forest** (Box 63, Laconia, NH 03247,
Hampshire tel. 603/528-8721) covers 770,000 acres of northern New Hampshire.

State Parks New Hampshire parklands vary widely, even within a region. Major recreation parks are at Franconia Notch, Crawford Notch, and Mt. Sunapee. Rhododendron State Park (Monadnock) has a singular collection of wild rhododendrons; Mt. Washington State Park (White Mountains) is on top of the highest mountain in the northeast. In addition, 23 state recreation areas provide vacation facilities that include camping, picnicking, hiking, boating, fishing, swimming, bike trails, winter sports, and food services. The **Division of Parks and Recreation** (Box 856, Concord 03302, tel. 603/271–3254) provides information.

Maine **Acadia National Park** (Box 177, Bar Harbor 04609, tel. 207/288–
National Park 3338), which preserves fine stretches of shoreline and the highest mountains along the East Coast, covers much of Mount Desert Island and more than half of Isle au Haut and Schoodic Point on the mainland. Camping is permitted at designated campgrounds; hiking, biking, carriage rides, and boat cruises are the most popular activities. Isle au Haut, accessible by mailboat, is the least crowded section; the Park Loop Road on Mount Desert is the busiest.

National Forest **White Mountain National Forest** (Evans Notch Ranger District, RFD 2, Box 2270, Bethel 04217, tel. 207/824–2134) has camping areas in rugged mountain locations, hiking trails, and picnic areas.

State Parks **Baxter State Park** (64 Balsam Dr., Millinocket 04462, tel. 207/723–5140) comprises more than 200,000 acres of wilderness surrounding Katahdin, Maine's highest mountain. Campgrounds are at sites near the park's dirt road and in remote backcountry sections; reservations are strongly recommended. Hiking and moose-watching are major activities at Baxter. The **Allagash Wilderness Waterway** (Maine Department of Conservation, Bureau of Parks and Recreation, State House Station 22, Augusta 04333, tel. 207/287–3821) is a 92-mile corridor of lakes and rivers surrounded by vast commercial forest property. Canoeing the Allagash is a highly demanding activity that requires advance planning and the ability to handle white water. Guides are recommended for novice canoers. Other major state parks in Maine include **Camden Hills State Park** (tel. 207/236–

3109), with hiking and camping; **Crescent Beach State Park** (Rte. 77, Cape Elizabeth, tel. 207/767–3625), with a good sand beach and picnic area; **Grafton Notch State Park** (north of Bethel, tel. 207/824–2912), with spectacular White Mountain scenery, hiking, and picnic area; **Lamoine State Park** (Rte. 184, 8 mi from Ellsworth, tel. 207/667–4778), with camping and swimming on Frenchman Bay near Acadia; **Lily Bay State Park** (Moosehead Lake, tel. 207/695–2700), with lakeside camping, boat ramps, and a hiking trail; **Popham Beach State Park** (Rte. 209 near Phippsburg, tel. 207/389–1335), with a sand beach and picnic area; **Rangeley Lake State Park** (tel. 207/864–3858), with lakeside camping, boat ramps, showers, and swimming beach; **Reid State Park** (Rte. 127 near Bath, tel. 207/371–2303), with a broad sand swimming beach; and **Sebago Lake State Park** (Rte. 302, Naples, tel. 207/693–6613), with nature trails, boat ramp, sand beach, and camping.

Dining

Seafood is king throughout New England. Clams, quahogs, lobster, and scrod are prepared here in an infinite number of ways, some fancy and expensive, others simple and moderately priced. One of the best ways to enjoy seafood is "in the rough," off paper plates on a picnic table at a real New England clamboil or clambake—or at one of the many shacklike eating places along the coast, where you can smell the salt air!

At inland resorts and inns, traditional fare—rack of lamb, game birds, familiar specialties from other cultures—dominates the menu. Among the quintessentially New England dishes are Indian pudding, clam chowder, fried clams, and cranberry anything. You can also find multicultural variations on old themes, such as Portuguese *chouriço* (a spicy red sausage that transforms a clamboil into something heavenly) and the mincemeat pie made with pork in the tradition of the French Canadians who populate the northern regions.

Dress in restaurants is generally casual, except at some of the distinguished restaurants of Boston, Newport, Maine coast towns such as Kennebunkport, and occasionally in the Berkshires and in Litchfield and Fairfield counties in Connecticut.

Lodging

Hotel and motel chains provide standard rooms and amenities in major cities and at or near traditional vacation destinations. Otherwise you'll stay at small inns where each room is different and the amenities vary in number and quality. Price isn't always a reliable indicator here; fortunately, when you call to make reservations, most hosts will be happy to give all manner of details about their properties, down to the color scheme of the handmade quilts—so ask all your questions before you book. Don't expect telephone, TV, or honor bar in your room; you might even have to share a bathroom. Most inns offer breakfast—hence the name bed-and-breakfast—yet this formula varies, too; at one B&B you may be served muffins and coffee, at another a multicourse feast with fresh flowers on the table. Many inns prohibit smoking, which is a fire hazard in older buildings, and some are wary of children. Almost all say no to pets.

Many larger resorts and inns with restaurants either offer or require participation in a menu plan. The American Plan (AP) includes all three meals; the Modified American Plan (MAP), breakfast and dinner. Some resorts will credit guests credit for meals taken elsewhere.

Inexpensive accommodations are hard to find in downtown Boston and in the desirable resort areas, especially during high season, but accommodation packages for weekend getaways, local sports, or cultural events are frequently available, and it can pay to ask about them.

Home Exchange You can find a house, apartment, or other vacation property to exchange for your own by becoming a member of a home-exchange organization, which then sends you its annual directories listing available exchanges and includes your own listing in at least one of them. Arrangements for the actual exchange are made by the two parties to it, not by the organization. For more information contact the **International Home Exchange Association** (IHEA, 41 Sutter Street, Suite 1090, San Francisco, CA 94104, tel. 415/673–0347 or 800/788–2489). Principal clearinghouses include **Intervac International** (Box 590504, San Francisco, CA 94159, tel. 415/435–3497), with three annual directories; membership is $62, or $72 if you want to receive the directories but remain unlisted. **Loan-a-Home** (2 Park La., Apt. 6E, Mount Vernon, NY 10552, tel. 914/664–7640) specializes in long-term exchanges; there is no charge to list your home, but the directories cost $35 or $45 depending on the number you receive.

Apartment and Villa Rentals If you want a home base that's roomy enough for a family and comes with cooking facilities, a furnished rental may be the solution. It's generally cost-wise, too, although not always; some rentals are luxury properties (economical only when your party is large). Home-exchange directories do list rentals—often second homes owned by prospective house swappers—and some services search for a house or apartment for you (even a castle if that's your fancy) and handle the paperwork. Some send an illustrated catalogue, and others send photographs of specific properties, sometimes at a charge; up-front registration fees may apply.

Among the companies are **Rent a Home International** (7200 34th Ave. NW, Seattle, WA 98117, tel. 206/789–9377 or 800/488–7368) and **Vacation Home Rentals Worldwide** (235 Kensington Ave., Norwood, NJ 07648, tel. 201/767–9393 or 800/633–3284). **Hideaways International** (767 Islington St., Box 4433, Portsmouth, NH 03802, tel. 603/430–4433 or 800/843–4433) functions as a travel club. Membership ($99 yearly per person or family at the same address) includes two annual guides plus quarterly newsletters; rentals are arranged directly between members, not by the club staff.

Credit Cards

The following credit card abbreviations have been used: AE, American Express; D, Discover; DC, Diners Club; MC, MasterCard; V, Visa. It's always a good idea to call ahead and confirm an establishment's credit card policy.

Great Itineraries

The following recommended itineraries, arranged by theme, are offered as a guide in planning individual travel.

Scenic Coastal Tour

From southwestern Connecticut through Rhode Island and Massachusetts to Maine, New England's coastline is a picturesque succession of rocky headlands, sand-rimmed coves, and small towns built around shipbuilding, fishing, and other seaside trades. For more detailed information, follow the tours entitled "The Coast" in individual state chapters.

Duration Six to 10 days

The Main Route **One to two nights:** Travel through such classic Connecticut towns as Old Lyme and Mystic, passing through Rhode Island's South County to end up in Newport, with its magnificent turn-of-the-century mansions open for tours.

One to three nights: Stop off in the historic whaling port of New Bedford, Massachusetts, then head for one of the charming summer resort towns of Cape Cod.

One night: Drive north to Boston, one of the country's oldest thriving port cities.

One night: Head north through such historic North Shore fishing towns as Marblehead, Gloucester, and Rockport; visit sea captains' mansions in Newburyport.

Two to three nights: Swing through the Kennebunks and Portland to the small towns and islands around Penobscot Bay.

Factory Outlet Shopping

While this tour generally follows the same coastline as the preceding tour, its focus is less on picturesque surroundings and more on the challenge of finding bargains at New England's wealth of factory outlet stores.

Duration Four days

The Main Route **One night:** Norwalk, Connecticut, has several outlet stores; Mystic, Connecticut, has opened a factory outlet mall off Route 95, across from the Olde Mistick Village mall.

One night: Follow I–95 through Providence, and pick up I–195 to visit the Fall River and New Bedford areas, where there are several outlet malls.

Two nights: Drive north on Route 24 to rejoin I–95. Bypass Boston and head north for the Maine towns of Kittery, Freeport, Wells, and Searsport, where outlet shopping abounds.

Historical Preservations

Although they appear to be simply villages that time forgot, these meticulously preserved hamlets are the products of years of research and painstaking restoration, providing a living lesson in American history that's surprisingly free of commercial gloss. Tour escorts are likely to be immensely learned, and costumed interpreters on site give the eerie impression of having just stepped out of a time machine.

Duration Four to six days

The Main Route **Two nights:** From a base in Boston, venture south on Route 3 to Plimoth Plantation for a glimpse of the lives of the first Puritan settlers. Then refresh your sense of Colonial history by following the

Freedom Trail, a route of fine historic sites in the middle of busy modern Boston.

One night: Head west on the Massachusetts Turnpike to Old Sturbridge Village, which brings to life a prosperous farm town of the 1830s.

One night: I–395 will take you south to Mystic, Connecticut, and Mystic Seaport, a large, lively restoration that focuses on the whaling and shipbuilding industries of the mid- and late 19th century. Some may wish to end this tour here.

One night: A half-day's drive to Hartford and then up I–91 into western Massachusetts will take you to Old Deerfield, a tranquil pre-Revolutionary settlement preserved as a National Historic District.

One night: Take either the Massachusetts Turnpike or the more scenic Mohawk Trail (Rte. 2) west, then take Route 7 to Hancock, Massachusetts, where the Hancock Shaker Village offers a historic glimpse of a way of life that has always stood apart from America's mainstream.

College Towns

As one of the first settled areas in the United States, New England was the site of some of the nation's first colleges and universities. As those fine institutions were joined by others over the years, they enshrined in the American imagination an image of imposing ivy-clad buildings on green, shady campuses. College towns have an added attraction in that they usually offer excellent bookstores and museums, great inexpensive restaurants, and plenty of friendly, casual street life.

Duration Five to 10 days

The Main Route **One to three nights:** In the greater Boston area, perhaps the premier "college town" in the United States, visit the Cambridge campuses of Harvard University and the Massachusetts Institute of Technology and the busy urban campus of Boston University, centered on Kenmore Square. Head to the suburbs to visit Tufts University (Medford), Brandeis University (Waltham), Boston College (Newton), or Wellesley College (Wellesley).

One to two nights: Drive west to the five-college region of the Pioneer Valley, where you can visit Amherst College, Hampshire College, and the University of Massachusetts in Amherst; Mount Holyoke College in the quaint village of South Hadley; and Smith College in the bustling county seat of Northampton.

One to two nights: Head west to Williamstown, home of Williams College, in the Berkshires. Then swing north on Route 7 into Vermont to Bennington, where you'll find Bennington College.

One to two nights: Travel east on Route 9 to Keene State College, in Keene, New Hampshire, a well-kept college town with one of the widest main streets in the world. Head southeast through Worcester, Massachusetts, where Holy Cross is the most well known of several colleges in town, and on to Providence, Rhode Island, where Brown University and the Rhode Island School of Design share a fine hillside site. **One night:** An eastward drive along I–95 will take you to New Haven, Connecticut, the home of Yale University, with its gothic-style quadrangles of gray stone.

Kancamagus Trail

This circuit takes in some of the most spectacular parts of the White and Green mountains, along with the upper Connecticut River Valley. In this area the antiques hunting is exemplary and the traffic is often almost nonexistent. The scenery evokes the spirit of Currier & Ives—or at least the opening sequence of the *Newhart* TV series.

Duration Three to six days

The Main Route **One to three days:** From the New Hampshire coast, head northwest to Wolfeboro, perhaps detouring to explore around Lake Winnipesaukee. Take Route 16 north to Conway, then follow Route 112 west along the scenic Kancamagus Pass through the White Mountains to the Vermont border.

One to two days: Head south on Route 10 along the Connecticut River, past scenic Hanover, New Hampshire, home of Dartmouth College. At White River Junction, cross into Vermont. You may want to follow Route 4 through the lovely town of Woodstock to Killington, then travel along Route 100 and I–89 to complete the loop back to White River Junction. Otherwise, simply proceed south along I–91, with stops at such pleasant Vermont towns as Putney and Brattleboro.

One to two days: Take Route 119 east to Rhododendron State Park in Fitzwilliam, New Hampshire. Nearby is Mt. Monadnock, the most-climbed mountain in the United States; in Jaffrey take the trail to the top. Dawdle along back roads to visit the preserved villages of Harrisville, Dublin, and Hancock, then continue east along Route 101 to return to the coast.

Cape Cod and the Islands

Cape Cod, Martha's Vineyard, and Nantucket are favorite resort areas in and out of season. Because the Cape is only some 70 miles from end to end, day trips from a single base are easily managed. A visit to Martha's Vineyard or Nantucket takes about two hours each way from Hyannis (and it's only 45 minutes to the Vineyard from Woods Hole), so you may want to plan to stay overnight on an island, though a day trip is certainly feasible.

Duration Three to five days

The Main Route **One day:** Drive east on Route 6A to experience old Cape Cod, sampling some of the Cape's best antiques and crafts shops and looking into the historic sites and museums that interest you. Here, too, are charming restaurants and intimate bed-and-breakfasts. A stop at Scargo Hill Tower in Dennis allows a view of the lake, the bay, and the village below.

One day: Take Route 6 east to Provincetown. Do a whale-watch in the morning, spend the afternoon browsing the shops and galleries of the main street, and at sunset go for a Jeep or horseback ride through the dunes of the Province Lands. Try one of Provincetown's fine restaurants—or drive south to Chatham for dinner and theater.

One day: Take Route 6 to the Salt Pond Visitor Center in Eastham and choose your activity: swimming or surf-fishing at Coast Guard or Nauset Light Beach, wandering the bike path, taking a self-guided nature walk, or joining in one of the National Seashore programs. On the way there, you might look into some of the galleries or crafts shops in Wellfleet.

Four to five days: From Hyannis, take a ferry to either Martha's Vineyard or Nantucket. If you choose the Vineyard, visit the Camp Meeting Grounds and the old carousel in Oak Bluffs, then head for the sunset at Gay Head Cliffs before returning on the evening ferry; if you stay over, explore a nature preserve or the historic streets of Edgartown the next day. In Nantucket, you might explore the Whaling Museum, the mansions, and the shops; if you stay over, bike or take a bus to 'Sconset for a stroll around this village of rose-covered cottages and perhaps a swim at a fairly uncrowded beach.

2 Skiing New England

Updated by Craig Altschul, Peggi F. Simmons, and Marty Basch

For close to 100 years the softly rounded peaks of New England have attracted people who want to ski. When blanketed with snow, these mountains generate a quiet beauty that lingers in the mind long after one has left them.

In the beginning you had to climb a mountain in order to realize the experience of skiing down it. Then came the lifts; the first rope tow in the United States was installed at Suicide Six in Woodstock, Vermont. T-bars and chair lifts soon followed, and gondolas and tram cars enclosed and protected skiers from the elements on long rides to mountaintops. Today's high-speed chair lifts move skiers up the mountain in half the time of the older lifts.

Ski lifts made the sport widely accessible, and the continuing development of technology for manufacturing and treating snow when nature fell short has made skiing less dependent on weather conditions. The costs of these facilities—and those of safety features and insurance—are borne by the skier in the price of the lift ticket.

Lift Tickets

Although lift tickets come in many configurations, most people (including the media) make the mistake of listing the single-day, weekend-holiday adult lift pass as the "guidepost." It is always the highest price, and astute skiers look for package rates, multiple days, stretch weekends (a weekend that usually includes a Monday or Friday), frequent-skier programs, season-ticket plans, and off-site purchase locations to save their skiing dollars. Add to this list of bargains the newest lures—specially priced Sunday full and half-day rates for families and computerized data tickets at several resorts.

But, for comparison purposes, a single-day adult lift ticket throughout New England ranges from a low of about $20 to a high of $45. A good bet is that the bigger and more famous the resort, the higher the lift ticket. Be sure to check for senior discounts (over-70s usually ski free) and junior pricing.

On the positive side of things, skiing remains one of the more inexpensive sports, even at resorts that demand top-of-the-line rates. Divide six hours of skiing time into $45 (for a high-end full-day lift ticket), and the price is $7.50 per hour. Considering the costs of the transportation system (lifts) and the snow farming (making snow and grooming it), skiing somehow remains a sports bargain . . . even though it doesn't seem that way anymore.

Lodging

Lodging is among the most important considerations for skiers who plan more than a day trip. While some of the ski areas described in this chapter are small and draw only day trippers, often from nearby towns, most ski areas offer a variety of accommodations—lodges, condominiums, hotels, motels, inns, bed-and-breakfasts—close to or at a short distance from the action. Because of the general state of the New England economy the past few years, some prices have tended to drop a bit to lure skiers back to the hills. There might be a pleasant surprise or two awaiting your pocketbook.

Weekend accommodations can be arranged easily by telephone; for a longer vacation, one should request and study the resort area's accommodations brochure. For stays of three days or more, a package rate may offer the best deal. Packages vary in composition, price, and availability throughout the season; their components may include a room, meals, lift tickets, ski lessons, rental equipment, transfers to the mountain, parties, races, and use of a sports center. Tips and taxes may also be included. Most packages require a deposit upon making the reservation, and a penalty for cancellation usually applies.

Equipment Rental Rental equipment is available at all ski areas, at ski shops around resorts, and even in cities far from ski areas. Shop personnel will advise customers on the appropriate equipment for an individual's size and ability and on how to operate the equipment. It's a good idea to rent ski equipment until you're certain you will stick with the sport and you're competent enough on skis to manage at least easy slopes. Good skiers should ask to "demo" or test premium equipment.

First-time skiers may find that the best way to start is a one-day outing as close to home as possible. On arrival at the ski area, go to the base lodge and ask at an information desk (general information, ski school, or lift-ticket sales) about special arrangements for beginners. Packages usually include basic equipment (rental skis with bindings, ski boots, ski poles), a lesson lasting one hour or more, and a lift ticket that may be valid only on the beginners' slopes.

Trail Rating Ski areas have devised standards for rating and marking trails and slopes that offer fairly accurate guides. Trails are rated Easier (green circle), More Difficult (blue square), Most Difficult (black diamond), and Expert (double diamond). Keep in mind that trail difficulty is measured relative to other trails *at the same ski area*, not to those of an area down the road, in another state, or in another part of the country; a black-diamond trail at one area may rate only a blue square at a neighboring area. Yet the trail-marking system throughout New England is remarkably consistent and reliable.

Lessons Within the United States, the Professional Ski Instructors of America (PSIA) have devised a progressive teaching system that is used with relatively little variation at most ski schools. This allows skiers to take lessons at ski schools in different ski areas and still improve. Class lessons usually last 1½–2 hours and are limited in size to 10 participants. Some ski areas have specific workshops such as "Centered Skiing" (Sugarbush, VT) and "Perfect Turn" (Sunday River, ME; Jiminy Peak, MA).

The skill-transfer feature also applies to children taking lessons. Most ski schools have adopted the PSIA teaching system for children, and many also use SKIwee, which awards progress cards and applies other standardized teaching approaches. Classes for children are normally formed according to age and ability. Many ski schools offer half-day or full-day sessions in which the children ski together with an instructor, eat together, and take their breaks together.

Child Care Nurseries can be found at virtually all ski areas, and some accept children as young as 6 weeks and as old as 6 years. Parents must usually supply formula and diapers for infants; some youngsters may want to bring their own toys. Reservations are advisable. Although skiing may be offered for children at age 3, this activity is geared more to play than to serious learning.

Safety A few words about safety: The cartoon image of a person with a leg in a cast lounging before a fireplace at a ski resort seems to stick in people's minds and is a picture many nonskiers associate with the sport. That image is a carryover from the days of stiff skis, soft boots, and nonreleasing bindings, aggravated by icy slopes and a thin snow cover. Equipment and facilities have improved even in the last 10 years; according to statistics, skiing today is no more hazardous than most other participant sports. Yet accidents occur and peo-

Vermont

Ascutney Mountain Resort, **11**
Bolton Valley Resort, **4**
Bromley Mountain, **13**
Burke Mountain, **5**
Jay Peak, **1**
Killington, **9**
Mad River Glen, **7**
Mt. Snow (Mt. Snow-Haystack), **15**
Okemo Mountain, **12**
Pico Ski Resort, **8**
Smugglers' Notch Resort, **3**
Stowe Mountain Resort, **2**
Stratton, **14**
Sugarbush, **6**
Suicide Six, **10**

New Hampshire

Attitash, **22**
Balsams/Wilderness, **16**
Black Mountain, **20**
Bretton Woods, **17**
Cannon Mountain, **19**
Gunstock, **26**
King Pine Ski Area at Purity Spring Resort, **25**
King Ridge, **27**
Loon Mountain, **21**
Mt. Cranmore, **23**
Mt. Sunapee, **28**
Pats Peak, **29**
Waterville Valley, **24**
Wildcat Mountain, **18**

Maine

Big Squaw Mountain (Moosehead Resort), **30**
Mt. Abram, **34**
Saddleback Ski and Summer Lake Preserve, **32**
Shawnee Peak, **35**
Sugarloaf/USA, **31**
Sunday River, **33**

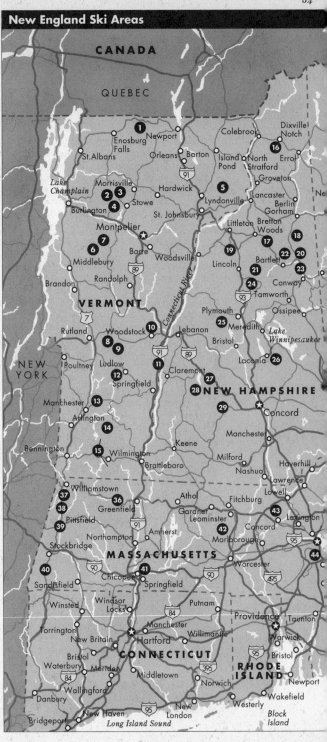

New England Ski Areas

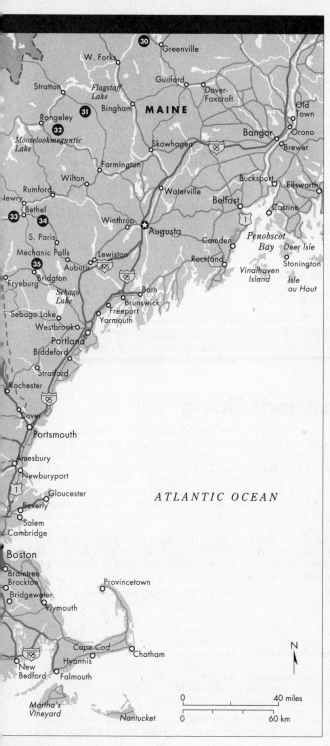

MAINE

W. Forks

Greenville

Stratton

Guilford

Dover-
Foxcroft

*Flagstaff
Lake*

Bingham

Rangeley

Old
Town

*Mooselookmeguntic
Lake*

Skowhegan

Bangor

Orono

Brewer

Farmington

Wilton

Bucksport

Ellsworth

Rumford

Waterville

Newry

Bethel

Belfast

Castine

S. Paris

Winthrop

Augusta

*Penobscot
Bay*

Deer Isle

Camden

Mechanic Falls

Lewiston

Auburn

Rockland

Stonington

*Vinalhaven
Island*

*Isle
au Haut*

Bridgton

Fryeburg

*Sebago
Lake*

Bath

Brunswick

Sebago Lake

Freeport

Yarmouth

Westbrook

Portland

Biddeford

Stratford

Rochester

Dover

Portsmouth

Amesbury

Newburyport

Gloucester

ATLANTIC OCEAN

Beverly

Salem

Cambridge

Boston

Braintree

Brockton

Provincetown

Bridgewater

Plymouth

New
Bedford

Cape Cod

Chatham

Hyannis

Falmouth

*Martha's
Vineyard*

Nantucket

N

0   40 miles

0   60 km

ple are hurt. All ski areas in the United States have trained Ski
Patrolers ready to come to the aid of injured skiers.

Other Activities There is a proliferation of outlet or factory-direct shopping developing in or near New England's ski country. Hundreds of outlets are located in the Mt. Washington Valley town of North Conway, New Hampshire (ski at Cranmore, Wildcat, Attitash, and Black Mountain), and at Manchester Center, Vermont (ski at Bromley and Stratton). In Maine, be sure to stop at Kittery and Freeport (L. L. Bean) on the way in or out. Attractive shopping villages can be found directly at some of the larger resorts, such as Waterville Valley, New Hampshire; Sugarloaf, Maine; and Stratton, Vermont. Nonskiers might also enjoy sports centers at major ski areas (for activities such as indoor tennis, racquetball, and swimming), and there's usually a cross-country ski touring center nearby.

Lodging The following rate categories apply to the hotels and inns described in this chapter. Usually, Very Expensive lodging is slopeside—often a convenience that's worth the money.

Category	Cost*
Very Expensive	over $150
Expensive	$100–$150
Moderate	$60–$100
Inexpensive	under $60

All prices are for a standard double room during peak season, with no meals unless noted, and excluding any service charge and local taxes.

Vermont Skiing

By Craig Altschul and Peggi F. Simmons

The Green Mountains run through the middle of Vermont like a bumpy spine, visible from almost every point in the state, and generous accumulations of snow make the mountains an ideal site for skiing. Today Vermont has 21 Alpine ski resorts with nearly 900 trails and some 4,000 acres of skiable terrain. Together, the resorts offer some 175 lifts and have the capacity to carry a total of more than 200,000 skiers per hour. In addition, the area offers a wide variety of accommodations and dining options, from inexpensive dormitories to luxurious inns, at the base of most ski mountains or within an easy drive. Though grooming is sophisticated at all Vermont areas, conditions usually range from hard pack to icy, with powder a rare luxury. The best advice for skiing in Vermont is to keep your skis well tuned.

Route 100 is well known as the "Skier's Highway," passing by 13 of the state's ski areas. Vermont's major resorts are Stowe, Jay Peak, Sugarbush, Killington, Okemo, Mt. Snow, and Stratton. Midsize, less hectic areas to consider include Ascutney, Bromley, Bolton Valley, Smugglers' Notch, Pico, Mad River Glen, and Burke Mountain. All have less- and more-expensive packages.

Ascutney Mountain Resort
Rte. 44 (Box 699), Brownsville 05037
Tel. 802/484–7711; lodging, 800/243–0011

Rescued by an extraordinary auction, Ascutney launched its 1993–94 season after being closed for several years due to bankruptcy. It's now owned by the Plausteiner family, whose patriarch, John, was instrumental in operations at Mt. Snow, Vermont, and White Face Mountain at Lake Placid, New York. Now with a low debt load, Ascutney's future appears to be much brighter, with its real estate development—once its downfall—now its centerpiece. There's a resort village in five buildings, with hotel suites and condominium units spread throughout. Perhaps the best feature for weary travelers is that the resort is right off I-91.

Downhill Skiing Thirty-one trails with varying terrain are covered by nearly 60% snowmaking. Like a stereotypical ski mountain cutout, this one reaches a wide peak, and gently slopes to the bottom. Beginner and novice skiers stay toward the base, while intermediates enjoy the band that wraps the mid-section; and for experts there are tougher black diamond runs topping the mountain. One disadvantage to Ascutney, however, is that there is no easy way down from the summit, so novice skiers should not make the trip. For intermediate and advanced skiers, though, the Summit Chair is an enjoyable ride up. Trails are serviced by one double and three triple chairs. Ascutney is popular with families because it offers some of the least expensive junior lift tickets in the region.

Cross-Country Skiing Ascutney Mountain Resort offers 32 kilometers (18 miles) of groomed cross-country trails, and provides lessons, clinics, and rentals. Daytime and nighttime guided tours are offered.

Other Activities Ascutney Mountain Resort Hotel has its own sports and fitness Center with full-size indoor and outdoor pools, racquetball, aerobics facilities and classes, weight training, and massage, as well as ice skating on the pond. With public meeting rooms and conference facilities accommodating 40–400 people, it's also an ideal site for meetings and conferences.

Child Care Day care is available for children ages 6 months to 6 years, with learn-to-ski options and rental equipment available for toddlers and up (children 6 and under ski free). The Mountain Ducks are for children 3–6, who have never skied, while the Flying Ducks (also for 3- to 6-year-olds) are for graduates of the Mountain Ducks. You can enroll your child in a half- or full-day session, and most are held on the Duck Soup Trail.

Lodging **Ascutney Mountain Resort Hotel.** One of the big attractions of this five-building resort hotel–condo complex is that the lift is literally outside the main door, making it a ski-in/ski-out property. The comfortable, well-maintained hotel suites come in different configurations and sizes, including three bedrooms with kitchen, fireplace, and deck. The Ascutney Harvest Inn, an attractive restaurant serving Continental and traditional cuisine, is within the complex. Slopeside multilevel condos have three bedrooms, three baths, and private entries to each unit. The entire complex operates more like a resort than a traditional hotel. *Box 699, Brownsville, 05037, tel. 802/ 484–7711 or 800/243–0011, fax 802/484–3117 or 800/243–0011. 240 suites and condos. Facilities: restaurant, 2 lounges, billiard room, separate sports and fitness center. Packages available. AE, MC, V. Expensive–Very Expensive.*

Millbrook Bed And Breakfast. This Victorian farmhouse was built in 1880 and is located directly across from the ski slopes. Within the property are five sitting rooms eclectically decorated with antiques and contemporary furnishings. *Rte. 44 (Box 410), Brownsville 05037, tel. 802/484–7283. 8 rooms, 4 with private bath, 2 with shared bath, and 1 family suite with 2 rooms. Facilities: hot tub, Jacuzzi on* *deck. Full breakfast and afternoon snacks included. MC, V. Inexpensive.*

Additional accommodations selections will be found under Windsor Lodging in the Central Vermont section of the Vermont chapter.

Nightlife **Crow's Nest Club** (tel. 802/484–7711), located in the Ascutney Mountain Resort Hotel, has live entertainment on weekends. **Destiny** (tel. 802/674–6671) in the town of Ascutney, has rock entertainment with live bands during the week and a DJ on Sundays.

Bolton Valley Resort
Box 300, Bolton 05477
Tel. 802/434–2131 or 800/451–3220

Although some skiers come for the day, most people who visit Bolton Valley stay at one of the hotels or condominium complexes at the base of the mountain, all within an easy walk of the ski lifts. Because of this proximity and the relatively gentle skiing, Bolton attracts more family groups and beginners than singles. The mood is easygoing, the dress and atmosphere casual; there is a ski shop, a country store, deli, post office, eight restaurants and lounges, sports club, and meeting and convention space. Package vacation plans, a specialty at Bolton Valley, range from the All-Frills Vacation for two to five days (with hotel accommodations, breakfast and dinner, lift tickets, daily ski lessons, use of the sports center, night skiing, and cross-country skiing) to a Super Saver low-season package that provides accommodations, lift tickets, and sports-club membership. Bolton Valley is in northern Vermont, 20 miles west of Montpelier.

Downhill Skiing Many of the 48 interconnecting trails on Bolton's two mountains, each with a vertical drop of 1,625 feet, are rated intermediate and novice. However, some 23% of the Bolton terrain is rated expert. In fact, as a note of credibility, the DesLauriers brothers of Warren Miller–movie fame ski and work here. Timberline Peak trail network, with a vertical of 1,000 feet, is where you'll find some of the wider slopes and more challenging terrain. Serving these trails are one quad chair, four doubles, and one surface lift—enough to prevent long lift lines on all but the most crowded days. Top-to-bottom trails are lit for night skiing 4–10 PM every evening except Sunday.

Cross-Country Skiing Bolton Valley has 100 kilometers (62 miles) of cross-country trails. Lessons and rentals (including telemark) are available.

Other Activities The sports center has an indoor pool, Jacuzzi, sauna, one indoor tennis court, and an exercise room. Weekly events and activities include sleigh rides, parties, recreational competitions, races, and special family programs. In summer there are eight outdoor tennis courts and a nature center offering guided tours of the region.

Child Care The HoneyBear child care center offers supervised play and games, indoors and outdoors, for infants and children up to 6 years old. Child care is also available three nights per week. For children who want to learn to ski, there's a Bolton Cubs program for ages 5–7, Bolton Bears for ages 6–12, and Mountain Explorers for ages 11–15.

Lodging **Bolton Valley Resort.** Like the ski area, this self-contained resort is geared to families. Hotel units are ski-in, ski-out, and have either a fireplace or a kitchenette; condominium units have as many as four bedrooms. *Bolton Valley 05477, tel. 802/434–2131, fax 804/434–4547. 146 rooms with bath. Facilities: 5 restaurants, deli, pub, fitness center, 9 tennis courts, indoor and outdoor pools, sauna, whirlpool. AE, D, DC, MC, V. Moderate.*

Black Bear Inn. Within the walls of this mountain-top country inn are 24 guest rooms, each with special touches such as quilts made by the innkeeper, in-room movies (a different one each night), and you guessed it—bears! Be sure to ask for a room with a balcony—many of which overlook the Green Mountains and ski trails. *Mountain Rd., Bolton Valley 05477, tel. 802/434–2126 or 800/395–6335, fax 802/434–5761. 24 rooms with bath. Facilities: restaurant, access to sports club, outdoor pool. Ski packages available. MC, V. Inexpensive–Moderate.*

Nightlife   The Bolton Valley Resort's **James Moore Tavern** (tel. 802/434–2131) has live entertainment, and the **Sports Center** (tel. 802/434–2131) organizes social activities and tournament games.

Bromley Mountain
Box 1130, Manchester Center 05255
Tel. 802/824–5522

Venerable Bromley, whose first trails were cut in 1936, is where thousands of skiers learned to ski and learned to love the sport. Today, Bromley attracts families who enjoy its low-key atmosphere as well as experienced skiers who seek their skiing roots. The area has a comfortable red-clapboard base lodge with a large ski shop and a condominium village adjacent to the slopes. Bromley completed a major overhaul of its snowmaking system in 1994.

Downhill Skiing   While most ski areas are laid out to face the north or west, Bromley faces south and east, making it one of the warmer spots to ski in New England. The bulk of its 35 trails are beginner (35%) and intermediate (34%), with some surprisingly good advanced-expert terrain (31%) serviced by the Blue Ribbon quad chair on the east side. The vertical drop is 1,334 feet. Five double chair lifts, one quad lift, a J-bar, and two surface lifts for beginners provide transportation. A reduced-price, two-day lift pass is available. Kids are still kids (price-wise) up to age 14, but they ski free with a paying adult on nonholiday weekdays.

Other Activities   Snowboarding and telemark skiing lessons are offered by the ski school. On weekends the area holds a variety of ski races. In summer an Alpine Slide with mountain rides is a major attraction for adults and children, and the Bromley Village condominiums have a heated outdoor pool and tennis courts.

Child Care   Bromley was one of the first ski areas to have a nursery, and it has maintained its reputation as one of the region's best places to bring children. Besides a nursery for children from one month to age 6 with half-day and all-day sessions, there is ski instruction in the Mighty Moose Club for children ages 3–5. Children 6–14 can attend the All-Day Mountain Club, which includes lunch.

Lodging   The town of Manchester, a center of activity for the resorts of Bromley Mountain and Stratton, offers a large variety of accommodations; additional selections will be found under Manchester Lodging in the Southern Vermont section of the Vermont chapter.

Barrows House. A long-time favorite with Bromley skiers who want to escape the commercial hustle of Manchester, is Jim and Linda McGinniss' 200-year-old inn, located about 8 miles away in nearby Dorset. Ask for one of the five rooms with a fireplace. The dining here is superb. *Rte. 30, Dorset 05251, tel. 802/867–4455 or 800/639–1620. 28 rooms and suites, 7 cottages with bath. Facilities: restaurant, tavern, sauna, outdoor pool, tennis, summer music festival. Full breakfast included; MAP available. MC, V. Expensive.*

The Highland House. "No request is too big" could be the credo of innkeepers Michael and Laurie Gayda and the staff of this 1842 country inn, situated 10 minutes by car from Bromley Mountain, on 32 private acres. The 17 individually decorated rooms contain reproduction furniture, dried-flower wall ornaments, bed quilts, and other country details. Included in the room rate is a hearty New England-style breakfast; in the evenings the six-table dining area becomes a candlelit room. *Rte. 100, Londonderry 05148, tel. 802/824–3019, fax 802/824–3657. 9 rooms in main house, 8 in additional building overlooking pool; all with bath. Facilities: restaurant, 5 km of cross-country ski trails on premises, tennis, outdoor heated pool. Full breakfast included. AE, MC, V. Moderate.*

Johnny Seesaw's. In the central living room of this Adirondack-style shingled cottage are a circular fireplace, a games room with pool table, and a raised alcove dubbed the "seducerie." Rustic rooms vary from small private units and suites to individual cottages with working fireplaces. The inn retains the flavor of the legendary roadhouse it once was. *Rte. 11 (½ mi from slopes), Peru 05152, tel. 802/824–5533 or 800/424–CSAW, fax 802/824–5533. 25 rooms with bath. Facilities: restaurant, tennis, outdoor pool. Closed Apr.–mid-May, late Oct.–Thanksgiving. MC, V. Moderate.*

Nightlife Après-ski action is largely located in Manchester. **Park Bench Café** (tel. 802/362–2557) has live entertainment on Friday and Saturday nights; **Mulligan's Pub & Restaurant** (tel. 802/362–3663) has a DJ on Friday and Saturday nights. The **Marsh Tavern** (tel. 802/362–4700) at the Equinox Hotel has more subdued pop and cabaret music on weekends. (Also, *see* Nightlife in Stratton, *below*.)

Burke Mountain
Box 247, East Burke 05832
Tel. 802/626–3305; lodging, 800/541–5480; snow conditions, 800/922–BURK

Burke has a reputation for being a low-key, family mountain that draws most of its skiers from Massachusetts and Connecticut. In addition to having plenty of terrain for tenderfeet, and intermediate skiers, experts, racers, telemarkers, and snowboarders are stimulated here, as well. Burke also has slopeside lodging and vacation packages, many of which are significantly less expensive than those at other Vermont areas. Burke Mt. Academy has contributed a number of notable racers to the U.S. Ski Team, including Olympians Diann Roffe-Steinrotter, Julie Parisien, Matt Grosjean, and Casey Puckett.

Downhill Skiing With a 2,000-foot vertical drop, Burke is something of a sleeper among the larger eastern ski areas. Although there is limited snowmaking (35%), the mountain's northern location and exposure assure plenty of natural snow. It has one quad, one double chair lift, and two surface lifts. Lift lines, even on weekends and holidays, are light to nonexistent.

Cross-Country Skiing Burke Mountain Ski Touring Center has more than 60 kilometers (37 miles) of groomed trails, some leading to high points with scenic views of the countryside.

Child Care The nursery here takes children ages 6 months to 6 years. SKIwee lessons through the ski school are available to children ages 4–8. Bear Chasers is for ages 9–12, and Ski Max is for ages 13–16.

Lodging **Burke Mountain Resort.** A variety of modern accommodations are available at this resort, from economical to luxurious, fully furnished slopeside studios and one-, two-, three-, and four-bedroom town houses and condominiums with full kitchens and TVs. Some have fireplaces, others have wood-burning stoves. *Box 247, East Burke 05832, tel. 800/541–5480, fax 802/626–3364. Two-night minimum stay required. AE, MC, V. Moderate.*

Old Cutter Inn. Only ½ mile from the Burke Mountain base lodge is this small converted farmhouse with a two-bedroom apartment in a separate building. The restaurant features superb Continental cuisine. *R.R. 1 (Box 62), East Burke 05832, tel. 802/626–5152. 9 rooms, 5 with bath. Facilities: restaurant, lounge, outdoor pool. MAP available. Closed Apr., Nov. MC, V. Inexpensive.*

Nightlife **Burke Mountain Resort** (tel. 802/626–3305) lounge is open most nights and has live dance bands on weekends. In nearby Lyndonville, **Gumby's** (tel. 802/626–3064) and **The Packing House** (tel. 802/626–8777) occasionally have live music.

Jay Peak
Rte. 242, Jay 05859
Tel. 802/988–2611 or 800/451–4449

Jay Peak boasts the most natural snow of any ski area in the East. Sticking up out of the flat farmland, Jay catches an abundance of precipitation from the Maritime provinces of Canada. Its proximity to Québec gives an international flavor to the area—French-speaking and English-speaking skiers mix on the slopes, in the base lodges, at the Hotel Jay, and at the adjacent Jay Peak condominiums. Although Jay is a popular weekend outing for Montréalers, its distance from metropolitan centers along the Eastern seaboard has led to the availability of bargain midweek packages designed to entice skiers to drive the extra hour beyond other northern Vermont areas. In January, for instance, guests of the Hotel Jay ski free Monday through Friday.

Downhill Skiing Jay Peak is in fact two mountains with 45 trails, the highest reaching nearly 4,000 feet with a vertical drop of 2,153 feet, served by a 60-passenger tram (the only one in Vermont). The area also has a quad, a triple, and a double chair lift and two T-bars. The smaller mountain has more straight-fall-line, expert terrain, while the tram-side peak has many curving and meandering trails perfectly suited for intermediate and beginning skiers. Every morning at 9 AM the ski school offers a free tour, from the tram down one trail.

Cross-Country Skiing A touring center at the base of the mountain has 40 kilometers (25 miles) of cross-country trails.

Child Care An indoor nursery for youngsters 2–7 is open from 9 to 4 at the mountain Child Care Center. Guests of Hotel Jay or the Jay Peak Condominiums get this nursery care free, as well as evening care and supervised dining at the hotel. Children 5–12 can participate in an all-day SKIwee program, which includes lunch.

Lodging **Hotel Jay.** Ski-lodge simplicity sets the tone here, with wood paneling in the rooms, built-in headboards, and vinyl wallpaper in the bathroom. This ski-in/ski-out hotel is located right at the lifts, so it's very convenient for people who plan to spend most of their time on the slopes. Rooms on the southwest side have a view of Jay Peak, those on the north overlook the valley, and upper floors have balconies. Summer rates are very low. *Rte. 242, Jay 05859, tel. 802/988–2611 or 800/451–4449, fax 802/988–4049. 48 rooms with bath. Facilities: restaurant, bar, tennis, outdoor pool, games room, sauna, Jacuzzi. Rates are MAP and include lift tickets. AE, D, DC, MC, V. Expensive.*

Jay Peak Condominiums. The 84 condominiums have fully equipped

1–3 bedrooms with modern kitchens, washers/dryers, and spacious living areas with fireplaces. Most are slopeside. *Rte. 242, Jay 05859, tel. 802/988–2611 or, outside VT, 800/451–4449; fax 802/988–4049. 84 units. Facilities: fireplace. Packages include lift tickets and meals. AE, D, DC, MC, V. Expensive.*

Snowline. Situated ¼ mile from the slopes is this small lodge whose hallway was, in part, a building exterior before it was enclosed. Look for early '70s funishings and hooked-rug wall hangings. There's a common room with a TV. The small restaurant offers steaks and burgers. *Rte. 242, Jay 05859, tel. 802/988–2822. 10 rooms with bath. Facilities: restaurant, lounge. AE, D, MC, V. Inexpensive–Moderate.*

Nightlife The **International** restaurant at the ski area base (tel. 802/988–2611) has entertainment on Saturday nights during ski season, and there's often a pianist in the hotel's **Sports Lounge.**

Killington

400 Killington Rd., Killington 05751
Tel. 802/422–3333; snow conditions, 802/422–3261

"Megamountain," "Beast of the East," and just plain "big" are appropriate descriptions of Killington. Considering that this is the largest ski resort in the East—with the most slopes and the greatest number of skiers—Killington manages its crowds very well. Despite its extensive facilities and terrain, lift lines on weekends (especially holiday weekends) can be long, but they move quickly. It has the longest ski season in the East and some of the best package plans anywhere. With a single telephone call (tel. 800/372–2007), skiers can select price, date, and type of ski week they want; choose accommodations; book air or railroad transportation; and arrange for rental equipment and ski lessons. Killington's new Vacation Center offers a marvelous, non-intimidating introduction to the sport. More than 100 lodging establishments serve the Killington region (including Pico and Rutland), though only a few of them are within walking distance of the lifts. On the Bear Mountain side, there are slopeside condominiums in the Sunrise Mountain Village. Some lodges have free shuttles to the area, and there is a scheduled mountain bus service. Six base lodges serve the mountains, and there's a cafeteria-style restaurant on Killington Peak.

Downhill Skiing It would probably take a skier a week to test all 155 trails on the six mountains of the Killington complex, even though everything interconnects. About 63% of the 829 acres of skiing can be covered with machine-made snow, and that's still more snowmaking than any other area in the world can manage. Transporting skiers to the peaks of this complex are a 3½-mile gondola plus seven quads, four triples, and five double chair lifts, as well as two surface lifts. That's a total of 19 ski lifts, a few of which reach the area's highest elevation, at 4,220 feet off Killington Peak, and a vertical drop of 3,150 feet to the base of the gondola. The range of skiing includes everything from Outer Limits, one of the steepest and most challenging trails anywhere in the country, to the 10-mile-long, super-gentle Juggernaut Trail.

Other Activities Killington proper is for skiing, but elsewhere in the region—up and down the access road—there are health clubs, indoor tennis and racquetball courts, ski touring centers, ice skating, and sleigh rides. In summer, Killington has an 18-hole golf course adjacent to a condominium complex; outdoor tennis courts and a tennis school; a concert series; and ballet, theater, and chamber music performances. There is a lift-accessed 37-mile mountain-bike trail system as well. Rutland is one of Vermont's largest and least charming cities, but it's handy, with several malls and movie theaters.

Child Care Nursery care is available for children from infants to 8 years old. For youngsters 3–8, the First Tracks program provides an hour of instruction in the morning or afternoon. The Superstars Program for children 6–12 has all-day skiing, with a break for lunch.

Lodging **Cortina Inn.** The large luxury lodge and miniresort features diverse activities including small-scale exhibits by local artists. About two-thirds of the rooms have private balconies, but the views aren't spectacular. However, the inn is very comfortable and the location is prime—providing easy access to either Killington or Pico. Enjoy sleigh rides, ice skating, and guided snowmobile tours. New England Culinary Institute is in residence. *Rte. 4, Mendon 05751, tel. 802/773–3331 or 800/451–6108, fax 802/775–6948. 98 rooms with bath. Facilities: restaurant, lounge, shuttle service to slopes, 8 tennis courts, indoor pool, fitness center with whirlpools, saunas. AE, D, DC, MC, V. Expensive.*

The Inn at Long Trail. This 1938 inn, with a Gaelic charm (Guinness beer is on tap at the pub) is situated just ¼ mile from the Pico ski slopes. The unusual decor consisting of boulders inside and outside, makes nature a prevailing theme. *Rte. 4 (Box 267), Killington 05751, tel. 802/775–7181 or 800/325–2540. 16 country bedrooms, 6 suites with fireplaces. Facilities: restaurant, bar. Closed June, mid-Oct.–Thanksgiving. MC, V. Expensive.*

Summit Lodge. Located on an access road, just 3 miles from Killington Peak, is this rambling, rustic two-story country lodge that caters to a varied crowd of ski enthusiasts who are warmly met by the lodge's mascots—a pair of Saint Bernards. Country decor and antiques blend with modern conveniences to create a relaxed atmosphere. Two restaurants allow formal and informal dining. *Killington Rd., Killington 05751, tel. 802/422–3535 or 800/635–6343, fax 802/422–3536. 45 rooms with bath, 2 suites. Facilities: 2 restaurants, racquetball, saunas, Jacuzzi, massage, recreation rooms, fireplace lounge, live entertainment, ice-skating pond, outdoor heated pool. AE, DC, MC, V. Expensive.*

Killington Village Inn. A fieldstone fireplace dominates the living room of the chalet-style ski lodge. There's a complimentary shuttle to the mountain's base, a mile away. This country inn is cozy and warm and attracts a good mix of families and singles. *Killington Rd., Killington 05751, tel. 802/422–3301 or 800/451–4105, fax 802/422–3971. 26 rooms with private bath; 2 double dorm rooms with shared bath. Facilities: restaurant, pub, tennis, Jacuzzi. Full breakfast included. AE, D, DC, MC, V. Moderate.*

Mountain Inn. This may be a ski lodge, but it has the feeling of a small luxury resort, and it's within walking distance of Killington's lifts. Rooms are clean, comfortable, motel-style standards. *R.R. 1 (Box 2850), Killington 05751, tel. 802/422–3595. 50 rooms with bath. Facilities: restaurant, lounge, whirlpool, sauna, games room. AE, D, MC, V. Moderate.*

Additional accommodations selections will be found under Rutland Lodging in the Central Vermont section of the Vermont chapter.

Nightlife Try the hot, spicy chicken wings to warm up after skiing at **Casey's Caboose** (tel. 802/422–3795) halfway up the access road. Among the many music-oriented night spots on Killington Road are the **Pickle Barrel** (tel. 802/422–3035), which offers live entertainment on weekends; the **Wobbly Barn** (tel. 802/422–3392), with dancing to blues and rock during ski season; and the **Nightspot/Outback Pizza** (tel. 802/422–9885), a singles-oriented dance club. Outback has acoustic music and brick oven pizza. Near Pico, the lounge at the **Inn at Long Trail** (tel. 802/775–7181) features Irish music on weekends.

Mad River Glen
Rte. 17, Waitsfield 05673
Tel. 802/496–3551; snow conditions, 802/496–2001 or 800/696–2001

Mad River Glen was developed in the late 1940s and has changed relatively little since then; the single chair lift may be the only lift of its vintage still carrying skiers. There is an unkempt aura about this place that for 40 years has attracted core groups of skiers from among wealthy families in the East as well as rugged individualists looking for a less-polished terrain. Remember that most of Mad River's trails are covered only by natural snow (85%) . . . when there is natural snow. The apt area motto is "Ski It If You Can."

Downhill Skiing Mad River is steep. Terrain changes constantly on 33 interactive trails, of which 75% are intermediate to superexpert. Intermediate and novice terrain are regularly groomed. Four chairs (including the famed single) service the mountain's 2,000-foot vertical.

Child Care The Cricket Club nursery (tel. 802/496–2123) takes children 3 weeks to 5 years while the ski school has classes for children 4–12. Junior Racing is available weekends and during holiday periods.

Lodging and Nightlife For information on these, *see* Lodging and Nightlife in Sugarbush, *below*.

Mt. Snow–Haystack
400 Mountain Rd., Mt. Snow 05356
Tel. 802/464–3333 or 802/464–8501; snow conditions, 802/464–2151; lodging, 800/245–SNOW

Mt. Snow is a place where ordinary people can be comfortable and confident and have a good time skiing. The resort is unpretentious, and it makes you feel like part of the skiing community. Mt. Snow was among the first in the east to add a snowboard park. Established in the 1950s, Mt. Snow has come a long way since the 1960s, when its dress-up-and-show-off ski scene earned it the nickname Mascara Mountain. Purchased in 1977 by SKI, Ltd., which also owns Killington (90 minutes away), Mt. Snow reveals its parent's highly professional management from the parking lot and ticket booths to the day-care center and ski-rental area. You may encounter crowds at the ski lifts (and on a weekend you most certainly will), but Mt. Snow knows how to handle them. There's also a bounty of skiing. Your lift ticket can be used not only at Killington (and vice versa) but also at Haystack Mountain (2½ miles away), which Mt. Snow is currently leasing and marketing. A free shuttle connects the two areas by road, and the trail networks merge seamlessly, so that unless you know Mt. Snow well, you never have the sense of moving from one ski area to another. Particularly if you do most of your skiing in small, local areas in the East, the overwhelming sensation is of the sheer size of the place—the combined trail count is 127.

At Mt. Snow, both the bustling Main Base Lodge and the Sundance Base Lodge have food service and other amenities. The Carinthia Base Lodge (site of the old Carinthia ski area, absorbed by Mt. Snow in 1986) is usually the least crowded and most easily accessible from the parking lot. Mt. Snow attracts a good mix of families and single skiers, and it often holds theme weeks such as the popular "Teddy Bear Ski Week" for families. A hotel and several condominiums are within walking distance of the lifts.

Haystack—the southernmost ski area in Vermont—is much smaller than Mt. Snow, but offers a more personal atmosphere, and relatively inexpensive packages are available for families and students; these contain lift tickets that are good only on Haystack. There is a modern, new base lodge close to the lifts, and a condominium village at the base of the mountain and three condo complexes around the golf course provide on-site accommodations; a free shuttle connects skiers to all services.

Downhill Skiing

Mt. Snow is a remarkably well-formed mountain. From its 1,700-foot vertical summit, most of the trails down the face are intermediate, wide, and sunny. Toward the bottom and in the Carinthia section are the beginner slopes; most of the expert terrain is on the North Face. In all, there are 84 trails, of which about two-thirds are intermediate. The trails are served by two quad, six triple, and eight double chair lifts, plus two surface lifts. The ski school's EXCL instruction program is designed to help advanced and expert skiers. On the Lower Exhibition trail, skiers can be videotaped and critiqued free of charge; for a fee, they can then take a 45-minute class with one or two other skiers who need the same type of instruction.

Most of the 43 trails at Haystack are pleasantly wide with bumps and rolls and straight fall lines—good cruising, intermediate runs. There's also a section with three double-black-diamond trails—very steep but short. A beginner section, safely tucked below the main-mountain trails, provides a haven for lessons and slow skiing. Three triple and two double chair lifts and one T-bar service Haystack's 1,400 vertical feet.

Cross-Country Skiing

Four cross-country trail areas within 4 miles of the resort provide more than 100 kilometers (62 miles) of varied terrain.

Other Activities

Sleigh rides and winter nature walks head the list of nonskiing winter activities at Mt. Snow. In summer, Mt. Snow has an 18-hole golf course and from May through September the resort holds a golf school. The area also conducts Vermont's leading mountain-biking instruction program and rents bikes for use on its trails.

Child Care

The lively, well-organized Pumpkin Patch (reservations only) takes children ages 6 weeks through 12 years in three separate sections: a pretty, cheerful nursery for those under 18 months, a comfortable, well-equipped playroom complex for toddlers up to 30 months, and, adjacent, an even bigger room for older kids. Each is well-equipped with age-appropriate toys and balances indoor play, including arts and crafts, with trips outdoors (except when the weather's nasty). Most youngsters over 8 as well as many younger than that sign up for full- or half-day sessions of the ski school–sponsored SKIwee program, designed for youngsters between 4 and 12.

Lodging

Inn at Sawmill Farm. The Williams family's small, aristocratic inn, 3 miles from Mt. Snow, has a distinctive look that's at once rustic and polished, with strong hand-hewn beams and a massive stone fireplace in counterpoint to the attractive traditional furnishings. Life here is on the formal side: Men must wear jackets in public areas after 6 PM. The largest rooms are the 10 in the cottages around the main inn, which include both studios with sitting areas and suites with separate bedrooms; all have working fireplaces. The dining room's menu and extensive wine list are renowned in New England. *Rte. 100, West Dover 05356, tel. 802/464–8131, fax 802/464–1130. 20 rooms with bath. Facilities: outdoor pool, tennis court. AE, MC, V. MAP only. Very Expensive.*

The White House of Wilmington. The grand staircase in this Federal-style mansion leads to spacious rooms that are individually decorated and have antique bathrooms, brass wall sconces, mah-jongg sets, and in some cases the home's original wallpaper. The newer section has more contemporary plumbing; some rooms have fireplaces and lofts. The inn is set back from busy Route 9, so road noise is no problem. A description of the public rooms—heavy velvet drapes, tufted leather wingchairs—suggests formality, yet the atmosphere is casual and comfortable. Although it's just a 10-minute drive to Mt. Snow–Haystack, the White House is primarily a cross-country ski touring center, with a rental shop and 43 kilometers (about 28 miles) of trails. Instruction is also available. *Rte. 9, Wilmington 05363, tel. 802/464–2135 or 800/541–2135. 12 rooms with bath. Facilities: restaurant, lounge, Jacuzzi, sauna, indoor and outdoor pools. AE, DC, MC, V. Breakfast and MAP available. Very Expensive.*

The Hermitage. Everywhere you look in this 19th-century inn—located 3 miles from Mt. Snow, and just ½ mile from Haystack—you'll see evidence of owner Jim McGovern's passion for decoys, wine, and Michel Delacroix prints. (Note the duck pond and roaming game birds.) Rooms are in the vintage main inn, where every room has a fireplace; in the adjacent Wine House built in 1980; and about ½ mile down the road in the Brook Bound Inn, which has more modest rooms and is much less expensive. *Coldbrook Rd. (Box 457), Wilmington 05363, tel. 802/464–3511. 15 rooms with bath in the main inn, 14 rooms with bath at Brook Bound. Facilities: 50 km (31 mi) of cross-country touring tracks, rental equipment, lessons, restaurant, lounge, sauna, tennis court. AE, DC, MC, V. Rates are MAP. Expensive–Very Expensive.*

Nutmeg Inn. This cozy inn, 10 minutes from the slopes at Haystack and Mt. Snow, has all the Colonial touches appropriate to a two-centuries-old farmhouse: an old butter churn, antique dressers, rag rugs, mason jars with dried flowers, and hand-hewn beams in the low-ceiling living room. Equally pleasing are the quilts on the brass beds and the thick carpeting. Three suites in the barn are the largest options; one of them, the king suite, has a private balcony with a terrific view of Haystack Mountain, but all three have a fireplace. *Rte. 9 W, Wilmington 05363, tel. 802/464–3351, fax 802/464–7331. 13 rooms, 9 with wood-burning fireplaces. AE, D, MC, V. Rates include full breakfast. Moderate–Expensive.*

Nightlife The **Snow Barn** (tel. 802/464–3333), near the base of Mt. Snow, has live entertainment weekends during the season; a little farther down Route 100, **Deacon's Den Tavern** (tel. 802/464–9361) and the **Sitzmark** (tel. 802/464–3384) have live bands on weekends. In nearby Wilmington, **Poncho's Wreck** (tel. 802/464–9320) is lively on weekends. For a quieter après-ski experience, there's **Le Petit Chef** (tel. 802/464–8437) or the **Dover Forge** (tel. 802/464–2114).

Okemo Mountain
RFD 1, Ludlow 05149
Tel. 802/228–4041 or 802/228–5571; snow conditions, 802/228–5222

Okemo has evolved and emerged in recent years to become popular as a major resort and an ideal ski area for families with children. The main attraction is a long, broad, gentle slope with two beginner lifts just above the base lodge. All the facilities at the bottom of the mountain are close together, so family members can regroup easily during the ski day. Deluxe slopeside condominiums are located at the base and along some of the lower trails. The net effect of the village area is efficient and attractive. It even boasts today's obligatory clock tower.

Downhill Skiing Above the broad beginner's slope at the base, the upper part of Okemo has a varied network of trails: long, winding, easy trails for beginners, straight fall-line runs for experts, and curving cruising slopes for intermediates. The 72 trails are served by an efficient lift system of six quads, two triple chair lifts, two surface lifts, and 95% are covered by snowmaking. From the summit to the base lodge, the vertical drop is 2,150 feet. The ski school offers a complimentary Ski Tip Station, where intermediate or better skiers can get an evaluation and a free run with an instructor.

Child Care The area's nursery, for children 6 weeks–8 years of age, has a broad range of indoor activities plus supervised outings. Children 3 and up can get brief introduction-to-skiing lessons. All-day or half-day SKIwee (ages 4–8) lessons are available.

Lodging **Okemo Mountain Lodge.** The three-story, brown-clapboard building has balconies and fireplaces in all guest rooms, and the one-bedroom condominiums clustered around the base of the ski lifts are close to restaurants, shops, and the resort's clock tower. Also available are Kettlebrook and Winterplace slopeside condominiums, run by Okemo Mountain Lodging Service. *Rte. 100, RFD 1, Ludlow 05149, tel. 802/228–5571, 802/228–4041, or 800/780–KEMO; fax 802/228–2079. 76 rooms with bath. Facilities: restaurant, lounge, shuttle bus to Ludlow. AE, D, MC, V. Expensive.*

Nightlife **Sitting Bull Lounge** (tel. 802/228–2800), at the base of the mountain, has entertainers; **Dadd's** (tel. 802/228–9820) has electronic games and weekend bands for a little harder rocking.

Pico Ski Resort
2 Sherburne Pass, Rutland 05701
Tel. 802/775–4346; snow conditions, 802/775–4345; lodging, 800/848–7325

Although it's only 5 miles down the road from Killington, venerable Pico has long been a favorite among people looking for uncrowded, low-key skiing. When modern lifts were installed and a village square was constructed at the base, some feared that friendly patina would be threatened, but the relatively new condo-hotel, restaurants, and shops have not altered the essential nature of Pico.

Downhill Skiing From the area's 4,000-foot summit, most of the trails are advanced to expert, with two intermediate bail-out trails for the timid. The rest of the mountain's 2,000 feet of vertical terrain is mostly intermediate or easier. The lifts for these slopes and trails are two high-speed quads, two triples, and three double chairs, plus two surface lifts.

Other Activities A sports center at the base of the mountain has fitness facilities, a 75-foot pool, aerobics section, Jacuzzi, saunas, a nursery, and a massage room.

Child Care The nursery takes children from 6 months through 6 years old and provides indoor activities, outdoor play, and optional ski instruction. The ski school has an Explorer's instruction program for children 3–6 and Mountaineers classes for ages 6–12; either can be taken for full- or half-day periods.

Lodging **Pico Resort Hotel.** This resort at the base of Pico Mountain, a stone's throw from the ski lift, offers condominiums with hotel services. Condos have full kitchen, modern bath, fireplace, daily maid service, and use of the sports center. There are two restaurants—one serves American cuisine, the other pizza—and there's a convenience store on the premises. Live entertainment is scheduled daily in the late afternoon in the base lodge. *Sherburne Pass 05701, tel. 802/747–3000 or 800/848–7325, fax 802/773–3849. 150 units. Facilities: 2 restaurants, base lodge food service, 75-foot indoor lap pool, sports center, Jacuzzi, sauna, TV lounge, conference facilities. AE, MC, V. Moderate–Expensive.*

Additional accommodations selections will be found under Rutland Lodging in the Central Vermont section of the Vermont chapter.

Nightlife *See* Nightlife in Killington, *above.*

Smugglers' Notch Resort
Smugglers' Notch 05464
Tel. 802/644–8851 or 800/451–8752

This resort complex has condominiums, restaurants, a grocery store, sports shops, meeting and convention facilities, and even a post office at the base of the lifts. Most skiers stay at the resort, and a large majority take advantage of the reasonably priced package plans that include lift tickets and daily lessons. Smugglers' has long been respected for its family programs and, therefore, attracts such clientele.

Downhill Skiing Smugglers' is made up of three mountains. The highest, Madonna, with a vertical drop of 2,610 feet, is in the center and connects with a trail network to Sterling (1,500-foot vertical). The third mountain, Morse (1,150-foot vertical), is more remote, but you can visit all three without removing your skis. The tops of each of the mountains have expert terrain—a couple of double black diamonds make Madonna memorable—while intermediate trails fill the lower sections. Morse specializes in beginner trails. The 56 trails are served by five double chair lifts, including the new Mogul Mouse Magic Lift in 1993, and one surface lift. The area has improved its grooming and snowmaking capabilities in recent years and has added a 6.5-million-gallon reservoir and 4 miles of additional snowmaking pipe. There is now top-to-bottom snowmaking on all three mountains.

Cross-Country Skiing Thirty-seven groomed and tracked kilometers (23 miles) of cross-country trails have been laid out.

Other Activities Management committed itself to developing an activities center long before the concept was adopted by other ski resorts. The self-contained village has ice skating, sleigh rides, and horseback riding. For indoor sports, there are hot tubs, tennis courts, and a pool. In summer, Smugglers' offers a water playground, miniature golf, shuffleboard, outdoor tennis courts, and an outdoor pool.

Child Care The Alice's Wonderland Child Care Center is a spacious facility that takes children from 6 weeks through 6 years old. The Discovery Ski Camp gives children 3–6 lessons, movies, games, and story-time entertainment. Adventure Ski Camp for ages 7–12 has all-day skiing and other activities. For teens ages 13–17 there's the Explorer Program, which runs daily, beginning at noon.

Lodging **Smugglers' Notch Resort.** The large year-round resort offers contemporarily furnished condos, most of them with fireplaces and decks. Ski or family packages offer deals for guests who stay several nights. *Rte. 108, Jeffersonville 05464, tel. 802/644–8851 or 800/451–8752, fax 802/644–5913. 350 condo units. Facilities: 3 restaurants, lounge, 2 indoor and 8 outdoor tennis courts, hot tub, indoor pool, exercise equipment, saunas, outdoor ice rink, child-care center, games room, 3 water slides. AE, DC, MC, V, Expensive–Very Expensive.*

The Highlander Motel. Although most of the rooms are motel-style, the Highlander also offers three inn-style, antiques-filled units that look onto the mountain. No matter what configuration you choose, you won't be far from Smugglers' Village, 2½ miles away. For breakfast and dinner you can enjoy your meal by fireside. *Rte. 108 S, Jeffersonville 05464, tel. 802/644–2725 or 800/367–6471, fax 802/644–2725. 15 rooms. Facilities: restaurant, games room. Packages available. MC, V. Moderate.*

Nightlife Most après-ski action centers in Smugglers' Village, where there are afternoon bonfires and nightly live entertainment in the **Meeting House** (tel. 802/644–8851) or **Smugglers' Lounge** (Village Restaurant, tel. 802/644–2291). Sleigh rides, fireworks, and torchlight parades occur twice weekly. **The Brewski** (tel. 802/644–5432), on Route 108 just outside the village, has occasional entertainment. Good dining is available nearby at **Café Banditos** (tel. 802/644-8884), **Crown and Anchor** (tel. 802/644–2900), and **Three Mountain Lodge** (tel. 802/644–5736).

Stowe Mountain Resort

5781 Mountain Rd., Stowe 05672
Tel. 802/253–3000 or 800/247–8693; snow conditions, 802/253–2222

To be precise, the name of the village is Stowe, the name of the mountain is Mt. Mansfield, but to generations of skiers, the area, the complex, and the region are just plain Stowe. This classic resort, steeped in tradition, dates to the 1930s, when the sport of skiing was a pup. Even today the area's mystique attracts more serious skiers than social skiers. In recent years, on-mountain lodging; free shuttle buses that gather skiers from lodges, inn, and motels along the Mountain Road; improved snowmaking; and new lifts have added convenience to the Stowe experience. Yet the traditions remain: the Winter Carnival in January, the Sugar Slalom in April, ski weeks all winter. So committed is the ski school to improvements that even noninstruction package plans include one free ski lesson. Three base lodges provide plenty of essentials, including two on-mountain restaurants.

Downhill Skiing Mt. Mansfield, with a vertical drop of 2,360 feet, is one of the giants among Eastern ski mountains. Its symmetrical shape allows skiers of all abilities long, satisfying runs from the summit. The famous Front Four runs (National, Liftline, Starr, and Goat) are the intimidating centerpieces for tough, expert runs, yet there is plenty of mellow intermediate skiing and one long beginner trail from the top that ends at the Toll House, where there is easier terrain. Mansfield's satellite sector is a network of intermediate and one expert trail off a basin served by a gondola. Spruce Peak, separate from the main mountain, is a teaching hill and a pleasant experience for intermediates and beginners. In addition to the new high-speed, eight-passenger gondola, Stowe has one quad, one triple, and six double chair lifts, plus one handle tow and poma, to service its 45 trails. Night skiing has been added on a three-year trial basis and trails are accessed by the gondola.

Cross-Country Skiing The resort has 40 kilometers (24 miles) of groomed cross-country trails and 40 kilometers (24 miles) of back-country trails. There are four interconnecting cross-country ski areas with over 100 kilometers of groomed trails within the town of Stowe, including the famed Trapp Family Lodge.

Other Activities In addition to sleighing and tobogganing facilities, Stowe boasts a public ice-skating rink with rental skates.

Child Care   The Kanga's Pocket infant care center takes children ages 2 months through 6 years; Pooh's Corner day-care center takes ages 3–12. Children's Adventure Center on nonthreatening Spruce Peak is headquarters for all children's programs, ages 3-12.

Lodging   **Stowe Mountain Resort.** This is the lodging closest to the lifts, owned and operated by the same company that built the ski operation. The resort includes an inn, townhouses, and 40 upscale one- to three-bedroom condominiums. The inn, which was converted from a motel in the 1960s and recently renovated, has folk-art prints. Most of the 34 hotel rooms have balconies. *5781 Mountain Rd., Stowe 05672, tel. 802/253–3000 or 800/253–4754, fax 802/253–2546. 74 rooms with bath. Facilities: 2 restaurants, tavern, tennis, golf, outdoor pool, exercise equipment, whirlpool, sauna, trout pond. Rates are MAP. AE, D, DC, MC, V. Very Expensive.*

Topnotch at Stowe. The 20-year-old resort, situated just 3 miles from the base, is one of the state's most posh. Floor-to-ceiling windows, a freestanding circular stone fireplace, and cathedral ceilings make the lobby an imposing setting, appropriate for the afternoon tea served from a rolling cart. Rooms have thick rust-color carpeting, a small shelf of books, and perhaps a barnboard wall or an Italian print. The restaurant is renowned, and there's a health spa. *Mountain Rd., Stowe 05672, tel. 802/253–8585 or 800/451–8686, fax 802/253–9263. 92 rooms with bath, 14 2–3 bedroom town homes, 8 suites. Facilities: 3 restaurants, lounge, 4 indoor and 10 outdoor tennis courts, indoor and outdoor pools, stables. AE, D, MC, V. Very Expensive.*

The Gables Inn. The converted farmhouse is a rabbit warren of charming, antiques-filled rooms. The four rooms in the carriage house have cathedral ceilings, fireplaces, TVs, whirlpool tub, and are open year-round. There is a porch with comfortable chairs on which you can enjoy the view of Mt. Mansfield. The tiny plant-filled sunroom is fine for lazy mornings, and the innkeepers are known for generous breakfasts. *Mountain Rd., Stowe 05672, tel. 802/253–7730 or 800/422–5371, fax 802/253–8989. 17 rooms with bath. Facilities: TV, lounge, hot tub, outdoor pool, room equipped for people with disabilities. Rates are MAP. AE, D, MC, V. Expensive–Very Expensive.*

Stowe Inn At Little River. The former Yodler Hotel, located in Stowe Village, has been totally renovated and restored, and is considered one of Stowe's top lodging properties. Moreover, a trolley to the lifts comes to the front door, so you won't need a car. The unpretentious, 40-room inn is now owned by veteran resort hosts Linda and Bruce Watson. Choose from accommodations in the Main Inn with 18 rooms, all with private bath; or in the 22-units Carriage House, where several of the rooms have fireplaces. American cuisine is served in the contemporary dining area. There's even a full-scale Weather Station in the lobby. *123 Mountain Rd, Stowe 05672, tel. 802/253–4836 or 800/227–1108, fax 802/253–7308. 40 rooms with bath, 4 efficiencies, 5 luxury suites. Facilities: restaurant, hot tub, outdoor pool, clay tennis court. AE, MC, V. Moderate–Expensive.*

Additional nearby accommodations are described under Stowe Lodging in the Northern Vermont section of the Vermont chapter.

Nightlife   The **Matterhorn Night Club** (tel. 802/253–8198) has music for dancing. The **Rusty Nail Saloon** (tel. 802/253–9444) and **BK Clark's** (tel. 802/253–9300) also provide live music. Other options include the lounges at **Topnotch at Stowe** (tel. 802/253–8585) for live weekend entertainment, and the less-expensive **Stoweflake Inn** (tel. 802/253–7355).

Stratton

Stratton Mountain 05155
Tel. 802/297–2200 or 800/843–6867; snow conditions, 802/297–4211

Since its creation in 1961, Stratton has undergone several physical transformations and upgrades, yet the area's sophisticated character has been retained. It has been the special province of well-to-do families and, more recently, young professionals from the New York–southern Connecticut corridor. Since the mid-80s, an entire village, with a covered parking structure for 700 cars, has arisen at the base of the mountain. Adjacent to the base lodge are a condo-hotel, restaurants, and about 25 shops lining a pedestrian mall. Beyond that complex are many ski-in, ski-out villas and several condominiums and town houses minutes away from the slopes. Across the main road and accessible by shuttle are three more good-size hotel-inns. Package plans are available, and conventions and meetings can be accommodated. Stratton is a self-contained center 4 miles up its own access road off Route 30 in Bondville, and about 30 minutes from Manchester's popular shopping zone.

Downhill Skiing   Stratton's skiing comprises three sectors. The first is the lower mountain directly in front of the base lodge-village-condo complex; a number of lifts reach mid-mountain from this entry point, and practically all skiing is beginner or low-intermediate. Above that, the upper mountain, with a vertical drop of 2,000 feet, is graced with a high-speed, 12-passenger gondola, *Starship XII*. Down the face are the expert trails, while on either side are intermediate cruising runs with a smattering of wide beginner slopes. The third sector, the Sun Bowl, is off to one side with two quad chair lifts and two new expert trails, a full base lodge, and a lot of intermediate terrain. A new Ski Learning Park with 10 trails and 5 lifts has its own "Park Packages" available for novice skiers. In all, Stratton has 92 slopes and trails served by the gondola and four quad, one triple, six double chair lifts, and two surface lifts.

Cross-Country Skiing   The Stratton area has 22 kilometers (12 miles) of cross-country skiing on the Sun Bowl side of the mountain.

Other Activities   The area's sports center has two indoor tennis courts, three racquetball courts, a 25-meter indoor swimming pool, a Jacuzzi, a steam room, a fitness facility with Nautilus equipment, and a restaurant. The summertime facilities include 15 additional outdoor tennis courts, 27 holes of golf, horseback riding, and mountain biking. Instruction programs in tennis and golf are offered. The area hosts a summer entertainment series and is home of an LPGA golf tournament and the Women's Hardcourt Tennis Championships.

Child Care   The day-care center takes children ages 6 weeks through 5 years for indoor activities and outdoor excursions in mild weather. The ski school has a Little Cub program for ages 4–6 and Big Cub for 7–12; both are daylong programs with lunch. SKIwee instruction programs are also available for ages 4–12. A junior racing program and special instruction groups are aimed at more-experienced junior skiers.

Lodging   The town of Manchester, a center of activity for the resorts of Stratton and Bromley Mountain, offers a large variety of accommodations; additional selections will be found under Manchester Lodging in the Southern Vermont section of the Vermont chapter.

Windham Hill Inn. In the converted, turn-of-the-century dairy barn, two rooms share an enormous deck that overlooks the West River Valley. Rooms in the main building (some have a balcony) are more formal, but personal touches abound throughout the inn, including antiques-adorned rooms and a restored Steinway piano for guests to plunk. Guests can dine alone or at a communal table for dinner. The inn is reserved for nonsmokers. *West Townshend 05359, tel. 802/874–4080, fax 802/874–4702. 15 rooms with bath. Facilities: restaurant, lounge, fireplaces in common areas, skating pond, 10 km (6 mi) cross-country trails (equipment, instruction). Closed in early spring and Nov.–Thanksgiving. AE, MC, V. Very Expensive.*

Stratton Mountain Inn and Village Lodge. The complex includes a 125-room inn—the largest on the mountain—and a 91-room lodge built in 1985, which has studio units. Ski packages that include lift tickets bring down room rates. *Stratton Mountain Rd., Stratton Mountain 05155, tel. 802/297–2500 or 800/777–1700, fax 802/297–1778. 216 rooms with bath. Facilities: 2 restaurants, golf, outdoor pool, racquetball, tennis, sauna, 2 Jacuzzis. AE, D, DC, MC, V. Expensive–Very Expensive.*

Nightlife One of the better lounges at Stratton Mountain is **Mulligan's** (tel. 802/297–9293), which has three bars on three floors, American cuisine, and dancing to DJs and live bands in the late afternoon and on weekends. **Haig's** (tel. 802/297–1300) in Bondville, 5 miles from Stratton, has a unique indoor simulated golf course for those who can't wait for summer. **The Red Fox Inn** (tel. 802/297–2488), 5 miles from the ski area, has a DJ and occasional live music in the tavern. (*See also* Nightlife in Bromley, *above*.)

Sugarbush
Box 350, Warren 05674
Tel. 802/583–2381; snow conditions, 802/583–7669; lodging, 800/53–SUGAR

In the early 1960s Sugarbush had the reputation of being an outpost of an affluent and sophisticated crowd from New York. While that reputation has faded, Sugarbush has maintained a with-it aura for the smart set—not that anyone would feel uncomfortable here. The base of the mountain has a village of condominiums, restaurants, shops, bars, and a sports center, and just down the road is the Sugarbush Inn, recently acquired by the ski area.

Downhill Skiing Sugarbush is two distinct mountain complexes. The Sugarbush South area is what old-timers recall as Sugarbush Mountain: With a vertical of 2,400 feet, it is known for formidable steeps toward the top and in front of the main base lodge. In recent years, intermediate trails that twist and turn off most of the lifts have been widened and regraded to make them more inviting. This sector has three triple, four double, and two surface lifts that together serve 110 trails. The Sugarbush North peak offers what the South side has in short supply—beginner runs. North also has steep fall-line pitches and intermediate cruisers off its 2,600 vertical feet. This mountain has three quads (including a high-speed version), two double chair lifts, and two surface lifts. Snowmaking improvements to Sugarbush South have doubled capacity, greatly improving early and late season skiing. There are plans to connect the two mountains with a series of lifts and trails, but for the present a shuttle bus takes skiers back and forth. Top-level racers seem to spew out of the Green Mountain Academy in Waitsfield.

Cross-Country Skiing More than 25 kilometers (15 miles) of marked cross-country trails are adjacent to the Sugarbush Inn.

Other Activities Two sports centers near the ski lifts have Nautilus and Universal equipment; indoor and outdoor tennis, squash, and racquetball courts; Jacuzzi, sauna, and steam rooms; an indoor pool; and outdoor skating. In summer there are 36 outdoor tennis courts, 9 outdoor pools, and an 18-hole golf course on the Sugarbush property.

Child Care The Sugarbush Day School accepts children ages 6 weeks through 6 years; older children have indoor play and outdoor excursions. The Minibear Program introduces children ages 4–5 to skiing as an adjunct to the nursery. For children 6–11 years, the Sugarbear instruction program operates half days or full days.

Lodging **Sugarbush Inn.** This yellow-clapboard country inn is the centerpiece of the entire resort, with activities to interest all family members. The plant-filled public areas are spacious, and bedrooms have been remodeled recently. The large enclosed porch is used as a dining area. *R.R. 1 (Box 350), Warren 05674, tel. 802/583–3333 or 800/53–SUGAR, fax 802/583–3209. 46 rooms with bath. Facilities: 3 restaurants, 11 tennis courts, golf, weight room, games room, complete sports pavilion with indoor swimming pool. AE, D, DC, MC, V. Moderate–Very Expensive.*

PowderHound Resort. Most of the rooms in this farmhouse-turned-inn that dates back more than 100 years, are two-room suites with a living area, bath, and kitchenette. *Rte. 100 (Box 369), Warren 05674, tel. 802/496–5100 or 800/548–4022. 44 units with bath. Facilities: restaurant, lounge, tennis, volleyball, croquet, shuttle to lifts, outdoor pool, hot tub. Ski packages available. MC, V. Moderate–Expensive.*

Mad River Barn. Maintaining its 1940s ski-lodge style ambience is this inn, situated in nearby Waitsfield, and decorated with pine-panelling and otherwise simple furnishings. The guest rooms are large, and there are additional quarters in the renovated farmhouse. A trail from Mad River Glen runs to the lodge. *R.R. 1 (Box 88), Waitsfield 05673, tel. 802/496–3310; no fax. 15 rooms with bath. Facilities: restaurant, bar, lounge, game room, sundeck. MC, V. MAP. Moderate.*

Christmas Tree Inn. Situated on the access road is this modern country-style inn that's only 3 miles from Sugarbush and 7 miles from Mad River. In addition to the 12 country-yet-contemporary rooms there are 29 condos, each with one or three bedrooms, fireplace, cable TV, full kitchen, and telephones. Antiques and Laura Ashley accents set the tone throughout, and seem to appeal to the mostly couples and families who stay here. Breakfast is served in the inn's dining room. Handmade jigsaw puzzles are set out around the large fireplace in the main room to challenge guests. *Sugarbush Access Rd., Warren 05674, tel. 802/583–2211 or 800/535–5622. 12 rooms with bath, 29 condos. Facilities: sports bar, 2 outdoor pools, tennis. Full breakfast included for inn guests only. AE, MC, V. Inexpensive–Moderate.*

Golden Lion Riverside Inn. At the base of the road to the Sugarbush ski area, is this small, riverside family motel that's guarded by a golden chainsaw-carved lion. The fireside lobby, where hearty country breakfast is served, is cozy; rooms are standard motel decor. *Rte. 100 at Access Rd. (Box 336), Warren 05674, tel. 802/496–3084. 12 rooms with bath; 1 efficiency; 1 apartment. Facilities: riverside beach. Full breakfast included; packages available. AE, D, MC, V. Inexpensive–Moderate.*

Nightlife In Sugarbush Village, **Chez Henri** (tel. 802/583–2600), a trailside restaurant open for lunch and dinner, has long been the leading dance spot. The **Blue Tooth** (tel. 802/583–2656) has a variety of live entertainment and dancing during ski season and is popular with the singles crowd; it's on the access road to Sugarbush.

Suicide Six
Woodstock 05091
Tel. 802/457–1666; snow conditions, 802/457–1622

Suicide Six, site of the first ski tow in the United States, is owned and operated by the Woodstock Inn and Resort. The inn, located in lovely Woodstock Village, 3 miles from the ski area, offers package plans that are remarkably inexpensive, considering the high quality of the accommodations. In addition to skiers interested in exploring Woodstock, the area attracts students and racers from nearby Dartmouth College.

Downhill Skiing Despite Suicide Six's short vertical of only 650 feet, the area offers challenging skiing. There are several steep runs down the mountain's face and intermediate trails that wind around the hill. Beginner terrain is mostly toward the bottom. The 19 trails are serviced by two double chair lifts and one surface lift.

Cross-Country Skiing The ski touring center has 60 kilometers (37 miles) of trails. Equipment and lessons are available.

Other Activities A sports center at the Woodstock Inn and Resort (tel. 802/457–1100) has an indoor lap pool; indoor tennis, squash, and racquetball courts; whirlpool, steam, sauna, and massage rooms; and exercise and aerobics rooms. Outdoor tennis courts, lighted paddle courts, croquet space, and an 18-hole golf course are available in the summer.

Child Care Although the ski area has no nursery, baby-sitting can be arranged; lessons for children are given by the ski-school staff. Children's ski-and-play park has been added for ages 3–7.

Lodging Accommodations selections will be found under Quechee and Woodstock Lodging in the Central Vermont section of the Vermont chapter.

Nightlife Bentley's (tel. 802/457–3232) in Woodstock has a DJ and dancing on weekends. There is often live entertainment in **Richardson's Tavern** at the **Woodstock Inn and Resort** (tel. 802/457–1100).

New Hampshire Skiing

Magnificent Mt. Washington, which looms like a beacon over the White Mountains, may have been the original attraction in the northern region of New Hampshire. Scandinavian settlers who came to the high, handsome, rugged peaks in the late 1800s brought their skis with them. But skiing got its modern start in the Granite State in the 1920s, with the cutting of trails on Cannon Mountain.

Today there are 28 ski areas in New Hampshire, ranging from the old, established slopes (Cannon, Cranmore, Wildcat) to the most contemporary (Attitash, Loon, Waterville Valley). Whatever the age of the area, traditional activities—carnivals, races, ski instruction, family services—are important aspects of the skiing experience. On the slopes, skiers encounter some of the toughest runs in the country alongside some of the gentlest, and the middle range is a wide one.

The New Hampshire ski areas participate in a number of promotional packages allowing a sampling of different resorts. There's Ski 93 (referring to resorts along I–93), Ski New Hampshire, Ski the Mt. Washington Valley, and more.

Attitash
Rte. 302, Bartlett 03812
Tel. 603/374–2368

In the 1980s a new, savvy management at Attitash directed the resort's appeal to active young people and families. Keeping a high and busy profile, the area hosts many activities, race camps, and demo equipment days. Lodging at the base of the mountain is available in condominiums and motel-style units a bit away from the hustle of North Conway. Attitash has a computerized lift ticket system; skiers now go through turnstiles on their way to the lifts. In essence, the Smart Ticket allows you to pay by the run. Skiers can share the ticket, which is good for two years (including summer when it can be used on the slides). Attitash expects a new infusion of capital, which will ultimately lead to further improvements.

Downhill Skiing Enhanced with massive snowmaking, the trails and lifts have expanded significantly in recent years. There are expert pitches at the top of the mountain (try Idiot's Option, for example), but the bulk of the skiing is geared to advanced-intermediates and below, with wide fall-line runs from mid-mountain. Beginners have a share of good terrain on the lower mountain. Serving the 22 miles of trails and the 1,750-foot vertical drop are two triple and four double chair lifts.

Other Activities Attitash has two Alpine Slides and five water slides in summertime; and concerts, stock theater, rodeo, and a horse show are held on premises. There's also horseback and pony riding, a golf driving range, and a scenic chairlift to the White Mountain observation tower.

Child Care Attitots Clubhouse takes children ages 6 weeks through 5 years. Children's programs are Attitots Plus (3 years of age), Mini Attiteam (4–5 years of age), Attiteam (6–8 years of age), Attidudes (9–12 years of age), and Attiteens (13–16 years of age). Children's programs are all housed at the Attitash Children's Center.

Lodging **Attitash Mountain Village.** This condo-motel complex—just across the street from the mountain, via a tunnel under the road—has a glass-enclosed pool and units that will accommodate 2–14 people. Those quarters with fireplaces and kitchenettes are especially good for families. The style is Alpine-contemporary; the staff, young and enthusiastic. *Rte. 302, Bartlett 03812, tel. 603/374–6501 or 800/862–1600, fax 603/374–6509. 250 rooms with bath. Facilities: restaurant, pub, games room, indoor pool, sauna, whirlpool. AE, D, MC, V. Expensive.*

Best Western Storybook Resort Inn. This family-owned, family-run motor inn is well suited to families, particularly because of its large rooms on the hillside. Copperfield's Restaurant has gingerbread, sticky buns, farmer's omelets, and a children's menu. *Box 129, Glen Junction 03838, tel. 603/383–6800 or 800/528–1234, fax 603/374–6509. 78 rooms with bath. Facilities: restaurant, indoor and outdoor pool, sauna. AE, DC, MC, V. Inexpensive–Moderate.*

More than 100 hotels, lodges, and motels are located in the Mt. Washington Valley. Many can be reached through the Mount Washington Valley Chamber of Commerce Travel and Lodging Bureau (tel. 800/223–SNOW).

Nightlife *See* Nightlife in Mt. Cranmore and Wildcat, *below.*

Balsams/Wilderness
Dixville Notch 03576
Tel. 603/255–3400 or 800/255–0600; in NH, 800/255–0800; snow conditions, 603/255–3951

Maintaining the tradition of a grand resort hotel is the primary goal at Balsams/Wilderness. Skiing was originally provided as an amenity for hotel guests, but the area has since become popular with day trippers, as well. Restoration and renovation of the large, sprawling structure that dates to 1866 has been continuous since the early 1970s. Guests will find many nice touches: valet parking, gourmet meals, dancing and entertainment nightly, cooking demonstrations, and other organized recreational activities.

Downhill Skiing Sanguinary, Umbagog, Magalloway are the tough-sounding slope names that are really only moderately difficult, leaning toward intermediate. There are trails from the top of the 1,000-foot vertical drop for every skill level. One double chair lift and two T-bars carry skiers up the mountain.

Cross-Country Skiing Balsams/Wilderness has 70 kilometers (45 miles) of cross-country skiing, tracked and also groomed for skating (a cross-country ski technique), with natural-history markers annotating some trails.

Other Activities In winter, the area offers ice skating, hayrides, sleigh rides, snowshoeing, and snowmobiling. In summer, the resort has 27 holes of golf; six tennis courts; two trap fields; a heated outdoor pool; boating, swimming, and fly fishing on Lake Gloriette; and trails for hiking and climbing.

Child Care The nursery takes children up to age 6 at no charge to hotel guests, however, there is a fee for day-trippers. Wind Whistle lessons are designed to introduce skiing to children 3–5 years old. For those 5 and up, group lessons are available.

Lodging A full review of the Balsams Grand Resort Hotel will be found under Dixville Notch Dining and Lodging in the White Mountains section of the New Hampshire chapter.

Black Mountain
Rte. 16B, Jackson 03846
Tel. 603/383–4490; in NH, 800/698–4490

The setting is 1950s, the atmosphere is friendly and informal, and skiers have fun here. There's a country feeling at the big base building, which resembles an old farmhouse, and at the skiing facilities, which generally have no lines. Black has the essentials for families and singles who want a low-key skiing holiday. The Family Passport allows two adults and two juniors to ski at discounted rates. Midweek rates here are usually the lowest in Mt. Washington Valley.

Downhill Skiing The bulk of the terrain is easy to middling, with intermediate trails that wander over the 1,100-vertical-foot mountain. Devil's Elbow on the Black Beauty trail—once a real zinger—has been expanded and is no longer as difficult to ski. The lifts are a triple and a double chair lift and two surface tows. Most of the skiing is user-friendly, particularly for beginners. The southern exposure adds to the warm atmosphere.

Cross-Country Skiing Black is near some of the finest cross-country skiing in the East. Contact the Jackson Ski Touring Foundation (Box 216, Jackson Village, NH 03846, tel. 603/383–9355). JSTF has about 154 kilometers (94 miles) that wind through Jackson Village, along the Ellis River, and up into the backcountry.

Other Activities In addition to having access to ski trails, snowboarders can also use the halfpipe to practice their freestyle stunts.

Child Care The nonski nursery takes children up to 6 years old. The ski school offers Penguin Peak Skiing Nursery for ages 3–6, and the 1st Mountain Division for ages 6–12.

Lodging **Nordic Village.** The light wood and white walls of these deluxe condos are as Scandinavian as the snowy views. The Club House has a pool and spa, and there is a nightly bonfire at Nordic Falls. Fireplaces, full kitchens, and Jacuzzis can be found in the larger units; some economy cottages have wood stoves and kitchenettes. *Rte. 26, Jackson 03846, tel. 603/383–9101 or 800/472–5207, fax 603/383–9823. 135 apartments. Facilities: heated indoor and outdoor pools, therapy spa, steam room, skating area, sleigh rides, whirlpool, Jacuzzi. AE, MC, V. Moderate–Very Expensive.*

Whitneys' Village Inn. The Bowman family brings more than 30 years of inn-keeping experience to this classic country inn at the base of Black Mountain. You'll find antiques in the living room, period pieces in the one-of-a-kind bedrooms (some with sitting area), and suites that can take the bang of ski-week families. The windows of the dining room look out onto the slopes. *Box W, Jackson 03846, tel. 603/383–8916 or 800/677–5737. 28 rooms with bath, 2 cottages. Facilities: restaurant, games room, pond. Rates are MAP. AE, DC, MC, V. Moderate–Expensive.*

Additional accommodations selections will be found under Jackson Dining and Lodging in the White Mountains section of the New Hampshire chapter.

Nightlife The **Shovel Handle Pub** in Whitneys' Village Inn (tel. 603/383–8916) is the après-ski bar adjacent to the slopes.

Bretton Woods

Rte. 302, Bretton Woods 03575
Tel. 603/278–5000; information, 800/232–2972; lodging, 603/278–1000

Bretton Woods offers comfort and convenience in the attractive three-level open-space base lodge, the drop-off area, the easy parking, and the uncrowded setting that make skiing a pleasant experience for families. On-mountain town houses are available with reasonably priced packages through the resort. The spectacular views of Mt. Washington itself are worth the visit; the scenery is especially beautiful from the new on-mountain Top o' Quad restaurant.

Downhill Skiing The skiing on the 30 trails is mostly gentle, with some intermediate pitches near the top of the 1,500-foot vertical, and a few expert runs. One quad, one triple, and two double chair lifts, and one T-bar service the trails. The area has night skiing Friday, Saturday, and holidays. A limited lift-ticket policy helps keep lines short.

Cross-Country Skiing A short distance from the base of the mountain is a large cross-country center with 86 kilometers (51 miles) of groomed and double-track trails.

Other Activities A recreation center has racquetball, saunas and whirlpools, indoor swimming, an exercise room, and a games room. In summer the mountain is turned into a summer park, with in-line skating and mountain biking, as well as 27 holes of golf, 12 tennis courts, an outdoor pool, fly fishing, and hiking are available at the Mount Washington Hotel (tel. 603/278–1000).

Child Care The nursery takes children ages 2 months through 3 years. The Hobbit Ski School, and all-day program for ages 4–12, uses progressive instructional techniques. Rates include lifts, lessons, equipment, lunch, and supervised play.

Lodging **Bretton Arms.** Built in 1896, this restored historic inn predates even the grande dame Mount Washington Hotel across the way, so you know that the trendsetters of the last century stayed here. Reservations are required in the dining room and should be made on arrival. Guests are invited to use the facilities of the historic Mount Washington Hotel during the summer and the Lodge at Bretton Woods year-round. *Rte. 302, Bretton Woods 03575, tel. 603/278–1000 or 800/258–0330, fax 603/278–3457. 34 rooms with bath. Facilities: restaurant, lounge, free shuttle service. MC, V. Expensive.*

Lodge at Bretton Woods. Rooms have contemporary furnishings, a balcony, and views of the Presidential Range. Darby's Restaurant serves Continental cuisine around a circular fireplace, and the bar is a hangout for après skiers. The lodge, across the road from the Mount Washington Hotel, shares its facilities in summer. *Rte. 302, Bretton Woods 03575, tel. 603/278–1000 or 800/258–0330, fax 603/278–3457. 50 rooms. Facilities: restaurant, indoor pool, spa pool, sauna, whirlpool, games room, lounge. MC, V. Moderate.*

Additional accommodations will be found under Bretton Woods Lodging in the White Mountains section of the New Hampshire chapter.

Cannon Mountain
Franconia Notch State Park, Franconia 03580
Tel. 603/823–5563; snow conditions, 603/823–7771 or 800/552–1234

Nowhere is the granite of the Granite State more pronounced than at Cannon Mountain, where you'll find the essentials for feeling the thrill of downhill. One of the first ski areas in the United States, the massif has retained the basic qualities that make the sport unique—the camaraderie of young people who are there for challenge and family fun. The New England Ski Museum is located adjacent to the base of the tramway. Cannon is owned and run by the state, and as a result, greater attention is being paid to skier services, family programs, snowmaking, and grooming.

Downhill Skiing The tone of this mountain's skiing is reflected in the narrow, steep pitches off the peak of the 2,146 feet of vertical rise. Some trails marked intermediate may seem more difficult because of the sidehill slant of the slopes (rather than the steepness). Under a new fall of snow, Cannon has challenges not often found at modern ski areas. There is an 80-passenger tramway to the top, one quad, one triple, and two double chair lifts, and one surface lift.

Cross-Country Skiing Nordic skiing is available on a 13-kilometer (8.2-mile) bicycle path through Franconia Notch State Park.

Child Care Cannon's Peabody Base Lodge takes children 1 year and older. All-day and half-day SKIwee programs are available for children 4–12, and season-long instruction can be arranged.

Lodging **Indian Head Resort.** Views of Indian Head Rock, the Great Stone Face, and the Franconia Mountains are available across the 180 acres of this resort motel. Take Exit 33 from I-93, then Route 3 north. *Rte. 3, North Lincoln 03251, tel. 603/745–8000 or 800/343–8000, fax 603/745-8414. 98 rooms with bath. Facilities: restaurant, games room, outdoor and indoor pools, sauna, whirlpool, tennis. AE, D, DC, MC, V. Moderate–Expensive.*

Horse and Hound Inn. Off the beaten path and yet convenient to the Cannon Mountain tram 2¾ miles away, is this traditional inn set on 8 acres surrounded by the White Mountain National Forest. Antiques and assorted collectibles offer guests a cheery atmosphere, and on the grounds are 10 kilometers (6 miles) of cross-country ski trails. *205 Wells Rd., Franconia 03580, tel. 603/823–5501. 10 rooms, 8 with bath; 2 suites. Facilities: restaurant, bar, lounge, pool table. Closed Apr. Full breakfast included. AE, DC, MC, V. Moderate.*

Additional accommodations will be found under Franconia Dining and Lodging in the White Mountains section of the New Hampshire chapter.

Nightlife   There's live nightly entertainment in the **Thunderbird Lounge** at the **Indian Head Resort** (tel. 603/745–8000). **Hillwinds** (tel. 603/823–5551), on Main Street in Franconia, offers live entertainment weekends.

Gunstock
Box 1307, Laconia 03247
Tel. 603/293–4341 or 800/GUNSTOCK; snow conditions, 603/293–4345

High above Lake Winnipesaukee, the pleasant, all-purpose ski area of Gunstock attracts some skiers for overnight stays and others—many from Boston and its suburbs—for the day's skiing. Gunstock allows skiers to return lift tickets for a cash refund for any reason—weather, snow conditions, health, equipment problems. That policy plus a staff of customer-service people give a bit of class to an old-time ski area; Gunstock dates to the 1930s.

Downhill   Some clever trail cutting, summer grooming, and surface sculpting
Skiing   have made this otherwise pedestrian mountain an interesting place for intermediates. That's how most of the 39 trails are rated, with designated sections for slow skiers and learners. The 1,400 feet of vertical has one quad, two triple, and two double chair lifts and two surface tows. Gunstock has also improved its night skiing facilities.

Cross-Country   The Gunstock ski area offers 32 kilometers (19 miles) of cross-coun-
Skiing   try trails.

Child Care   The nursery takes children from infants up. The ski school teaches the SKIwee system to children 3–12.

Lodging   **B. Mae's Resort Inn.** All the rooms in this resort and conference center are large; some one-bedroom condominiums have kitchens. *Rte. 11A, Gilford 03246, tel. 603/293–7526 or 800/458–3877, fax 603/293–4340. 82 rooms with bath. Facilities: restaurant, lounge, games room, exercise room, indoor pool, whirlpool. AE, D, DC, MC, V. Moderate–Expensive.*

Gunstock Inn and Health Club. This country-style resort and motor inn about a minute's drive from the Gunstock recreation area has rooms of various sizes furnished with American antiques, with views of the mountains and Lake Winnipesaukee. *580 Cherry Valley Rd. (Rte. 11A), Gilford 03246, tel. 603/293–2021 or 800/654–0180, fax 603/293–2050. 27 rooms with bath. Facilities: restaurant, health club, indoor pool, spa. AE, D, MC, V. Moderate–Expensive.*

King Pine Ski Area at Purity Spring Resort
Rte. 153, E. Madison, 03849
Tel. 603/367–8896 or 800/367–8897

King Pine, located a little more than 10 miles from Conway (past the white-steepled church town of Eaton), has been a family-run ski area for more than 100 years, and family is the key. The Hoyt family offers many ski-and-stay packages throughout the winter season, in addition to other activities such as swimming in the indoor pool, cross-country skiing, and dogsledding.

Downhill Skiing King Pine's gentle slopes make it an ideal area for families just learning to ski. Because most of the terrain is geared for beginner and intermediate skiers, experts won't be challenged here except for a brief pitch on the Pitch Pine trail. Sixteen trails are serviced by a triple chair, double chair, and two J-bars. Night skiing is offered on Tuesdays, Fridays, Saturdays, and holidays.

Cross-Country Skiing Ten kilometers (6.1 miles) of cross-country skiing is offered on the King Pine property.

Other Activities Ice skating and dogsledding rides are enjoyable activities for kids. Adults use the indoor pool and fitness complex, which provides pleasant water views to those using the pool and exercise room facilities. In summer guests canoe, hike, fish, and waterski.

Child Care Children of all ages are welcome at the nursery (open daily 9–4) on the second floor of the base lodge. Knee Hi ski lessons are offered to children ages 4–6.

Lodging For a full review of the Purity Springs Resort, see East Madison Lodging in the White Mountains section of the New Hampshire chapter.

King Ridge
41 King Ridge Rd., New London 03257
Tel. 603/526–6966; snow conditions, 800/343–1312

They call it a summit village, which accurately—if a bit dramatically—describes the base facilities at King Ridge. The lodge and all attendant services are located at the top of the ski area, with the trails spinning off to points below. Skiers and family groups who come here make the adjustment quickly and appreciate the efficient and agreeable skiing.

Downhill Skiing Upside down it may be, but King Ridge's 850 vertical feet has the right kind of challenge for novices and intermediate skiers. Most of the terrain is for beginners, but several long intermediate runs are rewarding, and three advanced trails are fun, too. Two triple and one double chair lift and four surface lifts transport skiers. Lift-ticket prices are low.

Other Activities The King Ridge Racquet Club offers tennis, racquetball, volleyball, and an indoor golf simulator. The Hatter House restaurant and lounge is open daily. The new family center features après ski activities for kids only, with puppet shows, storytelling, and sing-alongs. Also new is the business center, which offers office conveniences such as fax machines, computer access, and cellular phone rentals.

Child Care The Children's Center takes children 4 months through 6 years old and offers "Playtime on Skis" lessons to ages 4–6. On nonholiday weekdays, nursery care is free. All-day and half-day SKIwee lessons are available through the ski school for children 5–12.

Lodging **Follansbee Inn.** Built in 1840, this quintessential country inn on the shore of Lake Kezar is a perfect fit in the 19th-century village of North Sutton, about 4 miles south of New London. Common rooms and bedrooms alike are loaded with collectibles and antiques. You can ice-fish on the lake as well as ski across it. *Rte. 114, North Sutton 03260, tel. 603/927–4221. 23 rooms, 11 with bath. Facilities: sitting rooms with fireplaces, dining room (guests only), cross-country* *trails, skating, tobogganing. Full breakfast included. MC, V. Moderate.*

Pleasant Lake Inn. This quiet, family-run property is aptly named for its location and ambience. The herbs, preserves, and other yummy things found on the dining table were grown on the property; all the baked goods come from the inn's kitchen. The original farmhouse dates from 1790, and that early country look has been maintained with the fireplace and woodstove. There are even sheep in the barn. *125 Pleasant St., Box 1030, New London 03257, tel. 603/ 526–6271. 11 rooms with bath. Facilities: dining room (guests only). Full breakfast included. MC, V. Moderate.*

Additional accommodations will be found under New London Dining and Lodging in the Western and Central New Hampshire section of the New Hampshire chapter.

Loon Mountain
Kancamagus Hwy., Lincoln 03251
Tel. 603/745–8111; snow conditions, 603/745–8100; lodging, 800/ 229–STAY

On the Kancamagus Highway and the Pemigewasset River is the modern Loon Mountain resort. Loon opened in the 1960s, and saw serious development in the 1980s, when more mountain facilities, base lodges, and a large hotel near the main lifts at the bottom of the mountain were added. The result attracts a broad cross-section of skiers. In the base lodge and around the mountain are a large number of food services and lounge facilities. The first-rate Mountain Club Hotel has guest rooms within walking distance of the lifts, and there are on-slope and nearby condominium complexes.

Downhill Skiing Wide, straight, and consistent intermediate trails prevail at Loon, making makes it ideal for plain fun or for advancing one's skills. Beginner trails and slopes are set apart, so faster skiers won't interfere. Most advanced runs are grouped on the North Peak section farther from the main mountain. The vertical is 2,100 feet; a four-passenger gondola, two triple and five double chair lifts, and one surface lift serve the 41 trails and slopes.

Cross-Country Skiing The touring center has 35 kilometers (22 miles) of cross-country trails.

Other Activities The Mountain Club has a fitness center with a whirlpool, lap pool, saunas, steam rooms, an exercise room, and racquetball and squash courts. Massages and aerobics classes are available. Summmer facilities include an outdoor pool, tennis courts, horseback riding, archery, in-line skating, skeet shooting, mountain biking, and the gondola Skyride to the summit. For a thrilling adventure take a mountain bike to the top and ride down.

Child Care The Honeybear nursery takes children as young as 6 weeks. Nonintensive ski instruction is offered to youngsters of nursery age. The ski school has a Mountain Explorers program for children 9–12 and SKIwee for ages 3–8. Children 5 and under ski free every day, while those 6–12 ski free midweek during nonholiday periods when parents participate in a five-day ski week.

Lodging **The Mountain Club on Loon.** This slopeside resort hotel includes an assortment of accommodations, such as suites that sleep as many as eight; studios with Murphy beds; and 70 units with kitchens. There's a full range of activities offered to all guests, including live entertainment five nights a week in the lounge. Take Exit 32 from I–93 (Kancamagus Hwy.). *Rte. 112, Lincoln 03251, tel. 603/745–*

8111 or 800/433-3413, fax 603/745-2317. 234 rooms with bath. Facilities: restaurant, lounge, deli, convenience store, fitness center, garage, indoor pool, racquetball, squash, sauna. AE, D, DC, MC, V. Moderate-Very Expensive.

Mill House Inn. This hotel on the western edge of the Kancamagus Highway offers country-inn style along with free transportation to Loon and Waterville Valley during ski season. Nonskiers will have plenty to do, too: shopping, a four-screen cinema, and the North Country Center for the Performing Arts are nearby. *Box 696, Lincoln 03251, tel. 603/745-6261 or 800/654-6183, fax 603/745-6896. 96 rooms with bath, including 24 suites. Facilities: restaurant, nightclub, exercise room, outdoor and indoor pools, sauna, tennis, whirlpools. AE, D, DC, MC, V. Moderate-Expensive.*

Nightlife Après-ski activity will be found at the **Granite Bar** at the **Mountain Club** (tel. 603/745-8111), and there's dancing at the **Loon Saloon** at the ski area. **Dickens** (tel. 603/745-2278), in the Village of Loon, has live musical entertainment.

Mt. Cranmore
Box 1640, North Conway, 03860
Tel. 603/356-5543; snow conditions, 800/786-6754; lodging, 800/543-9206

The ski area at Mt. Cranmore, on the outskirts of North Conway, came into existence in 1938 when local residents saw an opportunity to make the most of their mountain. One early innovation, the clankety-clank Skimobile lift, has sadly been put out to museum pastures and no longer operates. An aggressive mountain-improvement program has been under way for several years, with new grooming equipment, a triple chair, expanded terrain, and base-restaurant services. A fitness center completes the "new" Cranmore with an indoor climbing wall.

Downhill Skiing The mountain and trail system at Cranmore is well laid out and fun to ski. Most of the runs are naturally formed intermediates that weave in and out of glades. Beginners have several slopes and routes from the 1,200-foot summit, while experts must be content with a few short but steep pitches. One triple and four double chair lifts carry skiers to the top. There is night skiing Fridays and Saturdays and during holiday periods.

Cross-Country Skiing Sixty-five kilometers (40 miles) of groomed cross-country trails weave through North Conway and the countryside along the MountWashington Valley Ski Touring Association Network (tel. 603/356-9920).

Other Activities Mt. Cranmore Recreation Center contains four indoor tennis courts, exercise equipment, an indoor pool, aerobics workout space, and a 40-foot indoor climbing wall. There is outdoor skating and, in summer, four outdoor tennis courts. There is a halfpipe for snowboarders.

Child Care The nursery takes children 1 year and up. For children 4-12, the SKIwee program offers all-day skiing and instruction from the expanded Children's Learning Center. The Rattlesnake Youth Development Program gives season-long ski instruction for children in the same age range.

Lodging **Eastern Slope Inn Resort and Conference Center.** Although this has been an operating inn for more than a century, recent restoration and refurbishing have updated its image and its facilities. The resort has the ambience of a historic site, and such modern amenities as an enclosed pool. Jackson Square, the inn's restaurant, serves traditional American fare in a glassed-in courtyard. There's also nightly entertainment. *Main St., North Conway 03860, tel. 603/356–6321 or 800/258–4708, fax 603/356–8732. 125 rooms with bath. Facilities: restaurant, pub, games room, indoor pool, sauna, whirlpool. AE, D, MC, V. Moderate.*

Additional accommodations will be found under North Conway Lodging in the White Mountains section of the New Hampshire chapter.

Nightlife For lively weekend entertainment go to **Barnaby's** (tel. 603/356–5781) or the **Cranmore Pub** (tel. 603/356–2472) in North Conway. **Horsefeather's** (tel. 603/356–2687), on Main Street in North Conway, is also hopping on the weekends. **The Red Jacket Mountain View Inn** (tel. 603/356–5411) has weekend and holiday entertainment. Also, *see* Nightlife for Wildcat Mountain, *below.*

Mt. Sunapee
Mt. Sunapee State Park, Rte. 103, Mt. Sunapee 03772
Tel. 603/763–2356; snow conditions, 800/322–3300; lodging, 603/763–2145 or 800/258–3530

Without glitz or glamour, state-run Sunapee remains popular among local residents and skiers from Boston, Hartford, and the coast for its low-key atmosphere and easy skiing. Two base lodges supply the essentials.

Downhill Skiing This mountain of 1,510 vertical feet, the highest in southern New Hampshire, has 19 miles of gentle-to-moderate terrain with a couple of pitches that could be called steep. A nice beginner's section is located beyond the base facilities, well away and well protected from other trails. Three triple and three double chair lifts and one surface lift transport skiers.

Child Care The Duckling Nursery takes children from 12 months through 5 years of age. Little Indians ski instruction gives ages 3 and 4 a taste of skiing, while SKIwee lessons are available for ages 5–12.

Lodging **Bradford Inn.** This delightfully old-fashioned country inn in the village of Bradford has two common rooms and a popular restaurant, J. Albert's, which features New England cooking. Rooms have details circa 1898, and there are family suites. Senior citizen discounts and facilities for people with disabilities are available. *Main St., Bradford 03221, tel. 603/938-5309 or 800/669-5309. 14 rooms with bath. Facilities: restaurant, outdoor pool, tennis court. Full breakfast included. MC, V. Moderate.*

Additional accommodations will be found under Lodging in the Western and Central New Hampshire section of the New Hampshire chapter.

Pats Peak
Rte. 114, Henniker 03242
Tel. 603/428–3245; snow conditions, 800/258–3218

Ideally located near Boston and the coastal metropolitan region, Mt. Sunapee is a feasible drive for families and is geared for such a clientele. Base facilities are rustic, and friendly personal attention is the rule.

Downhill Skiing Despite its size of only 710 vertical feet, with 19 trails and slopes, Pats Peak has something for everyone: New skiers are well served with a wide slope, chair lift, and several short trails; intermediates have wider trails from the top; and advanced skiers have a couple of real thrillers to choose from. One triple and two double chair lifts, two T-bars, and two surface lifts serve the runs.

Child Care The nursery takes children ages 6 months through 5 years. Special nursery ski programs for children ages 4–12 are offered on weekends and during vacations. All-day lessons for self-sufficient skiers ages 4–12 are scheduled throughout the season.

Lodging **Meeting House Country Inn.** This quiet, cozy 200-year-old farmhouse, located conveniently at the base of Pats Peak, serves a country breakfast in bed to guests. A solar-sided pub and restaurant occupy the old barn. *Rte. 114 (Flanders Rd.), Henniker 03242, tel. 603/428–3228. 6 rooms with bath. Facilities: restaurant, pub, hot tub, sauna. Full breakfast included. AE, D, MC, V. Moderate.*

Additional accommodations selections will be found under Henniker Loding in the Western and Central New Hampshire section of the New Hampshire chapter.

Waterville Valley
Waterville Valley 03215
Tel. 603/236–8311; snow conditions, 603/236–4144; lodging, 800/468–2553

Most everything in the valley belongs to or is licensed by the mountain company, effectively making the area an enclave, of sorts. There are inns, lodges, and condominiums; restaurants, taverns, small cafés; shops, boutiques, and a grocery store; conference facilities; a post office; and a sports center. Everything has been built with taste and regard for the New England sensibility, and the resort attracts skiers from Boston and environs. An array of three- to five-day vacation packages is available.

Downhill Skiing Mt. Tecumseh, a short shuttle ride from the Town Square and accommodations, has been laid out with great care and attention to detail. A good selection of the 53 trails offers most advanced skiers an adequate challenge, and there are slopes and trails for beginners, too. Yet the bulk of the skiing is intermediate: straight down the fall line, wide, and agreeably long. Still, the variety is great enough that no one will be bored on a weekend visit. The lifts serving the 2,020 feet of vertical rise include one high-speed, detachable quad; three triple and five double chair lifts; and four surface lifts. A second mountain, Snow's, about 2 miles away, is open on weekends and takes some of the overflow; it has five fairly easy natural snow trails and one double chair lift off a 580-foot vertical. This ski area has hosted more World Cup races than any other in the nation.

Cross-Country Skiing The cross-country network, with the ski center in the Town Square, has 105 kilometers (62 miles) of trails, 70 of them groomed.

Other Activities An ice-skating arena is adjacent to the Town Square. A snowboard park was added in 1994. The Sports Center has tennis, racquetball, and squash courts; a 25-meter indoor pool; jogging track; exercise equipment and classes; whirlpools, saunas, and steam rooms; massage service; and a games room. In summer, there is an outdoor pool, 18 tennis courts, nine holes of golf, biking, horseback riding, in-line skating, and water sports on Corcoran's Pond.

Child Care The nursery takes children 6 weeks through 4 years old. Children ages 6–12 who want to ski have a choice of group lessons or half-day or full-day SKIwee lessons. Petite SKIwee is designed for children 3–5, SKIwee is for ages 6–8, and Grand SKIwee is for ages 9–12. The Kinderpark, a children's slope, has a slow-running lift and special props to hold children's attention. Children 5 and under ski free anytime; midweek, those 12 and under ski and stay free with a parent on multiday packages. Evening child care is available for ages 6 weeks through 12 years.

Lodging **Black Bear Lodge.** The all-suite hotel has one- and two-bedroom units with full kitchens, heated indoor and outdoor pools, a sauna, a steam room, and bus service to the slopes. *Snow's Brook Rd. (Box 357), Waterville Valley 03215, tel. 603/236–4501 or 800/468–2553. 107 suites. Facilities: indoor and outdoor pools, access to sports center, saunas, steam room. AE, D, DC, MC, V. Expensive–Very Expensive.*

Golden Eagle Lodge. Waterville's premier lodging property is reminiscent of the grand hotels of an earlier era. There are 139 condominium suites in this four-year-old complex, with a two-story lobby and a front desk staff that provides all the services you'd find in a hotel. *Waterville Valley 03215, tel. 603/236–8311. 139 condominium suites. Facilities: kitchen, living/dining area, indoor pool, whirlpools, saunas, games room, shuttle to the slopes. AE, D, DC, MC, V. Expensive–Very Expensive.*

Snowy Owl Inn. The inn is cozy and intimate, and offers a variety of setups: The fourth-floor bunk-bed lofts are ideal for families; the first-floor rooms are suitable for couples who want a quiet getaway. Among the attractive features are a three-story-high central fieldstone fireplace (one of seven fireplaces), a surrounding atrium supported by single-log posts, and lots of prints and watercolors of snowy owls. Four restaurants are within walking distance. *Snow's Brook Rd. (Box 407), Waterville Valley 03215, tel. 603/236–8383 or 800/468–2553. 80 rooms with bath. Facilities: indoor pool, saunas, sports center access, whirlpool. Continental breakfast included. AE, D, DC, MC, V. Moderate–Expensive.*

Nightlife The valley has a number of popular lounges, taverns, and cafés. The **Comman Man** (tel. 603/236–8885), overlooking Corcoran's Pond, is known for a zesty cheese dip. Weekend and holiday entertainment can be found at **Legends 1291** (tel. 603/236–4678), Waterville's only year-round disco, and **Brookside Bistro** (tel. 603/236–4309).

Wildcat Mountain
Pinkham Notch, Rte. 16, Jackson 03846
Tel. 603/466–3326; snow conditions, 617/965–7991 or 800/552–8952

Wildcat has been working hard to live down its reputation of being a difficult mountain. On a clear day, there is no better view than those of Mt. Washington, the highest peak in the Northeast. Tuckerman Ravine, where skiers trek in spring to hike up and skidown, can also be seen. The 2.75-mile-long Polecat is where skiers who can hold a wedge should head, while experts can be found zipping down The Lynx, a run constantly voted by patrons of a local bar as the most popular in the Mt. Washington Valley. Trails are classic New England—narrow and winding.

Downhill Skiing Wildcat's expert runs deserve their designations and then some. Intermediates have newly widened midmountain-to-base trails, and beginners will find gentle terrain and a broad teaching slope. The 30 runs with a 2,100-foot vertical drop are served by a two-passenger gondola and one double and four triple chair lifts.

Child Care The Kitten Club Child Care Center takes children 18 months and up. All-day SKIwee instruction is offered to children 5–12. A separate slope is used for teaching children to ski.

Lodging **Eagle Mountain House.** When this country estate of 1879 was restored and modernized in 1986, it became a showplace and is now run by Colony Resorts. The public rooms are rustic-palatial, in keeping with the period of tycoon roughing-it; the bedrooms are large and furnished with period pieces. On a warm day, nurse a drink from a rocking chair on the wraparound deck. *Carter Notch Rd., Jackson 03846, tel. 603/383-9111 or 800/777-1700, fax 603/383-0854. 94 rooms with bath. Facilities: restaurant, health club, outdoor pool, saunas, whirlpool. AE, D, MC, V. Moderate.*

Wildcat Inn & Tavern. After a day of skiing, collapse on a comfy sofa by the fire in this tavern, situated in the center of Jackson Village. Although only 12 rooms are available in this small 19th-century inn, it's a lodestone for skiers in nearby condos and bed-and-breakfasts. The fragrance of home-baking permeates into guest rooms, which are full of interesting furniture and knickknacks. There's entertainment, too. *Rte. 16A, Jackson 03846, tel. 603/383-4245, fax 603/383-6456. 12 rooms, 10 with bath. Facilities: restaurant. Full breakfast included. AE, MC, V. Inexpensive–Moderate.*

Nightlife The **Wildcat Inn & Tavern** (tel. 603/383-4245) has weekend entertainment. In Glen, the **Bernerhof Inn** (tel. 603/383-4414) is the setting for an evening of fondue and soft music by the fireside, and the **Red Parka Pub** (tel. 603/383-4344) is nearby. The mountain's own **Tuckerman's Lounge** is a good place to have a drink while looking over the ski photos and memorabilia on display. Also *see* Nightlife in Mt. Cranmore, *above.*

Maine Skiing

By Marty Basch Weather patterns that create snow cover for Maine ski areas may come from the Atlantic or from Canada, and Maine may have snow when other New England states do not—and vice versa. In recent years ski-area operators in Maine have embraced snowmaking with a vengeance, and they now have the capacity to cover thousand-foot-plus mountains. In turn, more skiers have discovered Maine skiing, yet in most cases this has still not resulted in crowds, hassles, or lines. The exception is Sunday River, which has become a huge, well-managed attraction and one of New England's most popular ski destinations.

Further good news for Maine ski areas is the building of more and better lodging; best news of all is that skiers generally find lower prices here for practically every component of a ski vacation or a day's outing: lift tickets, accommodations, lessons, equipment, and meals. Nightlife activities at most resorts center on the ski areas and hotel bars and restaurants.

Big Squaw Mountain (Moosehead Resort)
Box D, Greenville 04441
Tel. 207/695-2272

Remote but pretty, Moosehead Resort and Ski Area at Big Squaw is an attractive place for family ski vacations and one that offers appealing package rates. A hotel at the base of the mountain, integrated into the main base lodge, has a restaurant, bar, and other services and offers ski packages.

Downhill Skiing Trails are laid out according to difficulty, with the easy slopes toward the bottom, intermediate trails weaving from midpoint, and steeper runs high up off the 1,750-vertical-foot peak. The 17 trails are served by one triple and one double chair lift and one surface lift.

Other Activities Moosehead Lake and other ponds and streams provide fishing, sailing, canoeing, swimming, and lake-boat cruising in summer. At the mountain there are two tennis courts, hiking, and lawn games. A recreation program for children functions midweek in summer.

Child Care The nursery takes children from infants through age 6 and provides skiing lessons for those who want them. The ski school has daily lessons and racing classes for children of all ages and abilities.

Lodging **Big Squaw Mountain Moosehead Resort.** From the door of the resort you can ski to the slopes and to cross-country trails. The motel-style units and dorm rooms have picture windows opening onto the woods or the slopes, and Katahdin and Moosehead Lake (6 miles away) can be seen from the lawn. The restaurant serves hearty family meals. Live entertainment is often offered on the weekends. American Plan and ski packages are available. *Rte. 15, Greenville 04441, tel. 207/695–2272 or, in ME, 800/348–6743. 58 rooms with bath. Facilities: restaurant, cafeteria, ski shop, ski school, nursery, playground, volleyball, tennis. AE, MC, V. Inexpensive.*

Mt. Abram
Rte. 26 (Box 120), Locke Mills 04255
Tel. 207/875–5003

This complete resort has a friendly, rustic Maine feeling and is known for its snow grooming, home-style cooking, and family atmosphere. Many skiers choose to stay in reasonably priced condominiums on the mountain road.

Downhill Skiing The mountain reaches just over 1,000 vertical feet, the majority of its terrain intermediate, with fall-line steep runs and two areas for beginning and novice skiers. The area has two double chair lifts and three T-bars. In addition to learn-to-ski classes, there are regular improvement clinics for all ability levels and age groups. The new management has a five-year plan, which includes 100-percent snowmaking coverage, a new chair lift to the top, and a new base facility.

Child Care The Ski Mt. Abram's Day Care Center takes children from 6 months through 6 years. The ski school offers class lessons on weekends and during vacation weeks to children 3–6 who are enrolled in the nursery. For juniors 6–16 there are individual classes plus a series of 10 two-hour lessons on weekends.

Saddleback Ski and Summer Lake Preserve
Box 490, Rangeley 04970
Tel. 207/864–5671; snow conditions, 207/864–3380; reservations, 207/864–5364

A down-home, laid-back atmosphere prevails at Saddleback, where the quiet and the absence of crowds, even on busy weekends, draw return visitors—many of them families. The base area has the feeling of a small community for the guests at trailside homes and condominiums. Midweek lift tickets and packages are attractively priced. With recent expansion and plans for more, Saddleback is becoming a major resort.

Downhill Skiing The expert terrain is short and concentrated at the top of the mountain, and an upper lift makes the trails easily accessible to more advanced skiers. The middle of the mountain is mainly intermediate, with a few meandering easy trails; the beginner or novice slopes are toward the bottom. Two double chair lifts and three T-bars (usually without lines) carry skiers to the 40 trails on the 1,830 feet of vertical. The T-bar to the summit can be a wintry (i.e., chilling) experience.

Cross-Country Skiing Forty kilometers (25 miles) of groomed cross-country trails spread out from the base area and circle Saddleback Lake and several ponds and rivers.

Other Activities More than 100 miles of maintained snowmobile trails in the Rangeley Region, along with ice skating, sledding, and tobogganing, are available in winter.

Child Care The nursery takes children ages 6 weeks through 8 years. For those who are new to skiing, Snoopy classes offer a half day or full day of lessons for children 4–7. The goal at Saddleback is to get children into the Junior Masters Program: Levels One and Two are for 5-year-olds and up with beginning and intermediate skiing skills; the Ski Meisters is for 9-year-olds and up who can ski in control. A Junior Racing Program serves three age groups: 9–11, 12–14, and 15 and up.

Lodging **Rangeley Inn and Motor Lodge.** From Main Street you see only the massive, three-story, blue inn building (ca. 1907), but behind it the newer motel wing commands Haley Pond, a lawn, and a garden. The traditional lobby and a smaller parlor have 12-foot ceilings, a jumble of rocking and easy chairs, and polished wood. Sizable guest rooms boast iron and brass beds, subdued wallpaper, and a clawfoot tub in the bath. Motel units contain Queen Anne reproduction furniture, velvet chairs, and a whirlpool bath. Gourmet meals are served in the spacious dining room with the Williamsburg brass chandeliers. *Main St., Rangeley 04970, tel. 207/864–3341 or 800/666–3687, fax 603/864–3634. 36 rooms with bath, 15 motel units with bath. Facilities: dining room, bar, conference and meeting room. MAP available. AE, MC, V. Inexpensive–Moderate.*

Town & Lake Motel. This complex of efficiencies, motel units, and cottages alongside the highway and on Rangeley Lake is just down the road from the shops and restaurants of downtown Rangeley. Two-bedroom cottages with well-equipped kitchens are farther from the highway, and some face Saddleback. Pets are welcome. *Rte. 16, Rangeley 04970, tel. 207/864–3755. 16 motel units with bath, 9 cottages. Facilities: swimming, canoes, boat rental in summer. AE, MC, V. Inexpensive–Moderate.*

Additional accommodations selections will be found under Rangeley Lodging in the Western Lakes and Mountains section of the Maine chapter.

Shawnee Peak
Box 734, Rte. 302, Bridgton 04009
Tel. 207/647–8444

Situated on the New Hampshire border, Shawnee Peak (formerly Pleasant Mountain) draws many skiers from the North Conway, New Hampshire, region 18 miles away and from Portland, Maine, 45 miles distant. It's a relative sleeper owned by the Shawnee Group, a resort enterprise whose aim is to attract families. Condominiums on the mountain and an upgraded base lodge point toward expansion, but it doesn't seem that Shawnee will lose its hospitable atmosphere.

Downhill Skiing Recent lighting installations have opened more trails for night skiing off the 1,300-foot vertical; this resort offers perhaps the most night-skiing terrain in New England. Most trails are pleasant cruisers for intermediates, with some beginner slopes and a few pitches suitable for advanced skiers. One triple and three double chair lifts service the 30 ski runs.

Child Care The area's nursery takes children from 6 months through 7 years. SKIwee instruction for children 4–12 lasts six hours a day and includes lunch. Children under 8 ski free when accompanied by a parent. The Youth Ski League has instruction for aspiring racers.

Lodging Accommodations selections will be found under Bridgton and Center Lovell Lodging in the Western Lakes and Mountains sections of the Maine chapter. Other condominium lodging in the area is available and may be booked through the Bridgton Group (tel. 207/647–2591).

Sugarloaf/USA
Kingfield 04947
Tel. 207/237–2000; snow conditions, 207/237–2000

The 1980s saw Sugarloaf emerge as a major ski resort, with two sizable hotels, a condominum complex, and a village cluster of shops, restaurants, and meeting facilities. Sugarloaf/USA likes to refer to itself as the "Snowplace of the East" because of the abundance of natural snow it usually receives, plus its ability to manufacture 20 tons of snow per minute (via an $11 million infusion into its snowmaking plant since 1986). Plenty of special packages and activities are offered at this sophisticated ski resort.

Downhill Skiing With a vertical of 2,837 feet, Sugarloaf is taller than any other New England ski peak, except Killington, Vermont. The advanced terrain begins with the steep snowfields on top (now facilitated by snowmaking), wide open and treeless. Coming down the face of the mountain, there are black-diamond runs everywhere, often blending into easier terrain. A substantial number of intermediate trails can be found down the front face, and a couple more come off the summit. Easier runs are predominantly toward the bottom, with a few long, winding runs that twist and turn from higher elevations. The 91 trails are served by Maine's only gondola, two quads, one triple, eight double chair lifts, and a T-bar. Skidder, the Loaf's famous bump run, now has snowmaking capabilities. The King Pine Bowl area has wide, joyous cruiser runs.

Cross-Country Skiing The Sugarloaf Ski Touring Center has 85 kilometers (53 miles) of cross-country trails that loop and wind through the valley. Trails connect to the resort.

Other Activities The Sugartree Sports and Fitness Club features an indoor pool, six indoor and outdoor hot pools, racquetball courts, weightlifting equipment, aerobics machines, saunas, steam rooms, a massage room, and a beauty salon. Use of club facilities is included in all lodging packages. For summer, there is an 18-hole golf course and six tennis courts.

Child Care A nursery takes children from 6 weeks through 6 years. Once they reach 3, children are allowed to try ski equipment for free. A night nursery is open on Wednesday and Saturday, 6–10 PM by reservation. Mountain Magic provides instruction for ages 4–6 on a half-day or full-day basis; and Mountain Adventure, with half-day and full-day instruction, is offered to ages 7–14. Nightly activities are free.

Lodging **Sugarloaf Inn Resort.** This lodge provides ski-on access to Sugarloaf/USA, a complete health club, and rooms that range from king-size on the fourth floor to dorm-style (bunk beds) on the ground floor. A greenhouse section of the Seasons restaurant affords views of the slopes and offers "ski-in" lunches. At breakfast the sunlight pours into the dining room, and at dinner you can watch the snow-grooming machines prepare your favorite run. Adult alpine and Nordic midweek lessons are available. *R.R. 1 (Box 5000), Kingfield 04947, tel. 207/237-2000 or 800/843-5623, fax 207/237-3773. 37 rooms with bath, 5 dorm rooms. Facilities: restaurant, lounge, health club, sauna, Jacuzzi, aerobics classes, video arcade, conference facilities. AE, MC, V. Moderate–Very Expensive.*

Sugarloaf Mountain Hotel. This six-story brick structure at the base of the lifts on Sugarloaf combines a New England ambience with full hotel service in the European manner. Oak and redwood paneling in the main rooms is enhanced by contemporary furnishings. Valet parking, ski tuning, lockers, and mountain guides are available through the concierge. *R.R. 1, Box 2299, Carrabassett Valley 04947, tel. 207/237-2222 or 800/527-9879. 90 rooms with bath, 26 suites. Facilities: restaurant, pub, spa, 2 hot tubs, sauna, tanning booth, massage. AE, MC, V. Moderate–Very Expensive.*

Lumberjack Lodge. Located on the access road, ½ mile from Sugarloaf, this informal lodge is the closest accommodation to the mountain. The Tyrolean-style building contains eight efficiency units, each with living and dining area, kitchenette, full bath, and bedroom, but no phone or TV. Units sleep up to eight people. A free shuttle to the lifts operates during the peak season. There are restaurants nearby. *Rte. 27, Carrabassett 04947, tel. 207/237-2141. 8 units. Facilities: recreation room with fireplace and cable TV, video games, sauna. Closed May–Sept. AE, MC, V. Inexpensive.*

Sunday River

Box 450, Bethel 04217
Tel. 207/824-3000; snow conditions, 207/824-6400; reservations, 800/543-2SKI

From a sleepy little ski area with minimal facilities, Sunday River came on in the 1980s like gangbusters. Today it is among the best managed, forward-looking ski areas in the East; in fact, expansion could be the resort's middle name. A ski train has been added to take skiers from Portland to Bethel, and new glade areas were opened last year. This resort will continue to grow rapidly.

Spread throughout the valley are three base areas, trailside condominiums, town houses, and a ski dorm that provide the essentials. Lots of imaginatively packaged ski weeks are geared toward a variety of interested groups, including college students, Canadians, and disabled skiers, among others. Beginners are offered a program that guarantees they will learn the basics of skiing in one day or their money will be refunded.

Downhill Skiing Billed as the steepest, longest, widest lift-served trail in the East, White Heat is the latest in a line of trails opened at Sunday River in recent years. At present the area has 90 trails, the majority in the intermediate range. Expert and advanced runs are grouped from the peaks, and most beginner slopes are located near the base of the area. Trails representing all difficulty levels spread down from six peaks (the tallest with a vertical drop of 2,001 feet), which are served by six quads, five triples, and one double chair lift. Each spring the area holds a "Bust n' Burn" mogul skiing contest on White Heat.

Other Activities Within the housing complexes are indoor pools, outdoor heated pools, saunas, and Jacuzzis for winter and summer. Sunday River added a new snowboard park last season. For summer, there are two tennis courts, a volleyball court, and mountain biking. Cyclists can take their bicycles on the lifts and ride down.

Child Care The nursery takes children ages 6 weeks through 2 years; the Day Care Center takes them from 2 through 6 years. The SKIwee program accommodates children 4–6, and Mogul Meister is available for ages 7–12. Both programs are available in half- or full-day sessions. All of these are located in the new Children's Center at the South Ridge base area.

Lodging **Summit Hotel and Conference Center.** Opened Christmas 1992, the condominium hotel was an instant hit with skiers. Already it has expanded from its original 140 slopeside rooms, 220 total units. A new 800-seat ballroom has been built, as well. Conference facilities give a great excuse to combine business and skiing for groups of 10–400. *Bethel 04217, tel. 207/824–3000 or 800/543–2SKI. Facilities: restaurant, lounge, valet parking, child care, heated outdoor pool, tennis, health club with sauna and steam room. AE, D, MC, V. Moderate–Expensive.*

Sunday River Inn. Located at the base of the Sunday River ski area, this modern chalet offers private rooms for families, and dorm rooms (bring your sleeping bag) for groups and students, but all within easy access of the slopes. Hearty meals are served buffet-style, and the comfy living room is dominated by a stone hearth. *Sunday River Rd., RFD 2 (Box 1688), Bethel 04217, tel. 207/824–2410. 12 rooms, 5 dorms, 1 apartment chalet with 4 rooms. Facilities: cross-country skiing, Finnish sauna. Rates are MAP. Closed Apr.–Thanksgiving. AE, MC, V. Inexpensive.*

Additional accommodations selections will be found under Bethel Lodging in the Western Lakes and Mountains section of the Maine chapter.

Massachusetts Skiing

By Marty Basch

The Massachusetts Berkshires are in fact foothills of the Green Mountains of Vermont, and many of the ski areas here have significant vertical drops of just over 1,000 feet, usually on gentle beginner-to-intermediate terrain. This can be the ideal environment for an introduction to skiing and for family outings on winter weekends. Although most skiers go to the Berkshires for day skiing, there are numerous places to stay overnight, and two ski areas can be visited comfortably in one weekend. Ski areas in Massachusetts have become expert at providing quality snowmaking, and when conditions are marginal in the north, staying put and skiing locally here is a good idea. In fact, with sophisticated full-service resorts (Jiminy Peak in particular) and plenty of skiing choices, skiers are now opting to make the Berkshires a serious destination, closer to home.

In the Boston and Springfield areas the hills may be smaller, but the numbers of skiers tend to rival those in the Berkshires. These ski areas offer the same mix of people—beginners, families, and bus groups—and provide excellent opportunities for learning the sport.

Berkshire East

Box 0, South River Rd., Charlemont 01339
Tel. 413/339–6617

Berkshire East has been around for some years, yet it seems to attract mostly a college crowd from the region and loyal families and youngsters interested in the area's racing program.

Downhill Skiing The 1,200-foot vertical was once considered more difficult than that of neighboring ski areas. Recent blasting, widening, and sculpting tamed many of the steeper trails, but you can still find steep pitches toward the top. Wide, cruisable intermediate slopes are plentiful, and beginner terrain is abundant. Four double chair lifts and one surface lift serve the 30 trails that are all covered by snowmaking. The new Little Beaver Novice Complex offers three easy trails. There's night skiing Wednesday, Friday, and Saturday, 4–10 PM.

Child Care   The nursery takes children from infants through 8 years on weekends; children under 6 ski free. For older children the ski school offers instructional classes. For aspiring racers, 5–18, the race-training program is Saturday and Sunday.

Lodging   **The Inn at Charlemont.** This rambling old inn just two minutes' drive from Berkshire East was reopened several years ago, and the new owners are in the renovation process. Guest rooms have uneven wood floors and rather basic furnishings; those that have been restored are more comfortable, with quilts and country-style decorations. Bunk beds are available, and individual packages, including lift-ticket discounts, can be arranged. *Rte. 2, Charlemont 01339, tel. 413/339–5796. 14 rooms share 7 baths. Facilities: restaurant, bar, TV lounge. AE, D, DC, MC, V. Inexpensive.*

Nightlife   **The Inn at Charlemont** is the main resource for skiers at Berkshire East, an area that hardly throbs with activity. On Friday and Saturday evenings blues and reggae bands perform; on Sunday there's a "warm-up" hour, with blues, piano, and saxophone entertainment beginning as skiers leave the slopes, at about 4 PM.

Blue Hills
Canton 02186
Tel. 617/828–7490; ski school, 617/828–5090; snow conditions, 617/828–5070

Situated just 30 minutes south of downtown Boston, Blue Hills is a day and night outpost for suburban skiers. On most midweek afternoons the slopes are filled with groups of children from schools and recreation programs taking part in beginner to junior classes. Evenings attract a cross-section of skiers; weekends see mostly families.

Downhill   The vertical is only 365 feet, but the terrain is surprisingly varied.
Skiing   Most of the slopes are easy; a double chair lift and three surface lifts carry skiers.

Bousquet Ski Area
Dan Fox Dr., Pittsfield 01201
Tel. 413/442–8316; snow conditions, 413/442–2436

In 1935, when skiing was a novelty sport, the installation of a state-of-the-art rope tow at Bousquet made it a true destination resort. Ski trains from New York City brought skiers by the hundreds throughout the winter. In 1936 a group of engineers from General Electric devised a way to light the slopes for night skiing, which further propelled Bousquet into the heady modern era of skiing. Today, while other areas have entered an era of glamour and high prices, Bousquet remains an economical, no-nonsense place to ski. Three current members of the U.S. Ski Team (twins Kim and Krista Schmidinger and Heidi Voelker) started racing here, and the gate-bashing is still a big part of Bousquet life. Bousquet remains a fixture in Pittsfield with its same-price-every-day lift-ticket policy; night skiing Monday through Saturday; and bargain packages in the area, which include lodging and lift tickets.

Downhill Skiing The Bosquet brochure discusses 21 trails, but that's counting every change in steepness, cutoff, and merging slope. There is, however, a good selection of beginner and intermediate runs, with a few steeper pitches, off a 750-foot vertical drop. The area has two double chair lifts and two surface lifts.

Other Activities A center across the road offers four handball courts, six indoor tennis courts, saunas, and a whirlpool.

Child Care Bous-Care Nursery serves toddlers and up. This is child care by the hour and reservations are suggested. Ski instruction classes are offered twice daily on weekends and holidays for ages 5 and up.

Lodging **Cliffwood Inn.** This classic Colonial Revival building sits unobtrusively on a residential street in Lenox. Six of the seven guest rooms have fireplaces (one in a bathroom!), and there are four more fireplaces in the public room, hall, and formal dining room downstairs. Much of the furniture comes from Europe—the innkeepers have lived in France, Belgium, and Italy—and most rooms have canopy beds. *25 Cliffwood St., Lenox 01240, tel. 413/637–3330. 7 rooms with bath. Facilities: dining room, music room, outdoor pool. Continental breakfast included in summer and on winter weekends. No credit cards. Expensive–Very Expensive.*
Cranwell Resort and Hotel. Here's a 100-year-old Tudor mansion with Colonial-style furniture, situated in the Lenox hills. Each of the 65 rooms has a private bath. The Wyndhurst dining room is open to the public, but only for dinner. The Music Room lounge has a bar with fireplace. There are cross-country touring trails on the golf course. *55 Lee Rd., Lenox 02140, tel. 413/637–1364 or 800/ CRANWELL, fax 413/637–4364. 65 rooms with private bath. Facilities: restaurant, lounge. Continental breakfast included. AE, D, DC, M, V. Moderate–Expensive.*

Additional accommodations will be found under Lenox and Pittsfield Lodging in the Berkshires section of the Massachusetts chapter.

Nightlife In addition to the many restaurants in the Lenox and Pittsfield area, **Brannigan's** (1015 South St., Lenox, tel. 413/443–6228) is a well-known nightclub, with a disco and DJ downstairs and live bands upstairs. **Tamarack Lounge** (tel. 413/442–8316) in the Bousquet base lodge has DJ entertainment on weekends during ski season.

Brodie

U.S. 7, New Ashford 01237
Tel. 413/443–4752 or 413/443–6597; snow conditions, 413/443–4751

Color it green and you might be skiing at Brodie, where the snow can be green, the beer is often green, and the decor is always green. Yet there's more here than an Irish ambience to attract young crowds to its weekend and night skiing. The base lodge has a restaurant and bar with live entertainment, lodging is within walking distance of the lifts, and RV trailers can be accommodated on the grounds.

Downhill Skiing Almost all trails are beginner and intermediate despite the black diamonds, which designate steeper (not expert) runs. They are served by four double chair lifts and two surface lifts, off 1,250 feet of vertical.

Cross-Country Skiing The area's cross-country skiing covers 25 kilometers (16 miles) of trails, half of which are groomed daily.

Other Activities A sports center (tel. 413/458–4677) 1 mile from the ski area has five indoor courts for tennis and five for racquetball, an exercise room, and a cocktail lounge.

Child Care The nursery takes infants through age 8 by the hour, half day, or full day. Afternoon ski-instruction programs teach techniques to youngsters from beginning to racing levels. Brodie Mountain Ski School offers Making Trax, a ski program that runs weekends and holidays, allowing parents to ski while children learn how.

Lodging **Best Western Springs Motor Inn.** This pleasant motel overlooks Brodie Mountain from across Route 7. Rooms have modern furnishings; those on the second tier are larger, with better views and furnishings. Some rooms have refrigerators; all have coffeemakers. It's close to Jiminy Peak (*see below*), as well. *Rte. 7, New Ashford 01237, tel. 413/458–5945 or 800/528–1234. 40 rooms with bath. Facilities: restaurant, lounge, breakfast shop, outdoor pool, games room. AE, D, DC, MC, V. Moderate.*

Field Farm Guest House. Built in 1948 on 254 acres of private grounds, the house was designed primarily to exhibit its owner's art collection (which went to the Williams College Museum of Art on the owner's death). Guest rooms are large, some of them huge, with big windows and expansive views over the grounds and pond. Three rooms have private decks, two have working fireplaces decorated with tiles depicting animals, birds, and butterflies. The place resembles a modern museum: Most of the furniture was handmade by the owner-collector, and there are sculptures in the garden. Cross-country ski trails begin at the door. *554 Sloan Rd. (off Rte. 43), Williamstown 01267, tel. 413/458–3135. 5 rooms with bath. Facilities: dining room, lounge, outdoor pool, tennis. No credit cards. Moderate.*

Nightlife The **Blarney Room** (tel. 413/443–4752) on the top floor of the main lodge has entertainment nightly and live music weekends and Sunday afternoon. **Kelly's Irish Pub,** on the first floor, has Irish entertainment on weekends.

Butternut Basin
Great Barrington 01230
Tel. 413/528–2000; ski school, 413/528–4433

The friendly Butternut Basin has good base facilities, pleasant skiing, and tasty food in the base lodge, attracting skiers by the score. Skiers from New York's Long Island and Westchester County and Connecticut's Fairfield County continue to flock to the area.

Downhill Skiing Only a steep chute or two interrupts the mellow intermediate terrain. There are slopes for beginners and something for everyone off the area's 1,000-foot vertical. One triple and five double chair lifts plus two surface lifts keep skier traffic spread out.

Cross-Country Skiing Butternut Basin has 7 kilometers (4 miles) of groomed cross-country trails.

Child Care The nursery takes children ages 2½–6 for indoor and outdoor activities on weekends and holidays. The ski school's highly successful SKIwee program is for children 4–12. During midweek, youngsters can get group lessons.

Lodging **Mountain View Motel.** This is the closest motel to Butternut, situated a mile west of the ski area on Route 23. Rooms have in-room coffee and Norman Rockwell prints. *304 State Rd. (Rte. 23E), Great Barrington 01230, tel. 413/528–0250. 16 rooms with bath, 1 suite, 1 efficiency. AE, MC, V. Moderate–Very Expensive.*

Weathervane Inn. The open fireplace and beehive oven in the lounge of this friendly, family-run inn date to the 1760s, when the original building was constructed. The more formal parlor has striking reproduction wallpaper, and guest rooms are pleasantly decorated with stencils, country curtains, wreaths, Norman Rockwell prints, and rocking chairs. The inn has had a varied past; at one period it served as dog kennels, and one of the guest bathrooms has inherited an original dog-size bathtub! *Rte. 23, South Egremont 01258, tel. 413/528–9580, fax 413/528–1713. 10 rooms with bath. Facilities: 2 dining rooms, lounge, TV lounge, outdoor pool. Full breakfast included; MAP available. Closed Dec. 20–26. AE, MC, V. Moderate–Very Expensive.*

Turning Point Inn. Located ½ mile east of Butternut Basin, this 200-year-old inn used to be the Pixie Tavern, a stagecoach stop. The whole of the upstairs—now guest rooms—was then a ballroom. Guests share a sitting and living room, with two fireplaces and a piano, as well as a kitchen area. Bedrooms, with uneven, wide-board floors, are of varying sizes, and several have sloping roofs; they are furnished with antiques. Breakfasts are a specialty—the hosts are natural-foods advocates and serve up multigrain hot cereals, frittatas with fresh garden vegetables, buckwheat pancakes, eggs, and home-baked muffins or cakes. The barn was recently converted into a two-bedroom cottage, which has modern furnishings, a full kitchen, living room, and winterized porch. *Rte. 23 and Lake Buel Rd., R.D. 2 (Box 140), Great Barrington 01230, tel. 413/528–4777. 7 rooms, 1 with bath, 1 cottage. Facilities: kitchen, lounge, cross-country ski trail. Full breakfast included (except in cottage). No credit cards. Expensive.*

Nightlife Sampling the cuisine at a nearby inn is probably the principal evening entertainment at Butternut. Those who are determined to seek out more active nightlife should head for the **Lion's Den**, beneath the **Red Lion Inn** (tel. 413/298–5545) in Stockbridge, which has live entertainment and is located 15 minutes from the ski area by car. The Red Lion is one of the most famous inns in the region.

Jiminy Peak
Corey Rd., Hancock 01237
Tel. 413/738–5500; snow conditions, 413/738–PEAK

Jiminy Peak has all the amenities of a major mountain resort and is located just 2½ hours from New York City or three hours from Boston. Condominiums and an all-suites country inn are within walking distance of the ski lifts; more condominium complexes are nearby; and two restaurants and bars are at the slopes. These services attract nearby residents, as well as families, for day and night skiing. Rentals are available nightly, weekly, or on a seasonal basis. Jiminy Peak is a popular choice for conference and convention business because of its self-contained nature and Berkshire location.

Downhill Skiing With a vertical of 1,140 feet, Jiminy can claim big-time status. The steeper black-diamond sections are toward the top of the mountain, and there is enough good intermediate terrain to satisfy most skiers. A quad chair—dubbed "Q1" because it is the first in Massachusetts—serves Jiminy's slopes. The area also has one triple and three double chair lifts and one surface lift for its 26 trails. Night skiing is an option every night of the week.

Other Activities Jiminy has seven outdoor tennis courts in summer, four outdoor pools, an Alpine Slide, an 18-hole putting course, and a pond stocked for fishing. Tennis instruction is available for one or a series of lessons, and tennis camps operate from May through October. There is a new snowboard park and an old-fashioned ice rink.

Child Care The nursery takes children from 6 months. Children 4–12 can take daily SKIwee lessons, and for ages 6–15 the Mountain Adventure program offers a series of eight weekends of instruction with the same teacher. The Jiminy Cricket Children's Center has been expanded, plus there is now a new kid's ski area, Chipmunk, with its own Mighty Mite lift.

Lodging **The Country Inn at Jiminy Peak.** The massive stone fireplaces in the lobby and lounge give this year-round hotel a ski-lodge atmosphere. All rooms are modern, condo-style suites, and have neat kitchenettes—separated from the living area by a bar and high stools—that are supplied with crockery, electric range, dishwasher, and refrigerator. Rooms at the rear of the building overlook the slopes. *Corey Rd., Hancock 01237, tel. 413/738–5500, fax 413/738–5513. 105 suites. Facilities: restaurant, lounge, heated outdoor pool, 2 saunas, 2 hot tubs, exercise room, 7 tennis courts, minigolf, Alpine Slide, meeting rooms. AE, D, DC, MC, V. Expensive–Very Expensive.*

Hancock Inn. The inn dates to the late 1700s and provides cozy Old World accommodations a mile from Jiminy Peak. Dinner at the inn's restaurant is well recommended. *Rte. 43, Hancock 01237, tel. 413/738–5873. 6 rooms with bath. Facilities: 2 dining rooms, bar, lounge. Full breakfast included. AE, MC, V. Expensive.*

Nightlife The Country Inn's **Drummond's Restaurant** overlooks the slopes, has an adjoining bar-lounge, and is open throughout the evening. (*See also* Nightlife in Brodie, *above.*)

Mt. Tom
Rte. 5, Holyoke 01041
Tel. 413/536–0516; ski school, 413/536–1575

Just minutes from Springfield and several colleges, Mt. Tom attracts skiers for day and night skiing, and offers a five-week series of ski-lesson packages for children and adults. In addition, the area holds races and special events for local groups. There is a restaurant, cafeteria, and ski and rental shop.

Downhill Skiing Slopes and trails at Mt. Tom tend to be extra wide, if not long, off the vertical of 680 feet. The trails are mostly for intermediates and beginners, with a few steeper pitches. Serving the 15 trails are three double chair lifts, two T-bars, and two surface lifts.

Other Activities Summer amusements available at Mt. Tom include a wave pool, an Alpine Slide, and a water slide.

Child Care In addition to daily group lessons on weekends, day camps provide an entire day of instruction for children 6–14. During vacation periods in December and February, five-day lesson programs are offered. Mt. Tom also has midweek instruction programs for schoolchildren.

Lodging **Holiday Inn.** This typical Holiday Inn property is located 5 miles from the ski area. Samuel's Restaurant and bar, inside, is handy enough, and the huge Ingleside shopping mall and movie theaters are next door. *Exit 15 off I–91, Holyoke, 01040, tel. 413/534–3311. 219 rooms. Facilities: restaurant, bar. AE, D, DC, MC, V. Moderate.*

Suisse Chalet. This chain motel, 2 miles from Mt. Tom, provides comfortable modern furnishings. The 37-year-old facility has no restaurant, but there is one within walking distance. *Rte. 5, Holyoke*

01040, tel. 413/536–1980 or 800/258–1980. 52 rooms with bath. AE, MC, V. Inexpensive.

Nightlife If asked for nightlife recommendations, local residents may suggest a visit to the **Ingleside Shopping Mall**. There is **Tom's Tavern** at the base, but those who seek something on the order of a nightclub should head north to Northampton.

Nashoba Valley
Power Rd., Westford 01886
Tel. 508/692–3033

Close to Boston, Nashoba attracts suburban families for day and night skiing. Package instruction programs are offered to adults in the morning and evening, and to children in the afternoon.

Downhill Skiing Nashoba offers 10 ski trails of mostly novice–intermediate terrain. There is a newly designed 300-foot half-pipe for snowboarders. One double chair, two triple chair lifts, and five surface lifts provide transport. Though the hill is short, each year it's host to a major slalom race, as part of the U.S. Pro Ski Tour. Snowmaking has increased by 30%.

Child Care For children ages 4 and 5, a series of four consecutive one-hour morning classes is offered Monday through Friday. For students in grades 1–12, six consecutive one-hour lessons are offered midweek in the afternoon and on Saturday and Sunday mornings. For children in grades 7–12, the series is also offered on Friday and Saturday evenings.

Lodging **The Westford Regency.** Just five minutes' drive from Nashoba Valley's slopes, this luxurious hotel offers ideal facilities for the skier—a sauna, Jacuzzi, steam room, and indoor pool—and the choice of formal or informal dining. Guest rooms have either modern furnishings or reproduction antiques. *219 Littleton Rd., Rte. 110, Westford 02886, tel. 508/692–8200 or 800/543–7801. 193 rooms with bath, 5 suites. Facilities: 2 dining rooms, bar, pool, Jacuzzi, steam room, exercise room, racquetball, massage, tanning, meeting rooms. AE, DC, MC, V. Moderate–Expensive.*

Nightlife The **Outlook Restaurant and Lounge** upstairs in the base lodge is open year-round, serving lunch and dinner daily. At night the Outlook hops with skiers and local businesspeople.

Wachusett Mountain
499 Mountain Rd., Princeton 01541
Tel. 508/464–2300; snow conditions, 800/SKI–1234.

Wachusett, one hour from Boston, offers a good-size mountain and a large base lodge with facilities usually found only at bigger resorts. It attracts family skiers for day skiing and provides numerous ski-instruction programs for school groups midweek and on weekends. Skiing is available daily until 10 PM.

Downhill Skiing Wachusett has two peaks, the higher with a vertical drop of 1,000 feet. The more difficult terrain is located toward the top of the higher peak; most of the rest is intermediate. Beginner slopes are separated from the main traffic. The area has two triples, a double chair lift, surface lift, and a poma. There are 18 trails; the longest is 1 mile. Steep trails such as 10th Mountain and Smith Walton, plus 10 or so blue cruisers, keep skiers coming back.

Cross-Country Skiing Twenty-five kilometers (16 miles) of cross-country trails circle the mountain.

Child Care At the Polar Club Den in the base building, children meet for classes, take hot-chocolate breaks, and have lunch. The Polar Cub ski instruction program for children 3–12 offers full-day SKIwee lessons on weekends.

Lodging **Westminster Village Inn.** This bed-and-breakfast with efficiencies and suites (some with fireplaces) and 40-year-old cottages is located about 10 minutes away from the ski area. *9 Village Inn Rd. and Rte. 2, Westminster 01473, tel. 508/874–5351. 72 rooms with bath. Facilities: restaurant, indoor pool, sauna, recreation room. Continental breakfast included. AE, DC, MC, V. Moderate–Expensive.*
Harrington Farm. One can ski cross-country to Wachusett from this bed-and-breakfast, and it's only three minutes by car. The farmhouse, built in 1763, has Colonial-style furnishings, antiques, and hand-stenciling on the walls. *178 Westminster Rd., Princeton 01541, tel. 508/464–5600 or 800/736–3276. 7 rooms, 2 with bath. Facilities: dining room. Full breakfast included. MC, V. Moderate.*

Nightlife The lodge at Wachusett Mountain, open late, offers a cafeteria, coffee shop, and the **Black Diamond Restaurant** and **Coppertop Lounge** (with live entertainment on special occasions). The area's next best bet is **Abigail's Restaurant** in the **Days Inn** (Betty Spring Rd., Gardner, tel. 508/630–2500), where a DJ or live bands perform Friday and Saturday nights.

3 Connecticut

*By Andrew
Collins*

*Connecticut-
bred Andrew
Collins is a
freelance
writer who
has edited
and
contributed to
numerous
Fodor's
guides.*

Connecticut has very few sidewalks. Except for a dozen midsize metropolises, Connecticut's towns and villages exist, for now anyway, without those concrete emblems of urbanity—the brackets that crisscross much of America at right angles, defying nature's alluvial and undulating boundaries: the rivers and ridges, mountains and meadows. In such a densely populated state—only three states have more residents per square mile—visitors are typically taken aback by the seeming wealth of space and the seeming distance and inaccessibility between the homes of neighbors.

Nearly every Connecticut town is anchored by a glorious elm-shaded town green, a throwback to a forgotten era but evidence that today's "nutmeggers" still hold precious the ever-elusive commodity of elbow-room and the rich and verdant gifts of nature. Zoning laws in most towns forbid abutting edifices—at least in residential neighborhoods—and 2-acre zoning is the norm in many towns.

This is not to say Connecticut Yankees are unfriendly, or even aloof. It is a state of decidedly civilized and proper persons. But glowing behind this somewhat frosty veneer is a hospitable, if not garrulous, soul. Seldom is a friendly gesture unreturned, though it is usually the non-Yankee who makes the initial overture. And if we rely on the trusty measure of how well Connecticutters respond to distressed drivers seeking directions, the state scores well. Not only will you be told how to get where you're going, but you will also endure the presentation of a complicated but scenic shortcut, the enactment of which is executed with hand gestures, furrowed brows, and ponderous gazes. The directions may get you lost, but the ensuing adventure will be well worth the inconvenience.

People here are inventive, particular, and quirky: History has seen the manufacture of locks, clocks, guns, hats, submarines, bicycle spokes, and numerous tools and innovative mechanisms. There was a time when scheming merchants whittled blocks of wood to resemble rounds of nutmeg and sold them as such to unsuspecting buyers.

Of course, the aforementioned stereotypes speak mostly of the state's natives—and this fraction of the population is dwindling rapidly. Remember the state motto: "He who transplanted still sustains." Outsiders move here, often to build or renovate their dream house in the sticks, and as in any proud land, locals generally resent the throngs of city-dwellers invading the countryside like locusts. Starting in the southwest corner and fanning out a little farther every year, urban sprawl is attacking. Hillside after hillside is taken, stripped of its flora and fauna, and developed. And even with all those zoning laws, things are getting a bit crowded. Some developments even have sidewalks. The immigration is not without its financial advantages, but most natives would gladly trade wealth, which many already have, for privacy.

Connecticut *is* the richest state in the country. A troublesome aspect of this wealth is its uneven distribution. From the top of Yale University's ivory-like Harkness Tower, you can look in no direction without seeing evidence of a deeply troubled city, New Haven, too much of which trudges along below the poverty level. Winding country roads flow arterially from Connecticut's struggling cities into prosperous satellite communities. Many fear that if out of disrespect we allow our once vibrant cities to fall away in disrepair, the lifeblood of every small thriving town will cease to flow, and the state as a whole will suffer. The notions of ethnic integration and urban renewal are hotly discussed at town meetings these days, as residents find ways to keep Connecticut a desirable gateway to New England.

Connecticut

Essential Information

Visitor Information

Department of Economic Development (865 Brook St., Rocky Hill 06067, tel. 203/258–4200, or, for a brochure, tel. 800/282–6863).

Tour Groups

General-
Interest
Tours
Classics Limited (855 Ridge Rd., Wethersfield 06109, tel. 203/563–0848, fax 203/257–9161) offers individual and group tours throughout Connecticut and Southern New England by private car, limousine, van, and coach.

Special-
Interest
Tours
Unique Auto Tours (Box 879, Canton 06019, tel. 203/693–0007; July–Oct.) helps you design a four- or seven-day itinerary through New England, then sends you and a pal off in an antique Rolls-Royce or '50s Cadillac. The cost ranges from $1,600 to $2,100.

"Pick Your Own" Farms

Searching for A-1 apples? the juiciest raspberries? the sweetest blueberries? The experts know: You have to pick 'em yourself. The **Connecticut Department of Agriculture** (165 Capitol Ave., Hartford 06106, tel. 203/566–4865) distributes a list of farms where you can do it.

Arriving and Departing

By Plane
Bradley International Airport (tel. 203/627–3000), 12 miles north of Hartford and New England's second-largest airport, has scheduled daily flights by most major U.S. airlines. **Igor Sikorsky Memorial Airport** (tel. 203/576–7498), 4 miles south of Stratford, is served by Business Express, USAir, and Continental. **Tweed/New Haven Airport** (tel. 203/787–8283), 5 miles southeast of the city, is served by USAir and Continental.

By Car
From New York City, head north on I–95, which hugs the Connecticut shoreline into Rhode Island or, to reach the Litchfield Hills and Hartford, head north on I–684, then east on I–84. From Springfield, Massachusetts, go south on I–91, which bisects I–84 in Hartford and I–95 in New Haven. From Boston, take I–95 south through Providence or take the Massachusetts Turnpike west to I–84. I–395 runs north–south from southeastern Connecticut to Massachusetts.

By Train
Amtrak (tel. 800/872–7245) runs from New York to Boston, stopping in Greenwich, Stamford, Bridgeport, and New Haven before heading either north to Hartford or east to New London. **Metro North** (tel. 212/532–4900 or 800/638–7646) stops locally between Greenwich and New Haven, and a few trains head inland to New Canaan, Danbury, and Waterbury.

By Bus
Greyhound (tel. 800/231–2222) and **Bonanza Bus Lines** (tel. 800/556–3815) join Hartford, Middletown, New London, Stamford, Bridgeport, New Haven, and smaller towns with Boston and New York. **Connecticut Limo** (tel. 800/472–5466) has bus service between Connecticut and the New York airports.

Getting Around Connecticut

By Car The interstates are quickest. But they are busy and ugly. If time allows, skip them in favor of the historic, winding Merritt Parkway (Rte. 15), which runs between Greenwich and Middletown; Routes 7 and 8, extending between I–95 and the Litchfield Hills; and Route 9, which heads south from Hartford through the Connecticut River Valley to Old Saybrook. State maps are available free from the **Connecticut Department of Economic Development** (*see* Visitor Information, *above*).

Dining

Call it the fennel factor. Or the arugula influx. Or the proscuitto preponderance. However you wish to characterize it, southern New England has witnessed a gastronomic revolution in recent years. Preparation and ingredients now reflect the culinary trends of nearby Manhattan and Boston. And while a few traditional favorites remain, such as New England clam chowder, Yankee pot roast, and grilled haddock, Grand Marnier is now favored on ice cream over hot fudge sauce, duck is often served boneless minus its rich, gooey orange glaze, and wilted field greens and grilled seasonal vegetables now complement meat dishes. In cities you'll find a burgeoning selection of Indian, Vietnamese, Thai, Japanese, and Mexican restaurants. Perhaps most astounding is the renaissance of the once thick and greasy pizza pie, something for which Connecticut has long been known. Traditional deep-pan Grecian-style pizzas are being slowly eclipsed in popularity by thin, crispy, gourmet pies, topped by, you guessed it, fennel, arugula, prosciutto, and the like. The drawback of this turn in cuisine is that finding an under-$10 entrée (or even under-$10 14″ pizza) is proving difficult. Dress is casual unless noted otherwise.

Highly recommended restaurants are indicated by a star ★.

Category	Cost*
Very Expensive	over $35
Expensive	$25–$35
Moderate	$12–$25
Inexpensive	under $12

average cost of a three-course dinner, per person, excluding drinks, service, and 6% sales tax

Lodging

Connecticut offers a variety of accommodations. Where major chain hotels are concerned, we've tried to mention the best and the most popular, but many are nondescript, located in busy cities, and appealing mostly to business travelers. We pay more attention to those unusual inns, resorts, bed-and-breakfasts, and country hotels you might not spy from the fast lane of I–95. You'll pay dearly for rooms in summer on the coast and in autumn in the hills, where thousands peek at the peaking foliage. In winter, rates are lowest, but so is the windchill factor—leaving verdant spring as the best time for bargain seekers unwilling to dress in wool and mufflers. The **Nutmeg Bed & Breakfast Agency** (tel. 203/236–6698) is a reliable statewide reservation service for B&Bs and small inns.

Highly recommended lodgings are indicated by a star ★.

Category	Cost*
Very Expensive	over $160
Expensive	$110–$160
Moderate	$60–$110
Inexpensive	under $60

*All prices are for a standard double room during peak season, with no meals unless noted, and excluding service charge and 12% state lodging tax.

Southwestern Connecticut

In terms of both money and personality, southwestern Connecticut, just 50 miles outside of midtown Manhattan, is a rich swirl of old New England and new New York. Encompassing all of Fairfield County, it consistently registers the highest cost of living and most expensive homes of any community in the country. Its bedroom communities are home primarily to white-collar executives; some still make the nearly two-hour mad dash to and from Gotham, but most enjoy a more civilized morning drive to Stamford, which is reputed to have more corporate headquarters per square mile than any other U.S. city. Strict zoning has preserved a certain privacy and rusticity uncommon in other such densely populated areas, and numerous celebrities—Paul Newman, David Letterman, Ron Howard, Ivan Lendl, and Dustin Hoffman among them—call Fairfield County home. The combination of drivers, winding roads, and heavily wooded countryside has resulted in at least one major problem: According to a survey in central Fairfield County, nearly 50% of area drivers have struck a deer.

Venture away from the wealthy communities, and you'll discover four cities in different stages of urban renewal: Stamford, Norwalk, Bridgeport, and Danbury. The cities do have some of the region's best cultural and shopping opportunities, but the economic disparity between Connecticut's tony towns and troubled cities is perhaps nowhere more visible than in Fairfield County, and by most accounts the gulf is widening.

Important Addresses and Numbers

Visitor Information **Housatonic Valley Tourism Commission** (Box 406, Danbury 06813, tel. 203/743–0546 or, outside CT, 800/841–4488). **Yankee Heritage District** (297 West Ave., The Gate Lodge–Matthews Park, Norwalk 06850, tel. 203/854–7825 or 800/866–9255).

Emergencies **Norwalk Hospital** (34 Maple St., Norwalk, tel. 203/852–2000).

Pharmacy **CVS Pharmacy** (235 Main St., Norwalk, tel. 203/847–6057 is open 24 hours).

Getting Around Southwestern Connecticut

By Car Merritt Parkway and the coastal I–95 are the region's main arteries; both are subject to harrowing rush hour snarls. Route 7 is the main road between Norwalk and Danbury, a 40-minute proposition when traffic is behaving. But the best way to see the region is via back roads, so grab a good map and dig around. Travel time from Greenwich to Bridgeport is roughly 35 minutes, Greenwich to New Haven an hour.

By Bus **Connecticut Transit** (tel. 203/327–7433) has local service in Stamford and Norwalk. **Westport Transit** (tel. 203/226–7171) serves the Westport area.

Exploring Southwestern Connecticut

Numbers in the margin correspond to points of interest on the Southwestern Connecticut map.

❶ In **Greenwich,** you'll probably want to start off on Route 1 by buying a Ferrari or Aston Martin at **Miller Motor Cars** (273 W. Putnam Rd., tel. 203/629–8830). The cars are housed in an imposing 1920s stone mansion with leaded-glass windows and beautiful slate floors. And if you can't plunk down $200,000, the going rate for a low-end Aston Martin, you can inspect the walls of the sales room, which are covered with a terrific collection of sepia-tone prints of classic autos. Continuing along Route 1, a thoroughfare of ritzy car dealers, Euro-chic clothing shops, and other posh emporiums, you'll have no trouble believing that Greenwich is one of the wealthiest towns in the United States, if not the world.

❷ Glitzy office buildings, chain hotels, and major department stores have revitalized much of **Stamford** and made it the most dynamic city on the southwestern shore—though a view of several depressed neighborhoods reflects off the glass of its shiny skyscrapers. Here is one of the country's most unusual churches: The fish-shaped **First Presbyterian Church** (1101 Bedford St., tel. 203/324–9522; open daily 9–5), which has beautiful stained-glass windows and a humongous mechanical-action pipe organ. The top cultural attraction is the **Whitney Museum of American Art Champion.** Exhibits of primarily 20th-century American painting and photography change every 10 to 12 weeks, often featuring works from the Whitney's permanent collection in New York City. *Atlantic St. and Tresser Blvd., tel. 203/ 358–7652. Admission free. Open Tues.–Sat. 11–5.*

The northern half of town is much quieter, epitomizing the affluence of the rest of the county. Here, the 118-acre **Stamford Museum and Nature Center** has permanent exhibits of farm tools, local Native American life, and Early American artifacts, and an observatory and planetarium. *39 Scofield Town Rd., tel. 203/322–1646. Admission to grounds free; planetarium: $4 adults, $3 senior citizens and children; observatory: $2 adults, $1 senior citizens and children. Grounds open Mon.–Sat. 9–5, Sun. 1–5; planetarium shows Sun. 3:30; observatory Fri. 8 PM–10 PM.*

❸ A drive through **Darien** may leave you thinking the entire town is one enormous country club. The small downtown area on Route 1, in and around the train station, has a variety of little shops and restaurants. South of town via Route 136 are the small yachting enclaves of **Noroton** and **Rowayton,** two villages that retain the low-key blue-blood atmosphere you expect to find on Nantucket or eastern Long Island.

❹ **Norwalk** is the home of Yankee Doodle Dandies: In 1756, Colonel Thomas Fitch threw together a motley crew of Norwalk soldiers and led them off to fight at Fort Crailo, near Albany. Supposedly, Norwalk's women gathered feathers for the men to wear as plumes in their caps in an effort to give them some appearance of military decorum. Upon the arrival of these shoddily clad warriors, one of

Southwestern Connecticut

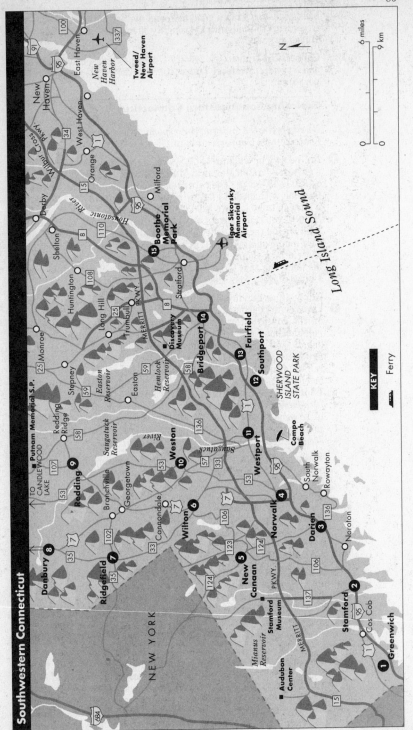

Long Island Sound

KEY

▬▬▬ Ferry

N

0 — 6 miles
0 — 9 km

the British officers sarcastically dubbed them "Macaronis"—slang for fops or dandies. The saying caught on, and so did the song: "Yankee Doodle came to town/Riding on a pony/Stuck a feather in his hat/ And called it macaroni..."

In the 19th century, Norwalk became a major New England port and manufactured pottery, clocks, watches, shingle nails, and paper. It then fell into a state of neglect, in which it remained for much of this century. During the past decade, however, its coastal business district has been the focus of a major redevelopment project, the **SoNo commercial district,** an avenue containing several art galleries, restaurants, and trendy boutiques—the cornerstone of which is the **Maritime Center.** Built around a restored 19th-century redbrick factory on the west bank of the Norwalk River, the 5-acre waterfront center brings to life the ecology and history of Long Island Sound. A huge aquarium competes for attention with such actual marine vessels as the 56-foot oyster sloop *Hope.* The screen of the 340-seat IMAX theater rises six stories and extends 80 feet in width. Although not as popular as Mystic Seaport, the Maritime Center is one of the state's most worthwhile attractions—especially for families. *10 N. Water St., tel. 203/852–0700 or 800/243–2280. Admission: $7.50 adults, $6.50 senior citizens and children; IMAX theater: $5.50 adults, $4.50 senior citizens and children; combined: $11.50 adults, $9.50 senior citizens and children. Open daily 10–5.*

⑤ North of town on Route 124 is **New Canaan,** an even neater, inland version of Darien. So rich and elegant is the landscape that you may want to invest in a local street map and spend the afternoon driving around the estate-studded countryside. Routes 7 and 106, next
⑥ door, cut through the equally dapper community of **Wilton,** which is home to Connecticut's first National Historic Site, **Weir Farm.** It's also the first property of its kind dedicated to the legacy of an American painter, J. Alden Weir. Hikers and picnickers will enjoy the property's 60 heavily wooded acres. A gallery is planned, but for now only tours of Weir's former studios are offered. *735 Nod Hill Rd. (off Rte. 33), Wilton, tel. 203/761–9945 or 203/834–1896. Admission free. Open daily 8:30–5.*

New Yorkers have been known to stay at one of the rambling inns in
⑦ **Ridgefield** rather than drive all the way to comparatively remote Litchfield County, 40 miles north. In Ridgefield, you'll find northwestern Connecticut's atmosphere within an hour of Manhattan. The town center, which you approach from Wilton on Route 33, is still a largely residential sweep of lawns and majestic homes.

An outstanding sculpture garden is the major draw of the **Aldrich Museum of Contemporary Art,** a first-rate collection of contemporary artwork that rivals any small collection in New York. *258 Main St., tel. 203/438–4519. Admission: $3 adults, $2 senior citizens. Open Tues.–Sun. 1–5.*

⑧ Now a middle-class slice of suburbia, **Danbury** was the hat capital of America for nearly 200 years, until the mid-1950s. Rumors persist that the term "mad as a hatter" originated here. It *is* known that hat makers suffered widely from the injurious effects of mercury poisoning, a fact that is said to explain the resultant "madness" of veteran hatters. You can still learn a great deal about the town's hat-making history by visiting the **Scott-Fanton Museum,** a complex that includes a re-created hat shop, a house decorated in 1785 period decor, and the late-18th-centruy house that was birthplace of composer Charles Ives, also with period decor. *43 Main St., tel. 203/ 743–5200. Donation suggested. Open Wed.–Sun. 2–5.*

From Danbury's Route 53, turn east onto Route 302, then south onto Route 58, taking it to its junction with Route 107. Here you'll pass **Putnam Memorial State Park** (tel. 203/566–2304), now a beautiful place for hiking and cross-country skiing, but formerly the site of General Israel Putnam's camp, then known as "Connecticut's Valley Forge."

9 Follow Route 107 through **Redding,** the home of Mark Twain's estate, Stormfield, which burned to the ground. Little has changed since Twin described the area as "one of the loveliest spots in America." From Redding, take Route 53 south as it borders the Saugatuck
10 Reservoir into **Weston,** the home of more writers and painters than you can shake a stick at.

11 Follow Route 53 south and then bear left onto Route 57 to **Westport,** an artists' mecca since the turn of the century. Even today, despite commuters and corporations, Westport remains more arty and cultured than its neighbors: If the rest of Fairfield County is stylistically five years behind Manhattan, Westport lags by just five months.

From Route 1, follow signs to Sherwood Island State Park, and make a left onto Greens Farms Road, following it east along what's commonly dubbed Connecticut's Gold Coast. Here, hiding behind creeper-covered fortress walls of varying sizes and colors, are Gatsbyesque mansions (F. Scott Fitzgerald summered here in the early '20s), whose architectural inconsistency is jarring—one com-
12 pound is even hot pink. The road leads into the village of **Southport,** on the Pequot River, an enclave of sailing enthusiasts and old money.

13 The road from Southport leads into **Fairfield,** a town that was settled well before Westport and still has many old Dutch and postmedieval English Colonials on the network of roads north of Route 1 (Post Rd.).

14 **Bridgeport,** a city that has fallen lately on hard times, is unsafe at night and rather unappealing by day. Three of its attractions, however, definitely bear visiting. The **Barnum Museum,** associated with past resident and former mayor P. T. Barnum, has exhibits depicting the great showman's career, which feature such characters as General Tom Thumb and Jenny Lind, the Swedish Nightingale. You can also tour a scaled-down model of Barnum's legendary three-ring circus. This is one of the most visited attractions in the state. *820 Main St., tel. 203/331–1104. Admission: $5 adults, $4 senior citizens, $3 children. Open Tues.–Sat. 10–4:30, Sun. noon–4:30.*

Beardsley Park and Zoological Gardens, north of downtown, is an extremely pleasant surprise. Connecticut's largest zoo is contained within the grounds, which sprawl over 30 acres. Its indoor walk-through South American rain forest, the only one in New England, alone justifies a visit. In the rest of the zoo you'll find 350 species of animals. A smaller children's zoo offers pony rides. *Noble Ave., tel. 203/576–8082. Admission to zoo: $3.75 adults, $2 children 5–12, $1 children 3–4; to grounds and park, per car: $5 out-of-state visitors, $3 CT residents. Open daily 9–4.*

Still north of Beardsley is the **Discovery Museum,** which touches all bases with an eclectic collection of art from the Renaissance to contemporary times, a planetarium, several hands-on science exhibits, a computer-art exhibit, and a children's museum. *4450 Park Ave., tel. 203/372–3521. Admission: $5.50 adults, $3.50 senior citizens and children. Open Tues.–Fri. 10–5, Sun. noon–5.*

15 East on the Merritt Parkway, in northern **Stratford,** is **Boothe Memorial Park,** a complex of several unusual buildings, including a blacksmith shop, carriage and tool barns, and a museum that includes a history of the trolley among its displays. There's also a beautiful rose garden and a children's playground. *Main St., tel. 203/378–9895. Admission free. Park open year-round, dawn–dusk; museum open June–Sept., Tues.–Fri. 11–1, weekends 1–4.*

Historic Homes and Small Museums

Hours of the following homes are usually limited to a few days a week, although most will open by appointment—always call ahead. Admission ranges from free to $3 unless otherwise noted.

Cos Cob The 1732 **Bush–Holley House** (39 Strickland Rd., tel. 203/869–6899; open Feb.–Dec.), a handsome central-chimney saltbox, now houses a wonderful collection of artwork by sculptor John Rogers, potter Leon Volkmar, and painters Childe Hassam, Elmer Livingstone MacRae, and John Twachtman. It was run as a boardinghouse during the early 20th century, and Hassam, Twachtman, Willa Cather, Lincoln Steffens, and other famous personages spent time here.

Greenwich The **Bruce Museum** (1 Museum Dr., tel. 203/869–0376; open year-round) has wildlife dioramas, a worthwhile small collection of American Impressionist paintings, and many exhibits on the area. The small, barn-red **Putnam Cottage** (248 E. Putnam Ave., Rte. 1, tel. 203/869–9697; open year-round) was built in 1690 and operated as Knapp's Tavern during the Revolutionary War. It was a frequent meeting room of Revolutionary War hero General Israel Putnam. Today you can meander through a lush herb garden and examine the cottage's Colonial furnishings and prominent fieldstone fireplace.

New Canaan The **Historical Society** (13 Oenoke Ridge, tel. 203/966–1776; open year-round), one of the best in Connecticut, operates several buildings in town, including the town house in which it's based, the John Rogers Sculpture Studio, a Colonial schoolhouse, a tool museum, a print shop, and a restored Georgian Colonial home.

North Darien The 1737 **Bates–Scofield Homestead** (45 Old Kings Hwy., tel. 203/655–9233; open year-round), a classic New England saltbox with a center chimney, contains period decor and has a lovely herb garden.

Norwalk Restoration continues at the **Lockwood-Matthews Mansion Museum** (295 West Ave., tel. 203/838–1434; admission $5 adults, $3 senior citizens; open mid-Feb.–mid-Dec.), a building that was slated for demolition in 1965 and is today an ornate tribute to Victorian decorating—it's hard not to be impressed by the octagonal rotunda and 50 rooms of gilt, fresco, marble, ornate woodwork, and etched glass.

Ridgefield A British cannonball is enlodged in the wall of the **Keeler Tavern Museum** (132 Main St., tel. 203/438–5485; open Feb.–Dec.), a historic inn and the former home of architect Cass Gilbert, which now houses a museum filled with furniture and Revolutionary memorabilia.

What to See and Do with Children

Barnum Museum, Bridgeport
Maritime Center, South Norwalk
Scott-Fanton Museum, Danbury

Shopping

Antiques, Crafts, and Objets d'Art
Route 7, which runs through **Wilton** and **Ridgefield,** has dozens of fine antiques sheds and boutiques. Of particular note is **Cannon Crossing** (just off Rte. 7, Cannondale, tel. 203/762–2233), a pre–Civil War farm village–turned–shopping complex restored by former child actress June Havoc. The **Barter Shop** (140 Main St., Norwalk, tel. 203/846–1242) has several buildings chock-full of bric-a-brac and both finished and unfinished furniture. **Washington Street** in South Norwalk (SoNo) has excellent galleries and crafts dealers; stop by the **Brookfield/SONO Crafts Center** (127 Washington St., tel. 203/853–6155)—a second branch is in Brookfield on Route 25 (tel. 203/775–4526). **The Elements Gallery** (14 Liberty Way, Greenwich, tel. 203/661–0014), one of the state's most exciting crafts galleries, exhibits the works of top crafts artists in a converted livery stable. **Our World Gallery** (The Stone Studio, 82 Erskine Rd., Stamford, tel. 203/322–7018) shows the work of international and local painters and sculptors. At northern Stamford's **United House Wrecking** (535 Hope St., tel. 203/348–5371), acres of architectural artifacts, decorative accessories, antiques, nautical items, lawn and garden furnishings, and other less valuable but certainly unusual items await you. The **Stratford Antique Center** (400 Honeyspot Rd., tel. 203/378–7754) shows the wares of about 120 dealers.

Food
The area's three **Hay Day** markets (1050 E. Putnam Ave., Greenwich, tel. 203/637–7600; 21 Governor St., Ridgefield, tel. 203/431–4400; 1385 Post Rd. E, Westport, tel. 203/254–1880) stock hard-to-find fresh produce, mouth-watering locally made sauces and salads, jams, cheeses, fresh baked goods, flowers, and much more. **Stew Leonard's Dairy** (100 Westport Ave., Rte. 1, Norwalk, tel. 203/847–7213; 99 Federal Rd., Danbury, tel. 203/790–1571), the self-billed "Disneyland of Supermarkets," is a great place to take children—large windows in the store allow you to see the milk-processing plant, and outside is a small petting zoo.

Shopping Malls and Districts
Upscale
The nine-story **Stamford Town Center** (100 Greyrock Pl., tel. 203/356–9700), which houses 130 shops, is the chic mall in which Woody Allen and Bette Midler's on-screen marriage crumbled in the film *Scenes from a Mall.* Its outdoor equivalent is Main Street in Westport, with **J Crew, Barney's, Ann Taylor, Eddie Bauer,** and dozens of other fashionable shops. The downtown areas of **New Canaan** and **Darien** and Route 1 in **Greenwich** are also renowned for their swank brand-name stores and boutiques.

Discount
Near the East Norwalk train station are the **Factory Outlets at Norwalk** (11 Rowan St., tel. 203/838–1349), with more than 20 brand-name outlet shops, including the **Royal Doulton Shoppe** and **Bass. Decker's** (666 West Ave., Norwalk, tel. 203/866–5593) sells Polo clothing, along with several other fashionable labels, at discount prices. The **Danbury Fair Mall** (where Rte. 7 and I–84 intersect, tel. 203/743–3247) and **Trumbull Mall** (just off the Merritt Pkwy., tel. 203/372–4500) have scores of shops ranging from discount to mainstream.

Sports and Outdoor Activities

Beaches
In summer, visitors to Westport congregate at **Sherwood Island State Park** (I–95, exit 18, tel. 203/226–6983). In addition to its long sweep of sandy beach, it has two water's-edge picnic groves and several food concessions. Sunbathing, swimming, and fishing are the chief attractions. New Fairfield's **Squantz Pond State Park** (western

shore of Candlewood Lake, Rte. 39, tel. 203/566–2304) is crowded in summer but still pretty; it has boat and canoe rentals, fishing and bait shops, picnicking, and hiking trails.

Fishing **Bareboats** are available at **Yacht Haven** (Washington Blvd., Stamford, tel. 203/359–4500) and **Stratford Marina** (Broad St., Stratford, tel. 203/377–4477). **Fishing boats** can be chartered from **Norwalk Cove Marina** (Norwalk, tel. 203/838–2326).

Golf *Golf Digest* recently rated Danbury's **Richter Park Golf Course** (Aunt Hack Rd., tel. 203/792–2550) one of the top 10 public courses in the country. Also try **H. Smith Richardson Golf Course** (Morehouse Hwy., Fairfield, tel. 203/255–5016), **Sterling Farms Golf Course** (Newfield Ave., Stamford, tel. 203/329–8171), and **Ridgefield Golf Club** (Ridgebury Rd., tel. 203/748–7008). All are 18-hole courses.

Hiking and Nature Centers In northern **Greenwich** is the 485-acre **Audubon Center** (613 Riversville Rd., tel. 203/869–5272), with 8 miles of hiking trails and exhibits about the local environment. The **Connecticut Audubon Society** in **Fairfield** (2325 Burr St., tel. 203/259–6305) maintains a 160-acre wildlife sanctuary that includes 6 miles of rugged hiking trails and special walks for people with visual impairments and mobility problems. The society operates a smaller **Birdcraft Sanctuary** nearby (314 Unquowa, Fairfield, tel. 203/259–0416), which has a children's activity corner along with 6 acres of trails and a pond that attracts waterfowl during their spring and fall migrations; the 1935 chimney was built to attract the very chimney swifts that nest in it. In **Weston** 1,660 acres of woodlands, wetlands, and rock ledges await intrepid hikers at **Devil's Den Preserve** (tel. 203/226–4991). Several trails traverse the 62-acre **Nature Center for Environmental Activities** in **Westport** (10 Woodside La., tel. 203/227–7253). **New Canaan Nature Center** (44 Oenoke Ridge, tel. 203/966–9577) has hands-on exhibits, live animals, programs on conservation and solar power, and beautiful gardens. Still more hiking is available at the **Weir Farm National Historical Site** in **Wilton,** the **Stamford Nature Center,** and the **Putnam Memorial State Park** in **Redding** (*see* Exploring in Southwestern Connecticut, *above*).

Water Sports You can rent sailboards and surfboards at **Rick's Surf City** (570 Boston Post Rd., Milford, tel. 203/877–4257), sailboats at the **Longshore Sailing School** (Longshore Club Park, 260 S. Compo Rd., Westport, tel. 203/226–4646).

Spectator Sports

Jai Alai **Bridgeport Jai Alai** (255 Kossuth St., tel. 203/576–1976, 800/972–9471, or, outside Ct, 800/243–9490; open Dec.–May) and **Milford Jai Alai** (311 Old Gate La., tel. 203/877–4242 or 800/243–9660; open June–Nov.) host the fast-moving sport popular with gamblers.

Dining and Lodging

Darien **Comfort Inn.** This is a perfectly clean and safe rendition of the typical chain motel—in an unusually nice town. Southwestern Connecticut's major attractions are all within a 30-minute drive. *50 Ledge Rd., 06820, tel. or fax 203/655–8211 or tel. 800/221–2222. 99 rooms with bath. AE, D, DC, MC, V. Moderate.*
Lodging

Greenwich **Bertrand.** The spectacular brick vaulting in this former bank building on the town's main street sets the scene for classic and nouvelle
Dining
★ French cuisine. Owner-chef Christian Bertrand was sous-chef at

Lutèce, one of Manhattan's best French restaurants. The confit of duck with sorrel sauce and the salmon in a pastry crust seem more at home here than stacks of money bags, and financial matters are forgotten with the arrival of the nougat ice cream—until the check comes. *253 Greenwich Ave., tel. 203/661–4618. Reservations advised. Jacket and tie required. AE, DC, MC, V. No lunch Sat. Closed Sun. Very Expensive.*

★ **Restaurant Jean-Louis.** Roses, Villeroy & Boch china, and crisp, white tablecloths with lace underskirts complement extraordinary food, carefully served. Specialties include quail-and-vegetable ragout with foie gras sauce, scaloppine of salmon on a bed of leeks with fresh herb sauce, and, for dessert, lemon and pear gratin. *61 Lewis St., tel. 203/622–8450. Reservations advised. Jacket and tie required. AE, D, DC, MC, V. Closed Sun. Very Expensive.*

Pasta Vera. The tiny, plain white dining space of this shop-cum-restaurant belies the splendor of its many variations on simple pasta. Try the wild mushroom ravioli or the deliciously imaginative *pesto torte* (layers of zucchini pesto in puff pastry topped with tomato sauce). *88 E. Putnam Ave., tel. 203/661–9705. No reservations. No credit cards. Closed Sun. Inexpensive–Moderate.*

Dining and Lodging
★ **Homestead Inn.** This enormous Italianate wood-frame house, in a posh residential neighborhood not far from the water, is an architectural treasure with its cupola, ornate bracketed eaves, and wraparound Victorian porch, now enclosed. Rooms are decorated individually with antiques and period reproductions. Those in the nearby 19th-century outbuilding have 20th-century decor but still plenty of charm. But it's for Jacques Thiebeult's cuisine that the Homestead is best known: The appetizers mostly involve exquisitely prepared shellfish, and such entrées as veal kidney finished with brandy, cream, and mustard represent some of the best French cuisine in the area. *420 Field Point Rd., 06830, tel. and fax 203/869–7500. 17 rooms with bath, 6 suites. Facilities: restaurant (reservations advised, jacket required), Continental breakfast included. AE, DC, MC, V. Inn: Moderate–Expensive. Restaurant: Very Expensive.*

Greenwich Harbor Inn. Thanks to the major renovation that its new management undertook in 1993, this informal harborside inn looks better than ever. Rooms are done in soft Colonial colors, with floral bedspreads and reproductions of 18th-century antiques. Make no mistake, though—this is more like an upscale chain hotel than a rambling inn. Still, it's clean and within walking distance of the railroad station and the Greenwich Avenue boutiques. The Atlantis Restaurant, which has an outdoor deck overlooking the harbor, serves such seafood dishes as Mediterranean shellfish stew and yellowtail snapper with roast tomatoes and fennel. *500 Steamboat Rd., 06830, tel. 203/661–9800, fax 203/629–4431. 96 rooms. Facilities: restaurant (reservations advised), patio bar, meeting facilities, dockage. AE, DC, MC, V. Inn: Moderate–Expensive. Restaurant: Expensive–Very Expensive.*

Lodging
★ **Hyatt Regency Greenwich.** At one time the Condé Nast publishing empire was ruled from the four-story turreted tower of this modern edifice. Inside, a vast but comfortable atrium boasts its own flourishing lawn and abundant flora. The rooms are spacious, with all the amenities, including modem-compatible telephones. The pleasantly clublike Condé's restaurant serves interesting renditions of classic dishes. *1800 E. Putnam, 06870, tel. 203/637–1234 or 800/233–1234, fax 203/637–2940. 353 rooms with bath. Facilities: 2 restaurants, jazz bar, atrium lounge, valet parking, indoor pool, health club,*

steam room, open-air sun court. AE, D, DC, MC, V. Very Expensive.

Stanton House Inn. This large, Federal mansion within walking distance of downtown underwent considerable redesign by Stanford White in 1899. It has been carefully redone with a mixture of antiques and tasteful reproductions. *76 Maple Ave., 06830, tel. 203/ 869–2110, fax 203/629–2116. 25 rooms, 2 share a bath. Continental breakfast included. AE, MC, V. Moderate–Expensive.*

New Canaan
Lodging

The Maples Inn. This white-trim, yellow-clapboard structure— which is just a short drive form downtown—has 13 gables, most of which are veiled by a canopy of aged maples. Bedrooms are furnished with antiques and canopied, queen-size beds. Mahogany chests, gilt frames, and brass lamps gleam with energetic polishing, and the imaginative use of fabrics and paper fans is an education in design. *179 Oenoke Ridge, 06840, tel. 203/966–2927, fax 203/966– 5003. 6 double rooms with bath, 4 suites, 6 apartments. MC, V. Expensive–Very Expensive.*

Norwalk
Dining

Meson Galicia. Somehow good Spanish restaurants are rare in this region. But the tapas served in this restored trolley barn in downtown Norwalk are extraordinary, inventive, and electrifying to the taste buds: Ingredients used include sweetbreads, capers, asparagus, chorizo . . . the list goes on. Come with an empty stomach and an open mind, and let the enthusiastic staff spoil you. No greasy paellas here. *10 Wall St., tel. 203/866–8800. Reservations advised. AE, MC, V. No lunch weekends. Closed Mon. Moderate–Expensive.*

Dining and
Lodging
★

Silvermine Tavern. Though best known for its restaurant, this establishment also offers lodgings, parts of which date to 1642 and which represent one of the better values in the region. Each of the cozy rooms is configured and furnished differently, with hooked rugs and antiques as well as some modern touches. The large low-ceiling dining room is romantic, with its Colonial decor and numerous windows overlooking a waterfall. Traditional New England favorites are given some new slants: The duckling is semi-boneless and served in lingonberry sauce, and the rainbow trout is prepared with white wine, diced tomatoes, and lime. Sunday brunch is a local tradition. *194 Perry Ave., 06850, tel. 203/847–4558, fax 203/847–9171. 10 rooms with bath. Facilities: restaurant (reservations advised.). Continental breakfast included. AE, DC, MC, V. Closed Tues. Inn: Moderate. Restaurant: Expensive.*

Lodging

Marriott Courtyard. This is an unusually clean and well-run modern hotel on a rather bleak corporate stretch of Main Avenue, just north of the Merritt Parkway. Within the courtyard, a gazebo is surrounded by a perfectly groomed lawn and a pool. *474 Main Ave., 06851, tel. 203/849–9111 or 800/321–2211, fax 203/849–8144. 133 rooms with bath, 12 suites. Facilities: restaurant, lounge, health club, whirlpool, indoor pool. AE, DC, MC, V. Expensive.*

Days Inn. This late-'80s motel is next door to the Marriott and also well kept. The small lobby is efficient, if not cheery, and rooms contain modern furnishings in soft colors. Pick any room—all the views are equally blah. *426 Main Ave., 06851, tel. 203/849–9828 or 800/ 325–2525, fax 203/846–6925. 119 rooms with bath. Facilities: restaurant, lounge, health club. AE, DC, MC, V. Inexpensive–Moderate.*

Ridgefield
Dining
★

Hay Day Cafe. This small sunlit eatery is popular for both lunch and dinner. It's noteworthy for two things: Every menu selection, including the appetizers and even a few desserts, is listed with an appropriate wine, and nearly every item is intended to show off the incredible selection of gourmet groceries sold in an adjoining country market (*see* Shopping, *above*). If you just love the poached salmon with lemon thyme risotto and sauce verte you had for dinner, the friendly staff will tell you which ingredients to buy and how to make it. The food is New American all the way, and the selection changes all the time. *21 Governor St., tel. 203/438–2344. Reservations accepted. MC, V. Moderate–Expensive.*

Dining and Lodging

Stonehenge. When this famous 18th-century inn burned to the ground a few years ago, everybody wondered if a rebuilt Stonehenge could ever equal the original. Alas, much of the old charm is lost. Although this white-clapboard imposter is lavishly decorated, it feels more like a luxury hotel than a cozy and characterful inn. One thing that has improved is the restaurant, which presents a solid but pricey menu of Continental classics, including duck with orange sauce, sirloin steak with onion rings—there are no surprises here. *Box 667, Rte. 7, 06877, tel. 203/438–6511, fax 203/438–2478. 14 rooms with bath, 2 suites. Facilities: restaurant (reservations advised; jacket and tie required), outdoor pool. AE, DC, MC, V. Inn: Expensive–Very Expensive. Restaurant: Very Expensive.*

The Elms. The best rooms are in the impressive frame house, built by a Colonial cabinetmaker in 1760, near the site of the Battle of Ridgefield. Rooms in the adjacent 1850 building are nondescript. With its mix of antiques, reproductions, and modern fixtures, the inn is a comfortable stopping-off place. The recently refurbished restaurant is brighter now and churns out dependable Continental cuisine, including local game specialties and, in January, wild boar. *500 Main St., 06877, tel. 203/438–2541. 15 rooms with bath, 5 suites. Facilities: restaurant (reservations advised), meeting facilities, pub, Continental breakfast included. AE, DC, MC, V. Moderate–Expensive.*

Stamford Dining ★

Hacienda Don Emilio. The decor of this Mexican restaurant is definitely more upscale Spanish than Americanized south-of-the-border—there are no streamers here. But the real draw is the imaginative and authentic cuisine. *Pollo en mole poblano* (chicken mole) is a favorite and not to be confused with the bland version of the dish you usually find around the state. Try the *tacos pibil*, a Yucatán specialty consisting of shredded pork marinated in a delicious roasted-tomato salsa. *222 Summer St., tel. 203/324–0577. Reservations advised. AE, DC, MC, V. No Sun. lunch. Moderate–Expensive.*

Il Forno Ristorante. The two-story dining room is decorated like a Venetian piazza. The list of specials always seems more extensive than the menu, which itself offers everything from seafood and veal dishes by the dozen to crisp-crusted, brick-oven pizzas with imaginative toppings. It's within easy walking distance of Stamford's theaters. *45 Atlantic St., tel. 203/357–8882. Reservations advised. AE, MC, V. Moderate.*

Lodging

Stamford Marriott. The Marriott stands out for its convenience to trains and airport buses and for its up-to-date facilities. Furnishings throughout are modern and comfortable, if unmemorable. The large, busy lobby is a favorite meeting place of the city's movers and shakers, who frequently head for one of several meeting rooms or to Le Carrousel, the state's only revolving rooftop restaurant. *2 Stamford Forum, 06901, tel. 203/357–9555 or 800/228–9290, fax 203/324–6897. 500 rooms with bath, 7 suites. Facilities: 2 restaurants, 2 lounges, health club, jogging track, indoor and outdoor pools, racquetball. AE, DC, MC, V. Expensive.*

Stamford Sheraton. The drive leading to the ultramodern entrance of this downtown luxury hotel should prepare you for the dramatic atrium lobby inside, with its brass-and-glass-enclosed gazebo—high-tech haywire to some. Attractive, contemporary furnishings in the rooms are complemented by spacious bathrooms. *1 First Stamford Pl., 06901, tel. 203/967–2222 or 800/325–3535, fax 203/967–3475. 471 rooms with bath, 34 suites. Facilities: 2 restaurants, lounge, health club, indoor pool. AE, DC, MC, V. Expensive.*

Stamford Super 8 Motel. The furnishings in this link of the national hotel chain are modern but nondescript, but the property is clean and convenient to all local attractions. *32 Grenhart Rd., 06902, tel. 203/324–8887 or 800/843–1991. 92 rooms, 7 suites. Facilities: coffee shop. AE, DC, MC, V. Inexpensive–Moderate.*

Westport
Dining

Le Chambord. Tiny oil lamps cast a romantic glow on each almond-colored tablecloth and make the silver and crystal gleam. Service is attentive yet unobtrusive, and the kitchen staff is accomplished in its renditions of such trusted French classics as canard à l'orange and baby rack of lamb with vegetables. *1572 Post Rd. E, tel. 203/255–2654. Reservations advised. AE, DC, MC, V. No lunch Sat. Closed Sun. and Mon. Very Expensive.*

Allen's Clam House. Here's a classic New England seafood house, in this case overlooking a 17-acre mill pond. Stop in for one thing: fresh seafood. The lobster is wonderful, but consider also the salmon in dill sauce and the crabmeat au gratin. *191 Hillspoint Rd., tel. 203/226–4411. Reservations advised. Closed Mon. AE, MC, V. Expensive.*

★ **Cafe Christina.** One of the more recent reasons Westport now rivals Greenwich as Connecticut's culinary capital is this outstanding take on Tuscan-Provençal cooking. Installed in Westport's turn-of-the-century former library, it is bright and colorful, a recent collaboration of 17 local artists and craftspersons, with faux columns and other trompe l'oeil touches on the muraled walls. You might start with baked polenta or an arugula-and-portobello mushroom risotto fritter. The striped bass with stewed tomatoes stars among the entrées, which include a few filling pasta dishes. *1 Main St., tel. 203/221–7950. Reservations required. AE, DC, MC, V. Closed Mon. Expensive.*

★ **Meeting Street Grill.** In this unassuming green-shingled, white-trim house on Post Road next to the Westport Inn, about the last thing you expect to find is both the jazziness and down-home zest of the Garden District, but here it is: Only the clang of the St. Charles Streetcar is missing. With ceiling fans, historic prints of Louisiana, gold drapes, and lace curtains, the Grill sets the scene without overdoing it. And when you've tasted the crawfish-and-crab cakes topped with lemon-and-fennel remoulade, the pecan-Creole mustard chicken, and the apple-blueberry cobbler, you'll think you've died and gone to Dixie heaven. Loosen your belt for Sunday's hearty jazz brunch. *1563 Post Rd. E, tel. 203/256–3309. Reservations advised. AE, MC, V. Closed Mon. Expensive.*

Dining and
Lodging
★

The Inn at National Hall. The self-important name belies the whimsical and exotic interior of this towering redbrick Victorian on the downtown banks of the Saugatuck River. Each room is a study in innovative restoration, wall-stenciling, and decorative design. The furniture collection is exceptional, from the 300-year-old Swedish grandfather clock in the lobby to the chandelier in the conference room, which once hung in London's Savoy Hotel. Rooms and suites are magnificent—some with sleeping lofts and 18-foot windows. They are also, often, amusing: One might carry out a folk theme, another has its own commode-cum-reading room, fully stocked with books. With its Corinthian columns and tasseled curtain swags,

Restaurant Zanghi, on the lushly decorated first floor, sets the stage for Continental fare, including venison and rabbit. *2 Post Rd. W, 06880, tel. 203/221–1351 or 800/NAT–HALL, fax 203/221–0276. 7 rooms, 8 suites. Facilities: restaurant (reservations required), meeting facilities, VCRs and refrigerators in all rooms, kitchenette and fireplace in one suite. AE, DC, MC, V. Inn: Very Expensive. Restaurant: Expensive–Very Expensive.*

Lodging **The Cotswold Inn.** Honeymooners often nest at this elegant cottage in the heart of downtown Westport's chic shopping area. Though the steep gabled roof and stone porches recall England's Cotswold region, rooms capture the essence of 18th-century Connecticut, with reproduction Chippendale and Queen Anne furnishings—highboys, mule chests, wing chairs. Two rooms have canopy beds; one has a fireplace. It's more museumlike than it is homey. *76 Myrtle Ave., 06880, tel. 203/226–3766. 3 rooms with bath, 1 suite. Continental breakfast included. AE, MC, V. Very Expensive.*

★ **The Inn at Longshore.** This small, late-19th-century mansion is on one of the most beautiful sites on the Connecticut shore. The drive up the long road lined with stately oaks is the perfect prelude to a romantic weekend at this classy inn of reproduction antiques and rooms with water and park views. *260 S. Compo Rd., 06880, tel. 203/ 226–3316, fax 203/226–5723. 9 rooms with bath, 3 suites. Facilities: restaurant, tennis, handball, golf, outdoor pool, sailing, windsurfing. AE, DC, MC, V. Expensive.*

The Westport Inn. Bedrooms of this upscale motor lodge have been refurbished with attractive contemporary furniture and several excellent restaurants are within walking distance. Rooms surrounding the large indoor pool are set back nicely and are slightly larger than the rest. *1595 Post Rd. E, 06880, tel. 203/259–5236 or 800/446– 8997, fax 203/254–8439. 112 rooms with bath, 2 suites. Facilities: restaurant, health club, indoor pool. AE, DC, MC, V. Moderate– Expensive.*

The Arts and Nightlife

All of the four excellent theaters in the region mount professional Broadway-style shows. The **Stamford Center for the Arts** (307 Atlantic St., tel. 203/323–2131), which recently presented Al Pacino in *Chinese Coffee,* and the **Downtown Cabaret Theatre** (263 Golden Hill St., Bridgeport, tel. 203/576–1636), which has an excellent children's theater, are open year-round. The **Gateway's Candlewood Playhouse** (Rte. 37 at Rte. 39, New Fairfield, tel. 203/746–4441) runs between April and December, and the **Westport Playhouse** (25 Powers Court, tel. 203/227–4177) is a summer theater.

Musical performances are given at the outdoor **Levitt Pavilion** (off Jesup Green, tel. 203/226–7600) in Westport. Stamford's **Palace Theatre** (61 Atlantic St., tel. 203/325–4466) presents the **Stamford Symphony Orchestra** (tel. 203/325–1407), the **Connecticut Grand Opera and Orchestra** (tel. 203/327–2867), and other fine musical performances. The **Fairfield Symphony Orchestra** (tel. 203/972–7400) has its symphonic series at the Norwalk Concert Hall (125 East Ave.) and a chamber series at Greenwich's Bruce Museum (1 Museum Dr.).

Bars are plentiful around these parts, and most have a tavernlike atmosphere. The best are near the railroad station and on Main Street in **Westport,** in the SoNo district of **South Norwalk,** and around Main Street in **Ridgefield.**

The Connecticut River Valley

It was along the meandering Connecticut River that westward expansion in the New World began. Dutch explorer Adrian Block first checked things out in 1614, and in 1633 a trading post was set up in what is now Hartford. Within five years, throngs of restive Bay colonists had settled in this fertile valley. What followed was more than three centuries of barque building, shad hauling, and river trading with ports as far away as the West Indies and the Mediterranean.

Far less touristy than the coast and northwest hills, the Connecticut River Valley is an unspectacular stretch of small river villages and uncrowded state parks punctuated by a few small cities and one large one: Hartford. Of all the regions in Connecticut, this is the one seemingly designed for travelers just passing through. It's seldom the goal of a journey. Hartford, the Connecticut River's major port, is known to most as the insurance capital of America. Its small but lively downtown and dramatic skyline of distinctive office towers belie what is actually just an enormous suburban settlement that continues to outgrow itself. To the south, with the exception of industrial Middletown, a slew of genuinely quaint hamlets vie for a share of Connecticut's tourist crop, offering antiques shops, scenic drives, trendy restaurants, and museums—most of the latter with only local appeal.

Important Addresses and Numbers

Visitor Information **Connecticut Valley Tourism Commission** (393 Main St., Middletown 06457, tel. 203/347–6924). **Farmington Valley/West Hartford Visitors Bureau** (Box 1550 Old Avon Village, 41 E. Main St., Avon 06001, tel. 203/674–1035). **Greater Hartford Convention and Visitors Bureau** (1 Civic Center Plaza, Hartford 06103, tel. 203/728–6789). **Olde Towne Tourism District** (105 Marsh St., Wethersfield 06109, tel. 203/257–9299).

Emergencies **Hartford Hospital** (80 Seymour St., tel. 203/524–2525). **Middlesex Hospital** (28 Crescent St., Middletown, tel. 203/347–9471).

Late-Night Pharmacies **CVS** (1099 New Britain Ave., West Hartford, tel. 203/236–6181). **Community Pharmacy** (197 Main St., Deep River, tel. 203/526–5379).

Getting Around the Connecticut River Valley

By Car I–84, I–91, Route 2, Route 202, and Route 44 intersect in Hartford. The major road through the valley is Route 9, which extends from just south of Hartford at I–91 to I–95 at Old Saybrook. Farmington is reached from Hartford on Route 4.

By Taxi **Airport Taxi** (tel. 203/627–3210) has limo service between Bradley International Airport and downtown Hartford.

By Train and Bus Hartford's attractively renovated **Union Station** (1 Union Pl., tel. 203/727–1776) is the main terminus for **Amtrak** (tel. 800/872–7245) trains as well as **Greyhound** (tel. 800/231–2222), **Bonanza** (tel. 800/556–3815), and **Peter Pan** (tel. 203/724–5200) buses. Bus and train service is available to most major northeastern cities. **Connecticut Transit** (tel. 203/525–9181) provides local Hartford bus service; the fare is 75¢.

Guided Tours

Heritage Trails (Box 138, Farmington, tel. 203/677–8867) runs daily city tours of Hartford and candlelight dinner tours and it sells self-guided driving tours on tape for $9.95. **Chester Charter** (Chester Airport, 61 Winthrop Rd., Chester, tel. 203/526–4321) hosts 15-minute scenic orientation flights over the lower Connecticut River valley, weather permitting. The cost is $20. The **Greater Hartford Architecture Conservancy** (278 Farmington Ave., tel. 203/525–0279; weekends July–Aug.) sponsors *Hartford on Tour*, one- and two-hour walking tours of historic sights, and sells tape tours for $7.99.

Between May and October the **Valley Railroad** (Exit 3 off Rte. 9, Essex, tel. 203/767–0103) carries you by rail along the Connecticut River and lower valley, then, if you wish to continue, by riverboat up the river. The train trip lasts an hour, the riverboat ride 90 minutes. The train fare is $8.50 for adults, $4.25 for children; a combined train–boat fare costs $14 for adults, $7 for children.

Exploring the Connecticut River Valley

Numbers in the margin correspond to points of interest on the Connecticut River Valley and Downtown Hartford maps.

1 **Essex,** a few miles north of I–95 on Route 9, looks much now as it did in the mid-19th century, at the height of its shipbuilding prosperity. So important to a young America was Essex's boat manufacturing, that the British burned more than 40 ships here during the War of 1812. Gone are the days of steady trade with the West Indies, when the aroma of imported rum, molasses, and spices hung heavy in the air. Now its main street is lined with charming whitewashed houses—many the former roosts of weary sea captains—and shops selling clothing, antiques, paintings and prints, and sweets. On the river are wood- and aluminum-mast yachts, and the **Connecticut River Museum** (Steamboat Dock, tel. 203/767–8269; admission: $3 adults; open Tues.–Sun. 10–5). In addition to pre-Colonial artifacts and displays, there's a full-size reproduction of the world's first submarine, the *American Turtle;* the original was built by David Bushnell in 1775.

2 **Ivoryton,** on the other side of Route 9, was named for its steady import of elephant tusks from Kenya and Zanzibar during the 19th century. What was Ivoryton's leading *export* during this time? Piano keys. At one time, the Comstock-Cheney piano manufacturers processed so much ivory that Japan regularly purchased Ivoryton's surplus, using the scraps to make souvenirs. The Depression closed the lid on Ivoryton's pianos and what remains is a sleepy, shady hamlet. The **Museum of Fife and Drum** on Main Street has a lively collection of martial sheet music, instruments, and uniforms chronicling America's history of parades, from the Revolutionary War to the present. Live musical performances are given in summer. *62 N. Main St., tel. 203/767–2237. Admission: $1 adults, 50¢ senior citizens. Open May, June, Oct., weekends 1–5; July–Sept., Fri.–Sun. 1–5.*

3 Farther along Route 9 is **Deep River**, which, like Essex, has a small main street lined with antiques shops. It too was famous for many
4 years as a manufacturer of piano keys. Across the river in **Hadlyme**, perched high on a cliff overlooking the river, is the state's leading oddity, **Gillette Castle State Park.** The outrageous, some might say tacky, 24-room, oak-and-granite hilltop castle was built by the eccentric actor William Gillette between 1914 and 1919—modeled af-

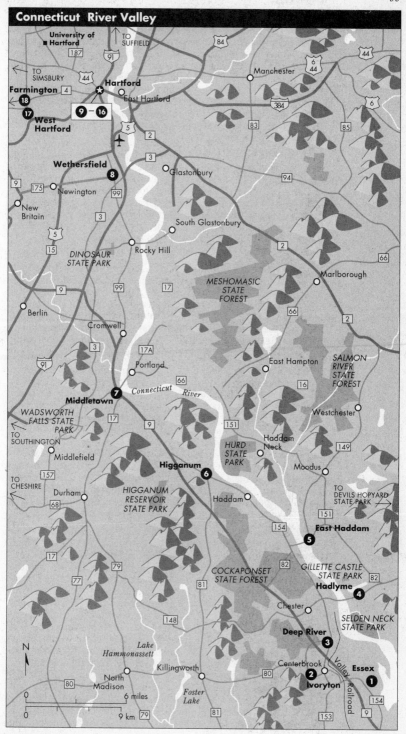

Connecticut River Valley

University of Hartford

TO SUFFIELD

187 91 84 44

TO SIMSBURY

44 6 44 Manchester

TO
SIMSBURY

Farmington 4 Hartford 6

18 East Hartford 384

17 West
Hartford 9 – 16 83 85

5

Wethersfield 2 6

8 3 Glastonbury

9 175 Newington 94

99

New
Britain 3 South Glastonbury

5

15 Rocky Hill 2 66

DINOSAUR
STATE PARK 99 MESHOMASIC
STATE
FOREST Marlborough

9 17 66 2

Berlin Cromwell 17A East Hampton SALMON
RIVER
STATE
FOREST

91 3 Portland 16

9 Connecticut River Westchester 149

Middletown 66

WADSWORTH
FALLS STATE
PARK 17 151 HURD
STATE
PARK Haddam
Neck Moodus

TO
SOUTHINGTON Middlefield 9

TO
CHESHIRE 157 Higganum 154 TO
DEVILS HOPYARD
STATE PARK

68 Durham 6 Haddam 151

HIGGANUM
RESERVOIR
STATE PARK East Haddam

17 COCKAPONSET
STATE FOREST 82 5 GILLETTE CASTLE
STATE PARK 82

79 81 Hadlyme 4

77 148 Chester SELDEN NECK
STATE PARK

N Lake
Hammonassett Deep River 3

80 Killingworth 80 Centerbrook Essex 1

0   6 miles North
Madison 2 154

0   9 km 79 Foster
Lake 81 Ivoryton 9

153

ter the medieval castles of the Rhineland. You can tour the castle and see the remains of the 3-mile private railroad that chugged about the property until the owner's death in 1937. Gillette, in his will, demanded that the castle not fall into the hands of "some blithering saphead who has no conception of where he is or with what surrounded." To that end, the castle and 117-acre grounds were designated a state park, and there's excellent hiking and picnicking. *67 River Rd. (off Rte. 82), tel. 203/526–2336. Admission: $4 adults, $2 children. Castle open Memorial Day–Columbus Day, daily 10–5; Columbus Day–mid-Dec, weekends 10–4. Grounds open year-round.*

⑤ Take Route 82 north to **East Haddam,** a former fishing, shipping, and musket-making concern—and the only town in the state with banks on both sides of the Connecticut River. Here, the upper floors of the 1876 gingerbread **Goodspeed Opera House** have served as a venue for theatrical performances for more than 100 years. From 1960 to 1963 the Goodspeed underwent a restoration that included the stage area, the Victorian bar, the sitting room, and the drinking parlor. *Rte. 82, tel. 203/873–8668. Tour admission: $1 adults, 50¢ children. Tours July–Oct., Mon. 1–3. Performances Apr.–Dec.*

Within walking distance, you'll find **St. Stephen's Church,** whose belfry is fitted with a 9th-century Spanish church bell that is believed by the folks at St. Stephen's to be the oldest in the Western Hemisphere. Also nearby is the **schoolhouse** where Nathan Hale taught from 1773 to 1774. On display are some of his possessions and other items of local history. *Rte. 149 (rear of St. Stephen's Church), tel. 203/873–9547. Admission: 25¢. Open Memorial Day–Labor Day, weekends 2–4.*

Return to Route 9, and at Exit 9 take a right onto Route 81, which
⑥ leads to **Higganum,** the town name a variation on a Native American word *higganumpus* (fishing place). Indeed, it was home for many years to several important shad fisheries. From Route 81, turn right onto Brault Hill Road and follow signs to the **Sundial Herb Garden.** The 1970 restoration of this Colonial farmstead led to the development of its three unusual gardens—a knot garden of interlocking hedges, a typical 18th-century geometric garden with central sundial, and a topiary garden. In the barn shop you'll find herbs, books, and gourmet items. Call ahead for information on the different light and high teas held at the farm throughout the year. *59 Hidden Lake Rd., tel. 203/345–4290. Admission free. Open weekends 10–5; Nov.–Dec. 24, daily 10–5.*

⑦ North on Route 9 is the once-bustling river city of **Middletown,** so named for its location halfway between Hartford and Long Island Sound—interestingly enough, it's also halfway between New York City and Boston. From about 1750 to 1800, Middletown was the wealthiest town in the state. Unfortunately, for a variety of reasons, it's fallen further and further downhill every year since. The imposing campus of **Wesleyan University** (tel. 203/347–9711), founded here in 1831, is traversed prominently by High Street, which Charles Dickens once called the loveliest Main Street in America—even though Middletown's actual Main Street runs parallel to it a few blocks east. It is an impressive and architecturally eclectic thoroughfare. Note the massive, fluted Corinthian columns of the Greek Revival Russell House (ca. 1828) at the corner of Washington Street, near the pink Mediterranean-style Davison Arts Center, built just 15 years later; farther on are gingerbreads, towering brownstones, Tudors, and Queen Annes. A few hundred yards up Church Street, which intersects High Street, is the impressive Olin

Library. Designed in 1928 by Lincoln Memorial architect Henry Bacon, the building was later ingeniously enlarged to allow the original structure to remain intact within the walls of the addition.

8 Head up I–91 to **Wethersfield,** a vast Hartford suburb dating from 1634. As was the case throughout early Connecticut, the Native Americans indigenous to these lands fought the arriving English with a vengeance; here their struggles culminated in the 1637 Wethersfield Massacre, when Pequot Indians killed nine settlers. Three years later, the citizens held a public election, America's first defiance of British rule, for which they were fined £5.

Hartford The so-called Insurance City, located at the intersection of I–84
9 with I–91, is where America's insurance industry was born in 1810—largely in an effort to protect the Connecticut River Valley's tremendously important shipping interests. Throughout the 19th century, insurance companies expanded their coverage to include fires, accidents, life, and in 1898, automobiles. At that time, the premium on a $5,000–$10,000 policy was $11.25—how times have changed. Through the years, Hartford industries have included the inspection and packing of the northern river valley's once prominent tobacco industry and the manufacture of everything from bed springs to artificial limbs to pool tables to coffins. Today, 50,000 Connecticutters are employed by the headquarters of more than 40 insurance companies. For the most part, it's a dull city of uninspired office blocks and tenements, made bearable by a few outstanding cultural, historic, and architectural offerings: Hartford's individual parts are of far greater interest than the city as a whole.

10 The Federal **Old State House,** a distinctive building with an elaborate cupola and roof-balustrade, was designed by Charles Bulfinch, architect of the U.S. Capitol, and occupied by the state legislature from 1796 to 1878. The restored Senate chamber contains a Gilbert Stuart portrait of George Washington that still remains in its commissioned location. *800 Main St., tel. 203/522–6766. Admission free. Open Mon.–Sat. 10–5, Sun. noon–5.*

Nearby looms the **Travelers Insurance Tower,** the hallmark of Hartford's skyline. This 527-foot beacon, capped by a pyramidal roof and gold-leafed cupola, was once the tallest building in New England.

11 Farther down the street is the **Wadsworth Atheneum,** the first public art museum in the country. Today, its 40,000-item collection spans 5,000 years, and includes paintings from the Hudson River School, the Impressionists, and 20th-century painters; the museum also mounts changing exhibits of contemporary art. Exhibits in its Lions Gallery of the Senses were designed for people with visual impairments. The Fleet Gallery of African-American Art, opened in 1993, is already one of the nation's best collections. *600 Main St., tel. 203/ 247–9111. Admission: $3 adults, $1.50 senior citizens; free to all Sat. 11–1 and Thurs. Open Tues.–Sun. 11–5.*

12 Nearby is the **Center Church and Ancient Burying Ground** (Main and Gold Sts., tel. 203/249–5631, open by appointment), built in 1807 and patterned after London's Church of St. Martin-in-the-Fields—though the parish itself dates to 1632. Five of the stained-glass windows were created by Louis Tiffany.

13 **Bushnell Park,** which fans out from the State Capitol building, was the first public space in the country with natural landscaping rather than with a traditional village green. The park was created by the firm of Frederick Law Olmsted, the Hartford landscape architect

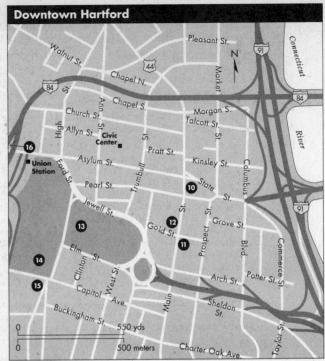

Downtown Hartford

who designed New York City's Central Park. On Bushnell's 40 acres you'll find 150 varieties of trees as well as such landmarks as the 100-foot-tall, 30-foot-wide medieval-style **Soldiers and Sailors Memorial Arch,** dedicated to Civil War soldiers.

⑭ Rising above the park and visible citywide is the grandiose **State Capitol,** a leviathan comprised of wholly disparate architectural elements. Built in 1879 of marble and granite—to a tune of $2.5 million—this gilt-dome wonder is replete with crockets, finials, and pointed arches. It currently houses the governor's office and legislative chambers and displays historic murals, statuary, flags, and furnishings. *210 Capitol Ave., tel. 203/240–0222. Admission free. Open weekdays 9–3. Weekday tours 9:15–1:15; tours also Sat. 10:15–2:15 Apr.–Oct.*

⑮ Across from the Capitol building is the **Raymond E. Baldwin Museum of Connecticut History,** with exhibits of Connecticut memorabilia that include its original Colonial charter. It also contains the vast collection of Samuel Colt firearms—the so-called Arm of Law and Order was first manufactured in Hartford. *231 Capitol Ave., tel. 203/566–3056. Admission free. Open weekdays 9–4:45, Sat. 9–12:45.*

A couple of miles west on Farmington Avenue, at its intersection with Forest Street, is the spot where Samuel Langhorne Clemens, **⑯** better known as Mark Twain, built his Victorian mansion at **Nook Farm** in 1874. The neighboring cottage, erected in 1871, was the home of Harriet Beecher Stowe, the author of one of 19th-century America's most popular novels, *Uncle Tom's Cabin.* During his residency at Nook Farm, Twain published seven major novels, including

Tom Sawyer, Huckleberry Finn, and *The Prince and the Pauper.* Personal memorabilia and original furnishings of both writers are on display. A visitor center serves both houses. *351 Farmington Ave., tel. 203/525–9317. Admission to both houses: $10 adults, $4.50 children. Open June–Columbus Day and Dec., Mon.–Sat. 9:30–4, Sun. noon–4; Jan.–May, Tues.–Sat. 9:30–4, Sun. noon–4.*

⑰ Farther west on Farmington Avenue, in **West Hartford,** is the **Science Museum of Connecticut,** which includes an aquarium with a tank you can reach into, a mini-zoo, and a planetarium. You're greeted at the museum's entrance by a life-size, walk-through replica of a 60-foot sperm whale. There are daily animal and planetarium shows plus changing exhibits on subjects ranging from the human heart to computers. *950 Trout Brook Dr., tel. 203/236–2961. Admission: $5 adults, $4 senior citizens and children. Weekend laser shows: $2. Open Tues.–Fri. 9–5, Sat. 10-5, Sun. 1–5.*

The University of Hartford's **Museum of American Political Life** has a broad range of displays, including artifacts of U.S. presidents and their campaigns and memorabilia of the temperance crusade and the women's rights and other political movements. *200 Bloomfield Ave., tel. 203/243–4090. Donation suggested. Open Tues.–Fri. 11–4, weekends noon–4.*

⑱ Nearby **Farmington,** incorporated in 1645, is a classic river town with lovely estates, a perfectly preserved main street, and the prestigious Miss Porter's School (Jacqueline Kennedy Onassis's alma mater).

Historic Homes and Small Museums

Hours of the following homes are usually limited to a few days a week, although most will open by appointment—always call ahead. Admission ranges from free to $3 unless otherwise noted.

Deep River The 19th-century **Stone House** (245 S. Main St., tel. 203/526–1449; open July–Aug.) has a charter-oak piano, Native American artifacts, and locally made cut glass.

Essex The **Pratt House** (19 West Ave., tel. 203/767–1191; open June–Labor Day), a central-chimney Colonial dwelling that dates from 1732 to 1734, contains an extensive collection of 17th- to 19th-century furnishings, notably Connecticut redware and Chinese courting mirrors.

Farmington The **Hill-Stead Museum** (35 Mountain Rd., tel. 203/677–4787; admission $5 adults, $4 senior citizens, $2 children; open mid-Feb–mid-Jan.) was converted from a private home into a museum by its unusual owner, Theodate Pope, the woman who helped Stanford White design it. A Colonial Revival farmhouse, it contains a superb collection of Impressionist art. Its drawing room may be the only one in America with Monet haystacks at either end and Manet's *The Guitar Player* in the middle.

Hartford The Federal **Butler-McCook Homestead** (396 Main St., tel. 203/247–8996 or 203/522–1806; open May 15–Oct. 15) was built in 1782 and was occupied continuously by the same family until 1971. Its entrance is dominated by four fluted columns. Now its furnishings show the evolution of tastes over time, with the Victorian era predominating. There's also an extensive collection of East Asian artifacts.

Manchester   The **Cheney Homestead** (106 Hartford Rd., tel. 203/643–5588; open by appointment) documents the birth of the state's silk industry and contains 18th- and 19th-century furnishings.

Middletown   The Federal **General Mansfield House** (151 Main St., tel. 203/346–0746; open year-round) houses 18th- and 19th-century decorative arts, Civil War memorabilia and firearms, and local artifacts.

Suffield   The **Hatheway House,** about 20 miles north of Hartford (55 S. Main St., tel. 203/247–8996; open mid-May–mid Oct.), is one of the finest architectural specimens in New England. The walls of its neoclassical north wing (1794) display their original 18th-century French hand-blocked wallpaper. The main house (1761) is typical of Connecticut Valley homes with its double-front doors and gambrel roof. An ornate picket fence fronts the property.

West Hartford   The **Noah Webster House and Museum** (227 S. Main St., tel. 203/521–5362; open year-round) is the birthplace of the famed author of the *Blue-Backed Speller* and the *American Dictionary*. An 18th-century farmhouse, it contains Webster memorabilia and period furnishings along with changing exhibits.

Wethersfield   The **Joseph Webb House, Silas Deane House,** and **Isaac Stevens House** (203, 211, 215 Main St. [exit 26 off I–91], tel. 203/529–0612; admission $6 adults, $2.50 children 12–18, $1 children 5–11; open year-round), all built in the mid- to late 1700s, jointly form one of the state's best historic house-museums. Well-preserved examples of Georgian and Federal architecture, they also reflect their individual owners' lifestyles as a merchant, a diplomat, and a tradesman, respectively. The Webb House was the site of the strategy conference between Washington and Rochambeau that led to the British defeat at Yorktown. The **Buttolph-Williams House** (249 Broad St., tel. 203/529–0460 or 203/247–8996; open May 15–Oct. 15), built in 1692, has a remarkable hand-hewn overhanging eave and small casement windows that suggests postmedieval English Colonial architecture. The kitchen is one of the best preserved in New England.

What to See and Do with Children

Science Museum of Connecticut, West Hartford
Valley Railroad, Essex (*see* Guided Tours, *above*)

Off the Beaten Track

In a building beside Bradley International Airport in Windsor Locks, the **New England Air Museum** displays more than 80 craft dating to 1909. *Tel. 203/623–3305. Admission: $6 adults, $2.50 children 6–11. Open daily 10–5.*

East Windsor's **Connecticut Trolley Museum** has more than 50 trolleys and a 3-mile antique-trolley ride. A special "Electric Sleigh" ride is offered each Christmas. *58 North Rd., tel. 203/627–6540. Admission: $6 adults, $5 senior citizens, $3 children 5–11. Open weekends noon–5.*

The **Lock 12 Historical Park** is a restored section of the long-gone Farmington Canal (1828–1874) and has a museum, lock-keeper's house, and helicoidal bridge open free to the public. *487 Brooksvale Rd., Cheshire, tel. 203/272–2743. Admission free. Open Mar.–Nov., daily 9–5.*

Shopping

Arts and
Antiques

Deep River seems like an enormous antiques fair, with its concentration of dealers on Main Street and at the intersection of Routes 80 and 145. Chester's **The Artisans** (1 Spring St., tel. 203/526–5575), a crafts gallery cooperative, makes and sells fine pottery, jewelry, and folk art. In Hartford, the **100 Pearl Street Gallery** (100 Pearl St., tel. 203/242–6880) is renowned for the exhibits it mounts year-round. Simsbury's **Arts Exclusive Gallery** (690 Hopmeadow St., tel. 203/651–5824) is equally esteemed. Varied shows are staged at the **Saltbox and Clubhouse Gallery** (37 Buena Vista Rd., West Hartford, tel. 203/521–3732). The **Farmington Valley Arts Center** (25 Arts Center La., Avon, tel. 203/675–5630) shows the work of nationally known artists. The **Wesleyan Potters** (350 Main St., Middletown, tel. 203/347–5925) have pottery and weaving studios that you can tour; all of the products are for sale.

Food

You can pick your own fruits and vegetables at **Lyman Orchards** (jct. Rtes. 147 and 157, Middlefield, tel. 203/349–3673), just south of Middletown, from June through October—berries, peaches, pears, apples, even sweet corn.

Shopping
Malls

In Hartford, the **Civic Center** (1 Civic Center Plaza, tel. 203/275–6100) has more than 60 shops as well as a 16,500-seat sports and performing arts arena. **The Richardson Mall** (942 Main St., tel. 203/525–9711) has more than 40 shops selling everything from hats to video games, and the art deco–style **Pavilion** (State House Sq., tel. 203/241–0100) has 25 shops. About 7 miles west is **Westfarms Mall** (I–84, Exit 40, tel. 203/561–3024), with 140 shops.

Sports and Outdoor Activities

Camping

Try **Markham Meadows Campground** (7 Markham Rd., East Hampton, tel. 203/267–9738) and **Nelson's Family Compound** (71C Mott Hill Rd., East Hampton, tel. 203/267–4561).

Canoeing

Down River Canoes (Box 283, Haddam 06438, tel. 203/345–8355; Mar.–Nov.) offers trips of one to three days with barbecues. Instruction, guides, and equipment are available.

Skiing

Mt. Southington (Southington, tel. 203/628–0954, or, for conditions, 800/982–6828), an easy drive from Hartford, has night skiing and racing camps. The 12 trails off the 425 feet of vertical range from basic beginner to low intermediate, with a bit of steeper stuff here and there. The trails at **Powder Ridge** (Powder Hill Rd., Middlefield, tel. 203/349–3454) drop straight down from the 500-foot-high ridge for which it's named. There is night skiing every day.

Spectator Sports

Baseball

See the next Roger Clemens at a game of the **New Britain Red Sox** (Field Willow Brook Park, tel. 203/224–8383; Apr.–Sept.), the Boston Red Sox double-A farm club.

Hockey

The NHL's **Hartford Whalers** (tel. 203/728–6637) play at the Civic Center in Hartford.

Jai Alai

Hartford Jai Alai (89 Weston St., tel. 203/525–8611) is where jai alai was introduced in the Northeast.

State Parks

The 15,652-acre **Cockaponset** (Rte. 148, Chester, tel. 203/345–8521) is Connecticut's second-largest state forest. Sixty-foot cascades flow down Chapman Falls at the 860-acre **Devil's Hopyard** (3 mi north of junction of Rtes. 82 and 156, tel. 203/873–8566). The park has 20 campsites. **Hurd State Park** (Rte. 151, Haddam Neck, no tel.), which sits high on the east bank of the Connecticut River, has excellent views in spring and summer. **Wadsworth Falls** (Rte. 157, Middlefield, tel. 203/344–2950), near Wesleyan University, has a beautiful waterfall and 285 acres of forest. **Talcott Mountain** (Rte. 185, Simsbury, tel. 203/242–1158) offers views of four states from the 165-foot Heublin Tower, a former private home that's just a 1-mile hike from the parking lot.

The **Dinosaur State Park,** north of Middletown in Rocky Hill, is roughly where dinosaurs once roamed. Tracks dating from the Jurassic period, 185 million years ago, are preserved under a giant geodesic dome here, and you can even make plaster casts of them. *West St., tel. 203/529–8423. Admission: $2 adults, $1 children. Exhibits open Tues.–Sun. 9–4:30.*

Dining and Lodging

Centerbrook
Dining
★

Fine Bouche. This gray Victorian mansion, complete with latticework and a touch of gingerbread trim, serves some of the finest contemporary French food in the state. Villeroy & Boch china accents the white napery on the tables of the handsome candlelit dining room. For starters consider the lobster bisque with Cognac, then try the sautéed sliced breast of duck with cranberries and cassis. The wine list is exceptional and reasonably priced. By day, a shop in the back known as Sweet Sarah's sells delicious desserts. *78 Main St., tel. 203/767–1277. Reservations advised. AE, MC, V. No lunch. Closed Mon. Expensive–Very Expensive.*

Chester
Dining

Restaurant du Village. A black wrought-iron gate beckons you away from the tony antiquaries of Chester's quaint Main Street and an off-white awning draws you through the the door of this classic little Colonial storefront, painted in historic Newport blue and adorned with flower boxes. Here you can sample exquisite classic French cuisine—escargots in a puff pastry, filet mignon—while recapping the day's shopping coups. *59 Main St., tel. 203/526–5301. Reservations advised. AE, MC, V. Expensive–Very Expensive.*

Inn at Chester. This hulking gambrel-roofed inn, about 5 miles west of downtown Chester, successfully captures that warm-and-cozy atmosphere for which New England hostelries are known. There are several dining rooms—the largest inside a rebuilt 19th-century barn with chandeliers and original beams, another on a glassed-in porch with a flagstone floor. The food is far tastier than is suggested by its nondescript monikers (Goat Cheese Salad, Pork Medallions). *318 W. Main St. (Rte. 148), tel. 203/526–9541. Reservations advised. AE, MC, V. Expensive.*

Fiddler's. Purists may scoff at the location (20 miles inland)—it doesn't matter. Where freshness and preparation are concerned, Fiddler's is as fine a fish house as exists. House specialties are the rich bouillabaisse and the lobster with peaches, shallots, mushrooms, peach brandy, and cream sauce. Blond bentwood chairs, lacy stenciling on the walls, prints of famous schooners, and the amber glow of oil lamps lend a gentrified air—further confounding those purists. *4 Water St., tel. 203/526–3210. Reservations advised. MC, V. No lunch Sun. Closed Mon. Moderate–Expensive.*

Deep River
Lodging
★

Riverwind. Each guest room in the restored Victorian town house has been faithfully decorated in period style, from the canopied four-poster bed in the Willow Room to the red, white, and blue furnishings of the Smithfield Room. An enormous homemade breakfast is served beside a cozy hearth on the main floor. *209 Main St., 06417, tel. 203/526–2014. 8 rooms with bath. AE, MC, V. Moderate–Expensive.*

East Haddam
Lodging

Bishopsgate Inn. This Federal inn around the bend from the landmark Goodspeed Opera House is filled with pictures of guests who have graced the Goodspeed stage. The rooms are cozy and inviting, furnished with period reproductions, a smattering of antiques, and crisp curtains. An irresistible breakfast specialty is Molly's stuffed French toast—recipe available. *7 Norwich Rd., Rte. 82, 06423, tel. 203/873–1677. 6 rooms with bath, 1 suite. Facilities: working fireplaces in some rooms, sauna in suite; full breakfast included. D, MC, V. Moderate.*

Essex
Dining and Lodging

Griswold Inn. The Gris, which has been offering rooms since 1776, sometimes goes overboard in its efforts to sustain its nautical character. Bedrooms have original beam ceilings, antique and reproduction furnishings—and push-button telephones (but no TVs or radios). With its worn floorboard and exposed ceiling beams, the dining room is probably the most Colonial. The menu offers no-frills, traditional American fare such as fried oysters, roast duckling, baked stuffed shrimp, and ribs; portions are hearty. *36 Main St., 06426, tel. 203/767–1776, fax 203/767–0481. 23 rooms with bath. Facilities: dining room (reservations advised), taproom, library. AE, MC, V. Moderate–Expensive.*

Farmington
Lodging

Barney House. This former mansion, now a thriving B&B, is on a quiet street just a few miles from downtown Hartford, amid 4½ acres of formal gardens. Spacious guest rooms mix modern furnishings with antiques; baths are oversize. *11 Mountain Spring Rd., 06032, tel. 203/677–9735. 7 rooms with bath. Facilities: outdoor pool, tennis; Continental breakfast included. MC, V. Moderate–Expensive.*

Hartford
Dining

Frank's Restaurant. This family-run restaurant opposite the Civic Center has been a favorite among Hartford politicians for nearly half a century. The menu offers traditional Italian and Continental specialties, but the kitchen is best with its pasta dishes and tomato sauce, which you can also buy in jars. Also worth a try is the San Francisco *cioppino* (fresh fish and shellfish baked with an oreganato or tomato sauce and served over linguine). Ceilings are high, and the lighting is soft and soothing; even when crowded, calm prevails. *185 Asylum St., tel. 203/527–9291. Reservations advised. AE, DC, MC, V. Moderate–Expensive.*

Max on Main. Calamari and carpaccio come with spicy touches here, and the designer pizza pies are mouth-watering; try the version with smoked chicken, pancetta, sweet peppers, scallions, and Monterey Jack cheese—a favorite of the late-night crowd. Or try the version topped with shrimp, sun-dried tomatoes, pesto, calamata olives, and two cheeses. There's a great oyster bar. *205 Main St., tel. 203/522–2530. Reservations advised. AE, DC, MC, V. No lunch Sat. Closed Sun. Moderate–Expensive.*

★ **Peppercorns Grill.** This trendy storefront bistro pulses with energy. Tubes of neon snake about the ceiling and windows like swirls of day-glo paint, and bright red Windsor chairs encircle tables laid with traditional white linen. The decor and boisterous crowds make for a vibrant though noisy dining experience. The Continental cuisine reflects current trends—lots of designer pizzas, creatively adorned pastas, and chicken and fish dishes. A large bottle of San Pellegrino water and a basket of fresh bread with olive oil are placed on every table. *357 Main St., tel. 203/547–1714. Reservations advised. No lunch weekends. AE, DC, MC, V. Moderate–Expensive.*

Kashmir. Although all dishes are flavorful at this traditionally furnished Indian restaurant, the meat vindaloos are the only truly spicy dishes. The *dopiaz* curries (simmered with tomatoes and onions) are a strong point on the menu. Tandoori chicken is juicy and naturally colored, not dry and lobster-pink as it is elsewhere. Nor are portions as obscenely enormous as you usually get at Indian restaurants. *481 Wethersfield Ave., tel. 203/296–9685. Reservations advised. AE, MC, V. No lunch Sun. Moderate.*

★ **First and Last Tavern.** What looks to be a simple neighborhood joint is actually one of the state's most hallowed pizza grounds. The long, old-fashioned wooden bar in one room is jammed most evenings with suburbia-bound daily-grinders shaking off their suits; the main dining room is just as noisy, its brick outer wall covered with the requisite array of celebrity photos. Pie toppings are refreshingly untrendy. It's a few miles south of downtown. *939 Maple Ave., tel. 203/956–6000. No reservations. AE, DC, MC, V. Inexpensive.*

Dining and Lodging
★ **The Hotel at Goodwin Square.** The only truly grand city hotel in Connecticut, this establishment looks a little odd in the downtown business district—its dark red, ornate classical facade is dwarfed by the Civic Center. Considering its stately exterior, rooms are nondescript. Still, they are large and tastefully decorated—and are the best in town. Suites have all-marble baths. Noteworthy is the hotel's imposing four-story and barrel-vaulted atrium. The clubby, mahogany-panel Pierpont's Restaurant serves commendable new American fare; along with an unsurprising selection of steak, chicken, and fish dishes, you can order such unusual sides as celery-root chips, huckleberry sauce, and chanterelle mushrooms. *1 Haynes St., 06103, tel. 203/246–7500 or 800/922–5006, fax 203/247–4576. 113 rooms with bath, 11 suites. Facilities: restaurant (reservations advised), meeting rooms, health club. AE, D, DC, MC, V. Hotel: Moderate–Very Expensive. Restaurant: Expensive.*

Lodging **Sheraton-Hartford.** At 15 stories, this is the city's largest hotel. It's not sumptuous, but there are touches of elegance, such as the lobby abloom with fresh flowers at street level. Connected to the Civic Center by an enclosed bridge, it's within easy walking distance of the downtown area. The preferred rooms are on floors 1 through 9, which are furnished with period reproductions. *315 Trumbull St. at the Civic Center Plaza, 06103, tel. 203/728–5151 or 800/325–3535, fax 203/240–7247. 400 rooms with bath, 6 suites. Facilities: restaurant, lounge, health club, indoor pool. AE, D, DC, MC, V. Moderate–Expensive.*

Ramada Inn. Situated beside Bushnell Park, this two-decade-old hotel has an unobstructed view of the Capitol. However, rooms facing the rear overlook the train station around the corner, a parking lot, and a busy highway. Its new restaurant, the Cafe on the Park, is run by the New England Culinary Institute and as a result offers much better food than you would expect in a chain hotel. *440 Asylum St., 06103, tel. 203/246–6591 or 800/228–2828, fax 203/728–1382. 96 rooms with bath, 4 suites. AE, D, DC, MC, V. Inexpensive–Moderate.*

Ivoryton Dining **The Ivory Room.** The main dining room of the otherwise ordinary Ivoryton Inn, its walls painted in creamy hues and stenciled in floral patterns, has joined the ranks of Connecticut kitchens churning out trendy new American cuisine. Fresh locally grown produce is beautifully presented and accented with sun-dried tomatoes, ginger, avocado, and fresh coriander. Specialties include grilled leg of lamb, duckling in champagne sauce, chateaubriand for two with bordelaise sauce, and lobster-and-corn chowder. *115 Main St., tel. 203/767–0422. Reservations advised. AE, MC, V. Expensive–Very Expensive.*

Dining and Lodging
★
Copper Beech Inn. A magnificent copper beech tree shades the imposing main building of this Victorian inn, once the residence of ivory importer A. W. Comstock. The entire inn is furnished in period pieces. Each of the four guest rooms in the main house has an old-fashioned tub; the nine rooms in the Carriage House have private decks and large Jacuzzis. Seven acres of wooded grounds and groomed terraced gardens create an atmosphere of privileged seclusion. Dining rooms are decidedly romantic. Highlights of the distinctive country French menu are the country pâté and game dishes, served in fall. Crepes filled with chocolate mousse top it off. *46 Main St., 06442, tel. 203/767–0330. 13 rooms with bath. Facilities: dining rooms (reservations required; jacket and tie suggested; closed Mon. and, Jan.–Mar., Tues.), lounge. Continental breakfast included. AE, DC, MC, V. Inn: Expensive. Restaurant: Expensive–Very Expensive.*

Manchester Dining
Cavey's. The 20 minutes it takes to get here from Hartford is time well spent. Downstairs is a formal French restaurant decorated with priceless antiques; the cuisine is classic all the way, and dishes such as squab and herb-crusted roast bass are hallmarks. Upstairs is a casual Italian dining room with Palladian windows, rush-seated wooden chairs, and contemporary art on the walls; spiced shrimp with gnocchi made from sun-dried tomatoes and broccoli rabe typify the menu's offerings. *45 E. Center Rd., tel. 203/643–2751. Reservations advised in the Italian restaurant, required in the French. Jacket and tie required in French restaurant. AE, MC, V. Italian: Moderate–Expensive. French: Very Expensive.*

Middletown Dining
O'Rourke's Diner. For a university town, Middletown has surprisingly few worthy eateries. This stainless-steel greasy-spoon, which has a line at the door most weekend mornings, is a cut above any of the "real" restaurants, despite the fact that it serves only breakfast and lunch. The usual diner fare is featured, along with such regional delicacies as steamed cheeseburgers, and it's all unusually good. It opens at 4:30 AM. *728 Main St., tel. 203/346–6101. No credit cards. No dinner. Inexpensive.*

Newington Dining
Ruth's Chris Steak House. Let's face it: Although a salad of wilted field greens with a delicate raspberry vinaigrette may be good for you, it pretty much tastes and looks like a pile of hedge-clippings. True satisfaction is biting into a juicy T-bone steak—such as are found, deliciously, at this Newington branch of the famed national chain with the harsh discordant name. The dark-shingle roadhouse exterior and location on the ticky-tacky Berlin Turnpike belie the excellent renditions of good red meat to be found inside: Every steak comes precisely as specified, sizzling on a stainless platter and dripping with flavorful butter. So much for cholesterol. *2513 Berlin Tpk., tel. 203/666–2202. Reservations advised. No lunch. AE, D, DC, MC, V. Expensive.*

West Hartford Dining
Butterfly Chinese Restaurant. The live piano entertainment suggests that this is not your ordinary order-by-number Chinese restaurant; indeed, the food is authentic, the staff gracious and outgoing. Entrées are mostly Cantonese with a fair representation of Szechuan; specialties include Peking duck and shrimp with wal-

nuts. *831 Farmington Ave., tel. 203/236-2816. Reservations accepted. AE, MC, V. Moderate-Expensive.*

The Arts and Nightlife

The Arts East Haddam's prestigious **Goodspeed Opera House** (Rte. 82, tel. 203/873-8668) presents an annual season of revivals, neglected great musicals, and other shows on their way to Broadway. In Chester, there's **Goodspeed at Chester,** where the East Haddam company presents new works or works in progress at the **Norma Terris Theatre** (N. Main St., Rte. 82, tel. 203/873-8668), as well as the **National Theatre of the Deaf** (5 W. Main St., tel. 203/526-4971), which originates here the spectacular productions it takes on tour throughout the country. In Middletown, Wesleyan University's **Center for the Arts** (between Washington Terr. and Wyllys Ave., tel. 203/347-7944) is the frequent host of concerts, theater, films, and art exhibits. The **Little Theater of Manchester** (177 Hartford Rd., tel. 203/645-6743), built in 1867, is the state's oldest theater and, though drawing on local talents, is highly professional.

In Hartford, the Tony Award–winning **Hartford Stage Company** (50 Church St., tel. 203/527-5151) turns out plenty of future Broadway hits as well as innovative productions of Shakespeare, the classics, and several new plays. **Theatreworks** (233 Pearl St., tel. 203/527-7838), the Hartford equivalent of Off Broadway, presents a series of theater works including experimental new dramas. The **Hartford Ballet** (166 Capitol Ave., tel. 203/525-9396) presents classical and contemporary productions, including a holiday presentation of the *Nutcracker.* The Hartford Symphony and tours of major musicals headline at **The Bushnell** (166 Capitol Ave., tel. 203/246-6807), while **Chamber Music Plus,** one of Connecticut's better chamber groups, performs at **Cathedral Theatre** (45 Church St., Hartford, tel. 203/232-0085). Both **Hartford Camerata Conservatory** (834 Asylum Ave., Hartford, tel. 203/246-2588) and the **Real Art Ways Music Series** (tel. 203/232-1006) present numerous recitals. The former tends to feature more traditional works, the latter the most modern and experimental.

Nightlife **Hartford** offers the most varied options. **Brown Thomson's Last Laugh Club** (942 Main St., tel. 203/525-1600) showcases comics from Boston and New York on weekend evenings. **Bourbon Street North** (70 Union Pl., tel. 203/525-1014) features a large dance floor and tunes ranging from New Orleans jazz to Motown. **The 880 Club** (880 Maple Ave., tel. 203/956-2428), the oldest jazz club in Hartford, presents live acts in an intimate atmosphere. **The Russian Lady Cafe** (191 Ann St., tel. 203/525-3003) swings into the wee hours with rock, R&B, and pop music. **The Arch Street Tavern** (85 Arch St., tel. 203/246-7610) presents local rock bands.

The Litchfield Hills

Two scenic highways, I-84 and Route 8, form the southern and eastern boundaries of the region. New York, to the west, and Massachusetts, to the north, complete the rectangle. Here, in the foothills of the Berkshires, is some of the most spectacular and unspoiled scenery in the state. Grand old inns—most of them fairly expensive—are plentiful as are surprisingly sophisticated eateries. Rolling farmlands abut thick forests, and engaging trails traverse the state parks and forests. Two rivers, the Housatonic and the Farmington, attract anglers and canoeing enthusiasts, and there are two sizable lakes, Waramaug and Bantam. Towns such as Litchfield, New Milford, and Sharon are anchored by sweeping town greens and stately homes; Kent, New Preston, and Woodbury draw avid antiquers; and Washington, Salisbury, and Norfolk offer a glimpse of quiet, New England village life as it might have existed two centuries ago.

Important Addresses and Numbers

Visitor Information
Litchfield Hills Travel Council (Box 1776, Marbledale 06777, tel. 203/868–2214).

Emergencies
New Milford Hospital (Elm St., tel. 203/355–2611). **Sharon Hospital** (Hospital Hill Rd., tel. 203/364–4141). **Winsted Memorial Hospital** (71 Spencer St., tel. 203/738–6600).

Pharmacy
CVS Pharmacy (127 Farmington Ave., Bristol, tel. 203/572–8167 is open 24 hours).

Getting Around the Litchfield Hills

By Car
Northwestern Connecticut is a Sunday driver's paradise. Narrow roads wind over precarious ridges, past antiques shops and soup-and-sandwich pantries, and through the occasional covered bridge. From New York, take I–684 to I–84, from which Exits 7 through 18 lead you northward into the Hills. From Hartford, it's most direct to follow Routes 44 west and 6 south. Favorite roads for admiring fall foliage and sprawling farmsteads are Route 7, from New Milford through Kent and West Cornwall to Canaan; Routes 41 to 4 from Salisbury through Lakeville, Sharon, Cornwall Bridge, and Goshen to Torrington; and Routes 47 to 202 to 341 from Woodbury through Washington, New Preston, Lake Waramaug, and Warren to Kent. Roads and intersections are well marked, but a good map is helpful.

Exploring the Litchfield Hills

Numbers in the margin correspond to points of interest on the Litchfield Hills map.

1 **New Milford** is a practical starting point. It was also a starting point of sorts for a young cobbler named Roger Sherman, who, in 1743, opened his shop where Main and Church streets meet. A Declaration of Independence signatory, he also helped draft the Constitution and the Articles of Confederation.

Route 7/202 is, up to its junction with Route 67, a dull stretch of shopping centers and consistently ugly storefronts. But where the road crosses the Housatonic River, you'll find old shops, galleries, and eateries all within a short stroll of New Milford green—one of the longest in New England.

2 In tiny **Northville,** 4 miles north of the New Milford green on Route 202, is **The Silo** (44 Upland Rd., tel. 203/355–0300). New Yorkers who miss Zabar's and Balducci's feel right at home in this silo and barn packed with objets de cookery and crafts; the array of gourmet goodies and sauces is unbelievable. Band leader Skitch Henderson and his wife, Ruth, own and operate this bazaar, whose success proves there's a great desire for sophisticated, urbane ingredients, even under the elms.

3 Three miles north on Route 202 is **New Preston,** a one-horse village perched on the Aspetuck River. It's packed with antiques shops, many specializing in folk furniture and fine prints. Just north of here
4 on Route 45 is **Lake Waramaug,** an area that reminds many of Aus-

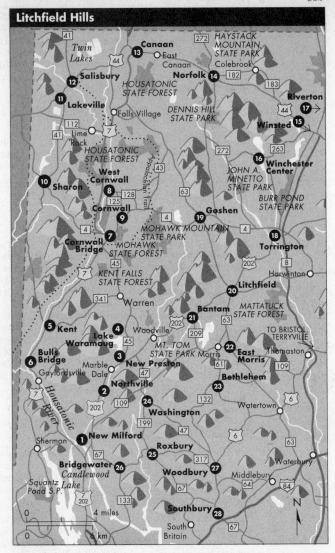

Litchfield Hills

Twin Lakes

41 · Canaan · 13 · 272 · HAYSTACK MOUNTAIN STATE PARK

44 · East Canaan · Colebrook

12 · Salisbury · Norfolk · 14 · 182 · 183

HOUSATONIC STATE FOREST

11 · Lakeville · Riverton · 17

Falls Village · DENNIS HILL STATE PARK · 44 · Winsted · 15

112 · 7 · 263

41 · Lime Rock · 272 · 16 · Winchester Center

HOUSATONIC STATE FOREST

West Cornwall · 8 · 43 · JOHN A. MINETTO STATE PARK · BURR POND STATE PARK

10 · Sharon · 128 · 63 · Goshen · 19

125 · Cornwall · 9 · 4 · 4 · 18

Cornwall Bridge · 7 · MOHAWK MOUNTAIN STATE PARK · Torrington

4 · MOHAWK STATE FOREST · 202 · 8

45 · Harwinton

7 · KENT FALLS STATE FOREST · Litchfield · 20

341 · Warren · Bantam · MATTATUCK STATE FOREST

Kent · 5 · 4 · Woodville · 21 · 63

Lake Waramaug · 202 · 209 · TO BRISTOL TERRYVILLE

6 · Bulls Bridge · 45 · MT. TOM STATE PARK · Morris · 22 · East Morris · Thomaston

Marble Dale · 3 · New Preston · 61 · 109

Gaylordsville · 47 · Bethlehem

7 · Northville · 2 · 23

202 · 109 · 24 · 132 · Watertown

Housatonic River

1 · New Milford · Washington · 199 · 47 · 6 · 63

Sherman · 67 · Roxbury · 25 · 317 · Waterbury

Bridgewater · 26 · Woodbury · 27 · Middlebury

Candlewood Lake · 64 · 84

Squantz Pond S.P. · 7 · 202 · 67

133 · Southbury · 28

0 — 4 miles · South Britain · 67

0 — 6 km · **N**

---

tria and Switzerland—though it's actually named for Chief
Waramaug, one the most revered figures in Connecticut's Native
American history. Drive completely around the lake (8 miles), admiring the beautiful homes and inns—a few of which now serve delicious Continental food. The state park of the same name, at the
northwest tip, is an idyllic 75-acre spread, great for picnicking.

⑤ Kent, reached from New Milford on Route 7 or from New Preston on
Route 341, has the area's greatest concentration of art galleries,
some nationally renowned. Kent is also home to the prestigious prep
school of the same name, a long history of ironworks, and the
Schaghticoke Indian Reservation. During the Revolutionary War,
100 Schaghticokes helped defend the Colonies: They transmitted
messages of army intelligence from the Litchfield Hills to Long Is-

land Sound, along the hilltops, by way of shouts and tom-tom beats. Today, these prominent ridges tower above downtown Kent's bookshops, bakeries, and antiques shops.

6 A few miles south of Kent on Route 7 is **Bulls Bridge,** one of the state's two covered bridges still open to cars. Bulls Bridge is said to be where George Washington's horse slipped on a rotted plank and tumbled into the roaring river.

7 Heading up Route 7 to **Cornwall Bridge,** you'll pass the entrance to **Kent Falls State Park,** where you can hike a short way to one of the most impressive waterfalls in the state.

8 Oddly, Connecticut's most romantic covered bridge is not in Cornwall Bridge, but several miles up Route 7 in **West Cornwall.** (The covered bridge in Cornwall Bridge smashed to bits during the great flood of 1936.) The wooden, barn-red, one-lane bridge was built in 1841 and has since carried travelers into this small village, which is also the site of a few notable crafts shops and restaurants.

9 **Cornwall** is halfway between its aforementioned cousins, at the intersection of Routes 125 and 4. Here, among the virgin pines and thick forest, fleeting pockets of civilization came and went throughout the 18th and 19th centuries. Starvation and cold stole the lives of most who settled here in the eerily named communities of Mast Swamp, Wildcat, Great Hollow, Crooked Esses, and Ballyhack. Unfortunately, a severe tornado ripped through here in 1989, and most of the pines snapped like matchsticks—the devastation is most easily seen at **Mohawk Mountain State Park,** which is off of Route 4, a mile from Cornwall.

10 Follow Route 4 west from Route 7 and up the winding hill to the well-preserved Colonial town of **Sharon.** Here is one of the best places to hike in Connecticut: the **Northeast Audubon Center.** In addition to various trails and nature walks, the 684-acre sanctuary is home to a center for orphaned wildlife, a shop, and a library. *Rte. 4, tel. 203/364–0520. Admission: $4 adults, $2 children. Open Mon.–Sat. 9–5, Sun. 1–5; trails open dawn–dusk.*

Time Out   Just south of the Audubon Center is **Ellsworth Farm** (Rte. 4, tel. 203/364–0249), where you can pick your own berries, apples, and veggies and buy fresh cider, pies, and other treats.

Sharon's history is one of Colonial manufacturing—everything from munitions and oxbows to wooden mousetraps were made here. There was even an attempt to introduce the silkworm; it failed because of New England's unwelcoming climate, but the mulberry trees that were planted as part of the experiment still line Main Street. Perhaps the strangest sight in town is the elaborate Hotchkiss Clock Tower, which looms importantly above the intersection of Routes 4 and 41. It was built in 1885 of native gray granite as a memorial to town son and inventor of the Hotchkiss explosive shell, Benjamin Berkeley Hotchkiss.

On to the lovely towns of Lakeville and Salisbury, you definitely begin to see more signs of urban invasion—fancier inns and restaurants, chic shops.

11 You can usually spot an original Colonial home in **Lakeville** by looking for the grapevine design cut into the frieze above the front door of many houses—the apparent trademark of whomever built the town's first homes. The lake of Lakeville is **Lake Wononscopomuc,** whose shoreline is lined with attractive weekend homes, well hidden in the foliage. Here and there, as you drive along Routes 44 or 41, you catch a glimpse of its sparkling waters. Off Route 41 is the Town Grove, where a lawn shaded by huge trees rolls right down to the water's edge; its small beach provides the only public access to the lake (and it's not very public at that—on weekends in summer, only residents and guests at local inns are admitted). From the water's edge here, you can just make out some of the buildings of Hotchkiss, one of the nation's most prestigious prep schools, which anchors the opposite shore.

⓬ Nearby **Salisbury,** were it not for the obsolescence of its ironworks, might today be the largest city in Connecticut. Instead, it settles for having both the state's highest mountain, Bear Mountain (2,355 feet), and its highest point, the shoulder of Mount Frissel (2,380 feet)—whose peak is actually in Massachusetts. There's a spot on Mt. Frissel where you can place various limbs in Connecticut, Massachusetts, and New York.

Iron was discovered here in 1732, and for the next century, the slopes of Salisbury's Mount Riga produced the finest iron in America—Swiss and Russian immigrants, and later Hessian deserters from the British army, worked the great furnaces. These dark, mysterious people inbred and lived in squalor inside tiny hillside cabins in these parts until well into the 20th century, long after the last forge cast a glow in 1847. "Raggies," as they were known, are cloaked in a legend of black magic and suspicion—believed to be responsible for various ghostly sightings, mishaps, and even an unexplained spell of rock and mortar bombardment on three of the city's homes back in 1802. As for the ironworks, the spread of rail transport opened up better and more accessible sources of ore, the region's lumber supply was eventually depleted, and the Bessemer process of steel manufacturing—partially invented by Salisbury native Alexander Holley—all put an end to Salisbury's pride. Today you can hike and drive all through the region, though most signs of cinder heaps and slag dumps are long gone, replaced by grand summer homes and gardens. The easiest way to hike the region is to travel along a stretch of the Appalachian Trail, which runs clear over Bear Mountain (*see* Sports and Outdoor Activities, *below*).

Time Out No trip through the region is complete without a brief stop at **Chaiwalla** tea house (1 Main St., tel. 203/435–9758), just across from the grand White Hart Inn. At Chaiwalla you can choose from among 19 different kinds of tea and sample some of owner Mary McMillan's scrumptious desserts.

⓭ The next town over, **Canaan,** is one of the more developed in the region: It has a McDonald's. Canaan was the site of some important late-18th-century industry, including a gun-barrel factory and a paper mill, and it's also the home of Captain Gershom Hewitt, who's credited with securing the plans of Fort Ticonderoga for Ethan Allen. Visit the **Canaan Union Station** (Rtes. 44 and 7, tel. 203/824–0339), built in 1871 and the oldest station in continuous use in America. From Canaan Union, you can take a tour, in vintage train cars, on the **Housatonic Valley Railroad,** which runs from Canaan to Cornwall between Memorial Day and October.

⓮ Continuing along Route 44 you'll soon reach **Norfolk,** which, thanks to its severe climate and terrain, is one of the best preserved villages in the Northeast. Notable industrialists have been summering here for two centuries, and several enormous homesteads still exist. At the junction of Routes 182 and 44 is the striking town green. At its southern corner is a fountain, designed by Augustus Saint-Gaudens and executed by Stanford White, a memorial to Joseph Battell, who turned this town into a major trading center 200 years ago. The northwest corner of the green is anchored by the Music Shed on the grounds of the magnificent Ellen Battell Stoeckel Estate, which for years has been the site of the **Norfolk Chamber Music Festival** (*see* The Arts and Nightlife, *below*).

⑮ **Winsted** still looks a bit like the set of a Frank Capra movie, with its rows of old homes and businesses, seemingly untouched since the 1940s. Although far less fashionable than its neighbor Norfolk to the west, it's still worth a brief stop. Here you can contemplate the devastation wreaked upon the town in 1955, when a major flood destroyed many homes and took lives. Or you can drive around the hills and alongside the reservoirs, hoping to glimpse the notorious "Winsted Wild Man," who has been described during sightings that span a couple centuries as possessing everything from cloven feet to an upright, eight-foot and hairy, 300-pound frame. Authorities explain away these stories as black bear sightings, but you never know.

⑯ A 4-mile drive from Winsted on Route 263 to **Winchester Center** takes you to the **Kerosene Lamp Museum,** which occupies a former gristmill. The more than 500 hanging and standing kerosene-powered lamps date mostly from 1852 to 1880. *100 Old Waterbury Tpk. (Rte. 263), tel. 203/379–2612. Admission free. Open daily 9:30–4.*

⑰ Almost every New Englander has sat in a Hitchcock chair, and visitors still drive up to **Riverton,** formerly Hitchcockville, to see where Lambert Hitchcock built the first one in 1826. The Farmington and Still rivers meet in this tiny hamlet, and it's one of the more unspoiled regions in the Hills, great for hiking and driving. The **Hitchcock Museum** is in the gray granite Union Church. *Rte. 20, tel. 203/379–4826. Admission free. Open late Mar.–Nov., Wed.–Sun. noon–5.*

From here, you're within 15 minutes of several scenic drives around **Barkhamstead Reservoir,** through **People's State Forest,** over **Saville Dam,** and through **Tunxis State Forest,** where you can hike and picnic.

⑱ Having now skirted the Massachusetts state line from Salisbury to Barkhamstead Reservoir, head down Route 8 to the raggedly industrial city of **Torrington,** birthplace of abolitionist John Brown and of Gail Borden, who developed the first successful method for the production of evaporated milk. Torrington's pines were for years used for shipbuilding, and factories produced such products as brass kettles, needles, pins, and bicycle spokes—its heyday was largely prior to World War II. Nowadays it seems as though most of the attractive homes here are funeral parlors, and strip malls are the only sign of progress. The drive west between Pie and Brandy hills leads to little **⑲** **Goshen,** once a dairy farming center and still host, on Labor Day weekend, of one of the best agricultural fairs in the Northeast.

⑳ The area's wealthiest and most noteworthy town is **Litchfield,** a few miles south of Goshen on Route 63. Everything here seems to exist on a larger scale than in neighboring towns: Enormous white Colonials line broad, majestic elm-shaded streets. **Litchfield Green** is surrounded by old shops and restaurants and is the most impressive green for miles around. This is the town where Aaron Burr, Horace Mann, John C. Calhoun, and Noah Webster earned law degrees. It's also where Harriet Beecher Stowe and Henry Ward Stowe were born and raised, and where, during the infamous Stove Wars of the late 18th century, worshipers vehemently debated the burning issue of whether a church would retain its sanctity if heated by a stove. Near the green is the Tapping Reeve House, America's first law school, which was founded in 1773 and is now a museum. In addition to the prominent graduates listed above, alums include six U.S. cabinet members, 26 U.S. senators, more than 100 congressmen, and dozens of Supreme Court justices, governors, and college presidents. *South St., tel. 203/567–4501. Admission: $2 adults, children under 16 free. Open mid-May–mid-Oct., Tues.–Sat. 11–5, Sun. 1–5.*

Opposite the Tapping Reeve House on South Street is the **Oliver Wolcott House,** now a private residence. During the Revolution, a lead statue of George III was hauled by zealous patriots in an oxcart from New York to the garden of this house, where Litchfield's local women melted and transformed the image of their enemy into 42,088 patriot bullets—a vengeful recycling program.

Three miles south of town on Route 63, watch for **White Flower Farms,** the home base of a mail-order operation where much of America buys its perennials and bulbs. Whether to buy or to browse, a stroll through these grounds is a pleasure for any gardening lover. *Rte. 63, tel. 800/888–7756. Open Apr.–Oct.*

A mile east of Litchfield on Route 118 is the **Haight Vineyard and Winery,** which flourishes despite the town's severe climate. Stop in for vineyard walks, winery tours, and tastings. *Chestnut Hill Rd., tel. 203/567–4045. Admission free. Open Mon.–Sat. 10:30–5, Sun. noon–5.*

Lourdes of Litchfield Shrine, also on Route 118, a short drive from the green, was built and is operated by the Montfort Missionaries. The 35-acre complex contains a replica of the famous grotto at Lourdes, France, and during pilgrimage season, May through mid-October, outdoor services are held Sunday at 3. Picnickers are welcome any time. *Rte. 118, Litchfield, tel. 203/567–1041. Grounds open year-round.*

Two miles west of the green, on Route 202, stop by the 4,000-acre **White Memorial Foundation,** the state's largest nature center and wildlife sanctuary. Besides 35 miles of hiking, cross-country skiing, and horseback-riding trails, the sanctuary has fishing areas, and bird-watching platforms. The main conservation center has children's exhibits, a library, and gift shop. *Rte. 202, tel. 203/567–0857. Admission to grounds free; conservation center: $1 adults, 50¢ children. Grounds open daily; conservation center open spring–fall, Tues.–Sat. 9–5, Sun. 11–5; winter, Tues.–Sat. 8:30–4:30, Sun. 11–5.*

㉑ From Litchfield, take Route 202 west to **Bantam,** a small, not especially picturesque village that yet has some good antiques and crafts shops and boutiques. Turn left here on Route 209, driving along the shore of Bantam Lake. Next, turn left again on Route 109, which **㉒** leads to **East Morris,** a picturesque cluster of mostly former summer homes—at one time, nearly three-fourths of the town's local taxes were paid by nonresidents.

Of course, come Christmas, one town in Connecticut is more popular than any other, and that is **Bethlehem,** just south of Morris. Cynics **㉓** say that towns such as Canaan, Goshen, and Bethlehem were named primarily with the hope of attracting prospective residents and not truly out of religious deference. In any case, the local post office has its hands full postmarking the 220,000 pieces of holiday greetings mailed from this town every December. In midmonth, the **Bethlehem Christmas Town Festival** (tel. 203/266–5702) draws quite a crowd, and yes, there's even a **Christmas Shop** (18 East St., tel. 203/266–7048) that year-round hawks the trimmings and trappings of happy holidays.

24 Like Norfolk, **Washington,** which is a few miles west of Bethlehem and south of New Preston, is one of the best-preserved Colonial towns in the state. The beautiful buildings of the Gunnery Prep School mingle with stately Colonials and churches, all set together on a sunny mound of old New England money. The newly renovated and reopened Mayflower Inn, just south of the Gunnery on Route 47, attracts an exclusive clientele. Washington was settled in 1734, and in 1779 became the first town in our young nation to be named for our heroic statesman and general.

Time Out Past the Gunnery, at the intersection of routes 47 and 109, you'll discover not only one of the best bookstores in the region, the **Hickory Stick Bookshop** (tel. 203/868–0525), but behind it a small clapboard deli called simply, **The Pantry** (Titus Sq., tel. 203/868–0258), where you can find all the makings of a gourmet picnic lunch. A little more atmospheric and warm, especially on a winter day, is **Green's General Store** (5 Kirby St., tel. 203/868–7324), which serves delicious homemade soups and sandwiches.

Between Roxbury and Washington, off Route 199 and at the end of a forested residential road (just follow the signs), is the **American Indian Archaeological Institute.** This is an excellent and thoughtfully arranged collection of exhibits and displays—even a replicated longhouse and nature trails detailing the state's history of Native American life. *Curtiss Rd., tel. 203/868–0518. Admission: $4 adults, $2 children. Open Mon.–Sat. 10–5, Sun. noon–5.*

25 There's really not a whole lot to do or see in **Roxbury.** But you can drive around hoping to spot one of this artist colony's prestigious residents, who include Richard Widmark, William Styron, Arthur Miller, Walter Matthau, and Philip Roth. A couple centuries ago, you might have bumped into a Revolutionary hero or two, including the likes of Ethan Allen, Seth Warner, and the not-easily-forgotten Remember Baker. If you don't happen to brush with fame, you'll at least spot several outstanding examples of Colonial architecture, mostly around the intersections of Routes 317, 67, and 199.

26 You might make the short side trip to tiny **Bridgewater,** a few miles southwest of Roxbury, just to see the dozens of restored Colonial homes in this tiny hamlet. Bridgewater is best known as the home of Charles B. Thompson, father of the mail-order business. In the late 18th century, Thompson began selling dolls, toys, housewares, and lotions out of his home, a novel practice that soon caused the town's diminutive post office to burst at the seams from the ensuing flood of orders. Today the ornately Victorian general store and post office out of which Thompson's store was run is an architectural landmark. Locals still remember the days when a dungaree-clad Marilyn Monroe, then married to Arthur Miller, bought her groceries here.

27 **Woodbury,** east of Roxbury on Route 317, is known these days for two things: its antiques and its churches. There may very well be more antiques shops in this quickly growing town than in the rest of the Litchfield Hills combined. The five magnificent churches that line Route 6, as well as the Greek Revival **King Solomon's Temple,** formerly a Masonic lodge, were all built between 150 and 200 years ago and represent some of the finest preserved examples of Colonial church architecture in New England.

28 Continuing down Route 6 to **Southbury,** you'll find a number of well-preserved Colonial homes and even a few more antiques shops. Unfortunately, you'll also find that this former agricultural community has been heavily developed and, like New Milford to the west, the town now acts as the bridge between southern Connecticut's modern suburbanity and the Litchfield Hills' pre-20th-century charm.

Historic Homes and Small Museums

Hours of the following homes are usually limited to a few days a week, although most will open by appointment—always call ahead. Admission ranges from free to $3 unless otherwise noted.

Kent The **Sloane–Stanley Museum** (Rte. 7, tel. 203/927–3849 or 203/566–3005; open mid-May–Oct.) was built by the author and artist Eric Sloane, whose work celebrates Early American woodworking and craftsmanship. Tools and implements, many from the 17th century, are on display. The ruins of the Kent Iron Furnace, in operation from 1826 to 1892, are also on the grounds.

Lakeville The **Holley-Williams House** (Upper Main St., tel. 203/435–2878; open July–Nov. 1), an early Classical Revival and Federal mansion that dates to 1808, contains fine furniture, Colonial art, and exquisite glass, silver, and china. John Milton Holley made his money running the Mt. Riga Iron Furnace and later founded the Holley Manufacturing Company, which was the nation's first pocketknife factory (which is around the corner; now restored, it houses offices).

Litchfield The **Litchfield Historical Society Museum** (jct. Rtes. 63 and 118, tel. 203/567–4501; open mid-Apr.–Oct.) has several well-organized galleries exhibiting decorative arts, paintings, and antique furnishings, as well as an extensive reference library. You can also find information on the town's many historic buildings, including Harriet Beecher Stowe's birthplace; the Sheldon Tavern, where George Washington slept on several occasions, and the Pierce Academy, America's first school for girls.

Norfolk The **Norfolk Historical Society Museum** (The Green, tel. 203/542–5761; open mid-June–mid-Sept.) is housed in the former Norfolk Academy, which was built about 1840. Exhibits include early American furnishings, maps, paintings, and documents related to Norfolk's history.

Torrington The **Hotchkiss-Flyer House** (192 Main St. tel. 203/482–8260; open year-round), a turn-of-the-century Victorian, is one of the better house-museums in the state, containing 16 rooms of elegant mahogany period pieces and hand-stenciled walls.

Winsted History buffs should see the 1813 **Solomon Rockwell House** (225 Prospect St. [Rte. 263 west off Rte. 44], tel. 203/379–8433; open mid-June–mid-Sept.),an immense Greek Revival structure housing an extensive collection of fine furniture, along with mostly regional books and other memorabilia.

Woodbury The **Glebe House** (Hollow Rd., tel. 203/263–2855; open Apr.–Nov.) is the large gambrel-roofed Colonial in which Dr. Samuel Seabury was elected America's first Episcopal bishop in 1783. Inside is an excellent collection of antiques; outside is a noteworthy garden, designed by renowned horticulturist Gertrude Jekyll.

What to See and Do with Children

Housatonic Valley Railroad, Canaan
Northeast Audubon Center, Sharon
White Memorial Conservation Center, Litchfield

Off the Beaten Track

The **American Clock and Watch Museum,** a collection of more than 1,800 New England–made clocks and watches, documents the rise, fall, and many innovations of the now-unwound clock-making industry of Bristol, the self-acclaimed clock capital of 19th-century America. Try to arrive on the hour, when 300 clocks strike at once. *100 Maple St., south of Rte. 6, Bristol, tel. 203/583–6070. Admission: $3 adults, $2.50 senior citizens, $1.50 children, $8 families. Open Mar.–Nov., daily 10–5.*

In Terryville, 13 miles southeast of Litchfield, you can explore the **Lock Museum of America,** America's largest collection of locks, keys, and ornate hardware in America. *Rte. 6, 130 Main St., Terryville, tel. 203/589–6359. Admission: $2 adults. Open May–Oct., daily 1:30–4:30.*

Waterbury, today one of America's least picturesque cities, is nevertheless home to one of the state's largest and most diverse historic districts. The 60-acre downtown district, which flourished around the turn-of-the-century as the cradle of the U.S. brass industry, comprises nearly 50 important buildings, including the dramatic 240-foot **Clock Tower** (389 Meadow St.), modeled after the city hall of Siena, Italy. The self-guided walking tour, available from the **Waterbury Convention and Visitors Commission** (83 Bank St., 06721, tel. 203/597–9527) or at the **Mattatuck Museum** (1 W. Main St., tel. 203/753–0381) is detailed, the walk fascinating—even if you aren't an architecture buff. The Mattatuck has a fine collection of 19th- and 20th-century Connecticut art, decorative arts, and memorabilia documenting the state's rich industrial history. *Admission free. Open year-round Tues.–Sat. 10–5 and, except July–Aug., Sun. noon–5.*

Shopping

Antiques   Best bets for antiquing are New Preston's little town center, Route 6 in Woodbury and Southbury, and the area of West Cornwall just over the covered bridge. Kent has prestigious art galleries and craft shops.

Gilyard's Antiques (Rte. 202, Bantam, tel. 203/567–4204) sells 18th- and 19th-century country furniture and decorative items. **Gooseboro Brook Antiques** (Old Turnpike Rd., Bantam, tel. 203/567–5245) carries antique furniture, baskets, quilts, stoneware, and collectibles. **Goshen Antiques Center** (North St., Goshen, tel. 203/491–2320) contains the varied wares of 28 antiques dealers. **Three Ravens** (1 E. Main St., Salisbury, tel. 203/435–9602) sells American folk art and country furniture. **Molly Bloom Vintage Clothing** (Sharon Goshen Tpk., West Cornwall, tel. 203/672–4947) offers the threads and accessories of yesteryear. **British Country Antiques** (50 Main St. N, Woodbury, tel. 203/263–5100) imports polished pine and country furniture from England and France. **Country Loft Antiques** (88 Main St. N, Woodbury, tel. 203/266–4500) also imports English and French furniture and rare Oriental rugs. **Monique Shay** (920 Main St. S, Woodbury, tel. 203/263–3186) carries Canadian country antiques.

Art Galleries Kent's **Bachelier-Cardonsky Gallery** (Main St., tel. 203/698–2382) and the **Paris–New York–Kent Gallery** (Kent Station, off Rte. 7, tel. 203/927–3357) are two of the foremost galleries in the Northeast specializing in contemporary works.

Crafts **Cornwall Bridge Pottery Store** (Rte. 128, West Cornwall, tel. 203/672–6545) sells pottery, glass by Simon Pearce, and paintings by local artists. **Ian Ingersoll Cabinetmakers** (River Rd., West Cornwall, tel. 203/672–6344) offers reproduction Shaker-style rockers and chairs. The **Connecticut Woodcarvers Gallery** (Rte. 44, East Canaan, tel. 203/824–0883) specializes in the work of professional woodcarvers and stocks Colonial-style eagles, pineapples, birds, clocks, and mirrors. **Kent Carved Signs** (Kent Station Sq., tel. 203/927–3013) sells hand-carved signs. **Housatonic Trading Co./Country Things** (27 Kent Rd., Kent, tel. 203/927–4411) offers the folk art of more than 200 local craftspeople. **Artisans Guild** (Greenwoods Rd. E, Norfolk, tel. 203/542–5487) carries local crafts—from personalized enameled eggs to unique arrangements of wild and cultivated flowers.

Sports and Outdoor Activities

Camping Try **White Pines Campground** (232 Old North Rd., Winsted, tel. 203/379–0124), **Lone Oak Campsites** (Rte. 44, East Canaan, tel. 203/824–7051 or 800/422–2267), **Valley in the Pines** (Lucas Rd., Box 5, Goshen, tel. 203/491–2032), and **Hemlock Hill Camp Resort** (Box 828, Litchfield, tel. 203/567–0920). Most campgrounds are closed between November and April.

Canoeing **Clarke Outdoors** (Rte. 7, Box 302, West Cornwall 06796, tel. 203/672–6365) offers canoe and kayak rentals as well as 10-mile trips from Falls Village to Housatonic Meadow State Park. **Main Stream Canoe Corp.** (Rte. 44, Box 448, New Hartford 06057, tel. 203/379–6657 or 203/693–6791) does flatwater and whitewater day trips on the Farmington River and moonlight trips on summer evenings. Equipment rentals are available March through November, weekends only. **Riverrunning Expeditions** (Main St., Falls Village 06031, tel. 203/824–5579 or 203/824–5286) offers the Housatonic River crowd rentals, instruction, guides, and trips that begin in Falls Village and end at Cornwall Bridge.

Fishing Trout season runs from mid-April through February, and a license is required. Pick up some gear at **Bantam Sportsman** (Lake Rd., Litchfield, tel. 203/567–8517) or **Housatonic Meadows Fly Shop** (Rte. 7 at Cornwall Bridge, Cornwall, tel. 203/672–6064).

Horse-and-Carriage Rides **Gems Morgan** (75 N. Poverty Rd., Southbury, tel. 203/264–6196) and the **Horse & Carriage Livery Service** (Loon Meadow Rd., Norfolk, tel. 203/542–6085) give horse-drawn sleigh and carriage rides—the former using registered Morgan horses.

Horseback Riding **Rustling Wind Stables** (Mountain Rd., Falls Village, tel. 203/824–7634) gives lessons and takes riders along the beautiful trails of Canaan Mountain. **Lee's Riding Stables** (57 E. Litchfield Rd., Litchfield, tel. 203/567–0785) gives trail and pony rides.

Hot-Air Ballooning Rides above the Hills are offered year-round by **Balloon Hollow, Inc.** (Newtown, tel. 203/426–4250), **Watershed Balloons** (Watertown, tel. 203/274–2010), and **Steppin' Up Balloons** (Southbury, tel. 203/264–0013).

Skiing **Mohawk Mountain** (Cornwall, tel. 203/672–6100 or, for conditions, tel. 203/672–6464) is a busy place midweek, with junior racing programs and special discount days; weekends attract families from nearby metropolitan areas. The 23 trails, ranged down 660 vertical feet, include a lot of terrain for beginners and intermediates, and there are a few steeper sections toward the top of the mountain. **Ski Sundown** (New Hartford, tel. 203/379–9851, or, for conditions, 203/379–SNOW) has some neat touches—a sundeck on the mountain and a Mountaineers social club for skiers 57 and older—as well as excellent facilities and equipment. The mountain is impressive for Connecticut. The vertical drop is 625 feet, and most trails (15 lighted at night) are for beginners and intermediates, although there's one advanced run.

Tubing **North American Canoe Tours** (65 Black Point Rd., Niantic 06357, tel. 203/739–0791) offers exhilarating tubing tours along the Farmington River from Memorial Day through June on weekends only and daily from June through Labor Day.

Spectator Sports

Auto Racing **Lime Rock Park** (Rte. 112, Lakeville, tel. 203/435–2571 or 203/435–0896) has been home to the best road racing in the Northeast for nearly four decades. Races take place on Saturday and holidays, and amphitheater-style lawn seating allows for great views all around.

State Parks

The best in the area are **Kent Falls** (Rte. 7, Kent), **Macedonia Brook** (Rte. 341, Kent), **Mt. Tom** (Rte. 202, Litchfield), **Dennis Hill** (Rte. 272, Norfolk), **Haystack Mountain** (Rte. 272, Norfolk), **Campbell Falls** (Rte. 272, Norfolk), **Housatonic Meadows** (Rte. 7, Sharon), and **Burr Pond** (Rte. 8, Torrington). For detailed information, contact the **Bureau of Parks and Forests** (Dept. of Environmental Protection, 165 Capitol Ave., Hartford 06106, tel. 203/566–2305).

Dining and Lodging

Canaan **Cannery Cafe.** Folks from all over come to enjoy the Cajun cooking at
Dining the Cannery, a little storefront eatery in downtown Canaan. Try
★ grilled shrimp over angel-hair pasta with lemon-butter sauce or sample the mixed grill, a combo of beef tenderloin, duck, Cajun sausage, and pork loin. Dessert might be chocolate decadence, a rich torte-like truffle with ganache icing, served with a light raspberry cream. *85 Main St. (Rtes. 44 and 7), tel. 203/824–7333. Reservations advised. MC, V. No lunch Sun. Closed Sun. and Mon. in winter. Moderate.*

Litchfield **West Street Grill.** The creative chef here, James O'Shea, and the
Dining friendly staff are always roving about, making sure their customers
★ are not just satisfied, but enraptured. This small, unpretentious dining room on Litchfield's quaint shopping street is the favorite of local glitterati, but newcomers are warmly welcomed, too. If you start off with the grilled peasant breads topped with roasted tomatoes and goat cheese or a Parmesan aioli, you'll have a tough time making room for one of the imaginative grilled fish, poultry, and lamb dishes, served with fresh vegetables and pasta. The crème brûlée is stellar. *43 West St. (Rte. 202), tel. 203/567–3885. Reservations advised. AE, MC, V. No dinner Sun. Expensive.*
Village Restaurant. The folks who run this storefront eatery in a charming redbrick town house claim that competitors get more than their share of attention. They have a point. The food here is as tasty as any in town, and the management has had the good sense to offer

inexpensive pub grub in one room, so-called new New England cuisine in the other. Whether you order burgers or polenta with wild mushrooms, you'll get plenty to eat—and what you get will be good. *25 West St., tel. 203/567–8307. Reservations advised. AE, DC, MC, V. Inexpensive–Expensive.*

Dining and Lodging

Tollgate Hill Inn and Restaurant. The 250-year-old Tollgate, formerly a way station for weary Colonials stagecoaching between Hartford and Albany, retains a definite romantic tavern atmosphere. The menu, however, is clearly contemporary: grilled salmon in a white port chutney, juicy half duckling in pear almond sauce. The wine list is extensive. Rooms in the main building, in a nearby schoolhouse, and in a modern building constructed in 1990 are decorated Colonial-style; many have canopy beds and working fireplaces. The only drawback is being a few miles from the town center on an extremely busy road. Still, the road is not visible through the dense evergreens surrounding the property. *Rte. 202 (2 mi east of Litchfield Center), tel. 203/567–4545. 15 rooms with bath, 5 suites. Facilities: restaurant (reservations required; closed Tues. Nov.– Mar.); Continental breakfast included. AE, DC, MC, V. Inn: Expensive. Restaurant: Expensive–Very Expensive.*

New Milford Dining
★

Maison LeBlanc. Energetic proprietors Rose and Pierre LeBlanc serve nonpareil French cuisine—an evenhanded representation of country, classic, and nouvelle—in this simply but authentically decorated 1775 Federal Colonial with high ceilings, four working fireplaces, wide-plank floors, and an original beehive oven. The prix fixe menu rotates weekly, showing off the likes of fillet of salmon en croute, venison meat pie, duck with a cranberry and brandy sauce, and wonderful apple-and-rum crepes for dessert. At $32.50, dinner of this caliber is a bargain—and you don't have to dress to the nines. *Rte. 7, New Milford, tel. 203/354–9931. Reservations advised. No lunch Sun. and Mon. AE, D, MC, V. Expensive.*

Charles Bistro. This bright storefront eatery has wide-wood plank floors, baskets on the walls, and white-linen tablecloths. Service can be slow, but then this is not the sort of place where you want to rush through a meal. Try the excellent overstuffed smoked salmon or mozzarella omelette with tomato chutney and spicy saffron home fries. For dinner try the steamed mussels followed by blackened bluefish or roasted Cornish game hen. *51 Bank St., tel. 203/355–3266. Reservations advised. AE, MC, V. Moderate–Expensive.*

Lodging

The Heritage Inn. Housed in a long and rambling former tobacco warehouse alongside the railroad tracks, the Heritage Inn's industrial history makes it one of the more unusual country hotels in Connecticut. Rooms are large, high-ceilinged, and tastefully decorated. Though the views are nothing to speak of, good restaurants and shops are within walking distance, and the restored New Milford railroad depot, which sees little locomotive action, is just across the street. *34 Bridge St., 06776, tel. 203/354–8883. 20 rooms with bath. AE, MC, V. Moderate.*

The Homestead Inn. High on a hill overlooking New Milford's town green, the Homestead was built in 1853 and opened as an inn in 1928. Life is casual here, and the owners, Rolf and Peggy Hammer, are always game for a leisurely chat. The extensive complimentary Continental breakfast is served in a large, cheery living room, where you can sit by the fire or admire the Steinway piano. The eight rooms in the main house have more personality than those in the motel-style structure next door. *5 Elm St., 06776, tel. 203/354–4080. 14 rooms, all with bath. AE, D, DC, MC, V. Moderate.*

New Preston
Dining

The Café. The patio here is pleasant in summer, with its view of the colorful antiques-and-crafts village of New Preston; in winter come sit before the crackling fire in the dining room, which is cozy but with an intentionally lived-in look. Everything from the salmon cakes to the pasta to the many homemade sweets are available for takeout, or you can come for afternoon tea and light fare between 4 and 5. *Rte. 45, tel. 203/868–1787. Reservations advised. No credit cards. BYOB. Closed Tues., Wed. Moderate–Expensive.*

★ **Doc's Trattoria.** Though set in a small nondescript house across from Lake Waramaug, this is not your ordinary pizzeria—as you may guess when you see the fancy cars in the tiny parking lot. Inside, mismatched green chairs and tables covered with butcher's paper carry on the charade, but the menu reveals the truth: This place serves sophisticated Northern Italian food. Although the designer pizzas are predictable, everything else is delicious, and the sautéed salmon and tuna with sun-dried tomatoes, roasted peppers, leeks, and lemon is unrivaled. Portions are large, and several choice salads and side dishes are available. *Rte. 45 and Flirtation Ave., tel. 203/868–9415. Reservations required. No credit cards. BYOB. Moderate–Expensive.*

Dining and
Lodging

★ **Boulders Inn.** This is the most idyllic and prestigious of the inns along Lake Waramaug's uneven shoreline. The Boulders opened in 1940 but still looks like the private home it was at the turn of the last century. Apart from the main house, a carriage house and four guest houses sit just across a country road, commanding panoramic views of the lake and countryside. Rooms contain a varied assortment of Victorian antiques and interesting odds and ends. The Boulders's window-lined, stone-wall dining room is outstanding. The menu includes pâté with pickled vegetables, shellfish risotto, and herb-grilled chicken with rosemary jus and garlic mashed potatoes. *East Shore Rd. (Rte. 45), 06777, tel. 203/868–0541. 10 double rooms with bath, 7 suites. MAP required on weekends. Facilities: restaurant (reservations advised; no lunch; closed Tues. in winter), lake, swimming, boating, tennis. AE, MC, V. Inn: Very Expensive. Restaurant: Expensive.*

The Inn on Lake Waramaug. Frequent changes in ownership during the 1980s kept the inn from living up to its potential, but the current innkeepers have things under control. From many of the antiques-filled bedrooms, some with working fireplaces, you can see Lake Waramaug sparkling through a grove of century-old sugar maples. In the candlelit dining room, new American accents are given to the likes of breast of pheasant and grilled New York strip steak. *North Shore Rd., 06777, tel. 203/868–0563 or 800/LAKE–INN, fax 203/868–9173. 23 rooms with bath. Facilities: restaurant (reservations advised), indoor pool, game room, tennis. MAP required on weekends. AE, DC, MC, V. Inn: Very Expensive. Restaurant: Expensive.*

★ **Hopkins Inn.** This grand Victorian, built in 1847 on a hill overlooking Lake Waramaug and originally run as a boardinghouse, is now one of the best bargains in the Hills. Rooms are furnished with plain white bedspreads, simple antiques, and pastel floral wallpaper; some share a bath. In winter, the whole inn smells of burning firewood; year-round, it is redolent of the aromas coming from the rambling dining rooms, which serve outstanding Swiss and Austrian dishes—calves brains in black butter, wiener schnitzel, sweetbreads Viennese. When the weather is kind, you can dine on the terrace overlooking the lake. *22 Hopkins Rd. (1 mi off Rte. 45), 06777, tel. 203/868–7295, fax 203/868–7464. 7 rooms with bath, 2 rooms share bath.*

Facilities: restaurant (reservations advised). No credit cards. Inn: Inexpensive–Moderate. Restaurant: Moderate–Expensive.

Norfolk
Lodging
★

Greenwoods Gate. This neatly preserved Federal Colonial is possibly the state's foremost romantic hideaway. Innkeeper Deanne Raymond is a cheerful host with a penchant for playing cupid. In each of the three suites, beds are covered in starched white linens. The Levi Thompson Suite is the most interesting: Its entrance is marked by a short flight of stairs leading to a small sitting area with a cathedral ceiling; from here, two additional staircases, which have solid cherry hand-tapered railings, lead to either side of an enormous master bed. *105 Greenwoods Rd. E (Rte. 44), Norfolk 06058, tel. 203/542–5439. 3 suites. Facilities: gift shop. Full breakfast included. MC, V. Expensive–Very Expensive.*

Riverton
Lodging

Old Riverton Inn. This rickety blue Colonial, built in 1796 and overlooking the Still River and the Lambert Hitchcock Chair Factory just a few miles from the Massachusetts border, is a wonderfully peaceful weekend retreat. Rooms are small—except for the fireplace suite—and the decorating is ordinary, but the inn always delivers, as promised, "hospitality for the hungry, thirsty, and sleepy." The inviting dining room serves ordinary traditional New England fare. *Rte. 20, Box 6, 06065, tel. 203/379–8678. 11 rooms with bath, 1 suite. AE, D, DC, MC, V. Moderate.*

Salisbury
Dining and Lodging
★

White Hart Inn. This celebrated 1815 country inn is furnished throughout with Chippendale reproductions and country pine pieces. Print wallcoverings and fabrics by Waverly complement soft-rose or muted-blue carpeting; period brass lamps and fixtures contribute to the Colonial ambience. There are two wonderful, distinctly different restaurants here: The Tap Room is a convivial, publike space where you can quaff a pint of Guinness while dining on creative cuisine befitting far fancier restaurants. The cushy, elegant Sea Grill—the more expensive of the duo—serves such expertly prepared dishes as tea-smoked lobster with red pepper flan and onion-and-horseradish crusted salmon. *The Village Green, 06068, tel. 203/435–0030, fax 203/435–0040. 23 rooms with bath, 3 suites. Facilities: restaurant and pub (reservations advised for both), meeting facilities. AE, DC, MC, V. Inn: Expensive–Very Expensive. Restaurants: Moderate–Very Expensive.*

Under Mountain Inn. The nearest neighbors of this white-clapboard farmhouse are the horses grazing in the field across the road. Indoors, there are antiques, knickknacks, and objets d'art in every corner, and the hospitality has a pronounced British flavor. Dinner, too, recalls Britain, with a variety of authentic game dishes and hearty steak-and-kidney pie. *482 Under Mountain Rd. (Rte. 41), 06068, tel. 203/435–0242. 7 rooms, 6 with bath. Facilities: pub, walking trail. MC, V. May be closed mid-Mar.–mid-Apr. Expensive.*

Lodging

Ragamont Inn. The tall white pillars of the 165-year-old downtown edifice signal a cozy country inn and fine restaurant. Five rooms are furnished in the Colonial style with assorted antiques; three contemporary rooms in the annex have king-size beds, color TV, and air-conditioning; a small suite has a charming sitting room with a fireplace. *Main St., 06068, tel. 203/435–2372. 9 rooms with bath. Facilities: restaurant. No credit cards. Closed Nov.–Apr. Moderate.*

Yesterday's Yankee Bed & Breakfast. Three upstairs guest rooms with braided rugs, down comforters, and air-conditioning share one bath in this Cape Colonial home built in 1744. Filling breakfasts (with home-baked muffins, rolls, or bread) are served at a large trestle table before the fireplace. *Main St. (Rte. 44), Box 442, 06068, tel.*

203/435–9539. 3 rooms. Facilities: box lunches prepared. AE, MC, V. Moderate.

Southbury

Dining

★ **Bacci's.** This bright and sunny Colonial-style restaurant serves the finest northern Italian food around, and the service is impeccable. Try the radicchio, endive, and goat-cheese salad as a starter, and you will still have room for deftly prepared rigatoni with a feather-light tomato sauce spiked with capers, olives, anchovies, garlic, and Parmesan cheese. Desserts are artistic renderings: sweet sauces decorate your plate of Italian pastries or ice cream. *900 Main St. S, tel. 203/262–1250. Reservations advised. AE, MC, V. Moderate–Expensive.*

Lodging

The Heritage Inn. You may be disappointed if you come here expecting to find a quaint country inn, which the slogan "Welcome to New New England" may suggest. Rooms and public areas have a contrived rusticity about them, and the restaurant, Timbers, is a cavernous banquet hall guarded overhead by bizarre chandeliers in hideous wooden cages. Still, as far as resorts go, the Heritage has plenty to offer, including a variety of reasonably priced packages for everything from golf to hot air ballooning, rock climbing to scuba certification. *Heritage Village, 06488, tel. 204/264–8200 or 800/932–3466. AE, DC, MC, V. Facilities: restaurant, bar, game room, golf, tennis. Moderate–Expensive.*

Torrington

Dining

Harvest Roasterie. Culinary whiz Randy Nichols left the West Street Grill in 1993 to start up his own place. By most accounts, it's a hit. Away from the din of downtown and actually closer to Winsted then to Torrington, the restaurant is a jolting hot-peach brick structure with a mansard roof, under which hangs a burgundy-and-white stripe awning; the interior is more conventionally stylish and contemporary. The food here, though, is anything but conventional—dishes include sublime spicy crab cakes and delectable mussels over pasta and calamari. *2404 Winsted Rd., tel. 203/496–9796. Reservations advised. AE, MC, V. Closed Mon. Moderate–Expensive.*

Lodging

Yankee Peddlar Inn. This brick-trim century-old inn, in the heart of a somewhat glum little city, underwent a major renovation a couple years ago, and rooms are now modern and even characterful, if a little musty. It's nothing fancy, but it's a good value and is run by friendly folks who have clearly worked hard to keep it running all these years. *93 Main St., 06790, tel. 203/489–9226 or 800/777–1891, fax 203/482–7851. 60 rooms with bath. Facilities: restaurant, bar. AE, D, DC, MC, V. Moderate–Expensive.*

Washington

Dining and Lodging

The Mayflower Inn. Though certain suites at this inn will set you back $475 a night, the place is always booked well ahead (and with guests who are only a tad livelier than the Joshua Reynolds portrait in the living room). Streams and trails crisscross the 28-acre grounds. The inn was completely rebuilt in 1992, and rooms are impeccably decorated with fine antiques and four-poster canopied beds; walls are hung with noteworthy prints and paintings, and papered in Regency stripes. The mouth-watering cuisine of renowned chef, John Farnsworth, includes roasted monkfish, New York strip steak, and braised lamb shank. *Rte. 47, Washington 06793, tel. 203/868–9466, fax 203/868–1497. 17 rooms with bath, 7 suites. Facilities: restaurant (reservations advised), tennis, meeting facilities, pool, health club. AE, MC, V. Very Expensive.*

West Cornwall

Dining

★ **Freshfields.** Artwork from the nearby Harris Gallery adorns the walls of this neat and homey restaurant, set within view of the historic covered bridge that spans the Housatonic River—in warm weather, you can even dine on a deck overlooking a waterfall. Even if

you're not in the market for a painting, stop in for some of the best
new American cuisine in the area. Incomparable is the Tuscan salad,
with roast garlic, black olives, polenta croutons, sun-dried tomatoes, and mozzarella. There is also usually a good selection of pasta
and a few superb chicken and fish dishes, all served with warm
homemade bread. *Rte. 128 (off Rte. 7, just over bridge), tel. 203/672–
6601. Reservations advised. MC, V. Closed Tues.–Wed. Moderate.*

Woodbury   **The Good News Cafe.** Carole Peck is a kitchenhold name in these
Diningz   parts and thus her decision to open a restaurant in Woodbury in late
★   1993 was met with cheers by all. The emphasis is on healthy, innovative fare: free-range chicken with wok veggies, grilled swordfish
and pumpkin ravioli with raisins and sunflower seeds. Or, you can
just bounce in for cappuccino and munchies—there's a separate
room just for this purpose, decorated with a fascinating collection of
vintage radios. Prices are extremely fair for such tasty creations,
and sharing is encouraged for but a nominal fee. There's also a terrific selection of imported and regional beers. *694 Main St., S, tel.
203/266–4663. Reservations advised. AE, MC, V. Moderate–Expensive.*

Woodbury Pizza Castle. The dining room's soothing pastel hues and
blond wood furniture are a relative improvement over the greasy
booths you find in most pizza joints, but then this isn't some ordinary
dive. This family-run parlor in a new wood-frame building serves delicious and filling deep-pan pizzas—try the Grecian-style pies with
sliced tomatoes, black olives, and feta cheese. *40 Sherman Hill Rd.,
tel. 203/263–2566. MC, V. Inexpensive.*

Lodging   **Curtis House.** Connecticut's oldest inn (1754), located at the foot of
Woodbury's antiques row, may also be its cheapest (some rooms,
even with private bath, are under $50). If you arrive with modest
expections, you should have a great time. The inn has seen dozens of
alterations and renovations over the years, but the floorboards still
creak like whoopie cushions, and the TVs in some rooms look to be
from the Ed Sullivan era. A fireplace roars downstairs and the furnishings vary from genuinely antique to just plain old. The restaurant serves heavy and filling steak-and-potato-type dishes in an
ancient dining room. *Main St. (Rte. 6), 06798, tel. 203/263–2101. 8
rooms with bath, 6 rooms share bath. Facilities: restaurant. MC, V.
Inexpensive–Moderate.*

The Arts and Nightlife

In most of the northwest corner of the state, after-dark entertainment means listening to the bug-zapper on the front porch, but in
Torrington, there's **Water Street Station** (131 Water St., tel. 203/
496–9872) with live rock, R&B, and jazz groups, both local and national, Thursday through Saturday. The **Gilson Cafe and Cinema**
(345 Main St., Winsted, tel. 203/379–6069), a refurbished Art Deco
movie house, serves food and drinks unobtrusively during the movie, evenings Tuesday through Sunday. You must be 21 or older to attend.

Music Mountain (Falls Village, tel. 203/496–2596) presents chamber
music concerts on weekends with such distinguished guest artists
as the Manhattan String Quartet, from mid-June to mid-September. The **Yale School of Music and Art** summer session and the **Norfolk Chamber Music Festival** (tel. 203/432–1966 or 203/542–5537)
perform Friday and Saturday evenings, and some Sunday afternoons, at Norfolk Green. The **Warner Theatre** (68 Main St., Torrington, tel. 203/489–7180 or 203/489–1219), a former Art Deco movie

palace, presents live Broadway musicals, ballet, and concerts by touring pop and classical musicians.

New Haven and the Southeastern Coast

As you drive east along I–95, culturally rich New Haven is the final urban obstacle between southwestern Connecticut's overdeveloped coast and southeastern Connecticut's quieter shoreline villages. The remainder of the jagged coast, which stretches all the way to the Rhode Island border, consists of small seafaring villages, quiet hamlets, and undisturbed beach. Along this mostly undeveloped seashore, the only interruptions are the industry and piers of New London and Groton. Mystic, Stonington, Old Saybrook, and Guilford claim the bulk of antiques and boutiques aficionados. North of Groton, in the heretofore seldom-visited town of Ledyard, the Mashantucket Pequots Reservation now owns and operates Foxwoods, the controversial casino that has quickly become the East Coast's greatest gaming facility outside of Atlantic City.

Important Addresses and Numbers

Visitor Information **Mystic and Shoreline Visitor Information Center** (Olde Mistick Village, Mystic, 06355, tel. 203/536–1641). **Southeastern Connecticut Tourism District** (27 Masonic St., Box 89, New London 06320, tel. 203/444–2206 or, outside CT, 800/222–6783).

Emergencies **Lawrence & Memorial Hospital** (365 Montauk Ave., New London, tel. 203/442–0711). **Yale-New Haven Hospital** (20 York St., tel. 203/785–2222).

Late-Night Pharmacy CVS (1168 Whalley Ave., New Haven, tel. 203/389–4714) is open until 10 on weeknights, 9 on weekends.

Getting Around Southeastern Connecticut

By Car From New Haven to the Rhode Island border, I–95 and Route 1, which run mostly parallel but sometimes intertwine, are the principal routes through the coastal area.

By Train **Connecticut Department of Transportation** (tel. 800/842–8299 or, outside CT, 800/243–2855) has commuter rail service (weekdays, westbound in the morning, eastbound in the evening) connecting the towns from Old Saybrook to New Haven. **Amtrak** (tel. 800/872–7245) makes stops in New London and Mystic.

By Bus **Southeastern Area Transit** (tel. 203/886–2631) has local bus service between East Lyme and Stonington.

By Ferry From New London, **Cross Sound Ferry** (tel. 203/443–5281; runs year-round) has passenger and car service to and from Orient Point, Long Island, NY; **Fishers Island Ferry** (tel. 203/443–6851) has passenger and car service to and from Fishers Island, NY; and **Montauk Passenger Ferry** (tel. 516/668–5709; runs May–Oct.) has passenger service to and from Montauk, Long Island, NY.

By Taxi **Airport Taxi** (tel. 203/627–3210) has limo service between Bradley International Airport and downtown New Haven. **Metro Taxi** (tel. 203/777–7777) serves New Haven and environs.

Exploring Southeastern Connecticut

*Numbers in the margin correspond to points of interest on the
Southeastern Connecticut map.*

❶ **New Haven** is a city of extremes: Although the historic area
surrounding **Yale University** and the shops, museums, theaters, and
restaurants on nearby **Chapel Street** prosper, roughly 20% of the
city's residents live below the poverty level. Stay near the campus
and city common, especially at night, and get a good map of the city.

New Haven enjoys a reputation as a manufacturing center dating to
the 19th century, but the city owes its fame to Elihu Yale. In 1718, a
donation by wealthy Yale enabled the Collegiate School, founded in
1701, to settle in New Haven, where it changed its name to **Yale University** to honor its benefactor. The university provides knowledgeable guides for one-hour walking tours that include Connecticut
Hall in the Old Campus, which once housed the young Nathan Hale,
William Howard Taft, and Noah Webster, not to mention George
Bush. *344 College St., Phelps Gateway, tel. 203/432–2300. Tours giv-
en weekdays at 10:30 and 2, weekends at 1:30.*

Sterling Memorial Library (120 High St., tel. 203/432–2798) and the
Beinecke Rare Book Library (121 Wall St., tel. 203/432–2977) house
major collections, including a Gutenberg Bible, illuminated manuscripts, and original Audubon bird prints. The **Yale Art Gallery**, the
country's oldest college art museum, contains American, African,
and Near and Far Eastern art, as well as Renaissance paintings and
European art of the 20th century. Don't miss the remarkable reconstruction of a Mithraic shrine. *1111 Chapel St., tel. 203/432–0600.
Admission free. Open Tues.–Sat. 10–5, Sun. 2–5.*

The **Peabody Museum of Natural History** opened in 1876 and has
amassed more than 9 million specimens and grown into one of the
largest natural history museums in the nation. Some of the best exhibits cover dinosaurs, meteorites, and Andean, Mesoamerican, and
Pacific cultures. Other notable displays cover Connecticut wildlife,
geology, and anthropology. *170 Whitney Ave., tel. 203/432–5050.
Admission: $2.50 adults, $2 senior citizens, $1.50 children; free
weekdays 3–5. Open Mon.–Sat. 10–4:45, Sun. 1–4:45.*

The **Yale Center for British Art** has probably the best collection of
British art outside of Britain itself. The center's skylit galleries, designed by Louis I. Kahn, are graced by original works by Constable,
Hogarth, Gainesborough, Reynolds, and Turner, to name but a few.
You'll also find rare books and paintings documenting English history from the 16th century to the present. *1080 Chapel St., tel. 203/
432–2800. Admission free. Open Tues.–Sat. 10–5, Sun. 2–5.*

Time Out   The cheerful **Atticus Bookstore-Cafe** (1082 Chapel St., tel. 203/776–
4040), adjacent to the Yale Center for British Art, is a funky hangout for hungry bookworms and cappuccino lovers—and it's open daily until midnight (9 PM Sun.). Lower of brow but far higher of culinary
significance, **Louis' Lunch** (Crowne St., between High and College
Sts., tel. 203/562–5507), a minuscule redbrick box with batten doors
and postmedieval windows, looks as if it might house some secret
Yale society; in fact it is the birthplace of America's beloved ham-
burger.

The most notable example of the campus's traditional university-
style Gothic architecture is the **Harkness Tower,** with its famous
motto, sometimes described as the world's greatest anticlimax: "For

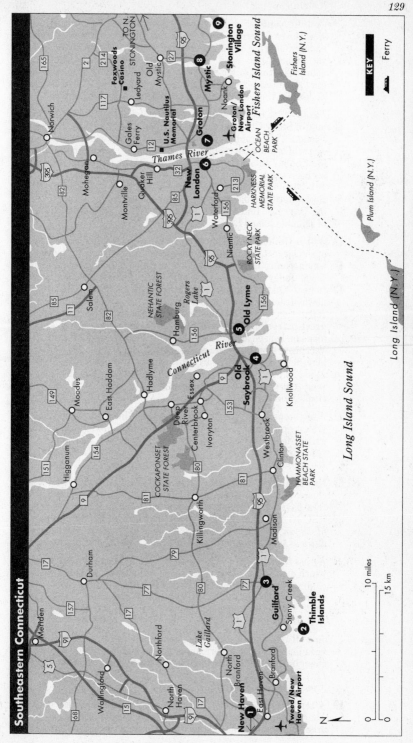

Southeastern Connecticut

KEY

Ferry

Fishers Island Sound

Fishers Island (N.Y.)

Stonington Village

⑨

⑧ Mystic

Old Mystic

TO N. STONINGTON

214

2

Foxwoods Casino

165

Ledyard

117

Norwich

Gales Ferry

U.S. Nautilus Memorial

Noank

Groton ⑦

Groton/ New London Airport

OCEAN BEACH PARK

Thames River

95

27

395

82

Mohegan

Quaker Hill

32

New London ⑥

85

Montville

Waterford

213

HARKNESS MEMORIAL STATE PARK

Plum Island (N.Y.)

1

156

Niantic

ROCKY NECK STATE PARK

85

111

Salem

82

NEHANTIC STATE FOREST

Rogers Lake

11

95

156

Old Lyme ⑤

149

Moodus

East Haddam

Hamburg

156

Connecticut River

Hadlyme

151

Higganum

154

Essex

Deep River

Centerbrook

Ivoryton

Old Saybrook ④

9

153

1

Knollwood

COCKAPONSET STATE FOREST

80

Westbrook

17

Durham

81

81

Killingworth

Clinton

HAMMONASSET BEACH STATE PARK

157

79

80

Madison

95

1

77

Northford

Lake Gaillard

77

1

Guilford ③

Stony Creek

② Thimble Islands

Wallingford

5

15

North Haven

17

91

North Branford

Branford

1

North Haven

Meriden

91

East Haven

① New Haven

Tweed/New Haven Airport

68

17

Long Island Sound

Long Island (N.Y.)

N

10 miles

15 km

0

0

God, for country, and for Yale." Across from the old campus, the **New Haven Green** offers impressive architecture as well as a superb example of urban planning. As early as 1638, village elders set aside the 16-acre plot as a town common. Three early-19th-century churches—the Gothic-style Trinity Episcopal Church, the Georgian-style Center Congregational Church, and the predominantly Federalist United Church—contribute to its present appeal.

② Take I-95 to Exit 56 and follow Leetes Island Road south to the village of Stony Creek, the departure point for cruises to the **Thimble Islands.** This group of 365 tiny islands was named for their abundance of thimbleberries, which are similar to gooseberries. Legend has it that Captain Kidd buried pirate gold on one island. Two sightseeing vessels vie for your patronage, the *Volsunga III* (tel. 203/481-3345 or 203/488-9978) and the *Sea Mist* (tel. 203/481-4841). Both offer trips daily between 10 and 4, early May through Columbus Day only. Both depart from Stony Creek Dock, found at the end of Thimble Island Road.

③ Stop in **Guilford,** home of nearly 500 historic sites and homes and one of the largest and oldest town greens in New England, before con-**④** tinuing on to **Old Saybrook,** once a lively shipbuilding and fishing town. Today the bustle comes mostly from its many summer vaca-**⑤** tioners. On the other side of the Connecticut river is **Old Lyme,** renowned among art lovers throughout the world. Central to its reputation is the **Florence Griswold Museum,** the former home of a great patron of the arts. Built in 1817, the well-preserved Federal mansion housed an art colony that included Willard Metcalfe, Clark Voorhees, and Childe Hassam. Many of their works are still on display here, along with early furnishings and decorative items. *96 Lyme St., tel. 203/434-5542. Admission: $3 adults, $2 senior citizens. Open June–Oct., Tues.–Sat. 10–5, Sun. 1–5; Nov.–May, Wed.–Sun. 1–5.*

A few steps away is the **Lyme Academy of Fine Arts,** housed in a Federal-style former private home built in 1817. Today it's a popular gallery featuring works by contemporary artists. *84 Lyme St., tel. 203/434-5232. $2 donation suggested. Open weekdays 9–5, Sat. 10–4, Sun. 1–4.*

⑥ **New London** is home to the **U.S. Coast Guard Academy.** The 100-acre cluster of traditional redbrick buildings includes a museum and visitors' pavilion with a gift shop. The three-masted training bark, the USCGC *Eagle* (tel. 203/444-8595), may be boarded when in port. *15 Mohegan Ave., tel. 203/444-8270. Admission free. Academy open daily 9–5. Museum open weekdays 9–5, Sat. 10–5, Sun. noon–5.*

Across from the academy entrance is the **Lyman Allyn Art Museum,** which displays a small, selective collection of art and antiques—including an impressive array of dolls, dollhouses, and toys—dating from the 18th and 19th centuries. *625 Williams St., tel. 203/443-2545. Donation suggested. Open Tues., Thurs., Fri., Sun. 1–5, Wed. 1–9, Sat. 11–5.*

Just off Williams Street is the **Thames Science Center,** a regional science museum with a permanent "Time and the River" exhibit and changing presentations focusing on river basin ecology. *Gallows La., tel. 203/442-0391. Admission: $3 adults, $1 children. Open Mon.–Sat. 9–5, Sun. 1–5.*

⑦ After crossing the river to **Groton,** you're in submarine country. There's no escaping the impact of the **U.S. submarine base** on the area. Just outside the entrance to the base is the U.S. *Nautilus* Sub-

marine Force Library and Museum. The world's first nuclear-pow-ered submarine, the *Nautilus*, launched from Groton in 1954, is now permanently berthed here and welcomes you aboard. The adjacent library-museum contains submarine memorabilia, artifacts, and displays, including working periscopes and controls. *Rte. 12, tel. 203/449–3174 or 203/449–3558. Admission free. Open Wed.–Mon. 9–4 (until 5 PM Apr. 15–Oct. 14).*

The best way to see the subs is by boat. The *River Queen II* conducts sightseeing and sunset cruises past the *Nautilus*, the sub base, the Coast Guard's *Eagle* when it's in home port, the Coast Guard Acade-my, and a panoply of local craft. Evenings get a little jazzier with dinner and Dixieland as part of the scene. *193 Thames St. (departs from Thames Harbor Inn), tel. 203/445–9516. Harbor tour fare: $6 adults, $3.50 children. Tours: Memorial Day weekend–mid-June, mid-Sept.–Columbus Day, weekends 11:15–3; mid-June–Labor Day, daily 10–3.*

Ft. Griswold Battlefield State Park (Monument St. and Park Ave., tel. 203/445–1729) contains historic battle emplacements and histor-ic displays marking the site of the massacre of American defenders by Benedict Arnold's British troops in 1781. From the top of the me-morial tower you get a sweeping view of the shoreline.

8 A few miles east, **Mystic** has tried with dedication to recapture (al-beit with excessive commercialism) the spirit of the 18th and 19th centuries. Some people think the name of the town is **Mystic Sea-port,** and it very well might be, given the lure of the museum that goes by that name. It is the nation's largest maritime museum, and its 17 riverfront acres feature authentic 19th-century sailing vessels you can board, a maritime village with historic homes, working craftspeople who give demonstrations, steamboat cruises, small-boat rentals, shops, restaurants, art exhibits, and special events in keeping with the seasons. *50 Greenmanville Ave. tel. 203/572–0711. Admission: $15 adults, $9 children. Open May–Oct., 9–5 (until 8 PM July–Aug.); Nov.–Apr., 10–4.*

Time Out It's hard to say who benefitted most from the success of the 1988 sleeper film *Mystic Pizza:* then budding actress Julia Roberts or the pizza parlor on which the film is based (none of the scenes was actual-ly filmed here). **Mystic Pizza** (56 W. Main St., tel. 203/536–3737) does serve terrific, inexpensive pizza, garlic bread, and grinders, but beware seething summertime crowds. Just as reputable, though not as full of character, is **Angie's** (25 Roosevelt Ave., jct. Rtes. 1 and 27, tel. 203/536–7300), which is a roll down the grassy hill from the Inn at Mystic. For dessert, venture into **Mystic Drawbridge Gourmet Ice Cream** (W. Main St.), a cozy little wood-floor nook where you can munch on scones, flavored coffees, homemade breads, and ice cream, all the while watching sailboats glide down the Mystic.

Nearby is the **Mystic Marinelife Aquarium** with more than 6,000 specimens and 50 live exhibits of sea life, including the new Penguin Pavilion. Seal Island, a 2½-acre outdoor exhibit, shows off seals and sea lions from around the world. At the Marine Theater, dolphins and sea lions perform every hour on the half hour. *55 Coogan Blvd., tel. 203/536–3323 or 203/536–9631. Admission: $8 adults, $7 senior citizens, $5 children. Open July–Labor Day, 9–5:30; Labor Day–June, 9–4:30.*

Be sure to stroll through the center of town and cross over the old drawbridge into West Mystic. The area has several well-preserved houses, and West Main Street is crowded with shops and eateries.

⑨ Little **Stonington Village** is your final peek at Connecticut's coastline, and some say the most memorable. Poking into Fisher's Island
Sound, Stonington remains a quiet fishing community clustered
around white-spired churches, far less commercial than neighboring
Mystic. Wander around the historic buildings that line the town
green and border both sides of Water Street until you reach the imposing **Old Lighthouse Museum,** which overlooks the Atlantic Ocean
and Fishers Island. Built in 1823, it was moved not long afterwards
to higher ground, where it remains today, displaying a wealth of
shipping, whaling, and early village artifacts. Climb to the top of the
tower for a spectacular view of the sound and the Atlantic Ocean. *7
Water St., tel. 203/535–1440. Admission: $2 adults, $1 children.
Open daily, July–Aug., 11–5; May, June, Sept., Oct., Tues.–Sun.
11–5, or by appointment.*

Within the same borough are the **Stonington Vineyards,** a small
coastal winery that has grown premium vinifera and French hybrid
grape varieties since 1979. Visitors are welcome to tour the winery,
stroll through the vineyard, and sample its wines. *Taugwonk Rd.,
tel. 203/535–1222. Admission free. Open daily 11–5.*

Historic Homes and Small Museums

Hours of the following homes are usually limited to a few days a
week, although most will open by appointment—always call ahead.
Admission ranges from free to $3 unless otherwise noted.

Branford The restored two-story clapboard **Harrison House** (124 Main St., tel.
203/488–8835; open June–Aug.), built in 1774, has a fine collection of
late-18th- and early-19th-century furnishings and a Colonial-style
herb garden.

Clinton The Marquis de Lafayette stayed at the **Stanton House** (63 E. Main
St., tel. 203/669–2132; open June–Sept.) in 1824, in a bed still displayed in its original surroundings. Built about 1790, the house was
once a general store and now exhibits items it might have sold back
then as well as a large collection of antique American and Staffordshire dinnerware.

Groton **Ebenezer Avery House** (Ft. Griswold, tel. 203/446–9257; open Memorial Day–Labor Day), a center-chimney Colonial built by a local
Revolutionary War hero, has a well-furnished restored kitchen and a
weaving room.

Guilford Right on the village green, New England's oldest stone house, the
Whitfield House Museum (Old Whitfield St., tel. 203/453–2457 or
203/566–3005; open mid-Jan.–mid-Dec.) was built by the Reverend
Henry Whitfield, an English vicar who settled here in 1639. The
late-medieval-style building has 17th-century furnishings. In the
same neighborhood is the **Hyland House** (84 Boston St., tel. 203/453–
9477; open June–Sept.) a Colonial saltbox built in 1660. Its hand-
hewn floorboards are still held together by the original handwrought nails and bolts. A 1720 addition contains a sophisticated
Bolection molding around the fireplace. Farther down the street is
another Colonial saltbox, the **Thomas Griswold House** (171 Boston
St., tel. 203/453–3176 or 203/453–5452; open mid-June–Columbus
Day), built in 1774. On display are farm tools, clothing, furniture,
and memorabilia. There's also a restored blacksmith shop and Colonial garden.

Madison The **Allis–Bushnell House and Museum** (853 Boston Post Rd., tel.
203/245–4567 or 203/245–7891; open June–Labor Day), built about

1785, has an early furnished doctor's office, along with period rooms containing antique furnishings and costumes.

Mystic   In the cluster of attractions in downtown Mystic is **Whitehall** (Rte. 27, tel. 203/536–8845; open May–Oct.), a country mansion that dates to the 1770s. It has been restored with authentic furnishings, and the kitchen contains a very rare "trimer arch," a brick-built arch that supports the hearthstone of the fireplace in the room directly above.

New Haven   The **Pardee–Morris House** (325 Lighthouse Rd. [Exit 50 off I–95], tel. 203/562–4183; open June–Aug.), built in 1750, was burned by the Redcoats in 1779, then rebuilt in 1780 on the original foundation. Furnishings are early-19th-century American.

New London   The **Joshua Hempsted House** (11 Hempsted St., tel. 203/443–7949 or 203/247–8996; open mid-May–mid-Oct.), built in 1678, is the oldest house in New London; today it showcases Early American furnishings. Nearly a century later, Nathaniel Hempsted built the nearby cut-stone house and its outdoor stone beehive bake oven, where occasional demonstrations of open-hearth cooking are given. The stone **Shaw-Perkins Mansion** (305 Bank St., tel. 203/443–1209; open year-round) has unique, paneled-cement fireplace walls. Built in 1756, it was visited during the Revolutionary War by Washington and Lafayette, to the delight of the Shaw family, whose furnishings and portraits abound. **Nathan Hale Schoolhouse** (foot of State St., tel. 203/426–3918; open mid-June–Aug.) is where the state's Revolutionary War hero taught prior to his military service. The **Monte Cristo Cottage** (325 Pequot Ave., tel. 203/443–0051; open Apr.–mid-Dec.) was the boyhood home of playwright Eugene O'Neill and was named for his actor-father's greatest role, as the literary count. The setting figures in two of O'Neill's landmark plays, *Ah, Wilderness!* and *Long Day's Journey into Night.*

Niantic   The **Thomas Lee House** (230 W. Main St., tel. 203/739–0761; open June–Sept.), built in 1660, is the oldest wood-frame house in Connecticut still on its original site. Also on the grounds is **Little Boston School** (ca. 1734), which is the oldest in the state. Both contain period furnishings.

Norwich   At the 1660 **John Baldwin House** (210 W. Town St., tel. 203/889–5990; open by appointment), you see a working Colonial household in action: Witness actual spinning, bread baking, soap making, and herb drying amid authentic period furnishings. Industrialist Christopher Leffingwell built the now restored **Leffingwell Inn** (348 Washington St., tel. 203/889–9440; open May–Oct.) in 1675. It went on to serve as a meeting point for patriots during the revolution.

Old Saybrook   The Georgian-style **General William Hart House** (350 Main St., Old Saybrook, tel. 203/388–2622; open mid-June–mid-Sept.), once the residence of a prosperous merchant and politician, was built about 1767.

What to See and Do with Children

Children's Museum of Southeastern Connecticut. This excellent museum, which opened in 1993, uses a hands-on approach to engage kids in the fields of science, math, and current events. Rotating exhibits and special programs are planned throughout the year. *409 Main St., Niantic, tel. 203/691–1255. Admission: $3 adults, $1.50 children under 12. Open Thurs. 10–4, Fri. 10–8, Sat. 11–5, Sun. 1–5.*
Mystic Marinelife Aquarium, Mystic

Mystic Seaport, Mystic
Peabody Museum of Natural History, New Haven
The **Shoreline Trolley Museum,** which houses more than 100 classic trolleys, among them the oldest rapid transit car and the world's first electric freight locomotive, is in nearby East Haven. Admission includes 3-mile rides aboard a vintage trolley. *17 River St., East Haven, tel. 203/467–6927. Admission: $5 adults, $4 senior citizens, $2 children. Open Memorial Day–Labor Day, daily 11–5; May, Sept., Oct., and Dec., weekends 11–5; Apr. and Nov., Sun. 11–5.*
Thames Science Center, New London

Off the Beaten Track

The **Comstock Bridge** (off Rte. 16, about 15 mi northwest of New London), in Colchester, is one of the few remaining covered bridges in the state.

Shopping

The New Haven and New London areas have typical concentrations of shopping centers. Downtown Mystic has a more interesting collection of boutiques and galleries, as well as factory-outlet stores. **Olde Mistick Village** (Coogan Blvd., tel. 203/536–1641), a re-creation of what an American village might have looked like about 1720, is at once hokey and picturesque. Here stores sell crafts, clothing, souvenirs, and food.

Art and Antiques In Mystic, both **Tradewinds Gallery** (20 W. Main St., tel. 203/536–0119) and **Framers of the Lost Art Gallery** (48 W. Main St., tel. 203/536–8339) have nautical prints, maps, and other rare artwork. **The Antiques Village** (985 Middlesex Tpk., tel. 203/388–0689) in **Old Saybrook** has more than 80 dealers. The **Goldsmith Gallery** (845 Boston Post Rd., Madison, tel. 203/245–7800) has six showrooms dedicated to contemporary painting in the impressionist mode. Norwich's **Arts Council Gallery** (60 Broadway St., tel. 203/887–2789) is the working space of 20 local potters, painters, printmakers, sculptors, and photographers. **Old Lyme, Guilford,** and **Stonington** are also strong on antiques.

Books True bibliophiles will head for the **Arethusa Book Shop** (87 Audubon St., New Haven, tel. 203/624–1848) and its large selection of out-of-print, used, early, and first editions. Here you can also get a handy guide to the many new and used bookstores that thrive in this university town.

Crafts **Branford Craft Village** (779 E. Main St., tel. 203/488–4689), set on the 150-year-old 85-acre Bittersweet Farm, has 25 crafts shops and studios in a village setting as well as a small play area and a café. The **Guilford Handcrafts Center** (411 Church St., tel. 203/453–5947) has changing exhibitions.

Discount Outlets At the **Mystic Factory Outlets** (Coogan Blvd., tel. 203/443–4788), nearly two dozen stores offer discounts on famous-name clothing and other merchandise.

Shopping Malls Opposite the New Haven Green, the **Chapel Square Mall** (900 Chapel St., tel. 203/777–6661) has 63 shops and a parking garage. New Haven's **Broadway** is an avenue of great little shops and eateries, including the **Yale Co-op** (tel. 203/772–2200), an enormous campus bookstore, which carries Yale goods and a vast stock of books. **Cutler's Records** (tel. 203/777–6271), also on Broadway, has a large collection of cassettes and compact discs, especially classical labels.

Sports and Outdoor Activities

Biking **Haley Farm** (Brook St., off Rte. 215, Groton) offers an 8-mile bike trail that winds through shoreline farm property.

Camping **Riverdale Farm Campsites** (111 River Rd., Clinton, tel. 203/669–5388), **River Road Campground** (13 River Rd., Clinton, tel. 203/669–2238).

Fishing Southeastern Connecticut is the charter- and party-boat capital of New England. Charter fishing boats take passengers for half-day, full-day, and some overnight trips at fees from $20 to $35 per person; tuna-fishing trips may cost as much as $100 a day. Party fishing boats, which are open to the public on a first-come basis, include the *Sunbeam Express* (15 1st St., Waterford, tel. 203/443–7259) and the *Hel-Cat II* (181 Thames St., Groton, tel. 203/445–5991). Private charter boats, whose rentals range from $275 to $375 for a half day, to $450 and up for a full day, are available in Mystic at **Brewer Yacht Yard** (tel. 203/536–2293); in New London at **City Pier** (tel. 203/442–1777) and **Burr's Yacht Haven** (tel. 203/443–8457); in Noank at **Noank Village Boatyard** (tel. 203/536–1770); and in Waterford at **Captain John's Dock** (tel. 203/443–7259).

Golf Popular 18-hole courses in the area include **Elmridge Country Club** (Elmridge Rd., Pawcatuck, tel. 203/599–2248) and **Shennecosset Golf Course** (Plant St., Groton, tel. 203/445–0262).

Hayrides **Davis Farm** (Greenhaven Rd., Pawcatuck, tel. 203/599–5841) offers hayrides in horse-drawn wagons along the Pawcatuck River.

Hot-Air Ballooning If you're crazy—or just curious—consider bungee jumping from one of the hot-air balloons of **Mystical Balloon Flights** (43 Forest Dr., Salem, tel. 203/537–0025). Rides high above the countryside, complete with champagne brunch, are available, too. **Mystic River Balloon Adventures** (17 Carriage Dr., Stonington, tel. 203/535–0283) offer similar trips.

Water Sports Surfboards and sailboards can be rented from **Action Sports** (324 W. Main St., Branford, tel. 203/481–5511) and **Sunset Bay Surf Shop** (192 Boston Post Rd., Westbrook, tel. 203/669–7873). Boats can be rented or chartered from **Colvin Yachts** (Hammock Dock Rd., Westbrook–Old Saybrook, tel. 203/399–9300), **Dodson Boat Yard** (184 Water St., Stonington, tel. 203/535–1507), **Sea Sprite Charters** (113 Harbor Pkwy., Clinton, tel. 203/669–9613), and **Shaffer's Boat Livery** (Mason's Island Rd., Mystic, tel. 203/536–8713).

Wildlife-Watching Spend the day here spotting whales, seals, or eagles aboard the 100-foot *Sunbeam Express*. Naturalists from Mystic Aquarium sail with you and answer questions. Contact **Captain John's Sports Fishing** (15 1st St., Waterford, tel. 203/443–7259).

State Parks

Harkness Memorial State Park (Rte. 213, Waterford, tel. 203/443–5725), a former summer estate, contains formal gardens, picnic areas, a beach for strolling and fishing (not swimming), in addition to the Italian villa–style mansion, Eolia. Come for the summer music festival in July and August.

Beaches

Hammonasset Beach State Park (I–95, Exit 62, tel. 203/245–2785), the largest of the state's shoreline sanctuaries, has a 2-mile beach and facilities for swimming, camping, picnicking, fishing, and scuba diving. The 82-acre **Lighthouse Point** (end of Lighthouse Rd., tel. 203/787–8005), in southeastern New Haven, has a public beach, nature trails, a picnic grove, and an antique carousel in a turn-of-the-century beach pavilion. **Ocean Beach Park** (Ocean Ave., New London, tel. 203/447–3031 or 800/962–0284) has an Olympic-size outdoor pool with a triple water slide; the park also includes minigolf, food concessions, a picnic area, a boardwalk, great Sound views, and an amusement park. The mile-long crescent-shape strand at **Rocky Neck State Park** (Rte. 156, Niantic, tel. 203/739–5471) is one of the finest beaches on Long Island Sound. Facilities include family campgrounds, picnicking sites, food concessions, fishing, and public bath houses.

Dining and Lodging

Branford **Riviera Cafe.** This tiny but tony eatery, by the Long Island Sound
Dining community of Indian Neck, opened in 1993 to rave reviews. The food
★ is strictly Mediterranean, with lots of capers and black olives, except in dishes like lamb served with pineapple-and-mango chutney. With everything dusted with generous pinches of herbes de Provence, the usual veal, chicken, and seafood grills are transformed here into works of art, and, after feasting here, one literally expects to stumble out the door onto a pebbly beach in Nice. *3 Linden Ave., tel. 203/481–7011. Reservations advised. AE, MC, V. Moderate–Expensive.*

Guilford **The Stone House.** Refurbished and reopened in 1992, this friendly
Dining waterside establishment now sparkles with floral-print table linens, red-tile floors, and wicker or striped rush-seated chairs. Seafood and pasta dishes make up the bulk of the menu, though grilled pizzas and a few chicken and veal entrées are offered, too. The grilled tuna with peach salsa is a nice choice. *506 Whitfield St., tel. 203/453–2566. No reservations. AE, MC, V. Inexpensive–Expensive.*

Mystic **The Inn at Mystic.** The highlight of this 90-year-old inn, which
Dining and sprawls over 15 hilltop acres and overlooks picturesque Pequotsepos
Lodging Cove, is the five-bedroom, Georgian Colonial mansion in which
★ Lauren Bacall and Humphrey Bogart honeymooned. Almost as impressive are the rambling four-bedroom gatehouse and the unusually attractive motor lodge. Mansion rooms are the best and most expensive; two have fireplaces. A number of rooms in various buildings have Jacuzzis, and each is furnished differently. This is perfect for families and long-term guests. The Floodtide Restaurant has a convivial, sun-filled dining room and specializes in traditional New England fare: clam chowder, beef Wellington, and veal française are typical. Brunchaholics flock here on Sunday. *Jct. Rtes. 1 and 27, 06355, tel. 203/536–9604 or 800/237–2415, fax 203/572–1635; restaurant tel. 203/536–8140. 68 rooms with bath. Facilities: restaurant (reservations advised), dockage, canoes, sailboats, outdoor pool and hot spa, tennis. AE, D, DC, MC, V. Inn: Moderate–Very Expensive. Restaurant: Very Expensive.*

The Whaler's Inn and Motor Court. This property on the east side of the Mystic River is the perfect compromise between a chain motel and a country inn. Rooms in the inn's four separate buildings are clean and attractive, and the public rooms are furnished with lovely antiques. Of the four, the 1865 house has the nicest accommodations, but the inn is good, too. You're near shops and restaurants. The restaurant, Bravo Bravo, was recently revamped, its roster of Italian standbys given a few nouvelle touches: Black pepper fettuccine comes with grilled scallops, roasted tart apples, fresh thyme, sun-dried tomatoes, and a gorgonzola cream sauce, for instance. But you can still get ossobuco the way it's prepared in Italy. *20 E. Main St., 06355, tel. 203/536–1506 or 800/243–2588, fax 203/572–7697. 41 rooms with bath. Facilities: restaurant (reservations advised), minifridges in some rooms. AE, D, DC, MC, V. Moderate–Expensive.*

Lodging **The Steamboat Inn.** It's not your typical, creaky old Connecticut inn. This establishment with rooms named after famous Mystic schooners feels very new—and is. As a result, every room has a fireplace, whirlpool bath, and dramatic river view, and looks as though it's posing for the cover of *House Beautiful.* Despite the inn's busy downtown location, within earshot of the eerie hoot of the Bascule Drawbridge and the chatter of tourists, its rooms are the most luxurious and romantic in town. *73 Steamboat Wharf (off W. Main St.), 06355, tel. 203/536–8300. 7 rooms with bath. AE, MC, V. Expensive–Very Expensive.*

Comfort Inn. This version of the prototypical chain motel is near all of Mystic's attractions. *48 Whitehall Ave., 06355, tel. 203/572–8531 or 800/228–5150, fax 203/572–9358. 120 rooms with bath. Facilities: exercise room. Continental breakfast included. AE, D, DC, MC, V. Moderate–Expensive.*

New Haven
Dining
Azteca's. This elegant restaurant serves the standard chimichangas and chile rellenos, but what really makes it outstanding are its more exotic—purists will say trendy—dishes: baked shellfish quesadillas, baked roasted chiles, chevre-filled tortillas, and pecan-crusted catfish with apple chutney, chorizo rice, and sugar snap peas. The artwork on the walls changes monthly; the innovative menu changes somewhat less frequently. *14 Mechanic St., tel. 203/624–2454. Reservations advised. MC, V. No lunch. Closed Sun. Moderate–Expensive.*

Bagdon's. On the scene only since 1992, this corner storefront has quickly made itself one of New Haven's favorites. The decor is clean, simple, and refined, with black wooden chairs, crisp white napery, and white brick walls. The New American menu lacks the esoteric pretensions of some others; entrées include rock Cornish game hen with a Dijon mustard sauce and seafood ragout. *9 Elm St., tel. 203/777–1962. Reservations advised. No lunch weekends. AE, MC, V. Moderate–Expensive.*

★ **Leon's.** It was in 1938 that the enthusiastic, down-to-earth Varipapa family started this traditional Italian restaurant, with red-vinyl booths and rough-plaster walls. They've been running it in the same location ever since, and have garnered countless awards from critics and local newspaper polls; it has also become a hangout of celebs and hotshots. The menu is extensive; not only are there 10 varieties of veal, for instance, but there are also a number of specialties you won't find anywhere outside of Italy. Portions are enormous and most of the appetizers are meals in themselves. Located not far from Yale–New Haven Hospital, it's a little tricky to find; call first. *321 Washington St., tel. 203/777–5366. Reservations advised. No lunch Sat. Closed Mon. AE, DC, MC, V. Moderate–Expensive.*

Saigon City. Vietnamese cuisine incorporates some of the best ingredients of Chinese, Thai, and Indian cultures, and Saigon City does it as well as any. Try king charbroiled shrimp, mushroom sauté with chicken, or spicy beef curry. *Corner of Chapel and Park Sts., tel. 203/865–5033. No reservations. AE, MC, V. Moderate–Expensive.*

Union League Cafe. Occupying what was once the Union League Club and until 1993 housed Robert Henry's—a premier French dining room—this establishment is presided over by the next generation of the former restaurant's owners. The haute French cuisine is not altogether gone, but the menu offers such new twists as the smoked salmon terrine with pesto sauce, offered as an appetizer, and touches of Provençal cuisine come through in dishes like the roast duck with white beans and flank steak with shallot sauce. The food is now more affordable; some say it has improved. The wine list is still among the state's best. *1032 Chapel St., tel. 203/562–4299. Reservations advised. AE, MC, V. No lunch weekends. Moderate–Expensive.*

Bruxelles. Whatever your price range, this sophisticated downtown brasserie is a good spot to grab pre-theater grub. Entrées include apple chicken and herb-roasted game hen; the pizzettes come with such toppings as Peking duck, sun-dried tomatoes, black olives, and mozzarella. The dining room, which is on the second floor, is at once formal and madcap, with starched cloth napkins standing at attention in stemmed glasses on top of tablecloths covered with butcher's paper that you can doodle on—crayons are provided. *220 College St., tel. 203/777–7752. No reservations. AE, MC, V. Inexpensive–Expensive.*

★ **Frank Pepe's.** Is this really the best pizza in the world—as critics from all over have been known to say? Of course not, but it's damn close, and it's the only thing on the menu, which is actually just a chalkboard on the wall. So don't ask for garlic bread, or one of the smart-mouthed waitresses will groan at you. Wooster Street is a fairly long walk from the more fashionable Chapel West neighborhood, so consider driving here—there is off-street parking. Expect to wait an hour or more for a table—or, on weekend evenings, go after 10. *157 Wooster St., tel. 203/865–5762. No reservations. No credit cards. No lunch Mon., Wed., and Thurs. Closed Tues. Inexpensive.*

Sally's. This is Frank Pepe's main competition—the debate continues as to which makes the best pizza. If you're lucky, you'll have the chance to try them both. With rows of tightly spaced tables, Sally's is a bit more cramped than Pepe's. *237 Wooster St., tel. 203/624–5271. No reservations. No credit cards. Inexpensive.*

Lodging
★ **The Inn at Chapel West.** This 1847 Victorian mansion, despite its bordering a questionable neighborhood, is one of the most polished small inns in the state. The rooms are furnished individually, in styles ranging from Victorian to country home to contemporary; all are luxurious. The staff knows all the great nearby eateries and points of interest, and the inn is steps away from Yale's campus and New Haven's theater district. A popular afternoon tea, with home-baked scones and breads, is open to the public by reservation. *1201 Chapel St., 06511, tel. 203/777–1201, fax 203/776–7363. 10 rooms with bath. Afternoon refreshments and Continental breakfast included. AE, D, DC, MC, V. Very Expensive.*

Colony Inn. In this establishment in the center of the Chapel Street hotel district, the lobby is eclectic, with its ornate chandelier—part grand Baroque, part Victorian. Guest rooms are furnished with Colonial reproductions and have attractive modern baths; some of those on the higher floors overlook the Yale campus. There's sidewalk dining in the inn's glass-enclosed Greenhouse Restaurant. *1157 Chapel St., 06511, tel. 203/776–1234 or, outside CT, 800/458–8810; fax 203/772–3929. 80 rooms with bath, 6 suites. Facilities: restaurant, lounge. AE, DC, MC, V. Moderate–Expensive.*

New London **Recovery Room.** It's a favorite game of Connecticut pizza parlors to
Dining declare: "We're as good as Pepe's"—a reference to the famed godfather of the pizza pie in New Haven. But this white Colonial storefront eatery, presided over by the friendly Cash family, lives up to

its claim. Plenty of "boutique" toppings are available, but you're advised not to ruin a great pizza with too many flavors. Perfection is realized by the three-cheese 'za with grated Parmesan, romano, and gorgonzola. *443 Ocean Ave., tel. 203/443–2619. Reservations accepted. MC, V. Inexpensive.*

Lodging **Lighthouse Inn.** This establishment, located in a residential neighborhood with splendid views of Long Island Sound, is the quintessential grand seaside inn: nothing more, nothing less. The 24 rooms in the carriage house are furnished with canopy beds and wingback arm chairs; their odd configuration is pleasantly quirky. Rooms in the turn-of-the-century mansion, more expensive, have similar furnishings and equally odd layouts but better views. All are clean, if a tad stuffy. Grounds and public areas are well cared for. The restaurant serves unremarkable seafood. *6 Guthrie Pl., tel. 203/443–8411. 51 rooms. Facilities: restaurant, lounge. AE, DC, MC, V. Expensive–Very Expensive.*

Queen Anne Inne and Antiques Gallery. This turreted, three-story mansion has floral-patterned wallpaper, stained-glass windows, fireplaces, and antique furniture that dates from the inn's founding in 1903. If any of the antiques and paintings strike your fancy, you're in luck—they're for sale. *265 Williams St., 06320, tel. 203/447–2600 or 800/347–8818. 10 rooms, 8 with bath. Full breakfast and afternoon tea included. V. Moderate–Very Expensive.*

Radisson Hotel. A downtown location makes this property convenient to State Street, I–95, and the Amtrak station. Rooms have nondescript modern furnishings but are quiet and spacious. *35 Gov. Winthrop Blvd., 06320, tel. 203/443–7000 or 800/333–3333, fax 203/443–1239. 114 rooms with bath, 4 suites. Facilities: restaurant, lounge, exercise room, Jacuzzi, indoor pool. AE, DC, MC, V. Moderate–Expensive.*

Noank **Abbott's Lobster in the Rough.** If you want some of the state's best
Dining lobster, mussels, crab, or clams on the half shell, grab a bottle of
★ wine and slip down to this unassuming seaside lobster shack in sleepy Noank (it's BYOB). Seating is outdoors or on the dock, and views are magnificent. It's a terrific spot for a clamfest with a crowd and for intimate evenings alike. *117 Pearl St., tel. 203/536–7719. Reservations advised. Open daily Memorial Day–Labor Day; weekends Labor Day–Columbus Day. MC, V. Moderate–Expensive.*

North **Randall's Ordinary.** This inn is famed for its open-hearth cooking.
Stonington Arrive by 7 PM; then watch some of the open-fire preparations before
Dining and sitting down at simple old wood tables. The fixed-price menu changes
Lodging daily but consists of three courses with choices such as loin of pork and
★ Nantucket scallops. Waiters dress in Colonial garb. The original structure, the 17th-century John Randall House, provides bare, simple accommodations on the second floor, and the three public rooms have working fireplaces. The Jacob Terpenning Barn, built in 1819, was transformed in 1987 into wonderfully irregular guest rooms, all with fireplaces and authentic, early Colonial decor. *Rte. 2, Box 243, 06359, tel. 203/599–4540. 15 rooms with bath. Facilities: restaurant (reservations required for dinner, advised for lunch), whirlpool bath. Continental breakfast included. AE, MC, V. Inn: Moderate–Very Expensive. Restaurant: Expensive.*

Lodging **Antiques & Accommodations.** The English influence is evident in the
★ Georgian formality of this Victorian country home, built about 1861. Exquisite furniture and accessories, all for sale, decorate all the common and guest rooms. The 1820 house in the rear contains similarly furnished two- and three-bedroom suites. Breakfast,

served by candlelight at the formal dining table, includes seasonal fruits, local eggs, and home-baked goods. Aromatic candles and fresh flowers create a warm and inviting atmosphere. *32 Main St., 06359, tel. 203/535–1736 or 800/554–7829. 4 rooms, 3 with bath; 2 suites. Full breakfast included. DC, MC, V. Moderate–Very Expensive.*

Old Lyme
Dining and Lodging

Bee & Thistle Inn. This establishment just down the street from the Old Lyme Inn is a bit homier than its neighbor; it's also farther out of the shadows of I–95. Innkeepers Bob and Penny Nelson have furnished this two-story 1756 Colonial on the Lieutenant River with period antiques and plenty of warm touches. Most bedrooms have canopy or four-poster beds and private baths. The outstanding American cuisine is served in one of the most romantic dining rooms around. *100 Old Lyme St., 06371, tel. 203/434–1667. 11 rooms, 9 with bath; cottage. Facilities: restaurant (reservations advised; jacket requested). AE, DC, MC, V. Closed first 2 weeks in Jan. Inn: Moderate–Very Expensive. Restaurant: Expensive.*

Old Lyme Inn. This gray-clapboard farmhouse, built in the 1850s, serves the best American cuisine in the area. Innkeeper, local historian, and antiques collector Diane Atwood has filled the spacious bedrooms with a harmonic assortment of Empire and Victorian furnishings, including canopy beds and Rococo Revival settees; bathrooms are contemporary. Some of her collection is also on display in the bright and airy common rooms and in the restaurant, where you might sample Norwegian salmon, boneless loin of rabbit, or sliced loin of venison or antelope. *85 Old Lyme St. (just north of I–95), Box 787, 06371, tel. 203/434–2600, fax 203/434–5352. 5 rooms with bath, 8 suites. Facilities: restaurant (reservations advised). Continental breakfast included. AE, D, DC, MC, V. Closed first 2 weeks in Jan. Inn: Moderate–Expensive. Restaurant: Very Expensive.*

Old Saybrook
Lodging

Saybrook Point Inn. This establishment, which opened in 1989, feels more like a small hotel than the inn it purports to be. Rooms are furnished with traditional British reproductions, floral-print spreads, and Impressionist- and classical-style art. The health club and pools overlook the inn's marina and the Connecticut River. *2 Bridge St., 06475, tel. 203/395–2000. 62 rooms, including 7 suites, all with bath. Facilities: restaurant, meeting rooms, marina, spa, health club, indoor and outdoor pools, Jacuzzi. AE, D, DC, MC, V. Very Expensive.*

Stonington
Lodging

Sea Breeze Motel. Behind the vibrant mustard-and-white facade are basic, modern rooms, each with two double beds, simple contemporary furnishings, and a bathroom with stall shower. *Rte. 1, 06378, tel. 203/535–2843. 25 rooms with bath. Facilities: cable TV. AE, MC, V. Moderate–Expensive.*

Stonington Village
Dining

Harborview. Nouvelle influences are making themselves felt in the kitchen here, which has a longstanding commitment to classic French cuisine. Still, the formal dining room, with fine crystal, china, and white napery, is one of the most romantic in southeastern Connecticut. The large, old-fashioned taproom in front offers a contrast, with its bare wood floor and kegs hung from the ceiling. Specialties in the dining room include *homard Melanie* (pan-roasted lobster with bourbon and chervil-butter) and *ris de veau Guesclin* (braised veal sweetbreads with wild mushrooms in a puff pastry shell). Burgers and salads are popular in the taproom. *60 Water St. (Cannon Sq.), tel. 203/535–2720. Reservations advised. AE, DC, MC, V. Moderate–Very Expensive.*

Skipper's Dock. This seafood restaurant is on the dock behind the

Harborview parking lot, and is under the same management. Surrounded by nautical artifacts as you are here, you might well choose the kettle of fisherman's stew Portuguese (clams, mussels, shrimp, native fish, and chorizo sausage in broth with tomato and peppers). On the weekend, prime rib is served in two generous sizes. *66 Water St. (on the pier), tel. 203/535–2000. No reservations. AE, DC, MC, V. Closed Jan.–mid-Mar. Moderate–Expensive.*

Lodging **Lasbury's Guest House.** This modest establishment occupies a frame house and the small, red Colonial building a few steps behind it. It's on a quiet side street, disturbed only by the occasional speeding Amtrak train, with a salt marsh to the rear. A nautical theme, along with framed posters for the annual Stonington Fair, provides the decoration. A Continental breakfast is delivered to each room in a tiny basket. *24 Orchard St., 06378, tel. 203/535–2681. 3 rooms, 1 with bath. Continental breakfast included. No credit cards. Moderate.*

Westbrook **Aleia's.** This large late-19th-century house on Post Road, which
Dining looks quite ordinary from the outside, is surprisingly elegant with
★ its dark wainscoting and bentwood chairs, its classic dark green-and-white color scheme, and its walls painted with images of plants. The eclectic menu has several nouvelle-inspired pasta, veal, and poultry dishes, such as grilled chicken with artichokes and roasted tomatoes over couscous. The food is superb, the service personal but laid back. *1353 Boston Post Rd., tel. 203/399–5050. Reservations advised. AE, MC, V. Closed Mon. Moderate–Expensive.*

Lodging **Water's Edge Inn.** With its spectacular setting on Long Island
★ Sound, this traditional weathered gray-shingle compound is one of the Connecticut shore's premier resorts. The main building has warm and bright public rooms furnished with antiques and reproductions, and its upstairs bedrooms, with wall-to-wall carpeting and clean, modern bathrooms, afford priceless Sound views. Though larger and ideal for business trade, the suites in the surrounding outbuildings are not as nicely kept and lack the fine views. *1525 Post Rd., 06498, tel. 203/399–5901 or 800/222–5901, fax 203/399–6172. 100 rooms and suites. Facilities: restaurant, tennis, indoor and outdoor pools, Jacuzzi, volleyball, lounge, meeting rooms, beach. AE, D, DC, MC, V. Expensive–Very Expensive.*

Talcott House. This 1890 cedar-shingle beach cottage is now an attractive shoreline B&B with a spacious main salon offering an expansive ocean view. Bedrooms feature polished wood floors topped with a scattering of bright carpets, some brass beds, hobnail spreads, and pale painted walls bordered with stenciling. Continental breakfast includes homemade muffins, breads, and tarts. *161 Seaside Ave., Box 1016, 06498, tel. 203/399–5020. 7 rooms, 4 with bath. Continental breakfast included. MC, V. Moderate–Expensive.*

The Arts and Nightlife

New Haven is where many shows work out the kinks before heading to Broadway. The **Long Wharf Theatre** (222 Sargent Dr., tel. 203/787–4282) and the **Yale Repertory Theatre** (Chapel and York Sts., tel. 203/432–1234) both stage major star-studded dramas year-round, and the **Shubert Performing Arts Center** (247 College St., tel. 800/955–5566) presents an array of musical, operatic, and dramatic performances, usually following their run in the Big Apple. In New London, Connecticut College's **Palmer Auditorium** (Mohegan Ave., tel. 203/439–2787) presents both dance and theater programs, and the **Garde Arts Center** (325 Captain's Walk, tel. 203/444–6766) hosts the Eastern Connecticut Symphony Orchestra, a Broadway-style theater series, innovative dance programs, and a number of well-known performers. **Shoreline Alliance for the Arts** (tel. 203/453–3890) sponsors concert offerings throughout the western part of the region. **East Haven Cultural Arts Council** produces a concert series at the East Haven Community Center (91 Taylor Ave., tel. 203/468–2963). In Branford, the **Branford Folk Music Society** (Box 441, tel. 203/488–7715) presents music on the green at Trinity Church. In Stony Creek, **Puppet House Theatre** (128 Thimble Island Rd., tel. 203/773–8080) has a lively season of comedy, drama, and musical productions by three companies.

Yale University's Woolsey Hall (College and Grove Sts.) hosts performances of the **Yale School of Music** (tel. 203/432–4157) and the **New Haven Symphony Orchestra** (tel. 203/865–0831), which celebrated its centennial season in 1993–1994 and has been presenting its delightful Young People's Concerts—the country's leading music program for children—for 62 years. New London's **El 'n' Gee Club** (86 Golden St., tel. 203/443–9227) has different programs nightly—heavy metal, reggae, local bands, and occasionally nationally known acts.

In Ledyard, on the Mashantucket Indian Reservation, the **Foxwoods Casino** (Rte. 2, tel. 203/885–3000 or 800/752–9244) has the state's first—and New England's largest—gambling operation. It's open daily around the clock. This surprisingly attractive skylit Colonial-style compound draws more than 20,000 visitors daily and will eventually include hotels, restaurants, showrooms, golf courses, and of course, more gambling options. Slot machines were added in March 1993.

4 Rhode Island

By Deborah Kovacs and Marjorie Ingall, with an introduction by William G. Scheller

Updated by Anne Merewood

Rhode Island, which shares with New Jersey the distinction of being one of the two most densely populated states in the Union, has at least one other characteristic in common with the Garden State: All too often it is a place people pass through on their way to somewhere else. The culprit in both cases is I–95, but for Rhode Island the problem is compounded by its size. With dimensions of 48 by 37 miles, the state can come and go without the notice of someone who is humming along to the car radio. Just about everyone seems to know Rhode Island is the smallest of the 50 states. What is less known is that the state is home to 20% of the country's National Historic Landmarks and has more restored Colonial and Victorian buildings than any other destination in the United States.

To experience Rhode Island as an end rather than a means, stay off the interstate. Traveling the city streets and blacktop roads reveals a place where changes in landscape and character come abruptly.

Take the 5 miles or so of Route 1 just above Wickford. On the face of it, this is a crass and tacky example of modern strip-mall Americana. But if you turn off the highway onto a discreetly marked drive in North Kingstown, you'll pass through a grove of trees and enter the 17th-century world of Smith's Castle, a beautifully preserved saltbox plantation house on the quiet shore of an arm of Narragansett Bay. Little appears to have changed here since Richard Smith built his "castle" after buying the surrounding property from Rhode Island's founder, Roger Williams, in 1651. Follow Route 1 a bit farther south to Route 1A, and the scene will change once again: The bayside town of Wickford is the kind of almost-too-perfect, salty New England period piece that is usually conjured up only in books and movies—and rumor says that this was John Updike's model for the New England of his novel *The Witches of Eastwick*.

So there it is: a run of tawdry highway development, a restored relic of a house that was once the seat of a 17,000-acre plantation, and a picture-perfect seacoast town that may or may not have suggested the locale for a novel of contemporary witchcraft. Pick the Rhode Island you want; all are cheek by jowl and none is visible from I–95. Nor is the 2,600-acre Great Swamp south of Kingston, the Victorian shore resort of Watch Hill, or the exquisite desolation of Block Island, way out in Long Island Sound.

Essential Information

Visitor Information

Rhode Island Department of Economic Development, Tourism Division (7 Jackson Walkway, Providence 02903, tel. 401/277–2601 or 800/556–2484).

Tour Groups

Stumpf Balloons (Box 1143, Providence, tel. 401/253–0111) offers fall foliage tours of Rhode Island by balloon—with champagne.

Arriving and Departing

By Plane **Theodore Francis Green State Airport** (tel. 401/737–4000), north of Warwick, has scheduled daily flights by seven major U.S. airlines and additional service by regional carriers.

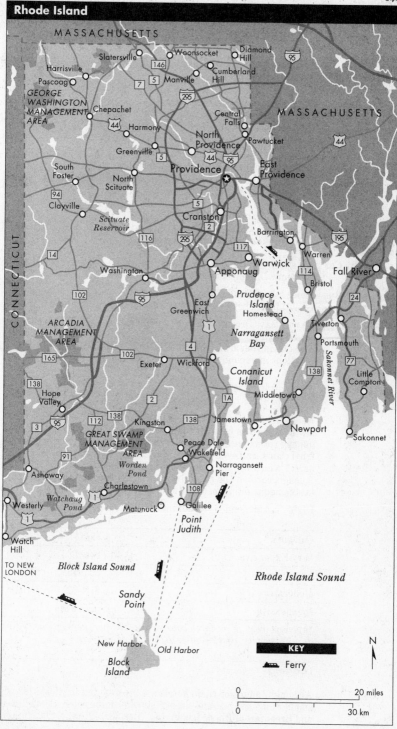

Rhode Island

MASSACHUSETTS

Harrisville
Pascoag
Slatersville
146
7
5
Manville
Woonsocket
Diamond Hill
95
Cumberland Hill
MASSACHUSETTS

GEORGE WASHINGTON MANAGEMENT AREA

Chepachet
44
Harmony
295
Central Falls
44

North Providence
Pawtucket

Greenville
5
Providence
44
95
East Providence

South Foster
North Scituate

94
Clayville

Scituate Reservoir

116
Cranston
5
2
295
Barrington
195
Warren

14

117
Warwick
114
Fall River
Bristol

Washington
Apponaug

102
95

East Greenwich
1

Prudence Island
Homestead

Narragansett Bay

Tiverton
Portsmouth

4
Conanicut Island
138
Sakonnet River
77
Little Compton

ARCADIA MANAGEMENT AREA

165
102
Exeter
Wickford

138
Hope Valley
3
95

112
138
Kingston

2
GREAT SWAMP MANAGEMENT AREA

138
Middletown
1A

Jamestown
Newport
24

91
Worden Pond

Ashaway
Peace Dale
Wakefield

Charlestown
1
Narragansett Pier

Westerly
Watchaug Pond

1
Matunuck
108
Galilee
Point Judith
Sakonnet

Watch Hill
1

TO NEW LONDON

Block Island Sound

Rhode Island Sound

Sandy Point

CONNECTICUT

New Harbor
Old Harbor

Block Island

KEY

Ferry

N

0   20 miles

0   30 km

By Car I–95 cuts diagonally across the state, the fastest route to Providence from Boston, coastal Connecticut, and New York City. I–195 links Providence with New Bedford and Cape Cod. I–295 links Providence with Worcester and I–90. Route 1 follows much of the Rhode Island coast east from Connecticut before turning north to Providence.

By Train Amtrak (tel. 800/872–7245) service between New York City and Boston makes stops at Westerly, Kingston, and Providence's **Union Station** (100 Gaspee St.). **MBTA commuter rail service** (tel. 617/722–3200) connects Boston and Providence during weekday morning and evening rush hours at about half the cost of Amtrak.

By Bus **Greyhound Lines** (tel. 800/231–2222) and **Bonanza Bus Lines** (tel. 800/556–3815) link cities of the northeastern United States with the **Providence Bus Terminal** (Bonanza Way, off Exit 25 from I–95, tel. 401/751–8800). A shuttle service connects the terminal with Kennedy Plaza in downtown Providence. Bonanza also runs a bus from Boston's Logan Airport to Providence.

Getting Around Rhode Island

By Car Get a free official state map from the Rhode Island Department of Economic Development (*see above*).

By Bus **Rhode Island Public Transit Authority** (tel. 401/781–9400) has service within and between the state's major cities.

By Ferry Ferries leave Providence for Newport and Block Island from the **India Street Pier** (tel. 401/483–4613). Ferries from Point Judith to Block Island depart from **Galilee State Pier** (tel. 401/783–4613). Reservations are required for cars, and service is curtailed in the off-season.

Dining

Rhode Island is home to much traditional regional fare. Johnnycakes are a sort of corn cake cooked on a griddle, and the native clam, the quahog (pronounced KO-hog), is served in chowder, stuffed clams, fried clams, and even clam pie. Particularly popular are "shore dinners," which include clam chowder, steamers, clam cakes, baked sausage, corn-on-the-cob, lobster, watermelon, and Indian pudding (a steamed pudding made with cornmeal and molasses).

Highly recommended restaurants are indicated by a star ★.

Category	Cost*
Very Expensive	over $35
Expensive	$25–$35
Moderate	$15–$25
Inexpensive	under $15

average cost of a three-course dinner, per person, excluding drinks, service, and 7% sales tax

Lodging

Although the major chain hotels are represented in Rhode Island, smaller inns and bed-and-breakfasts offer more color. Contact **Bed and Breakfast of Rhode Island, Inc.** (Box 3291, Newport 02840, tel.

401/849–1298), the state's reservation service. Rates are very much seasonal; in Newport, for example, winter rates are often half those of summer.

Highly recommended lodgings are indicated by a star ★.

Category	Cost*
Very Expensive	over $150
Expensive	$100–$150
Moderate	$60–$100
Inexpensive	under $60

All prices are for a standard double room during peak season, with no meals unless noted, and excluding 12% hotel and sales taxes.

Providence

Founded by Roger Williams in October 1635 as a refuge for free-thinkers and religious dissenters, Providence remains a community that tolerates difference and fosters cultural inquiry and diversity. Brown University, the Rhode Island School of Design (RISD), and the Trinity Square Repertory Company are major forces in New England's intellectual and cultural life.

After Roger Williams, the most significant name in Providence history may have been Brown. Four Brown brothers played a major part in the city's development in the 18th century. John Brown traded in slaves, opened trade with China, and aided the American Revolution; his mansion on the East Side is a must-see. Joseph Brown's designs—including his brother's mansion and the First Baptist Meeting House—changed the face of the city. Moses Brown, an abolitionist and a pacifist, funded the Quaker School that bears his name. Nicholas Brown rescued the failing Rhode Island College—known today as Brown University.

Although Providence suffered in the 1940s and '50s with the decline of its two main industries, textiles and costume jewelry (the city was once the nation's chief producer of the glittering baubles), a number of restoration and renewal projects are currently underway, bringing downtown back to life: Historic buildings once neglected are being renovated, and the city's new Convention Center opened in December 1993. Surrounding the center city are diverse neighborhoods attractive for strolling: Fox Point's Portuguese community, Federal Hill's Italian section, the historically Yankee and now predominantly Jewish East Side, and the young and hip College Hill. Providence is also a culinary center and home to the prestigious Johnson and Wales University Culinary Institute. Local restaurants include several that have won national recognition and quite a few that reflect the panoply of cuisines of the city's ethnic populations. Many residents will argue that it is this ethnicity that makes Providence special.

Important Addresses and Numbers

Visitor Information **Greater Providence Convention and Visitors Bureau** (30 Exchange Terr., 02903, tel. 401/274–1636; open weekdays 8:30–5.)

Emergencies **Rhode Island Hospital** (593 Eddy St., tel. 401/444–4000) is the city's
Hospital main hospital.

Late-Night   CVS (681 Reservoir Ave., Cranston, tel. 401/943–7186) has
Pharmacy   branches throughout the Providence region.

Getting Around Providence

By Car   Overnight parking is not allowed on Providence streets, and the
gaping potholes and countless diversions of ongoing urban renewal
render downtown driving a nightmare. Providence is small, so try to
find a central lodging with parking, forget your car, and walk or take
buses. On the plus side, I–95 cuts right through the city, so access is
easy.

By Bus   **Rhode Island Public Transit Authority** (tel. 401/781–9400 or, in RI,
800/244–0444; TDD 401/461–9400) runs around town, as well as out
to the airport; the fare is 75¢–$2.50. A free trolley (painted green
and orange) circles the downtown area from 11 AM to 2 PM weekdays,
making a loop every 15 minutes between Davol Square and the State
House, and calling also at Kennedy Plaza, where most of the city's other bus lines begin.

By Taxi   Try **Airport Taxi** (tel. 401/737–2868), **Checker Cab** (tel. 401/273–
2222), **East Side Taxi Service** (tel. 401/521–4200), and **Yellow Cab**
(tel. 401/941–1122). Fare is $1.20 at the flag drop, then $1.60 per
mile. The ride from the airport takes about 15 minutes and costs
about $20.

Guided Tours

Providence Preservation Society (21 Meeting St., tel. 401/831–7440)
offers two 90-minute cassette tours, one of College Hill (including
Brown University and the Rhode Island School of Design), and one
of the downtown area. The society runs popular Historic Houses
tours the first week of June, which allow visitors to explore
stunningly furnished private homes. Three additional tours visit
historic houses with architecture ranging from pre-Revolutionary
to Federal, Greek Revival to Victorian.

Exploring Providence

*Numbers in the margin correspond to points of interest on the Cen-
tral Providence map.*

❶   Begin your exploration of Providence at the **admissions office of
Brown University** (45 Prospect St., tel. 401/863–2378; call ahead–reduced hours in summer) where you can orient yourself to the history
and layout of the university and even join a tour of the National Historic Landmark campus, dominated by Gothic and Beaux-Arts
structures. Founded in 1764, Brown University is the country's sev-
enth oldest college. A walk on Thayer Street will acquaint you with
the campus's principal commercial thoroughfare.

Time Out   **Peaberry's** (258 Thayer St., tel. 401/861–2727) is a comforting little
shop that sells tempting varieties of fresh-brewed coffee and rich
homemade pastries. Here you can sit and watch the students debate
esoteric points of academia.

❷   Leave the campus via Prospect Street, where you'll face the **John
Hay Library.** This 1910 structure, named for Abe Lincoln's secretary, houses 11,000 items related to the 16th president. The library
also has American drama and poetry collections, 500,000 pieces of
American sheet music, the Webster Knight Stamp Collection, the

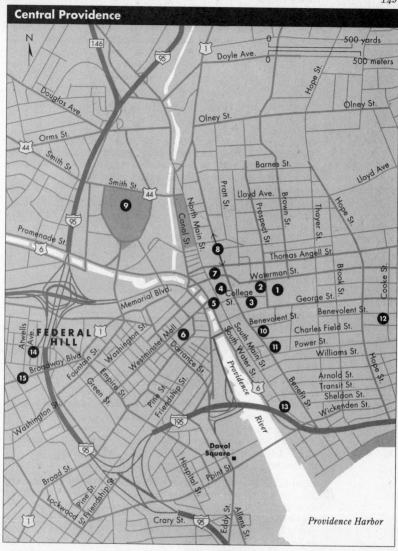

Central Providence

Providence Harbor

Admissions office,
Brown University, **1**
The Arcade, **6**
Benefit Street, **8**
Broadway, **15**
Federal Hill, **14**
First Baptist Church in
America, **7**
First Unitarian Church
of Providence, **10**
Fox Point, **13**

John Brown House, **11**
John Hay Library, **2**
Market House, **5**
Museum of Rhode
Island History, Aldrich
House, **12**
Providence
Athenaeum, **3**
Rhode Island School of
Design Museum of
Art, **4**
State House, **9**

letters of the early horror and science-fiction writer H. P. Lovecraft, military prints, and a collection of toy soldiers. *20 Prospect St., tel. 401/863–2146. Admission free. Open weekdays 9–5.*

❸ Walk two blocks down College Street and turn left onto Benefit Street. The **Providence Athenaeum,** housed in an imposing 1838 Greek Revival, was established in 1753 and is among the oldest lending libraries worldwide. Here Edgar Allan Poe, visiting Providence to lecture at Brown, met and courted Sarah Helen Whitman, who was said to be the inspiration for his poem "Annabel Lee." Whitman lived nearby at 88 Benefit Street. The library has a collection of Rhode Island art and artifacts, as well as an original set of elephant folio *Birds of America* prints by John J. Audubon. *251 Benefit St., tel. 401/421–6970. Admission free. Open June–Labor Day, weekdays 8:30–5:30; Labor Day–May, weekdays 8:30–5:30 (until 8:30 Wed.), Sat. 9:30–5:30, Sun 1–5.*

❹ Just down the street, the small **Rhode Island School of Design Museum of Art** is amazingly comprehensive nonetheless. In addition to about 25 exhibitions that change annually, many involving textiles (a long-standing native industry), the permanent holdings contain the Abby Aldrich Rockefeller collection of Japanese prints, Paul Revere silver, 18th-century porcelain, and French Impressionist paintings. Especially popular with kids are the 10-foot statue of Buddha and the mummy from the Ptolemaic period (ca. 300 BC). The RISD Museum is connected to **Pendleton House,** a replica of an early-19th-century Providence house, with period furnishings. *224 Benefit St., tel. 401/454–6100. Admission: $2 adults, $1 senior citizens, 50¢ children under 18; free Sat. Open summer, Wed.–Sat. noon–5; fall–spring, Tues.–Wed., Fri.–Sat. 10:30–5, Thurs. noon–8, Sun. 2–5.*

❺ Follow College Street west to South Water Street and **Market House** (Market Sq., South Main St.), designed by Joseph Brown. Opening onto the Providence River, this brick structure was central to Colonial Providence's trading economy. Tea was burned here in March 1775, and the upper floors were used as a barracks during the Revolutionary War. Afterward Market House was the seat of city government from 1832 to 1878. A plaque shows the height reached by floodwaters during the Great Hurricane of 1938.

❻ Head north on South Water Street, turn west onto Westminster Mall, and you'll soon reach **the Arcade,** America's very first indoor shopping mall. Built in 1828 and now a National Historic Landmark, the Greek Revival arcade has cast-iron railings, a facade with six gigantic Ionic columns, and three tiers of shops: The shops on the lower level have clothing, furnishings, jewelry (be sure to stop in the eclectic Copacetic Rudely Elegant Jewelry), paper goods, and toys. The Weybosset Street and Westminster Street facades differ—one has a pediment, the other stone panels. The reason for this discrepancy is that the man who owned only half the land on which his arcade was to be built could not agree with the other owners on an architect, so they hired two—each of whom insisted on carrying out his own conception. *65 Weybosset St., tel. 401/272–2340. Open Jan.–Nov., Mon.–Sat. 10–6; Thanksgiving–Christmas, weekdays 10–8, Sat. 10–6, Sun. noon–5.*

Time Out The **Providence Cookie Co.** (tel. 401/272–5742) on the ground floor of the Arcade has chocolate chip for traditionalists, white chocolate–macadamia nut for the more adventurous.

7 Head back over to North Main Street and walk north until you cross Waterman Street, and the **First Baptist Church in America** will be on your right. Designed by Joseph Brown and built in 1775 for a congregation established in 1638 by Roger Williams and his fellow dissenters, the church has carved wood, a "meeting-house sage" decor, and features a Waterford crystal chandelier and graceful but austere Ionic columns. It was rebuilt by ships' carpenters in 1775, and so it survived the Gale of 1875 and the 1938 hurricane. *75 North Main St., tel. 401/751–2266. Admission free (donations accepted). Open weekdays 9–4, self- or guided tours from 10–3; Sun. guided tours at 10:45 (July–Aug.), 12:15 (Sept.–June); Sat. guided tours by appointment.*

8 Turn left onto **Benefit Street,** the "Mile of History." A bumpy cobblestone sidewalk leads past a long row of early Federal and 19th-century candy-color houses, crammed shoulder-to-shoulder, on a steep hill overlooking downtown Providence. Here is a reminder of the wealth brought to Rhode Island by the triangular trade of slaves, rum, and molasses in Colonial times—and a reminder that neighborhoods long thought past their prime can be brought back to fashion, given a timely influx of ambitious "rehabbers." Throughout the 1980s, much of Providence beyond Benefit Street was discovered by erstwhile Bostonians looking for drastically cheaper real estate even though it meant enduring an hour-plus commute. Try to stroll here at dusk, when there is still some daylight but the old-fashioned streetlights have already lighted up.

9 Head west on Smith Street to Rhode Island's **State House,** built in 1900, and the first unsupported marble dome in the United States. The dome is the world's second-largest, after St. Peter's Basilica in Rome, on which Rhode Island's version was modeled. The ornate white Georgian marble exterior is topped by the gilded statue of *Independent Man,* designed by George T. Brewster. The interior features a full-length portrait of George Washington by Rhode Islander Gilbert Stuart, the same artist who created the likeness on the $1 bill. You'll also see the original parchment charter granted by King Charles to the colony of Rhode Island in 1663 and military accoutrements of Nathanael Greene, Washington's second-in-command during the Revolutionary War. *82 Smith St., tel. 401/277–2357. Open weekdays 8:30–4:30; tours given 9:30–3:30.*

10 Return to Benefit Street and walk south. The **First Unitarian Church of Providence,** on the corner of Benefit and Benevolent streets, was built in 1816. The bell tower houses the largest bell ever cast in Paul Revere's foundry, a 2,500-pounder. *1 Benevolent St., tel. 401/421–7970. Admission free. Service Sun. 10:30 in Meeting House or by appointment.*

Walk another block down Benefit Street to Power Street and the **John Brown House,** designed by Joseph Brown for his brother in 1786. This three-story Georgian mansion suggests that the slave trade was good to John; John Quincy Adams called it "the most magnificent and elegant mansion that I have ever seen on this continent." Abolitionist brother Moses wasn't impressed; through his organization, the Anti-Slavery Society, Moses brought charges against John for illegally engaging in the buying and selling of human lives. In addition to opening trade with China, John is famous for his role in the burning of the British customs ship *Gaspee.* George Washington slept here—and he probably found it lovely: The house is replete with elaborate woodwork and filled with examples of decorative arts, furniture, silver, pewter, glass, linens, and Chinese porcelain from the late 18th and early 19th centuries. Children may enjoy the antique doll collection. *52 Power St., tel. 401/331–8575. Admission: $5 adults, $3 senior citizens, $2 children 7–17. Open Mar.–Dec., Tues.–Sat. 11–4, Sun. 1–4; Jan.–Feb. by appointment.*

Across the street, Ambrose Burnside's now rather dilapidated mansion (314 Benefit St.), a redbrick Victorian with a turret, was built in 1866. Burnside was the Civil War general who led the Rhode Island army in defense of Washington and later became governor. Today he is best remembered for his facial hair: Sideburns are named after him. Walk east on Charles Field Street to Hope Street. Turn left, and then right onto Benevolent Street. The **Museum of Rhode Island History, Aldrich House,** has no permanent collection but offers two to five exhibits a year on the history, culture, architecture, and crafts of Rhode Island. *110 Benevolent St., tel. 401/331–8575. Admission: $2 adults, $1.50 senior citizens, $1 children 7–17. Open Tues.–Fri. 9–5, weekends for special exhibitions.*

⑬ Walk south on Hope Street to Wickenden Street. **Fox Point** used to be a Portuguese neighborhood, but gentrification is rapidly changing its character, and Wickenden Street is now chockablock with antiques stores, galleries, and trendy cafés. Nonetheless, many of the houses along Wickenden, Transit, Gano, and neighboring streets are painted the pastel colors of Portuguese homes, and people still sit out on their stoops on hot summer evenings. Follow Wickenden across the Point Street Bridge to **Davol Square** (*see* Shopping, *below*).

Time Out | **Taj Mahal** (230 Wickenden St., tel. 401/331–2442) and **Taste of India** (221 Wickenden St., tel. 401/421–4355) are dueling Indian restaurants, both cheap, across the street from each another. The hours and prices are the same (the owners used to be in business together); choose the one that has no wait for a table.

⑭ The Italian community is vital to Providence's culture and sense of self, and **Federal Hill** is its center. Entering the neighborhood via Atwells Avenue might make you think you're walking down a main street in a small Italian town: You're as likely to hear Italian as English. The stripe down the middle of the avenue is repainted each year in red, white, and green, and a huge *pigna* (pinecone), an Italian symbol of abundance, hangs on an arch soaring over the street and adorns the decorative fountain. The hardware shops may sell boccie sets and the corner store may sell little china statues of saints, but the Avenue, as locals call it, isn't cutesy. The St. Joseph's and Columbus Day seasonal celebrations, with music, street food, and parades, are not to be missed.

Places to visit include the **Grotta Azzura** (210 Atwells Ave., tel. 401/272–9030), a great Old World restaurant, and **Plaza Grille** (64 DePasquale Ave., tel. 401/274–8684), on a side street off the Avenue. The former is for more formal dining, the latter serves bistro-style burgers and omelets in a cozy, pink, exposed-brick setting.

⑮ **Broadway** is a Victorian boulevard first developed in the 1830s by Irish immigrants. They built the large, rambling gingerbread houses frosted with external bric-a-brac and such details as porticoes, turrets, towers, and small stained-glass windows. Toward the turn of the century, the Broadway gradually turned Italian, like neighboring Federal Hill. "Barnaby's Castle," the huge mansion at No. 229—adorned with a four-story, 12-sided tower—was owned by J. B. Barnaby, "The Rhode Island Clothing Prince." Barnaby's wife was the victim in a famous murder, which came to trial in 1891, when her doctor sent her a New Year's present of whiskey laced with arsenic. Other particularly stunning houses are at No. 514 and No. 78. The houses vary in style from Greek Revival to Italianate to Queen Anne to Gothic Revival; there's even a row of brownstones (rare in Providence).

Providence for Free

Athenaeum
Brown University
John Hay Library
State House

What to See and Do with Children

The **Children's Museum of Rhode Island** is a "please touch" museum. Great-Grandmother's Kitchen encourages children to rifle through cabinets filled with Victorian utensils, letting them see what cooking was like long ago; they can also explore "our house," which is a small replica of the museum, play in the shape-lab math exhibit, and visit a room-size map of Rhode Island. *58 Wolcott St., Pawtucket, tel. 401/726–2590. Admission: $3.50; free 1st Sun. of each month. Open Tues.–Sat. 9:30–5, Sun. 1–5.*

The **Roger Williams Park and Zoo** is popular with children and dogs. With 430 acres, there's plenty of room to run, tumble, and shriek. Have a picnic, take out a paddleboat, feed the ducks in the lakes, take a pony ride. There's even tennis in warmer months. At the zoo you can see giraffes and elephants, watch the penguins, and pet the animals in the petting zoo (but do not feed Norton and Trixie, the polar bears). At nearby Carousel Village, kids can ride the vintage carousel or a miniature train, explore the playground, then mellow out with the family in the restful Japanese Garden. The museum on the grounds has exhibits on local history, wildlife, and Narragansett Bay. *Elmwood Ave., tel. 401/785–3510. Admission: $3.50 adults, $1.50 children 3–12. Zoo open summer, daily 9–5; winter, daily 9–4. Museum open Tues.–Fri. 10–4, weekends noon–4.*

Slater Mill Historic Site. The first factory in America to successfully produce cotton yarn from water-powered machines was built in 1793 by Samuel Slater and two Providence merchants, William Almy and Smith Brown. The mill now houses classrooms, a theater with a slide show, and machinery used to illustrate the conversion of raw cotton to finished cloth. Marvel at the 16,000-pound waterwheel that powers the operating 19th-century mill, and visit the worker's cottage, built in 1758. The mill offers such classes as weaving, chair-caning, and basketry. *727 Roosevelt Ave., Pawtucket, tel. 401/725–8638. Admission: $4 adults, $3 senior citizens, $2 children 6–14. Open June–Labor Day, Tues.–Sat. 10–5, Sun. 1–5; Mar.–May and Labor Day–Dec. 21, weekends 1–5.*

Off the Beaten Track

Kind of seedy, kind of musty, the **Cable Car Cinema** is a relic from another time. Sit on old couches, munch popcorn and Steve's ice cream, and watch low-budget, foreign, and cult films you can't see anywhere else in Providence. Before the show, watch the street-theater artists perform. *204 S. Main St., tel. 401/272–3970. Admission: $6.*

Shopping

Malls If you're Christmas shopping, avoiding the rain, or into indiscriminate spending, try **the Arcade** (*see* Exploring Providence, *above*), or **Davol Square** (Point and Eddy Sts., tel. 401/273–6278), which is housed in a former rubber factory built about 1874. This appealing brick building now bustles with restaurants, carts of inexpensive little items to buy on whim, and small (generally expensive) boutiques like **Talbots**. Unlike the Arcade, it's still bopping into the night.

Specialty Stores

Antiques Wickenden Street has the greatest concentration of antiques stores, as well as several art galleries. **The Cat's Pajamas** (227 Wickenden St., tel. 401/751–8440) specializes in 1920s–1960s jewelry, linens, housewares, accessories, and small furnishings. **Cav Coffee House & Bistro** (14 Imperial Pl., tel. 401/751–9164) brings together an eclectic blend of fine rugs, tapestries, prints, portraits, and antiques in a coffeehouse located in a restored factory. A nice place to relax and listen, from time to time, to local music. **Off Broadway** (432 Broadway, tel. 401/274–3150) is the place to find Art Deco and 1950s- and '60s-era furniture and collectibles. Great for funky kitchen appliances, lava lamps, and salt and pepper shakers. **Roxy Deluxe** (286 Thayer St., tel. 401/861–4606) sells such glamorous antique duds as beaded sweaters from the 1950s, Edwardian women's underwear and gowns, and men's vests, hats, and overcoats.

Art **The Alaimo Gallery** (301 Wickenden St., tel. 401/421–5360) specializes in ephemera: antique posters, hand-colored engravings, magazine and playbill covers, political cartoons, antique prints, book pages, and box labels. The gallery is run by the former director of the picture collection of the library at RISD. **JRS Fine Art** (218 Wickenden St., tel. 401/331–4380) sells contemporary jewelry, paintings, and sculpture, including some Southwest-inspired work. **The Peaceable Kingdom and Black Crow** (116 Ives St., tel. 401/351–3472) offers folk art, with strengths in Native American jewelry and crafts, kilims, and brilliantly colored, finely detailed, embroidered Hmong story cloths. (The state has a large Hmong community, and Joan Ritchie, the owner of the store, has written about the cloths made by these people from Laos.)

Foods The **Providence Cheese Shop** (178 Atwells Ave., tel. 401/421–5653) on Federal Hill sells homemade pasta, bread, pizza, pastries, and a large selection of cheeses. Gourmands will enjoy **Tony's Colonial** (311 Atwells Ave., tel. 401/621–8675), a neighborhood grocery store that has dried pasta of every conceivable shape, color, and size; Abruzzese sausage; Parma ham; extra-virgin olive oil; fresh mozzarella; and a wide assortment of such freshly prepared foods as stuffed peppers, eggplant parmigiana, and chicken cacciatore. You can create your own Italian feast at home if you stop by **Venda's** (265 Atwells Ave., tel. 401/421–9105) to take out some fresh, homemade ravioli or gnocchi.

Jewelry **Copacetic Rudely Elegant Jewelry** (the Arcade, 65 Weybosset St., tel. 401/273–0470) sells the work of a group of diverse artists. Expect the unusual, and you will not be disappointed—anything from glass to precious metal and from holograms to computer-designed jewelry may be on display.

Maps **The Map Center** (671 N. Main St., tel. 401/421–2184) has an extensive selection of wall maps, world maps, U.S. topographical maps, nautical charts, road and street maps, and U.S. and foreign atlases.

Men's Clothing **Briggs Ltd.** (61 Weybosset St., tel. 401/331–5000) features men's suits, shirts, and dresswear both off-the-rack and custom-made.

Zuccolo's Fine Men's Clothing (200 Atwells Ave., tel. 401/521–0646) has fine leather and silk garments.

Toys **The Game Keeper** (67 Arcade Building, 65 Weybosset St., tel. 401/351–0362), on the third floor of the Arcade, sells board games, puzzles, and many little spur-of-the-moment gadgets.

Women's Clothing **Urban Cargo** (224 Thayer St., tel. 401/421–7179), smack in the middle of collegeland, features young, casual, and moderately priced clothing and a selection of costume jewelry.

Sports and Outdoor Activities

Biking For information on city trails, call the **Department of Public Parks** (tel. 401/785–9450). For a bike map of Providence, write to the **Rhode Island Bicycle Coalition** (Box 4781, Rumford 02916). Biking from Providence, you can easily get to the farm country of Seekonk in Massachusetts and to the shores of Narragansett Bay.

Boating In addition to the Roger Williams Park paddleboats, boating is available on the Seekonk River and in Narragansett Bay. For more information, contact the **Narragansett Boat Club** (River Rd., Providence, tel. 401/272–1838).

Jogging Try the 3-mile tree- and bench-lined Blackstone Boulevard, where Brown's track team works out.

Spectator Sports

Baseball The **Pawtucket Red Sox,** the Boston Red Sox triple-A farm team, plays spring–fall at McCoy Stadium (Pawtucket, I–95S to Exit 2A; follow Newport Ave. for 2 mi, then turn right onto Columbus at light, tel. 401/724–7300).

Football Brown's mediocre but enthusiastic team plays at **Brown Stadium** (Elmgrove and Sessions Sts., Providence, tel. 401/863–2236). The NFL Patriots train in July and August at **Bryant College** (Smithfield, tel. 401/232–6070).

Other Sporting Events The **Providence College Friars** play Big East basketball at the Providence Civic Center (1 LaSalle Sq., tel. 401/331–6700). The **Boston Celtics** (basketball) and **Boston Bruins** (hockey) play exhibition games at the Civic Center, and there are regularly scheduled wrestling and boxing matches there.

Dining

Providence restaurants are less expensive than those of Boston and Manhattan, and the city's many ethnic groups are well represented. Dress is casual unless noted.

American ★ **Troye's Southwestern Grill.** There's a definite trendiness here, with bovine-print chairs, exposed pipes, and cacti galore, but the feeling of a neighborhood restaurant remains—and they're nice to kids! Gazpacho, blue-corn nachos, tortilla pizzas, and Cajun calamari are among the offerings. Savor your vegetarian black-bean chili and think what you'd pay for the same food in New York City. *404 Wickenden St., tel. 401/861–1430. AE, D, DC, MC, V. BYOB. No lunch. Closed Mon. Moderate.*

Wes' Rib House. Sure, they serve vegetable kebabs for vegetarians, but this Providence institution is really for those who want to tear into sticky, meaty viands. Order wood-fire barbecued ribs by the piece, damn your cholesterol count, and dig in. Late diners appreciate the 2 AM weeknights, 4 AM weekends closing times. *38 Dike St., tel. 401/421–9090. Reservations accepted for 6 or more. D, MC, V. Moderate.*

Continental   **Al Forno.** This restaurant cemented Providence's reputation as a cu-
★   linary center in New England. George Germon and Johanne Killeen's combined talents draw upon Italian recipes to make the most of New England's fresh produce. The menu changes according to the season and what's freshest at the market that day. Wood-grilled pizza could be your appetizer, followed by a clam roast with spicy sausage served in a tomato broth or charcoal-seared tournedos with mashed potatoes and onion rings. Desserts range from crepes with apricot purée and crème anglaise to fresh cranberry tart with walnuts and brown sugar. *577 S. Main St., tel. 401/273–9760. No reservations; expect to wait on weekends. AE, MC, V. Closed Sun.–Mon.; Dec. 24–Jan. 4. Expensive.*

Ethnic   **Andreas.** This popular spot, with lots of windows, brass rails, light wood, and booths and tables, is in the center of the College Hill shopping district. Gyros, souvlaki, Greek salads, and plenty of options for vegetarians make Andreas a healthy resource. In the warmer months small sidewalk tables offer the best seating. *268 Thayer St., tel. 401/331–7879. Reservations advised for 10 or more. AE, DC, MC, V. Moderate–Expensive.*

Thailand Restaurant. What's a nice Thai restaurant doing smack in the middle of a staunchly Italian neighborhood? It's introducing the Italian community to the wonders of *tom ka gai* (chicken soup in a coconut-and-lime broth with cilantro and ginger) and *pla rard prik* (deep-fried fish in fiery chili sauce). The decor is minimalist: white tables and a few flowers. *244 Atwells Ave., tel. 401/331–0346. Reservations advised. MC, V. BYOB. No lunch Sun. Moderate.*

Cecilia's West African Restaurant. The neighborhood isn't particularly inviting, but the Liberian food and reggae on weekends make it worth the trip. Steaming stews and meat in exotic sauces—cassava and palm butter—are served in wood bowls. *486 Friendship St., tel. 401/621–8031. Reservations advised. No credit cards. No lunch. Inexpensive.*

European   **Rue de l'Espoir.** This restaurant's eclectic menu often blends ethnic preparations to offer such tempting appetizers as chicken-and-cashew spring rolls or fried calamari with hot-pepper relish. You may follow with an entrée of roasted pork porterhouse crusted with mustard and pepper and served with caponata and fresh sage oil, or any of the creative pasta specialties. In addition to lunch and dinner, Rue de l'Espoir serves breakfast beginning at 7:30 (brunch on weekends). Eye-pleasing art, including a great mural on the walls around the bar, and homey decor add to the appeal. The crusty bread from Palmieri's is a local institution. *99 Hope St., tel. 401/751–8890. Reservations advised. AE, D, DC, MC, V. Closed Mon. Moderate.*

Italian   **Adesso.** Upscale California-influenced Italian, including the requi-
★   site enthusiasm for radicchio, reigns here. The wood-oven pizzas are big enough to share, but you might not want to, especially if you order the one with garlicky eggplant, red onion, oregano, parmigiano, mozzarella, chopped fresh tomato, and fresh basil. Tuna cooked on the mesquite grill is also a good bet. For dessert, the tiramisu is to swoon for. Despite the erratic qualities of the more exotic dishes, such luminaries as Diana Ross can be seen dining here. Be prepared to wait for a table on weekends. *161 Cushing St., tel. 401/521–0770. No reservations. AE, MC, V. No lunch Sun. Moderate–Expensive.*

In-Prov. Overlooking the interior of the financial district's Fleet Center, this is a great spot to watch the city's movers and shakers in action. The restaurant has marble floors, tapestries, mahogany, and a 20-foot ceiling. Having recently dropped its tapas menu, In-Prov now specializes in Italian dishes; highlights include gnocchi gorgonzola, grilled yellowfin tuna, and linguine frutte di mare. *Fleet Center, 50 Kennedy Plaza, tel. 401/351–8770. Reservations advised. AE, MC, V. No lunch Sat. Closed Sun. Moderate–Expensive.*

Angelo's Civita Farnese. On Federal Hill, in the heart of Little Italy, this family-run place has vinyl booths, oil paintings of the family, and fresh and simply prepared pasta. The portions are large, the place loud. *141 Atwells Ave., tel. 401/621–8171. No reservations. No credit cards. Inexpensive.*

Seafood **Hemenway's.** When you want to marvel at the city's revitalizing
★ downtown, this is one of the bright spots. The seafood is superb, the lighting makes everyone look good, and the atmosphere is loud and cheerful. New England Clambake (a seafood sampler), seasonal stone or softshell crabs, and Norwegian salmon are commendable. *1 Old Stone Sq., tel. 401/351–8570. Reservations advised for 6 or more. AE, D, DC, MC, V. Expensive.*

Ocean Express. The neon lobster and fish out front beckon youngsters and adults alike, and even the most finicky child usually finds something appealing to eat here. The house promises the freshest seafood, oysters, clams, and lobster, with a raw bar. Oak and brass furnishings are brightened by green and burgundy decor, and there are plants everywhere. *800 Allens Ave., tel. 401/461–3434. Reservations advised for 6 or more. AE, MC, V. Inexpensive–Moderate.*

Lodging

Expensive **Marriott Hotel.** Although it lacks the Omni Biltmore's old-fashioned elegance (*see below*), some travelers (especially those on business) will prefer the Marriott's larger size and modern conveniences. Rooms, renovated in 1993, are modern, decorated in tones of peach, green, and jade. The two swimming pools are a draw. *Charles and Orms Sts., near Exit 23 on I–95, tel. and fax 401/272–2400 or 800/ 937–7768. 339 rooms, 6 suites. Facilities: restaurant, indoor and outdoor pools, health club, saunas, free parking, meeting facilities. AE, D, DC, MC, V.*

Old Court Bed & Breakfast. Located on historic Benefit Street, this three-story Italianate inn was built in 1863 as a rectory. Elegant antique furniture, chandeliers, richly colored wallpaper, and memorabilia throughout the house reflect the best of 19th-century decor. Rooms are generally large with high ceilings, several have marble, nonworking fireplaces, and some have views of the state house and downtown. A few of the well-worn rugs could be replaced, but overall there's a sedate, elegant atmosphere. Continental breakfast is served buffet-style in the large dining room with a marble fireplace and a glass chandelier. *144 Benefit St., tel. 401/751–2002. 10 rooms with bath, 1 suite. Free parking. Continental breakfast included. AE, MC, V.*

★ **Omni Biltmore Hotel.** The Biltmore, completed in 1922, has a sleek Art Deco exterior, Old World charm, and an external glass elevator that offers attractive views of Providence at night. The personal attentiveness of its staff, the downtown location, and the many new amenities make this hotel the best base from which to explore the city. *Kennedy Plaza, tel. 401/421–0700 or 800/843–6664, fax 401/ 421–0210. 217 rooms, 21 suites. Facilities: restaurant, café, parking garage, meeting facilities, health club. AE, D, DC, MC, V.*

Moderate **C. C. Ledbetter's.** At about half the price of the Old Court Bed & Breakfast, and across the street from the John Brown House, the

unmarked, somber green exterior of C. C.'s Benefit Street home belies its vibrant interior—the place is filled with two English spring-
er spaniels, lively art, books, photographs, quilts, and a homey
blend of contemporary furnishings and antiques. C. C. serves Continental breakfast in her modern yet cozy dining room with a marvelous "new antique" pine table. Book early for Brown University's
parents' and graduation weekends. *326 Benefit St., tel. and fax 401/
351–4699. 1 room with bath, 4 rooms share 2 baths. Free parking.
Continental breakfast included. No credit cards.*

Day's Hotel on the Harbor. Despite its small lobby (modern, with
marble floors and ficus trees), Providence's newest hotel affords a
sense of openness: You can even watch the chef at work. Guest rooms
feature contemporary furnishings in pastel colors; half the rooms offer views of the harbor, and the other rooms overlook speeding traffic on I–95. A few rooms have their own whirlpool bath. *220 India St.
tel. or fax (ext. 199) 401/272–5577. 136 rooms with bath. Facilities:
restaurant, free garage parking, exercise room, Jacuzzi, meeting
rooms, free shuttle to airport and downtown. AE, D, DC, MC, V.*

Holiday Inn. This high-rise hotel is conveniently close to Exit 21 on
I–95, the Providence Civic Center, and the new Rhode Island Convention Center. The comfortable lounge (Early American decor,
with nautical overtones), off the lobby, encourages relaxed conver-
sation. Spacious rooms are decorated in shades of green and purple,
with shiny Colonial furniture, and have great city views and all the
amenities (room service, phones, cable TV) endemic to good chain
hotels. *21 Atwells Ave., tel. 401/831–3900 or 800/465–4329, fax 401/
751–0007. 274 rooms with bath. Facilities: restaurant, lounge, indoor pool, Jacuzzi, exercise room, free garage parking, meeting
rooms, free airport shuttle. AE, D, DC, MC, V.*

★ **State House Inn.** Beautifully restored rooms of this classy, convenient inn are furnished with Shaker or Colonial-style pieces, and
some have canopy beds and working fireplaces. In addition, all have
phones and TVs: Frank and Monica Hopton, who renovated the
large 1880s house in 1990, have done a fine job of combining Old
World style with the conveniences that befit a city inn just a few
blocks from the state house. Some rooms are on the small side, but
that's the only caveat about this inviting inn. Breakfast is served in a
country-style dining room with wide-plank floors, a brick fireplace,
and a carved mantel. *43 Jewett St., tel. 401/785–1235. 9 rooms with
bath. Facilities: breakfast room, free parking. Full breakfast included. AE, MC, V.*

Inexpensive **Lansing House.** This bed-and-breakfast is in a quiet neighborhood, a
short bus ride or a very long walk from downtown. The pink three-
story house with gambrel roof was built in 1904, and the current
owner "derenovated" the '50s interior when she bought it—uncov-
ering large brick fireplaces and reinstating a floor-to-ceiling wooden
sideboard, which was languishing in the basement. The staircase
has an art nouveau stained-glass oriel window; guest rooms, on the
second floor, are decorated with Laura Ashley wallpaper and contain Victorian antiques. Three rooms share a gloriously old-fashioned bathroom with the original pedestal sink, stolid tub, and
enormous faucets. *Box 2441 (call for physical address), tel. 401/
421–7194. 3 rooms share 1½ baths. Continental breakfast included.
AE, MC, V.*

The Arts

See the *Providence Journal*, the *Newpaper* (available free in restaurants and bookstores; extensive rock/funk/blues coverage), and

Rhode Island Magazine. Look for free speakers and performances at Brown and RISD.

Music **Providence Civic Center** (1 LaSalle Sq., tel. 401/331–6700) with 14,500 seats, hosts touring rock groups, including the very pro-Providence Grateful Dead. **Providence Performing Arts Center** (220 Weybosset St., tel. 401/421–2787) is a 3,200-seat hall that is home to touring Broadway shows, concerts, and other large-scale happenings. Opened in 1928, its lavish interior is filled with painted frescoes, Art Deco chandeliers, gilt, bronze moldings, and marble floors. The **Rhode Island Philharmonic** (222 Richmond St., tel. 401/831–3123) presents 10 concerts at the Providence Performing Arts Center between October and May. **Veterans Memorial Auditorium** (Brownell St., tel. 401/277–3150) hosts concerts, children's theater, and ballet—both traveling productions and short-run performances.

Theater **Trinity Square Repertory Company** (201 Washington St., tel. 401/351–4242) has become nationally known for Tony Award–winning plays. In the renovated old Majestic Movie House downtown, the Rep generally offers a varied season: classics, foreign plays, new works. Audiences from all over New England support the repertory actors in what can be unusual and risky works.

Several smaller companies stage contemporary works: **Alias Stage** (Atlantic Mill, 120 Manton Ave., tel. 401/831–2919), an ambitious offshoot of Trinity, presents original works. **Brown University** (Leeds Theatre, 77 Waterman St., tel. 401/863–2838) mounts productions that range from contemporary works to classics to avant-garde and student pieces. **New Gate Theatre** (134 Mathewson St., tel. 401/421–9680). **Second Story Theatre Company** (75 John St., tel. 401/421–5776).

Nightlife

The Hot Club (575 S. Water St., tel. 401/861–9007; live jazz Sun. and Wed.) is just that, a hip place—with plants, a jukebox, and nice lighting—that was an early entry in the movement to revive nightlife on the city's waterfront. **Oliver's** (83 Benevolent St., tel. 401/272–8795), with a pool table, bar, and jukebox upstairs as well as good pub food, booths, and brass downstairs, is a hangout for Brown students. **Manhattan** (1 Throop Alley, tel. 401/861–1996) offers mostly jazz and blues bands, Tuesday through Saturday nights. **Sh-Booms** (108 N. Main St., tel. 401/751–1200) has a 1950s theme, good dance music, a pink Cadillac as part of the decor, and some hairy chests and chains. **AS220** (71 Richmond St., tel. 401/831–9327), a gallery and performance space, features paintings, plays, and performance art primarily for the young at heart. Musical styles run the gamut from techno-pop, hip-hop, and jazz to traditional Hmong folk music and dance. **The Last Call Saloon** (15 Elbow St., tel. 401/421–7170) is a good spot for rock and blues. **Desperado's Contemporary Country Night Club** (180 Pine St., tel. 401/751–4263) offers country and western music, dancing, and country dancing lessons. **Gerardo's** (1 Franklin Sq., tel. 401/274–5560) is a popular gay and lesbian disco.

South County

When the principal interstate traffic shifted from the coastal Route 1 to the new I–95, coastal Rhode Island—known within the state as South County—was left behind in time, largely escaping the advance of malls and tract-housing developments that has overtaken other, more accessible areas. More popular with visitors today than in recent years, this region of rolling farmland is still undervisited compared to other parts of New England; its vast stretches of sandy beaches, wilderness, and colorful historic sites escape the crush of tourists.

With 19 preserves, state parks, beaches, and forest areas, including Charlestown's Burlingame State Park and Ninigret Park National Wildlife Refuge, South County is a region that respects the concept of wilderness.

Important Addresses and Numbers

Visitor Information For information, contact **South County Tourism Council** (4808 Tower Hill Rd., Wakefield 02879, tel. 401/789–4422 or 800/548–4662). Or stop by the **Charlestown Chamber of Commerce** (Old Post Rd., Charlestown, tel. 401/364–3878; open Memorial Day–Columbus Day, daily 9–5; rest of year, weekdays 9 AM–11:30 AM), the **Greater Westerly Chamber of Commerce** (74 Post Rd., Rte. 1, Westerly, tel. 401/596–7761 or 800/732–7636; open May–Oct., weekdays 9–5, weekends 9–2), the **Narragansett Chamber of Commerce** (The Towers, Rte. 1A, Narragansett Pier, tel. 401/783–7121; open May–Sept., daily 9–4; Oct.–Apr., weekdays 9–3), or the **Visitor Information Center** (I–95 at the CT border; open daily 8:30–4:30; Memorial Day–Columbus Day until 6:30).

Emergencies **South County Hospital** (100 Kenyon Ave., Wakefield, tel. 401/782–
Hospitals 8000). **Westerly Hospital** (Wells St., Westerly, tel. 401/596–6000).

Late-Night **Granite Drug** (Granite Shopping Center, Westerly, tel. 401/596–
Pharmacy 0306).

Getting Around South County

By Car I–95 passes just north of Westerly before heading inland toward Providence. Routes 1 and 1A follow the coastline up into Narragansett Bay and are the more scenic coastal routes.

Exploring South County

Numbers in the margin correspond to points of interest on the Rhode Island Coast map.

1 Just over the Connecticut border, **Westerly** is a busy little railway town that grew up in the late 19th century around a major station on what is now the New York–Boston Amtrak corridor. Victorian and Greek Revival mansions line many streets just off the town center. **Wilcox Park** (71½ High St., Westerly, tel. 401/596–8590), designed in 1898 by Warren Manning, an associate of Frederick Law Olmsted and Calvert Vaux, is an 18-acre park in the heart of town with a garden designed for people with visual impairments and other disabilities. Here signs in Braille identify the plantings of carnations, mint, chives, thyme, bay leaves—as well as coconut-, apple-, lemon-, and rose-scented geraniums—to touch, smell, and taste.

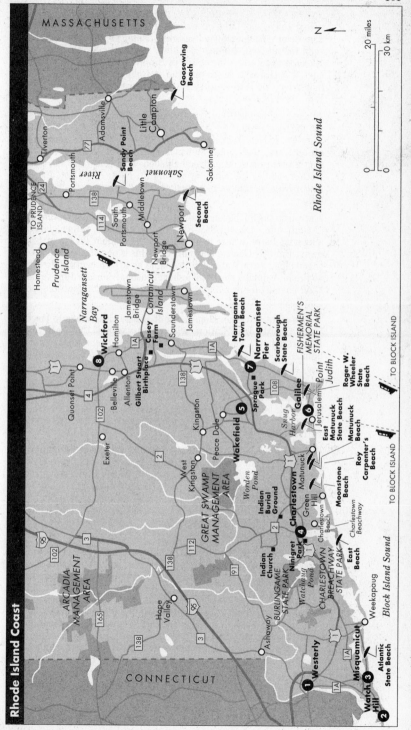

Rhode Island Coast

② South of Westerly on Route 1A, **Watch Hill,** a pretty Victorian-era resort town, has miles of beautiful beaches, a number of Native American settlements, and an active fishing port; it's a good place to shop for jewelry, summer clothing, and antiques. On Bay Street you'll be greeted by the **statue of Ninigret,** a chief of the Rhode Island Niantics who first appeared in Colonial history in 1637. The model for this 19th-century statue was part of Buffalo Bill Cody's Wild West Review.

At the beach end of Bay Street, the **Flying Horse Carousel,** the oldest merry-go-round in America, was built by the Charles W. F. Dare Co. of New York in about 1867. The horses, suspended from a center frame, swing out when in motion. Each is hand-carved from a single piece of wood and embellished with real tails and manes, leather saddle, and agate eyes. *Bay St. Fare: 75¢. Open June 15– Labor Day, weekdays 1–9, weekends and holidays 11–9. Children only.*

A stroll up the hill beyond the carousel will bring you to **Ocean House** (2 Bluff Ave., tel. 401/348–8161), a resplendent, yellow-clapboard Victorian hotel, whose immensity will just about take your breath away. Built by George Nash in 1868, this is one of the grand hotels that helped earn Watch Hill its fame as a 19th-century resort. If you're here during the hotel's short season, from late June to Labor Day, have a bite or a drink on the magnificent 200-foot-long porch that faces the Atlantic.

To the right of Ocean House, Light House Road leads to the **U.S. Coast Guard Light Station,** with great views of the ocean and of Fishers Island, New York. There's a tiny museum here about the light. *No tel. Admission free. Open May–Sept., Tues. and Thurs. 1–3.*

Beyond the carousel end of Bay Street, a path leads to **Napatree Point,** one of the best long beach walks in the entire state. A sandy spit lying between Watch Hill's Little Narragansett Bay and the ocean, Napatree Point is a protected conservation area teeming with wildlife.

③ From Watch Hill, coastal Route 1A heads east toward **Misquamicut,** where Victorian hotels cede graciously to legions of 20th-century strip motels. In their midst lies **Atlantic Beach Park** (tel. 401/322–0504), a mile-long beach featuring an amusement park, giant water slide, carousel, minigolf, roller rink, and fast-food stands: Kids from 2 to 92 will love it. The beach is accessible year-round, but most amusements close by late September, leaving an eerie, abandoned atmosphere off-season.

Sandy beaches line the Rhode Island coast for miles here: The next posse of motels and summer chalets lies in wait 10 miles east of **④** Misquamicut, around the scattered community of **Charlestown,** which straggles along the Old Post Road and is bisected by Route 1. Most visitors come here for the excellent beaches, though a couple of large parks offer a chance to sample the inland outdoors: Just northwest of Charlestown, on Kings Factory Road, you'll find **Burlingame State Park** (tel. 401/322–7337 or 401/322–7994), a 2,100-acre park offering freshwater swimming, camping, and picnic areas, as well as boating and fishing on Watchaug Pond. **Ninigret Park** (tel. 401/365–1222), off Route 1A just before Charlestown proper, is a 172-acre park with picnic grounds, ball fields, a bike path, tennis, nature trails, and the Frosty Drew Observatory and Nature Center (tel. 401/364–9508), which runs nature and astronomy programs on Friday evenings.

Long before tourists, Dutch traders, and Christopher Columbus showed up, the region was inhabited by the Narragansett, a powerful Native American tribe that occupied the lands and islands of Narragansett Bay. The Niantics, ruled by Chief Ninigret, were one branch of this tribe. Many of the Narragansett still live in the Charlestown area, but their historical sites are unmarked and easy to miss. The **Indian Burial Ground,** resting place of sachems (chiefs) and Narragansetts, is on the left side of Narrow Lane just north of Route 1: You'll recognize it by the tall fences, but there's no sign and it's not open for visits. Narrow Lane crosses Route 2/112 and becomes a dirt lane known as the Lewis Trail. Follow this about a mile to see the **Indian Church,** built in 1859 and still used for Sunday morning services by the community. The church is the site of the annual Narragansett meeting, usually the second Sunday in August, when tribal members from around the nation convene for costumed dancing and rituals; visitors are welcome.

Beyond Charlestown, Route 1 barrels eastward again for a few miles to the next major "beach exit," rowdy Matunuck Beach—marked by fast-food stands, a large trailer park, and a good surf. Next, follow ❺ Route 1 north to **Wakefield,** a small mill town (like its northern England namesake) and home to several big shopping malls, as well as the old **Washington County Jail.** Built in 1792, it now houses the Pettaquamscutt Historical Society. Here you can see jail cells and rooms from the Colonial period, a Colonial garden, and changing exhibits that depict South County life during the last 300 years. *1348 Kingstown Rd., tel. 401/783–1328. Admission free. Open May–Oct., Tues., Thurs., and Sat. 1–4.*

The Narragansett town line takes in the peninsula east of Point Judith Pond and the Pettaquamscutt River, and the two villages of Galilee and Narragansett Pier. **Galilee,** south of Route 1 on Route 108, is a busy, workaday fishing port, offering visitors whale-watching and fishing trips, good seafood restaurants, plenty of fish, and, as one local put it, "the smell," which may or may not be your idea of heaven. The only year-round **ferry to Block Island,** run by the Interstate Navigation Company (Galilee State Pier, Point Judith, tel. 401/783–4613) leaves from Galilee, and the **Southland Ferry** (tel. 401/783–2954) offers a 1¾-hour tour of Point Judith, Galilee, and Jerusalem. From the port it's a short drive to the **Point Judith Lighthouse** and a beautiful ocean view. *1460 Ocean Rd., tel. 401/789–0444. Open during daylight.*

Taking Ocean Road north from Galilee, you'll loop around the peninsula, past Scarborough State Beach, with its vast parking lot and ❼ beach facilities, to reach **Narragansett Pier.** Now a languid little town, at the turn of this century it was a posh resort linked by rail with New York and Boston and a major stop on the New York–Newport steamboat line. The well-to-do traveled in from those cities and beyond, many of them headed for the Narragansett Pier Casino. Designed by McKim, Mead, and White in 1885, the casino was the center of social activity, with bowling, billiards, tennis, a rifle gallery, a theater, and a ballroom. The great structure, and a six-story Victorian hotel nearby, burned to the ground in September 1900. Now only **The Towers** (tel. 401/783–7121), the grand stone-turreted entrance to the former casino, remains, spanning the road and housing the Narragansett Chamber of Commerce.

Time Out   The locals claim there's no better breakfast than at **Dad's Place** (142 Boon St., Narragansett, tel. 401/783–6420). The eggs Benedict are legendary.

Just inland of the Towers, at **Sprague Park** (Kingstown Rd. and Strathmore St.), you can see the **Narragansett Indian Monument.** Donated to the town by the sculptor Peter Toth, the 23-foot monument weighs 10,000 pounds and is made from a single piece of wood, the trunk of a giant Douglas fir. To create the sculpture, Toth worked with hammer and chisel 12 hours a day for two months, then applied 100 coats of preservative.

As you leave Narragansett Pier on Route 1A north, stop by **South County Museum,** on the grounds of Canonchet Farm, to see reconstructions of typical New England buildings. Exhibits include a general store, a cobbler's shop, a tack shop, a print shop, a children's nursery, and vintage vehicles. The museum hosts special events throughout the season. *Canonchet Farm, tel. 401/783–5400. Admission: $2.50 adults, $1.50 children 6–16. Open May–Oct., Wed.–Sun. 11–4.*

Following Route 1A north will take you through "plantation country," with a number of farms dating to the Colonial era, some of which are open to the public. The **Silas Casey Farm** still functions much as it has since the 18th century. Home to the Casey family (prominent in military and political affairs), it was also the home of Thomas Lincoln Case, engineer of the Washington Monument, and is a prominent Revolutionary War site. The farmhouse contains original furniture, prints, paintings, and political and military documents from the 18th to 20th centuries. The 360-acre farmstead is surrounded by nearly 30 miles of stone walls and has many barns. *Boston Neck Rd., Rte. 1A, Saunderstown, tel. 401/294–9182. Admission: $3. Open June–Oct., Tues.–Thurs. 1–5, Sun. 1–5.*

Continue north on Route 1A to Gilbert Stuart Road, turn left, and follow the signs for 2 miles down a pleasant country road to the **Gilbert Stuart Birthplace.** Built in 1751, the home of America's foremost portraitist of George Washington has been completely restored. The adjacent 18th-century snuff mill was the first in America. *Tel. 401/294–3001. Admission: $1.50 adults, $1 children. Open Apr.–Oct., Sat.–Thurs. 11–4:30.*

For a quick but scenic detour, follow Gilbert Stuart Road west, turn south onto Route 1, and follow it a short way to the first stoplight. Here you can climb the 100-foot, open-air **Observation Tower,** at the top of McSparren Hill. Your reward: a beautiful panoramic view of the Rhode Island coastline.

8 Return to Route 1A and follow it north to the Colonial village of **Wickford,** which has an attractive little harbor, dozens of 18th- and 19th-century homes, and a tempting assortment of antiques, furniture, and curiosity shops. Wickford's **Old Narragansett Church,** built in 1707, is one of the oldest Episcopal churches in America. *Tel. 401/294–4357. Open mid-June–Labor Day, Fri. 11–5, Sat. 10–5, for Sunday worship, and by appointment.*

Time Out   **Wickford Gourmet Foods** (21 W. Main St., tel. 401/295–8190) proffers homemade and specialty foods to eat in its comfortable loft, outside on the patio, or to take for a picnic. It's only a short walk down historic Brown Street to the Municipal Wharf, where beaches and lawns provide a lovely view of the harbor and its fishing activities.

Drive north beyond Wickford, turn north onto Route 1, then turn right onto Richard Smith Drive to reach **Smith's Castle,** built in 1678 by Richard Smith, Jr. This home was the site of many orations by Roger Williams, Rhode Island's most famed historical figure. A major restoration project is planned through 1994; call ahead to be sure it's open. *Tel. 401/294–3521. Admission: $3 adults, $1 children under 12. Open May and Sept., Fri.–Sun. 12–4; June–Aug., Thurs.– Mon. 12–4.*

What to See and Do with Children

Adventureland in Narragansett has bumper boats, minigolf, and other games and rides. *Rte. 108, Narragansett, tel. 401/789–0030. Combination tickets: $1.50–$9.50. Open June 15–Labor Day, daily 10–10; Labor Day–Oct. and Apr. 15–May 30, weekends 10–10.*
Flying Horse Carousel, Watch Hill
Silas Casey Farm, Saunderstown
South County Museum, Narragansett

Shopping

Antiques are a specialty of the region, with more than 30 stores within an hour's drive. The best places to browse are Wickford, Charlestown, and Watch Hill.

Specialty
Stores
Antiques

Artists Guild and Gallery (5429 Post Rd., Rte. 1, Charlestown, tel. 401/322–0506) exhibits 19th- and 20th-century art, and the staff will help with conservation, frame repair, and gilding. **Book and Tackle Shop** (7 Bay St., Watch Hill, tel. 401/596–0700), buys, sells, and appraises old and rare books, prints, autographs, and photographs. **Dove and Distaff Antiques** (365 Main St., Wakefield, tel. 401/783–5714) is a good spot for Early American furniture and accessories; restoration and refinishing and an upholstery and drapery workshop are held here, too. **Fox Run Country Antiques** (Rtes. 1 and 2, Crossland Park, Charlestown, tel. 401/364–3160 or 401/377–2581) has for years sold old jewelry, lighting devices, Orientalia, country primitives, and a large selection of china and glassware. **Mentor Antiques** (7512 Post Rd., Rte. 1, Wickford, tel. 401/294–9412) receives monthly shipments of English furniture—mahogany, pine, and oak—and has an extensive inventory of armoires. **Peter Pots Authentic Americana** (494 Glen Rock Rd., West Kingston, tel. 401/783–2350) features stoneware, period furniture, and collectibles. **Wickford Antiques Center I** (16 Main St., tel. 401/295–2966) vends wooden kitchen utensils and crocks, country furniture, china, glass, linens, and jewelry. **Wickford Antiques Center II** (93 Brown St., tel. 401/295–2966) sells antique furniture from many periods and fine art.

Art Galleries

The small and friendly **Artists' Gallery of Wickford** (5 Main St., Wickford, tel. 401/294–6280) shows the work of regional artists, some of whom are usually on hand to talk about their work. **Hera Gallery** (327 Main St., Wakefield, tel. 401/789–1488), established as a women's art cooperative in 1974, exhibits the work of emerging local artists, often dealing with ethnic or other provocative themes.

*Children's
Clothing*

Gabrielle's Originals (1 Fort Rd., Watch Hill, tel. 401/348–8986) sells better-quality cotton goods, locally produced hand-knit sweaters, and Mousefeather clothing. **Teddy Bearskins** (17 Brown St., Wickford, tel. 401/295–0282) has an extensive selection of children's clothing, as well as fine toys and stuffed animals.

Crafts

Needlepoint pillows, fabric-bound books, Florentine leather books, lamps, and woven throws are just a few of the elegant gifts and home furnishings you'll find at **Askham and Telham Inc.** (12 Main St., Wickford, tel. 401/295–0891). At **The Fantastic Umbrella Factory** (Rte. 1A, Charlestown, tel. 401/364–6616), three rustic shops are built around a spectacular wild garden in which peacocks, pheasants, and chickens parade; the factory sells its own hardy perennials and unusual daylilies as well as greeting cards, kites, and other wares. An outdoor café serves organic food in the summer. **Puffins of Watch Hill** (84 Bay St., tel. 401/596–1140) offers Halcyon Days enamels, Perthshire paperweights, Arthurcourt Designs, Seagull pewter, garden statuary and fountains, and handcrafted jewelry and gifts. At **Small Axe Productions** (at The Fantastic Umbrella Factory, Rte. 1A, Charlestown, tel. 401/364–1060), local artisans sell stained glass, blown glass, and pottery, along with imported textiles, leather crafts, and jewelry.

Sportswear   **Green Ink** (17 Brown St., Wickford, tel. 401/294–6266) has a fine selection of women's clothing, shoes, and accessories. **John Everets** (114 Bay St., Watch Hill, tel. 401/596–2229) features evening wear, daytime dresses, jewelry, lingerie, sportswear, and accessories. **Wilson's of Wickford** (35 Brown St., Wickford, tel. 401/294–9514) sells traditional clothing for men and women.

Sports and Outdoor Activities

Canoeing   Many small rivers and ponds in the South County are perfect for canoeing. The **Quaker Lane Bait Shop** (4019 Quaker La., North Kingston, tel. 401/294–9642) has advice and rentals.

Fishing   Tackle shops in the area include **Ocean House Marina** (60 Town Dock Rd., Charlestown, tel. 401/364–6040), **Quaker Lane Bait Shop** (4019 Quaker La., North Kingston, tel. 401/294–9642), and **Wickford Bait and Tackle** (1 Phillips St., Wickford, tel. 401/295–8845). The **Frances Fleet** (2 State St., Galilee, tel. 401/783–4988 or 401/783–8513) offers day and overnight fishing trips. **Snug Harbor Marina** (Snug Harbor, Gooseberry Rd., Galilee, tel. 401/783–7766) can put you in touch with captains who skipper fishing boats.

Hiking   One of the best trail guides for the region is the *AMC Massachusetts and Rhode Island Trail Guide*, available at local outdoors shops or from the Appalachian Mountain Club (5 Joy St., Boston, MA 02114, tel. 617/523–0636). The **Rhode Island Audubon Society** (12 Sanderson Rd., Smithfield 02917, tel. 401/231–6444) offers interesting hikes and field expeditions. The **Sierra Club** (3 Joy St., Boston, MA 02114, tel. 617/227–5339) and the **Appalachian Mountain Club** both have active groups in Rhode Island. **Great Swamp** (near West Kingston), a temporary home to migrating waterfowl, has a network of trails; pick up a map from park headquarters.

Water Sports   **Ocean House Marina, Inc.** (60 Town Dock Rd., Charlestown, tel. 401/364–6060), is a full service marina. **Narragansett Surf & Sports** (Pier Village, Narragansett, tel. 401/789–2323) rents sailboards, surfboards, and diving equipment.

Whale-Watching   The Frances Fleet offers whale-watching aboard the ***Lady Frances***, leaving Point Judith at 1 PM and returning at 6 PM. *2 State St., Galilee, tel. 401/783–4988 or 401/783–8513. Open July–Sept., Mon., Tues., and Thurs.–Sat. Cost: $30 adults, $20 children.*

National Wildlife Refuge

Ninigret Park National Wildlife Refuge is a 400-acre park that borders Ninigret Pond, Rhode Island's largest salt pond (separated from Block Island Sound by a long barrier of sand dunes) and home to many species of waterfowl. In addition to the smaller recreational area, the refuge has about 2½ miles of trails from which more than

1,250 species of birds have been sighted. Walking along the outer barrier of the pond is advised only at low tide, and then only with sturdy shoes. *Charlestown, tel. 401/364–9124. Open daily, dawn–dusk.*

Beaches

The south coast of Rhode Island has miles of beautiful ocean beaches, many of which are open to the public. The beaches are sandy, for the most part, and their water is clear and clean—in some places, the water takes on the turquoise color of the Caribbean Sea.

Charlestown   The **Charlestown Town Beach** (Charlestown Beach Rd.) can have high waves; the water is turquoise and warm. **East Beach** (East Beach Rd.) comprises two miles of dunes backed by the crystal-clear waters of Ninigret Pond, making this beach a treasure, especially for the adventurous beach goer willing to hike a distance from the car.

Narragansett   **Narragansett Town Beach** (Rte. 1A) has a boardwalk, good surf, and is within walking distance of many Narragansett hotels and guest houses. Its pavilion has changing rooms, showers, and concessions. **Roger W. Wheeler State Beach** (Cove Wood Dr.) has picnic areas, a playground, mild surf, and swimming lessons. It's near Galilee. With high surf, a bathhouse, and concessions, **Scarborough State Beach** (Ocean Dr.) becomes crowded with teenagers on weekends. *Rhode Island Monthly* says: "Big hair, hard muscles, and more mousse and mascara than Factor 15. Definitely not for the timid or self-conscious."

Matunuck   **East Matunuck State Beach** (Succotash Rd.), also called Daniel O'Brien State Beach, is popular with the college crowd for its white sand, picnic areas, and bathhouse. Unpredictable high waves make **Matunuck Beach** (Matunuck Beach Rd.) a good spot for surfing and raft-riding. **Roy Carpenter's Beach** (Matunuck Beach Rd.) is quiet, private, and secluded, yet there's food and drink within walking distance.

Misquamicut   A haven for young people, the lively, friendly **Atlantic State Beach at Misquamicut** draws crowds in the summer.

Dining and Lodging

Casual wear is the rule in the restaurants and dining rooms of South County.

Charlestown   **The General Stanton Inn.** For helping pay the ransom of an Indian
Dining and   princess in 1655, the Narragansetts rewarded Thomas Stanton with
Lodging   the land where this inn now stands. Stanton, a trader from England, first ran it as a schoolhouse for African and Native American children. The family opened it up later as an inn, and it has operated as such since the 18th century, offering dining and lodging in an authentic Colonial atmosphere. Guest rooms have low ceilings, uneven floorboards, and small windows; they're done in period antiques and wallpapers; some have nonworking fireplaces. The restaurant dining rooms have brick fireplaces, beams, and wooden floors, and the menu offers traditional New England fare—steaks, lobster, scrod, rack of lamb—as well as pasta and salads. *Old Post Rd. (Rte. 1A), 02813, tel. 401/364–0100, fax 401/364–5021. 16 rooms with bath. Facilities: restaurant (reservations advised in summer), tavern. Full breakfast included. MC, V. Moderate.*

Galilee **Aunt Carrie's.** This tremendously popular, family-owned place has
Dining been serving up traditional Rhode Island shore dinners, clam cakes
and chowder, and meat dinners for more than 60 years—and there's
a children's menu. At the height of the season you may find a line;
one alternative is to order from the take-out window and picnic on
the grass nearby. Try the enormous but light clam cakes; for the
more adventurous, there's the squid burger, served on homemade
bread. Indian pudding à la mode is a favorite dessert. *Rte. 108 and
Ocean Rd., Point Judith, tel. 401/783–7930. No reservations. No
credit cards. Closed Labor Day–Memorial Day. Moderate.*

★ **Champlin's Seafood.** Come to this casual, self-service restaurant for
the best fried scallops in South County. Other possibilities are
boiled lobster, fried oysters, and the snail salad. Take a seat out on
the oceanfront deck and look down on the fishing trawlers tied to the
docks below, or sit at one of the wood tables inside. Take-out service
is offered. *Port of Galilee, tel. 401/783–3152. No reservations. MC,
V. Moderate.*

George's of Galilee. The lines around the building on summer Saturday nights baffle local residents, who speculate that it might be because of the location at the end of a spit of land in a busy fishing
harbor. They insist that it's certainly not the atmosphere (frantic
and noisy) or the food (much better, they say, elsewhere in Galilee).
Yet it's hard to argue with success, and George's has been a "must"
for tourists since 1948. The restaurant offers several chowders and
hosts barbecues on the beach on summer weekends. *Port of Galilee,
tel. 401/783–2306. No reservations. D, MC, V. Closed Nov.–Dec.;
weekdays, Jan.–Feb. Moderate.*

Lodging **Dutch Inn by the Sea.** A windmill, a tropical terrace, talking par-
★ rots, and a fountain in the lobby—kinda crazy, but the kids will love
this stellar motel. The large indoor pool (with slide) is surrounded
by palm trees and tropical birds; there are also pool tables, pinball
machines, and outdoor tennis. Some rooms overlook the pool, and
many have been refurbished luxuriously with deep green carpeting,
white furniture, and king-size beds; others are in beige and brown.
The motel, which has a large, family-oriented restaurant, is across
the street from the Block Island Ferry Terminal and is open year-
round. *Port of Galilee, Narragansett, 02882, tel. 401/789–9341 or
800/335–6662, fax 401/789–1590. 100 rooms with bath. Facilities:
restaurant, bar, indoor pool, sauna, exercise room, whirlpool, tennis, games. AE, D, DC, MC, V. Inexpensive–Expensive.*

Matunuck **Admiral Dewey Inn.** Listed on the National Historic Register, the
Lodging building was constructed as a seaside hotel in 1898 and restored by
its current owners, Joan and Hardy DeBel, in the late 1980s. The 10
rooms are furnished with Victorian antiques; some have views of the
ocean, others are tucked cozily under the eaves. The inn is part of a
summer community just across the road from Matunuck Beach.
Smoking is permitted only on the wraparound veranda, which is
filled with old-fashioned rocking chairs. *668 Matunuck Beach Rd.,
02881, tel. 401/783–2090. 8 rooms with bath, 2 rooms share 1 bath.
Continental breakfast included. MC, V. Moderate.*

Misquamicut **Paddy's Seafood Restaurant.** Leather booths line the walls of the big
Dining square dining room of this beachside restaurant. It's a friendly, family-style, no-frills place, as befits its setting, but the food is good and
portions are generous. Seafood dishes star on the menu—lobster,
scrod, stuffed shrimp, and grilled tuna—but there's also pasta, a
choice of salads, and an extensive children's menu. *159 Atlantic
Ave., Misquamicut Beach, tel. 401/596–2610. Reservations advised*

in summer. AE, D, MC, V. Closed Jan.–Apr.; Oct.–Dec., Tues.–Wed. Moderate.

Lodging
★ **Breezeway Motel.** The roads around Misquamicut are thick with strip motels—this is probably the best. The Bellone family takes great pride in its business and offers a variety of accommodations: villas with fireplaces and Jacuzzis, suites, efficiencies, and standard rooms, but the standard is always high. Also on site are a swing set, shuffleboard, and a couple of floodlit fountains. The decor varies from room to room: The new, "junior suites" are resplendent in dark green and white with king-size beds. *Box 1368, 70 Winnapaug Rd., 02891, tel. 401/348–8953 or 800/462–8872. 44 rooms with bath, 8 suites, 2 villas. Facilities: outdoor pool, game room, refrigerators in rooms. Continental breakfast included. AE, D, DC, MC, V. Closed Nov.–Apr. Moderate–Expensive.*

Narragansett Pier
Dining

Basil's Restaurant. Within walking distance of the Towers, Basil's presents French and Continental cuisine in an intimate setting. Dark, floral wallpaper and fresh flowers decorate the small dining room, which seats 30. The specialty is milk-fed baby veal topped with a light cream and mushroom sauce; fine fresh fish dishes and duck à l'orange are also featured. The desserts are homemade. *22 Kingstown Rd., tel. 401/789–3743. Reservations advised. AE, DC, MC, V. No lunch. Closed Mon. and, Oct.–June, Tues. Expensive.*

★ **Coast Guard House.** This restaurant, which dates to 1888 and which served for 50 years as a life-saving station, was severely damaged by Hurricane Bob in 1991; commemorative plaques high on the walls record the storm's incredible water levels. The restaurant also displays interesting photos of bygone Narragansett Pier and the casino. Tables are candlelit and picture windows overlook the ocean on three sides. The menu offers a range of typical American fare—seafood, pasta, veal, steak, and lamb entrées. Friday and Saturday nights see entertainment in the Oak Room and a DJ in the upstairs lounge. *40 Ocean Rd., tel. 401/789–0700. Reservations accepted for 8 or more. AE, D, DC, MC, V. Expensive.*

Spain Restaurant. Rhode Island's only true Spanish restaurant is in a somewhat unlikely setting—on the ground floor of the modern, very American, Village Inn hotel. The interior, though, is appropriately dark and atmospheric, the air pungent with garlic and spices. Enjoy such appetizers as shrimp in garlic sauce, stuffed mushrooms, and Spanish sausages; the main courses are variations on lobster, steak, paella and mariscada, and other meat dishes. *Village Inn, 1 Beach St., tel. 401/783–9770. Reservations advised on Sat. AE, D, DC, MC, V. Expensive.*

Lodging
The Richards. Imposing and magnificent, this English manor–style mansion, built of granite quarried on the site, was the brainchild of Joseph Peace Hazard, scion of one of the founding families of Rhode Island. The home has a broodingly Gothic mystique that is almost the antithesis of a summer house. From the wood-panel common rooms downstairs, French windows look out onto a lush landscape, with a grand swamp oak the centerpiece of a handsome garden. A fire crackles in the library fireplace on chilly afternoons. Breakfast consists of fresh fruit and baked goods as well as such main courses as eggs Florentine and oven pancakes. Some rooms are furnished with 19th-century English antiques, floral-upholstered furniture, and fireplaces; two have private baths. *144 Gibson Ave., 02832, tel. 401/789–7746. 2 rooms with bath, 2 rooms share a bath, 1 2-bedroom suite. Full breakfast included. No credit cards. Moderate–Expensive.*

Stone Lea. The spacious house, more than 100 years old and filled with period furniture collected by the owners, is a bed-and-breakfast in a wonderful location with lawns down to the sea. The atmosphere is rather stiff and stilted, but the ocean-facing rooms have panoramic views, the most striking in Nos. 1 and 7; No. 5 has a sitting room attached. *40 Newton Ave., 02882, tel. 401/783–9546. 7 rooms with bath. Facilities: lounge with pool table, player piano. Continental breakfast included. MC, V. Moderate–Expensive.*

Wakefield
Dining

Larchwood Inn. The owners call this "a country inn with a Scottish flavor." More than 150 years old, the original building is set in a grove of larch trees. Ask for a table near the fireplace in winter, and try for a patio spot under the larch trees in summer. On the menu are halibut stuffed with scallops; and seafood, chicken, beef, and veal preparations. *521 Main St., Wakefield, tel. 401/783–5454. Reservations advised. AE, D, DC, MC, V. No lunch Sun. Expensive.*

★ **South Shore Grille.** The restaurant has a wood-fired grill and waterfront views: One wall, overlooking Marina Bay, is all windows. Favorites on the constantly changing menu include crispy fried chicken, herb-grilled swordfish, and fillet of beef. In summer, the patio deck opens for an informal lunch and snacks from noon to dusk. *210 Salt Pond Rd., Wakefield, tel. 401/782–4780. Reservations advised. MC, V. Closed Mon.–Wed. Jan.–Mar. Expensive.*

Watch Hill
Dining

Olympia Tea Room. Step back in time to a small restaurant, first opened in 1916, where the soda fountain has a long marble counter and there are varnished wood booths. Try a marshmallow sundae— or an orangeade. For dinner sample ginger chicken or mussels steamed in white wine. On the dessert menu, the "world famous Avondale swan" is a fantasy of ice cream, whipped cream, chocolate sauce, and puff pastry. *30 Bay St., tel. 401/348–8211. No reservations. AE, MC, V. Closed Dec.–Easter. Expensive.*

Lodging

Ocean House. The grand—if enormous—old lady may appear a bit down-at-the-heels, yet hers is one of the best seaside porches in New England. The casual, relaxing, quiet place has a reassuring if faded elegance. The furniture could be called "maple eclectic," with oldish mattresses, blankets, and sheets; those considerations pale next to the beautiful ocean view (ask for a good one). The Ocean House serves three meals a day; MAP rates are offered. The porch offers great sunset views, and a set of splintery stairs leads to an excellent private beach. *2 Bluff Ave., 02891, tel. 401/348–8161. 59 rooms with bath. Facilities: restaurant, lounge, private beach. MAP available. MC, V. Closed Sept.–June. Expensive.*

Weekapaug
Lodging

Weekapaug Inn. The building seems more a mansion than an inn, with a peaked roof, stone foundation, and huge wraparound porch. It's perched on a peninsula surrounded on three sides by salty Quonochontaug Pond; just beyond a barrier beach is Block Island Sound. As if on a set from "Father Knows Best," there's a comfy tidiness about the furnishings in the common rooms and bedrooms, where every surface looks freshly painted, waxed, or varnished. Room decor is cheerful, if not particularly remarkable, and each room is big and bright, with wide windows offering impressive views. Many guests are regulars—some for as long as 45 or 50 years—although newcomers are more than welcome. Standards in the restaurant are very high; a new menu every day features four to six entrées, emphasizing seafood, and a full-time baker makes all the desserts, breads, and rolls. Thursday-night cookouts feature swordfish, steak, and chicken, as well as seasonal vegetables. *15 Spring Ave., 02892, tel. 401/322–0301. 54 rooms with bath. Facilities: restaurant, boat rentals. No credit cards. Very Expensive.*

Grandview Bed and Breakfast. This large home on a rise above Route

1A offers clean, comfortable rooms at the lowest prices in the area. Guest rooms, some with shared baths, are furnished with a mixture of wicker and family hand-me-downs; front rooms have ocean views, and there's a small guest sitting room with TV and VCR. Breakfast is served on the porch in summer or in the family dining room out of season. It's friendly, relaxed, and affordable—just like the original British version of a B&B. Although the mailing address is Westerly, it's closer to Weekapaug. *212 Shore Rd., Westerly, 02891, tel. 401/596–6384. 12 rooms, 6 with private bath. AE, MC, V. Inexpensive.*

Westerly
Dining and
Lodging
★

Shelter Harbor Inn. In a quiet rural setting not far from the beach, this begs a romantic weekend getaway ruled by simple comforts and privacy. The original 19th-century house has been renovated, as have several outbuildings. Several rooms have both a working fireplace and a deck, and there's another deck, with a barbecue and a hot tub, on the roof. The corner room, No. 9, is a particular favorite. At the excellent restaurant, the frequently changing menu might include smoked scallops and capellini or pecan-crusted duck breast. The wine list is extensive, and a bowl of warm, buttery Indian pudding makes a solid finish to any dinner. Breakfast is good any day, but Sunday brunch is legendary. Although the address is Westerly, the inn is about six miles east of downtown. *Rte. 1, Westerly, 02892, tel. 401/322–8883. 24 rooms with bath. Facilities: restaurant (reservations advised), lighted paddle tennis, croquet, hot tub, van service to beach. Full breakfast included. AE, DC, MC, V. Inn: Moderate–Expensive. Restaurant: Expensive.*

The Arts and Nightlife

The Chorus of Westerly (119 High St., Westerly, tel. 401/596–8663) performs a variety of choral works year-round. **Colonial Theatre** (1 Granite St., Westerly, tel. 401/596–0810) presents professional musicals, comedies, and dramas throughout the year. **South County Players Children's Theater** (South Kingstown High School, tel. 401/783–6110) gives performances by children for children. The barn-style **Theatre-by-the-Sea** (Cards Pond Rd., off Rte. 1, Matunuck, tel. 401/782–8587), built in 1933 and listed on the National Register of Historic Places, presents musicals and plays in summer.

South County isn't exactly famous for nightlife—the area around Misquamicut and Atlantic Beach Park is about the liveliest for summer visitors: The **Windjammer** (Atlantic Ave., Westerly, tel. 401/322–0271) offers oceanfront dining and dancing to rock bands in a room that holds 1,500. Recent performers have included Jefferson Airplane, Roomful of Blues, and John Cafferty and the Beaver Brown Band. There are a few nightclubs in **Wakefield,** and at nearby **Narragansett Pier,** you can find weekend entertainment, including live bands, at the **Coast Guard House** (*see* Dining, *above*).

Newport

Perched gloriously on the southern tip of Aquidneck Island and bounded on three sides by water, Newport is one of the great sailing cities of the world and the host to world-class jazz, blues, and classical music festivals.

Newport's first age of prosperity was in the late 1700s, when it was a major port city almost on a par with Boston and New York. Dozens of Colonial homes still stand today, most of them restored, in the historic "Point District."

By the 19th century Newport became a summer playground for the wealthiest families in America. These riches were not made in Rhode Island but imported by the titans of the Gilded Age and translated into the fabulous "cottages" overlooking the Atlantic. The masters and mistresses of such estates as Marble House and the Breakers lived in luxury that would be unimaginable even to New York developers today; ironically, the same sorts of local citizens whom one society matron once referred to as "footstools" weathered the days of ersatz feudalism and now earn a good deal of their tourism income from visitors to the palaces by the sea.

Newport in summer can be exasperating, its streets jammed with visitors and the traffic slowed by the procession of air-conditioned sightseeing buses. Yet the quality of Newport's arts festivals persuades many people to brave the crowds. In fall, winter, and spring, you stand a much better chance of soaking in Newport's merits without the migraine of standing in long lines. The weather is pleasant well into November, and the city goes all out to attract visitors in December with the many "Christmas in Newport" activities.

Important Addresses and Numbers

Visitor Information   **Newport County Convention and Visitors Bureau** (23 America's Cup Ave., tel. 401–849–8048 or 800/326–6030; open May–Sept., daily 9–7, Oct.–Apr., daily 9–5.), one of the best centers of its kind, shows an orientation film and provides maps, cassette tours, and advice.

Emergencies
Hospital   **Newport Hospital** (Friendship St., Newport, tel. 401/846–6400) is the largest in the region.

Late-Night Pharmacy   **Douglas Drug** (7 E. Main Rd., Middletown, tel. 401/849–4600) is open until 9 PM.

Arriving and Departing by Plane

Newport State Airport (tel. 401/846–2200), 3 miles northeast of the city, has connecting flights by charter companies to Theodore Francis Green State Airport in Warwick. **Cozy Cab** (tel. 401/846–2500) runs a frequent shuttle service ($13) between the airport and the visitors bureau downtown, and some Newport hotels provide free airport shuttle service to guests.

Getting Around Newport

By Car   With the exception of Ocean Drive and Bellevue Avenue, Newport is a walker's city. A car is a liability in summer, when traffic thickens on the city's narrow one-way streets. Once in town, it's worth parking in one of the many pay lots and forgetting about your car for the rest of your stay.

By Bus   **Rhode Island Public Transit Authority** (tel. 401/847–0209 or, in RI, 800/221–3797) serves the Newport area.

Guided Tours

Old Colony & Newport Railway follows an 8-mile route along Narragansett Bay from Newport to Portsmouth's Green Animals Topiary Gardens. The round-trip takes a little over three hours, with a 1¼-hour stop at the garden. *19 America's Cup Ave., tel. 401/624–6951. Admission: $6 adults, $5 senior citizens, $3 children 2–14, $15 fam-*

*ilies. Departs May–mid-June and mid-Sept.–mid-Nov., Sun.
12:30; mid-June–mid-Sept., weekends 12:30.*

The Spirit of Newport (tel. 401/849–3575) gives one-hour mini-
cruises of Newport Harbor and Narragansett Bay, departing from
the Newport Harbour Inn (America's Cup Ave.) every 90 minutes
from June through Labor Day and less frequently out of season.

Viking Bus and Boat Tours of Newport (Brick Marketplace, tel. 401/
847–6921) runs Newport tours on air-conditioned buses and one-
hour cruises of Narragansett Bay.

Walking Tours   The **Newport Freedom Trail** makes a loop through the downtown
area, beginning at the Historical Society on Touro Street and finishing at the Automobile Museum. **Newport Historical Society** (82
Touro Street, tel. 401/846–0813) sponsors walking tours on Friday
and Saturday in summer. **Newport on Foot** (Box 1042, tel. 401/846–
5391) organizes mile-long walks through Colonial Newport.

Exploring Newport

*Numbers in the margin correspond to points of interest on the
Downtown Newport and Greater Newport maps.*

This tour begins with Colonial Newport, the northwestern section
of the city, clustered around the harbor; the second half of the tour
turns to the Newport of the Gilded Age, the southern part of town,
where many of the city's stunning mansions stand. Newport residents have worked carefully alongside such organizations as the
Newport Preservation Society and the Newport Historical Society
to restore important buildings and open them to the public.

➊ A walk around **Colonial Newport,** which should give you a good idea
of what the town was like in Revolutionary times, begins at **Hunter
House** (ca. 1748) on Washington Street—on the outskirts of the historic Point District. Notice the carved pineapple over the doorway;
throughout Colonial America the pineapple was a symbol of hospitality, from the days when a seaman's wife placed a fresh pineapple
at the front door to announce that her husband had returned from
the sea. The elliptical arch in the central hall is a typical Newport
detail. Much of the house is furnished with pieces made by Newport
craftsmen Townsend and Goddard. *54 Washington St., tel. 401/847–
1000. Admission: $6 adults, $3 children 6–11. Open May–Sept.,
daily 10–5; Apr. and Oct., weekends 10–5.*

Walk north on Washington Street and make a right onto Popular
Street. This leads to Farewell Street, lined with ancient cemeteries.
➋ The oldest is the 18th-century **Common Burial Ground** on Warner
Street—a continuation of Popular Street once you cross Farewell
Street. The tombstones are fine examples of Colonial stone carving,
much of it the work of John Stevens.

Walk south on Farewell Street to Thames Street (pronounced
Thaymes), the main street of Colonial Newport. Continue south on
➌ Thames Street to Washington Square. The **Brick Market,** built in
1760, was designed by Peter Harrison, who was also responsible for
the Touro Synagogue and the Redwood Library. From 1793 to 1799
it was used as a theater, and if you look closely at the east wall, you'll
find a trace of one of the theatrical scenes—a seascape of ships. In
later years the building was used as a town hall, and today it's surrounded by some 40 shops and curio stores that make up the Brick
Market Place. In December 1993, the original market building, once
used for slave trading, was converted into the **Museum of Newport**

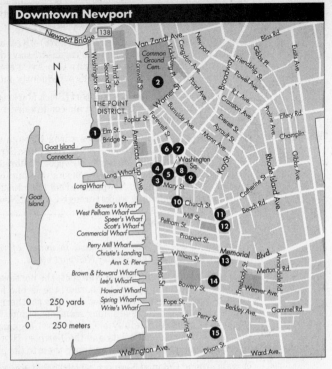

History, a multimedia exhibit with audiovisual programs exploring Newport's past. *Thames St., tel. 401/841–8770. Admission: $5 adults, $4 senior citizens, $3 children. Open Wed.–Mon. 10–5.*

4 Facing the Brick Market on Washington Square is the **Old Colony House,** built in 1739. The headquarters of the Colonial and state governments, it was from the balcony of this building that the succession of George III was announced and the Declaration of Independence read to Newporters. George Washington met here with General Rochambeau. *Washington Sq., tel. 401/846–2980 or 401/277–2669. Tours by appointment.*

5 Walk northeast from Washington Square on Broadway to reach Newport's oldest house, the **Wanton-Lyman-Hazard House,** which displays a "two-room" plan typical of the time. It also has a Colonial garden, and there are demonstrations of 18th-century cooking. *17 Broadway, tel. 401/846–0813. Admission: $4 adults, children under 12 free. Open mid-June–Sept., Tues.–Sat. 10–4.*

6 Continue up Broadway and turn left on Farewell Street to Marlborough Street and the **White Horse Tavern** (tel. 401/849–3600). In operation since 1687, the White Horse claims to be the oldest tavern in America. Its low, dark-beam ceiling, cavernous fireplaces, uneven plank floors, and cozy, yet elegant, tables epitomize Newport's Colonial charm.

7 Also on this corner stands the **Friends Meeting House.** Built in 1699, this is the oldest Quaker meeting house in America. With its wide-plank floors, simple benches, balcony, and beam ceiling (considered lofty by Colonial standards), this two-story, shingle structure reflects the elegance, quiet reserve, and steadfast faith of Colonial Quakers. *29 Farewell St., tel. 401/846–0813. Tours by appointment.*

8 Return to Washington Square, crossing it to Touro Street. Here, the oldest surviving synagogue in the country, **Touro Synagogue,** was designed by Peter Harrison and dedicated in 1763. Very simple on the outside, the building has an elaborate interior. Notice the way its design combines the ornate columns and moldings of the Georgian style with Jewish ritualistic requirements. *85 Touro St., tel. 401/847–4794. Admission free. Guided tours on the ½ hour in summer, Sun.–Fri. 10–4; the rest of the year, Sun. 1–2:30 or by appointment.*

9 At 82 Touro Street you'll find the headquarters of the **Newport Historical Society,** the departure point for walking tours of Newport. The building is also a museum featuring a large collection of Newport memorabilia, furniture, and maritime items. *82 Touro St., tel. 401/846–0813. Admission free. Open Tues.–Fri. 9:30–4:30.*

10 South of Washington Square, at the corner of Spring and Church streets, you'll find **Trinity Church,** a Colonial beauty built in 1724 and modeled after many of Sir Christopher Wren's churches in London. A special feature of the interior is the three-tiered wineglass pulpit, the only one of its kind in America. *Queen Anne Sq., tel. 401/846–0660. Admission free. Open June–Oct., daily 10–4; Nov.–May, daily 10–1.*

11 Turn up Church Street to the beginning of Bellevue Avenue and the **Redwood Library,** built in 1748—the nation's oldest library in continuous use. Another magnificent example of the architecture of Peter Harrison, the building, although made of wood, was designed to look like a Roman temple, the original exterior paint mixed with sand to resemble stone. The library houses a wonderful collection of paintings by such important Early American artists as Gilbert Stuart and Rembrandt Peale. *50 Bellevue Ave., tel. 401/847–0292. Admission free. Open Mon.–Sat. 9:30–5:30.*

12 On the next block you'll find the **Newport Art Museum and Art Association.** Permanent and changing exhibits of historic contemporary art of Rhode Island and New England are displayed in a stick-style Victorian building designed by Richard Morris Hunt. *76 Bellevue Ave., tel. 401/848–8200. Admission: $4 adults, $3 senior citizens, children under 18 free. Open Memorial Day–Labor Day, daily 10–5; Labor Day–Memorial Day, Tues.–Sat. 10–4, Sun. 1–5.*

A left on Memorial Boulevard brings you to Easton's Beach and the beginning of the 3-mile **Cliff Walk,** which runs south along Newport's cliffs to Bailey's Beach and offers a water view of many Newport mansions. This is a challenging walk, not recommended for the infirm or for children under six, but it promises breathtaking vistas.

13 Farther south on Bellevue Avenue is the **International Tennis Hall of Fame** and the **Tennis Museum.** Housed in a magnificent building by Stanford White, the museum features photographs and other memorabilia of more than a century of tennis history. The first National Tennis Championships were held here in 1881. *Newport Casino, 194 Bellevue Ave., tel. 401/849–3990. Admission: $6 adults, $3.50 senior citizens, $3 children 6–12, $12 family. Open daily 10–5.*

We turn now to **Gilded Age Newport,** which is seen largely in the splendid mansions of the turn of the century. You may find a car useful here in covering the considerable distances between the grand homes, for you'll have plenty of walking to do inside the mansions themselves, and free parking is available at each site.

It is hard to imagine the sums of money possessed by the wealthy elite who made Newport their summer playground in the late 1800s and early 1900s. The "cottages" they built are almost obscenely grand, laden with ornate rococo detail and designed with a determined one-upmanship.

Six Newport mansions are maintained by the **Preservation Society of Newport County** (tel. 401/847–1000). A combination ticket—available at any of the society's properties or at the visitors bureau—gives you a discount. Each mansion provides a guided tour that lasts about an hour.

⑭ We begin at **Kingscote,** just west of Bellevue Avenue, on Bowery Street. Built in 1839 for George Noble Jones, a Savannah, Georgia, plantation owner, this mansion serves to remind us that Newport was popular with Southerners before the Civil War. Today it is furnished with antique furniture, glass, and Asian art. It also has a number of Tiffany windows. *Bowery St., off Bellevue Ave. Admission: $6 adults, $3 children 6–11. Open May–Sept., daily 10–5; Apr. and Oct., weekends 10–5.*

⑮ Head south on Bellevue Avenue and look to your right for **The Elms,** one of Newport's most graceful mansions. The Elms pays homage to the classical design, broad lawn, fountains, and formal gardens of the Château d'Asnières near Paris; it was built for Edward Julius Berwind, a bituminous-coal baron, at the turn of the century. *Bellevue Ave. Admission: $7 adults, $3 children 6–11. Open May–Oct., daily 10–5; Apr., weekends 10–4.*

⑯ A few blocks south is **Chateau-sur-mer,** the first of Bellevue Avenue's stone mansions. Built in 1852 and enlarged by Richard Morris Hunt for William S. Wetmore, a China-trade tycoon, the mansion houses a toy collection. Compared to the more opulent homes built during the 1890s, this one seems rather modest today. A December visit will find the home decorated for a Victorian Christmas. *Bellevue Ave. Admission: $6 adults, $3 children 6–11. Open May–Oct., daily 10–5; Nov.–Apr., weekends 10–4.*

⑰ Turn left on Victoria Avenue and continue to Ochre Point Avenue and **the Breakers.** It's easy to understand why it took more than 2,500 workmen two years to create this structure, the most magnificent of the Newport mansions. Built in 1893 for Cornelius Vanderbilt II and his small family, the Breakers has 70 rooms and required 40 servants to keep it running. Just a few of the marvels within the four-story limestone villa are a gold-ceiling music room, a blue marble fireplace, rose alabaster pillars in the dining room, and a porch whose mosaic ceiling took Italian craftsmen six months, lying on their backs, to install. If it were possible to build the Breakers today, according to recent estimates, it could cost $400 million. *Ochre Point Ave. Admission: $7.50 adults, $3.50 children 6–11. Open May–Oct., daily 10–5; Nov.–Apr., weekends 10–4.*

⑱ Return to Bellevue Avenue and continue south to **Rosecliff.** Built for Mrs. Hermann Oelrichs, this romantic mansion was completed in 1902. Modeled after the Grand Trianon at Versailles, the 40-room home includes the Court of Love (inspired by a similar room at Versailles) and a heart-shape staircase designed by Stanford White. It has appeared in several movies, including *The Great Gatsby. Bellevue Ave. Admission: $6 adults, $3 children 6–11. Open daily Apr.–Oct. 10–5.*

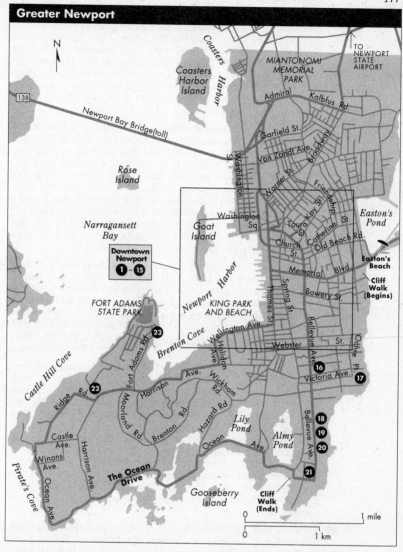

Greater Newport

The Astors'
Beechwood, **19**

Belcourt Castle, **21**

The Breakers, **17**

Chateau-sur-mer, **16**

Hammersmith
Farm, **22**

Marble House, **20**

Museum of
Yachting, **23**

Rosecliff, **18**

⑲ Farther down Bellevue Avenue is **The Astors' Beechwood,** where a succession of actors, dressed in period costume, plays the parts of members of the Astor family (including Mrs. Astor, the belle of New York and Newport society), servants, and household guests. The guides involve visitors in much banter, such as noticing a woman's knee-length skirt and asking, "Do your clothes have a shrinkage problem?"! *580 Bellevue Ave., tel. 401/846-3772. Admission: $7.75 adults, $6 senior citizens and children 6-12, $30 families. Open May-mid-Dec., daily 10-5; Feb.-Apr., Fri.-Sun. 10-4.*

⑳ Continue down Bellevue Avenue, and on your left will be **Marble House,** with its extravagant gold ballroom, the gift of William Vanderbilt to his wife, Alva, in 1892. Alva divorced William in 1895 and married Oliver Perry Belmont to become the lady of Belcourt Castle (just down the road). When Oliver died in 1908, she returned to Marble House. Mrs. Belmont was involved with the suffragist movement and spent much of her time campaigning for women's rights. In the kitchen you'll see plates marked Votes for Women. The lovely Chinese teahouse behind the estate was built in 1913 by Mrs. Belmont. *Bellevue Ave. Admission: $6 adults, $3 children 6-11. Open Apr.-Oct., daily 10-5; Jan.-Mar., weekends 10-4.*

㉑ Farther along the avenue is **Belcourt Castle,** designed by Richard Morris Hunt based on Louis XIII's hunting lodge. The castle contains an enormous collection of European and Oriental treasures. Sip tea and admire the stained glass and carved wood, and don't miss the Golden Coronation Coach. *Bellevue Ave., tel. 401/846-0669 or 401/849-1566. Admission: $6.50 adults, $5 senior citizens, $2 children 6-12. Open Apr.-Oct., daily 10-5; Nov.-Dec. and Feb.-Mar., daily 10-4; Jan., weekends 10-3.*

㉒ Take Ocean Drive all the way along the coast to **Hammersmith Farm,** the childhood summer home of Jacqueline Bouvier Kennedy Onassis, the site of her wedding to John F. Kennedy, and a summer White House during the Kennedy Administration. It is also the only working farm in Newport. Loaded with Bouvier and Kennedy memorabilia, the house is so comfortable that it seems as though its owners have just stepped out of the room. The elaborate gardens were designed by Frederick Law Olmsted, and there are breathtaking views of the ocean. *Ocean Dr., near Ft. Adams, tel. 401/846-7346. Admission: $6.50 adults, $3 children. Open Memorial Day-Labor Day, daily 10-7; Mar.-Memorial Day and Labor Day-mid-Nov., daily 10-5. Closed mid-Nov.-Feb., with special openings around Christmas.*

㉓ Turn left onto Ft. Adams Road to reach the **Museum of Yachting.** Here are four galleries of pictures: Mansions and Yachts, Small Craft, America's Cup, and the Hall of Fame for Single-handed Sailors. *Ft. Adams, Ocean Dr., tel. 401/847-1018. Admission: $2.50 adults, $2 senior citizens, children under 12 free. Open May-Oct., daily 10-5.*

Newport for Free

Jazz and folk **concerts** are held in Newport parks, and popular music concerts and events such as clambakes are held at **Newport Beach Rotunda** on Memorial Boulevard throughout the summer.

Kite flying is a popular pastime on Newport's beaches and in its parks. **Price's Neck** along Ocean Drive is a wonderful spot for a picnic, within sight of the ships at sail in summer and early fall.

What to See and Do with Children

The Children's Theatre (Box 144, Newport, tel. 401/848–0266) puts on several major productions for children each year.

Norman Bird Sanctuary. The 450-acre sanctuary has nature trails, guided tours, and a small natural history museum. *583 Third Beach Rd., Middletown, tel. 401/846–2577. Admission: $2 adults, children under 12 and senior citizens free. Open Tues.–Sun. 9–5.*

Off the Beaten Track

Between the city of Newport and the Massachusetts border to the east there are two areas that deserve a visit and make a lovely drive: Portsmouth and the Sakonnet lands.

About 4 miles north of Newport on Route 138, turn east onto Sandy Point Avenue to reach **Sandy Point Beach,** where the calm surf of the Sakonnet River creates a choice spot for families and beginning windsurfers. Leaving the beach area, continue north on Route 138, and, just before Portsmouth, look out for the signs that direct you to **Green Animals,** a topiary garden filled with plants sculpted to look like an elephant, a camel, a giraffe, and even a teddy bear. The main Victorian house, which, along with the small estate, was left to the Preservation Society in 1972, contains toy collections and a plant shop. *Cory La., tel. 401/847–1000. Admission: $6 adults, $3.50 children 6–12. Open May–Oct., daily 10–5.*

Just north of Green Animals, on Route 138, lies **Portsmouth,** which has seen much development in recent years, a departure from its somewhat rural past. Route 138 continues beyond Portsmouth across the Sakonnet River and into the Sakonnet lands; turn south after the bridge and take Route 77 to **Tiverton.** On Lawton Avenue, turn right to reach the remains of **Ft. Barton,** named for Colonel William Barton, who captured Newport's British commander during the Revolutionary War. A climb of the observation tower will give you a view of Aquidneck Island.

As you drive the 12 miles south on Route 77 from Tiverton to the town of **Little Compton,** the landscape becomes more rural, and the road, lined with fruit and vegetable stands, passes turkey, tree, and pumpkin farms, as well as a vineyard. A left onto Meetinghouse Lane leads to Little Compton commons, at the edge of which is a lofty United Congregational Church built in 1832. Gravestones in the nearby burial ground, laid out in 1675, include that of Benjamin Church, the Indian fighter who took part in the Great Swamp Fight and the execution of King Philip. Across the commons is a Big Toy playground structure: a wooden castle incorporating turrets, bridges, tunnels, and a dragon.

Shopping

Newport is a shopper's—but not a bargain hunter's—city. Specialties include antiques, traditional clothing, and marine supplies. Many of Newport's arts and antiques shops are found on Thames Street or near the waterfront; others are located on Spring Street, Franklin Street, and at Bowen's and Bannister's wharves. The Brick Market area—between Thames Street and America's Cup Avenue—has more than 40 shops.

Department Stores Leys (Long Wharf Mall, opposite Gateway Center, tel. 401/846–2100), America's oldest department store (established in 1796), sells clothing, linens, home furnishings, and souvenirs. **Josephson's**

Clothing (1 Bannister's Wharf, tel. 401/847–0303) sells Polo, leather, cashmere, and silk fashions for men and women.

Specialty Stores

Antiques

Aardvark Antiques (475 Thames St., tel. 401/849–7233) has architectural pieces: mantels, doors, garden ornaments, and stained glass. **John Gidley House** (22 Franklin St., tel. 401/846–8303) features Continental furnishings from the 18th and 19th centuries. The store's own chandeliers and marble are a reminder of what Newport was like in the Gilded Age. **The Nautical Nook** (86 Spring St., tel. 401/846–6810) stocks an unusual combination of antiques and collectibles related to ships: maps, navigational instruments, model boats, and ships in bottles. **The Old Fashion Shop** (38 Pelham St., tel. 401/847–2692) sells American furniture and accessories, including elegant china, kitchenware, quilts, and glass—and Orientalia.

Art

The Liberty Tree (104 Spring St., tel. 401/847–5925) has contemporary folk art, furniture, carvings, and paintings. **MacDowell Pottery** (220 Spring St., tel. 401/846–6313) is a studio/shop where you can not only purchase the wares of many New England potters, but also see a potter's wheel in use. **Native American Trading Company: Indian Territory** (138–40 Spring St., tel. 401/846–8465) sells paintings and artifacts. **Thames Glass** (688 Thames St., tel. 401/846–0576) sells delicate and dramatic blown-glass gifts, designed by Matthew Buechner and handmade in the adjacent studio. Don't miss the selection of slight imperfects. **William Vareika Fine Arts** (212 Bellevue Ave., tel. 401/849–6149) exhibits and sells American paintings and prints from the 18th through 20th centuries and offers appraisal and consulting.

Books

Anchor & Dolphin Books (30 Franklin St., tel. 401/846–6890) buys, sells, and appraises rare books, libraries, and collections. The store is especially rich in garden history, architecture, and design. **The Armchair Sailor** (543 Thames St., tel. 401/847–4252) stocks marine and travel books, charts, and maps.

Clothing

World View Graphics (11 Christies Landing, tel. 401/847–8120) displays hand-painted T-shirts in vibrant colors; its wares illustrate nautical, environmental, and pop-culture themes.

Crafts

Tropea-Puerini (391 Thames St., tel. 401/846–3344) calls itself the Alternative Bridal Registry and offers interesting pottery, sculpture, jewelry, and functional home accessories.

Flags

Ebenezer Flagg Co. (corner of Spring and Touro Sts., tel. 401/846–1891) has a large selection of flags, banners, and wind socks, as well as in-shop manufacturing and custom design.

Home Furnishings

Rue de France (78 Thames St., tel. 401/846–3636) specializes in French lace: curtains, pillows, and table linens.

Jewelry

J. H. Breakell & Co. (69 Mills St., tel. 401/849–3522) shows original designs in gold and silver.

Men's Clothing

JT's Ship Chandlery (364 Thames St., tel. 401/846–7256) is a major supplier of marine hardware, equipment, and clothing. **Native American Trading Company: Explorer's Club** (138 Spring St., tel. 401/846–8465) features quality outdoor sportswear with British and American labels.

Women's Clothing

Native American Trading Company: Ladies' Division (140 Spring St., tel. 401/846–8465) sells quality shearlings and leathers and other outdoor wear.

Sports and Outdoor Activities

Biking **Ten Speed Spokes** (18 Elm Street, tel. 401/847–5609) and **Firehouse Bicycle** (25 Mill St., tel. 401/847–5700) rent bikes for $15 per day. **Fun Rentals** (1 Commercial Wharf and Goat Island, tel. 401/846–4374) offers Rollerblades at $10 for two hours, bikes at $15 per day, and mountain bikes and mopeds for $40 per day. The 15-mile swing down Bellevue Avenue and along Ocean Drive and back is a great route to ride your rented wheels. For a long country ride, cycle across the bridge over the Sakonnet River and through the small villages of Tiverton and Little Compton (*see* Off the Beaten Track, *above*).

Boating **Old Port Marine Services** (Sayer's Wharf, tel. 401/847–9109) offers harbor tours, daily and weekly yacht charters, and rides on a harbor ferry. **Sight Sailing of Newport** (Bowen's Wharf, tel. 401/849–3333) organizes one- and two-hour sailing tours of Newport Harbor in a six-passenger sailboat with a U.S. Coast Guard–licensed captain; they also run a sailing school and charter captained yachts for longer periods. **Sail Newport** (Ft. Adams State Park, tel 401/846–1983) rents sailboats by the hour.

Fishing No license is required for saltwater fishing, although anglers should check with local bait shops, such as **Sam's Bait** (936 Aquidneck Ave., tel. 401/848–5909), **Edwards Bait** (36 Aquidneck Ave., tel. 401/846–4521), and **Beachfront Bait Shop** (103 Wellington Ave., tel. 401/849–4665) for minimum size requirements. Charter fishing boats depart daily from Newport, spring–fall. Contact **Black Horse Fishing Charter** (Long Wharf Moorings, tel. 401/841–8848).

Spectator Sports

Newport Jai Alai (150 Admiral Kalbfus Rd., tel. 401/849–5000) has its season from May to mid-October.

Beaches

Middletown **Sachuest Beach,** or Second Beach (Sachuest Point area), is a beautiful sandy beach adjacent to the Norman Bird Sanctuary. Dunes and a campground make it popular with singles as well as surfers. **Third Beach** (Sachuest Point area), on the Sakonnet River, with a boat ramp, is a favorite of windsurfers.

Newport **Easton's Beach** (Memorial Blvd.), also known as First Beach, is popular for its carousel for the kids and for minigolf. **Ft. Adams State Park** (Ocean Dr.), a small beach with a picnic area and lifeguards during the summer, has beautiful views of Newport Harbor. **King Park** (Wellington Ave.), with lifeguards patrolling in summer, is a haven for scuba divers.

Dining

Dress is casual unless otherwise noted.

American **The Black Pearl.** At this popular waterfront restaurant with a nautical decor, diners choose between the casual tavern and the very formal Commodore's Room. The latter offers such appetizers as black-and-blue tuna with red pepper sauce. Entrées might include swordfish with Dutch pepper butter or duck breast with green peppercorn sauce. *Bannister's Wharf, tel. 401/846–5264. Commodore Room: Reservations and jacket required. AE, MC, V. Very Expensive.*
Clarke Cooke House. Formal dining is on the upper level; its timber-

ceiling room has water views, dark green latticework, richly patterned pillows, and wood model hulls, which combine to pay homage
to Colonial, nautical, and Gilded Era Newport. The menu includes
rack of lamb and *seafood nage* (a fresh seafood stew). The first two
levels, the Candy Store and the Bistro, feature American fare and
casual dining in pleasant, airy, white-beam sections with large windows facing the marina and the bustling pedestrian traffic of the
wharf. *Bannister's Wharf, tel. 401/849–2900. Reservations advised;
required in summer. Jacket required upstairs. AE, D, DC, MC, V.
Expensive.*

Newport Star Clipper Dinner Train. This five-course, 22-mile journey
along Narragansett Bay features such delicacies as prime rib and
swordfish, while providing fine water views and murder-mystery
entertainment on selected journeys (call for exact schedule). Make
reservations for lunch or dinner well in advance for the three-hour
trip. *102 Connell Hwy., tel. 401/849–7550 or 800/462–7452. Reservations required. AE, D, MC, V. Operates Mar.–Nov., daily; Nov.–
Mar., Fri.–Sun. Expensive.*

Brick Alley Pub. Low ceilings, small tables, plants, and American
memorabilia give this place a friendly atmosphere. An extensive
menu includes fresh fish, chowder, steaks, and homemade pasta.
The enthusiastic owner, Ralph Plumb, keeps the tavern hopping until 1 AM, and you can eat lightly or fatten up on a full dinner. On summer
evenings, the outdoor bar and patio throb with activity. *140 Thames
St., tel. 401/849–6334. Reservations advised. AE, D, DC, MC, V.
Inexpensive–Moderate.*

Ocean Coffee Roasters. Known around here as the Wave Café, this
place attracts coffee aficionados, who come for the fresh-roasted coffee (the restaurant will ship its blends) and gladly indulge in the
fresh-baked muffins and bagels, salads, and homemade Italian
soups. For late risers, breakfast is served until 3 PM. *22 Washington
Sq., tel. 401/846–6060. No reservations. MC, V. Inexpensive–Moderate.*

Franklin Spa. Omelets, shepherd's pie, and turkey sandwiches star
on the menu of this neighborhood luncheonette that looks as though
it's been preserved in a 1950s time capsule. *229 Spring St., tel. 401/
847–3540. No reservations. No credit cards. Inexpensive.*

Gary's Handy Lunch. Come to this fisherman's hangout—its long
counter lined with chrome stools—for homemade soup, BLT sandwiches, and delicious fresh-brewed coffee. *462 Thames St., tel. 401/
847–9480. No reservations. No credit cards. No dinner. Inexpensive.*

Continental
★
White Horse Tavern. Supposedly the nation's oldest operating tavern, the White Horse offers a setting conducive to intimate dining.
Lobster and beef Wellington are served here, along with more exotic
entrées such as honey-and-cinnamon roast duckling and Thai
poached shrimp. The food is fine—but what you're really paying for
is the historical ambience of the tavern. On Sunday there's a champagne brunch. *Marlborough and Farewell Sts., tel. 401/849–3600.
Reservations required. Jacket required. No lunch Tues. AE, D, DC,
MC, V. Expensive.*

French
La Petite Auberge. This romantic Colonial home offers exquisite
French cuisine in intimate rooms with lace tablecloths; in summer,
you can dine on the patio. The colorful, feisty, owner-chef (once the
maître d' for General de Gaulle) prepares such delicacies as trout
with almonds, duck flambé with orange sauce, and medallions of
beef with goose liver pâté. *19 Charles St., tel. 401/849–6669. Reservations advised. AE, MC, V. Expensive.*

Le Bistro. This chic haven on Newport's busy waterfront produces

French country cuisine in a friendly, informal atmosphere. The third floor offers the best harbor views. Enjoy such specialties as grilled duck with figs, fillet of sole meunière, and roast rack of lamb. The less expensive luncheon menu features soups, fancy sandwiches, salads, and pizza. *Bowen's Wharf, tel. 401/849–7778. Reservations advised. AE, D, DC, MC, V. Expensive.*

Italian   **Puerini's.** The aroma of garlic and basil greets you as soon as you enter this friendly neighborhood restaurant with soft-pink walls covered with black-and-white photographs of Italy and lace curtains on the windows. The long and intriguing menu presents such selections as green noodles with chicken in marsala wine sauce; tortellini with seafood; and cavatelli in four cheeses. An expansion of the upstairs dining room has eased the summer wait for tables. Smoking is not allowed. *24 Memorial Blvd., tel. 401/847–5506. No reservations. No lunch. Closed Mon. in winter. No credit cards. Moderate.*

Seafood   **Anthony's Seafood & Shore Dinner Hall.** The large, light room with the panoramic views of Newport Harbor is a cafeteria-style restaurant serving lobsters, fried clams, fish-and-chips, and other seafood at reasonable prices. Families find the atmosphere congenial. The adjoining seafood shop sells fresh specialties. *Lower Thames St., at Waites Wharf, tel. 401/848–5058. No reservations. AE, MC, V. Closed Dec.–Mar.; Mon.–Wed. Oct–Nov. Moderate.*

★   **The Lobster Pot.** A glass wall provides a view looking onto Narragansett Bay, and the menu offers grilled lobster, crab cakes, and smelt. Meat and chicken dishes are also on the menu, but people come here for the freshness of the fish. *119–121 Hope St., Bristol, tel. 401/253–9100. Reservations advised. AE, MC, V. Closed Mon.; Feb. Moderate.*

The Moorings. In fine weather, dine on the enclosed patio overlooking the yachts moored in the harbor; on chilly winter evenings take advantage of the open fire in the sunken interior room. The menu ranges from meats to seafood, and lobster lovers find this crustacean delectable and reasonably priced. *Sayer's Wharf, tel. 401/846–2260. Reservations accepted on weekdays. AE, D, DC, MC, V. Moderate.*

★   **Salas'.** Movie posters, red-and-white plastic tablecloths, and lines of waiting customers create a lively, good-natured waterfront dining spot that is great for families. Pastas, lobster, clams, and corn-on-the-cob are the principal fare. Spaghetti and macaroni are served by the ¼, ½, and full pound. In the summer there's a raw bar and dining room on the ground floor, and quieter dining upstairs; in winter only the upstairs stays open. *341 Thames St., tel. 401/846–8772. No reservations. AE, DC, MC, V. Moderate.*

Lodging

Expensive–   **Cliffside Inn.** Near Newport's Cliff Walk and downtown, on a quiet,
Very   tree-lined street, this elegant 1880 Victorian home offers an atmos-
Expensive   phere of grandeur and comfort. The wide front porch has a view of the lawn, the foyer is welcoming and dramatic, and the tastefully appointed rooms—filled with Victorian antiques and some with bay windows—are light and airy. Annette and Norbert Mede bought the inn in January 1992 and have been refurbishing ever since: One room in the attic has a cathedral ceiling, skylights, and a king-size bed, plus a bathroom lined with mirrors and a whirlpool bath. Five other rooms also have whirlpool baths, and five have working fireplaces. *2 Seaview Ave., 02840, tel. 401/847–1811 or 800/845–1811. 12 rooms with bath. Facilities: porch, meeting area. Full breakfast included. AE, D, DC, MC, V.*

The Inntowne. This small town-house hotel is in the center of Newport and 1½ blocks from the harbor. Another plus is the staff's personal attention; they greet you warmly on your arrival and are on hand throughout the day to give sightseeing advice. The neatly appointed rooms are decorated in floral motifs with low-hung pictures; light sleepers may prefer rooms on the upper floors, which let in less traffic noise. *6 Mary St., 02840, tel. 401/846–9200, fax 401/846–1534. 26 rooms, 25 with bath. Facilities: parking for a nominal fee (free in off-season). Continental breakfast and afternoon tea included. AE, MC, V.*

The Marriott. The luxury hotel on the harbor at Long Wharf has an atrium lobby with marble floors and a gazebo. Rooms, bordering the atrium or overlooking the skyline or the water, are decorated in mauve and seafoam, with either a king-size bed or two double beds. Fifth-floor rooms facing the harbor have sliding French windows opening onto a large deck. Rates vary greatly according to season and to whether your room overlooks the harbor. The visitors bureau is right next door. *25 America's Cup Ave., 02840, tel. 401/849–1000 or 800/228–9290, fax 401/849–3422. 307 rooms, 12 suites. Facilities: restaurant, lounge, disco, indoor pool, outdoor sundeck, sauna, racquetball, health club, Jacuzzi, conference rooms, parking. AE, D, DC, MC, V.*

Moderate–Very Expensive
★

The Francis Malbone House. The design of this stately whitewashed 1760 house is attributed to the architect responsible for the Touro Synagogue and the Redwood Library. Beautifully restored with highly polished original wide-plank flooring, the inn is furnished in period reproductions. Guest rooms are large, have a corner position (with two windows), and face either the garden or across the street to the harbor. The suite is on the ground floor with its own entrance from Thames Street and from the garden. For lounging, guests have three salons. Breakfast is served in a country-style kitchen. *392 Thames St., Newport 02840, tel. 401/846–0392. 8 rooms with bath, 1 suite. Facilities: 6 rooms with working fireplaces. Full breakfast and afternoon tea included. AE, MC, V.*

★ **The Inn at Castle Hill.** Perched on an oceanside cliff 3 miles from the center of Newport and close to the Bellevue mansions, this rambling inn was built as a summer home in 1874, and much of the original furniture remains. Despite some recent refurbishments and an enthusiastic staff, the inn remains a bit shabby and could use further renovation. Nevertheless, bookings well in advance are necessary. The public areas have tremendous charm, and the views over the bay are enthralling. The inn is famous for its Sunday brunches—be sure to reserve ahead. *Ocean Dr., 02840, tel. 401/849–3800. 10 rooms, 7 with bath. Facilities: restaurant (closed Nov.–Mar.), 3 private beaches. Continental breakfast included. AE, MC, V.*

★ **Ivy Lodge.** The only bed-and-breakfast in the mansion district, this grand Victorian (small by Newport's standards but mansionesque anywhere else) bristles with gables and a Gothic turret. Inside, the rooms are large, lovely, and private, but even the brass and four poster beds, clawfoot tubs, window seats, and glorious antiques pale beside the home's greatest feature: a 33-foot gothic paneled oak entry with a three-story turned baluster staircase. A fire burns brightly on fall and winter afternoons in the huge brick fireplace shaped like a Moorish arch. *12 Clay St., 02840, tel. 401/849–6865. 10 rooms, 8 with bath. Facilities: parlor, parking. Full breakfast included. AE, MC, V.*

Victorian Ladies. This bed-and-breakfast is sumptuously decorated with Victorian antiques and is within walking distance of Newport's shops. Bedrooms have either pencil four-poster, brass, or rice beds—all with down quilts. Windows are trimmed with lace curtains and balloon shades. Most rooms have pedestal sinks. The house's insulation muffles the city's sounds significantly. *63 Memorial Blvd., 02840, tel. 401/849–9960. 11 rooms with bath. Facilities: off-street parking. Full breakfast included. MC, V.*

Moderate   **Newport Islander Doubletree Hotel.** Set on Goat Island, just across from the Colonial Point District, the Doubletree has great views of the harbor and Newport Bridge. About 80% of the rooms have water views. There's free parking, and although it's a 15-minute walk to Newport's center, bike and moped rentals are nearby. In 1992, all rooms were renovated with oak furnishings and multicolor jewel-tone fabrics. *Goat Island, 02840, tel. 401/849–2600 or 800/528–0444, fax 401/846–7210. 250 rooms. Facilities: 2 restaurants, indoor and outdoor pools, health center, sauna, beauty salon, tennis, racquetball, marina, conference rooms. AE, D, DC, MC, V.*

Inexpensive   **Harbor Base Pineapple Inn.** This basic, clean motel is about the least expensive lodging in Newport. All rooms, decorated in shades of blue, contain two double beds. Close to the Navy Base and Jai Alai, it's a five-minute drive from downtown. *372 Coddington Hwy., 02840, tel. 401/847–2600. 48 rooms. Facilities: some efficiencies. AE, D, DC, MC, V.*

The Arts

Newport County Convention and Visitors Bureau (23 America's Cup Ave., tel. 401/849–8048 or 800/326–6030) has listings of concerts, shows, and special events, as do the Newport and Providence newspapers.

Theater   Murder-mystery plays are performed Thursday evening July–October at the **Astors' Beechwood mansion** (580 Bellevue Ave., tel. 401/846–3772). **Rhode Island Shakespeare Theater** (tel. 401/849–7892) performs classic plays at several spaces in Newport.

Nightlife

Clark Cooke House (Bannister's Wharf, tel. 401/849–2900) has two discos (daily in summer, weekends off-season), one downstairs and another upstairs overlooking the harbor. **Thames Street Station** (337 America's Cup Ave., tel. 401/849–9480) plays high-energy dance music and videos and offers live progressive rock bands Monday through Thursday in summer. **David's** (28 Prospect Hill St., tel. 401/847–9698) is a mainly gay bar with a DJ daily in season and weekends in winter.

Block Island

Situated 13 miles off the coast, Block Island's 11-square-mile area has been a popular tourist destination since the 19th century. Despite the large number of visitors who come here each summer, the island's beauty and privacy have been preserved; its 365 freshwater ponds make it a haven for more than 150 species of migrating birds.

Block Island's original inhabitants were the Native Americans who called it Manisses, or Isle of the Little God. In 1524 Verrazano renamed it Claudia, after the mother of the French king. Revisited in 1614 by the Dutch explorer Adrian Block, the island was given the name Adrian's Eyelant, which later became Block Island. In 1661 the island was settled by colonists seeking religious freedom; they established a farming and fishing community that still exists today.

Most tourism here occurs between May and September—at other times, the majority of restaurants, inns, stores, and visitor services close down.

Important Addresses and Numbers

Visitor **Block Island Chamber of Commerce** (Drawer D, Water St., 02807,
Information tel. 401/466–2982; open Apr.–mid-Oct., daily 10–5; mid-Oct.–Mar., Mon.–Sat. 10–4). A second tourist information booth at the Old Harbor opens for ferry arrivals.

Arriving and Departing by Plane

New England Airlines (tel. 401/596–2460 or 800/243–2460) provides air service from Westerly State Airport to Block Island. **Action Air** (tel. 203/448–1646 or 800/243–8623) has flights from Groton, Connecticut, to Block Island from June through October. Several hotels run courtesy vans from the airport. Taxis are also available (*see* By Taxi, *below*).

Arriving and Departing by Car and Ferry

Interstate Navigation Co. (Galilee State Pier, Point Judith, tel. 401/ 783–4613) has ferry service from Galilee (1 hr, 10 min; make auto reservations well in advance) and passenger boats from Providence via Newport. Passengers cannot make reservations but should arrive 45 minutes ahead in high season as the boats do fill up.

From Montauk, Long Island (NY), the *Jigger III* (tel. 516/668–2214) has passenger ferry service (2 hrs.), June–September, and **Viking Ferry Lines** (tel. 516/668–5709) has passenger and bicycle service (1 hr., 45 min), mid-May–mid-October.

Nelseco Navigation (tel. 203/442–7891) runs an auto ferry from New London, Connecticut (2 hrs.), in summer; reservations are advised.

Getting Around Block Island

By Car Because most inns, restaurants, and shops are in or near the Old Harbor area, and bicycling to any point on the island is a joy, there's no need to have a car. If you do want to rent one, try **Block Island Car Rental** (tel. 401/466–2297).

By Bicycle The best way to cover the island effectively *and* make the most of its
and Moped natural beauty is by bicycle or moped. **The Sea Crest Inn** (tel. 401/ 466–2882; bikes only), **Esta's at Old Harbor** (tel. 401/466–2651), **Old Harbor Bike Shop** (tel. 401/466–2029), **Block Island Boat Basin** (tel. 401/466–2631), and **Moped Man** (tel. 401/466–5011) have rentals: Bikes cost about $15 per day, mopeds about $40, and most places have child seats for bikes. Most rental places close at summer's end; Moped Man is open through October. Operating a motorcycle between midnight and 6 AM is forbidden, and mopeds are prohibited on dirt roads.

By Taxi Taxis are plentiful at both the Old Harbor and New Harbor ferry landings. The island's dispatch services include **O. J. Berlin** (tel. 401/ 466–2872), **A. Ernst Taxi** (tel. 401/466–7739), and **Wolfie's Taxi** (tel. 401/466–5550).

Exploring Block Island

Numbers in the margin correspond to points of interest on the Block Island map.

Block Island has two harbors, Old Harbor and New Harbor. The Old Harbor commercial district extends along Water and Dodge streets. Approaching Block Island by sea from Newport or Point Judith, you'll see the Old Harbor and its group of Victorian hotels.

The Old Harbor area is the island's only village. A concentration of shops, boutiques, restaurants, inns, and hotels, it's a short walk from the ferry landing and near most of the interesting sights of Block Island.

1 Begin at the **Block Island Historical Society,** where permanent and special exhibits have described the island's farming and maritime past since the society opened in 1942. You'll be given a short introduction to the house (an 1850 structure with a mansard roof, furnished with many original pieces), and then you may look around on your own; the house is well worth a visit. *Old Town Rd., tel. 401/466–2481 or 401/466–5009. Admission: $2 adults, $1 senior citizens and children. Open July–Aug., daily 10–4; June and Sept., weekends 10–4.*

Head east on Old Town Road, and a short walk north on Corn Neck Road brings you to a string of beautiful beaches known collectively
2 as **Crescent Beach.** The Fredrick J. Benson Town Beach, in the middle of Crescent Beach, is patrolled by lifeguards and good for a
3 swim. Continue north on Corn Neck Road to find the **Clay Head Nature Trail,** leading first to the east, where you'll hike along oceanside cliffs, then to the north. Meander down side trails for the best views and wildlife spotting. Guided tours are available in summer.

If you follow the trail to its end (or take Corn Neck Rd. north to its
4 end), you'll find the stone of **Settler's Rock** on the shores of Chaqum Pond. Erected in 1911, the stone lists the names of the original settlers and marks the spot where they first landed in 1661. On this narrow strip of land straddling the pond and Rhode Island Sound, there's a sense of openness and quietness.

5 Walk along the sand to the **North Light** at Sandy Point, the northernmost tip of Block Island. Built in 1867 of Connecticut granite hauled across the island to the site by oxen, it was restored and opened as a maritime museum in 1993. *Admission: $2. Open July–Aug., daily 10–4; June and Sept., weekends 10–4.*

Follow Corn Neck Road all the way back to town, turn right onto
6 Beach Avenue and then right again onto Ocean Avenue. **New Harbor,** on the inland side of the Great Salt Pond, provides safe anchor for the many small craft that call at Block Island and is the arrival and departure point for the ferry from Montauk. The harbor also has a few shops and marina facilities.

Turn right off Ocean Avenue onto West Side Road and climb to the
7 top of Job's Hill. Here the **Block Island Historical Cemetery** houses the remains of island residents since the 1700s. Not only will you recognize the names of quite a few longstanding Block Island families (Ball, Rose, Champlin) at this well-maintained, sprawling cemetery, you'll also get a wonderful view of New Harbor and Great Salt Pond.

Continue on West Side Road for about 2 miles, and make a left onto
8 Cherry Hill Road. Down the road on your right is **Rodmans Hollow,**

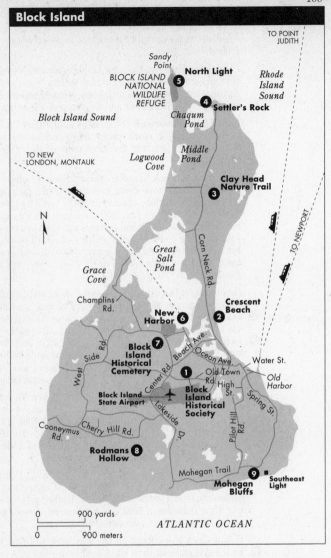

Block Island

TO POINT JUDITH

Sandy Point

North Light

BLOCK ISLAND NATIONAL WILDLIFE REFUGE

Rhode Island Sound

Settler's Rock

Chaqum Pond

Block Island Sound

Middle Pond

Logwood Cove

TO NEW LONDON, MONTAUK

Clay Head Nature Trail

Corn Neck Rd.

TO NEWPORT

Great Salt Pond

Grace Cove

Champlins Rd.

New Harbor

Crescent Beach

Block Island Historical Cemetery

Beach Ave.

Ocean Ave.

Water St.

West Side Rd.

Center Rd.

Old Town Rd.

Block Island Historical Society

Old Harbor

Block Island State Airport

High St.

Spring St.

Lakeside Dr.

Cherry Hill Rd.

Pilot Hill Rd.

Cooneymus Rd.

Rodmans Hollow

Mohegan Trail

Mohegan Bluffs

Southeast Light

0   900 yards
0   900 meters

ATLANTIC OCEAN

one of Block Island's five wildlife refuges and a natural wonder: a ravine formed by a glacier. You can follow the deep cleft in the hills along many winding paths all the way down to the ocean; then have a picnic on the rocky beach, beneath sandstone cliffs, as you watch the boats go by.

Follow Cherry Hill Road east and turn right onto Lakeside Drive. Next turn left onto and follow the Mohegan Trail to the southern tip of the island, the top of **Mohegan Bluffs**. Here you'll get dramatic ocean views, and you'll see the **Southeast Light**, a redbrick building with gingerbread detail built in 1873. Originally surrounded by fields, the lighthouse was repositioned by erosion and sat precariously close to the edge of a 200-foot cliff until 1993, when it was moved to a safer location away from the precipice.

Continue east toward Old Harbor along South East Light Road and then Spring Street. This peaceful walk yields beautiful views wherever you look: to your right, rocky coastline and dark blue ocean, punctuated by jetties; inland, lush, rolling green lawns sprinkled with lovely private homes, behind old low stone walls and white picket fences.

What to See and Do with Children

The owners of the 1661 Inn and Hotel Manisses run a small **Animal Farm,** with a collection of llamas, emus, cows, goats, ducks, and the like coexisting happily in a large meadow next to the hotel. Tourists are free to view or pet the animals. *Spring St., tel. 401/466–2063. Admission free. Open dawn–dusk.*

Shopping

General Stores   **Esta's at Old Harbor** (Water St., tel. 401/466–2651) has art supplies and video rentals as well as resort wear, sun products, beach supplies, and souvenirs. **Star Department Store** (Water St., tel. 401/466–5541), the self-proclaimed "general store of Block Island," stocks saltwater taffy, film, toys, gifts, shoes, hats, sportswear, and the island's largest selection of T-shirts and sweatshirts.

Specialty   **Block Island Blue Pottery** (Dodge St., tel. 401/466–2945; closed win-
Stores   ter), true to its name, sells handmade bowls, mugs, pins, and wind
Art and Crafts   chimes—mostly in blue. The shop is housed in a 1790 building with a central brick chimney. **Ragged Sailor** (Water St., tel. 401/466–7704) shows paintings, crafts, porcelain, folk art, and photographs. **The Red Herring** (Water St., tel. 401/466–2540), on the second floor of **The Shoreline** (the two stores share the same owner), sells distinctive folk art and crafts—pottery, jewelry, home furnishings—much of which is made by local artists. **Scarlet Begonia** (Dodge St., tel. 401/466–5024) offers unusual jewelry, and crafts (including place mats and handmade quilts; closed winter). **Spring Street Gallery** (Spring St., tel. 401/466–5374), an artist's cooperative, shows and sells hand-knit baby clothing, stained glass, serigraphs, and other work of island artists and craftspeople.

Books   **The Book Nook** (Water St., tel. 401/466–2993) stocks paperbacks (mostly beach reading, with a few more substantial contemporary titles thrown in, plus a rack of classics and a children's section), posters, magazines, and newspapers.

Irish Imports   **Island House, the Irish Shoppe** (Water St., tel. 401/466–2309), specializes in imported Irish merchandise, hand-knit sweaters, jewelry, and cassettes of Irish music.

Water-Sports   **Block Island Boatworks & Block Island Kite Co.** (Corn Neck Rd., tel.
Gear   401/466–2033) occupies two buildings, one filled with boogie boards and kites, the other with snorkeling gear, bathing suits, casual clothing, and fine garden furniture.

Women's   **The Shoreline** (Water St., tel. 401/466–2541; Fish Head Bldg., Ocean
Clothing   Ave., tel. 401/466–5800) on Water Street has contemporary clothing by Patagonia, Esprit, Kiko, Cambridge Dry Goods, and B. D. Baggies. The branch in the Fish Head Building stocks rugged sportswear, beachwear, and surfboards. (Both closed weekdays, Oct.–Apr.)

Sports and Outdoor Activities

Boating **Block Island Boat Basin** (tel. 401/466–2631) and **Captain John Neill** (tel. 201/337–7929) offer charters. **Block Island Club** (tel. 401/466–5939) rents sailboats. **Oceans & Ponds** (tel. 401/466–5131) rents and sells kayaks and canoes. **Twin Maples** (tel. 401/466–5547) has rowboats for rent.

Fishing **Oceans & Ponds** (tel. 401/466–5131) offers charters. Shellfishing without a license is illegal; licenses may be obtained at the police station.

Water Sports Sailboard rentals and lessons are available from **Island Moped** (tel. 401/466–2700) and **Oceans & Ponds** (tel. 401/466–5131).

Dining

Dress is casual.

★ **Manisses.** Dine inside by the long oak bar, which once graced a Boston waterfront establishment; under the canopy on the outdoor deck; or in the glassed-in garden terrace. Try the smoked fish or meats from the smokehouse, or enjoy the raw bar for an appetizer. Main courses include local seafood and beef, pork, and veal dishes. Pasta and light fare such as gourmet pizzas and littleneck clams Dijonnaise are also featured. Fresh vegetables are grown in the hotel's garden, and delicious homemade desserts are prepared by the pastry chef. *Spring St., tel. 401/466–2421. Reservations advised. AE, MC, V. Closed Nov. 1–May 14, Mon.–Thurs. No lunch. Very Expensive.*

★ **Ballard's Inn.** The place to go for lobster, Italian food, or family-style dinners, this noisy, lively spot caters especially to the boating crowd. The enormous dining room has flags from around the world hanging from the ceiling among the wood rafters, and the waiters are just as informal and quirky as the decor. Come here if you're looking for a place to polka. *Old Harbor, tel. 401/466–2231. MC, V. Closed mid-Oct.–May. Moderate.*

Finn's Seafood Bar. Eat inside or out on the deck, which offers a panoramic view of the harbor. The smoked bluefish pâté is wonderful. A popular lunch order is the Workman's Special platter—a burger, coleslaw, and french fries. Take-out orders are also available. *Ferry Landing, tel. 401/466–5391. No reservations. AE, MC, V. Closed mid-Oct.–May. Moderate.*

Harborside Inn. This cheerful and noisy restaurant in the heart of town features excellent, fresh native seafood, as well as steaks, and an extensive salad bar. Order the scallops sautéed in butter or the lobster, swordfish, or steak, and enjoy the view of the harbor from the pleasant, bustling outdoor terrace. *Water St., tel. 401/466–5504. Reservations advised. AE, MC, V. Closed Nov.–Apr. Moderate.*

The BeacHead. This is a favorite local spot where you can play pool, catch up on local gossip, or sit at the bar and stare out at the sea. Food and service is unpretentious—burgers come on paper plates with potato chips and pickles—but the food is satisfying, the price is right, and you won't feel like a tourist. The spicy chili is also a good bet. *Corn Neck Rd., tel. 401/466–2249. No reservations. No credit cards. No dinner in winter. Inexpensive.*

Old Harbor Take-out. This is a great place to stop for lunch or a snack when taking a break from the beach or exploring the Old Harbor area. Orders are placed at the roadside shanty, and seating is outdoors, overlooking the ferry dock, at blue picnic tables with big blue umbrellas. The light, fresh sandwiches are a cut above the usual take-out fare, and the clam chowder is packed with big chunks of juicy clams. This place offers the best value in the Old Harbor district. *Water St., tel. 401/466–2935. No reservations. No credit cards. Closed Oct.–May. Inexpensive.*

Lodging

★ **1661 Inn and Guest House.** If you're celebrating a special occasion, choose the 1661 Inn and splurge for the Edwards Room, an enormous, luxurious, split-level suite with a Jacuzzi in the loft, a king-size canopy bed, and a huge private terrace with spectacular views of marshes, swans, and the sea beyond. This is one of New England's loveliest inns, and all the guest rooms, named for the settlers of 1661, are exquisite. Decorated in pastel shades with thick carpets, they contain Victorian antiques and four-poster or canopy beds; some are huge and have decks or Jacuzzis. Across the small parking lot, the Nicholas Ball cottage, a replica of St. Ann's Church (blown down in the hurricane of 1938), houses three split-level rooms, each with a fireplace and a Jacuzzi. A motel-style room in the adjacent 1661 Inn Guest House might be your best option if the kids tend to demolish Victorian antiques (though children are welcome). A sumptuous buffet breakfast—bluefish, Boston baked beans, and Belgian waffles—is served in the dining room or outdoors on a canopied deck. *Spring St., 02807, tel. 401/466–2421, fax 401/466–2858. 21 rooms, 19 with bath. Facilities: picnic lunches, playground, parking, island tours. AE, MC, V. Full breakfast and afternoon tea included. Inn closed mid-Nov.–mid-Apr.; guest house and cottage open year-round. Expensive–Very Expensive.*

Atlantic Inn. Built in 1879, the Atlantic Inn is a long, white, classic, gray-roofed Victorian resort that bravely fronts the elements on a hill above the ocean (and that is duly rewarded with panoramic views of the sunset, the harbor, beaches, and bluffs). Big windows, high ceilings, and a sweeping staircase contribute to the breezy atmosphere. Guest rooms are lined up on long, straight hallways. The inn is furnished with turn-of-the-century furniture, much of it golden oak. The generally austere feel of the place is softened by predominantly pastel colors, and the large pink-and-white dining room displays local artwork, which rotates seasonally. The restful ambience accords well with the bracing effect of the clean ocean air. The inn welcomes children and has a wooden swing set and model of the hotel. *Box 188, High St., 02807, tel. 401/466–5883, fax 401/466–5678. 21 rooms with bath. Facilities: restaurant, tennis, croquet, playground, meeting facilities. Continental breakfast included. AE, MC, V. Closed Nov.–Easter. Expensive.*

Hotel Manisses. This 1870 mansion was fully restored by the Abrams family in the 1970s. Many of the rooms, named after famous shipwrecks, are filled with unusual Victorian pieces, such as the multilevel bureau in the Princess Augusta Room, and intriguing knickknacks occupy every available bit of space. Some small rooms are almost overpowered by the furniture—if you prefer light and airy to dark and formal, stay at the Abrams's other property, the nearby 1661 Inn (*see above*). The many extras include afternoon tea in a romantic parlor overlooking the garden, a copious buffet breakfast (served at the 1661 Inn), picnic baskets, gourmet cooking, and an animal farm with llamas, emus, geese, and a donkey (*see* What to See and Do with Children, *above*)! *Box 1, Spring St., 02807, tel. 401/ 466–2063, fax 401/466–2858. 17 rooms with bath. Facilities: restaurant, ceiling fans, Jacuzzi in some rooms. Full breakfast and afternoon tea included. AE, MC, V. Expensive.*

Rose Farm Inn. Just outside the village of Old Harbor, next to the

Atlantic Inn, Rose Farm is convenient to downtown and the beaches. The wallpapered rooms are furnished with antiques, and all have views. Porch and sundeck offer society and relaxation. In July 1993 the owners opened the Captain Rose House, across the driveway, with nine more rooms, four of which boast Jacuzzi tubs. *Box E, Roslyn Rd., 02807, tel. 401/466–2021, fax 401/466–2053. 17 rooms with bath, 2 share 1 bath. Buffet breakfast included. AE, MC, V. Closed mid-Oct.–Apr. Moderate–Very Expensive.*

Sea Breeze Inn. A few minutes' walk from Old Harbor, on a hill overlooking the ocean, the Sea Breeze comprises a cluster of renovated shingle-style cottages and a more weathered main house, also shingle-style. The individually decorated cottage rooms, distinguished by cathedral ceilings, are not huge but are spotless, bright, and airy. They have an island feel, created by colorful bedspreads, rugs, and upholstery; brass beds or beds with carved-wood headboards; polished pine floors; blond-wood interior shutters; and contemporary art. Rooms in the main house have been thoughtfully decorated in a similar style but are smaller, more modest, and share baths. *Spring St., 02807, tel. 401/466–2275 or 800/786–2276. 10 rooms, 5 share baths. Continental breakfast included. MC, V. Moderate–Very Expensive.*

Blue Dory Inn. This restored hotel, with three small additional houses, is decorated with Victorian-era antiques. Rooms are not large, but each is tastefully furnished and has either an ocean or harbor view. The small, cozy living room has a wood steamer trunk, small writing desk, and lots of books and magazines; the window, looking out to the street, has white lace curtains. Continental breakfast is served each morning in a homey kitchen facing the ocean; the inn is open year-round. *Box 488, Dodge St., 02807, tel. 401/466–2254. 14 rooms with bath. Continental breakfast included. AE, MC, V. Moderate–Expensive.*

National Hotel. This classic Block Island hotel has been renovated throughout and the original furniture of the guest rooms restored. The front porch commands a view of Old Harbor and the Atlantic Ocean and is the setting for breakfast, lunch, and afternoon cocktails. Indoors, the dining room offers seafood and entertainment. The hotel's central location makes it fairly busy, especially during high season; you won't find the tranquillity that some seek for a romantic getaway weekend (especially if your room is above the bar). The spare, motellike rooms (all with cable TV and phones) have no character, but the front ones do have nice ocean views. Probably not your first choice, but a good standby. *Box 189, Water St., 02807, tel. 401/466–2901 or 800/225–2449, fax 401/466–5948. 44 rooms with bath. Facilities: restaurant, bar with live entertainment, gift shop. Closed Nov.–Mar. AE, MC, V. Moderate–Expensive.*

Surf Hotel. This hotel seems to have changed very little over the years; it's not hard to imagine what the Surf was like when it first opened, in 1876. The lobby, a study in cheerful chaos, has dark blue floral wallpaper, white lace curtains, a birdcage with chirping residents, card tables, a chess set, TV, shelves of books, and red-leather armchairs and couches. Rooms are simply furnished with Victorian antiques and ceiling fans, and, with Crescent Beach at the back door, back rooms have terrific ocean views (front rooms have harbor views). The spacious front porch with rockers overlooks Old Harbor, and decks in back let you take in the ocean. Only the three guest rooms in the annex have private baths; other rooms, lining long corridors, share dormitory-style bathrooms, but no one seems to mind. *Box C, Dodge St., 02807, tel. 401/466–2241. 38 rooms, 3 with bath. Facilities: barbecue grills. Continental breakfast included. Closed mid-Oct.–Apr. MC, V. Inexpensive–Moderate.*

Nightlife

The National Hotel (Water St., tel. 401/466–2901) has live music in the bar every evening in summer and Saturday nights off-season. **McGovern's Yellow Kittens Tavern** (Corn Neck Rd., tel. 401/466–5855), established in 1876, features live music, with reggae, rock, and R & B bands every night in season.

5 Massachusetts

By Anne
Merewood
and Candice
Gianetti, with
an introduc-
tion by
William G.
Scheller

The author of
two travel
guides to
Greece, Anne
Merewood
writes
frequently on
health and
travel for
major
American
magazines.

Updated by
Susan Bain,
Tara
Hamilton,
and Anne
Merewood

Americans tend to see Massachusetts not just as postcard views of pretty villages and Beacon Hill streetscapes, but as a center of social and political thought. Conservatives derisively call it the People's Republic of Massachusetts; liberals remember it fondly as the only state to vote for George McGovern in the presidential election of 1972. At the same time, the commonwealth is often stereotyped as a bastion of reactionaries, of thin-lipped Yankees who banned books and condemned Sacco and Vanzetti in the 1920s. Yet the image of puritanical rectitude is accompanied by memories of the roguish Boston mayor James Michael Curley, who for most of the first half of this century ran a crony-ridden fiefdom as reform-proof as any Chicago machine.

Unlike the other New England states, Massachusetts is populous enough, rich enough, and influential enough to conceive of itself as playing a substantial role in the scheme of the nation—and to trouble itself over just what that role might be. For generations the Bay State has amounted to something of a national resource, offering brains and conscience in much the same way that the desert yields borax or the Pacific Northwest contributes salmon and logs. (Massachusetts once had marketable supplies of salmon and logs, too, but they ran out years ago.) Great eras of shipping, manufacturing, high technology, investment banking, and insurance have followed one upon the other in the centuries since the first settlers built an economy based on primary resources, and throughout all these epochs ideas have been Massachusetts's greatest stock-in-trade.

The list of Massachusetts men and women who have helped to define American culture—either as builders of a mainstream consensus or as often-cantankerous consciences of the nation—is long indeed. The short list would have to include Cotton Mather, Anne Hutchinson, Benjamin Franklin (even though he moved to Philadelphia early in his career), John Adams, William Ellery Channing, Ralph Waldo Emerson, Henry David Thoreau, Margaret Fuller, Nathaniel Hawthorne, William Lloyd Garrison, Henry Adams, Francis Parkman, Oliver Wendell Holmes, Samuel Eliot Morison, and John F. Kennedy.

How could one small state, even if it is one of the oldest in the Union, have produced so many citizens who made such a difference in our national life? The easiest answer, and perhaps the one most often put forward, is education: Massachusetts has more than a hundred institutions of higher learning, surmounted by the twin pinnacles of Harvard University and the Massachusetts Institute of Technology. Even more important, it has a long tradition of deeply valuing education at all levels, a tradition that dates to the Puritan founders of the Bay Colony.

Yet education alone did not create this galaxy of memorable individuals. Having a hundred colleges and universities is all very well, but the rigor of debate is what has kept Massachusetts intellectually vital, and we honor its heroes not only for what they knew but for the ways in which they often challenged received wisdom. Massachusetts has always been a fertile ground for intellectual controversy, a place where contentious people have had at each other with all the erudition and moral ardor they could muster. In the beginning it was hard-line Calvinists against the theologically unorthodox who in later generations would spark the Unitarian and Transcendentalist movements. In politics the liberal, conservative, and radical elements fought their way to and through the Revolution; in its aftermath, Federalists and Democrats debated the merits of a weak versus a strong central government, the mercantile versus the agrarian control of economic policy.

The 19th century saw the great debate over slavery, and, while Massachusetts is usually remembered as a hotbed of abolitionism, powerful forces opposed the new movement in a state where fortunes had been built on the slave trade. William Lloyd Garrison, remember, was physically attacked when he spoke in Boston early in his career as an antislavery crusader. In later years the Yankees and the ascendant Irish struggled for power in a clash that was less a contest of ideas than an opposition of temperament and will.

In the end it may not matter what stamp the rest of America puts on the ideas that come out of the state. Massachusetts will live on in the national imagination as a place where people think—and where they make a lot of noise when they do.

Essential Information

Visitor Information

Massachusetts Office of Travel and Tourism (100 Cambridge St., Boston 02202, tel. 617/727–3201 or 800/447–6277).

Package Deals for Independent Travelers

Amtrak (tel. 800/321–8684) offers a Boston package including hotels and a city tour.

Arriving and Departing

By Plane Boston's **Logan International Airport,** the largest airport in New England, has scheduled flights by most major domestic and foreign carriers.

Bradley International Airport, in Windsor Locks, Connecticut, 18 miles south of Springfield on I–91, has scheduled flights by major U.S. airlines.

Hyannis's **Barnstable Municipal Airport** is Cape Cod's air gateway, with flights from **Business Express/Delta Connection** (tel. 800/345–3400), **Cape Air** (tel. 800/352–0714), **Nantucket Airlines** (tel. 508/790–0300 or 800/635–8787), and **Northwest Airlink** (tel. 800/225–2525). **Provincetown Municipal Airport** is served by **Cape Air.**

Martha's Vineyard Airport is served by **Cape Air** and **Continental Express** (tel. 800/525–0280). **Nantucket Memorial Airport** is served by all the above-mentioned airlines, as well as **Island Airlines** (tel. 508/775–6606 or 800/248–7779) and **Nantucket Airlines** (tel. 508/790–0300 or 800/635–8787).

By Car Boston is the traffic hub of New England, with interstate highways approaching it from every direction and every major city in the northeast. New England's chief coastal highway, I–95, skirts Boston, while I–90 leads west to the Great Lakes and Chicago. Interstate 91 brings visitors to the Pioneer Valley in western Massachusetts from Vermont and Canada in the north and Connecticut and New York to the south.

By Train **Amtrak's Northeast Corridor** service (tel. 800/872–7245) links Boston with principal cities between it and Washington, DC. The *Lake Shore Limited*, which stops at Springfield and the Berkshires, carries passengers from Chicago to Boston. On summer weekends, Hyannis is served by the *Cape Codder* from New York, with connecting service to Washington, D.C., Philadelphia, and other points.

By Bus **Greyhound** (tel. 800/231–2222) and **Peter Pan Bus Lines** (tel. 800/237–8747) connect Boston and other major cities in the state with cities throughout the United States. **Bonanza** (tel. 800/556–3815) serves Boston and the eastern part of the state from Providence with connecting service to New York.

Dining

Apart from the seafood specialties that the state shares with other New England regions, Massachusetts claims fame for inventing the fried clam, a revolutionary event that apparently took place in Essex. Fried clams, therefore, appear on many North Shore menus, especially around the salt marshes of Essex and Ipswich, and on Cape Cod, where clam chowder is another specialty. Eating seafood "in the rough" (from paper plates in shacklike wooden buildings dominated by deep-fryers) is a revered local custom.

Nantucket Island has plenty of first-rate gourmet restaurants (with price tags to match), as does Brewster on the Cape. On the North Shore, Rockport is a "dry" town, though you can almost always take your own alcohol into restaurants; most places charge a nominal corking fee. This law leads to early closing hours—many Rockport dining establishments are shut by 9 PM. Martha's Vineyard also has dry towns.

Dining in the state is generally casual, except at certain inns, particularly in the Berkshires, which require formal dress at dinner.

Highly recommended restaurants are indicated by a star ★.

Category	Cost*
Very Expensive	over $40
Expensive	$25–$40
Moderate	$15–$25
Inexpensive	under $15

average cost of a three-course dinner, per person, excluding drinks, service, and 5% sales tax

Lodging

Highly recommended lodgings are indicated by a star ★.

Category	Boston, the Cape, and the Islands*	Other Areas*
Very Expensive	over $150	over $100
Expensive	$95–$150	$70–$100

Massachusetts

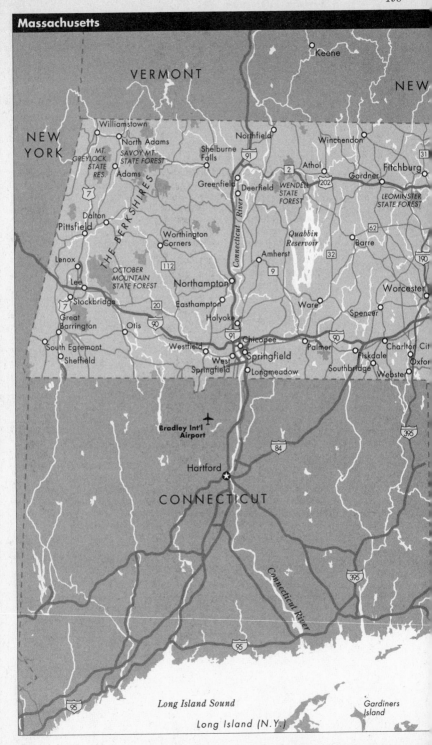

VERMONT

Keene

NEW

NEW
YORK

Williamstown

North Adams
MT.
GREYLOCK
STATE
RES.

SAVOY MT.
STATE FOREST

Shelburne
Falls

Northfield

Winchendon

Adams

Greenfield

Deerfield

WENDELL
STATE
FOREST

Athol

Gardner

Fitchburg

31

LEOMINSTER
STATE FOREST

Dalton

Pittsfield

THE BERKSHIRES

Worthington
Corners

Quabbin
Reservoir

Barre

62

190

Lenox

OCTOBER
MOUNTAIN
STATE FOREST

112

Amherst

32

Lee

Stockbridge

Northampton

20

Easthampton

9

Ware

Spencer

Worcester

Great
Barrington

Otis

Holyoke

90

Westfield

Chicopee

Palmer

Fiskdale

Charlton Cit

South Egremont

West
Springfield

Springfield

Southbridge

Oxfor

Sheffield

Longmeadow

Webster

Bradley Int'l
Airport

84

395

Hartford

CONNECTICUT

395

Connecticut River

95

Long Island Sound

Gardiners
Island

Long Island (N.Y.)

Connecticut River

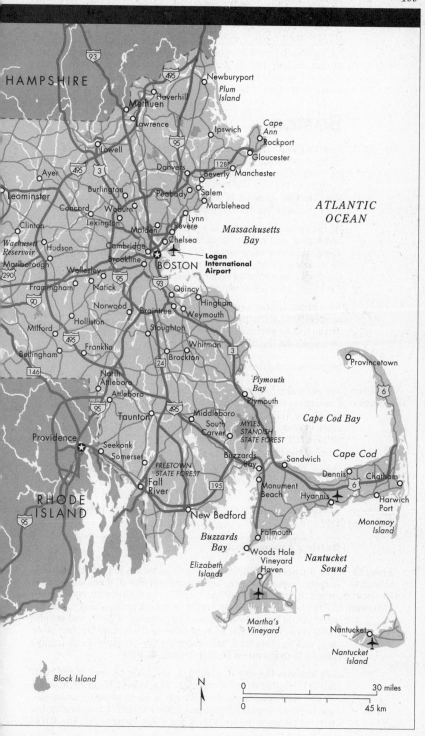

NEW HAMPSHIRE

Newburyport
Plum Island
Haverhill
Methuen
Lawrence
Ipswich
Cape Ann
Rockport
Lowell
Gloucester
Danvers
128
Manchester
Ayer
Beverly
Burlington
Peabody
Salem
Leominster
Concord
Woburn
Marblehead
Clinton
Lexington
Lynn
ATLANTIC OCEAN
Wachusett Reservoir
Hudson
Malden
Revere
Massachusetts Bay
Marlborough
Cambridge
Chelsea
290
Brookline
BOSTON
Logan International Airport
Wellesley
Framingham
Natick
Quincy
90
Norwood
Hingham
Milford
Holliston
Braintree
Weymouth
Bellingham
Franklin
Stoughton
Whitman
146
24
Brockton
3
North Attleboro
Provincetown
Attleboro
Plymouth Bay
6
Taunton
Middleboro
Plymouth
South Carver
MYLES STANDISH STATE FOREST
Cape Cod Bay
Providence
Seekonk
Buzzards Bay
Sandwich
Cape Cod
Somerset
Dennis
Chatham
FREETOWN STATE FOREST
195
Fall River
Monument Beach
6
Hyannis
Harwich Port
RHODE ISLAND
New Bedford
Monomoy Island
95
Palmouth
Buzzards Bay
Woods Hole
Nantucket Sound
Elizabeth Islands
Vineyard Haven
Martha's Vineyard
Nantucket
Nantucket Island
Block Island
N
0   30 miles
0   45 km

| Moderate | $70–$95 | $40–$70 |
| Inexpensive | under $70 | under $40 |

All prices are for a standard double room during peak season and do not include tax or gratuities. Some inns add a 15% service charge. The state tax on lodging is 5.7%; individual towns can impose an extra tax of up to 10% more.

Boston

New England's largest and most important city, the cradle of American independence, Boston is 360 years old, far older than the republic it helped to create. Its most famous buildings are not merely civic landmarks but national icons; its great citizens are not the political and financial leaders of today but the Adamses, Reveres, and Hancocks who live at the crossroads of history and myth.

At the same time, Boston is a contemporary center of high finance and higher technology, a place of granite and glass towers rising along what once were rutted village lanes. Its enormous population of students, artists, academics, and young professionals has made the town a haven for foreign movies, late-night bookstores, squash, Thai food, alternative music, and unconventional politics.

Best of all, Boston is meant for walking. Most of its historical and architectural attractions are in compact areas, and its varied and distinctive neighborhoods reveal their character and design to visitors who take the time to stroll through them.

Important Addresses and Numbers

Visitor Information For general information and brochures, contact the **Greater Boston Convention and Visitors Bureau** (Box 490, Prudential Tower, Boston 02199, tel. 617/536–4100; open Mon.–Fri. 8:30–5) or the **Boston Welcome Center** (140 Tremont St., Boston 02111, tel. 617/451–2227 or, outside MA, 800/765–4482; open daily 9–5). The latter has a second office at the Park Street subway station.

Emergencies **Police, fire, ambulance** (tel. 911); **Massachusetts General Hospital** (tel. 617/726–2000); **dental emergency** (tel. 508/651–3521); **poison control** (tel. 617/232–2120); **rape crisis center** (tel. 617/492–7273).

Late-Night Pharmacy **Phillips Drug Store** (155 Charles St., tel. 617/523–1028 or 617/523–4372).

Getting Around Boston

From the Airport to Downtown Boston Only 3 miles—and Boston Harbor—separate Logan International Airport from downtown, yet it can seem like 20 miles when you're caught in one of the many daily traffic jams at the two tunnels that go under the harbor. Boston traffic is almost always heavy, and the worst conditions prevail during the morning (6:30–9) and evening (3:30–7) rush hours. For 24-hour information on parking, bicycle access, and bus, subway, and water shuttle transport, call Logan's **Ground Transportation Desk** (tel. 800/235–6426).

Cab fare into the city is about $15, including tip; call **MASSPORT** (tel. 617/561–1919) for information. The **Airport Water Shuttle** (tel. 800/235–6426) crosses Boston Harbor in about seven minutes, running between Logan Airport and Rowes Wharf (a free shuttle bus operates between the ferry dock and airline terminals). The **MBTA**

Blue Line to Airport Station is one of the fastest ways to reach downtown from the airport (free shuttle buses connect the subway station with all airline terminals; tel. 800/235-6426). **City Transporation** (tel. 617/321-2282) is a scheduled van service that runs between Logan Airport and area hotels. If you are driving from Logan to downtown, take the Sumner Tunnel; if that's not passable, try Route 1A north to Route 16, then to the Tobin Bridge and into Boston.

By Bus   Bus, trolley, and subway service is provided by the Massachusetts Bay Transportation Authority (MBTA). The MBTA bus routes crisscross the metropolitan area and extend farther into the suburbs than those of the subways and trolleys. Fares on MBTA local buses are 60¢ for adults, 30¢ children 5-11; longer suburban bus trips cost more. For general travel information, call 617/722-3200 or 800/392-6100 (TDD 617/722-5146), weekdays 6:30 AM-11 PM, weekends 9-6; for 24-hour recorded service information, call 617/722-5050.

Visitor passes are now available for three- or seven-day periods. The fares are $9 for a three-day pass and $18 for a seven-day pass. The passes are good for unlimited travel on city buses and subways. These passes are not sold at every station, so call 617/722-3200 for a nearby location.

A free map of the entire public transportation system is available at the Park Street Station information stand (street level), open daily 7 AM-10 PM.

By Subway and Trolley   The MBTA, or "T," operates subways, elevated trains, and trolleys along four connecting lines. The **Red Line** has points of origin at Braintree and Mattapan to the south; the routes join near South Boston and proceed to Harvard and to suburban Arlington. The **Green Line** is a combined underground and elevated surface line, originating at Cambridge's Lechmere and heading south through Park Street to divide into four major routes: Boston College (Commonwealth Avenue), Cleveland Circle (Beacon Street), Riverside, and Arborway. Green Line trains are actually trolleys that travel major streets south and west of Kenmore Square and operate underground in the central city. The **Blue Line** runs from Bowdoin Square (near Government Center) to the Wonderland Racetrack in Revere, north of Boston. The **Orange Line** runs from Oak Grove in north suburban Malden to Forest Hills near the Arnold Arboretum. Trains operate from about 5:30 AM to about 12:30 AM. The fare is 85¢ for adults, 40¢ for children 5-11. An extra fare is required for the distant Green and Red Line stops.

By Car   Those who cannot avoid bringing a car into Boston should be able to minimize their frustration by keeping to the main thoroughfares and by parking in lots—no matter how expensive—rather than on the street. Parking on Boston streets is a tricky business.

The major public parking lots are at Government Center and Quincy Market; beneath Boston Common (entrance on Charles Street); beneath Post Office Square; at the Prudential Center; at Copley Place; and off Clarendon Street near the John Hancock Tower. Smaller lots are scattered through the downtown area. Most are expensive, especially the small outdoor lots; a few city garages are a bargain at about $6-$10 a day.

By Taxi   Cabs are not easily hailed on the street, except at the airport; if you need to get somewhere in a hurry, use a hotel taxi stand or telephone for a cab. Companies offering 24-hour service include **Checker** (tel. 617/536-7000), **Independent Taxi Operators Association** or ITOA (tel. 617/426–8700), **Green Cab Association** (tel. 617/628–0600), **Town Taxi** (tel. 617/536–5000), and, in Cambridge, **Cambridge Taxi** (tel. 617/547–3000). The current rate is about $1.60 per mile.

Guided Tours

Orientation Tours
By Land

Beantown Trolleys (435 High St., Randolph, tel. 617/236–2148) covers the Freedom Trail among its many stops. One ticket allows you to get on and off at will all day long. The narration runs 1½ hours total. Fare is $15 adults, $11 senior citizens, $5 children 5–11; trolleys run every 15 minutes, 9 AM–dark. **Brush Hill/Gray Line** (39 Dalton Ave., tel. 617/236–2148) has buses leaving from several downtown hotels twice daily from March to November for 3½-hour tours of Boston and Cambridge. **Old Town Trolley** (329 W. 2nd St., tel. 617/269–7010) takes you on a 1½-hour narrated tour of Boston or an hour-long tour of Cambridge. You can catch it at major hotels, Boston Common, Copley Place, or in front of the New England Aquarium on Atlantic Avenue.

By Water

Boston Harbor Cruises (1 Long Wharf, tel. 617/227–4320) has tours from mid-April through October. The **Charles River Boat Co.** (100 Cambridgeside Pl., Cambridge, tel. 617/621–3001) offers a 50-minute narrated tour of the Charles River Basin. It departs from the Galleria and Museum of Science dock on the hour from noon to 5 daily, June–September, and on weekends in April, May, and October.

Special-Interest Tours

The **Bay State Cruise Company** (67 Long Wharf, tel. 617/723–7800) offers whale-watch cruises Saturday and Sunday from late April to mid-June, Saturday during the summer.

Walking Tours

The **Black Heritage Trail** (tel. 617/742–5415), a 90-minute walk exploring the history of Boston's 19th-century black community, passes 14 sites of historical importance on Beacon Hill. Guided tours are available by appointment in the winter, and from April to October at 10, noon, and 2 daily from the Shaw Memorial in front of the State House on Beacon Street. Maps and brochures can be obtained for self-guided tours.

The mile-and-a-half **Freedom Trail** (tel. 617/242–5642) is marked in the sidewalk by a red line that winds its way past 16 of Boston's most important historic sites. The walk begins at the Freedom Trail Information Center on the Tremont Street side of Boston Common, not far from the MBTA Park Street Station. Sites include the State House, Park Street Church, Old State House, Boston Massacre Site, Paul Revere House, and Old North Church.

Tour 1: Boston Common and Beacon Hill

Numbers in the margin correspond to points of interest on the Boston map.

① Nothing is more central to Boston than its **Common** (ca. 1630), the oldest public park in the United States and undoubtedly the largest and most famous of the town commons around which all New England settlements were once arranged.

Start your walk at the **Park Street Station,** on the common on the corner of Park and Tremont streets. This is the original eastern terminus of the first subway in America, opened in 1897 against the warnings of those who believed it would make the buildings along Tremont Street collapse. The copper-roof kiosks are National Historic Landmarks. A well-equipped **visitor information booth** is less than 100 yards from here. It serves as the starting point for the **Freedom Trail;** guide booklets are available at no charge.

② The Congregationalist **Park Street Church,** designed by Peter Banner and erected in 1809–1810, occupies the corner of Tremont and Park streets. Here, on July 4, 1831, Samuel Smith's hymn "America" was first sung, and here in 1829 William Lloyd Garrison began his long public campaign for the abolition of slavery. *Tel. 617/523–3383. Open to visitors last week in June–third week in Aug., Tues.–Sat. 9:30–3:30.*

③ Next to the church is the **Old Granary Burial Ground.** The most famous individuals interred here are heroes of the Revolution: Samuel Adams, John Hancock (the precise location of his grave is not certain), James Otis, and Paul Revere. Here, too, are the graves of the philanthropist Peter Faneuil, Benjamin Franklin's parents (Franklin is buried in Philadelphia), and the victims of the Boston Massacre. *Open daily 8–4:30.*

At the corner of Park and Beacon streets, at the summit of Beacon **④** Hill, stands Charles Bulfinch's magnificent **State House,** arguably the most architecturally distinguished of American seats of state government. The design is neoclassical, poised between Georgian and Federal; its finest features are the delicate Corinthian columns of the portico, the graceful pediment and window arches, and the vast yet visually weightless golden dome. The dome is sheathed in copper from the foundry of Paul Revere. During World War II, the entire dome was painted gray so that it would not reflect moonlight during blackouts. *Tel. 617/727–3676. Admission free. Tours weekdays 10–4. Research library open weekdays 11–5.*

Beacon Hill is the area bounded by Cambridge Street on the north, Beacon Street on the south, the Charles River Esplanade on the west, and Bowdoin Street on the east. The highest of three summits, Beacon Hill was named for the warning light (at first an iron skillet filled with tallow and suspended from a mast) set on its peak in 1634.

No sooner do you put the State House behind you than you encounter the classic face of Beacon Hill: brick row houses, nearly all built between 1800 and 1850 in a style never far divergent from the early Federal norm. Even the sidewalks are brick, and they shall remain so; in the 1940s residents staged a sit-in to prevent conventional paving. Since then, public law, the Beacon Hill Civic Association, and the Beacon Hill Architectural Commission have maintained tight controls over everything from the gas lamps to the color of front doors.

Chestnut and **Mt. Vernon,** two of the loveliest streets in America, are distinguished not only for the history and style of their individual houses but for their general atmosphere and character as well. **Mt. Vernon Street** is the grander of the two, its houses set back farther and rising taller; it even has a free-standing mansion, the Second **⑤** Otis House. Mt. Vernon opens out on **Louisburg Square,** an 1840s model for town house development that was never repeated on the Hill because of space restrictions. The little green belongs collectively to the owners of the homes facing it.

Chestnut Street is more modest than Mt. Vernon, yet in its trimness and minuteness of detail it is perhaps even more fine. Delicacy and grace characterize virtually every structure, from the fanlights above the entryways to the wrought-iron boot scrapers on the steps.

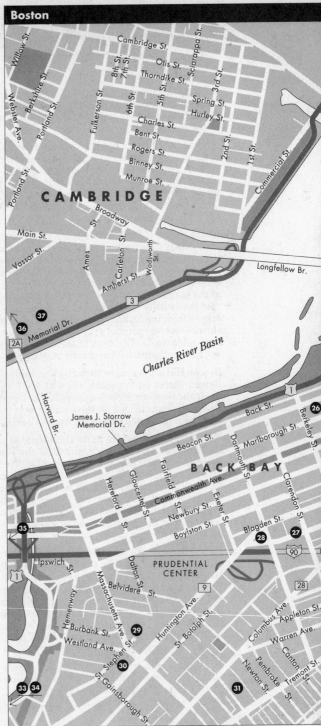

Boston

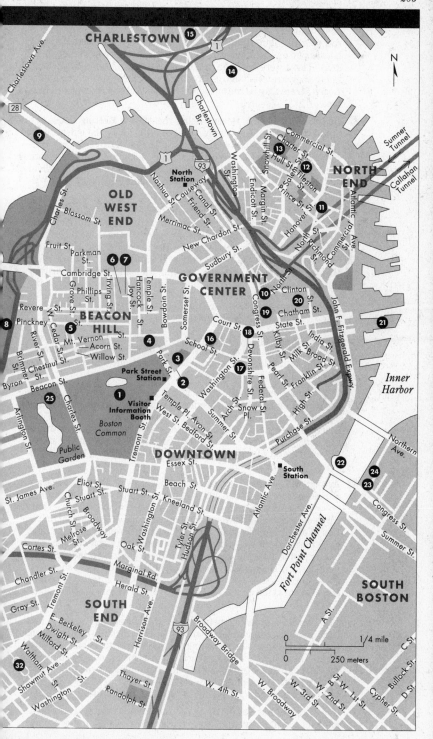

N

CHARLESTOWN

OLD WEST END

NORTH END

BEACON HILL

GOVERNMENT CENTER

DOWNTOWN

SOUTH END

SOUTH BOSTON

Inner Harbor

Boston Common

Public Garden

Park Street Station

Visitor Information Booth

North Station

South Station

Sumner Tunnel

Callahan Tunnel

Fort Point Channel

0   1/4 mile
0   250 meters

Running parallel to Chestnut and Mt. Vernon streets, half a block down Willow Street from Louisburg Square, is **Acorn Street,** a narrow span of cobblestones lined on one side with almost toylike row houses and on the other with the doors to Mt. Vernon's hidden gardens. These were once the houses of artisans and small tradesmen; today they are every bit as prestigious as their larger neighbors. Acorn Street may be the most photographed street of its size in Boston.

6 On the north slope of Beacon Hill is the **African Meeting House** at 8 Smith Court (near Joy and Myrtle), built in 1806, the oldest black church building still standing in the United States. It was constructed almost entirely with black labor, using funds raised in both the white and the black communities. In 1832 the New England Anti-Slavery Society was formed here under the leadership of William Lloyd Garrison.

Opposite the African Meeting House is the home (1799) of **William Nell,** a black crusader for school integration active in Garrison's circle. These sites and others are part of the **Black Heritage Trail,** a walking tour that explores the history of the city's black **7** community during the 19th century. The **Museum of Afro-American History** provides information on the trail and on black history throughout Boston. Daily tours of the African Meeting House begin here. *46 Joy St., tel. 617/742–1854. Suggested admission: $3 adults, $1.50 senior citizens. Open daily 10–4. Tours daily 10, noon, and 2.*

Charles Street, on the flat part of Beacon Hill, is home to Boston's antiques district and an assortment of bookstores, leather stores, small restaurants, and vintage-clothing boutiques. Stroll along the romantically lit street after dusk.

If you head east toward the river, you can cross over to the **8** **Esplanade** on the Arthur Fiedler Footbridge, named for the late maestro who conducted the Boston Pops for 50 years. Many of his concerts were given right here, in the **Hatch Memorial Shell,** where the Pops plays each summer. The Esplanade is one of the nicest places in the city for jogging, picnicking, and watching the sailboats along the Charles River.

9 Across the Charles River, and a short walk away, Boston's **Museum of Science** has more than 400 exhibits covering astronomy, anthropology, progress in medicine, computers, the organic and inorganic earth sciences, and much more. Many exhibits invite the participation of children and adults. The Transparent Woman's organs light up as their functions are described, newborn chicks hatch in an incubator, and a powerful generator produces controlled indoor lightning flashes. The museum has three restaurants and a gift shop. *Tel. 617/723–2500 or 617/523–6664). Admission: $7 adults, $5 senior citizens and children 4–14; free Wed. 1–5. Open daily 9–5, Fri. until 9.*

The **Charles Hayden Planetarium,** in the Museum of Science, features a planetarium projector and sophisticated multi-image system that combine to produce exciting programs on astronomical discoveries. Laser light shows, using a new visual technology complete with brilliant laser graphics and computer animation, are scheduled Friday–Sunday evenings. *Tel. 617/589–0270 or 617/723–2500. Admission: $6.50 adults, $4.50 senior citizens and children.*

The **Mugar Omni Theater** in the Museum of Science features a 76-foot, four-story domed screen, which wraps around and over you;

27,000 watts of power drive the sound system's 84 loudspeakers. *Tel. 617/523–6664. Admission: $6.50 adults, $4.50 senior citizens and children 4–14. Shows from 11 AM. Reduced-price combination tickets available for museum, planetarium, and Omni Theater.*

Tour 2: The North End and Charlestown

From **Government Center** walk northeast toward the raised central artery (the Fitzgerald Expressway) and you'll soon come upon the oldest commercial block in Boston, the Blackstone Block. In this block Boston's oldest restaurant, the **Union Oyster House,** has been operating since 1826. Around the corner on Friday and Saturday, come rain or sleet, Haymarket vendors hawk fruit, vegetables, meat, and fish.

Opposite the pedestrian tunnel beneath the expressway is the oldest neighborhood in Boston and one of the oldest in the New World. Men and women walked the narrow streets of the **North End** when Shakespeare was not yet 20 years dead and Louis XIV was new to the throne of France. In the 17th century the North End *was* Boston, for much of the rest of the peninsula was still under water or had yet to be cleared of brush.

The North End visible to us today is almost entirely a creature of the late 19th century, when brick tenements began to fill with European immigrants. The Irish and the Jews both had their day here, but the Italians, more recent arrivals, have stayed. For more than 60 years the North End has been Italian Boston. This is not only a district of Italian restaurants (there are dozens) but of Italian groceries, bakeries, churches, social clubs, cafés, festivals honoring saints and food, street-corner debates over soccer games, and encroaching gentrification.

Hanover Street is the main thoroughfare dividing the North End. Off Hanover Street is North Square, home to the **Paul Revere House**—the oldest house in Boston—built nearly a hundred years before Revere's 1775 midnight ride through Middlesex County. Revere owned it from 1770 until 1800, although he and his wife Rachel rented it out during the later part of that period. Attendants are available to answer questions. *19 North Sq., tel. 617/523–1676. Admission: $2.50 adults, $1.50 senior citizens, $1 children 5–17. Open daily 9:30–4:15. Closed Mon. Jan.–Mar.*

Time Out   The **Caffe Vittoria** (296 Hanover St., tel. 617/227–7606) serves cappuccino and special coffee drinks in an Old World café ambience. Next door, **Mike's Pastry** (300 Hanover St., tel. 617/742–3050) is the place for ricotta cannoli.

Past North Square on Hanover Street is **St. Stephen's,** the only one of architect Charles Bulfinch's churches still standing in Boston. At Hanover and Tileston streets, the **Prado,** or **Paul Revere Mall,** is lined with bronze plaques that tell the stories of famous North Enders. The centerpiece is Cyrus Dallin's equestrian statue of Paul Revere.

Continue on Tileston Street to Salem Street to see the church steeple where the two lanterns were hung as a signal to Paul Revere on the night of April 18, 1775. Christ Church, the **Old North Church** (1723), the oldest church building in Boston, was designed by William Price from a study of Christopher Wren's London churches. *Tel. 617/523–6676. Open daily 9–5. Sun. services at 9, 11, and 4.*

⓭ Walk uphill on Hull Street to reach the **Copp's Hill Burying Ground,** which incorporates four cemeteries established between 1660 and 1819. Many headstones were chipped by practice shots fired by British soldiers during the occupation of Boston, and a number of the musketball pockmarks can still be seen. Of all Boston's early cemeteries, Copp's Hill seems most to preserve an ancient and melancholic air. *Open daily 9–4.*

⓮ The view from Copp's Hill to the north encompasses the mouth of the Charles and much of Charlestown. The USS *Constitution* can be reached via the Charlestown Bridge, which is visible to the northwest.

The USS *Constitution*, nicknamed Old Ironsides for the strength of its oaken hull, not because of any iron plating, is the oldest commissioned ship in the U.S. Navy. She is moored at a national historic site, the **Charlestown Navy Yard,** one of six established to build warships. She was launched in 1797 in Boston, where Constitution Wharf now stands. During her principal service in Thomas Jefferson's campaign against the Barbary pirates, off the coast of North Africa, and in the War of 1812, she never lost an engagement. Sailors show visitors around the ship, taking them below decks to see the impossibly cramped living quarters as well as the guns where the desperate and difficult work of naval warfare under sail was carried out. *Tel. 617/426–1812. Admission to Constitution free. Admission to museum: $3 adults, $2 senior citizens, $1 children 6–16. Open daily 10–6. The ship will be in dry dock through Mar. 1996 for repairs. During this time 2 decks will be open for tours (tel. 617/242–5670) daily 9:30–sunset; a film of the tour will be shown at the adjacent museum.*

The phrase "Battle of Bunker Hill" is one of America's most famous misnomers. The battle was fought on Breed's Hill, and that is where Solomon Willard's 220-foot shaft of Quincy granite stands. The monument, for which the Marquis de Lafayette laid the cornerstone in 1825, rises from the spot where, on June 17, 1775, a citizen's militia, which had been commanded not to fire "till you see the whites of their eyes," inflicted more than 1,100 casualties on the British regulars (who eventually seized the hill).

⓯ Ascend the **Bunker Hill Monument** (Main St. to Monument St., then straight uphill) by a flight of 294 steps. There is no elevator, but the views from the observatory are worth the climb. At the base, four dioramas tell the story of the battle; ranger programs are given hourly. If you are in Boston on June 17, go to the hill to see a full-scale historical demonstration. *Tel. 617/242–5641. Admission free. Lodge open daily 9–5, monument until 4:30.*

Time Out Built in 1780, the **Warren Tavern** (2 Pleasant St., tel. 617/241–8142) is a restored Colonial neighborhood pub once frequented by George Washington and Paul Revere. This was the first building reconstructed following the Battle of Bunker Hill, which leveled the town. Stop in for a drink or for some American food with an international twist.

Tour 3: Downtown Boston

The financial district—what Bostonians usually refer to as "downtown"—is off the beaten track for visitors who are concentrating on following the Freedom Trail, yet there is much to see in a walk of an hour or two. There is little logic to the streets here; they were, after all, village lanes that only now happen to be lined with 40-story office towers. The area may be confusing, but it is mercifully small.

16 Just south of Government Center, at the corner of Tremont and School streets, stands **King's Chapel,** built in 1754 and never topped with the steeple that the architect Peter Harrison had planned. It took five years to build the solid Quincy granite structure. As construction proceeded, the old church continued to stand within the walls of the new, to be removed in pieces when the stone chapel was completed. The chapel's bell is Paul Revere's largest and, in his opinion, his sweetest-sounding. *Open June–Oct., Mon.–Sat. 9:30–4, Sun. noon–4; Nov.–May, Tues.–Wed. 11–1 and Sat. 10–4. Sun. service at 11. Music program Tues. 12:15–12:45.*

The adjacent **King's Chapel Burying Ground,** the oldest in the city, contains the remains of the first Massachusetts governor, John Winthrop, and several generations of his descendants. Here, too, are many other tombs of Boston worthies of three centuries ago.

Time Out   Rebecca's Café (18 Tremont St., tel. 617/227–0020), with an array of fresh salads, sandwiches, and homemade pastries, is a comfortable place to stop for a casual lunch.

Follow School Street down from King's Chapel and pass the **old City Hall,** with Richard S. Greenough's bronze statue of **Benjamin Franklin** (1855), which was Boston's first portrait sculpture. Franklin was born (1706) a few blocks from here on Milk Street and attended the Boston Latin School.

At the Washington Street corner of School Street stands the **Globe Corner Bookstore,** until recently a museum of old editions and now once again a working bookstore, thanks to the good offices of the *Boston Globe.* It was built in 1718, and throughout most of the 19th century it counted among its clientele the leading lights of literary society—Emerson, Holmes, Longfellow, Lowell.

17 The **Old South Meeting House** is a short block away, at the corner of Washington and Milk streets. Built in 1729, it is Boston's second-oldest church. Unlike the older Old North, the Old South is no longer the seat of an active congregation. (Its principal associations have always been more secular than religious.) Some of the fieriest of the town meetings that led to the Revolution were held here, including the one Samuel Adams called concerning some dutiable tea that activists wanted returned to England. *Tel. 617/482–6439. Admission: $2.50 adults, $2 senior citizens, $1 children 6–18. Open Apr. 1–Oct. 31, daily 9:30–5; Nov. 1–Mar. 31, weekdays 10–4, weekends 10–5. Lecture-concert series (free with admission) Oct.–Apr., Thurs. 12:15.*

Washington Street is the main commercial street of downtown Boston. You'll pass many of the area's major retail establishments (don't overlook the side streets) and the two venerable anchors of Boston's mercantile district, Filene's and Jordan Marsh.

Boston's **Theater District** is small: The Wilbur, Shubert, Emerson Majestic, and Colonial theaters and the Wang Center for the Performing Arts all cluster near the intersection of Tremont and Stuart streets. Yet the area does an increasingly lively business booking Broadway tryouts, road shows, and big-name recitals.

A right turn onto Washington Street from the doorstep of the Old South Meeting House will take you past the Globe Corner Bookstore once again, past Pi Alley (named after the loose type, or "pi," spilled from the pockets of printers when upper Washington Street was Boston's newspaper row—or after Colonial pie shops, depending on the story you believe) and to the rear of the Old State House near the intersection of Court Street.

18 The **Old State House** was the seat of the Colonial government from 1713 until the Revolution, and after the evacuation of the British from Boston in 1776 it served the independent Commonwealth until the new State House on Beacon Hill was completed. John Hancock was inaugurated here as the first governor under the new state constitution. After a two-year, $4 million federal preservation and renovation project, the Old State House has reopened and changed the focus of its exhibits. The permanent collection traces Boston's Revolutionary War history, while changing exhibits on the second floor address such contemporary issues as "Urban Renewal and Boston's West End." *206 Washington St., tel. 617/720–1713. Admission: $2.50 adults, $1.50 senior citizens, $1 children 6–16. Open daily 9:30–5.*

Turning left onto Congress Street, we encounter, first, an historic marketplace of ideas and, second, an old provisions market reborn as the emblem of downtown revitalization. Faneuil Hall ("the Cradle of Liberty") and the Quincy Market (also known as Faneuil Hall Marketplace) face each other across a small square thronged with people at all but the smallest hours.

19 **Faneuil Hall** (pronounced "Fan'l") was erected in 1742 to serve as both a place for town meetings and a public market. Though it has been rebuilt, enlarged, and remodeled over the years, the great balconied hall is still made available to citizen's groups.

20 **Quincy Market** consists of three structures and has served its purpose as a retail and wholesale distribution center for meat and produce for a century and a half. By the 1970s, though, the market area had become seedy. Some of the old tenants—the famous Durgin Park restaurant and a few butchers and grocers in the central building—had hung on through the years, but the old vitality had disappeared.

Thanks to a creative and tasteful urban-renewal project, the north and south market buildings, separated from the central market by attractive pedestrian malls with trees and benches, house retail establishments, offices, and restaurants. There may be more restaurants in Quincy Market than existed in all of downtown Boston before World War II. Abundance and variety, albeit of an ephemeral sort, have been the watchwords of Quincy Market since its reopening in 1976. Some people consider it all hopelessly trendy; but another 50,000 or so visitors a day rather enjoy the extravaganza. You'll want to decide for yourself. *Open Mon.–Sat. 10–9, Sun. noon–6. Restaurants and bars generally open daily 11 AM–2 AM.*

At the end of Quincy Market opposite Faneuil Hall, the newer **Marketplace Center,** between the market buildings and the expressway toward the waterfront, is also filled with shops and boutiques. Beyond is Columbus Park, bordering the harbor and several of Boston's restored wharves. **Lewis Wharf** and **Commercial Wharf,** which long lay nearly derelict, had by the mid-1970s been transformed into condominiums, apartments, restaurants, and upscale shops. **Long Wharf's** Marriott hotel was designed to be compatible with the old seaside warehouses. Sailboats and power yachts ride here at anchor; Boston's workaday waterfront is now located in three places: along the docks of South Boston, in East Boston (directly opposite Columbus Park), and in the huge containerized shipping facilities at the mouth of the Mystic.

Central Wharf, immediately to the right of Long Wharf as you face the harbor, is the home of one of Boston's most popular attractions, the **New England Aquarium.** Here you'll find seals, penguins, a variety of sharks and other sea creatures—more than 2,000 species in all, some of which make their home in the aquarium's four-story, 187,000-gallon observation tank. *Tel. 617/973–5200 (whale-watch information, 617/973–5277). Admission: $8.50 adults, $7.50 senior citizens, $4.50 children 3–15; free Thurs. after 3, Oct.–Apr. Open weekdays 9–5, Thurs. until 8, weekends 9–6.*

One corner of downtown that has been relatively untouched by high-rise development is the old **leather district,** which is nestled into the angle formed by Kneeland Street and Atlantic Avenue opposite South Station. This was the wholesale supply area for raw materials in the days when the shoe industry was a regional economic mainstay, and a few leather firms are still located here. The leather district is probably the best place in downtown Boston to get an idea of what the city's business blocks looked like in the late 19th century.

The leather district directly abuts **Chinatown,** which is also bordered by the Theater District and the buildings of the Tufts New England Medical Center. Chinatown's borders may be constrained, yet it remains one of the larger concentrations of Chinese-Americans in the United States, and it is a vibrant center for both the private and the public aspects of local Chinese culture. As in most American Chinatowns, it is the concentration of restaurants that attracts most visitors, and today the numerous Chinese establishments are interspersed with a handful of Vietnamese eateries—a reflection of the latest wave of immigration into Boston. Most Chinese restaurants, food stores, and retail businesses are located along Beach and Tyler streets and Harrison Avenue. The area around the intersection of Kneeland Street and Harrison Avenue is the center of Boston's textile and garment industry, and a number of shops here specialize in discount yard goods.

Time Out   It's a special treat to sample the Chinese baked goods in shops along Beach Street. Many visitors familiar with Cantonese and even Szechuan cookery will still be surprised and delighted with moon cakes, steamed cakes made with rice flour, and other sweets that seldom turn up on restaurant menus.

Along Atlantic Avenue, at the foot of Pearl Street, a plaque set into the wall of a commercial building marks the site of the **Boston Tea Party.** When you cross Fort Point Channel on the Congress Street Bridge, you encounter the *Beaver II,* a faithful replica of one of the Tea Party ships that was forcibly boarded and unloaded on the night Boston Harbor became a teapot. Visitors receive a complimentary cup of tea. *Tel. 617/338–1773. Admission: $6 adults, $5 senior citizens, $3 children 5–14. Open Mar.–mid-Dec. daily 9–5 (until 6 in summer).*

At the opposite end of the bridge is Museum Wharf, home of the popular **Boston Children's Museum.** The multitude of hands-on exhibits includes computers, video cameras, and exhibits designed to help children understand cultural diversity, their bodies, and disabilities. *300 Congress St., tel. 617/426–6500 or 617/426–8855. Admission: $7 adults, $6 senior citizens and children 2–15, $2 1-year-olds, $1 Fri. 5–9. Open Tues.–Sun. 10–5, Fri. until 9.*

24 Museum Wharf is also the home of the world's only **Computer Museum,** housing exhibits chronicling the spectacular development of machines that calculate and process information. The more than 75 exhibits include the two-story Walk-Through Computer ™. *300 Congress St., tel. 617/426-2800 or 617/423-6758. Admission: $7 adults, $5 senior citizens and children 5-18; ½ price Sun. 3-5. Open Tues.- Sun. 10-5, Fri. until 9 except in winter.*

Tour 4: The Back Bay and the South End

The Back Bay once was truly a bay, a tidal flat that formed the south bank of a distended Charles River in the 1850s. Beacon Street was built in 1814 to separate the Back Bay from the Charles River. At the rate of 3,500 railroad carloads of gravel a day, it took 30 years to complete the filling as far as the Fens. When the work was finished, the 783-acre peninsula of Boston had been expanded by approximately 450 acres. By 1900 the area was the smartest and most desirable in all Boston.

25 A walk through the Back Bay properly begins with the **Public Garden,** the oldest botanical garden in the United States. Its establishment marked the first phase of the Back Bay reclamation project, occupying what had been salt marshes on the edge of the Common's dry land. Its pond has been famous since 1877 for its **swan boats,** which make leisurely cruises during the warm months of the year.

The best place to begin exploring the streets of the Back Bay is at the corner of Commonwealth Avenue and Arlington Street, with a statue of Washington and his horse looking over your shoulder. The planners of the Back Bay were able to do something that had never before been possible in Boston: to lay out an entire neighborhood of arrow-straight streets. While other parts of Boston may be reminiscent of the mews and squares of London, the main thoroughfares of the Back Bay (especially Commonwealth Avenue) resemble nothing so much as they do Parisian boulevards.

Beginning at the Charles River, the main east-west streets are bisected by eight streets named in alphabetical order from Arlington to Hereford, with three-syllable street names alternating with two-syllable names. Service alleys run behind the main streets; they were built so that delivery wagons could be driven up to basement kitchens. That's how thorough the planning was.

Back Bay is a living museum of urban Victorian residential architecture. **26** The **Gibson House** offers a representative look at how life was arranged in—and by—these tall, narrow, formal buildings. One of the first Back Bay residences (1859), the Gibson House is relatively modest in comparison with some of the grand mansions built during the decades that followed. Unlike other Back Bay houses, the Gibson family home has been preserved with all its Victorian fixtures and furniture intact—not restored, but preserved: A conservative family scion lived here until the 1950s and left things as they were. Here you will understand why a squad of servants was a necessity in the old Back Bay. The Gibson House now serves as the meeting place for the New England chapter of the Victorian Society in America. *137 Beacon St., tel. 617/267-6338. Admission: $3. Tours May-Oct., Wed.-Sun. at 1, 2, and 3; Nov.-Apr., weekends at 1, 2, and 3.*

The Great Depression brought an end to the old Back Bay style of living, and today only a few of the houses serve as single-family residences. Most have been cut up into apartments and expensive condominiums.

Newbury Street is Boston's Fifth Avenue, with dozens of upscale specialty shops offering clothing, china, antiques, and art. It is also a street of beauty salons and sidewalk cafés. Boylston Street, similarly busy but a little less posh, boasts elegant apparel shops.

Time Out | The **Harvard Book Store Café** (190 Newbury St., tel. 617/536–0095) serves meals or coffee and pastry—outdoors in nice weather. Since it's a real bookstore, you can browse to your heart's content.

Boylston Street, the southern commercial spine of the Back Bay, separates the sedate old district (some say not effectively enough) from the most ambitious developments this side of downtown. One block south of Boylston, on the corner of St. James Avenue and Clarendon Street, stands the tallest building in New England: the 62-story **John Hancock Tower,** built in the early 1970s and notorious in its early years as the building whose windows fell out. The 60th-floor observatory is one of the three best vantage points in the city, and the "Boston 1775" exhibit shows what the city looked like before the great hill-leveling and landfill operations commenced. *Observatory ticket office, Trinity Pl. and St. James Ave., tel. 617/247–1977. Admission: $3 adults, $2.25 senior citizens and children 5–15. Open Mon.–Sat. 9 AM–10 PM, Sun. noon–10.*

The Hancock Tower stands at the edge of **Copley Square,** a civic space that is defined by three monumental older buildings. One is the stately, bowfronted **Copley Plaza Hotel,** which faces the square on St. James Avenue and serves as a dignified foil to two of the most important works of architecture in Boston, if not in the United States. At the left is **Trinity Church,** Henry Hobson Richardson's masterwork of 1877. In this church Richardson brought his Romanesque Revival to maturity.

Across the street from Copley Square stands the **Boston Public Library.** When this building was opened in 1895, it confirmed the status of McKim, Mead, and White as apostles of the Renaissance Revival and reinforced a Boston commitment to the enlightenment of the citizenry that goes back 350 years to the founding of the Public Latin School. In the older part of the building is a quiet courtyard with chairs around a flower garden, and a sumptuous main reference reading room. *Tel. 617/536–5400. Open Mon.–Thurs. 9–9, Fri.–Sat. 9–5.*

With a modern assertive presence, **Copley Place** comprises two major hotels (the high-rise Westin and the Marriott) and dozens of shops and restaurants, attractively grouped on several levels around bright, open indoor spaces. The scale of the project bothers some people, as does the fact that so vast a complex of buildings effectively isolates the South End from the Back Bay. *Shopping galleries open Mon–Sat. 10–7, Sun. noon–5.*

Down Huntington Avenue is the headquarters complex of the **Christian Science Church.** Mary Baker Eddy's original granite First Church of Christ, Scientist (1894) has since been enveloped by the domed Renaissance basilica added to the site in 1906, and both church buildings are now surrounded by the offices of the *Christian Science Monitor* and by I. M. Pei's complex of church administration structures completed in 1973. The 670-foot reflecting pool is a pleasant spot to stroll around. *175 Huntington Ave., tel. 617/450–3790. Open Tues.–Sat. 9:30–4, Sun. 11:15–2. Free tours on the hour in the church and every 10 minutes in the mapparium (closed Sun.). Services Sun. at 10 and 7, Wed. at 7:30 PM.*

The best views of the pool and the precise, abstract geometry of the entire complex are from the **Prudential Center Skywalk,** a 50th-floor observatory that offers fine views of Boston, Cambridge, and the suburbs to the west and south. *800 Boylston St., tel. 617/236–3318. Admission: $2.75 adults, $1.75 senior citizens and children 5–15. Skywalk open Mon.–Sat. 10–9:45, Sun. noon–9:45.*

③⓪ **Symphony Hall,** since 1900 the home of the Boston Symphony Orchestra, stands at the corner of Huntington and Massachusetts avenues, another contribution of McKim, Mead, and White to the Boston landscape. Acoustics, rather than exterior design, make this a special place. Not one of the 2,500 seats is a bad one. *301 Massachusetts Ave., tel. 617/266–1492. Tours by appointment with the volunteer office.*

From here you can walk southeast on Massachusetts Avenue to explore the South End or southwest on Huntington Avenue to the Fens and the Museum of Fine Arts. This tour finishes with a visit to the **South End,** a neighborhood eclipsed by the Back Bay more than a century ago but now solidly back in fashion, with upscale galleries and restaurants on Tremont Street catering to young urban professionals. The observation is usually made that while the Back Bay is French-inspired, the South End is English. The houses, too, are different. In one sense they continue the pattern established on Beacon Hill (in a uniformly bowfront style), yet they also aspire to a much more florid standard of decoration. Although it would take years to understand the place fully, you can capture something of the flavor of the South End with a short walk. To see elegant house restorations, go to **Rutland Square** (between Columbus Avenue and ③① ③② **Tremont Street)** or **Union Park** (between Tremont Street and Shawmut Avenue). These oases seem miles from the city around them.

There is a substantial black presence in the South End, particularly along Columbus Avenue and Massachusetts Avenue, which marks the beginning of the predominantly black neighborhood of Roxbury. The early integration of the South End set the stage for its eventual transformation into a remarkable polyglot of ethnic groups. You are likely to hear Spanish spoken along Tremont Street, and there are Middle Eastern groceries along Shawmut Avenue. At the northeastern extreme of the South End, Harrison Avenue and Washington Street connect the area with Chinatown, and consequently there is a growing Asian influence. Still another minority presence among the neighborhood's ethnic groups, and sometimes belonging to one or more of them, is the largest concentration of Boston's gay population.

Time Out   **Botolph's on Tremont** (569 Tremont St., tel. 617/424–8577) serves gourmet Italian cuisine in light and airy surroundings. The café atmosphere is achieved through the black, white, and red decor. Dishes range from $6 to $12.

Tour 5: The Fens

The Back Bay Fens mark the beginning of Boston's Emerald Necklace, a loosely connected chain of parks designed by Frederick Law Olmsted that extends along the Fenway, Riverway, and Jamaicaway to Jamaica Pond, the 265-acre Arnold Arboretum, and the zoo at Franklin Park. The Fens park consists of still, irregular, reed-bound pools surrounded by broad meadows, trees, and flower gardens.

㉝ The **Museum of Fine Arts,** the MFA, between Huntington Avenue and the Fenway, has holdings of American art that surpass those of all but two or three U.S. museums. The MFA boasts the most extensive collection of Asiatic art gathered under one roof, and European art is represented by works from the 11th through the 20th centuries. It has strong collections of textiles and costumes and an impressive collection of antique musical instruments. The museum's new West Wing, designed by I. M. Pei, is used primarily for traveling exhibitions and special showings of the museum's permanent collection. On the Fenway Park side of the Museum of Fine Arts, the **Tenshin Garden,** the "garden at the heart of heaven," allows visitors to experience landscape as a work of art. The museum has a good restaurant and a less formal cafeteria serving light snacks; both are in the West Wing. *465 Huntington Ave., tel. 617/267–9300 or 617/ 267–9377. Admission: $7 adults, $6 senior citizens, $3.50 children 6–17, free to all Wed. 4–9:45. Open Tues.–Sun. 10–4:45, Wed. until 9:45. West Wing open Thurs. and Fri. until 9:45, with admission reduced by $1. 1-hr tours available.*

㉞ Two blocks west of the MFA, on the Fenway, stands the **Isabella Stewart Gardner Museum,** a monument to one woman's taste—and despite the loss of a few masterpieces in a daring 1990 robbery, still a trove of spectacular paintings, sculpture, furniture, and textiles. There is much to see: *The Rape of Europa,* the most important of Titian's works in an American collection; paintings and drawings by Matisse, Whistler, Bellini, Van Dyck, Botticelli, and Rubens; John Singer Sargent's oil portrait of Mrs. Gardner herself, in the Gothic Room. At the center of the building is the magnificent courtyard, fully enclosed beneath a glass roof. *280 The Fenway, tel. 617/566– 1401 or 617/734–1359. Admission: $6 adults, $3 senior citizens and children over 12. Open Tues.–Sun 11–5.*

㉟ The Boston shrine known as **Fenway Park** is one of the smallest and oldest baseball parks in the major leagues. It was built in 1912, when the grass on the field was real—and it still is today. Babe Ruth pitched here when the place was new; Ted Williams and Carl Yastrzemski slugged out their entire careers here.

Kenmore Square, home to fast-food parlors, alternative rock clubs, an abundance of university students, and an enormous neon sign advertising gasoline, is two blocks north of Fenway Park. The neon sign is so thoroughly identified with the area that historic preservationists have fought successfully to save it—proof that Bostonians are an open-minded lot who do not require that their landmarks be identified with the American Revolution.

Tour 6: The "Streetcar Suburbs"

The 19th-century expansion of Boston was not confined to the Back Bay and the South End. Toward the close of the century, as the working population of the downtown district swelled and public transportation (first horsecars, then electric trolleys) linked outlying suburbs with the core city, development of the "streetcar suburbs" began. These areas answered the housing needs of both the rising native middle class and the second-generation immigrant families who were outgrowing the narrow streets of the North and West ends.

South Boston was a landfill project of the mid-1880s, and as such it is not a true streetcar suburb; its expansion predates the era of commuting. Some of the brick bowfront residences along East Broadway in City Point date from the 1840s and 1850s. But "Southie" came into its own with the influx of Irish Americans around 1900, and the Irish still hold sway here.

South Boston projects farther into the harbor than any other part of Boston save Logan Airport, and the views of the Harbor Islands from along Day Boulevard or Castle Island are fine. At L Street and Day Boulevard is the L Street Beach, where an intrepid group called the L Street Brownies swims all year long and celebrates New Year's Day with a dip in the icy Atlantic. **Castle Island Park** is no longer on an island, but **Fort Independence,** when it was built here in 1801, was separated from the mainland by water. The circular walk from the fort around Pleasure Bay is delightful on a warm summer day.

Near the juncture of the South Boston peninsula with the Dorchester mainland, off Telegraph Street, stands the high ground of Thomas Park, where you will find the **Dorchester Heights Monument** and National Historic Site. In 1776 Dorchester Heights commanded a clear view of downtown Boston, where the British had been under siege since the preceding year. *Thomas Park (near G St.), tel. 617/242–5642. Admission free. Grounds open daily.*

South of the Dorchester Heights Monument, on the other side of Columbus Park, a stark, white, prowlike building (designed by I. M. Pei) at a stunning harbor-surrounded site at the tip of Columbia Point pays homage to one of Washington's successors as president, a native Irish Bostonian named John F. Kennedy. The **Kennedy Library** is the official repository of his presidential papers. Several exhibits and video presentations that capture and interpret President Kennedy's life and legacy opened in late 1993. The harborfront site alone is worth a visit. *Columbia Point, tel. 617/929–4523. Admission: $6 adults, $4 senior citizens, $2 children 6–16. Open daily 9–5. Free shuttle bus every 20 min. from the T.*

Inland from Columbia Point are Dorchester, Roxbury, and Jamaica Plain, all rural retreats barely more than a century ago, now thick with tenements and the distinctive three- or six-family triple-decker apartment houses of Boston's streetcar suburbs. Both Dorchester and Roxbury are almost exclusively residential, tricky to navigate by car, and accessible by elevated train (the Red or Orange Lines) only if you know exactly where you are going. The two contiguous neighborhoods border on **Franklin Park,** an Olmsted creation of more than 500 acres noted for its zoo.

The 70-acre **Franklin Park Zoo,** near the Seaver Street–Blue Hill Avenue corner of the park, has been renovated during the past decade and has an especially fine walk-through aviary. The new Tropical Forest Pavilion has a gorilla exhibit and 32 other species of mammals, reptiles, birds, and fish. The park, 4 miles from downtown, is reached by Bus 16 from Forest Hills (Orange Line) or Andrew (Red Line). *Blue Hill Ave., tel. 617/442–2002 or 617/442–4896. Admission: $5 adults, $2.50 senior citizens and children 4–11. Open daily 9–4.*

During the growing season, no one with an eye for natural beauty and more than a couple of days to spend in Boston should pass up the **Arnold Arboretum.** This 265-acre living laboratory, administered by Harvard University, is open to pedestrians during daylight hours all year long. It can be reached by taking the #39 bus from Copley

Square or by taking the Orange Line to Forest Hills and then the #16 bus to the arboretum. *Rtes. 1 and 203, Arborway, tel. 617/524–1718. Admission free. Grounds open daily dawn–dusk; visitor's center open 10–4. Hour-long guided tours Sun. at 2, May–Nov.*

If you have the time and stamina for a jaunt of approximately 3½ miles, it is possible to walk almost the entire distance from the Arnold Arboretum to Kenmore Square within the Emerald Necklace. Just follow the Jamaicaway north from its beginning at the circle that marks the northern tip of the arboretum. Within one long block you'll reach Jamaica Pond. Continue along the Jamaicaway through Olmsted Park, past Leverett Pond. From a point just north of here, either Brookline Avenue or the Riverway will take you to the Fens and Kenmore Square. Along the way you will pass many of the spacious freestanding mansions built along the park borders of Jamaica Plain around the turn of the century, when this was the choicest of the streetcar suburbs.

From Kenmore Square it's just a few minutes on the MBTA Green Line to Coolidge Corner in Brookline, where a four-block walk north on Harvard Street takes you to the **John Fitzgerald Kennedy National Historic Site.** This was the home of the 35th president of the United States from his birth on May 29, 1917, until 1920, when the family moved to nearby Naples and Abbottsford streets. Rose Kennedy provided the furnishings for the restored 2½-story, wood-frame structure. *83 Beals St., tel. 617/566–7937. Admission: $1 adults, children under 17 and senior citizens free. Open Wed.–Sun. 10–4:30; tours every 45 min. from 10:45.*

Tour 7: Cambridge

Cambridge is an independent city faced with the difficult task of living in the shadow of its larger neighbor, Boston, while being overshadowed as well by the giant educational institutions within its own borders. It provides the brains and the technical know-how that, combined with Boston's financial prowess, have created the vibrant high-tech economy of which Massachusetts is so proud. Cambridge also continues to function as the conscience of the greater Boston area; when a new social experiment or progressive legislation appears on the local scene, chances are it came out of the crucible of Cambridge political activism.

36 Cambridge, just minutes from Boston by MBTA, is easily reached on the Red Line train to **Harvard Square.**

A good place to begin a tour is the **Cambridge Discovery** information booth near the MBTA station entrance, where you will find maps, brochures, and information about the entire city. The walking tour brochures cover Old Cambridge, East Cambridge, and Revolutionary Cambridge. Cambridge Discovery also gives a rewarding tour of Old Cambridge conducted by a corps of well-trained high school students. *Cambridge Discovery, Inc., Box 1987, Cambridge 02238, tel. 617/497–1630 or 617/495–1631. Open in winter, Mon.–Sat. 9–5, Sun. 1–5; in summer, daily 9–6.*

In 1636 the country's first college was established here. Named in 1638 for a young Charlestown clergyman who died that year, leaving the college his entire library and half his estate, Harvard remained the only college in the New World until 1693, by which time it was firmly established as a respected center of learning.

The Harvard University information office on the ground floor of Holyoke Center (1350 Massachusetts Ave., tel. 617/495–1573), run by students, offers a free hour-long tour (during the academic year, weekdays at 10 and 2, Sat. at 2; mid-June–Aug., Mon.–Sat. at 10, 11:15, 2, and 3:15, Sun. at 1:30 and 3:30) of Harvard Yard and maps of the university area. The tour does not include visits to museums, but it provides a fine orientation and will give you ideas for further sightseeing.

Harvard has two celebrated art museums, each a treasure in itself. The most famous is the **Fogg Art Museum,** behind Harvard Yard on Quincy Street, between Broadway and Harvard Street. Founded in 1895, it now owns 80,000 works of art from every major period and from every corner of the world. Its focus is primarily on European, American, and Far Eastern works; it has notable collections of 19th-century French Impressionist and medieval Italian paintings. Special exhibits change monthly. *32 Quincy St., tel. 617/495–9400. Admission: $4 adults, $2.50 senior citizens, children under 18 free; free to all Sat. 10–noon. Open daily 10–5.*

A ticket to the Fogg will gain you admission to the noted **Busch-Reisinger Museum** (Werner Otto Hall, tel. 617/495–2317), entered via the Fogg, and the **Arthur M. Sackler Museum** (tel. 617/495–9400), across the street. The former hosts collections specializing in Central and Northern European art. The Sackler exhibits Chinese, Japanese, ancient Greek, Egyptian, Roman, Buddhist, and Islamic works. Hours at both are the same as those at the Fogg.

Harvard also maintains the **Harvard University Museums of Natural History,** north of the main campus on Oxford Street. It contains four distinct collections: comparative zoology, archaeology, botany, and minerals. The most famous exhibit here is the display of glass flowers in the **Botanical Museum.** The **Peabody Museum of Archaeology and Ethnology** holds one of the world's outstanding anthropological collections; exhibits focus on Native American and Central and South American cultures. *26 Oxford St., tel. 617/495–3045. Admission: $4 adults, $3 senior citizens, $1 children 3–13; free to all Sat. 9–11. Open Mon.–Sat. 9–4:30, Sun. 1–4:30.*

Across Massachusetts Avenue, at the north end of the Cambridge Common, go down Appian Way through a small garden to the heart of **Radcliffe College.** Founded in 1897 "to furnish instruction and the opportunities of collegiate life to women and to promote their higher education," Radcliffe is an independent corporation within Harvard University.

From Harvard Square, follow elegant **Brattle Street** out to the **Long-fellow National Historic Site.** George Washington lived here throughout the siege of Boston. The poet Henry Wadsworth Long-fellow received the house in 1843 as a wedding gift and filled it with the exuberant spirit of his own work and that of his literary circle, which included Emerson, Thoreau, Holmes, Dana, and Parkman. *105 Brattle St., tel. 617/876–4491. Admission: $2 adults, under 16 and over 62 free. Open daily 10–4:30; last tour departs at 4.*

❸❼ An exploration of Cambridge would not be complete without a visit to the **Massachusetts Institute of Technology.** The 135-acre campus of MIT borders the Charles River, 1½ miles south of Harvard Square. Obviously designed by and for scientists, the MIT campus is divided by Massachusetts Avenue into the West Campus, which is devoted to student leisure life, and the East Campus, where the heavy work is done. The West Campus has some extraordinary buildings. The **Kresge Auditorium,** designed by Eero Saarinen with a curving roof and unusual thrust, rests on three instead of four points. The **MIT Chapel,** another Saarinen design, is lit primarily by a roof oculus that focuses light on the altar, as well as by reflections from the water in a small moat surrounding it, and it is topped by an aluminum sculpture by Theodore Roszak. **Baker House** was designed in 1947 by the Finnish architect Alvar Aaltoa in such a way as to give every room a view of the Charles River. MIT's East Campus buildings are connected by a 5-mile "infinite corridor," touted as the second-longest corridor in the country.

The Institute maintains an Information Center and offers free tours of the campus Monday–Friday at 10 and 2. *Building Seven, 77 Massachusetts Ave., tel. 617/253–4795. Open weekdays 9–5.*

Boston for Free

Boston's Travel Planner is available free (tel. 617/536–4100).

The **Hatch Shell** on the bank of the Charles River is the site of numerous concerts during the summer months, and the Boston Pops and the Boston Ballet are among the performers.

Although most museums charge admission, several museums schedule a period when admission is free to all: **the Museum of Fine Arts,** Wednesday 4–9:45; **the Museum of Science,** Wednesday 1–5, November–April; **the Aquarium,** Thursday after 3, October–March. In Cambridge, the **Harvard University Museums of Natural History, the Fogg Art Museum,** and the **Arthur M. Sackler Museum** are free Saturday morning.

What to See and Do with Children

Children who are interested in history will find much to enjoy in Boston. The city's historical legacy is vivid and accessible: Youngsters can see where Paul Revere's lanterns were hung, and they can walk the decks of an undefeated man-of-war.

Boston Children's Museum (*see* Tour 3: Downtown Boston) *T stop, South Station.*
The *Boston Parents Paper* (tel. 617/522–1515), published monthly and distributed free throughout the city, is an excellent resource for finding out what's happening.

Shopping

Boston's shops and stores are generally open Monday through Saturday from 9 or 9:30 until 6 or 7; many stay open until 8 late in the week. Some stores, particularly those in malls or tourist areas, are open Sunday from noon until 5. The state sales tax of 5% does not apply to clothing or food (except food bought in restaurants). Boston's two daily newspapers, the *Globe* and the *Herald*, are the best places to learn about sales; Sunday's *Globe* often announces sales for later in the week.

Shopping Districts Most of Boston's stores and shops are located in an area bounded by Quincy Market, the Back Bay, downtown, and Copley Square. There are few outlet stores in the area, but there are plenty of bargains, particularly in the world-famous Filene's Basement and Chinatown's fabric district. Charles Street in Beacon Hill is a mecca for antiques lovers from all over the country.

Boston **Copley Place** (617/375–4400), an indoor shopping mall connecting the Westin and Marriott hotels, has 87 stores, restaurants, and cinemas that blend the elegant, the glitzy, and the overpriced. **Downtown Crossing,** Boston's downtown shopping area at Summer and

Washington streets, has been spruced up: It's now a pedestrian mall with outdoor merchandise kiosks, street performers, and benches for people-watchers. Here are the city's two largest department stores, Jordan Marsh and Filene's. **Faneuil Hall Marketplace** has small shops, kiosks of every description, street performers, and one of the great food experiences, Quincy Market. The intrepid shopper must cope with crowds of people, particularly on weekends. **Marketplace Center,** where 33 stores on two levels ring a central plaza, is adjacent to Faneuil Hall Marketplace and smack in the middle of the "Walkway to the Sea" from Government Center to Boston's waterfront. **Newbury Street,** Boston's version of New York's Fifth Avenue, is where the trendy gives way to the chic and the expensive.

Cambridge **Cambridgeside Galleria** (100 Cambridgeside Place, tel. 617/621–8666), in East Cambridge, is a three-story mall accessible by the Green Line's Lechmere T stop. It encompasses more than 60 shops, including the anchor stores of Filene's, Lechmere, and Sears. **Harvard Square** in Cambridge has more than 150 stores within a few blocks. In addition to the surprising range of items sold in the square, Cambridge is a book lover's paradise.

Department **Filene's** (426 Washington St., tel. 617/357–2100), a full-service de-
Stores partment store, is known for its two-level bargain basement (tel. 617/348–7974), where items are automatically reduced in price according to the number of days they've been on the rack. The competition can be stiff for the great values on discontinued, overstocked, or slightly irregular items. The **Harvard Coop Society** (1400 Massachusetts Ave., tel. 617/499–2000; at MIT, 3 Cambridge Center, tel. 617/499–3200) was begun in 1882 as a nonprofit service for students and faculty; the Coop is now a full department store known for its extensive selection of records and books.

Food Markets Every Friday and Saturday, **Haymarket** (near Faneuil Hall Marketplace) is a crowded jumble of outdoor fruit and vegetable vendors, meat markets, and fishmongers. The fruit sold here is often very ripe, and you may have to discard some of it, but you will still end up with more for your money.

Specialty **Bova's Bakery** (76 Prince St., tel. 617/523–5601). This is the place
Stores for freshly baked rolls and bread and wonderful bakery-style pizza
Baked Goods as well. It's open 24 hours.

Books **Barnes and Noble** (395 Washington St., tel. 617/426–5502, and 607 Boylston St., tel. 617/236–1308). Boston's biggest discount bookseller specializes in reduced prices on recent best-sellers and tables heaped with remainders at bargain prices.

Clothing **Alan Bilzerian** (34 Newbury St., tel. 617/536–1001) is the only place to go for avant-garde and au courant men's and women's clothing in Boston. **Ann Taylor** (18 Newbury St., tel. 617/262–0763, and Faneuil Hall Marketplace, tel. 617/742–0031) sells high-quality fashions for both classic and trendy dressers. **Bonwit Teller** (500 Boylston St., tel. 617/267–1200) has imported and American designer clothing and accessories, and an International Boutique and Designer Salon. Go to **Brooks Brothers** (46 Newbury St., tel. 617/267–2600; 75 State St., tel. 617/261–9990) for traditional formal and casual clothing. The styling is somewhat more contemporary in the third-floor Brooksgate shop, but basically Brooks is Brooks: correct and durable through the ages. **Louis** (234 Berkeley St., tel. 617/262–6100) carries elegantly tailored designs and a wide selection of imported clothing and accessories, including many of the more daring Italian styles. They also have subtly updated classics in everything from linen to tweed.

Ice Cream **Herrell's** (15 Dunster St., Cambridge, tel. 617/497–2179) is run by local ice cream maven Steve Herrell. Nondairy ice cream and frozen yogurt complement the extensive variety of regular ice cream flavors, of which chocolate pudding is one of the more intense.

Jewelry **Shreve, Crump & Low** (330 Boylston St., tel. 617/267–9100). The finest jewelry, china, crystal, and silver. Also an extensive collection of clocks and watches. Shreve's, one of Boston's oldest and most respected stores, is where generations of Brahmin brides have registered their china selections.

Sporting Goods **Eastern Mountain Sports** (1041 Commonwealth Ave., Brighton, tel. 617/254–4250). New England's best selection of gear for the backpacker, camper, climber, skier, or all-round outdoors person.

Thrift Shops **Bargain Box** (117 Newbury St., tel. 617/536–8580). Operated by a nonprofit organization, Bargain Box sells donated or consignment high-quality, often designer-label clothing.

Tobacconists **L. J. Peretti Company** (2½ Park Square, corner of Boylston and Charles Sts., tel. 617/482–0218). A Boston institution since 1870, this is one of the few places that still makes pipes. Peretti sells its own blends of tobacco, a large selection of others, and handmade imported cigars.

Toys **F.A.O. Schwarz** (440 Boylston St., tel. 617/266–5101). This branch of the famed New York toy emporium offers the highest quality (and the highest-priced) toys.

Participant Sports and Fitness

The mania for physical fitness is big in Boston. Most public recreational facilities, including the many skating rinks and tennis courts, are operated by the Metropolitan District Commission (MDC; tel. 617/727–5114, ext. 555).

Biking The **Dr. Paul Dudley White Bikeway,** approximately 18 miles long, runs along both sides of the Charles River. **The Bicycle Workshop** (259 Massachusetts Ave., Cambridge, tel. 617/876–6555) rents bicycles, fixes flat tires while you wait, and delivers bicycles to your hotel.

Golfing The **Massachussetts Golf Association** (190 Park Rd., Weston, tel. 617/891–4300) provides information on courses open to the public and equipment rentals.

Jogging Both sides of the Charles River are popular with joggers. Many hotels have printed maps of nearby routes.

Physical **Fitness** The **Westin Hotel** (Copley Place, Back Bay, tel. 617/262–9600) has complete health club facilities. Nonguests are welcome to use the facilities for an $8 fee.

Spectator Sports

Sports are as much a part of Boston as are codfish and Democrats. Everything you may have heard about the zeal of Boston fans is true, and out-of-towners wishing to experience it firsthand have these choices:

Baseball: The **Boston Red Sox,** American League (tel. 617/267–8661 or 617/267–1700 for tickets), play at Fenway Park.

Basketball: The **Boston Celtics,** NBA (tel. 617/523–3030 or 617/931–2000 for tickets), shoot hoops at Boston Garden on Causeway Street.

Football: The **New England Patriots,** NFL (tel. 800/543–1776), play football at Sullivan Stadium in Foxboro, 45 minutes south of the city.

Hockey: The **Boston Bruins,** NHL (tel. 617/227–3223), are on the ice (the ice is under the Celtics' parquet) at Boston Garden.

Dining

*Updated by
Jonathon
Alsop*

Boston is a city that respects traditions. Old Boston dining haunts that have been around for centuries persist through the years by resisting innovation and hewing closely to the culinary line that has made them successful—namely, the bean and the cod, as they say, but also the lobster and the shellfish. New restaurants, on the other hand, pop up regularly and manage to remain open thanks to experimentation and evolution.

Boston is composed of several diverse, easy-to-reach neighborhoods, and that's where the best food is. Except for very few exceptions, avoid all tourist destinations, which in a nutshell means Faneuil Hall and the waterfront. Please don't take this as a condemnation of all downtown restaurants, but if you want a taste of the authentic Boston, seek out the growing number of bistros and trattorias that serve splendidly fresh fare, usually in cozy local storefronts tucked here and there.

Neat but casual dress is fine unless otherwise noted; only a few restaurants still require coats and ties for men.

Back Bay   **Aujourd'hui.** This formal dining room of the Four Seasons Hotel has become one of the city's power rooms. The food reflects an inventive approach to regional ingredients and New American cuisine. Some entrées, such as rack of Colorado meadow lamb with layered potato and lasagna, can be extremely rich, but the seasonal menu also offers low-calorie, low-cholesterol, "alternative cuisine" choices. Window tables overlook the Public Garden. *200 Boylston St., tel. 617/451–1392. Reservations required. Jacket and tie advised. AE, DC, MC, V. Very Expensive.*

★ **L'Espalier.** Since 1988, this very special restaurant has been run by Frank McClelland, one of America's top chefs. Fresh native ingredients dominate the daily menu of contemporary French and American cuisine. All dinners are prix fixe; $56 for the regular menu and $72 for the seven-course tasting menu. Specialties include roast native partridge with chanterelles and cappuccino chanterelle soup. In recent years, the general atmosphere has become more relaxed and the wait staff more casual. Unchanged are the excellent wine list and the decor of the three intimate but elegant dining rooms, all with well-spaced tables. *30 Gloucester St., tel. 617/262–3023. Reservations required. Jacket and tie advised. AE, D, MC, V. No lunch. Closed Sun. Very Expensive.*

★ **Mirabelle.** In January 1993, catering magnate Stephen Elmont sold a business that fed 50,000 people a day and opened this beautifully understated restaurant on fashionable Newbury Street. The dining room seats 40 on two levels: The upper level, almost even with the street, offers great opportunities for people-watching. The interior features soft goldenrod-color walls and smooth, rounded woodwork. The menu changes a couple of times a season, but especially tasty are the grilled portobello and shiitake mushroom appetizer and the savory roasted veal chop entrée stuffed with prosciutto and sage. *85 Newbury St., tel. 617/859–4848. Jacket advised. Reservations advised. AE, DC, MC, V. Expensive.*

★ **Biba.** Everything about Biba's makes it Boston's overwhelmingly favorite place to see and be seen, from the vividness of the dining room's rambling mural to the huge street-level windows of the downstairs bar. The menu encourages inventive, inexpensive combinations, and the gutsy fare mixes flavors from five continents. Dishes are as simple as pan-fried oysters on semolina blinis or as elaborate as fried cauliflower in peppery olive oil on grilled sirloin with English Stilton. The wine list emphasizes adventurous selections from lesser-known areas. Allow plenty of time for dining; service can be slow. *272 Boylston St., tel. 617/426–7878. Reservations advised. D, DC, MC, V. Moderate–Expensive.*

Rocco's. Rocco's serves Italian cuisine from all regions. Dinner begins with a basket of warm crusty rolls, with soft garlic for a spread and olive oil for a dip. Sicilian baked tuna and roasted chicken cacciatore are some of the treats offered. For dessert there's tiramisù and hazelnut torte. *5 Charles St. S, Transportation Bldg., tel. 617/723–6800. Reservations advised. AE, D, DC, MC, V. Moderate–Expensive.*

Legal Sea Foods. What began as a tiny adjunct to a fish market has grown into a restaurant of important status, with additional locations in Chestnut Hill, the Copley Place Mall, the Prudential, and Kendall Square in Cambridge. Always busy, Legal still does things its own way. Dishes are not allowed to stand until the orders for a table are completed but are brought when ready to ensure freshness. The style of food preparation is, as always, straightforward: you can order seafood raw, broiled, fried, steamed, or baked; fancy sauces and elaborate presentations are rare. Homemade ice creams are welcome desserts. Legal also has a shop in Terminal C at Logan Airport (tel. 617/569–4622). Stop in before your flight departs, and they will package for you their famous chowder, pâté, shellfish, and lobster. *35 Columbus Ave., next to Park Plaza Hotel, tel. 617/426–4444. Cambridge: 5 Cambridge Ctr. in Kendall Sq., tel. 617/864–3400. Cambridge Legal accepts reservations only for parties of 6 or more; all others, no reservations. AE, D, DC, MC, V. Moderate.*

Miyako. This ambitious little restaurant in a bilevel space on Newbury Street serves some of the most exotic sushi in town. Among its estimable hot dishes are *age-shumai* (shrimp fritters), *hamachi teriyaki* (yellowtail teriyaki), and *agedashi* (fried bean curd). The waitresses are uncommonly personable, too. Tatami seating is available. *297A Newbury St., tel. 617/236–0222. Reservations advised. AE, DC, MC, V. Moderate.*

Small Planet. This world-beat bistro blends global peasant cuisine with new American motifs for an interesting mix of intriguing food and exotic atmosphere. The dining room is colorful with a lively bar scene, eccentric animal sculptures, and a working waterfall. Specials include pizzas, homemade pastas and curries, paella, fresh grilled fish, and quesadillas. Best of all, Small Planet is a restaurant with a social conscience, and owner Frank Bell often overextends himself to support and host noble charity events. *565 Boylston St., tel. 617/536–4477. No reservations. AE, D, DC, MC, V. No lunch Sun. and Mon. Moderate.*

Thai Cuisine. Those who have business at Northeastern University, tickets for a Symphony Hall event, or simply an adventurous palate will welcome Thai Cuisine. Dishes can be very spicy, but the kitchen will make adjustments. The food is not merely exotica; it is well cooked, and the kitchen uses first-rate ingredients. A main course of half a duck is the only single-size entrée on the menu; the rest are the kind you order and share with two or three. *14A Westland Ave., tel. 617/262–1485. No reservations. AE, DC, MC, V. No lunch Sun. Inexpensive.*

Dining

Aujourd'hui, **26**

Bartley's Burger
Cottage, **8**

Biba, **25**

Blue Diner, **32**

The Blue Room, **3**

Bombay Club, **10**

Daily Catch, **41**

Durgin-Park, **38**

East Coast Grill, **2**

Grendel's Den, **11**

Hamersley's
Bistro, **27**

The Harvest, **6**

Ho Yuen Ting, **31**

Iruna, **7**

Jimmy's
Harborside, **33**

Legal Sea Foods, **25**

L'Espalier, **15**

Michela's, **13**

Mirabelle, **22**

Miyako, **16**

Restaurant Jasper, **40**

Ristorante Lucia, **42**

Rocco's, **29**

Seasons, **39**

Small Planet, **21**

Thai Cuisine, **17**

Union Oyster
House, **36**

Lodging

Boston Harbor Hotel
at Rowes Wharf, **34**

Boston International
Hostel, **18**

Bostonian, **37**

Cambridge House Bed
and Breakfast, **9**

The Charles Hotel, **4**

Copley Square
Hotel, **20**

Eliot Hotel, **14**

Four Seasons, **28**

Harborside Hyatt
Conference Center
and Hotel, **43**

Hotel Meridien, **35**

The Inn at
Harvard, **12**

Lenox Hotel, **19**

Ritz-Carlton, **24**

Sheraton
Commander, **5**

Susse Chalet Inn, **1**

Tremont House, **30**

Wyndham Copley
Plaza, **23**

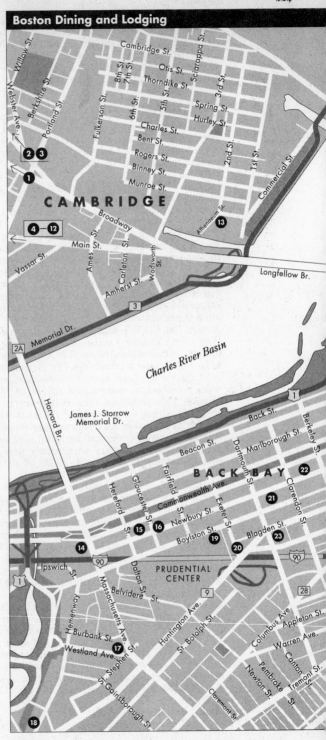

Boston Dining and Lodging

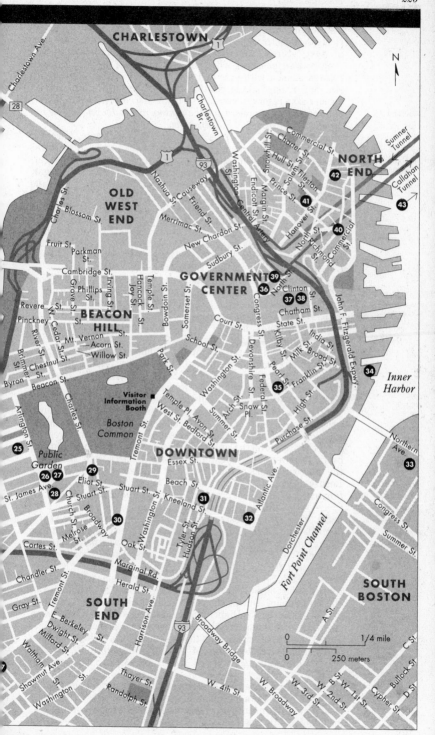

Cambridge
★

The Harvest. New owners and a new chef have brought few changes: The restaurant continues to emphasize ingredients that are native to Massachusetts and New England. The menu changes nightly but always features game and fresh fish. Current favorites include oven-roasted pheasant with wild rice and wild mushrooms, pan-roasted salmon with oats and maple-saffron sauce, and the outstanding roasted-garlic risotto. The less expensive café section doesn't take reservations. *44 Brattle St., tel. 617/492–1115. Reservations strongly advised for the dining room. Jacket and tie advised. AE, D, DC, MC, V. Expensive.*

Michela's. One of the city's most popular restaurants, Michela's boasts a menu that changes every eight weeks or so. It promises such imaginative dishes as pizza *margherita* (with five cheeses, caramelized onion, and truffle oil); roast duck with balsamic vinegar, olives, and duck liver *crostini* (toasted bits of bread); and lobster and Taylor Bay scallops in a broth with fennel, black pasta, and hot red peppers. All sauces, breads, and pastas are made fresh daily. The decor combines the building's industrial past (with exposed heating ducts) with soft, Tuscan colors. An atrium café serves a lighter menu, with all dishes less than $12. *1 Athenaeum St. (lobby of former Carter Ink Bldg.), tel. 617/225–2121. Reservations advised. Closed Sun. AE, DC, MC, V. Expensive.*

The Blue Room. Totally hip, funky, and Cambridge, the Blue Room blends together a world of ethnic cuisines. The emphasis is on lots of grilled or smoked fare and an eclectic blend of spices and ingredients. Dishes here focus on flavor rather than formality: Recommended favorites include the smoked duck leg and hominy appetizer, and the Latin Trio—a large platter of assorted specialties, such as chili-glazed shrimp, garlic and chicken chorizo, pork loin with spices, cornbread salad, black beans, pickled cole slaw, flour tortillas, and salsa. *1 Kendall Sq., tel. 617/494–9034. Reservations advised. No lunch. MC, V. Moderate–Expensive.*

★ **East Coast Grill.** The chef calls his food "equatorial cuisine," and rightly so: Ethnic dishes such as grilled tuna with black bean sauce, grilled sweetbreads, jerk chicken, and "pasta from Hell"—a pasta livened with hot sauce—share the menu with such Southern regional specialties as North Carolina barbecue. The dining room is small, bright, and very busy. Next door is Jake & Earl's Dixie Barbecue, the take-out branch of the East Coast Grill and home of the Inner Beauty sauces. *1271 Cambridge St., tel. 617/491–6568. Reservations accepted for 5 or more; go early or late to avoid a long wait. No lunch. MC, V. Moderate–Expensive.*

Iruna. This Spanish restaurant, popular with students for years, specializes in paellas and seafoods and has great salads. Outdoor dining, on a private patio, is possible in warm weather. Wine and beer only. *56 JFK St., tel. 617/868–5633. Reservations accepted. No credit cards. Closed Sun. Moderate.*

★ **Bombay Club.** Specializing in northern Indian cuisine with southern Indian dishes on Sunday, Bombay Club offers a beautiful view of Harvard Square. During the week, their luncheon buffet is a splendid bargain at $5.95. Dinner specials include kebabs of baby lamb chops, chicken tikka marsala, and many homemade cheese dishes. This is quietly becoming one of the Boston area's favorite ethnic restaurants and is not to be missed. *57 John F. Kennedy St., tel. 617/661–8100. Reservations advised. AE, D, DC, MC, V. Inexpensive–Moderate.*

Grendel's Den. Housed in a former Harvard College fraternity building, Grendel's has an unusually warm (three fireplaces), clubby atmosphere, a downstairs bar, and an eclectic assortment of cuisines, including Middle Eastern, Greek, Indian, Italian, and French. Diners are welcome to mix and match small-portion dishes, which generally include such diverse items as shish kebab, fettuccine, moussaka, hummus, and broiled fish. And there's a large salad bar. *89 Winthrop St., tel. 617/491–1160. No reservations. AE, D, DC, MC, V. Inexpensive–Moderate.*

Bartley's Burger Cottage. Famed for its 42 varieties of burgers and its fried onion rings, Bartley's is good, too, for salads and sandwiches. Daily specials might include baked meat loaf with mashed potatoes and a vegetable. The small, crowded tables and bustling waitresses qualify the place as a real burger joint. It's popular with students. *1246 Massachusetts Ave., tel. 617/354–6559. No reservations. Closed Sun. No credit cards. Inexpensive.*

Downtown **Blue Diner.** This original 1945 diner has genuine diner food as well as more sophisticated offerings. It gets rave reviews for such originals as pork loin stuffed with Granny Smith apples, and homemade corned beef hash, considered by many to be the best in Boston. Tuesday through Saturday, it's one of the few places in town that's open all night; it closes at midnight Sunday and Monday. *178 Kneeland St., tel. 617/338–4639. No reservations. AE, D, DC, MC, V. Open Tues.–Sat. 24 hours; Sun. and Mon. 7:30 AM–midnight. Moderate.*

★ **Ho Yuen Ting.** Every night a waiting line forms outside this Chinatown hole-in-the-wall. The reason is simple: Ho Yuen Ting serves some of the best seafood in town. The house specialty is a sole and vegetable stir-fry served in a spectacular whole, crisply fried fish. Come with friends so you can also enjoy the clams with black bean sauce, lobster with ginger and scallion, and whole steamed bass. *13A Hudson St., tel. 617/426–2316. Reservations accepted for 7 or more. No credit cards. Inexpensive–Moderate.*

Faneuil Hall **Seasons.** Popular with businesspeople and politicians (City Hall is ★ just a block away), this solarium-like restaurant on the fourth floor of the Bostonian Hotel overlooks the bustling Faneuil Hall Marketplace and is a good place to entertain when you want to impress. The cuisine of chef Anthony Ambrose is American with international influences, and it changes seasonally. Selections from the summer menu include steamed halibut with Oriental spices and apple paper, and for dessert, macadamia nut and coconut flan with mango sorbet. The wine list is exclusively American. *Bostonian Hotel, North and Blackstone Sts., tel. 617/523–3600. Reservations advised. No lunch. AE, DC, MC, V. Expensive.*

Union Oyster House. Established in 1826, the Union Oyster House is Boston's oldest restaurant. For nearly two decades its best feature has been a first-floor shellfish bar—a handy place to stop for a dozen fresh, well-chilled oysters or cherrystone clams on the half shell. The rooms at the top of the narrow staircase are dark and have low ceilings—very Ye Olde New England. A recent bar addition has a lighter feel. *41 Union St., tel. 617/227–2750. Reservations accepted. No lunch Sun. AE, D, DC, MC, V. Moderate.*

Durgin-Park. Diners here should be hungry enough to cope with enormous portions, yet not so hungry that they can't tolerate the inevitably long wait. Durgin-Park was serving its same hearty New England fare (Indian pudding, baked beans, and huge prime rib) back when Faneuil Hall was a working market instead of a tourist attraction. The atmosphere is uniquely Old Boston. *340 Faneuil Hall Marketplace (North Market Bldg.), tel. 617/227–2038. Reservations accepted for 15 or more. AE, MC, V. Inexpensive–Moderate.*

North End **Restaurant Jasper.** Jasper White trained a number of Boston's best
★ chefs, and his national reputation as the creator of contemporary
New England cuisine is well deserved. Dishes are as nouvelle as a
salad of grilled duck with cranberries and spiced nuts—or as traditional as a New England boiled dinner cooked to perfection. The exposed brick walls and red lacquer furniture create a contemporary
atmosphere, and the luscious desserts are anything but Puritan. *240
Commercial St., tel. 617/523–1126. Reservations advised. Closed
Sun., Mon. D, MC, V. Very Expensive.*

Ristorante Lucia. Some aficionados consider Lucia's the best Italian
restaurant in the North End. Its specialties from the Abruzzi region
include batter-fried artichoke hearts or mozzarella in carrozza as
appetizer and the chicken alla Lucia or *pollo arrabiatta.* Check out
the upstairs bar, with its pink marble and its takeoff on the Sistine
Chapel ceiling. *415 Hanover St., tel. 617/523–9148. Reservations accepted. No lunch Mon.–Thurs. AE, D, MC, V. Moderate.*

Daily Catch. Shoulder-crowding small, this storefront restaurant
specializes in calamari dishes, lobster fra diavolo, linguini with clam
sauce—at extremely reasonable prices that compensate for the almost always crowded atmosphere. A second restaurant has opened
at 261 Northern Avenue, across from Jimmy's Harborside, and a
third in Brookline at 441 Harvard Street. Hours of operation vary
greatly; call for times. *323 Hanover St., tel. 617/523–8567. No reservations. No credit cards. Inexpensive–Moderate.*

South End **Hamersley's Bistro.** Fiona and Gordon Hamersley have received
★ rave reviews since opening this dining spot in 1987. The restaurant
moved to a new location in late 1993, and it now includes a full bar, a
café area with 10 tables for walk-ins, and a larger dining room that's
a little more formal and decorative than the bar and café, though nowhere near stuffy. Specialties that have a permanent place on the
daily menu include a garlic and mushroom sandwich (served as an
appetizer) and roast chicken with garlic, lemon, and parsley. *553
Tremont St., tel. 617/423–2700. Reservations advised. D, MC, V.
Expensive.*

Waterfront **Jimmy's Harborside.** This exceedingly popular seafood establishment enjoys a solid reputation. The bright, three-tier main dining
room was designed to ensure that every table has an unobstructed
view of the harbor. In addition to the many fresh seafood preparations that have long been standard fare, the menu now offers such
specials as pasta primavera with a medley of sautéed shrimp, veal,
and pork tenderloin. As a change from chowder or traditional
bouillabaisse, try the scampi Luciana, a bouillabaisse made with
white wine, cream, and a variety of fresh fish and shrimp. The wine
list showcases American wines. The Boat Bar, the scene of high-
spirited camaraderie, is a favorite watering hole of politicians. *242
Northern Ave., tel. 617/423–1000. Reservations accepted. No lunch
Sun. AE, DC, MC, V. Moderate.*

Lodging

Many of the city's most costly lodging places offer attractively
priced weekend packages. These weekend rates (and their availability) will vary; for a free copy of the *Boston Travel Planner,* contact
the **Greater Boston Convention and Visitors Bureau** (Box 490, Prudential Tower, Boston, MA 02199, tel. 617/536–4100, fax 617/424–
7664).

Although Boston does not have a large number of bed-and-breakfasts, there are several, and they are usually very reasonable, with

daily rates in the $55–$120 per room range. Reservations may be made through **Bed and Breakfast Associates Bay Colony** (Box 57166, Babson Park Branch, Boston 02157, tel. 617/449–5302 or 800/347–5088, fax 617/449–5302).

Back Bay

★ **Four Seasons.** The only hotel (other than the Ritz) overlooking the Public Garden, the newer 15-story Four Seasons specializes in luxurious personal service, Old World elegance, and comfort. The rooms have king-size beds, individual climate control, minibars, and 24-hour room service. A room overlooking the Garden is worth the extra money. The antiques-filled public rooms include a relaxed piano lounge and Aujourd'hui (*see* Dining, *above*), a fine restaurant serving New American cuisine. *200 Boylston St., 02116, tel. 617/338–4400 or 800/332–3442, fax 617/423–0154. 288 rooms and suites. Facilities: lounge, concierge, heated indoor pool, sauna, exercise machines, whirlpool. AE, DC, MC, V. Very Expensive.*

★ **Ritz-Carlton.** Since 1927 this hotel overlooking the Public Garden has been one of the most luxurious and elegant places to stay in Boston, and many people consider it the only place in town. Its reputation for quality and service (there are two staff members for every guest) continues. All the rooms are traditionally furnished and equipped with bathroom phones and refrigerators. The most coveted rooms remain the suites in the older section, which have working fireplaces and the best views of the Public Garden. Public rooms include the elegant café, with a window on chic Newbury Street; the sumptuous second-floor main dining room; the sedate Street Bar; and The Lounge. *Arlington and Newbury Sts., tel. 617/536–5700 or 800/241–3333, fax 617/536–1335. 241 rooms, 48 suites. Facilities: affiliated with spa a block away, exercise room, laundry, barber salon. AE, DC, MC, V. Very Expensive.*

★ **Wyndham Copley Plaza.** The stately, bowfronted classic among Boston hotels, built in 1912, has been elegantly renovated. Guest rooms have carpeting from England, customized furniture from Italy, and new bathroom fixtures surrounded by marble tile. The Plaza Bar has seating to accommodate piano bar performances; Copley's Bar has just been renovated. A separate concierge area has been created. The hotel staff is multilingual, children under 18 stay free in their parents' room, and pets are welcome. *138 St. James Ave., 02116, tel. 617/267–5300 or 800/826–7539, fax 617/247–6681. 319 rooms, 51 suites. Facilities: 2 restaurants, 2 bars, beauty and barber salons. AE, DC, MC, V. Very Expensive.*

Copley Square Hotel. One of Boston's oldest hotels (1891), the Copley Square is still one of the best values in the city. It has recently undergone extensive renovations and a complete restoration of its facade, bringing it back to its turn-of-the-century look. The original Sport Saloon has also been entirely renovated. The hotel is popular with Europeans and is European in flavor. The rooms, which are set off long, circuitous hallways, vary tremendously in size from very small to spacious. Some of the furnishings have been replaced; others will be refurbished. If you want a quiet room, ask for one on the courtyard. The popular Café Budapest is downstairs. Children under 14 stay free in their parents' room. *47 Huntington Ave., 02116, tel. 617/536–9000 or 800/225–7062, fax 617/267–3547. 143 rooms. Facilities: use of a nearby health club for a small fee, coffee shop. AE, DC, MC, V. Expensive.*

Lenox Hotel. Constructed in 1900, the Lenox has long been a comfortable—if unexciting—hotel, but extensive renovations have given it a low-key elegance. The soundproof guest rooms have spacious walk-in closets, TV, and air-conditioning. The decor is Early American or Chinese on the lower floors, French provincial on the top floor. The lobby is ornate and handsome, trimmed in blues and golds and set off by a large, welcoming fireplace that evokes the ambience of a country inn. Diamond Jim's Piano Bar, with its loyal local clientele, has been remodeled, and an added wheelchair lift has improved accessibility to both Diamond Jim's and the main lobby. Children under 18 stay free in their parents' room. *710 Boylston St., 02116, tel. 617/536–5300 or 800/225–7676, fax 617/266–7905. 222 rooms. Facilities: 2 restaurants. AE, DC, MC, V. Expensive.*

Eliot Hotel. An ambitious renovation has brought a new elegance and lots of marble to a formerly modest nine-floor, European-style hotel. The upgraded, all-suite Eliot offers marble baths, period furnishings, and a marble-clad lobby. All rooms have air-conditioning and cable TV. An extensive breakfast is offered for a small fee. The popular Eliot Lounge is next door to the hotel. Children under 12 stay free in their parents' room. *370 Commonwealth Ave., 02215, tel. 617/267–1607, fax 617/536–9114. 12 rooms, 82 suites. Facilities: laundry. AE, DC, MC, V. Moderate–Expensive.*

Boston International Hostel. This is a youth-oriented hostel near the Museum of Fine Arts and Symphony Hall. Guests sleep in dormitories for three to five persons and must provide their own linens or sleep sacks (sleeping bags are not permitted). There are five family rooms available with reservations. The maximum stay is three nights in summer, seven nights off-season. Reservations are highly recommended. Doors close at 2 AM. Preference is given to AYH members in high season; contact the Greater Boston Council of American Youth Hostels (1020 Commonwealth Ave., Boston 02215, tel. 617/731–5430) for information. *12 Hemenway St., 02115, tel. 617/536–9455. Capacity 190 in summer, 100 in winter. MC, V. Inexpensive.*

Cambridge

★ **The Charles Hotel.** The Charles anchors one end of the Charles Square development, which is set around a brick plaza facing the Charles River. The architecture is sparse and modern, softened by New England antiques and paintings by local artists. Guest rooms have quilts, TVs in the bathroom, and an honor bar. The dining room, Rarities, serves new American cuisine. A Sunday buffet brunch is served in the Bennett Street Cafe. The Regattabar is one of the city's hottest spots for jazz. Children under 18 stay free in their parents' room. *1 Bennett St., 02138, tel. 617/864–1200 or 800/882–1818, fax 617/864–5715. 296 rooms. Facilities: full spa services, indoor pool, 24 shops. AE, DC, MC, V. Very Expensive.*

★ **Sheraton Commander.** A nicely maintained older hotel on Cambridge Common, its rooms are furnished with four-poster beds. Children under 17 stay free in their parents' room. All rooms have TV and air-conditioning, and some have kitchenettes. *16 Garden St., 02138, tel. 617/547–4800 or 800/325–3535, fax 617/868–8322. 176 rooms and suites. Facilities: restaurant, lounge, business center, concierge, fitness room. AE, DC, MC, V. Expensive.*

Cambridge House Bed and Breakfast. A gracious 1892 Greek Revival house listed on the National Register of Historic Places, Cambridge House offers 16 antiques-filled guest rooms, most with private baths. The site is convenient to the T and buses; there is also a reservations center here for host homes and short-term rentals in the metropolitan Boston area. Rates include a full gourmet breakfast and afternoon tea and sherry. *2218 Massachusetts Ave., 02140, tel. 617/491–6300 or 800/232–9989, fax 617/868–2848. AE, MC, V. Moderate.*

The Inn at Harvard. One of the newer hotels in the area, this understated four-story property sits on an island in the heart of Harvard Square. Owned by Harvard University and run by Doubletree Hotels, the inn was intended to house university visitors, but it welcomes tourists and business travelers as well. Each room has cable television and voice mail and, on the walls, original 17th- and 18th-century sketches on loan from the nearby Fogg Art Museum, as well as more contemporary watercolors. Many rooms have tiny balconies, and all rooms feature oversize windows with views of Harvard Square or Harvard Yard. Breakfast and dinner are served in the lobby to guests only. *1201 Massachusetts Ave., 02138, tel. 617/491–2222 or 800/528–0444, fax 617/491–6520. 113 rooms. Facilities: laundry and dry cleaning, meeting rooms, business center. AE, DC, MC, V. Moderate.*

Susse Chalet Inn. This is a typical Susse Chalet: clean, economical, and sparse. It's isolated from most shopping or sites, a 10-minute drive from Harvard Square, but it is within walking distance of the Red Line terminus, offering T access to Boston and Harvard Square. All rooms have TV and air-conditioning. *211 Concord Tpk., 02140, tel. 617/661–7800 or 800/258–1980, fax 617/868–8153. 78 rooms. AE, DC, MC, V. Inexpensive.*

Downtown **Boston Harbor Hotel at Rowes Wharf.** One of Boston's most elegant
★ luxury hotels is located right on the water, providing a dramatic entryway to the city for travelers arriving from Logan Airport via the water shuttle that docks at the hotel. The hotel is within walking distance of major sights. The guest rooms begin on the eighth floor, and each has either a city view or a water view; the decor has hints of mauve or green and cream, and the traditional furnishings include a king-size bed and a sitting area. Some rooms have balconies. Business travelers benefit from a new, fully equipped business center. The elegant and comfortable Rowes Wharf Restaurant offers seafood and American regional cuisine as well as sweeping harbor views. The spectacular Sunday brunch is expensive at $35 per person but worthwhile for those with healthy appetites or children under 12, who eat free. *70 Rowes Wharf, 02110, tel. 617/439–7000 or 800/752–7077, fax 617/330–9450. 204 rooms, 26 suites. Facilities: 2 restaurants, bar, health club and spa with pool, whirlpool, sauna, steam and massage rooms, gift shop, business center, marina. AE, DC, MC, V. Very Expensive.*

Bostonian. One of the city's smallest hotels and one of its most charming, the Bostonian epitomizes European-style elegance with fresh flowers in its rooms, private balconies, and French windows. The Harkness Wing, constructed originally in 1824, has rooms with working fireplaces, exposed-beam ceilings, and brick walls. The rooms tend to be small but are extremely comfortable. The service is attentive, and the highly regarded Seasons restaurant (*see* Dining, *above*) has a glass-enclosed rooftop overlooking the marketplace. Children under 12 stay free in their parents' room. *Faneuil Hall Marketplace, 02109, tel. 617/523–3600, 617/523–2454, or 800/343–0922. 152 rooms and suites. Facilities: restaurant, Jacuzzi in some suites. AE, DC, MC, V. Very Expensive.*

★ **Hotel Meridien.** The respected French chain refurbished the old downtown Federal Reserve Building, a landmark Renaissance Revival building erected in 1922. The rooms, including some cleverly designed loft suites, are airy and naturally lighted, and all have been recently redecorated. Most rooms have queen- or king-size beds; all rooms have a small sitting area with a writing desk, a minibar, modern furnishings, in-room movies, and two phones lines. Julien, one of the city's finest French restaurants, is here, as is the Café Fleuri, which serves a Saturday afternoon chocolate buffet and an elegant, award-winning Sunday brunch. There are two lounges. Some pets permitted. *250 Franklin St., 02110, tel. 617/451–1900 or 800/543–4300, fax 617/423–2844. 326 rooms, including several bilevel suites.*

Facilities: health club with whirlpool, dry sauna, and exercise equipment; indoor pool. AE, DC, MC, V. Very Expensive.

Logan Airport **Harborside Hyatt Conference Center and Hotel.** Although it is situated at Logan Airport, the city's newest hotel actually claims one of the most spectacular views of Boston's skyline, across the harbor from downtown. All rooms have a water view; half have a view of the city, while others look out over the harbor toward the sea. In addition to a private water shuttle, which crosses the harbor from the hotel to downtown, the Hyatt operates its own complimentary shuttle from the airport terminals and the airport T stop. Both the Harborside Grill restaurant and the lobby lounge have harbor and city views. Room amenities include turndown service, two phones, robes, video checkout, and soundproof windows. *101 Harborside Dr., 02128, tel. 617/568–1234 or 800/233–1234, fax 617/568–6080. 270 rooms. Facilities: health club, heated pool, sauna, outdoor jogging trail, business services. AE, D, DC, MC, V. Very Expensive.*

Theater District **Tremont House.** The once-popular 12-story Bradford Hotel (closed for three years and completely renovated by Choice Hotels International) is again a welcome constituent of the Boston hotel scene. Because the Bradford was built as national headquarters for the Elks Club in 1925, when things were done on a grand scale, its spacious lobby has high ceilings, marble columns, a marble stairway, and lots of gold leaf. The 16-foot, four-tier crystal chandelier is a replica of the original, which was made in West Germany (five similar chandeliers hang in the ballroom). The guest rooms tend to be small; they are furnished in 18th-century Thomasville reproductions and decorated with prints from the Museum of Fine Arts. Good news for deli lovers: One of New York's most popular spots for corned beef and blintzes, the Stage Delicatessen, has opened a deli here with a promise to truck in authentic Kosher pickles from the Big Apple. *275 Tremont St., 02116, tel. 617/426–1400 or 800/331–9998, fax 617/338–7881. 281 rooms. Facilities: laundry, nightclub, restaurant. AE, DC, MC, V. Expensive.*

The Arts

Boston is a paradise for patrons of all the arts, from the symphony orchestra to experimental theater and dance to Orson Welles film festivals. Thursday's *Boston Globe* Calendar and the weekly *Boston Phoenix* (published on Thursday) provide comprehensive listings of events for the coming week.

Bostix is Boston's official entertainment information center and the largest ticket agency in the city. Half-price tickets are sold here for the same day's performances. *Faneuil Hall Marketplace, tel. 617/723–5181. Open Tues.–Sat. 11–6, Sun. 11–4.*

CONCERTCHARGE (tel. 617/497–1118; open Mon.–Fri. 9–6, Sat. 9–5:30) and **Ticketmaster** (tel. 617/931–2000; open Mon.–Fri. 9 AM–10 PM, weekends 9–8) are ticket brokers for telephone purchases.

Theater First-rate Broadway tryout theaters are clustered in the theater district (near the intersection of Tremont and Stuart Sts.) and include the Colonial, the Shubert, the Wang Center for the Performing Arts, and the Wilbur. Local theater companies all over the city thrive as well.

The **Loeb Drama Center** (64 Brattle St., tel. 617/495–2668) has two theaters, the main one an experimental stage. This is the home of the American Repertory Theater, the long-established resident professional repertory. The highly respected ART produces both classic and experimental works. **Emerson Majestic Theatre** (219 Tremont St., tel. 617/578–8727), at Emerson College, the nation's only private institution devoted exclusively to communications and performing arts, has undertaken the extensive multimillion-dollar job of restoring this 1903 Beaux Arts building. The Majestic hosts professional productions from all walks of Boston's cultural scene, from avant-garde dance to drama to classical concerts. The **Huntington Theatre Company** (264 Huntington Ave., tel. 617/266–0800), under the auspices of Boston University, is Boston's largest professional resident theater company, performing five plays annually, a mix of established 20th-century plays and classics.

Music　For its size, Boston is the most musical city in America, unsurpassed in the variety and caliber of its musical life. Of the many contributing factors, perhaps the most significant is the abundance of universities and other institutions of learning. Boston's churches also offer outstanding, often free, music programs; check the Thursday and Saturday listings in the *Boston Globe*. Early music, choral groups, and chamber music also thrive.

Symphony Hall (301 Massachusetts Ave., tel. 617/266–1492) is one of the world's most perfect acoustical settings, home to the Boston Symphony Orchestra and the Boston Pops.

Dance　**Boston Ballet** (19 Clarendon St., tel. 617/695–6950), the city's premier dance company, performs at the Wang Center for the Performing Arts. **Dance Umbrella** (380 Green St., Cambridge, tel. 617/492–7578) is one of New England's largest presenters of contemporary dance. Performances are scheduled in theaters throughout Boston. The Umbrella also offers information on all dance performances in the Boston area.

Film　Cambridge is the best place in New England for finding classic, foreign, and nostalgia films.

The Brattle Theater (40 Brattle St., Cambridge, tel. 617/876–6837) is a recently restored landmark cinema for classic-movie buffs. **Harvard Film Archive** (Carpenter Center for the Visual Arts, 24 Quincy St., Cambridge, tel. 617/495–4700) programs the work of directors not usually shown at commercial cinemas; two screenings daily. **Loews Nickelodeon Cinema** (606 Commonwealth Ave., tel. 617/424–1500) is one of the few theaters in the city that shows first-run independent and foreign films as well as revivals.

Opera　The **Boston Lyric Opera Company** (114 State St., tel. 617/248–8660), a professional company, presents three fully staged productions each season. They have performed operas of Massenet, Mozart, Strauss, and others, and they always include a 20th-century work in their repertoire.

Nightlife

Boston restaurants, clubs, and bars, often clustered in distinct areas in various parts of the city, offer a broad spectrum of evening and late-night entertainment.

The Quincy Market area may be the center of the city's nightlife; it has been thronged with visitors from the day the restoration opened in 1976. Here in the shadow of historic Faneuil Hall you'll find international cuisine and singles bars among the specialty shops and boutiques.

Copley Square is the hub of another major entertainment area, and Kenmore Square, near the Boston University campus, has clubs and discos devoted to rock and alternative groups.

The most breathtaking views of the city at night are from the Top of the Hub Restaurant, 50 stories up atop the Prudential Center, and the Bay Tower Room at 60 State Street. Both have convivial bars and live music.

Thursday's *Boston Globe* Calendar, a schedule of events for the upcoming week, includes an extensive listing of live entertainment in the *Nightlife* section. The weekly *Boston Phoenix* (also published on Thursday) is another excellent source for entertainment.

Bars and Lounges The **Bull and Finch Pub** (84 Beacon St., tel. 617/227–9605), the original of which was dismantled in England, shipped to Boston, and reassembled here, is an obvious success and provided the inspiration for the TV series *Cheers*. **Daisy Buchanan's** (240a Newbury St., tel. 617/247–8516) is a favorite hangout of athletes; you might run into Cam Neely or Mike Greenwell at the bar. The jukebox is loud.

Cafés and Coffeehouses **Blacksmith House** (56 Brattle St., Cambridge), the original 18th-century house where Longfellow's blacksmith lived, is now operated by the Cambridge Center for Adult Education (tel. 617/547–6789). It houses an excellent German bakery (tel. 617/534–3036) with indoor tables and a warm-weather streetside café. Poetry readings, concerts, and plays are staged in the Spiegel Performance Center, located at the rear of the building. **Passim's** (47 Palmer St., Cambridge, tel. 617/492–7679), one of the country's first and most famous venues for live folk music, is by day a quiet basement setting for a light lunch or a coffee break. By night it's a gathering place for folk and bluegrass music or poetry readings.

Comedy **Catch a Rising Star** (Upstairs at the Wursthaus, 4 JFK St., Cambridge, tel. 617/661–9887 or 617/661–0167), run by the former New York club of the same name, has comedy seven nights a week. Nationally known acts appear Thursday–Saturday; new talents are showcased Sunday–Wednesday.

Disco Fast-paced **Avalon** (15 Lansdowne St., tel. 617/262–2424) is one of Boston's largest clubs. Near Kenmore Square, it features high-energy disco and a giant dance floor that can accommodate more than 1,000 people. House music pervades at **Quest** (1270 Boylston St., tel. 617/424–7747), a four-floor club that caters to a mixed gay/straight crowd Thursday, a gay male crowd on Friday and Saturday, and lesbians on Sunday. Quest is the only Boston club with a roof deck.

Jazz Some top names in jazz perform at **Regattabar** (Bennett and Eliot Sts., Cambridge, tel. 617/864–1200), a spacious and elegant club in the Charles Hotel. The **Boston Jazz Line** (tel. 617/787–9700) reports jazz happenings.

Rock **The Paradise** (967 Commonwealth Ave., tel. 617/254–2052 or 617/254–2053) is known for big-name talent, such as Sinéad O'Connor and Robin Trower. Rock, jazz, folk, blues, alternative pop/rock, and country all take turns on stage here, and the audience varies with the entertainment. This is a good venue for live shows; artists play here for the intimate setting. Tickets may be purchased in advance at Ticketmaster (tel. 617/931–2000) or at the box office.

Singles **Cityside Bar** (262 Faneuil Hall Marketplace, tel. 617/742–7390), a well-known singles haven, offers live entertainment nightly by local rock groups. It's a good spot, but it can be crowded and noisy. **Chaps** (27 Huntington Ave., tel. 617/266–7778), a popular gay men's bar and dance club, plays '70s oldies on Tuesday and pop and disco the rest of the week.

Excursion: Lexington and Concord

The events of April 19, 1775, the first military encounters of the American Revolution, are very much a part of present-day Lexington and Concord. In these two quintessential New England towns, rich in literary and political history, one finds the true beginning of America's Freedom Trail on the very sites where a Colonial people began their fight for freedom and a new nation.

Lexington To reach Lexington by car from Boston, cross the Charles River at the Massachusetts Avenue Bridge and proceed through Cambridge, bearing right for Arlington at Harvard Square. Continue through Arlington Center on Massachusetts Avenue to the first traffic light, turn left into Jason Street, and begin your tour. Travel time is 25 minutes one-way. The **MBTA** (tel. 617/722–3200) operates buses to Lexington and Boston's western suburbs from Alewife Station in Cambridge. Travel time is about one hour one-way.

As the Redcoats retreated from Concord on April 19, 1775, the Minutemen peppered the British with musket fire from behind low stone walls and tall pine trees before marching to the safety of Charlestown's hills. "The bloodiest half-mile of Battle Road," now Massachusetts Avenue in Arlington, began in front of the **Jason Russell House,** a Colonial farmhouse. Bullet holes are still visible in the house. *7 Jason St., Arlington, tel. 617/648–4300. Admission: $2 adults, 50¢ children under 13. Open Mon.–Fri. 1–5, weekends by appointment. 30-min tours available.*

Continuing west on Massachusetts Avenue (through Arlington Heights), you'll pass the **Old Schwamb Mill,** the **Museum of Our National Heritage,** and the **Munroe Tavern** (a pub of 1635 now open to the public) before coming to **Lexington Green.** On this 2-acre, triangular piece of land, the Minuteman Captain John Parker assembled his men to await the arrival of the British, who marched from Boston to Concord to "teach rebels a lesson" on the morning of April 19. Henry Hudson Kitson's renowned statue of Parker, the **Minuteman Statue,** stands at the tip of the Green, facing downtown Lexington. *Visitors Center (Lexington Chamber of Commerce), 1875 Massachusetts Ave., Lexington 02173, tel. 617/862–1450. Open June 1–Oct. 31, daily 9–5; Nov. 1–Nov. 30 and Jan. 1–May 31, daily 10–4; Dec., weekdays 10–4, weekends 10–2.*

On the right side of the Green is **Buckman Tavern,** built in 1690, where the Minutemen gathered initially to wait for the British on April 19. A 30-minute tour visits the tavern's seven rooms. *1 Bedford St., tel. 617/862–5598. Admission: $2.50 adults, 50¢ children 6–16. Open weekend nearest Apr. 1–Oct. 31, Mon.–Sat. 10–5, Sun. 1–5.*

A quarter-mile north of the Green stands the eight-room **Hancock-Clarke House,** a parsonage, built in 1698. Here the patriots John Hancock and Samuel Adams were roused from their sleep by Paul Revere, who had ridden out from Boston to "spread the alarm through every Middlesex village and farm" that the British were marching to Concord. A 20-minute tour is offered. *35 Hancock St., tel. 617/861–0928. Admission: $2.50 adults, 50¢ children 6–16. Open weekend nearest Apr. 19–Oct. 31, Mon.–Sat. 10–5, Sun. 1–5. The Lexington Historical Society offers a $5 combination ticket for* *the Munroe Tavern, the Buckman Tavern, and the Hancock-Clarke House.*

The town of Lexington comes alive each **Patriot's Day** (the Monday nearest April 19) to celebrate and re-create the events of April 19, 1775, beginning at 6 AM, when "Paul Revere" rides down Massachusetts Avenue shouting "The British are coming! The British are coming!" "Minutemen" groups in costume participate in events throughout the day.

Concord   To reach Concord from Lexington, take Routes 4/225 through Bedford and Route 62 west to Concord; or Route 2A west, which splits from Routes 4/225 at the Museum of Our National Heritage. The latter route will take you through parts of **Minute Man National Historical Park,** whose more than 750 acres commemorate the events of April 19; it includes Fiske Hill and the **Battle Road Visitors Center,** approximately 1 mile from the Battle Green on the right off Route 2A. *Tel. 617/862–7753. Admission free. Open mid-Apr.–Dec., daily 8:30–5. Audiovisual programs, printed material, lectures in summer.*

A short drive from Monument Square on Main Street to Thoreau Street, then left onto Belknap Street, takes you to the **Thoreau Lyceum,** where the writer and naturalist's survey maps, letters, and other memorabilia are housed. A replica of his Walden Pond cabin is here. *156 Belknap St., tel. 508/369–5912. Admission: $2 adults, 50¢ children under 12. Open Feb., Sat. 10–5, Sun. 2–5; Mar.–Dec., Mon.–Sat. 10–5, Sun. 2–5.*

At the **Old North Bridge,** a half-mile from Concord Center, Minutemen from Concord and surrounding towns fired "the shot heard round the world," signaling the start of the American Revolution. The National Historical Park's North Bridge Visitors Center is ½ mile down Monument Street. *174 Liberty St., tel. 508/369–6993. Open daily 8:30–5. Lectures Apr.–Oct.*

Next door is the **Old Manse,** built in 1769–1770. where Nathaniel Hawthorne and Ralph Waldo Emerson lived at different times. The house is filled with memorabilia from the Emerson family's more than 160 years here and Hawthorne's brief 3½-year stay. *Monument St., tel. 508/369–3909. Admission: $4 adults, $3.50 senior citizens, $2.50 children 6–12. Open mid-Apr.–late Oct., Mon. and Wed.–Sat. 10–4:30; Sun. 1–4:30.*

When Hawthorne returned to Concord in 1852, he bought a rambling structure called **The Wayside,** where visitors can now see his tower study. *455 Lexington Rd. (Rte. 2A), tel. 508/369–6975. Admission: $2 adults, under 16 and over 62 free. Open mid-Apr.–Oct. 31, Tues.–Sun. 10–5:30 (last tour leaves promptly at 5).*

On one side of The Wayside is Louisa May Alcott's family home, the **Orchard House,** where she wrote *Little Women*. Nothing is roped off in Orchard House, allowing visitors to get a good sense of what life was like for the Alcotts. *399 Lexington Rd., tel. 508/369–4118. Admission: $4 adults, $3 senior citizens, $2 children 6–12. Open Apr. 1–Sept. 15, Mon.–Sat. 10–4:30, Sun. 1–4:30; Sept. 16–Oct. 31., daily 1–4:30; Nov. and Mar., weekends only 1–4:30.*

On the other side of The Wayside, the yard of **Grapevine Cottage** (491 Lexington Rd.; not open to the public) has the original Concord grapevine, the grape that the Welch's jams and jellies company made famous.

After leaving the Old Manse, Emerson moved to what we know as the **Ralph Waldo Emerson House** at 28 Cambridge Turnpike. Here he wrote the famous *Essays* ("To be great is to be misunderstood"; "A foolish consistency is the hobgoblin of little minds, adored by little statesmen and philosophers and divines"). Furnishings are pretty much as Emerson left them, even down to his hat on the banister newel post. *28 Cambridge Tpk., on Rte. 2A, tel. 508/369–2236. Admission: $3 adults, $1.50 children 6–17. Open mid-Apr.–mid-Oct., Thurs.–Sat. 10–4:30, Sun. 2–4:30. 30-min tours.*

The original contents of Emerson's study and 15 period rooms are in the **Concord Museum**, ½ mile southeast on Route 2A heading into Concord, across the street from Emerson's house. *200 Lexington Rd., tel. 508/369–9609. Admission: $5 adults, $4 senior citizens, $2 children under 15. Open Mon.–Sat. 10–5, Sun. 1–5.*

Dining **Versailles.** An intimate French restaurant, the Versailles serves such specialties as brie with caviar baked in puff pastry and quiche Lorraine for lunch, rack of lamb and veal Oscar for dinner. *1777 Massachusetts Ave., Lexington, tel. 617/861–1711. Reservations advised. AE, DC, MC, V. No lunch Sun. Very Expensive.*
Colonial Inn. Traditional fare—from prime rib to scallops—is served in the gracious dining room of an inn of 1718. Lighter fare is offered in the lounge. Overnight accommodations are available in 54 rooms. *48 Monument Sq., Concord, tel. 508/369–9200. Reservations advised for dinner. Jacket advised at dinner. AE, DC, MC, V. Expensive.*
Walden Station. A casual restaurant situated in an old brick firehouse, Walden Station prepares American cuisine such as fresh seafood and beef fillets. The fresh desserts are made on premises. *24 Walden St., Concord, tel. 508/371–2233. Reservations accepted for 5 or more. AE, D, MC, V. Inexpensive–Moderate.*

The South Shore

Following the northward sweep of the New England coast, many travelers stay on I-95 as it makes its inland shortcut from Providence directly to Boston. In doing so, they bypass a large southeastern chunk of the state, sandwiched in between the Cape and the Boston suburbs. While it may not be as prosperous or as picturesque as other areas of Massachusetts, this is a region with its own strong historical associations—notably the great seafaring towns of Fall River and New Bedford, and the Pilgrims' colony at Plymouth. Even vacationers heading for the Cape all too often barrel past these towns, thus missing an important dimension of New England's past.

Important Addresses and Numbers

Visitor Information **Bristol County Convention and Visitor's Bureau** (70 N. 2nd St., New Bedford 02740, tel. 508/997–1250; open Mon.–Fri. 9–5). **New Bedford Office of Tourism** (47 N. 2nd St., New Bedford 02740, tel. 508/991–6200; open daily 9–4). **Plymouth County Development Council** (Box 1620, Pembroke 02359, tel. 617/826–3136). **Plymouth Visitor Information** (Rte. 3 [Exit 5], Plymouth, tel. 508/746–1150; open daily 8–4:30).

Emergencies **St. Luke's Hospital** (101 Page St., New Bedford, tel. 508/997–1515). **CVS** (2100 Achshnet Ave., New Bedford, tel. 508/996–2653) is open until 10 on weekdays, 9 on weekends.

Late-Night Pharmacy

Getting Around the South Shore

By Car   Fall River and New Bedford are connected by I–195, and from both cities the most direct route to Boston is Route 24, via Route 140 from New Bedford. I–93 connects Boston with Quincy; from here Route 3 is the quickest way to Plymouth.

By Bus   From Boston, **MBTA** buses (tel. 617/722–3200) serve both Quincy and Braintree, **American Eagle** (tel. 508/993–5040) serves New Bedford, and **Bonanza** (tel. 617/720–4110) serves Fall River.

By Train   The Boston subway (the "T") runs to Quincy; The **Plymouth and Brockton Street Railway Co.** (tel. 508/746–0378) calls at Plymouth en route to Cape Cod.

Guided Tours

Colonial Lantern Tours (Box 3541, Plymouth 02361, tel. 508/747–4161) runs 90-minute, lantern-lit strolls around Plymouth after dark, which take in Brewster Gardens, Plymouth Rock, and the site of the original Plimoth Plantation (not the re-created version). Tours leave from the John Carver Inn (25 Summer St; Apr., May, Sept., Oct. Fri.–Sun.; June–Aug. daily).

Plymouth Rock Trolley Co. (tel. 508/747–3419) offers narrated trolley tours of Plymouth, which make about 40 stops including Plimoth Plantation, the *Mayflower II*, and Plymouth Harbor. A one-day ticket (adults $5, children $2) allows unlimited reboarding; trolleys run every 20 minutes May–late November.

Captain John Boats (117 Standish Ave., Plymouth 02360, tel. 508/746–2643 or 800/242–2469) operates whale-watching cruises from Plymouth in spring, summer, and early fall; they also run daily 45-minute tours of Plymouth Harbor, June through September. All tours depart from either State Pier or the nearby Town Wharf.

Exploring the South Shore

Numbers in the margin correspond to points of interest on the South Shore map.

East of Rhode Island, as I–195 swings towards the Cape, the first Massachusetts city of interest is **Fall River.** It's hardly an inspiring town in terms of scenery—industrial docks and enormous factories recall the city's past as a major textile center in the 19th and 20th centuries. It also served as a port, however, and today the most interesting site is **Battleship Cove,** down beside the Taunton River in the shadow of the I–195 bridge. The cove harbors several museums and the 35,000-ton battleship USS *Massachusetts,* the battleship USS *Joseph P. Kennedy, Jr.,* and a World War II attack sub, the USS *Lionfish. Battleship Cove, tel. 508/678–1905. Admission: $8 adults, $6 senior citizens, $4 children 6–14. Open daily 9–5.*

In 1992, the **Fall River Carousel,** built in the 1920s, was rescued from the now-defunct Lincoln Amusement Park and moved to Battleship Cove. Both kids and adults marvel at this glorious restoration, which is now housed dockside. *Battleship Cove, tel. 508/324–4300. Rides: $1. Open Memorial Day–Labor Day, daily 10–10; Labor Day–Memorial Day, Fri.–Sun. 11–4.*

Nearby, the **Marine Museum at Fall River** celebrates the age of sail and steamship travel, especially the lavishly fitted ships of the Old Fall River Line, which operated until 1937 between New England

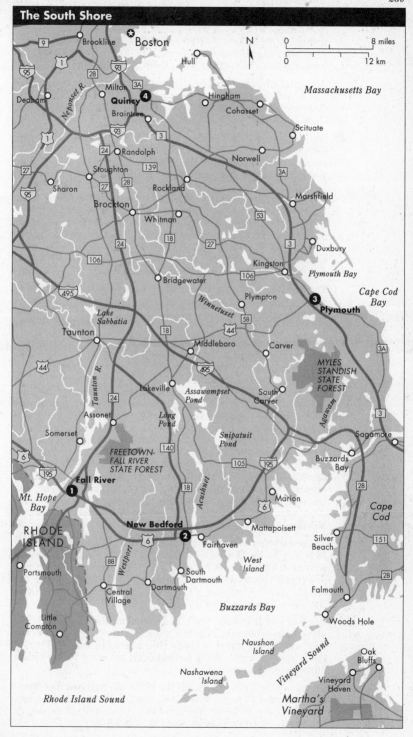

The South Shore

and New York City. The museum also contains the largest existing model of the *Titanic*—a 28-foot-long, 1-ton representation used in the famous 1952 movie. *70 Water St., tel. 508/674–3533. Admission: $3 adults, $2 children 6–14. Open May–Sept., weekdays 9–4:30, weekends 10–5; Oct.–Apr., Wed.–Fri 9–4, weekends 12–4.*

Also riverside, the **Fall River Heritage State Park** tells the story of Fall River's industrial past, focusing on the city's textile mills and their workers. *200 Davol St. W, tel. 508/675–5759. Admission free. Open July–Aug., daily 10–6; Sept.–June, daily 10–4.*

❷ Interstate–195 links Fall River to **New Bedford,** home of the largest fishing fleet on the East Coast. The historic district near the water is a delight; it was here that Herman Melville set his famous whaling novel, *Moby-Dick.* The **New Bedford Whaling Museum,** established in 1902, is the largest American museum devoted to the years of whaling, an era that lasted some 200 years in New Bedford. A 22-minute film depicting an actual whaling chase is shown twice daily July–August, once on weekends the rest of the year. Next door, you can see the **Seaman's Bethel,** the small chapel featured in *Moby-Dick. 18 Johnny Cake Hill, tel. 508/997–0046. Admission: $3.50 adults, $3 senior citizens, $2.50 children 6–14. Open Mon.–Sat. 9–5, Sun. 1–5 (from 11 AM on Sun. July and Aug.).*

The **New Bedford Preservation Society** publishes a series of excellent walking tours of the city's restored area. These and other brochures are available at the office of tourism (*see* Visitor Information, *above*).

East of New Bedford, I–195 intersects with I–495; here you may elect to head south to Cape Cod (*see* Cape Cod, *below*) or follow I–495 north toward Boston for one exit to Route 58. Take Route 58 north to Route 44, then head east to "America's hometown" of **❸** **Plymouth,** with its narrow streets, clapboard mansions, and antiques stores. Admire the picturesque waterfront, or browse and shop along the twisting main street. In December 1620, 102 weary Pilgrims disembarked on this spot, and today you can learn of their subsequent colonization at **Plimoth Plantation,** a reconstruction of the original settlement, where actors in period costume speak Jacobean English and carry on the daily life of the 17th century. In the furnished homes, "residents" demonstrate such household skills as soapmaking; you can also tour a meetinghouse, crafts center, and the vegetable gardens. *Warren Ave. (Rte. 3A), tel. 508/746–1622. Admission: $18.50 adults, $11 children 5–12 (includes entry to Mayflower II). Open Apr.–Nov., daily 9–5.*

At the waterfront is moored the *Mayflower II,* an exact replica of the 1620 *Mayflower.* The second version was built in England and sailed across the Atlantic in 1957; it, too, is staffed by costumed "Pilgrims" who regale visitors with tales of their trying journey. *State Pier, tel. 508/746–1622. Admission: $5.75 adults, $3.75 children 5–12. Open Apr.–Nov., daily 9–5 (until 7 in July and Aug.).*

Close by, on the shore, you'll find **Plymouth Rock,** popularly believed to have been the Pilgrims' stepping stone when they left the ship. Across the street is **Cole's Hill,** where the company buried their dead—at night, so the Indians could not count the dwindling numbers of survivors.

On top of Cole's Hill now stands the **Plymouth National Wax Museum,** containing 26 scenes with life-size models that tell the Pilgrims' story. *16 Carver St., tel. 508/746–6468. Admission: $5 adults, $2 children 5–12. Open mid-Feb.–Nov 30., daily 9–5.*

Away from the waterfront, the **Pilgrim Hall Museum** contains a sizable collection of household goods, books, weapons, and furniture used by the Pilgrims. *75 Court St. (Rte. 3A), tel. 508/746–1620. Admission: $5 adults, $4 senior citizens, $2.50 children 6–15. Open daily 9:30–4:30.*

Cranberry World, operated by Ocean Spray, tells the story of the one local crop and includes displays on harvesting, an outdoor working cranberry bog, and information about the natural inhabitants of the wetlands. *225 Water St., tel. 508/747–2350. Admission free. Open May–Nov., daily 9:30–5.*

4 Take scenic Route 3A along the coast north to **Quincy,** the only city in the United States with the birthplaces, homes, and final resting places of two U.S. presidents. The **Adams National Historic Site** comprises the Adams Mansion, residence of the Adams family for four generations; a short distance away, the birthplace of John Adams, second U.S. president; and the neighboring house where his son, John Quincy Adams, sixth U.S. president, was born. A guided tour of all three houses lasts about 1½ hours. *135 Adams St., tel. 617/773–1177. Admission: $2 adults, children under 16 free. Open mid-Apr.–mid.-Nov., daily 9–5.*

What to See and Do with Children

A&D Toy and Train Museum. Here's a great spot to take the kids on a rainy day. About 30 minutes inland of Plymouth by car, the museum houses various doll and toy collections but is devoted mainly to train sets: The star exhibit is a 34-foot-long model railway with 25 trains running on six levels. *49 Plymouth St., Middleboro 02346, tel. 508/947–5303. Admission $4.50 adults, $4 senior citizens, $3.50 children 4–12. Open July–Aug., Thurs.–Mon. 11–5; Sept.–Jun., Fri.–Sun. 11–5.*

Battleship Cove and **Fall River Carousel,** Fall River

Children's Museum. This museum contains many hands-on exhibits, including building blocks, bubbles, a display focused on Portuguese culture, and a wind farm model demonstrating different kinds of alternative energy. Outside are 60 acres of land with nature trails and picnic areas. *276 Gulf Rd., South Dartmouth 02748, tel. 508/993–3361. Admission: $3.75. Open Tues.–Sat. 10–5, Sun. 1–5.*

Mayflower II, Plymouth

Plimoth Plantation, Plymouth

Whaling Museum, New Bedford

Shopping

Antiques
A few antiques stores are on the South Shore, especially around Plymouth, but it is not a prime antiques-hunting area like the North Shore. For a brochure, contact **Southeastern New England Antiques Dealers Association** (Box 4416, East Providence, RI 02914, tel. 401/781–7222 or 508/993–4944).

Outlet Stores
Fall River is a haven for outlet-hopping. More than 100 of these small shops are housed in several old mills in the district north of downtown. For a brochure, contact the **Fall River Factory Outlet District Association** (683 Quequechan St., 02721, tel. 800/424–5519). In Plymouth a restored 19th-century rope mill is the site of a large shopping center: **Cordage Park** (Court St., Rte. 3A, tel. 508/746–7707) has 30 stores, 15 of which are factory outlets.

Dining and Lodging

Dress is casual and reservations are unnecessary unless otherwise noted.

Braintree
Lodging

Sheraton Tara. Brass statues of knights stand guard in the lobby of this huge, castle-fronted building. Room size and decor vary in the different wings, but all feature traditional furnishings, recliner chairs, and fanlight-shape headboards. Every evening the Sheraton offers live musical entertainment in the Irish tavern. The hotel lives up to the usual high standards of a Sheraton business hotel and is convenient to both Boston and the South Shore. *Rte. 128, Exit 6, 02184, tel. 617/848–0600. 377 rooms, 17 suites. Facilities: 2 restaurants, lounge, bar, health club, sauna, Jacuzzi, indoor and outdoor pool, meeting rooms, live entertainment. AE, D, DC, MC, V. Expensive–Very Expensive.*

Fall River
Dining

Leone's. Conveniently close to Battleship Cove on the waterfront, Leone's provides free docking space for customers in the summer months. Huge fish tanks, brass railings, and potted plants decorate the split-level, carpeted dining room, which is candlelit at night. Tables overlook the water, and the view is so pleasant you almost forget you're in Fall River. Specialties include lobster, prime rib, pasta, and chicken. *4 Davol St., Battleship Cove, tel. 508/679–8158. Reservations advised. AE, D, DC, MC, V. Moderate.*

T.A. Restaurant. This Portuguese-American restaurant is a friendly place in the center of Fall River. Spotlighting shows up light-pine wall panels hung with wicker decorations and plants. The menu—available in English or Portuguese—lists such specialties as tuna steak, red snapper, grilled *chaureo* (sausage), stewed octopus with potatoes in wine sauce, chicken, and steak. *408 S. Main St., tel. 508/673–5890. AE, D, DC, MC, V. Moderate.*

Lodging

Days Inn. This chain inn is just a couple of minutes' walk from Main Street and up the hill from Battleship Cove. Fairly spacious guest rooms have modern, comfortable furnishings in browns and greens, but views from the windows are grim. *332 Miliken Blvd., 02721, tel. 508/676–1991. 102 rooms. Facilities: restaurant, lounge, bar, outdoor pool, conference rooms. AE, D, DC, MC, V. Moderate–Expensive.*

New Bedford
Dining

Freestones. In the middle of the restored historic downtown area, this large, attractive restaurant is set in a refurbished bank, originally built in 1877. The interior is a strange but successful mix of marble floors, mahogany paneling, old church furniture (the front desk was once a pulpit), and modern curios. Entrées include Black Angus sirloin, broiled swordfish, lime barbecued chicken, and pasta dishes, as well as sandwiches and salads. *41 William St., tel. 508/993–7477. AE, DC, MC, V. Moderate.*

★ **Lisboa Antiga.** This outstanding Portuguese restaurant, at the Durant Sail Loft Inn but under different management, serves up generous portions of fish stew, baked fish in onion sauce, barbecued spring chicken, and steak prepared in an earthenware frying pan. It's a great find in a somewhat unauspicious location. *1 Merrill's Wharf, tel. 508/999–4495. AE, D, DC, MC, V. Moderate.*

Lodging

Durant Sail Loft Inn. The Durant Sail loft is convenient to the historic district, on the water, and the only full-service inn for miles. It's in an impressive, granite-block structure: the converted Bourne Counting House at the end of Merrill's Wharf. Jonathan Bourne, a successful 19th-century whaling merchant, used to watch his ships sail into harbor from the tall bay window on the second floor, now in the inn's Jonathan Bourne guest room. Though restaurant downstairs (*see* Lisboa Antiga, *above*) is excellent, the Sail Loft can't quite get it together: An excellent manager recently left, and this understaffed inn is currently up for sale—hopefully new ownership will restore it to its former reputation. *1 Merrill's Wharf, 02740, tel. 508/999–2700. 16 rooms. Facilities: restaurant, conference rooms. AE, D, DC, MC, V. Moderate.*

Plymouth
Dining

The Inn for All Seasons. Away from Route 3A up a long, winding drive, this restaurant backs onto pleasant gardens and has the charm of a faded country mansion. It was formerly the summer residence of a coal magnate from Pennsylvania. Three small dining rooms have large windows, frilled curtains, and decorative plates on racks; the bistro-style Pavilion room has an oak bar, fieldstone fireplace, and nightly entertainment. Try broiled scrod, chicken Milano baked with mozzarella, or veal parmigiana. *97 Warren Ave., tel. 508/746–8823. No lunch Tues.–Sat. Closed Mon. AE, DC, MC, V. Moderate.*

McGrath's Restaurant. This seafood place is decked with typical seafaring decor—the lights are either ship's-wheel chandeliers or have lobster-pot shades. The low-ceiling, square dining room has wood beams, and a closed-in patio looks toward the harbor. Traditional New England fare includes deep-fried fillet of sole, Ipswich clams, lobster cooked in five styles, and chicken and steak. *Water St. at Town Wharf, tel. 508/746–9751. AE, MC, V. Moderate.*

★ **The Station.** Housed in the former Plymouth fire station, this chic three-story bistro is anchored by a central staircase. The ceiling is of beautiful carved-wood panels, and tall windows in the exposed-brick walls overlook Plymouth's Main Street. Tables are candlelit, and unobtrusive live entertainment (barbershop quartets and the like) adds atmosphere. The menu cites a wide variety of seafood, pasta, steak, and chicken dishes. *51 Main St., tel. 508/746–1200. AE, MC, V. Moderate.*

★ **The Lobster Hut.** This casual oceanside restaurant is known for its great value. Order as you enter, then eat either in the small, bright dining room with modern, fast food–style furnishings, or at stone picnic tables on a deck overlooking the harbor. Best bets are fried lobster, clam chowder, fish-and-chips, and fried clams. Chicken and burgers are also served. *Town Wharf, tel. 508/746–2270. Closed Dec. 20–Jan. 31. No credit cards. Inexpensive.*

Lodging

Sheraton Plymouth at Village Landing. This is atypical of most Sheratons: The business atmosphere has been toned down, its setting in a modern shopping complex is unremarkable, and the exterior resembles a condominium block. Still, inside it's up to snuff. Most guest rooms, furnished with reproduction antiques, have balconies and surround the pool in a three-story atrium formation. The hotel is just one block from the ocean and convenient to all attractions. *180 Water St., 02360, tel. 508/747–4900 or 800/325–3535. 175 rooms, 3 suites. Facilities: restaurant, lounge, bar, indoor pool, Jacuzzi, sauna, exercise room, meeting rooms. AE, D, DC, MC, V. Expensive–Very Expensive.*

John Carver Inn. It would be hard for any inn to live up to the expectations raised by the massive pillared facade of this red-brick building, and the John Carver only just manages to do so. Although the public rooms and dining rooms are lavish, with period furnishings and stylish drapes, the bedrooms reveal the inn's 1969 construction: They are square and fairly small, with modern furnishings mixed with a few shiny reproductions. Newer refurbished rooms are a little more luxurious, with high-quality, business-style furnishings and matching floral-print fabrics. *25 Summer St., 02360, tel. 508/746–*

7100. 79 rooms. Facilities: restaurant, lounge, outdoor pool, meeting rooms. AE, D, DC, MC, V. Moderate–Expensive.

★ **Pilgrim Sands Motel.** Although it's a couple of miles south of downtown Plymouth, on Route 3A, this A-one motel is opposite Plimoth Plantation and has its own private beach. Choose a room with an ocean view—the sea practically laps against the walls. In fact, a major storm in 1991 virtually destroyed the first floor, and in 1992 the owners rebuilt and refurbished 14 rooms. Second-floor ocean-view rooms have balconies and deck chairs. The light, airy rooms are pleasantly furnished; some have refrigerators, and two large suites are luxuriously appointed. The friendly management tops off the experience. *150 Warren Ave., 02360, tel. 508/747–0900. 64 rooms, 2 suites. Facilities: coffee shop, lounge, indoor and outdoor pools, Jacuzzi, deck. AE, D, DC, MC, V. Moderate–Expensive.*

The Arts

Theater The **Zeiterion Theatre** (684 Purchase St., tel. 508/994–2900) in New Bedford is the only year-round performing arts center in southern Massachusetts. It draws a regular flow of well-known artists and attractions to the historic downtown location.

Cape Cod

Separated from the Massachusetts "mainland" by the 17.4-mile Cape Cod Canal, the Cape is always likened in shape to an outstretched arm bent at the elbow, its fist turned back at Provincetown toward the mainland. It's 70 miles from end to end, with 15 towns, each broken up into villages. The term Upper Cape refers to the towns of Bourne, Falmouth, Mashpee, and Sandwich; Mid-Cape, to Barnstable, Yarmouth, and Dennis; and Lower Cape, to Harwich, Chatham, Brewster, Orleans, Eastham, Wellfleet, Truro, and Provincetown.

The Cape is for relaxing—swimming and sunning, fishing and boating, playing golf and tennis, attending theater and hunting antiques. Despite summer crowds and overdevelopment, much remains unspoiled. Visitors continue to enjoy the Cape's charming old New England villages of weathered-shingle houses and white steepled churches, as well as its pine woods, grassy marshes, and rolling dunes.

Memorial Day through Labor Day (in some cases, Columbus Day) is high season on Cape Cod; you'll find good beach weather then, but high prices and crowds as well. Spring and fall are best for bird-watching, nature hikes, country drives, and lower prices at inns and specials at restaurants. In winter, many museums, shops, restaurants, and lodging places are closed; the intimate bed-and-breakfasts and inns that remain open—their tariffs greatly reduced—can make romantic winter retreats.

Important Addresses and Numbers

Visitor Information The main source of information on all of Cape Cod is the **Cape Cod Chamber of Commerce** (jct. Rtes. 6 and 132, Hyannis 02601, tel. 508/362–3225; open year-round, weekdays 8:30–5 and, Memorial Day–Columbus Day, weekends 9–4). Information booths are open daily 9–5, Memorial Day through Columbus Day, at the Sagamore Bridge rotary (tel. 508/888–2438) and just over the Bourne Bridge on Route 28 (tel. 508/759–3814) heading toward Falmouth.

Emergencies **Cape Cod Hospital** (27 Park St., Hyannis, tel. 508/771–1800); **Falmouth Hospital** (100 Ter Heun Dr., Falmouth, tel. 508/548–5300).

Late-Night Most of the Cape's 20 **CVS** stores, such as the one in the Cape Cod
Pharmacies Mall in Hyannis (tel. 508/771–1774), are open daily until 9 PM.

Getting Around Cape Cod

By Car From Boston (60 mi), take Route 3 south to the Sagamore Bridge. From New York (220 mi), take I–95 north to Providence; change to I–195 and follow signs for the Cape to the Bourne Bridge. Both roads connect to Route 6, running the length of the Cape. In summer, avoid arriving at the bridges in late afternoon, especially on holidays: All the major roads are heavily congested eastbound on Friday night and westbound on Sunday afternoon.

Barnstable's airport has the following car-rental agencies: **Avis** (tel. 508/775–2888), **Hertz** (tel. 508/775–5825), and **National** (tel. 508/771–4353).

By Bus The **Cape Cod Regional Transit Authority** (tel. 508/385–8326 or, in MA, 800/352–7155) offers its SeaLine service between Hyannis and Woods Hole, with stops at popular destinations; the buses can be flagged along the route. **Plymouth & Brockton Street Railway** (tel. 508/775–5524 or 508/746–0378) has service from Boston and Logan Airport, as well as between Sagamore and Provincetown, with stops at many towns in between. **Bonanza** (tel. 508/548–7588 or 800/556–3815) serves Bourne, Falmouth, Woods Hole, and Hyannis. All service is year-round.

By Bicycle The Cape will satisfy both the avid and the occasional cyclist. The terrain is fairly flat, and there are several bike trails. Rentals are available at **Arnold's** (329 Commercial St., Provincetown, tel. 508/487–0844), **Cascade Motor Lodge** (201 Main St., Hyannis, tel. 508/775–9717), **Idle Times** (off the Rail Trail, Rte. 6A, Brewster, tel. 508/896–9242), **The Little Capistrano** (across from Salt Pond Visitor Center, Rte. 6, Eastham, tel. 508/255–6515), **Outdoor Shop** (50 Long Pond Dr., South Yarmouth, tel. 508/394–3819), and **P&M Cycles** (across from canal path, 29 Main St., Buzzards Bay, tel. 508/759–2830).

Guided Tours

Cruises **Cape Cod Canal Cruises** (two or three hours, narrated) leave from Onset, just northwest of the Bourne Bridge. A Sunday jazz cruise, sunset cocktail cruises, and evening dance cruises are available Fridays and Saturdays. *Onset Bay Town Pier, tel. 508/295–3883. Cost: $6.50–$12 adults, $3.25–$6 children 6–12; $1 senior citizen discount Mon. and Fri. Tours May–mid-Oct.*

Hy-Line offers one-hour narrated tours of Hyannis Harbor, including a view of the Kennedy compound; sunset cruises also available. *Ocean St. dock, Pier 1, Hyannis, tel. 508/778–2600. Cost: $8 adults, $3.50 children 5–12 with adult. Tours mid-May–mid-Oct.*

Capt. John Boats offers excursions to Provincetown from Plymouth. *State Pier, Plymouth, tel. 508/747–2400 or, in MA, 800/242–2469. Cost, round-trip: $21 adults, $18 senior citizens, $14 children 2–11. Tours Memorial Day–Sept.*

| Train Tours | **Cape Cod Scenic Railroad** runs 1¾-hour excursions between Sagamore and Hyannis with stops at Sandwich and the Canal. The train passes ponds, cranberry bogs, and marshes. A dinner run is also offered some evenings; call for schedule. *Main and Center Sts., Hyannis, tel. 508/771-3788. Several departures daily (except Mon.) in each direction mid-June–Oct. Cost: $10.50 adults, $9.50 senior citizens, $6.50 children 3–12.* |

| Nature Tours | The **Massachusetts Audubon Society** (contact Wellfleet Bay Wildlife Sanctuary, Box 236, South Wellfleet 02663, tel. 508/349–2615) sponsors year-round, naturalist-led wildlife tours, including trips to Monomoy Island, canoe trips, bird-watching and insect-spotting walks, cruises, and hikes. |

The **Cape Cod Museum of Natural History** (Box 1710, Brewster, MA 02631, tel. 508/896–3867) offers four- and six-hour summer nature walks in Chatham's Monomy National Wildlife Refuge and an overnight in the island lighthouse. For a sedentary afternoon, take a two-hour boat ride through Nauset Marsh.

| Plane Tours | Sightseeing by air is offered by **Hyannis Air Service** (Barnstable airport, tel. 508/775–8171), **Cape Cod Flying Service** (Cape Cod Airport, 1000 Race La., Marstons Mills, tel. 508/428–8732), and **Cape Air** (Provincetown airport, tel. 800/352–0714). Cape Air also offers rides in a 1930 Stinson. |

| Dune Tours | **Art's Dune Tours** (tel. 508/487–1950 or 800/894–1951) gives hourlong narrated auto tours through the National Seashore and dunes around Provincetown. |

| Bike Tours | **Cape Cod Cycle Tours** (Box 1356, N. Eastham 02651, tel. 508/255–8281) arranges guided day trips. |

| Whale-Watching | Provincetown is close to the feeding grounds at Stellwagen Bank, 6 miles to the north. Several operators offer whale-watch tours from April through October, with morning, afternoon, or sunset sailings lasting three to four hours. Tickets are available at booths on MacMillan Wharf. **Dolphin Fleet** (tel. 508/349–1900 or 800/826–9300) tours are accompanied by scientists from Provincetown's Center for Coastal Studies, who provide commentary while collecting data on the whale population they've been monitoring for years. |

Out of Barnstable Harbor, there's **Hyannis Whale Watcher Cruises** (tel. 508/362–6088 or 800/287–0374; tours Apr.–Oct.), offering a fully narrated cruise on Cape Cod Bay.

Exploring Cape Cod

Numbers in the margin correspond to points of interest on the Cape Cod map.

Route 6, the Mid-Cape Highway, passes through the relatively unpopulated center of the Cape, characterized by a landscape of scrub pine and oak. Paralleling Route 6 but following the north coast is Route 6A, the Old King's Highway, in most sections a winding country road that passes through some of the Cape's best-preserved old New England towns. The south shore of the Cape, traced by Route 28, is heavily populated and the major center for tourism, encompassing Falmouth, Hyannis, and Chatham.

1 At the Cape's extreme southwest corner is **Woods Hole,** where ferries depart for Martha's Vineyard. An international center for marine research, it is home to the Woods Hole Oceanographic Institution (WHOI), whose staff led the successful search for the *Ti-*

tanic in 1985; the Marine Biological Laboratory (MBL); and the National Marine Fisheries Service, among other scientific institutions.

The **WHOI Exhibit Center** offers videos and exhibits on the institute and its projects. *15 School St., Woods Hole, tel. 508/457–2000, ext. 2663. Suggested donation: $1. Open Apr.–Oct, Tues.–Sat. 10–4:30, Sun. noon–4:30; Nov.–Dec., Fri.–Sun.; Feb.–Mar., Fri. and Sat. Call for off-season hours.*

The National Marine Fisheries Service has a public **aquarium** with two harbor seals in summer, tanks displaying regional fish and shellfish, plus hands-on tanks and microscopes for children. *Corner Albatross and Water Sts., Woods Hole, tel. 508/548–7684. Admission free. Open late June–mid-Sept., daily 10–4; mid-Sept.–late June, weekdays 9–4.*

The **Marine Biological Laboratory** (tel. 508/548–3705, ext. 423; call for reservations and meeting instructions) offers 1½-hour tours of its facilities, led by retired scientists, on weekdays in summer.

A free walking tour of the village is conducted one afternoon a week in July and August by the **Woods Hole Historical Collection** (Bradley House Museum, 573 Woods Hole Rd., tel. 508/548–7270). Before leaving Woods Hole, stop at **Nobska Light** for a great view of the Elizabeth Islands and Vineyard Sound.

② The village green in **Falmouth** was used as a military training field in the 18th century. Today it is the center of a considerable shopping district, flanked by attractive old homes, some fine inns, and the 1896 **First Congregational Church,** with a bell cast by Paul Revere.

The Falmouth Historical Society conducts free, docent-guided walking tours of the town in season. It also maintains two museums. The 1790 **Julia Wood House** has fine period architectural details (wide-board floors, leaded-glass windows, Colonial kitchen with wide hearth), plus embroideries, baby shoes and clothes, toys and dolls, and furniture. The **Conant House** next door, a 1794 half-Cape, has military memorabilia, whaling items, scrimshaw, sailors' valentines, silver, glass, and china. *Palmer Ave. at the Village Green, Falmouth, tel. 508/548–4857. Admission: $2 adults, 50¢ children under 13. Open mid-June–mid-Sept., weekdays 2–5.*

Outside town is the **Ashumet Holly and Wildlife Sanctuary,** a 45-acre tract of woods, ponds, meadows, and hiking trails supervised by the Massachusetts Audubon Society. The 1,000 holly trees include American, Oriental, and European varieties. *Ashumet Rd., off Rte. 151, East Falmouth, tel. 508/563–6390. Admission: $3 adults, $2 senior citizens and children under 13. Open daily sunrise–sunset.*

③ **Hyannis** is the Cape's year-round commercial hub. On its bustling Main Street, housed in the red-brick Old Town Hall, is the **John F. Kennedy Hyannis Museum,** which focuses on JFK's ties to the Cape through videos and artifacts from the presidential years. *397 Main St., tel. 508/775–2201. Admission: $1 adults, children under 17 free. Open daily 10–4.*

The **John F. Kennedy Memorial,** on Ocean Street overlooking Lewis Bay, is a plaque and fountain pool in memory of the president who **④** spent his summers nearby in the quietly posh village of **Hyannis Port.** The **Kennedy family compound**—best viewed from the Hy-Line cruise (*see* Guided Tours, *above*)—became the summer White House during the JFK administration.

The proliferation of motels, restaurants, and antiques shops continues past Hyannis on the south shore but thins out somewhat as you

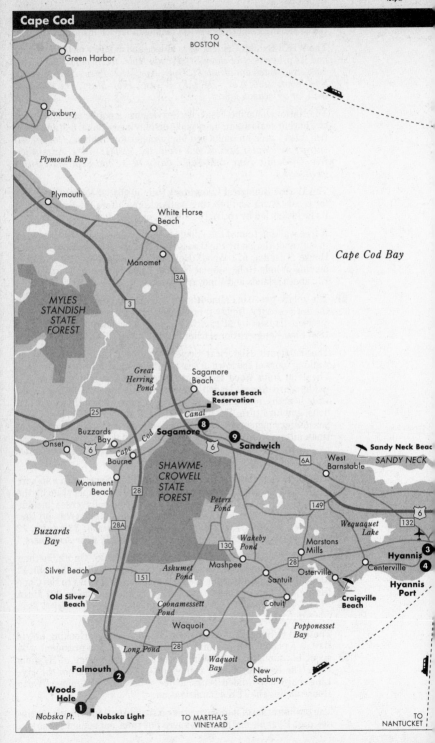

TO
BOSTON

Green Harbor

Duxbury

Plymouth Bay

Plymouth

White Horse
Beach

Manomet

3A

Cape Cod Bay

3

MYLES
STANDISH
STATE
FOREST

*Great
Herring
Pond*

Sagamore
Beach

**Scusset Beach
Reservation**

Canal

25

Buzzards
Bay

Cape

Cod **Sagamore** 8

9 **Sandwich**

6

6A

West
Barnstable

Sandy Neck Beac
SANDY NECK

Onset

6

Bourne

Monument
Beach

SHAWME-
CROWELL
STATE
FOREST

*Peters
Pond*

149

132

6

*Wequaquet
Lake*

28

*Buzzards
Bay*

28A

*Wakeby
Pond*

130

Marstons
Mills

28

Hyannis 3

4

Silver Beach

151

*Ashumet
Pond*

Mashpee

Santuit

Osterville

Centerville

**Hyannis
Port**

**Old Silver
Beach**

*Coonamessett
Pond*

Cotuit

**Craigville
Beach**

Waquoit

*Popponesset
Bay*

Falmouth 2

Long Pond 28

*Waquoit
Bay*

New
Seabury

**Woods
Hole** 1

Nobska Pt. **Nobska Light**

TO MARTHA'S
VINEYARD

TO
NANTUCKET

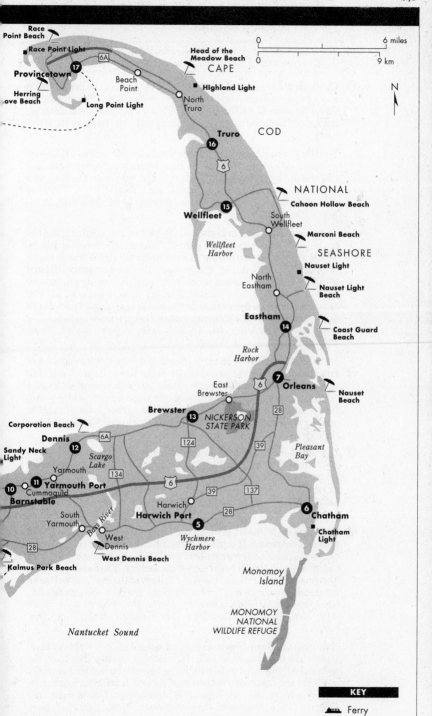

⑤ go east. At **Harwich Port,** a right turn onto Harbor Road will take you to scenic **Wychmere Harbor.**

Time Out The **Augustus Snow House** (528 Rte. 28, Harwich Port, tel. 508/430–0528) serves a full English tea in its Victorian parlors.

⑥ **Chatham** is a seaside town that is relatively free of the development and commercialism found elsewhere on the Cape. Wandering its tidy, attractive Main Street, which is lined with traditional clothing, crafts, and antiques shops, is a pleasant way to while away the afternoon.

The **Old Atwood House and Museums** includes a furnished 1752 house museum; collections of seashells, Sandwich glass, Parian ware, and antique dolls and toys; the old turret and lens from the Chatham Light; and more. *347 Stage Harbor Rd., Chatham, tel. 508/945–2493. Admission: $3 adults, $1 children under 12. Open mid-June–Sept., Wed.–Sat. 2–5.*

The view from **Chatham Light**—of the harbor, the sandbars, and the sea beyond—is spectacular. South of Chatham lies **Monomoy Island,** which was split in two during a fierce storm in 1958. A fragile barrier-beach area with dunes, it is protected as the **Monomoy National Wildlife Refuge.** The island provides nesting and resting grounds for 285 bird species. *Visitor Center: Morris Island, Chatham, tel. 508/945–0594. Ferry service is available from Morris Island mid-June–mid-Sept.; contact the Monomy Island Ferry, tel. 508/945–5450, or Stage Harbor Marine, tel. 508/945–1850, or see Guided Tours, above.*

⑦ From Chatham, Route 28 curves north and joins Routes 6 and 6A at **Orleans,** the busy commercial center of the Lower Cape. A left turn at the Main Street traffic light will take you to Rock Harbor Road, a winding street lined with gray-shingle Cape houses, white picket fences, and neat gardens; at the end is the harbor, a former packet landing and today base for a fishing fleet (both commercial and charter).

⑧ The north-shore segment of this tour begins at **Sagamore,** where you'll find a factory-outlet mall and a large Christmas tree shop (*see* Shopping, *below*), a fun place to browse for bric-a-brac. At **Pairpoint Crystal** you can watch colored lead crystal being hand-blown (weekdays 8:30–4:30), as it has been for 150 years, and buy the finished wares. *Rte. 6A, Sagamore, tel. 508/888–2344. Open daily 8:30–6.*

⑨ **Sandwich** is the oldest town on the Cape (founded 1637) and one of the most charming. It remains famous for the striking colored glass that was produced here from 1825 until 1888, when competition with glassmakers in the Midwest closed the factory. The **Sandwich Glass Museum** contains relics of the early history of the town, as well as an outstanding collection of Sandwich glass. *129 Main St., Sandwich, tel. 508/888–0251. Admission: $3 adults, 50¢ children 6–12. Open Apr.–Oct., daily 9:30–4:30; Nov.–Dec. and Feb.–Mar., Wed.–Sun. 9:30–4.*

Nearby is the **Hoxie House,** a restored shingle saltbox virtually unaltered since it was built in 1675. Overlooking Shawme Pond and the waterwheel-operated gristmill, it has been furnished authentically in period and features a collection of antique textile machines. *Rte. 130, Sandwich, tel. 508/888–1173. Admission: $1.50 adults, 75¢ children 12–16. Open mid-June–mid-Sept., Mon.–Sat. 10–5, Sun. 1–5.*

Heritage Plantation, set on 76 beautifully landscaped acres, is a complex of several museum buildings and gardens, including an extensive rhododendron dell. Its Shaker Round Barn showcases classic and historic cars. The Military Museum displays miniature soldiers and antique firearms. The Art Museum exhibits a Currier & Ives collection and a working 1912 carousel. *Grove and Pine Sts., Sandwich, tel. 508/888–3300. Admission: $7 adults, $6 senior citizens, $3.50 children 6–18. Open mid-May–Oct., daily 10–5.*

As you continue east on Route 6A, past fine views of meadows and the bay, you will come to **Barnstable,** a lovely town of large old homes. In **Yarmouth Port, Hallet's Store,** a working country drugstore and soda fountain, is preserved as it was 100 years ago. At Centre Street, take a left and follow signs to Gray's Beach, where the **Bass Hole Boardwalk** extends out over a marshy creek. In **Dennis,** past a string of small antiques shops, a right onto Old Bass River Road leads to **Scargo Hill,** offering a fine view of Scargo Lake and Cape Cod Bay.

Brewster, in the early 1800s the terminus of a packet cargo service from Boston, was home to many seafaring families. Many of mansions built for sea captains remain today, and quite a few have been turned into bed-and-breakfasts.

The **Cape Cod Museum of Natural History** has environmental and marine exhibits, guided field walks, and self-guided trails through 80 acres rich in wildlife. *Rte. 6A, Brewster, tel. 508/896–3867. Admission: $3.50 adults, $1.50 children 6–14. Open Mon.–Sat. 9:30–4:30, Sun. 12:30–4:30.*

At **Orleans,** Main Street leads east to **Nauset Beach,** which begins a virtually unbroken 30-mile stretch of barrier beach extending to Provincetown.

Three miles north on Route 6 is **Eastham.** Just beyond the village is the headquarters of the **Cape Cod National Seashore,** established in 1961 to preserve the Lower Cape's natural and historic resources. Within the Seashore are superb ocean beaches; great rolling dunes; forests, swamps, marshes, and wetlands; scrub and grasslands; and all kinds of wildlife.

The **Salt Pond Visitor Center** in Eastham has displays, literature, and an auditorium for nature films. *Off Rte. 6, tel. 508/255–3421. Open daily 9–4:30 (until 6 July–Aug.).*

From the center, roads and bicycle trails lead to **Coast Guard Beach, Nauset Light Beach,** and the **Nauset Light.** Hikes lead to a red-maple swamp, a marsh, and Salt Pond. From Memorial Day to Labor Day, park guides lead daily nature walks and lectures.

Five miles farther on Route 6 is the Seashore's **Marconi Station,** with a model of the first transatlantic wireless station erected on the U.S. mainland. From here, Guglielmo Marconi sent the first American wireless message to Europe on January 18, 1903. *South Wellfleet, tel. 508/349–3785. Open Jan.–Feb., daily 8–4:30; Mar.–Dec., weekdays 8–4:30.*

Wellfleet was once the site of a large oyster industry and, along with Truro to the north, a Colonial whaling and codfishing port. It is one of the more tastefully developed Cape resort towns, with fine restaurants, historic homes, and art and crafts galleries.

Truro is popular with writers and artists for its high dunes and virtual lack of development. The most prominent painter to have lived here was Edward Hopper, who found the Cape light ideal for his austere brand of realism. About 4 miles up Route 6, follow signs to the **Pilgrim Heights Area** of the National Seashore. *Mayflower* passengers explored this area for weeks before settling in Plymouth; a short walking trail leads to the spring where a Pilgrim party stopped to refill its casks.

Continue on Route 6 to the Seashore's **Province Lands Area,** comprising Race Point and Herring Cove beaches; bike, horse, and nature trails through forest and vast duneland; and a picnic area. The visitor center has films and exhibits. *Tel. 508/487–1256. Open mid-Apr.–Nov. daily 9–5 (until 6 July–Aug.)*

⑰ Provincetown offers spectacular beaches and dunes, as well as first-rate shops and galleries, lots of nightlife, and a wide variety of restaurants. Portuguese and American fishermen mix with painters, poets, writers, whale-watching tourists, and a steady nesting of gays and lesbians. During the early 1900s Provincetown became known as Greenwich Village North, and long before the 1960s local bohemians were shocking the more staid members of Provincetown society. Inexpensive summer lodgings close to the beaches attracted young rebels and artists, including John Reed, Sinclair Lewis, and Eugene O'Neill. Some of O'Neill's early plays were presented first in Provincetown. More recent glitterati include Robert Motherwell and Norman Mailer.

The Historical Society puts out a series of walking-tour pamphlets, available for less than $1 each at many shops in town, with maps and information on the history of many buildings and the famous folk who have occupied them. **MacMillan Wharf** is a center for whale-watching and fishing excursion boats.

Provincetown's main tourist attraction is the **Pilgrim Monument,** on a hill above the town center, commemorating the landing of the Pilgrims in 1620. From atop the 252-foot-high granite tower, there's a panoramic view of the entire Cape. At the base a historical museum has a diorama of the *Mayflower* and exhibits on whaling, shipwrecks, scrimshaw, and more. An exhibit of artifacts from the wreck of the 18th-century pirate ship *Whydah* and a working conservation lab. *Tel. 508/487–1310. Admission: $5 adults, $3 children 4–12. Open daily 9–4 (until 7 July–Sept.). May be closed some weekdays; call ahead.*

What to See and Do with Children

ZooQuarium offers sea-lion shows, a petting zoo with native wildlife, pony rides, wandering roosters and peacocks, a large seashell collection, aquariums, and a children's discovery center. *Rte. 28, West Yarmouth, tel. 508/775–8883. Admission: $7.50 adults, $4.50 children 2–9. Open mid-Feb.–late Nov. daily 9:30–5 (until 6:30 July–Aug.).*
Bassett Wild Animal Farm has lions, tigers, birds, monkeys, and llamas on 20 acres, plus hayrides, pony rides, and a picnic area. *Tubman Rd., between Rtes. 124 and 137, Brewster, tel. 508/896–3224. Admission: $5.50 age 12 and up, $3.75 children 2–11. Open mid-May–mid-Sept. daily 10–5.*
Four Seas (360 S. Main St., Centerville, tel. 508/775–1394) is a long-time favorite for ice cream. Around the corner is what would once have been called the penny-candy store, now stocked with nickel-and-dime candy.
Green Briar Nature Center and Jam Kitchen (off Rte. 6A, East Sandwich, tel. 508/888–6870) has a full summer program of nature walks, as well as weekday tours of the Jam Kitchen.

Pirate's Cove is the most elaborate of the Cape's many miniature-golf emporiums, with a hill, a waterfall, and a stream. *728 Main St. (Rte. 28), South Yarmouth, tel. 508/394–6200. Admission: $5.50 adults, $4.50 children under 12. Open daily 9 AM–11 PM in summer, 9:30 or 10–7:30 or 10 in spring and fall.*

Water Wizz Water Park has a 50-foot-high water slide, a river ride, a six-story tube ride, a kiddie water park, an arcade, volleyball, and minigolf. The new enclosed Black Wizard slide descends 75 feet in darkness. *Rtes. 6 and 28, Wareham (2 mi west of Bourne Bridge), tel. 401/596–0110. Admission: $16 adults, $10 children under 48" and senior citizens. Open Memorial Day–mid-June, weekends 11–4; mid-June–Labor Day, daily 10–6:30.*

Off the Beaten Track

At the 21,000-acre **Massachusetts Military Reservation** (known as Otis Air Base) in Bourne, an Air National Guard tour includes a film, a look into F–15 fighter planes, a tour of the aircraft museum, and sometimes observation of flying (tel. 508/968–4090). Tours of the reservation lasting 1½ or 3 hours are given by the Army National Guard (tel. 508/968–5975) and the Coast Guard (tel. 508/968–6316) on the first and third Thursdays of every month. Call ahead to reserve. An August open house features precision-flying teams, a military band, and static displays (tel. 508/968–4090 or 508/968–4003).

Shopping

Shopping Districts **Provincetown** has a history as an art colony and remains an important art center, with many fine galleries and exhibitions of Cape and non-Cape artists. Write for a free "Provincetown Gallery Guide" (Provincetown Gallery Guild, Box 242, Provincetown 02657). **Wellfleet** has emerged as a vibrant center for art and crafts as well, without Provincetown's crowds. Write for a free walking map of Wellfleet's art galleries and restaurants (Wellfleet Art Galleries Assoc., Box 916, Wellfleet 02667). **Hyannis's Main Street**—the Cape's largest—is lined with bookshops, gift shops, jewelers, clothing stores, summer wear and T-shirt shops, and ice-cream and candy stores, plus minigolf courses and fun eating places. The orientation is youthful, but everyone enjoys watching the summer parade. **Chatham's Main Street** is a pretty shopping area, with generally more upscale and conservative merchandise than Hyannis offers. Here you'll find galleries, crafts and clothing stores, and a few good antiques shops. **Falmouth** and **Orleans** also have a large number of shops.

Shopping Malls **Cape Cod Factory Outlet Mall** (Factory Outlet Rd., Exit 1 off Rte. 6, Sagamore, tel. 508/888–8417) has more than 20 outlets. **Cape Cod Mall** (Rtes. 132 & 28, Hyannis, tel. 508/771–0200), the Cape's largest, is where everyone congregates on rainy days. Its 90 shops include Jordan Marsh, Filene's, The Gap, Victoria's Secret, Sears, and restaurants. **Falmouth Mall** (Rte. 28, Falmouth, tel. 508/540–8329) has Bradlees, T. J. Maxx, and 30 other shops.

Flea Market **The Wellfleet Drive-In Theatre** (Rte. 6, Eastham–Wellfleet line, tel. 508/349–2520) is the site of a giant flea market (mid-Apr.–Oct., weekends and Mon. holidays 8–4; July–Aug., also Wed. and Thurs.). There's a snack bar and playground.

Pick-Your-Own Farm **Tony Andrews Farm and Produce Stand** (398 Old Meeting House Rd., East Falmouth, tel. 508/548–5257) lets you pick your own strawberries (mornings from mid-June), as well as peas, beans, and tomatoes (late June–late Aug.).

Specialty Stores
Antiques

Eldred's (1483 Rte. 6A, Box 796, East Dennis 02641, tel. 508/385–3116) has year-round auctions featuring top-quality antiques and art, as well as auctions of "general antiques and accessories" with less-expensive wares. **Eldred Wheeler** (866 Main St., Box 90, Osterville 02655, tel. 508/428–9049) is well-known for handcrafting fine 18th-century furniture reproductions. **H. Richard Strand** (Town Hall Sq., Sandwich, tel. 508/888–3230), in an 1800 home, displays fine pre-1840 and Victorian antique furniture, paintings, American glass, and more. **Kingsland Manor** (Rte. 6A, West Brewster, tel. 508/385–9741) is like a fairyland, with ivy covering the facade, fountains in the courtyard, and everything "from tin to Tiffany" from end to end. **Remembrances of Things Past** (376 Commercial St., Provincetown, tel. 508/487–9443) deals in jewelry, photographs, neon, telephones, and other articles from the 1920s to the 1960s. **The Spyglass** (618 Main St., Chatham, tel. 508/945–9686) carries telescopes, barometers, writing boxes, and antique maps.

Art

Blue Heron Gallery (Bank St., Wellfleet, tel. 508/349–6724) is one of the Cape's best, with representational contemporary art by regional and nationally recognized artists. **Cummaquid Fine Arts** (4275 Rte. 6A, Cummaquid, tel. 508/362–2593) has works by Cape Cod and New England artists, plus decorative antiques, beautifully displayed in an old home. **Hell's Kitchen Gallery** (439 Commercial St., Provincetown, tel. 508/487–3570) features photographer Joel Meyerowitz, painter John Dowd, and other Provincetown-associated artists. **Long Point Gallery** (492 Commercial St., Provincetown, tel. 508/487–1795) is a cooperative of several well-established artists, including Paul Resika and Varujan Boghosian.

Books

Parnassus Book Service (Rte. 6A, Yarmouth Port, tel. 508/362–6420) has a huge selection of Cape Cod, maritime, antiquarian, and other books in an 1840 former general store. **Provincetown Art Association and Museum** (460 Commercial St., tel. 508/487–1750) has a gift shop with many books on Provincetown and its artists. **Titcomb's Bookshop** (432 Rte. 6A, East Sandwich, tel. 508/888–2331) has used, rare, and new books, including a large collection of Cape and nautical titles. A children's book collection has been added.

Clothing

Hannah (47 Main St., Orleans, tel. 508/255–8234; Main St., Wellfleet, tel. 508/349–9884) has high-end women's fashions in unusual styles. **Northern Lights Leather** (361 Commercial St., Provincetown, tel. 508/487–9376) is a high-fashion leather boutique.

Crafts

The Blacks Handweaving Shop (597 Rte. 6A, West Barnstable, tel. 508/362–3955), in a barnlike building with the looms upstairs and down, makes and sells beautiful shawls, scarves, throws, and more in traditional and jacquard weaves. **Scargo Pottery** (off Rte 6A on Dr. Lord's Rd. S, Dennis, tel. 508/385–3894) has been a Cape favorite since 1953. In a pine forest, Harry Holl's unusual wares—such as his signature castle bird feeders—are displayed on tree stumps and hanging from branches. More pottery and the workshop and kiln are indoors. With luck you'll catch a potter at the wheel; watching is encouraged. **The Spectrum** (369 Rte. 6A, Brewster, tel. 508/385–3322; 342 Main St., Hyannis, tel. 508/771–4554) showcases imaginative American arts and crafts, including pottery, jewelry, stained glass, art glass, and more. **Sydenstricker Galleries** (Rte. 6A, Brewster, tel. 508/385–3272) features glassware handcrafted by a unique process, which you can watch in progress at the studio on the premises.

Tree's Place (Rte. 6A at Rte. 28, Orleans, tel. 508/255–1330), one of the Cape's most original shops, has handcrafted kaleidoscopes, art glass, hand-painted porcelain and pottery, handblown stemware, wood boxes, Russian lacquer boxes, imported tiles, and jewelry, as well as fine art.

Miscellaneous **Christmas Tree Shops** (Exit 1 off Rte. 6, Sagamore, tel. 508/888–7010; 6 other locations) are a Cape Cod tradition. Fun, not fancy, they offer discounted "stuff" of all kinds: paper goods, candles, home furnishings, kitchen items, you name it.

Sports and Outdoor Activities

Biking **Cape Cod Rail Trail,** the paved right-of-way of the old Penn Central Railroad, is the Cape's premier bike path. Running 20 miles, from Dennis to Eastham, it passes salt marshes, cranberry bogs, and ponds, and cuts through Nickerson State Park. The terrain is easy to moderate. The Butterworth Company (38 Rte. 134, South Dennis 02660, tel. 508/760–2000) sells a guide to the trail for $2.95.

On either side of the **Cape Cod Canal** is an easy 7-mile straight trail, offering a view of the bridges and canal traffic.

The **Shining Sea Bikeway** is a nice-and-easy 3½-mile coastal route between Locust Street, Falmouth, and the Woods Hole ferry parking lot.

The Cape Cod National Seashore maintains three bicycle trails. (A brochure with maps is available at visitor centers.) **Nauset Trail** is 1.6 miles, from Salt Pond Visitor Center in Eastham to Coast Guard Beach. **Head of the Meadow Trail** is 2 miles of easy cycling between sand dunes and salt marshes from High Head Road, off Route 6A in North Truro, to the Head of the Meadow Beach parking lot. **Province Lands Trail** is a 5¼-mile loop off the Beech Forest parking lot in Provincetown, with spurs to Herring Cove and Race Point beaches and Bennett Pond.

Camping There are many private campgrounds throughout the Cape, except within the National Seashore, where camping is not permitted. **Nickerson State Park** is a favorite tent and RV camping spot for its setting and wildlife, and **Shawme-Crowell State Forest** has tent, trailer, and motor-home sites on 742 acres (*see* National and State Parks, *below*).

Fishing Charter boats and party boats (per-head fees, rather than charters' group rates) take you offshore for tuna, mako and blue sharks, swordfish, and marlin. Get a license from tackle shops, such as **Eastman's Sport & Tackle** (150 Main St., Falmouth, tel. 508/548–6900) and **Truman's** (Rte. 28, West Yarmouth, tel. 508/771–3470), which rent gear. The Cape Cod Chamber of Commerce's *Fresh and Saltwater Fishing Guide* has lots of useful information.

Rental powerboats are available from **Cape Cod Boats** (also sailboats and canoes; Rte. 28 at Bass River Bridge, West Dennis, tel. 508/394–9268) and from **Cape Water Sports** and **Flyer's** (*see* Sailing and Water Sports, *below*).

Deep-sea fishing trips are operated on a walk-on basis by **Hy-Line** (Ocean St. dock, Hyannis, tel. 508/778–2600); **Cap'n Bill & Cee Jay** (MacMillan Wharf, Provincetown, tel. 508/487–4330 or 800/675–6723); and **Patriot Party Boats** (Falmouth Harbor, tel. 508/548–2826 or, in MA, 800/734–0088), which also offers sailing and sightseeing excursions. Some of these offer charters, which are also available at

Rock Harbor in Orleans (tel. 508/362–3908) and at Barnstable Harbor (tel. 508/255–9757 or, in MA, 800/287–1771).

Golf The Cape's mild climate makes golf possible year-round on most of its 20 public courses, though January and February do get nippy. **Ocean Edge Golf Course** (832 Villages Dr., Brewster, tel. 508/896–5911) is the top championship course, 18 holes. The semiprivate **New Seabury Country Club** (Shore Dr. W, New Seabury, tel. 508/477–9110) has 36 excellent holes. Other fine courses: **Captain's Golf Course** (1000 Freeman's Way, Brewster, tel. 508/896–5100), 18 holes; **Cranberry Valley Golf Course** (183 Oak St., Harwich, tel. 508/430–7560), 18 holes; and **Chatham Seaside Links** (the old Chatham Bars Inn course, now town-owned; tel. 508/945–4774), 9 holes—a good beginner's course.

Horseback Riding The **Province Lands Horse Trails are** three two-hour trails to the beaches through or past dunes, cranberry bogs, forests, and ponds; no area stables offer horse rentals. Cape stables that do hire out: **Deer Meadow Riding Stables** (Rte. 137, East Harwich, tel. 508/432–6580), **Haland Stables** (Rte. 28A, West Falmouth, tel. 508/540–2552). For private and semiprivate lessons try **Holly Hill Farm** (240 Flint St., Marstons Mills, tel. 508/428–2621).

Sailing and Water Sports **Arey's Pond Boat Yard** (off Rte. 28, South Orleans, tel. 508/255–0994) has a sailing school with individual and class lessons. **Flyer's** (131A Commercial St., Provincetown, tel. 508/487–0898) rents sailboats, Sunfish, canoes, outboards, and rowboats, and teaches sailing. **Cape Water Sports** (Rte. 28, Harwich Port, tel. 508/432–7079) has locations on several beaches for sailboat and sailboard rentals and lessons and canoe and powerboat rentals.

Tennis **Bissell's Tennis Courts** (Bradford St. at Herring Cove Beach Rd., Provincetown, tel. 508/487–9512) has five clay courts and offers lessons. **Mid-Cape Racquet Club** (193 White's Path, South Yarmouth, tel. 508/394–3511) has one outdoor all-weather and nine indoor tennis courts, two racquetball, and two squash; plus full health-club facilities. **Melrose Tennis Center** (792 Main St., Harwich Port, tel. 508/430–7012) offers three Omni and six Har-Tru courts, Rollerblade rentals, a pro shop, and lessons. The **Cape Cod Chamber of Commerce** (tel. 508/362–3225) has a listing of high schools and towns with public courts.

Beaches

Beaches fronting on Cape Cod Bay generally have colder water, carried down from Maine and Canada, and gentle waves. Southside beaches, on Nantucket Sound, have rolling surf and are warmer, because of the Gulf Stream. Open-ocean beaches on the Cape Cod National Seashore (*see* Exploring Cape Cod, *above*) are cold and have serious surf. Parking lots fill up by 10 AM or so. Those beaches not restricted to residents charge (sometimes hefty) parking fees; for weekly or seasonal passes, contact the local town hall.

All of the Atlantic Ocean beaches on the **National Seashore** are superior—wide, long, sandy, dune-backed, with great views. They're also contiguous: you can walk from Eastham to Provincetown almost without leaving sand. All have lifeguards and rest rooms; only Herring Cove has food.

Craigville Beach, a long, wide strip of beach near Hyannis, is extremely popular, especially with the roving and volleyball-playing young (hence the nickname "Muscle Beach"). It has lifeguards and a bathhouse, and food shops across the road.

Old Silver Beach, a beautiful white crescent in North Falmouth, is especially good for small children because a sandbar keeps it shallow at one end and makes tidal pools with crabs and minnows. There are lifeguards, rest rooms, showers, and food.

Sandy Neck Beach in West Barnstable, a 6-mile barrier beach between the bay and marshland, is one of the Cape's most beautiful: a wide swath of pebbly sand backed by grassy dunes extending forever in both directions.

West Dennis Beach is a long, wide, sandy beach on the warm south shore, across from marshland and Bass River, offering windsurfer rentals, all services, and lots of parking.

National and State Parks

Cape Cod National Seashore (*see* Exploring Cape Cod, *above*).

Nickerson State Park (3488 Main St., Brewster 02631, tel. 508/896–3491; map available on-site) is almost 2,000 acres of forest with eight freshwater kettle ponds stocked with trout for fishing. Other recreational options are camping, biking, canoeing, sailing, motorboating, bird-watching, and ice-skating and cross-country skiing in winter.

Scusset Beach Reservation (140 Scusset Beach Rd. off Rte. 3, Sandwich; Box 1292, Buzzards Bay 02532, tel. 508/888–0859), attracting primarily RV campers, comprises 490 acres near the canal, with a long beach on the bay. Its pier is a popular fishing spot; other activities include biking, hiking, picnicking, and swimming.

Shawme-Crowell State Forest (Rte. 130, Sandwich 02563, tel. 508/888–0351) is 742 acres near the canal. Activities include wooded tent and RV camping, biking, hiking, horseback riding, and swimming at Scusset Beach.

Monomoy National Wildlife Refuge (*see* Guided Tours and Exploring Cape Cod, *above*).

Dining

Malcolm Wilson of the Cape Cod Times wrote the reviews for Cape Cod and Nantucket.

New England cooking—hearty meat-and-potatoes fare—is the overwhelming cuisine of choice on the Cape, along with the ubiquitous milk-based clam chowder and fresh fish and seafood. Extraordinary gourmet restaurants can be found, along with occasional ethnic specialties, such as the Portuguese kale soup or linguiça. In the off-season many Cape restaurants advertise early-bird specials (reduced prices in the early evening) and Sunday brunches, often with musical accompaniment. Dress is casual unless otherwise noted.

Upper Cape **Coonamessett Inn.** Built in 1796, this elegant inn has lots of old-fashioned charm. The theme of the main dining room is the paintings by Ralph Cahoon; his signature hot-air balloons re-created in copper and enamel add a touch of whimsy to an otherwise subdued and romantic room. The regional American menu focuses on fresh fish and seafood—it's famed for the 1½-pound seafood-stuffed lobsters. *Corner of Jones Rd. and Gifford St., Falmouth, tel. 508/548–2300. Reservations advised. AE, DC, MC, V. Closed Mon. Jan.–Mar. Moderate–Expensive.*

★ **Dan'l Webster Inn.** The Colonial New England patina of this inn belies its 1971 construction. The glassed-in conservatory features luxuriant greenery; the main dining room has a traditional Colonial look; the third dining room is Victorian. The mostly regional American menu, served in all three, emphasizes seafood, such as lobster meat sautéed with chanterelle mushrooms in Fontina sauce on pasta. Hearty and elegant breakfasts and Sunday brunches are served. *149 Main St., Sandwich, tel. 508/888–3622. Reservations advised. AE, D, DC, MC, V. Moderate–Expensive.*

★ **The Bridge.** The several small dining rooms have recessed lighting, art on the walls, and linen tablecloths. The Yankee pot roast is the star of the eclectic menu, which also features *bijoux de la mer* (lobster, scallops, and shrimp with lemon and tarragon on spinach pasta with a smoky mushroom-cream sauce). *Rte. 6A, Sagamore, tel. 508/888–8144. Weekend reservations advised in season. D, DC, MC, V. Moderate.*

The Flume. This clean, plain fish house, decorated only with a few Native American artifacts and crafts (the owner is a Wampanoag chief), offers a small menu of simple dishes guaranteed to satisfy. The chowder is outstanding, perhaps the Cape's best. Other specialties are fried smelts, fried clams, Indian pudding, and fresh broiled fish. *Lake Ave. (off Rte. 130), Mashpee, tel. 508/477–1456. Reservations advised. MC, V. Closed some weekdays off-season. Moderate.*

★ **Stir Crazy.** Armed now with a liquor license and more seating, the owner of this Southeast Asian restaurant continues to serve authentic dishes from his native Cambodia. There are no tame flavors here. The Thai *me-siam* is sautéed minced pork, tofu, soybeans, coconut milk, and chili on a bed of bean sprouts and rice noodles, topped with peanut sauce; the deep-fried finger egg-roll appetizer is filled with chopped pork and vegetables and served with a very hot sauce. *626 MacArthur Blvd., Pocasset, tel. 508/564–6464. MC, V. No lunch Sun. Closed Mon. Inexpensive–Moderate.*

Mid-Cape **East Bay Lodge.** This casually elegant restaurant is set in an 1880 summer house with a glassed-in veranda. The Continental menu features Chateaubriand, Dover sole, salmon, and lobster, as in lobster Royale, sautéed with shrimp and scallops with tarragon-mustard sauce on green fettuccine. Sunday there's a lavish brunch buffet and an evening shellfish buffet. Renowned jazz pianist Eddie Perkins entertains in the lounge. *199 East Bay Rd., Osterville, tel. 508/428–5200. Reservations advised. Jacket requested. AE, D, DC, MC, V. Dinner and Sun. brunch only. Expensive.*

★ **The Regatta of Cotuit.** This sister restaurant to the renowned Regatta in Falmouth is set in a restored 18th-century stagecoach inn with eight intimate dining rooms. A specialty of the Continental and American menu is house-smoked salmon fillet with a honey glaze, as well as pâtés of rabbit, veal, or venison. Boneless rack of lamb *en chemise* (in pastry) with Cabernet sauce is outstanding, as is the wild mushroom strudel appetizer. The Tavern offers lighter fare on a lower-priced menu ($4.50–$12). *Rte. 28, Cotuit, tel. 508/428–5715. Reservations advised. AE, D, MC, V. No lunch. Expensive.*

★ **Abbicci.** This contemporary Italian restaurant is set in an 18th-century cottage with a bold, Mondrianesque decor. Chef Marietta Hickey makes light use of oils and fats, as in roast duck with vinegar-apricot sauce. Also offered are elegant pasta dishes and roast rack of lamb with a hazelnut crust and a roasted-shallot demiglace. *43 Main St. (Rte. 6A), Yarmouth Port, tel. 508/362–3501. Reservations advised. AE, D, DC, MC, V. Moderate–Expensive.*

★ **The Paddock.** Long the area's benchmark for consistent quality dining, this formal restaurant is decorated in Victorian style—from the dark, pubby bar to the airy summer-porch area filled with green wicker and potted plants. The main dining room blends dark beams, frosted-glass dividers, sporting art, and banquettes. The wine list is extensive. The Continental-American menu emphasizes regional seafood specialties. Steak au poivre, sautéed in shallot butter and flambéed with cognac, is popular. *W. Main St. Rotary (next to Melody Tent), Hyannis, tel. 508/775–7677. Reservations advised. AE, DC, MC, V. Closed mid-Nov.–Mar. Moderate–Expensive.*

Penguins Sea Grill. Formerly Penguins Go Pasta—the logo is a tuxedoed penguin—this sophisticated Northern Italian restaurant focuses on grilled seafood and homemade pastas. A signature dish is wood-grilled swordfish with either roasted pepper aioli or lime caper butter. The newly redecorated interior has a bistro look with linen tablecloths and dark tones. *331 Main St., Hyannis, tel. 508/775–2023. Reservations advised. AE, DC, MC, V. No lunch weekends. Moderate–Expensive.*

Red Pheasant Inn. The main dining room is pleasantly intimate and rustic, with antique pine floors, exposed beams, and two fireplaces. The cuisine is American regional with a refreshingly creative spin, one example being tuna pastrami. The large menu , though, always features lamb, seafood, game, and pastas. The wine list is long and select. *905 Main St. (Rte. 6A), Dennis, tel. 508/385–2133. Reservations advised. D, MC, V. No lunch. Moderate–Expensive.*

Baxter's Fish N' Chips. On busy Lewis Bay, Baxter's gets a lot of back-in boaters at its picnic tables for possibly the best fried clams on the Cape, as well as other fried, baked, and broiled fresh fish and seafood (plus burgers and chicken) and a raw bar. *Pleasant St., Hyannis, tel. 508/775–4490. No reservations. MC, V. Closed Oct.–Apr. Moderate.*

Inaho. Relocated from its Hyannis storefront to new quarters, Inaho offers traditional to Japanese fare in an attractive setting, complete with a sushi bar and Japanese screens. *157 Main St. (Rte. 6A), Yarmouth Port, tel. 508/362–5522. Reservations advised. AE, MC, V. No lunch. Moderate.*

Starbuck's. The decor is sort of Hard Rock Café without a theme—hanging from the rafters are flags, a sled, a miniature Fokker D-7, carved pigs, and lots more. The huge, eclectic menu includes fun ethnic selections, as well as seafood, barbecue, and exotic and frozen drinks. *645 Rte. 132, Hyannis, tel. 508/778–6767. Reservations advised weekends. AE, D, DC, MC, V. Moderate.*

★ **Up the Creek.** This casual spot with a busy hum about it serves fine food at very good prices. House specialties include seafood strudel—two pastries filled with lobster, shrimp, crab, and cheese—and baked stuffed lobster. *36 Old Colony Rd., Hyannis, tel. 508/771–7866. Reservations advised. AE, D, DC, MC, V. Inexpensive–Moderate.*

Lower Cape **Chillingsworth.** The Cape's best restaurant, this dramatically orchestrated, elegant spot offers award-winning French and nouvelle cuisine and an outstanding wine cellar. The frequently changing dinner menu is a five-course prix fixe and features such entrées as venison with celery root purée and fried pumpkin; or sweetbreads and foie gras with wild mushrooms and ham, asparagus, and smoky sauce. Lunch and an á la carte dinner menu are served in the more casual Greenhouse Lounge. *2449 Main St. (Rte. 6A), Brewster, tel. 508/896–3640. Reservations advised for dinner (seatings) and accepted for lunch. Jacket advised at dinner. AE, DC, MC, V. Open daily (except Mon.) mid-June–mid-Oct.; weekends only Memorial Day–mid-June and mid-Oct.–Thanksgiving. Closed Thanksgiving–Memorial Day. Very Expensive.*

High Brewster. A romantic country inn overlooking a pond, this restored farmhouse with dark exposed beams, wide paneling, gilt-frame oil paintings, and Oriental carpeting offers seasonal four-course prix-fixe menus; a fall menu might include pumpkin-and-sage bisque and tenderloin medallions with chives and cheese glaze. *964 Satucket Rd., Brewster, tel. 508/896–3636. Reservations required. Jacket advised. AE, MC, V. No lunch. May close Mon. and Tues. mid-Sept.–mid-June. Expensive.*

Captain Linnell House. Framed by huge trees, this neoclassical structure looks like an antebellum mansion. Inside are small dining rooms: one with a Normandy fireplace, exposed beams, and white plaster; another with a pecan-paneled fireplace, oil lamps, an Aubusson rug, and a ceiling rosette. Among offerings on the classic American menu are Wellfleet oysters with Champagne sauce and julienned vegetables; rack of lamb; and scrod in parchment with a lime-vermouth sauce. *137 Skaket Beach Rd., Orleans, tel. 508/255–3400. Reservations required in season. AE, MC, V. No lunch June–Oct. (except Sun. buffet brunch year-round). Moderate–Expensive.*

★ **Ciro's.** Opened in 1950, this stage-set Italian restaurant—raffia-covered Chianti bottles hanging from the rafters, walls of plaster and brick, strains of Italian opera in the air—plays out its role with the confidence of years on the boards. *Scampi alla Griglia* is grilled shrimp in lemon, parsley, garlic, butter, leeks, and shallots; veal and pasta dishes are specialties. *4 Kiley Court, Provincetown, tel. 508/487–0049. Reservations required summer, Sat. nights. MC, V. Closed Mon.–Thurs. Nov.–Memorial Day. Moderate–Expensive.*

★ **Land Ho!** Walk in, grab a newspaper from the rack, take a seat, and relax—since 1969 Land Ho! has been making folks feel right at home. This casual spot serves kale soup that has been noted by *Gourmet* magazine, plus burgers, hearty sandwiches, grilled fish in summer, and very good chicken wings, chowder, and fish and chips. *Rte. 6A and Cove Rd., Orleans, tel. 508/255–5165. No reservations. MC, V. Inexpensive.*

Lodging

In summer lodgings should be booked as far in advance as possible—several months for the most popular cottages and bed-and-breakfasts. Assistance with last-minute reservations is available at the **Cape Cod Chamber of Commerce information booths** by the two bridges in season. Off-season rates are much reduced, and service usually more personalized.

B&B reservations services include **House Guests Cape Cod and the Islands** (Box 1881, Orleans 02653, tel. 800/666–4678) and **Bed and Breakfast Cape Cod** (Box 341, West Hyannis Port 02672–0341, tel. 508/775–2772). **Provincetown Reservations System** (tel. 508/487–2400 or 800/648–0364) makes reservations year-round for accommodations, shows, restaurants, transportation, and condos.

Upper Cape **New Seabury Resort and Conference Center.** On a 2,000-acre point on Nantucket Sound, this vast self-contained resort (complete with a 20-shop marketplace and weekend concerts) offers houses and apartments with full kitchens, washer/dryers, and cable TV. In the oceanfront Maushop Village (Nantucket-look cottages with roses climbing white picket fences), interiors mix Cape-style and modern furnishings. The Mews, overlooking beautifully landscaped championship golf courses, features California-look condos with cathedral ceilings and some private pools and hot tubs. *Rock Landing Rd., Box 549, Mashpee 02649, tel. 508/477–9111 or 800/999–9033. 167 1- and 2-bedroom units. Facilities: 4 restaurants, health club, golf, tennis, water-sports-equipment and bike rentals, beach clubs, 2 outdoor pools, children's activities, soccer and baseball fields, jogging and bike trails, minigolf. AE, DC, MC, V. Very Expensive.*

★ **Coonamessett Inn.** This classic inn provides fine dining and gracious accommodations in a tranquil country setting. One- or two-bedroom suites are located in five buildings arranged around a landscaped lawn that spills down to a scenic wooded pond. Rooms are casually decorated, with bleached wood or pine paneling, New England antiques or reproductions, upholstered chairs, couches, and TVs. *Jones Rd. and Gifford St., Box 707, Falmouth 02541, tel. 508/548–2300. 25 suites, 1 cottage. Facilities: 2 restaurants, lounge, clothing shop. AE, DC, MC, V. Expensive.*

★ **Mostly Hall.** Set in a landscaped, parklike yard far back from the street, this 1849 house is imposing, with a wraparound porch and a dramatic cupola. Accommodations are in corner rooms, with large shuttered windows giving leafy views, reading areas, antique pieces and reproduction canopied queen beds, pretty floral wallpapers, Oriental accent rugs, and central air-conditioning. Inviting common areas include a cozy TV room in the cupola, a fireplaced parlor, and a backyard gazebo. *27 Main St., Falmouth 02540, tel. 508/548–3786 or 800/682–0565. 6 rooms. Facilities: bicycles, lending library, lawn games. AE, MC, V. Closed Jan.–mid-Feb. Full breakfast included. Expensive.*

Dan'l Webster Inn. This classy, traditional inn offers an excellent restaurant (*see* Dining, *above*) and guest rooms decorated with fine reproduction furnishings, including some canopy beds. All rooms have cable TV and air-conditioning; some suites have fireplaces or whirlpools. Morning coffee is served in the gathering room. *149 Main St., Sandwich 02563, tel. 508/888–3622 or 800/444–3566, fax 508/888–5156. 37 rooms, 9 suites. Facilities: outdoor pool, access to health club and golf, restaurant, lounge. AE, D, DC, MC, V. Moderate–Expensive.*

Earl of Sandwich Motor Manor. Single-story Tudor-style buildings form a U around a wooded lawn set with lawn chairs. The newer buildings (1981–1983) have air-conditioning, unlike the main building (1963). The rooms are a bit somber—dark paneled walls, exposed beams on white ceilings, olive leatherette wing chairs, Oriental throw rugs on slate or carpeted floors—but a good size, with large Tudor-style windows, small tiled baths, and telephones. *378 Rte. 6A, East Sandwich 02537, tel. 508/888–1415 or 800/442–3275. 24 rooms. AE, D, DC, MC, V. Inexpensive–Moderate.*

Mid-Cape **Ashley Manor.** Offering a relaxed and homey atmosphere, this
★ charming country inn dates back to 1699. Large, well-appointed rooms have private baths, working fireplaces, and pencil-post or canopy beds; the Garden Cottage has an efficiency kitchen. The sitting room offers a large fireplace, piano, antiques, Oriental rugs, handsome country furniture, and a view of the brick terrace, lovely grounds, and a fountain garden. *Box 856, 3660 Olde King's Hwy., Barnstable 02630, tel. 508/362–8044. 5 rooms with bath, 1 cottage. Facilities: tennis, complimentary beverages and snacks. Full breakfast included. AE, MC. V. Expensive–Very Expensive.*

★ **Tara Hyannis Hotel & Resort.** For its central-Cape location, beautiful landscaping, extensive services, and superior resort facilities, it's hard to beat the Tara. The lobby area is elegant, but room decor is a bit dull, with pale colors and standard contemporary hotel-style furnishings. Each room has a TV, a phone, and a private patio. Rooms overlooking the golf greens or the courtyard garden have the best views. *West End Circle, Hyannis 02601, tel. 508/775–7775 or 800/843–8272, fax 508/790–4221. 224 rooms, 2 suites. Facilities: restaurant, lounge, golf, tennis, indoor and outdoor pools, health club, roman bath, steam room, sauna, hair salon, business services,* *children's program. AE, D, DC, MC, V. Expensive–Very Expensive.*

★ **The Inn at Fernbrook.** The most striking feature of this inn is the grounds, originally landscaped by Frederick Law Olmsted, designer of New York's Central Park. Paths wind past duck ponds and blooming with water lilies; a heart-shaped sweetheart rose garden; a windmill; and a fern-rimmed brook. The house itself, an 1881 Queen Anne Victorian mansion on the National Register of Historic Places, is a beauty, from the turreted exterior to the fine woodwork and furnishings within. Some rooms have garden views; some have bay-windowed sitting areas, canopy beds, pastel Oriental carpets, and working fireplaces. *481 Main St., Centerville 02632, tel. 508/775–4334, fax 508/778–4455. 4 rooms, 1 suite, 1 cottage. AE, D, MC, V. Full breakfast and afternoon beverages included. Expensive.*

★ **Wedgewood Inn.** A handsome 1812 Greek Revival building, white with black shutters, houses this exceptional inn. The sophisticated country decor mixes fine antiques, cherry pencil-post beds with antique quilts, period wallpapers, large Stobart sporting prints, and Oriental and hand-hooked rugs on wide-board floors. Rooms are large and air-conditioned, with mostly large baths. The suites have canopy beds, fireplaces, and porches; one has a separate den. The recently added gazebo enhances the gardens. *83 Main St. (Rte. 6A), Yarmouth Port 02675, tel. 508/362–5157. 4 rooms, 2 suites. Full breakfast and afternoon tea included. AE, DC, MC, V. Expensive.*

Capt. Gosnold Village. An easy walk to the beach and town, this colony of efficiency units and motel rooms is ideal for families. Some units have been remodeled with walls painted in light and airy colors, and new kitchens, baths, and furniture. In others, walls are attractively paneled in knotty pine; floors are carpeted; furnishings are simple and pleasant. Units range from simple motel-style accomodations to three-bedroom, three-bath units with kitchens and living rooms. All but motel rooms have gas grills and phones; most have decks. *230 Gosnold St., Hyannis 02601, tel. 508/775–9111. 40 units in 18 buildings. Facilities: outdoor pool, basketball, game nets, picnic areas, gas grills, video library. MC, V. Closed Nov.–mid-Apr. Moderate–Expensive.*

Lower Cape
★ **Chatham Bars Inn.** An oceanfront resort in the old style, this Chatham landmark comprises the main building—with its grand lobby—and 26 one- to eight-bedroom cottages on 20 landscaped acres. The entire inn has been renovated to create a casual Cape Cod elegance. Some rooms have private ocean-view porches; all have TVs, traditional furnishings, upholstered armchairs, and wall-to-wall carpeting. Service is attentive and extensive. *Shore Rd., Chatham 02633, tel. 508/945–0096 or 800/527–4884, fax 508/945–5491. 152 rooms. Facilities: 3 restaurants, lounge, bar, beach, tennis, adjacent golf, outdoor pool, shuffleboard, launch service to North Beach, children's programs (July and Aug.). AE, DC, MC, V. Very Expensive.*

★ **Captain's House Inn.** Finely preserved architectural details, superb taste in decorating, opulent home-baked goods, and an overall feeling of warmth and quiet comfort are just part of what makes this one of the Cape's very best inns. Each room in the three inn buildings has its own personality. Some have fireplaces. The decor is mostly Williamsburg-style; the lovely, large rooms in the Carriage House have a somewhat more spare look. *371 Old Harbor Rd., Chatham 02633, tel. 508/945–0127, fax 508/945–0866. 14 rooms, 2 suites. Continental breakfast and afternoon tea included. AE, MC, V. Closed Jan.–mid-Feb. Expensive–Very Expensive.*

Best Western Chateau Motor Inn. Picture windows at this hilltop motel a longish walk to the center of town offer expansive views of marsh, dunes, and sea. Well-maintained modern rooms have cable TV, two phones, and air-conditioning. *Bradford St. W, Box 558, Provincetown 02657, tel. 508/487–1286 or 800/528–1234, fax 508/ 487–3557. 55 rooms. Facilities: outdoor pool; minifridges and room safes available. Children under 18 stay free with parents. AE, D, DC, MC, V. Closed Nov.–Apr. Expensive.*

Hargood House. This apartment complex on the water is a great option for longer stays and families. Most of the individually decorated units have decks and large water-view windows; all have kitchens and modern baths. Apartment 8 is on the water, with three glass walls, cathedral ceilings, and private deck; apartment 7 is its mirror image, on the ground floor. Rental is mostly by the week in season; nightly available off-season. *493 Commercial St., Provincetown 02657, tel. and fax 508/487–9133. 19 apartments. Facilities: private beach, barbecue grills. AE, MC, V. Expensive.*

★ **Captain Freeman Inn.** The ground floor of this 1866 Victorian is impressive, with 12-foot ceilings and windows, ornate plaster ceiling medallions, and seating around a marble fireplace. Other common areas include the wraparound veranda, a screened porch, a backyard bordered in wild grapes and berries, and a recently added health club and meeting room. Guest rooms feature high ceilings, grand windows, and antiques and Victorian reproductions. "Luxury suites" offer queen canopy beds, fireplaces, cable TVs and VCRs, minifridges, and glassed-in balconies with private hot-tubs. *15 Breakwater Rd., Brewster 02631, tel. 508/896–7481 or 800/843– 4664. 12 rooms (3 share a bath). Facilities: video library, heated pool, croquet, badminton, bikes. Full breakfast and afternoon tea included. AE, MC, V. Moderate–Expensive.*

The Fairbanks Inn. Just one block from Provincetown's busy Commercial Street, this comfortable inn offers cozy rooms filled with antique and reproduction furnishings. Rooms in the 1776 main house feature four-poster or canopy beds and Oriental rugs covering wideplank floors. Some rooms have cable TV, kitchens, or working fireplaces. *90 Bradford St., Provincetown 02657, tel. 508/487–0386. 13 rooms, 9 with bath; 1 efficiency, 1 2-bedroom apartment. Facilities: rooftop sun deck. Continental breakfast included. AE, D, MC, V. Moderate.*

The Arts

Theater Summer stock theater is popular throughout the Cape. The top venue, offering Broadway-style shows and children's plays, is the **Cape Playhouse** (off Rte. 6A, Dennis, tel. 508/385–3911). The **College Light Opera Company** (Highfield Theatre, Depot Ave. Ext., Falmouth, tel. 508/548–0668) features college music majors performing summer operetta and musical comedy. **Wellfleet Harbor Actors Theatre** (Wellfleet town pier, tel. 508/349–6835) offers a May–October season with more serious fare, including drama, farce, and satire.

Music **Cape Cod Melody Tent** (W. Main St., Hyannis, tel. 508/775–9100) presents such top musical and comedy performers as Willie Nelson and Joan Rivers in summer theater-in-the-round under a tent. The 100-member **Cape Cod Symphony** (Mattacheese Middle School, West Yarmouth, tel. 508/362–1111) gives regular and children's concerts, with guest artists, October through May. The **Cape & Islands Chamber Music Festival** (Box 2721, Orleans 02653, tel. 508/349–7709) presents three weeks of top-caliber performances and master classes in August.

Nightlife

Bars and Lounges Oliver's restaurant (Rte. 6A, Yarmouth Port, tel. 508/362–6062) has live guitar music weekends in its lounge. In summer **Guido Murphy's** (615 Main St., Hyannis, tel. 508/775–7242), with dancing to live and DJ music, and the **Chatham Squire** (487 Main St., Chatham, tel. 508/945–0945), with four bars, are rollicking places drawing a young crowd.

Jazz The Cape Cod Jazz Society operates a 24-hour hotline (tel. 508/394–5277) on jazz happenings on the Cape. **Bishop's Terrace** restaurant (Rte. 28, West Harwich, tel. 508/432–0253) has dancing to jazz nearly year-round.

Rock **The Compass** (Rte. 28, South Yarmouth, tel. 508/760–1616) is a large nightclub with dancing to country western, rock, and Top 40 tunes, plus laser light shows and a 15-foot video screen. **Sundancer's** (116 Rte. 28, West Dennis, tel. 508/394–1600) offers dancing to a DJ and live bands. The **Mill Hill Club** (164 Rte. 28, West Yarmouth, tel. 508/775–2580) has more live entertainment and some DJ, plus large-screen videos and sports. **Beachcomber** (Cahoon Hollow Beach, off Rte. 6, Wellfleet, tel. 508/349–6055) is a beachfront restaurant and dance club, open day and night for live rock and reggae in summer.

Country and Western **Bud's Country Lounge** (Bearse's Way and Rte. 132, Hyannis, tel. 508/771–2505) has pool tables and live entertainment year-round.

Martha's Vineyard

Much less developed than Cape Cod, yet more diverse and cosmopolitan than neighboring Nantucket, Martha's Vineyard has a split personality. From Memorial Day through Labor Day this island southeast of Woods Hole is a vibrant, star-studded event. Seekers of chic descend in droves on the boutiques of Edgartown and the main port of Vineyard Haven. Summer regulars return, including such celebrities as William Styron, Art Buchwald, Walter Cronkite, and Carly Simon.

But in the off-season the island becomes a place of peace and simple beauty. The beaches, always lovely, can now be appreciated in private. On drives along country lanes, there's time to linger over pastoral views, free from a throng of other cars, bikes, and mopeds. Though the pace is slower, cultural and recreational events continue, and a number of inns, shops, and restaurants remain open.

Important Addresses and Numbers

Visitor Information The **Martha's Vineyard Chamber of Commerce** publishes an excellent annual guidebook. *Box 1698, Beach Rd., Vineyard Haven 02568, tel. 508/693–0085. Open weekdays 9–5; also open Sat. 10–2 Memorial Day–Labor Day.*

Emergencies **Martha's Vineyard Hospital** (Linton La., Oak Bluffs, tel. 508/693–0410). **Vineyard Medical Services** (State Rd., Vineyard Haven, tel. 508/693–6399) provides walk-in care.

Late-Night Pharmacy **Leslie's Drug Store** (Main St., Vineyard Haven, tel. 508/693–1010) has pharmacists on 24-hour call.

Arriving and Departing by Ferry

If you plan to take a car to the island in summer or on popular weekends, you *must* reserve as far ahead as possible; spaces are often sold out months in advance. If you're without a reservation, get there very early, prepared to wait.

From Woods Hole The **Steamship Authority** (tel. 508/477–8600; on the Vineyard, 508/693–9130) operates the only car ferries, which make the 45-minute trip to Vineyard Haven year-round and to Oak Bluffs from late May through mid-September. (Guaranteed standby service for vehicles may be available in summer.) *Cost one-way: $4.75 adults, $2.40 children 5–12, $3 bicycles; cars: $38 mid-May–mid-Oct., $24 off-season.*

From Hyannis **Hy-Line** (Ocean St. dock, tel. 508/778–2600 for information; 508/778–2602 for reservations; on the Vineyard tel. 508/693–0112) makes the 1¾-hour run to Oak Bluffs from late May through October. *Cost one-way: $11 adults, $5.50 children 5–12, $4.50 bicycles.*

From Falmouth The *Island Queen* (Falmouth Harbor, tel. 508/548–4800) makes the 40-minute trip to Oak Bluffs from late May through Columbus Day. *Cost one-way: $5 adults, $2.50 children under 13, $3 bicycles; cost round-trip: $9 adults, $4.50 children, $6 bicycles.*

From New Bedford The *Schamonchi* (tel. 508/997–1688; on the Vineyard, tel. 508/693–2088) makes the 1½-hour trip from Billy Wood's Wharf to Vineyard Haven from mid-May to mid-October. *Cost one-way: $8.50 adults, $4.50 children under 12, $2.50 bicycles; round-trip same day: $15 adults, $7.50 children.*

From Nantucket **Hy-Line** (tel. 508/228–3949; on the Vineyard, tel. 508/693–0112) makes 2¼-hour runs to and from Oak Bluffs mid-June–mid-September. *Cost one-way: $10.50 adults, $5.25 children 5–12, $4.50 bicycles.*

Getting Around Martha's Vineyard

By Car Rentals can be booked through a courtesy phone at Woods Hole ferry terminal, or at the airport desks of **Budget** (tel. 508/693–7322) and **Hertz** (tel. 508/693–2402). **Adventure Rentals** (Beach Rd., Vineyard Haven, tel. 508/693–1959) rents mopeds and dune buggies.

By Bus and Trolley From mid-May to mid-October, shuttles operate between Vineyard Haven, Oak Bluffs, and Edgartown daily 7:30 AM–11:30 PM in high season, 7:30–7 other times. Cost one-way: $1.50–$3. Buses from Edgartown to Gay Head run frequently in July and August. Cost one-way: $1–$5. Trolley service around Edgartown (25¢) and from there to South Beach ($1.50) is also available mid-May to mid-September and can be hailed anywhere along their route. For transport information, call 508/627–7448.

By Bicycle and Moped The Vineyard is great for bicycling. For details on rentals and trails, *see* Biking in Sports and Outdoor Activities, *below*. Most of the bike-rental shops also rent mopeds, as does **Ride-On Mopeds** (Hy-Line Dock, Oak Bluffs, tel. 508/693–2076). A standard driver's license is required. Be careful: Skids on sand can cause accidents.

By Ferry The **On Time** ferry (Dock St., Edgartown, tel. 508/627–9427) makes the five-minute run to Chappaquiddick Island every day, 7:30 AM–midnight June–mid-October, less frequently off-season. *Cost round-trip: $4 car and driver, $2.50 bicycle and rider, $3.50 moped or motorcycle and rider, $1 individual.*

By Taxi Companies serving the island include **All Island** (tel. 508/693–3705), **Marlene's** (tel. 508/693–0037), and **Up Island** (tel. 508/693–5454).

Guided Tours

Orientation Three bus companies (tel. 508/693–1555, 508/693–4681, or 508/693–0058), now under one ownership, offer two-hour narrated tours of the island, with a stop at Gay Head Cliffs. Buses meet ferries in season; call at other times. *Cost: $11.50 adults, $3 children.*

Special-Interest Tours Sailplane tours are given in summer by **Soaring Adventures of America** (Katama Airfield, Herring Creek Rd., Edgartown, tel. 508/627–3833).

Day, sunset, and overnight sails to Nantucket or Cuttyhunk on the 54-foot ketch *Laissez Faire* (tel. 508/693–1646) are offered in season out of Vineyard Haven. Sunset cruises on the motor tour boat *Skipper* (tel. 508/693–1238), out of Oak Bluffs, promise glimpses of celebrities' homes (weather permitting).

Exploring Martha's Vineyard

Numbers in the margin correspond to points of interest on the Martha's Vineyard map.

The island is roughly triangular, with maximum distances of about 20 miles east to west and 10 miles north to south. Aside from the three main towns, much of its 130 square miles is undeveloped.

1 Most visitors to Martha's Vineyard arrive by ferry at **Vineyard Haven** (officially named Tisbury), the year-round commercial center of the island. Main Street, lined with shops and eating places, is just up the hill from the steamship terminal. The next block up from Main is **William Street,** a quiet, pretty stretch of white picket fences and Greek Revival houses, many of them built for prosperous sea captains. Now part of a National Historic District, the street was spared during the Great Fire of 1883, which claimed most of the old whaling and fishing town.

About 2 miles out on Main Street is **West Chop,** with an 85-acre conservation area, **West Chop Woods** (entrance on Franklin Street), and **2** a scenic overlook at the **West Chop Lighthouse.** Built in 1881 and moved back twice from the eroding bluff, the lighthouse is one of a pair guarding the entrance to Vineyard Haven harbor—in the 19th century, one of the world's busiest.

From town center, follow signs to Oak Bluffs and veer off toward the **3** 1876 **East Chop Lighthouse** for spectacular views of Nantucket Sound and a look at the expansive bluff-top summer "cottages" built in the breezy, porch-wrapped shingle style by the Boston and Newport rich in the late 19th and early 20th centuries. Continuing on **4** this road brings you to the heart of **Oak Bluffs.**

Once the setting for a number of grand hotels—the **Wesley Hotel** (1879) on Lake Avenue is the last of them—the still boat-filled and colorful Oak Bluffs harbor now specializes in guest houses and minimalls hawking fast food and souvenirs. On Oak Bluffs Avenue is the **Flying Horses,** a National Historic Landmark built in 1876. *Tel. 508/693–9481. Rides cost $1; $8 for a book of 10. Open mid-June–Labor Day, daily 10–10; spring and fall, weekends only.*

Circuit Avenue is the center of the action, with most of the town's shops, bars, and restaurants. Here you'll find the entrance to the **Oak Bluffs Camp Ground,** a warren of streets tightly packed with

Martha's Vineyard

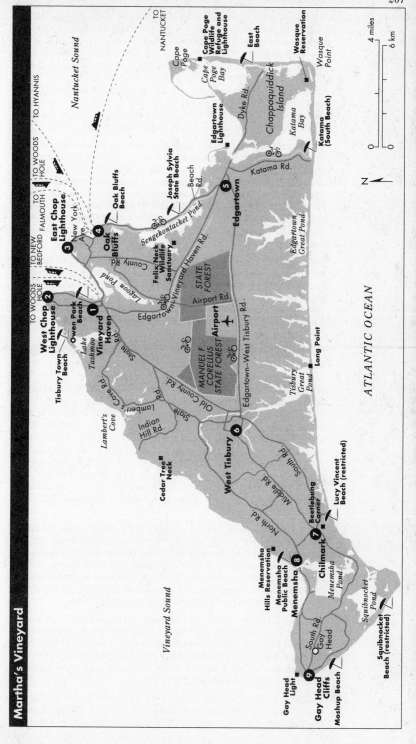

more than 300 Carpenter Gothic Victorian cottages, gaily painted in pastels and trimmed in lacy filigree. Methodist summer camp meetings have been held here since 1835; as the site's popularity grew, the original nine tents gave way to 500 tiny cottages by 1880. This development was compounded by an influx of fashionable folk who came on steamers from New Bedford, New York, and Boston for the bathing and sea air, creating a resort town known as Cottage City (now Oak Bluffs). Visitors are invited to a community sing held Wednesday at 8 PM, in season, at the **Tabernacle,** an impressive open-air structure of iron at the center of the campground.

The island's third main town is about 6 miles from Oak Bluffs via narrow, scenic Beach Road. **Edgartown** is tidy and polished, with upscale boutiques, elegant sea captains' houses, well-manicured lawns, and photogenic flower gardens. Two of the finest examples of Greek Revival architecture are on Main Street, between Pease's Point Way and Church Street: the **Old Whaling Church,** built in 1843 and now an arts center, with a 92-foot clock tower; and the roofwalk-topped **Dr. Daniel Fisher House** (1840) next door, now housing offices.

In back of the Fisher House is the oldest dwelling on the island: the 1672 **Vincent House,** a weathered-shingle farmhouse maintained as an architectural museum. Most of the original wide-board floors, glass, brick, and hardware remain; parts of walls are exposed to reveal construction techniques. Guided tours are offered. *Main St., Edgartown, tel. 508/627–8017. Admission: $2.50 adults, $1.50 children. Open June–Sept., weekdays 10–2.*

Head back toward the harbor, then right onto School Street; at the corner of Cooke Street (Edgartown's oldest) is a complex of buildings belonging to the **Dukes County Historical Society.** Built in 1765 with raised-wood paneling, wide-board floors, and great hearths, the Thomas Cooke House is a museum documenting the island's history through furniture, tools, costumes, and ship models. It is open in summer only, for docent-guided tours. Accessible year-round are a small whaling-oriented museum, a library, a collection of antique vehicles, a brick tryworks, and the 1,000-prism, 1854 Fresnel lens from the Gay Head Lighthouse. *Cooke and School Sts., Edgartown, tel. 508/627–4441. Admission: $5 adults, $3 senior citizens and children under 16; reduced admission off-season. Open July 5–Labor Day, Tues.–Sat. 10–4:30, Sun. noon–4:30; off-season, Wed.–Fri. 1–4, Sat. 10–4.*

The west end of the Vineyard—known as Up-Island, from the nautical expression of going "up" in degrees of longitude as you sail west—is more rural than the east. **West Tisbury** occupies the center of the island, including most of the 4,000-acre **State Forest,** several farms, and a small New England village, complete with agricultural hall and **Alley's General Store** (State Rd., tel. 508/693–0088), purveyor since 1858 of everything from hammers to dill pickles.

Past West Tisbury center is **Chilmark,** a rustic wooded area with scenic ocean-view roads and two beautiful (residents-only) beaches. At the crossroads called Beetlebung Corner, head toward the little fishing village of **Menemsha.** Along with the fishing shacks and fish markets you'll find a few summer boutiques and restaurants, a beach, and good fishing from the jetties.

Continue west for the **Gay Head Cliffs.** These dramatically striated walls of red clay are the island's major tourist site. The approach to the overlook—you can see the Elizabeth Islands across Vineyard

Sound—is lined with Native American crafts and food shops. Gay Head is a Wampanoag Indian township.

Time Out The **Aquinnah** (tel. 508/645–9654), at the end of the row of shops, perched over the cliffs, is a Native American–owned family-style restaurant with a wonderful view from the windy deck and great sunsets. The simple menu features burgers and sandwiches, fish, homemade chowder and pies, and elegant breakfasts.

Martha's Vineyard for Free

Vineyard Haven Town Band concerts take place on Sunday evening in summer, alternately at Owen Park in Vineyard Haven and at the gazebo on Beach Road in Oak Bluffs.
The Winery at Chicama Vineyards (Stoney Hill Rd., off State Rd., West Tisbury, tel. 508/693–0309) offers tours and wine tastings Memorial Day through Columbus Day, tastings only for the rest of the year (call for times).

What to See and Do with Children

In addition to the **Flying Horses Carousel** (*see* Exploring Martha's Vineyard, *above*), Oak Bluffs offers kids a 75-game arcade—**The Game Room** (Oak Bluffs Ave., tel. 508/693–5163)—**Dockside Minigolf** (Dockside Marketplace, Oak Bluffs harbor, tel. 508/696–7646), and other summer lures.

Children's Theatre (at the high school, Edgartown–Vineyard Haven Rd., Oak Bluffs, tel. 508/693–4060) has weekday classes for children, and **Vineyard Playhouse** (*see* The Arts, *below*) has theater-related activities for children and teens, both in summer.
Takemmy Farm (State Rd., North Tisbury, tel. 508/693–2486) is open for visits with llamas and miniature donkeys Wednesday and Saturday afternoons.

Shopping

Department Store **The Fligors** (27 N. Water St., Edgartown, tel. 508/627–8811) has varied offerings, including preppy clothing and gift items.

Food and Flea Markets A **flea market** is held on the grounds of the Chilmark Community Church (Menemsha Cross Rd., tel. 508/645–3177) Wednesday and Saturday in season from about 7 AM until 2:30 or 3. From spring into October, **farmers' markets** are held in West Tisbury at the Agricultural Hall on South Road Saturday 9–noon and at Up-Island Cronig's on State Road Thursday 3:30–6.

Specialty Stores
Antiques **Granary Gallery at the Red Barn Emporium** (Old County Rd., West Tisbury, tel. 508/693–0455 or 800/343–0471) has country antiques, as well as a gallery showcasing island artists and the photographs of Alfred Eisenstadt. **Soulagnet Collection** (Colonial Inn Shops, Edgartown, tel. 508/627–7759; Basin Rd., Menemsha, tel. 508/645–3735) has Americana, including furniture, folk art, and local photographs and prints.

Art **Edgartown Art Gallery** (20 S. Summer St., Edgartown, tel. 508/627–8508), across from the Charlotte Inn, has 19th- and 20th-century oils and watercolors, plus English antiques and sporting prints. **Hermine Merel Smith Fine Art** (548 Edgartown Rd., West Tisbury, tel. 508/693–7719) specializes in paintings and drawings by contemporary American impressionists and realists.

Books **Bickerton & Ripley Books** (Main St., Edgartown, tel. 508/627–8463) and the **Bunch of Grapes Bookstore** (Main St., Vineyard Haven, tel. 508/693–2291) carry new books, including many island-related titles, and sponsor book-signings. **Book Den East** (New York Ave., Oak Bluffs, tel. 508/693–3946) sells out-of-print, antiquarian, and paperback books in an old barn.

Clothing **Bramhall & Dunn** (Main St., Vineyard Haven, tel. 508/693–6437) has superb hand-knit sweaters, as well as fine English country pine antiques, crafts, linens, and housewares. **Island Children** (Main St., Vineyard Haven, tel. 508/693–6130) has hand-block-printed children's and women's clothing in 100% cotton. **Murray's of the Vineyard** (Main St., Vineyard Haven, tel. 508/693–2640) offers classic designer fashions and accessories.

Crafts **Chilmark Pottery** (off State Rd., West Tisbury, tel. 508/693–7874) is a workshop and gallery of stoneware and porcelain. **Edgartown Scrimshaw** (Main St., tel. 508/627–9439) has antique and new scrimshaw, Nantucket lightship baskets, and jewelry. **Sioux Eagle Designs** (Main St., Vineyard Haven, tel. 508/693–6537) features handcrafted jewelry in exotic designs.

Gifts **The Secret Garden** (148 Circuit Ave., Oak Bluffs, tel. 508/693–4759) has linens, lace, baby gifts, wicker furniture, and island watercolors. **Tashtego** (29 Main St., Edgartown, tel. 508/627–4300) is one of the island's most interesting shops, with small antiques, island crafts, and home furnishings.

Sporting Goods **Brickman's** (Main St., Vineyard Haven, tel. 508/693–0047; Main St., Edgartown, tel. 508/627–4700) has sports and surfer-type clothes and sports equipment. **Wind's Up!** (Tisbury Market Place, Beach Rd., Vineyard Haven, tel. 508/693–4340) sells swimwear, windsurfing and sailing equipment, and other outdoor gear.

Sports and Outdoor Activities

Biking Paths run along the coast road from Oak Bluffs to Edgartown, inland from Vineyard Haven to Edgartown, and from Edgartown to South Beach. Any of these connect with scenic paths that weave through the State Forest. Rent bikes in Oak Bluffs at **De Bettencourt's** (Circuit Ave. Ext., tel. 508/693–0011), in Vineyard Haven at **Martha's Vineyard Scooter and Bike Rental** (by the steamship terminal, tel. 508/693–0782), and in Edgartown at **R.W. Cutler Bike** (1 Main St., tel. 508/627–4052).

Fishing The party boat *Skipper* (tel. 508/693–1238) leaves from Oak Bluffs harbor in season. Companies offering charters include **Big Eye Charters** (Edgartown, tel. 508/627–3649) and **North Shore Charters** (Menemsha, tel. 508/645–2993). Rent gear at **Larry's Tackle Shop** (141 Main St., Edgartown, tel. 508/627–5088) or **Dick's Bait and Tackle** (New York Ave., Oak Bluffs, tel. 508/693–7669).

Golf **Farm Neck Golf Club** (Farm Neck Rd., Oak Bluffs, tel. 508/693–3057) is a semiprivate club with 18 holes. The public **Mink Meadows Golf Course** (off Franklin St., Vineyard Haven, tel. 508/693–0600), on elite West Chop, has nine.

Horseback Riding **Misty Meadows Horse Farm** (Old County Rd., West Tisbury, tel. 508/693–1870) has a large indoor riding area and offers trail rides and lessons. **Martha's Vineyard Riding Center** (across from the airport, West Tisbury, tel. 508/693–3770) offers English riding lessons, indoor and outdoor rings, a hunt course, and trails. Reservations are necessary.

Sailing Lessons and rentals are available at the **Harborside Inn** (S. Water St., tel. 508/627–4321) in Edgartown and **Wind's Up!** (Beach Rd., tel. 508/693–4252) on the lagoon in Vineyard Haven.

Shellfishing Each town hall issues shellfish licenses for the waters under town jurisdiction and will give information on good spots.

Water Sports **Wind's Up!** provides windsurfing and sailing lessons and rentals, plus an invaluable brochure on windsurfing, including best locations and safety tips. **Vineyard Boat Rentals** (Dockside Marina, Oak Bluffs, tel. 508/693–8476) offers Boston Whalers, Bayliners, and Jet Skis.

Beaches

East Beach, on Chappaquiddick Island, is accessible only by foot or by four-wheel-drive vehicle from the Wasque Reservation entrance or by boat; it offers heavy surf, good bird-watching, and relative isolation in a lovely setting. **Joseph A. Sylvia State Beach,** between Oak Bluffs and Edgartown, is a mile-long sandy beach popular with families for its calm, warm water and view of Cape Cod across Nantucket Sound. **Menemsha Public Beach** is a pebbly beach with gentle surf on Vineyard Sound, backed by dunes. A great place to catch the sunset is by the **fishing harbor** on the western side of the island. **Moshup Beach** is a long, beautiful stretch of sand below and left of the Gay Head Cliffs (from the cliffs' pricey parking lot, it's a five-minute walk). Negotiating large boulders and strong surf can make swimming tiring; a nude beach is under the cliffs. **South Beach,** the island's largest and most popular, is a 3-mile ribbon of sand on the Atlantic, with strong surf and sometimes riptides. From Edgartown, take the bike path or the trolley.

Nature Areas

Cape Poge Wildlife Refuge and Wasque Reservation on Chappaquiddick is a 709-acre wilderness of dunes, woods, salt marshes, ponds, and barrier beach that is an important migration stopover or nesting area for many bird species. You'll find good swimming at East Beach and good surf casting at Wasque Point. *Tel. 508/627–7260. Admission: $3 cars, $3 individuals in season. Jeep tours: tel. 508/627–3599.*

Cedar Tree Neck, 300 hilly acres of unspoiled West Tisbury woods, has wildlife, freshwater ponds, brooks, low stone walls, and wooded trails ending at a stony but secluded North Shore beach where swimming and sunbathing are prohibited. The guided nature walk, although written for children, is interesting for all ages. *Follow Indian Hill Rd., off State Rd., for 2 mi, then a rough dirt road downhill to right for 1 mi to parking lot. Tel. 508/693–5207. Admission free. Open daily 8:30–5:30.*

Felix Neck Wildlife Sanctuary, 3 miles out of Edgartown, comprises 350 acres, including 6 miles of trails traversing marshland, fields, woods, seashore, and a pond rich in wildfowl. It offers a full schedule of events, all led by naturalists, and a gift shop and exhibit center. *Off Edgartown–Vineyard Haven Rd., tel. 508/627–4850. Admission: $2 adults, $1 children under 13 and senior citizens. Open daily 8–4. Closed Mon. Nov.–May.*

Long Point offers 633 acres of grassland, dense heath, grassy dunes, freshwater and saltwater ponds, and a mile of South Beach, with swimming and surf fishing. *In season, turn left onto dirt road ⁹⁄₁₀ mi* *west of airport on Edgartown–West Tisbury Rd.; at end, follow signs to parking lot. Off-season, follow unpaved Deep Bottom Rd. (1.1 mi west of airport) for 2 mi to lot. Tel. 508/693–7392. Admission: $6 cars, $3 adults in season. Open daily 10–6.*

Dining

Only Edgartown and Oak Bluffs allow the sale of liquor. In the "dry" towns restaurants are glad to provide setups. Dress is casual unless otherwise noted.

Edgartown   **L'étoile.** Set in a glass-wrapped summerhouse, with English an-
★ tiques and gilt-frame oil paintings adding elegance, is the Charlotte Inn's popular restaurant. The contemporary French menu highlights imaginative native seafood and shellfish as well as game. Characteristic dishes from the prix-fixe dinner or Sunday-brunch menu include grilled swordfish with ginger, lime, and cilantro butter; or assiette of lobster, littlenecks, and scallops with a lobster, sweet pepper, and basil sauce. The wine list is extensive. *27 S. Summer St., tel. 508/627–5187. Reservations required. Jacket advised. AE, MC, V. No lunch. Closed Jan.–mid-Feb., weekdays off-season. Very Expensive.*

Andrea's. Served amid unpretentious surroundings in an old house are such northern Italian and Continental dishes as grilled veal chop and sirloin cardinale (with green-and-black-peppercorn sauce). Choose from a seat in the main room, the glassed-in porch, semiprivate rooms, the rose garden (in season), or the downstairs bistro. *137 Upper Main St., tel. 508/627–5850. Reservations advised. AE, D, MC, V. No lunch. Closed Nov.–Apr. Expensive.*

Menemsha   **Home Port.** Here you'll find very fresh fish and seafood simply
★ baked, broiled, or fried, served in prix-fixe menus with home-baked loaves of bread. The decor, too, is no-nonsense, with plain wood tables and a family atmosphere; window walls overlooking the harbor provide more than enough visual pleasure. The wait is often long, especially around sunset; take a seat outside and order from the raw bar, or wander around the fishing village. *North Rd., tel. 508/627–9968. Reservations required. AE, MC, V. No lunch. BYOB. Closed Nov.–Apr. Moderate.*

Oak Bluffs   **Le Grenier.** Owner Jean Dupon from Lyons serves such classic French fare as quail flamed with cognac and grapes, calf brains sautéed with black butter and capers, and grilled salmon with rosemary butter. The look of the second-floor restaurant is a mix of garret and garden room, with green latticework, a slanted, slatted ceiling, and a popular screened porch where painted vine tendrils climb posts to the roof. *Upper Main St., tel. 508/693–4906. Reservations advised. AE, MC, V. BYOB. No lunch. Expensive–Very Expensive.*

★ **Oyster Bar.** Subtitled "An American Bistro," the Oyster Bar (named for its 35-foot mahogany raw bar) has a sophisticated art-deco look, with faux-marble columns, tropical greenery, and a line of pink neon along the walls. Though the extensive menu includes pastas, pizzas, soups, and specials, the stars are the many varieties of fish available each night—including such exotic choices as mahimahi—cooked any way you like: broiled, sautéed, grilled, steamed, *wasabi*-glazed, blackened, or au poivre. *162 Circuit Ave., tel. 508/693–3300. Reservations advised. AE, MC, V. No lunch. Closed Dec.–mid-May. Expensive–Very Expensive.*

Giordano's. Bountiful portions of simply prepared Italian food (pizzas, pastas, cacciatores, cutlets) and fried fish and seafood at excellent prices keep Giordano's—run by the Giordano clan since 1930—a family favorite. Children's meals are available for under $6 (including milk and Jell-O). The ambience suits the clientele—hearty, noisy, and cheerful—with sturdy booths, bright green-topped wood tables, and hanging greenery. Lines wrap around the corner. *107 Circuit Ave., tel. 508/693–0184. No reservations. No credit cards. Closed late Sept.–early June. Moderate.*

★ **Zapotec.** Serving authentic and creative Mexican dishes with chunky, coriander-flecked salsa, Zapotec is an intimate place with heart and style. Highly recommended is the lobster quesadilla, crispy and flavorful with chunks of lobster. *10 Kennebec Ave., tel. 508/693–6800. No reservations. AE, MC, V. No lunch. Closed Thanksgiving–Easter. Moderate.*

Vineyard Haven **Black Dog Tavern.** An island landmark, the Black Dog serves basic chowders, pastas, fish, and steak, along with such dishes as grilled bluefish with avocado salsa or sirloin tips with aioli. The Black Dog Bakery (on Water St., across from the A&P) provides breads and desserts, and there's now a general store behind the bakery. The tavern theme is nautical, with rustic ship's-planking floors and pictures of ships; the glassed-in porch, lighted by ship's lanterns, looks directly out on the harbor. The wait for a table is often long; put your name on the list and walk around the harbor area to pass the time. *Beach St. Ext., tel. 508/693–9223. No reservations. BYOB. AE, D, MC, V. Expensive.*

West Tisbury **Lambert's Cove Country Inn.** The country-inn setting (*see* Lodging, ★ *below*), soft lighting and music, and fine Continental cuisine make this the coziest, most romantic dining spot on the island. The daily selection of six or seven entrées may include cioppino or herb-crusted halibut with the chef's choice of fresh vegetable. In summer a lavish Sunday brunch is served on the deck overlooking the orchard. *Off Lambert's Cove Rd., tel. 508/693–2298. Reservations required. AE, MC, V. BYOB. Closed weekdays off-season. No lunch. Expensive.*

Lodging

Martha's Vineyard and Nantucket Reservations (Box 1322, Lagoon Pond Rd., Vineyard Haven 02568, tel. 508/693–7200 or, in MA, 800/649–5671) and **Accommodations Plus** (RFD 273, Edgartown 02539, tel. 508/627–7374) book bed-and-breakfasts, hotels, and cottages.

Edgartown **Charlotte Inn.** Built as a whaling-company owner's home in the ★ 1860s, the Charlotte has grown into a five-building complex of meticulously maintained guest accommodations and is considered one of the finest inns in New England. The rooms are elegantly furnished with English antiques and reproductions; some have fireplaces. The beautifully landscaped grounds include an English garden. *27 S. Summer St., 02539, tel. 508/627–4751. 24 rooms, 2 suites. Facilities: restaurant, art gallery. AE, MC, V. Continental breakfast and (in summer) afternoon tea included. Very Expensive.*

Harbor View Hotel. A multimillion-dollar renovation of this full-service resort hotel, completed in 1991, maintained the historic architecture of the 1891 main building, but everything else is new. A Victorian theme is carried throughout, from the airy and elegant dining room to individual rooms, done with pastel carpeting and walls, painted wicker, pickled-wood armoires, and pastel floral drapes—plus telephones, air-conditioning, cable TV, minifridges, and wall safes (in-room fax machines and VCRs available). Additional buildings offer rooms and suites with cathedral ceilings, private decks, or kitchens. Located in a residential neighborhood just minutes from town, the hotel offers views of Edgartown Lighthouse and the ocean. Walk on the ¾-mile beach or catch bluefish from the jetty. Many packages are available. *131 N. Water St., 02539, tel. 508/ 627-7000 or 800/225-6005, fax 508/627-7845. 124 units. Facilities: restaurant, outdoor pool, tennis, golf privileges, lounge with enter- tainment, business services, children's program, baby-sitting, laundry. AE, DC, MC, V. Very Expensive.*

Daggett House. The flower-bordered lawn that separates the main house (1750) from the harbor makes a great retreat after a day of exploring town, a minute away. The fine restaurant preserves much of the tavern that it once was, including a secret stairway. This and two other buildings are decorated with fine wallpapers, antiques, and reproductions. One suite has its own kitchen, as well as a private roof-walk with a whirlpool and a superb water view. *59 N. Water St., Box 1333, 02539, tel. 508/627-4600 or 800/946-3400, fax 508/627- 4611. 23 rooms, 3 suites with kitchen. AE, MC, V. Expensive.*

Mattakesett. This community of three- and four-bedroom homes and condominiums is within walking distance of South Beach. Each unit is individually owned and decorated; some are superior, some just average. All have full kitchens, washer/dryers, decks, and cable TV; some have whirlpools or wood-burning stoves. The staff is extreme- ly attentive. *Katama Rd., RFD 270, 02539, tel. 508/627-4432. 92 units. Facilities: tennis, outdoor pool, swimming and tennis les- sons, bicycles, aerobics, children's program. No credit cards. Closed Columbus Day–Memorial Day. Expensive.*

Gay Head ★ **Outermost Inn.** Built by Hugh Taylor (brother of James) as his year- round home, this serene retreat by the Gay Head Cliffs offers spa- cious rooms with polished light-wood floors, white walls, local art, white-and-black tile baths, TVs (on request), and picture windows giving spectacular views of the lighthouse, the ocean, and surround- ing moorland; two rooms have private decks, and one has a Jacuzzi. A full breakfast is served on the veranda—a great place to watch the sunset—or in the dining room, with fireplace and window wall. It's a five-minute walk to the beach. *Off Lighthouse Rd., RR1, Box 171, 02535, tel. 508/645-3511, fax 508/645-3514. 6 rooms, 1 suite. Facili- ties: restaurant (open to public; BYOB) in season; charterable 50- foot catamaran. Full breakfast included. AE, D, MC, V. Very Ex- pensive.*

Menemsha **Beach Plum Inn.** The main draws of this 10-acre retreat are the woodland setting, the panoramic view of the Vineyard Sound and the Menemsha harbor, and the romantic gourmet restaurant that overlooks spectacular sunsets. The renovated 1890 Main House is surrounded by cottages; rooms on the second floor of the house have the best views. Both the cottages (one with Jacuzzi) and the inn rooms have New England country furnishings. *Beach Plum Rd., off North Rd., 02552, tel. 508/645-9454. 5 inn rooms, 6 rooms in 4 cot- tages. Facilities: restaurant, tennis, croquet, baby-sitting, bike ren- tals. AE, D, MC, V. Closed Nov.–Apr. Full breakfast included (MAP available). Very Expensive.*

Oak Bluffs ★ **Oak House.** The wraparound veranda of this pastel-front Victorian (1872) looks across a busy street to a wide strand of beach. Several rooms have private terraces; if you're bothered by noise, you might ask for a room at the back. The decor centers on well-preserved woods—some rooms have oak wainscoting from top to bottom— choice antique furniture, and nautical-theme accessories. *Sea View Ave., Box 299, 02557, tel. 508/693-4187, fax 508/696-7385. 8 rooms,*

2 suites. AE, MC, V. Closed mid-Oct.–mid-May. Continental breakfast and afternoon tea included. Expensive.

Sea Spray Inn. Separated from the same road and beach by a grassy park is this porch-wrapped summer house with an open, breezy feel. The simple and restful decor is highlighted by cheerful splashes of color, including pastel-painted furniture and floors. The Honeymoon Suite has lace-draped bay windows looking onto the park. The Garden Room offers a king-size bed with gauze canopy and a private porch. *2 Nashawena Park, Box 2125, 02557, tel. 508/693-9388. 7 rooms (2 with shared bath). MC, V. Continental breakfast included. Closed mid-Nov.–mid-Apr. Moderate.*

Vineyard Haven ★ **Thorncroft Inn.** Set on 3½ acres of woods about a mile from the ferry, the 1918 Craftsman bungalow is furnished with very fine Colonial and richly carved Renaissance Revival antiques and tasteful reproductions. The atmosphere is somewhat formal but not fussy. All rooms have air-conditioning and cable TV; some have wood-burning fireplaces, whirlpools, canopy beds, or minifridges; two have private screened porches with hot tubs. Breakfast is a gourmet, sit-down affair conducive to meeting and chatting. *278 Main St., Box 1022, 02568, tel. 508/693-3333 or 800/332-1236, fax 508/693-5419. 12 rooms, 1 suite. AE, D, DC, MC, V. Full breakfast and afternoon tea included. Expensive–Very Expensive.*

West Tisbury ★ **Lambert's Cove Country Inn.** The 1790 farmhouse is approached through pine woods and set in an apple orchard. It has elegance, with rich woodwork and large floral displays, yet makes you feel at home with firm beds and unpretentious furnishings in comfortably sized, recently refurbished guest rooms. Public areas include a gentleman's library with fireplace and a romantic gourmet restaurant where President and Mrs. Clinton dined in 1993. *Lambert's Cove Rd., West Tisbury (RR1 422, Vineyard Haven 02568), tel. 508/693-2298, fax 508/693-7890. 15 rooms. Facilities: restaurant, tennis. AE, MC, V. Continental breakfast included. Expensive.*

The Arts

Theater The **Vineyard Playhouse** (10 Church St., Vineyard Haven, tel. 508/693-7333) offers summer Shakespeare at an outdoor amphitheater, a summer season with a mostly Equity troupe, and winter community theater (tel. 508/693-6450).

Nightlife

Wintertide Coffeehouse (Five Corners, Vineyard Haven, tel. 508/693-8830) offers a varied program, including live folk and blues, teen nights, and a jazz DJ on Sunday. Some nights it is open just for light meals, playing games, sipping cappuccino, and listening to CDs.

The **Ritz Café** (Circuit Ave., Oak Bluffs, tel. 508/693-9851) has live blues and jazz on weekends, more often in season.

At **David's Island House** restaurant (Circuit Ave., Oak Bluffs, tel. 508/693-4516), renowned pianist David Crohan and special guests entertain dinner and lounge patrons with popular and classical music in summer. Two clubs offer a mix of live rock and reggae and DJ-spun dance music: the seasonal **Hot Tin Roof** (at the airport, tel. 508/693-1137) and the year-round **Atlantic Connection** (124 Circuit Ave., Oak Bluffs, tel. 508/693-7129).

Nantucket

Thirty miles southeast of Hyannis, in the open Atlantic Ocean, lies Nantucket. Settled in the mid-17th century by Quakers and others retreating from the repressive religious authorities of mainland Massachusetts, this 12-by-3-mile island became the foremost whaling port in the world during the golden age of whaling, in the early to mid-19th century. Shipowners and sea captains built elegant mansions that today remain remarkably unchanged, thanks to a very strict code regulating any changes to structures within the town of Nantucket, an official National Historic District. In addition, more than a third of the island's acreage is under protection from development.

Visitors on a day trip usually browse in the downtown's many art galleries, crafts shops, and boutiques, enjoy the architecture and historical museums, and sample the wealth of gourmet restaurants. Those who stay longer appreciate the breezy openness of the island. Its moors—swept with fresh salt breezes and scented with bayberry, wild roses, and cranberries—and its miles of clean, white-sand beaches make Nantucket a respite from the rush and regimentation of life elsewhere.

Important Addresses and Numbers

Visitor Information   **Chamber of Commerce** (Pacific Club Bldg., Main St., tel. 508/228–1700; open weekdays 9–5). **Nantucket Information Bureau** (25 Federal St., tel. 508/228–0925; open daily 9–6 in summer, Mon.–Sat. 9–4 off-season).

Emergencies   **Nantucket Cottage Hospital** (S. Prospect St., tel. 508/228–1200) has a 24-hour emergency room.

Arriving and Departing by Ferry

If you plan to take a car to the island in summer or on popular weekends, you *must* reserve as far ahead as possible; spaces are often sold out months in advance.

The **Steamship Authority** (on Nantucket, tel. 508/228–3274; on the Cape, tel. 508/477–8600) runs car-and-passenger ferries to the island from Hyannis year-round. The trip takes 2¼ hours. *Cost one-way: $10 adults, $5 children 5–12; cars, $90 mid-May–mid-Oct., $70 mid-Oct.–Nov. 30 and Mar. 1–mid-May, $50 Dec.–Feb., bicycles $5.*

Hy-Line (on Nantucket, tel. 508/228–3949; in Hyannis, tel. 508/778–2600) carries passengers from Hyannis from early May through October. The trip takes 1¾ to 2 hours. Cost one-way: $11 adults, $5.50 children 5–12, $4.50 bicycles. There is also service from Oak Bluffs on Martha's Vineyard (tel. 508/693–0112) mid-June to mid-September; that trip takes 2¼ hours and costs the same.

Getting Around Nantucket

By Car   Rent cars or four-wheel-drive vehicles at the airport desks of **Budget** (tel. 508/228–5666), **Hertz** (tel. 508/228–9421), and **Nantucket Windmill** (tel. 508/228–1227) or through the free phone at the Woods Hole ferry terminal.

By Bus   In season **Barrett's Tours** (20 Federal St., tel. 508/228–0174) runs shuttles to 'Sconset, Surfside, and Jetties beaches.

By Taxi Year-round taxi companies include **A-1 Taxi** (tel. 508/228–3330 or 508/228–4084), **All Points Taxi** (tel. 508/228–5779), and **Atlantic Cab** (tel. 508/228–1112).

By Bicycle Bikes and mopeds can be rented near Steamboat Wharf from **and Moped** **Young's Bicycle Shop** (tel. 508/228–1151; also cars) and **Nantucket Bike Shop** (tel. 508/228–1999; in season).

Guided Tours

Orientation **Barrett's Tours** (20 Federal St., tel. 508/228–0174) and **Nantucket Is-** **Tours** **land Tours** (Straight Wharf, tel. 508/228–0334) give 1½-hour narrated bus tours of the island, spring through fall; buses meet ferries.

Carried Away (tel. 508/228–0218) offers narrated carriage rides through the town historic district in season.

Gail's Scenic Rides (tel. 508/257–6557) offers a lively, intimate 1¾-hour van tour narrated by sixth-generation Nantucketer Gail Johnson.

Special- **Roger Young's historic walking tours** (tel. 508/228–1062; in season) of **Interest Tours** the town center are entertaining and leisurely.

Nantucket Whalewatch (Hy-Line dock, Straight Wharf, tel. 508/283–0313 or 800/942–5464) runs naturalist-led excursions in season.

Exploring Nantucket

Numbers in the margin correspond to points of interest on the Nantucket map.

❶ In **Nantucket town** the **Museum of Nantucket History,** in the old Thomas Macy Warehouse, tells the story of the island from its geologic beginnings, through the whaling era, to the its emergence as a summer colony. It is run by the Nantucket Historical Association (NHA); a visitor's pass allowing a single visit to all 14 NHA properties is available at any of the sites for $8 adults, $4 children 5–14. Audio and visual displays include photographs, ship models, a firefighting vehicle, and a 13-foot diorama of the waterfront before the Great Fire of 1846, when hundreds of buildings were lost. *Straight Wharf, tel. 508/228–1894. Admission: $3 adults, $2 children 5–14; or NHA Visitor's Pass. Open mid-June–Labor Day, daily 10–5; call for spring and fall hours.*

The **Whaling Museum** is a short walk away along South Water Street. Set in an 1846 factory for refining spermaceti and making candles, it traces Nantucket's whaling past through such exhibits as a fully rigged whale boat, harpoons and other implements, portraits of sea captains, a large scrimshaw collection, the skeleton of a 43-foot finback whale, and the original 16-foot-high glass prism light from the Sankaty Light. *Broad St., tel. 508/228–1736. Admission: $4 adults, $2 children 5–14; or NHA Visitor's Pass. Open mid-June–Labor Day, daily 10–5; call for spring and fall hours.*

Time Out At lunch and dinner the **Atlantic Cafe** (15 S. Water St., tel. 508/228–0570) offers a varied, inexpensive menu. Appetizers are great, including the quahog chowder and zucchini sticks sprinkled with cheese and served with a hot dipping sauce.

A walk up Main Street past the **Pacific National Bank,** at the corner of Fair Street, takes you out of the business district to the mansions that whaling built. At 93–97 Main Street are the well-known **"Three**

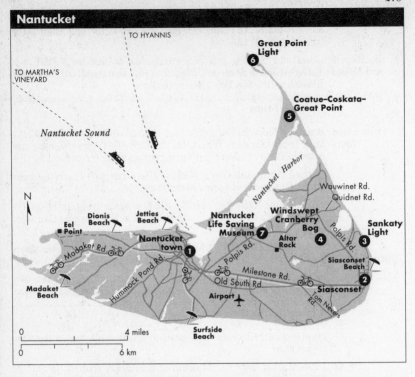

Nantucket

Bricks,"** identical redbrick mansions with columned Greek Revival porches at the front entrance. They were built between 1836 and 1838 by whaling merchant Joseph Starbuck for his three sons.

Across the street are two white, porticoed Greek Revival mansions built in 1845–46 by factory owner William Hadwen, the son-in-law of Joseph Starbuck, for himself and for the niece he and his wife adopted. One, called the **Hadwen House,** is now a house museum that reflects the affluence of Nantucket's whaling era. A guided tour points out the grand circular staircase, fine plasterwork, carved Italian marble fireplace mantels, and Regency, Empire, and Victorian furnishings. A recent refurbishment introduced additional period furnishings, wallpapers, and floor coverings. *96 Main St., tel. 508/228–1894. Admission: $3 adults, $2 children 5–14; or NHA Visitor's Pass. Open mid-June–Labor Day, daily 10–5; call for spring and fall hours.*

Continue up Main Street through the rotary, turn left onto Bloom Street, then right onto Vestal Street to the **Old Gaol,** an 1805 jailhouse in use until 1933. Walls, ceilings, and floors are bolted with iron; furnishings consist of rough-plank bunks and open privies. Don't feel too sympathetic, though: Most prisoners were allowed out at night to sleep in their own beds. *15R Vestal St., tel. 508/228–1894. Admission free. Open mid-June–Labor Day, daily 10–5; call for spring and fall hours.*

Backtrack to Hawden House and take a right onto Pleasant Street and another right onto South Mill Street for the **Old Mill,** a 1746 Dutch-style windmill built with lumber from shipwrecks and still worked with wood gears and wind power to grind cornmeal in season. *Tel. 508/228–1894. Admission: $3 adults, $2 children 5–14; or NHA Visitor's Pass. Open mid-June–Labor Day, daily 10–5; call for spring and fall hours.*

Other in-town sites not on this route are worth particular mention. The tower of the **First Congregational Church** provides the best view of Nantucket—for those who climb the 92 steps. Peek in at the church's 1850 trompe-l'oeil ceiling. *62 Centre St. Admission: $1.50 adults, 50¢ children under 15. Open mid-June–mid-Oct., Mon.–Sat. 10–4.*

The **Oldest House,** a 1686 saltbox also called the Jethro Coffin House, is the oldest house on the island. Its most striking feature is the massive central brick chimney with a giant brick horseshoe adornment. The sparsely furnished interior features leaded-glass windows and enormous hearths. *Sunset Hill, tel. 508/228–1894. Admission: $3 adults, $2 children 5–14; or NHA Visitor's Pass. Open mid-June–Columbus Day, daily 10–5; call for spring hours.*

② A lovely day trip from town by bike is the village of **Siasconset** (called 'Sconset). This beach community—first a fishermen's village, then an actors' colony—today offers an unhurried lifestyle in elementally beautiful surroundings. Here you'll find pretty little streets with rose-covered cottages and driveways of crushed white shells, a post office, a general store, a few restaurants, and a beach.

If you return to town via Polpis Road, rather than the 'Sconset bike **③** path, you'll pass the precariously perched **Sankaty Light** and large **④** areas of open moorland. The entrance to the 205-acre **Windswept Cranberry Bog,** open to walkers and bike riders, is also on Polpis, between Quidnet Road and Wauwinet Road.

⑤ Wauwinet Road takes you to the gateway of **Coatue–Coskata–Great Point,** an unpopulated spit of sand comprising three cooperatively managed wildlife refuges and entered only by foot or four-wheel-drive over-sand vehicle (tel. 508/228–2884 for information). Its beaches, dunes, salt marshes, and stands of oak and cedar provide a major habitat for such birds as marsh hawks, oystercatchers, terns, and herring gulls. Because of frequent dangerous currents and riptides and the lack of lifeguards, swimming is strongly discouraged, **⑥** especially around the **Great Point Light.**

⑦ A bit farther along on Polpis Road is the **Nantucket Life Saving Museum,** housed in a re-creation of an 1874 Life Saving Service station. It honors the men who valiantly lived by the service's motto: "You have to go out, but you don't have to come back." Exhibits include original rescue equipment and boats, photos, and accounts of daring rescues. *Polpis Rd., tel. 508/228–1885. Admission: $1. Open mid-June–mid-Oct., daily 9:30–4:30.*

What to See and Do with Children

Actors Theatre of Nantucket (*see* The Arts, *below*) has special matinees for children in July and August.
J.J. Clammp's (Nobadeer Farm and Sun Island Rds., off Milestone Rd., tel. 508/228–8977), an 18-hole minigolf course, also offers remote-control boats on ponds. There's a free shuttle from town in season.
Maria Mitchell Aquarium displays local marine life in saltwater and freshwater tanks. *28 Washington St., near Commercial Wharf, tel. 508/228–5387. Admission: $1. Open mid-June–Labor Day, Tues.–Sat. 10–4.*

Shopping

The island specialty is Nantucket lightship baskets—woven baskets of oak or cane, their covers adorned with scrimshaw or rosewood, that were first made on lightships by crew members between chores and are now used as preppy purses. Most shops are open only in season, though many make it through November.

Food Market Monday through Saturday in season, colorful farm stands are set up on Main Street to sell local produce and flowers.

Specialty Stores
Antiques **Forager House** (20 Centre St., tel. 508/228–5977) specializes in folk art and Americana, including whirligigs, maps and charts, and postcards. **Nina Hellman Antiques** (48 Centre St., tel. 508/228–4677) carries scrimshaw, ship models, nautical instruments, and other marine antiques and Nantucket memorabilia. **Tonkin of Nantucket** (33 Main St., tel. 508/228–9697) has two floors of fine English antiques, including furniture, china, art, and marine and scientific instruments.

Art **Janis Aldridge** (7 Centre St., tel. 508/228–6673) sells beautifully framed antique prints, including many botanicals. **Paul La Paglia** (38 Centre St., tel. 508/228–8760) has moderately priced antique prints, including Nantucket scenes and fish. **Robert Wilson Galleries** (34 Main St., tel. 508/228–6246) carries fine contemporary American art, most of it representational. **Sailor's Valentine Gallery** (40 Centre St., tel. 508/228–2011) features folk and contemporary art and exquisite sailor's valentines (intricate shell designs in glass boxes).

Books **Mitchell's Book Corner** (54 Main St., tel. 508/228–1080) offers the best selection of books on Nantucket; write for a brochure.

Clothing **Murray's Toggery Shop** (62 Main St., tel. 508/228–0437) carries top-name traditional clothing and footwear for all. **The Peanut Gallery** (60 Main St., tel. 508/228–2010) has a discriminating collection of children's clothing. **Zero Main** (0 Main St., tel. 508/228–4401) stocks stylishly classic women's clothing, shoes, and accessories.

Crafts **Artisans Store** (18 Broad St., tel. 508/228–4631) sells fine American art and crafts, such as quilts, jewelry, and sweaters. **Four Winds Craft Guild** (6 Straight Wharf, tel. 508/228–9623) carries a large selection of antique and new scrimshaw and lightship baskets, as well as ship models and duck decoys.

Gifts **Museum Shop** (Broad St., tel. 508/228–5785) has island-related books, antique whaling tools, toys, spermaceti candles, reproduction furniture, and local jellies. **Nantucket Vineyard** (3 Bartlett Farm Rd., tel. 508/228–9235) offers tastings of its wines and sells them year-round.

Jewelry **The Golden Basket** (44 Main St., tel. 508/228–4344) sells miniature lightship baskets in gold or silver, some with precious stones and pearls, as well as other fine jewelry.

Sports and Outdoor Activities

Biking Scenic and well-maintained bike paths lead to Madaket, 'Sconset, and Surfside beaches. **Nantucket Cycling Club** (tel. 508/228–1164) holds open races most of the year.

Fishing Bluefish and bass are the main catches. **Barry Thurston's Fishing Tackle** (Harbor Sq., tel. 508/228–9595) and **Bill Fisher Tackle** (14 New Lane, tel. 508/228–2261) rent equipment. Charters sail out of

Straight Wharf every day in season. For guided four-wheel-drive trips to remote areas for surf casting, contact **Whitney Mitchell** (tel. 508/228–2331).

Golf	**Miacomet Golf Club** (off Somerset Rd., tel. 508/228–8987) and **Siasconset Golf Club** (Milestone Rd., tel. 508/257–6596) are public nine-hole courses.
Health and Fitness Club	**Club N.E.W.** (10 Young's Way, tel. 508/228–4750) offers aerobics, dance, and yoga classes, a large complement of exercise machines and free weights, and personal trainers.
Tennis	**Town courts** (tel. 508/325–5334; closed Labor Day–mid-June) are at Jetties Beach. **Brant Point Racquet Club** (N. Beach St., tel. 508/228–3700; closed mid-Oct.–mid-May) has nine clay courts, lessons, and a pro shop.
Water Sports	**Indian Summer Sports** (Steamboat Wharf, tel. 508/228–3632) and **Force 5** (Jetties Beach, tel. 508/228–5358; 37 Main St., tel. 508/228–0700) rent all kinds of equipment and give lessons. **The Sunken Ship** (corner of Broad and S. Water Sts., tel. 508/228–9226) offers scuba lessons and equipment rentals, plus rentals of other sports equipment.

Beaches

Children's Beach, a calm harbor beach, is an easy walk from town and good for small children. It offers a park and playground, lifeguard, food service, and rest rooms. **Jetties Beach,** a short bike or shuttle ride from town, is the most popular beach for families because of its calm surf, lifeguards, bathhouse, snack bar, watersports rentals, and tennis. **Madaket Beach** is known for great sunsets. Reached by a 6-mile bike path, Madaket offers heavy surf, a lifeguard, rest rooms, and food nearby. **Siasconset Beach,** at the end of a 7-mile bike path, is an uncrowded sandy beach with surf, lifeguard, and playground. **Surfside Beach** is 3 miles from town on a bike path. It is the premier surf beach, with lifeguard, bathhouse, rest room, and snack bar.

Dining

Dress is casual unless otherwise noted.

Chanticleer. At his renowned restaurant in a rose-covered cottage in 'Sconset, owner-chef Jean-Charles Berruet has for two decades created sumptuous classic French fare using fresh island ingredients. Prix-fixe menus are offered at dinner (à la carte also available), which is served in the formal, fireplaced main dining room or in the casual upstairs room. The wine cellar is legendary, with hundreds of choices. Lunch in the rose garden is heavenly. *9 New St., Siasconset, tel. 508/257–6231. Reservations advised well in advance. Jacket required at dinner. AE, MC, V. Closed Wed. and Columbus Day– Mother's Day. Expensive–Very Expensive.*

★ **Club Car.** Superior Continental cuisine is served in a candlelit dining room with a wall of small-pane windows; in an attached old railway car is a cozy piano bar. The menu, often featuring seafood, changes with the season and includes game in fall. The rack of lamb glazed with honey mustard and herbs is highly recommended. *1 Main St., tel. 508/228–1101. Reservations advised. AE, D, DC, MC, V. Closed early Dec.–mid-May; Tues. and Wed. mid-May–June and mid-Sept.–early Dec. Expensive–Very Expensive.*

★ **Topper's.** Far from town at the exclusive Wauwinet resort, Topper's serves New American cuisine, including such choices as sautéed lobster with citrus, wild mushrooms, and roasted peppers in a Chardonnay beurre blanc. The interior reflects the inn's casual sophistication: hand-painted floors, fine wood paneling, oil paintings. The patio overlooking the water is a pleasant place for lunch or drinks, especially at sunset. *Wauwinet Rd., tel. 508/228–8768. Reservations required. Jacket advised at dinner. AE, DC, MC, V. Closed mid-Dec.–mid-May. Expensive–Very Expensive.*

Jared's. The formal restaurant of the Jared Coffin House is a large, elegant room, with salmon walls, pale green table linens and swag drapes, Federal antiques, and chandeliers. The American fare is equally elegant, such as sautéed chicken medallions and morel mushrooms with a rosemary pinot noir sauce; prix fixe meals are offered at under $30. *29 Broad St., tel. 508/228–2400. Reservations advised. Jacket advised. AE, D, DC, MC, V. No lunch. Breakfast only Jan.–Apr. Expensive.*

★ **American Seasons.** The creative regional American menu features such artfully presented dishes as grilled pork loin with pepper jelly and black-bean succotash, and a pancake appetizer of hickory-smoked lobster and wild mushrooms. Folk-art murals and tables hand-painted with decorative game boards are part of the relaxed decor. *80 Centre St., tel. 508/228–7111. Reservations advised. AE, MC, V. No lunch (Sun. brunch Sept.–Dec.). Closed Jan.–Mar. Moderate–Expensive.*

★ **The Brotherhood of Thieves.** Long lines are a fixture outside this very old-English pub restaurant. Inside is a dark, cozy room with low ceilings, a fireplace, and exposed brick and beams; much of the seating is at long, tightly packed tables. Dine happily on good chowder and soups, fried fish and seafood, burgers, jumbo sandwiches, and shoestring fries (the house specialty: long curls with the skins on). A convivial atmosphere prevails, thanks partly to the vast menu of spirits—ales, coffee drinks, brandies, mixed concoctions, etc. *23 Broad St. No reservations. No credit cards. Moderate.*

The Hearth at the Harbor House. The attractive dining room has a Colonial New England look, with a parquet floor, weathervane chandeliers, and antique-red walls. There or on an outdoor patio, dine on simply prepared New England fare, including surf-and-turf combinations. A lavish Sunday brunch buffet includes a raw bar. The four-course "sunset special" is an excellent deal, and children under 13 dine free with parents. *S. Beach St., tel. 508/228–1500. Reservations advised (required for Sun. brunch). AE, DC, MC, V. No lunch. Moderate.*

Lodging

Summer House. Here, across from 'Sconset Beach, are the little rose-covered cottages identified with Nantucket summers. Each one- or two-bedroom cottage is furnished in a blend of unfussy beach style and romantic English country, and has a marble bath with Jacuzzi. Some cottages have fireplaces or kitchens. *Ocean Ave., Box 313, Siasconset 02564, tel. 508/257–4577. 8 cottages. Facilities: 2 restaurants, outdoor pool and bar. AE, MC, V. Closed Nov.–late Apr. Continental breakfast included. Very Expensive.*

★ **Wauwinet.** A superb location (8 miles from town, surrounded by ocean and harbor beaches), fine furnishings, and extensive services and amenities make this recently renovated mid-19th-century property a luxurious perch. Each guest room—decorated in country style, with pine antiques—has a phone, air-conditioning, and TV with VCR; the most expensive have spectacular views of the sunset over the water. *120 Wauwinet Rd., Box 2580, 02584, tel. 508/228–0145 or 800/426–8718, fax 508/228–6712. 25 rooms, 5 cottages. Facilities: restaurant, bar, tennis, Sunfish and lessons, Great Point excursions and beach shuttle, croquet, business services, jitney service. AE, DC, MC, V. Closed Nov.–May. Full breakfast and afternoon snacks included. Very Expensive.*

★ **White Elephant.** Long a hallmark of service and style on the island, this newly renovated hotel offers a choice location, right on the harbor. From the pool, set on a lawn landscaped with roses, and from most rooms, guests enjoy the comings and goings of boats that moor just offshore. The Breakers is the hotel's ultraluxury arm, with coolly elegant rooms in sumptuous fabrics, half-canopy beds, and window walls or French doors opening onto private harborfront decks (plus minibars and minifridges). Main-inn rooms are done in English country style, with stenciled-pine armoires and florals. All rooms have phones and cable TV; some have VCRs and air-conditioning. *Easton St., Box 359, 02554, tel. 508/228–2500 or 800/475–2637. 48 rooms, 32 cottages (some with kitchens). Facilities: restaurant, lounge, heated outdoor pool/whirlpool, croquet, putting green, concierge, business services, boat slips, children's program. AE, D, DC, MC, V. Closed mid-Sept.–Memorial Day. Very Expensive.*

Jared Coffin House. This complex of four buildings is a longtime favorite with many visitors to Nantucket. The main building—a three-story, cupola-topped brick mansion built in 1845—has a historic feel that the others, pleasant as they are, don't have. The main house's common and guest rooms are beautifully furnished with Oriental carpets, lace curtains, and antiques (the other buildings, with reproductions); rooms across the street are larger. All rooms have cable TV (except in the main house) and phones; some have minifridges. Small, inexpensive single rooms are available. *29 Broad St., Box 1580, 02554, tel. 508/228–2405, 508/228–2400, or 800/248–2405. 60 rooms. Facilities: restaurant, tavern with patio. AE, D, DC, MC, V. Full breakfast included. Expensive–Very Expensive.*

Centerboard. White walls (some with pastel murals of moors and sky), natural or mauve-washed light woods, white furniture, and white lacy linens and comforters on featherbeds create a cool, dreamy atmosphere at this bed-and-breakfast. Antique quilts and stained glass add touches of color. The Victorian suite is a stunner, including fine antiques and a green-marble bath with whirlpool. All rooms have TVs and minifridges. *8 Chester St., Box 456, 02554, tel. 508/228–9696. 4 rooms, 1 suite, 1 studio. AE, MC, V. Continental breakfast included. Expensive.*

Corner House. Accommodations at this bed-and-breakfast range from tiny, rustic third-floor rooms in the 1790 main house—whose common rooms boast elaborate Colonial woodwork—to large rooms with cathedral ceilings in a new building nearby. Some rooms have sitting areas, TVs, or minifridges; all have antique brass or canopy beds, down pillows and comforters, and firm mattresses. *49 Centre St., 02554, tel. 508/228–1530. 14 rooms, 1 suite. MC, V. Continental breakfast and afternoon tea included. Moderate–Expensive.*

★ **76 Main Street.** Built in 1883 on a quiet part of Main Street, 76 Main carefully blends antiques and reproductions, Oriental rugs, handmade quilts, and lots of fine woods. Room 3, originally the dining room, has wonderful woodwork, a carved-wood armoire, and twin four-posters; spacious Room 1, considered the best room, has large windows, massive redwood pocket doors, and an eyelet-dressed canopy bed. Both are on the first floor. The motel-like annex rooms (available in season only) have low ceilings and are a bit dark but are large and good for families, with color TV and refrigerator. *76 Main*

St., 02554, tel. 508/228–2533. 18 rooms. No smoking. AE, MC, V. Continental breakfast included. Moderate–Expensive.

Youth Hostel **Star of the Sea AYH-Hostel.** A 3-mile ride on a bike path from town, with a great location at Surfside Beach, is the island's only budget accommodation (no camping is allowed on Nantucket). Set in a former lifesaving station, it offers a group kitchen and family rooms sleeping four. *Surfside, 02554, tel. 508/228–0433. 64 beds. No credit cards. Closed Columbus Day–Apr.*

The Arts

Concerts **Nantucket Chamber Music Center** (Coffin School, Winter St., tel. 508/228–3352) offers year-round choral and instrumental concerts as well as instruction. In July and August, the **Nantucket Musical Arts Society** (tel. 508/228–3735) offers Tuesday-evening concerts featuring internationally acclaimed musicians at the First Congregational Church (62 Centre St.), and **Noonday Concerts** on an 1831 Goodrich organ are held at the Unitarian Church (11 Orange St., tel. 508/228–5466) Thursday at noon.

Theater **Actors Theatre of Nantucket** (Methodist Church, Centre and Main Sts., tel. 508/228–6325) presents several plays each season (May–Oct.), plus children's matinees. **Theatre Workshop of Nantucket** (Bennett Hall, 62 Centre St., tel. 508/228–4305) offers community theater year-round.

Nightlife

Lounges **The Hearth** (5 Beach St., tel. 508/228–1500), the Harbor House hotel's restaurant, has dancing to live music (country, folk, oldies) in its lounge, with sports TV, darts and games, and a fun light menu. **The Regatta at the White Elephant** (Easton St., tel. 508/228–2500), a formal hotel restaurant lounge—proper dress advised—has a harbor view and a pianist playing show tunes.

Rock Two rock clubs open year-round are **The Box** (6 Dave St., tel. 508/228–9717) and **The Muse** (44 Atlantic Ave., tel. 508/228–6873 or 508/228–8801). All ages dance to rock, reggae, and other types of live or recorded music. The Muse has a pizza shop.

The North Shore

The slice of Atlantic coast known as the North Shore extends past grimy docklands, through Boston's well-to-do northern suburbs, to the picturesque Cape Ann region, and beyond the Cape to Newburyport, just south of New Hampshire. It takes in historic Salem, which thrives on a history of witches, millionaires, and maritime trade; Gloucester, the oldest seaport in America; quaint little Rockport, crammed with crafts shops and artists' studios; Newburyport with its redbrick center and rows of clapboard Federal mansions; and miles of sandy beaches. Bright and busy in the short summer season, the North Shore calms some between November and June, when most holiday-making facilities shut down.

Important Addresses and Numbers

Visitor Information The umbrella organization for the region is the **North of Boston Visitors and Convention Bureau** (248 Cabot St., Box 642, Beverly 01915, tel. 508/921–4990; open weekdays 9–4:30). The following cover more specific areas:

Cape Ann Chamber of Commerce (33 Commercial St., Gloucester 01930, tel. 508/283–1601; open weekdays 8–5 and, May–Oct., Sat. 10–6 and Sun. 10–4).

Essex North Chamber of Commerce (29 State St., Newburyport 01950, tel. 508/462–6680; open weekdays 9–5, Sat. 10–4, Sun. noon–4).

National Park Service Visitor Information (Museum Place, Essex St., Salem 02642, tel. 508/741–3648; open daily 9–5).

Rockport Chamber of Commerce (Box 67, 3 Main St., Rockport 01966, tel. 508/546–6575; open May–Oct., Mon.–Sat. 9–5; Nov.–Apr., weekdays 10–4).

Rockport Chamber of Commerce Information Booth (Rte. 127; open May 21–Oct. 16, Mon.–Sat. 11–5, Sun. noon–5).

Salem Chamber of Commerce and Visitor Information (32 Derby Sq., Salem 01970, tel. 508/744–0004; open weekdays 9–5).

Salisbury Chamber of Commerce (Town Hall, Beach Rd., Salisbury 01952, tel. 508/465–3581; open weekdays 9–4).

Emergencies   **Beverly Hospital** (Herrick St., Beverly, tel. 508/922–3000).

Late-Night Pharmacy   **Walgreen's** (201 Main St., Gloucester, tel. 508/283–7361) is open until 9 weeknights, 6 on weekends.

Getting Around the North Shore

By Car   The primary link between Boston and the North Shore is Route 128, which breaks off from I–95 and follows the coast northeast to Gloucester. If you stay on I–95, you'll reach Newburyport. A less direct route, but a scenic one once north of Lynn, is Route 1A, which leaves Boston via the Callahan Tunnel. Beyond Beverly, Route 1A goes inland toward Ipswich and Essex; at this point, switch to Route 127, which follows the coast to Gloucester and Rockport.

By Bus   From Boston to the North Shore, buses run less frequently than trains, but **Coach** (tel. 800/874–3377) offers service along Route 1 and an express commuter service from Boston to Newburyport.

On the Cape the **Cape Ann Transportation Authority** (CATA) (tel. 508/283–7916) covers the Gloucester/Rockport region.

By Train   **Massachusetts Bay Transportation Authority** (MBTA) (tel. 617/722–3200) trains leave Boston's North Station for Salem, Beverly, Gloucester, Rockport, and Ipswich.

By Boat   A boat leaves Boston for Gloucester daily between May 30 and Labor Day, at 10 AM (return boat leaves Gloucester at 3 PM). The three-hour trip costs $18 for adults, $10 for children under 12. Contact **A. C. Cruise Lines** (290 Northern Ave., Boston, tel. 617/261–6633 or 800/422–8419).

Guided Tours

The **Salem Trolley** (Trolley Depot, 191 Essex St., Salem, tel. 508/745–3003) gives one-hour narrated tours of the city. Tours depart from the Trolley Depot daily every hour from 10–4, April through December.

A whale-watching trip is a terrific way to spend the day from May to October, when four breeds of whale feed off the North Shore. Their abundance is such, you're practically guaranteed to see half-dozen—on ideal days you may see 40. Reputable operations include **Cape Ann Whale Watch** (415 Main St., Gloucester, tel. 508/283–5110), **Captain Bill's Whale Watch** (9 Traverse St., Gloucester, tel.

508/283–6995), **Newburyport Whale Watch** (54 Merrimac St., Newburyport, tel. 508/465–9885 or 800/848–1111), and **Yankee Fleet/Gloucester Whale Watch** (75 Essex Ave., Gloucester, tel. 508/283–0313).

Exploring the North Shore

Numbers in the margin correspond to points of interest on the North Shore map.

❶ **Marblehead,** with its ancient clapboard houses and narrow, winding streets, retains much of the character of the village founded in 1629 by fishermen from Cornwall and the Channel Islands. Today's fishing fleet pales in comparison to the armada of pleasure craft that anchors in the harbor. At one of New England's premier sailing capitals, Race Week (usually the last week of July) draws boats from all along the eastern seaboard. But merchant sailors, not weekend yachtsmen, made Marblehead prosper in the 18th century, and many of their impressive Georgian mansions still line downtown streets. Parking is notoriously difficult; try the 30-car public lot at the end of Front Street or along the street in metered areas.

Time Out To experience the fisherman's Marblehead, visit the **Driftwood** (Front St., tel. 617/631–1145), a simple, red-clapboard restaurant by the harbor. Fishnets drape from the ceiling and excellent, inexpensive breakfasts and lunches are served from 5:30 AM until 2 PM.

The town's Victorian municipal building, **Abbott Hall** (ca. 1876), is unremarkable except for the fact that it houses A. M. Willard's painting *The Spirit of '76,* one of America's treasured patriotic icons, depicting three Revolutionary veterans with fife, drum, and flag. *Washington St., tel. 617/631–0528. Open Mon.–Fri. 9–5, and June–Oct., Sat. 9–6, Sun. 11–6.*

❷ Follow Route 114 out of Marblehead, turn right onto Route 1A, and drive the short distance to **Salem.** Don't be put off by the industrial surroundings; the setting may be tarnished, but Salem is a gem, full of compelling museums, trendy waterfront stores and restaurants, a traffic-free shopping area, and a wide open common with a children's playground and jogging path. Settled in 1630, the town is known for the witchcraft hysteria of 1692, a rich maritime tradition, and the architectural splendor of its Federal homes. The frigates of Salem opened the Far East trade routes and provided the wealth that produced America's first millionaires. Numbered among its native sons were Nathaniel Hawthorne, the navigator Nathaniel Bowditch, and the architect Samuel McIntire.

One way to take in Salem's sights is to follow the Heritage Trail (a red line painted on the sidewalk) around the town. If you prefer to ride, the **Salem Trolley** (*see* Guided Tours, *above*) gives narrated tours of the city.

Salem unabashedly calls itself "Witch City." Decorations featuring witches astride broomsticks enhance the police cars; witchcraft shops, memorials, and at least one resident witch commemorate the city's infamous witchcraft trials of 1692, when religious zeal ran out of control and resulted in the hangings of 19 alleged witches. Visitors can see the story retold by waxworks at the **Salem Wax Museum** (288 Derby St., tel. 508/740–2929), by actors at the **Witch Dungeon Museum** (16 Lynde St., tel. 508/741–3570), or by multisensory presentation at the **Salem Witch Museum,** which stages a reenactment of the events using 13 different sets and life-size models. If you have

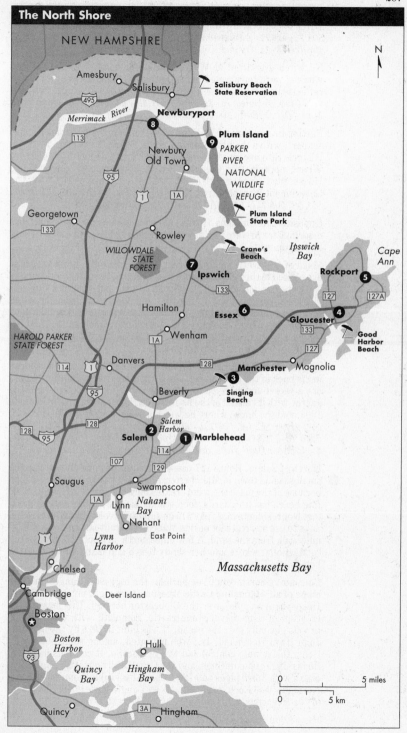

time for—or can stomach—only one such performance, the Salem Witch Museum is probably your best bet. *Washington Square N, tel. 508/744–1692. Admission: $4 adults, $3.50 senior citizens, $2.50 children 6–14. Open daily 10–5 (until 7 July–Aug.).*

No witch ever lived at **Witch House,** but more than 200 accused witches were questioned here. Authentic late-17th-century decor reflects the era when the trials were held. *310½ Essex St., tel. 508/744–0180. Admission: $4 adults, $1.50 children 5–16. Open mid-Mar.–Dec. 1, daily 10–4:30 (until 6 July–Aug.).*

Putting its macabre past behind it, Salem went on to become a major seaport, with a thriving overseas trade. **Salem Maritime,** a National Historic Site operated by the National Trust, is just beside Derby Wharf, opposite the Customs House. Tours take in the Customs House, made famous in Nathaniel Hawthorne's *Scarlet Letter;* the Government Warehouse; and historic shipowners' homes. *174 Derby St., tel. 508/744–4323. Admission free. Open daily 8:30–5.*

Opposite the Customs House, the restored **Pickering Wharf** has moorings for private boats, waterside gift stores, and a slew of bars and restaurants.

Much of the exotic spoils brought back by Salem's merchant ships are housed in the **Peabody and Essex Museum,** the oldest continuously operating museum in America. It also has exhibits on New England's whaling and fishing past and documents from the witch trials. For an additional fee, you can tour several historic mansions that belonged to shipowners and other wealthy merchants. *East India Sq., tel. 508/745–1876. Admission: $6 adults, $5 senior citizens, $3.50 children 6–16. Open Mon.–Sat. 10–5, Sun. noon–5.*

The **House of Seven Gables,** immortalized by Nathaniel Hawthorne in his book of the same name, should not be missed. Tour highlights are a secret staircase discovered during 1886 renovations and the garret with its model of the house. Hawthorne was born in Salem in 1804, and the house where he was born has been moved to this site. *54 Turner St., tel. 508/744–0991. Admission: $6.50 adults, $4 children 13–17, $3 children 6–12. Open July–Labor Day, daily 9:30–5:30; Labor Day–June, daily 10–4:30. Closed first week in Jan.*

North of Salem, Route 127 passes through Beverly en route to the small seaside town of **Manchester,** home of Singing Beach, so called because of the noise the wind creates blowing against the sand. This fine beach has lifeguards, food stands, and restrooms but no parking: Nonresidents must pay $15 on summer weekends or $8 on weekdays to use a private lot beside Manchester railroad station—a half-mile walk from the sand. A few miles north on Route 127 brings you to **Magnolia,** where another sandy beach and many smart summer homes await you.

Continuing north, you'll see perhaps the biggest, strangest seaside home of all: **Hammond Castle Museum** (turn right off Rte. 127 onto Hesperus Ave., just over the Gloucester border). This massive re-creation of a medieval stone castle, complete with drawbridge, broods gloomily over the ocean. It was built in 1926 by the inventor John Hays Hammond, Jr., who patented, among some 800 inventions, the remote control and the gyroscope. It contains medieval furnishings and paintings, and the Great Hall houses an impressive organ with 8,600 pipes and 126 stops. Also visible from the castle is **Norman's Woe Rock,** made famous by Longfellow's poem *The Wreck of the Hesperus. 80 Hesperus Ave., Gloucester, tel. 508/283–2080.*

Admission $5.50 adults, $4.50 senior citizens, $3.50 children 6–12. Open May–Oct., Wed.–Sun 10–5; Nov.–Apr., weekends 10–5.

❹ Route 127 continues along the coast, entering **Gloucester** along a fine seaside promenade. The first sight you'll see is the famous stat- ue of a man at a ship's wheel, eyes on the horizon, dedicated to those "who go down to the sea in ships." The statue was commissioned by Gloucester's citizens in 1923 in celebration of the seaport's 300th an- niversary. The oldest seaport in the nation, it is today a workaday town, a major fishing port, and home to **Rocky Neck,** the oldest working artists' colony in America.

Gloucester also has some of the best beaches on the north shore. **Wingaersheek Beach** (Exit 13 off Rte. 128) is a picture-perfect, well- protected cove of white sand and dunes, with the white Annisquam lighthouse in the bay. Parking here costs $10, and the lot fills on summer weekends by 10 AM. The same rules apply at **Good Harbor Beach** (signposted from Rte. 127A), a huge, sandy, dune-backed beach with a rocky islet just offshore. Just north of Good Harbor, **Long Beach,** off Route 127A on the Gloucester/Rockport town line, is another excellent place for sunbathing; parking here costs $5.

❺ **Rockport,** at the very tip of Cape Ann, derives its name from its granite formations, and many a Boston-area structure is made of stone from the town's long-gone quarries. Today, Rockport is a mec- ca for summer tourists attracted by its hilly rows of colorful clap- board houses, historic inns, artists' studios, and its beach (albeit rather small). In summer, parking in town is impossible; leave your car at the Tourist Information Center lot on Route 127, and take the **Cape Ann Trolley,** which leaves roughly once an hour daily in July and August, making 17 stops in and around town. While known pri- marily as a tourist haunt, Rockport has not gone overboard on T- shirt emporia and the other accoutrements of a summer economy: Shops sell crafts, clothing, and cameras, not trashy souvenirs, and restaurants serve quiche, seafood, or home-baked cookies rather than fast food. From downtown, walk out to the end of Bearskin Neck for an impressive view of the open Atlantic and the nearby lob- ster shack affectionately known as "Motif No. 1" because of its popu- larity as a subject for artists.

Time Out **Dock Square Coffee and Tea House** (25 Dock Square, tel. 508/546– 2525; closed Jan.) near Bearskin Neck serves up soups, breads, sal- ads, pastries, and cookies in a small, bright dining room with pol- ished floors, marble-top tables, and shelves packed with local pottery. The café also sells a variety of ground coffees.

---

❻ Head west out of Cape Ann on Route 128 and turn north on Route 133 for the village of **Essex.** Surrounded by salt marshes, the town has plenty of antiques stores and more than 15 seafood restaurants. The **Essex Shipbuilding Museum** displays exhibits from the 19th cen- tury, when the town was an important shipbuilding center; more twin-mast ships were built here than in any other locale. *Rte. 133, Essex, tel. 508/768–7541. Admission: $2 adults, $1.50 senior citi- zens. Open mid-May–mid-Oct., Thurs.–Sun. 11–4.*

Time Out **Woodman's of Essex** (Rte. 133, tel. 508/768–6451) claims to have fried the first clams in town back in 1916. Today, this large wood shack with unpretentious booths is *the* place for "seafood in the rough," and the menu includes lobster, a raw bar, clam chowder, and, of course, fried clams.

---

❼ Four miles north of Essex, **Ipswich,** settled in 1633 and famous for its clams, is said to have more 17th-century houses standing and occupied than any other place in America. More than 40 homes in town were built before 1725. A *Walking Tour Guide of Historic Ipswich* is available at the **Chamber of Commerce information kiosk** (Crane Beach Rd.; open June–Labor Day, daily 10–4).

Continuing north from Ipswich on Route 1A for 12 miles will take **❽** you past the salt marshes of **Rowley** and **Newbury** to **Newburyport.** Here Route 1A becomes High Street, which is lined with some of the finest examples of Federal (ca. 1790–1810) mansions in New England. You'll notice widow's walks, which afford a view of the port and the sea beyond, perched atop many houses. Like those in Salem, the homes were built for prosperous sea captains in this city that was once a leading port and shipbuilding center.

While Newburyport's maritime significance ended with the demise of the clipper ships (some of the best of which were built here), an energetic downtown renewal program has breathed new life into the town's redbrick center. Renovated buildings now house restaurants, taverns, and shops selling everything from nautical brasses to antique Oriental rugs. The civic improvements have been matched by private restorations of the town's housing stock, much of which dates from the 18th century, with a scattering of 17th-century homes in some neighborhoods. Massachusetts's smallest city is best seen on foot, and there's all-day free parking down by the water. A stroll through the **Waterfront Park and Promenade** gives a super view of the harbor and the fishing and pleasure boats that moor here. Walking to the left as you leave the parking lot will take you to the Classic Revival **Custom House Maritime Museum** (ca. 1835), which contains exhibits on maritime history, models, tools, and paintings. The audiovisual show is presented hourly. *25 Water St., tel. 508/462–8681. Admission: $3 adults, $2 senior citizens, $1.50 children 5–15. Open Apr.–Dec., Mon.–Sat. 10–4, Sun. 1–4.*

❾ A causeway leads from Newburyport to **Plum Island,** a narrow spit of land with a long, steeply descending public beach at one end and the **Parker River National Wildlife Refuge** at the other. The refuge has 4,662 acres of salt marsh, freshwater marsh, beaches, and dunes; it is one of the few natural barrier beach dune–salt marsh complexes left on the Northeast coast. The bird-watching, surf fishing, plum and cranberry picking, and swimming are wonderful. The refuge is quite popular in summer, and on weekends, cars begin lining up outside for the limited parking spaces before 7 AM. *Tel. 508/465–5753. Admission: $5 per car, $1 for walkers and bicyclists. Open ½ hr before sunrise–½ hr after sunset.*

What to See and Do with Children

The House of Seven Gables, Salem
Pioneer Village and Forest River Park, Salem, re-create the Salem of the 1630s, when it was the state capital. Costumed interpreters wander among replicas of thatched cottages, dugout homes, and wigwams. *Jct. Rtes. 1A and 129, tel. 508/745–0525. Admission: $4 adults, $3.50 senior citizens and children 13–17, $2.50 children 6–12. Open mid-May–Oct., daily 10–5.*
Salem Willows Park (at the eastern end of Derby St.), Salem, has picnic grounds, beaches, food stands, amusements, games, boat rentals, and fishing bait.
Salem Witch Museum, Salem
Salisbury Beach, Salisbury, has a number of honky-tonk family

amusement parks, water slides, food stalls, and various amusement arcades.

Tot Stop, at Museum Place Mall in Salem, is a haven for children up to 6 years old—and their weary parents. This huge indoor playground has slides, climbing frames, tunnels, pedal cars, a sandbox, and child-size rooms furnished as kitchens, bedrooms, and more. There are playhouses, rocking horses, and toys galore; a quiet room has board games, crayons, puzzles, and some electronic games. Parents can't leave children here, but there's a sitting area where grown-ups can work or read in relative peace. *Museum Place Mall, Church and Essex Sts., tel. 508/741–5704. Admission: $6 per child 8 months–6 years (parents free); maximum $14 per family. Open daily 9:30–5:30 (Thurs. until 8).*

Off the Beaten Track

Although Salem is world-famous as the witch hunt city, **Danvers** (Old Salem) is virtually unknown. Yet here are the real relics of the witchcraft episode. The house where the black slave Tituba told stories to two impressionable girls and began the whole business has been demolished, but the foundations were excavated in 1970 and can be viewed—they're located behind 67 Center Street.

The **Rebecca Nurse Homestead** was the home of aged, pious Rebecca, a regular churchgoer whose accusation caused shock waves, whose trial was a mockery (she was pronounced innocent, but the jury was urged to change its verdict), and who was hanged as a witch in 1692. Her family took her body afterward and buried her in secret on the grounds of this house. It has period furnishings and is gradually being developed as a model 18th-century farm. *149 Pine St., tel. 508/774–8799. Admission: $3.50 adults, $1.50 children under 12. Open June 15–Labor Day, Tues.–Sun. 1–4:30; Labor Day–May, weekends 1–4:30; or by appointment.*

Shopping

Antiques The greatest concentration of antiques stores on the North Shore is around **Essex,** but there are plenty sprinkled throughout **Salem** and **Cape Ann** as well. Members of the North Shore Antique Dealers Association guarantee the authenticity of their merchandise, and a leaflet listing their shops can be obtained from participating stores. Try the **Pickering Wharf Antique Gallery** in Salem, where five shops house 50 dealers.

Art An artist's colony, **Rockport** has a tremendous concentration of artists' studios and galleries selling work by local painters. *The Rockport Fine Arts Gallery Guide,* available from the Rockport Chamber of Commerce (*see* Visitor Information, *above*) lists around 30 reputable galleries in town. The Rocky Neck Arts Colony east of **Gloucester** is another good place to browse and buy.

Books **Toad Hall Bookstore** (51 Main St., Rockport, tel 508/546–7323) has a range of reading material for children and adults; **Pyramid Books** (214 Derby St., Salem, tel. 508/745–7171) stocks New Age and metaphysical books.

Clothing Several small-town clothing stores, stocking everything from kids' mittens to women's lingerie to men's sneakers can be found in Rockport; try the **Madras Shop** (37 Main St., tel. 508/546–3434) or the **John Tarr Store** (53 Main St., tel. 508/546–6524). For children's clothing the **Small Fry Shop** (18 Bearskin Neck, Rockport, tel. 508/

546–9354) has a great choice of dressy outfits, caps and hats, sweaters, and dresses at reasonable prices.

Specialty Items **Salem** is the center for a number of offbeat shops that have a distinct relationship to the city's witchcraft history. The best known such store is **Crow Haven Corner** (125 Essex St., tel. 508/745–8763), where Laurie Cabot, Salem's "official" witch, presides over a fabulous selection of crystal balls, herbs, tarot decks, healing stones, and books about witchcraft. **Gornigo** on Pickering Wharf (tel. 508/745–0552), complete with a black shop cat, sells a marvelous array of scented herbs, herbal teas, potion perfumes, runes, spirit lamps, and crystals. Crystals are a specialty at **The Crystal Chamber** (197 Derby St., tel. 508/745–9400).

Sports and Outdoor Activities

Boating Marblehead is the pleasure-sailing capital of the North Shore, but here and elsewhere it's not easy to find mooring space for your private yacht; many towns have waiting lists of several years. Town harbormasters will be able to inform you of nightly fees at public docks, when space is available.

Canoeing is less complicated; the best areas are on the Ipswich and Parker rivers. For saltwater canoeing and kayaking, the waters of the Essex River Estuary are generally calm and protected. The **Harold Parker State Forest** in North Andover and the **Willowdale State Forest** in Ipswich also permit canoeing.

Fishing Deep-sea fishing excursions are offered at various North Shore ports. In Gloucester try **Captain Bill's Deep Sea Fishing** (9 Traverse St., tel. 508/283–6995) for full- and half-day trips, and in Newburyport try **Newburyport Whale Watch** (54 Merrimac St., tel. 508/465–9885).

Surf casting is even more popular—bluefish, pollock, and striped bass can be taken from the ocean shores of Plum Island; permits to remain on the beach after dark are obtainable free of charge by anyone entering the refuge with fishing equipment in the daylight. You don't need a permit to fish from the public beach at Plum Island, and the best spot to choose is around the mouth of the Merrimac River. For freshwater fishing, the Parker and Ipswich rivers are both stocked with trout each spring, and many state parks permit fishing.

Hiking The best places to hike on the North Shore are in nature reserves with salt marshes. The Massachusetts Audubon's **Ipswich River Wildlife Sanctuary** (tel. 508/887–9264) offers a variety of trails through marshland hills, where there are remains of early Colonial settlements, as well as abundant wildlife. Get a self-guiding trail map from the office (closed Mon.). The Rockery Trail takes walkers to the perennial rock garden and Japanese garden; the Agawam Nature Trail focuses on local habitat. At the **Parker River National Wildlife Refuge** (Plum Island, tel. 508/465–5753), deer and rabbits share space with 25,000 ducks and more than 6,000 geese. The 2-mile Hellcat Swamp trail cuts through the marshes and sand dunes, taking in the best of the sanctuary. Trail maps are available at the office.

Spectator Sports

The one spectator sport of note on the North Shore is polo. The **Myopia Hunt Club** (South Hamilton, tel. 508/468–4433) stages polo matches on Sunday at 3 PM between late May and October at its grounds along Route 1A in Hamilton.

Beaches

Here are some of the best beaches on the North Shore: **Crane's Beach** (Ipswich), **Parker River Refuge** (Newbury), **Plum Island** (Newburyport), **Salisbury State Reservation** (Salisbury), **Singing Beach** (Manchester), and **Wingaersheek Beach, Long Beach,** and **Good Harbor Beach** (Gloucester).

National and State Parks

Of the numerous parks in the area, the following have particularly varied facilities: **Halibut Point State Park** (Rte. 127 to Gott Ave., Rockport, tel. 508/546–2997), **Parker River National Wildlife Refuge** (Plum Island, off Rte. 1A, Newburyport, tel. 508/465–5753), **Plum Island State Reservation** (off Rte. 1A, Newburyport, tel. 508/462–4481), **Salisbury Beach State Reservation** (Rte. 1A, Salisbury, tel. 508/462–4481), and the **Willowdale State Forest** (Linebrook Rd., Ipswich, tel. 508/887–5931).

Dining and Lodging

Dress is casual and reservations unnecessary unless otherwise noted.

Essex
Dining

Jerry Pelonzi's Hearthside. This 250-year-old converted farmhouse epitomizes coziness. Four small dining rooms have open fireplaces and exposed beams: The first is low-ceilinged with stencils on the walls; the others have cathedral ceilings with rough-panel walls and small windows. The newest eating area is in the loft. Entrées include baked stuffed haddock, seafood casserole, sirloin steak, lobster, and chicken. *Rte. 133, tel. 508/768–6002 or 508/768–6003. AE, MC, V. Moderate.*

Tom Shea's. Picture windows in this recently expanded, two-story, cedar-shingled restaurant overlook the salt marsh. Inside, walls are white, the rooms have mismatched wooden furniture, with many hanging plants. Seafood is the main fare, including shrimp in coconut beer batter, scallop-stuffed sole, Boston scrod, lobster, and, of course, the fried clams for which Essex is famous. *122 Main St., Rte. 133, tel. 508/768–6931. AE, D, MC, V. Moderate.*

Gloucester
Dining
★

White Rainbow. The dining room in this excellent restaurant is in the basement of a west-end store downtown, and candlelight sets a romantic mood. Specialties include Maui onion soup, grilled beef with a Zinfandel wine sauce, lobster *estancia* (lobster sautéed with tomatoes, artichoke hearts, olives, scallions, wine, and herb butter), and fresh fish of the day. *65 Main St., tel. 508/281–0017. AE, D, DC, MC, V. No lunch. Closed Mon. Expensive.*

★ **The Rhumb Line.** Despite its unimpressive location, this restaurant is worth the three-minute drive from the town center. The decor of the upstairs dining room gives one the impression of sitting on a ship's deck, with the wheel and compass at one end, rigging overhead, captain's chairs at the tables, and seascapes on the walls. Try seafood casserole of shrimp, crabmeat, and scallops in garlic-lemon butter and white wine; roast duckling glazed with Grand Marnier, honey, and marmalade sauce; and charbroiled steaks. The bar downstairs serves burgers, Mexican dishes, seafood, and steaks. *Railroad Ave., tel. 508/283–9732. AE, MC, V. Upstairs dining room closed mid-Feb.–Mar. Moderate–Expensive.*

★ **Evie's Rudder.** Quaint and quirky, as befits its ramshackle exterior and artists' colony location, Evie's has been dishing up good food and entertainment for almost four decades under the same ownership. The building dates from the 1890s, when it was used for fish packing, and has low ceilings, heavy beams, uneven floors, and shingle walls. You can also sit on a wharfside deck to feast on seafood, chicken, steak, and, as the menu puts it, "clam chowder New England–style—whoever heard of adding tomatoes? Manhattan-style? Do you see any skyscrapers out there????" Entertainment includes an invisible flaming baton twirling act by the owner's daughter and a retelling of *Pinderella and the Cince* by Evie herself. Don't miss it! *Rocky Neck, tel. 508/283–7958. D, MC, V. Closed Nov.–Mar., and Mon.–Wed., Apr. and Oct. Moderate.*

Lodging **Twin Light Manor.** This English Tudor mansion was built in 1905 as a private home, complete with an elevator, children's playhouse, and a seven-car garage equipped with a turntable! The most interesting guest rooms are those in the manor itself; some are enormous and have nonworking fireplaces, while newer buildings nearby offer different styles of accommodations, and the complex is set on 7 acres overlooking the ocean. Guests have golf privileges on a local course, and the hotel is affiliated with a Gloucester health club. *175 Atlantic Rd., 01930, tel. 508/283–7500. 63 rooms. Facilities: dining room, golf, health club, 2 outdoor pools, games room, bicycles, badminton, volleyball, croquet, shuffleboard, gardens. AE, D, DC, MC, V. Very Expensive.*

Back Shore Motor Lodge. This lodge in East Gloucester overlooks the ocean from a rocky headland. All guest rooms have sea views, and some have sliding doors onto decks at the front of the building. Furnishings are good-quality motor-lodge style, with some reproductions, and the color scheme is sea green. *85 Atlantic Rd., 01930, tel. 508/283–1198. 23 rooms. Facilities: dining room, outdoor pool. No credit cards. Expensive.*

Cape Ann Motor Inn. This wood-shingle, three-story motel is as close to the sands as they come, right on Long Beach on the Gloucester/Rockport border. Rooms are small, with queen-size beds and well-worn leather couches, but all have balconies and superb views over beach, sea, and the twin lights of Thatcher's Island. The suite contains modern furnishings, a whirlpool tub, and music center. The management is quite friendly. Some rooms have kitchenettes. *33 Rockport Rd., 01930, tel. 508/281–2900. 29 rooms, 1 suite. AE, D, MC, V. Moderate–Expensive.*

Magnolia **Tara.** On the town's fancy Shore Road, just north of the beach, Tara *Lodging* is the one of the most magnificent Queen Anne mansions in sight. Inside, bedrooms have good views and eclectic furnishings—a canopy bed here, a pink, pineapple four poster there; most could use a new coat of paint, but the faded glory upstairs is more than balanced by the elegant, and characterful, clutter below. There are books and seascapes everywhere, a painted grandfather clock, and no fewer than five silver coffee services in the dining room. It's a charming place to stay—and the price is right. Hosts Gladys and Hal Rundlett have lived here 37 years. *13–19 Shore Rd., 01930, tel. 508/525–3213. 6 rooms share 4 baths. Facilities: parlor, porch, dining room. Full breakfast included. No credit cards. Inexpensive–Moderate.*

Manchester **Old Corner Inn.** Built in 1865, and once used as the Danish Embassy, *Lodging* the Old Corner Inn is done in stylish trappings: Bedrooms with bird's eye maple floors have four-poster beds; some have working fireplaces, brass gaslight fixtures, feather mattresses, and claw foot tubs. A simple Continental breakfast is served in the lobby, where there's also a sitting area around the fireplace. The low rates reflect the fact that, although the country location is attractive, it's a mile's walk to the village center and a mile from the nearest beach. *2 Harbor St., 01944, tel. 508/526-4996. 6 rooms with private bath, 3 rooms share baths. Continental breakfast included. AE, MC, V. Inexpensive-Moderate.*

Marblehead
Dining

The Landing. Right on Marblehead harbor and still in the historic district, this pleasant, small restaurant offers outdoor dining on a balcony over the sea. Inside are wood chairs and tables, with lots of hanging plants. The chef prepares lobster, scallops primavera, seafood scampi, Atlantic sole florentine, Ipswich clams, and seafood kabob. A limited choice of steak and chicken dishes are also served. *Clark's Landing off Front St., tel. 617/631-6268. AE, D, DC, MC, V. Expensive.*

Lodging
★

Harbor Light Inn. This is the best place to stay in Marblehead and competes with the Clark Currier Inn in Newburyport as one of the most comfortable and authentic inns on the North Shore. Special features include five in-room Jacuzzis, skylights, rooftop decks, and spacious, modern bathrooms; traditional touches are found in the four-poster and canopy beds, carved arched doorways, sliding (original) Indian shutters, wide-board floors, and antique mahogany furnishings. In 1993, the innkeepers bought the building next door, adding eight big, beautiful bedrooms (with working fireplaces, four-poster beds, and painted-wood paneling) to the inn's roster. *58 Washington St., 01945, tel. 617/631-2186. 19 rooms, 1 suite. Facilities: outdoor pool, 2 parlors, breakfast room, conference room, courtyard garden. Continental breakfast included. AE, MC, V. Expensive-Very Expensive.*

Harborside House. Located in Marblehead's historic district, Harborside House was built in 1850 by a ship's carpenter. Susan Livingston has lived here for 28 years and has operated the house as a successful bed-and-breakfast since 1985. The downstairs living room has a working brick fireplace; bedrooms have polished wide-board floors with Oriental rugs, and two rooms overlook Marblehead harbor with its hundreds of sailboats. Susan, who works as a dressmaker, is a considerate and interesting host, and her home is convenient to all of Marblehead's attractions. *23 Gregory St., 01945, tel. 617/631-1032. 3 rooms. Facilities: parlor, breakfast room, parking. Continental breakfast included. No credit cards. Moderate-Expensive.*

Pleasant Manor Inn. Off the main road between Salem and Marblehead, this rambling Victorian mansion has large guest rooms (some with pineapple four-poster beds), and a carved mahogany staircase. The wallpaper is on the shabby side, but rooms are clean, the atmosphere relaxed and welcoming, and manager Lorraine French offers very reasonable rates. Amelia Earhart stayed in Room 32 in 1923, when the building first became an inn. *Rte. 114, 264 Pleasant St., 01945, tel. 617/631-5843. Facilities: VCRs, parlor, tennis, parking. Continental breakfast included. No credit cards. Moderate.*

Newburyport
Dining
★

Scandia. This restaurant is well known locally for its fine cuisine, and house specialties are veal and lobster sauté, and seafood linguine. The dining room is small and narrow and dimly lighted with candles on the tables and "candle" chandeliers. *25 State St., tel. 508/462-6271. Reservations advised. AE, D, DC, MC, V. Expensive.*

Dining and Lodging

Garrison Inn. This four-story Georgian redbrick building is set back from the main road on a small square. Guest rooms vary in size; all have handsome replicas. The best rooms are the top-floor suites, set on two levels: Spiral or colonial staircases lead up from the sitting room to the sleeping area above. The two restaurants, David's and Downstairs at David's, are top of the line for both food and service. If you dine upstairs, in a room furnished with chandeliers and white linen, damask chairs and drapes, such entrées as sautéed lobster with sea scallops and mushrooms in anise cream, and chicken breast medallions with roasted garlic can be yours. Downstairs at David's is less formal, with exposed brick arches, a bar, and a lighter menu of steak, burgers, and fish dishes. An advantage of these restaurants is their childcare facility, where, for a nominal fee, kids can play and eat while parents enjoy their own meal in peace. *11 Brown Sq., 01950, tel. 508/465–0910. 18 rooms, 6 suites. Facilities: 2 restaurants (tel. 508/462–8077; reservations advised), lounge, tavern. AE, DC, MC, V. Inn: Expensive. Restaurants: Moderate–Expensive.*

Lodging
★ **Clark Currier Inn.** This 1803 Federal mansion has been restored with care, taste, imagination, and enthusiasm, emerging as one of the best inns on the North Shore. Guest rooms are spacious and furnished with antiques: Some have pencil-post beds, one has a reproduction sea captain's bed complete with drawers below, and another contains a glorious sleigh bed dating from the late 19th century. There's a Federalist "good morning" staircase (so called because two small staircases join at the head of a large one, permitting family members to greet each other on their way down to breakfast). *45 Green St., 01950, tel. 508/465–8363. 8 rooms with bath. Facilities: TV lounge. Continental breakfast and afternoon tea included. AE, D, MC, V. Moderate–Expensive.*

Rockport
Dining
★ **Peg Leg Inn.** Lobster thermidor, lobster à la Newburg, lobster pie, lobster salad, and lobsters boiled, baked, or broiled—take your pick and enjoy this excellent restaurant. The flagstone floor and open kitchen create a comforting, "grandma's house" atmosphere, which is complemented by the traditional dress and friendliness of the staff. Also available: pasta, chicken pie, steak, and a host of other seafood dishes. *18 Beach St., tel. 508/546–3038. AE, DC, MC, V. BYOB. Closed Nov.–Apr. Expensive.*

★ **Brackett's Oceanview Restaurant.** A big bay window in this homey restaurant allows an excellent view across the beach. The menu includes scallop casserole, fishcakes, and other seafood dishes. *Main St., tel. 508/546–2797. AE, D, DC, MC, V. BYOB. Closed Mon. and mid-Nov.–Mar. Moderate.*

My Place by the Sea. By the sea it is—this tiny restaurant is perched at the very end of Bearskin Neck. Inside, the small dining area has white wicker chairs and rustic beams; outside, the lower deck has tables overlooking the ocean. The restaurant serves mainly seafood, including baked scrod, swordfish steak, seafood fettuccine, and sandwiches. *Bearskin Neck, tel. 508/546–9667. AE, DC, MC, V. BYOB. Closed mid-Dec.–May. Moderate.*

Portside Chowder House. This great little hole-in-the-wall restaurant is one of the few in Rockport that's open year-round. The tiny dining room with wood beams and low ceilings has partial sea views. Chowder is the house specialty; also offered are lobster and crab plates, salads, burgers, and sandwiches. *Bearskin Neck, no tel. No credit cards. No dinner Oct.–Apr. Inexpensive.*

Lodging
★ **Yankee Clipper Inn.** The imposing Georgian mansion that forms the main part of this impressive, perfectly set compound sits surrounded by gardens on a rocky point jutting into the sea. Built as a private home in the 1930s, it's been managed as an inn by one family for almost 50 years. Most rooms are spacious and have ocean views;

American Express offers Travelers Cheques built for two.

Cheques *for Two*^{SM} from American Express are the Travelers Cheques that allow either of you to use them because both of you have signed them. And only one of you needs to be present to purchase them.

Cheques *for Two* are accepted anywhere regular American Express Travelers Cheques are, which is just about everywhere. So stop by your bank, AAA* or any American Express Travel Service Office and ask for Cheques *for Two*.

Pack light.

Take the one number you need for any kind of call, anywhere you travel.

Checking in with your family back home? Calling for a tow truck? When you're on the road, the phone you use might not accept your calling card. Or you might get overcharged by an unknown telephone company. Here's the solution: dial 1 800 CALL ATT.[sm] You'll get flawless AT&T service, competitive calling card prices, and the lowest prices for collect calls from any phone, anywhere. Travel light. Just bring along this one simple number: 1 800 CALL ATT.

all are furnished with antiques and four-poster or canopy beds. In the newer Quarterdeck building, the spacious contemporary rooms have fabulous sea views through big picture windows. The nearby 1840 Greek Revival Bullfinch house is appointed with tasteful antiques but has less of a view. *96 Granite St., 01966, tel. 508/546–3407. 26 rooms, 6 suites. Facilities: restaurant, lounge, outdoor pool, gardens. Full breakfast included. AE, D, MC, V. Very Expensive.*

Seacrest Manor. The distinctive inn, surrounded by large gardens, sits atop a hill overlooking the sea. Two elegant sitting rooms are furnished with antiques and leather chairs; one has a huge wall mirror from the old Philadelphia Opera House. The hall and staircase are hung with paintings—some of which depict the inn—by local artists. Guest rooms vary in size and character and have a combination of traditional and antique furnishings—upstairs, two have large private decks with sea views. *131 Marmion Way, 01966, tel. 508/546–2211. 8 rooms, 2 with shared bath. Facilities: dining room, 2 lounges, gardens. Full breakfast included. No credit cards. Closed Dec. 1–Apr. 1. Expensive.*

★ **Addison Choate Inn.** This lovely, white clapboard inn sits inconspicuously among private homes, just a minute's walk from the center of town. The spacious rooms, with large bathrooms, are beautifully decorated; the navy and white captain's room has a dark-wood four-poster bed with a net canopy, handmade quilts, and Oriental rugs. Other rooms—all with polished pine floors—have Hitchcock rockers and headboards, spool or filigree brass beds, local seascape paintings, and antiques. The two luxuriously appointed duplex carriage-house apartments have skylights, cathedral ceilings, and exposed wood beams. *49 Broadway, 01966, tel. 508/546–7543. 7 rooms, 2 apartments, with bath. Facilities: parlor, outdoor pool. Continental breakfast included. D, MC, V. Moderate–Expensive.*

Bearskin Neck Motor Lodge. Set almost at the end of Bearskin Neck, the guest-room balconies here overhang the water. From the windows all you see is sea, and at night you can hear it lapping—or thundering—against the rocks below. Rooms are simply appointed with white and wood furniture and paneled walls. The exterior is gray cedar shingle, and guests can lie out on a large deck overlooking the sea. *Bearskin Neck, 01966, tel. 508/546–6677. 8 rooms with bath. No credit cards. Closed mid-Dec.–Mar. 30. Moderate–Expensive.*

★ **Inn on Cove Hill.** This Federal building on a picturesque hillside dates back to 1792, when it was reportedly constructed with money from a cache of pirates' gold. Some guest rooms are small, but all are cheerful, pretty, and carefully appointed with bright, flowery print paper, patchwork quilts, and old-fashioned beds—some are brass, others are canopy four-posters. Rooms have polished wide-board floors, iron latches, wood bathroom fixtures, and pastel-tone Oriental rugs. *37 Mt. Pleasant St., 01966, tel. 508/546–2701. 9 rooms with bath, 2 share a bath. Continental breakfast included. No credit cards. Closed mid-Oct.–mid-Mar. Moderate.*

★ **Sally Webster Inn.** Sally Webster was a member of Hannah Jumper's so-called hatchet gang, which smashed up the town's liquor stores in 1856 and turned Rockport into the dry town it remains today. Sally lived in this house for much of her life, and the guest rooms are named for members of her family. They contain rocking chairs; nonworking brick fireplaces; pineapple four-poster, brass, canopy, or spool beds; and pine wide-board floors with Oriental rugs. Bonnets and wickerwork hang on the walls; all rooms have candle-lanterns that can be lit in the evening. *34 Mt. Pleasant St., 01966, tel. 508/ 546–9251. 6 rooms. Facilities: dining room, lounge. MC, V. Full breakfast included. Closed Jan. Moderate.*

Salem　**Chase House.** This restaurant on Pickering Wharf overlooks the har-
Dining　bor and is extremely busy in summer. The main dining room has low
ceilings and exposed-brick walls. The menu has steak, squid, floun-
der, and "old-fashioned seafood dinners" of clams, scallops, shrimp,
fish, and lobster with onion rings. *Pickering Wharf, tel. 508/744–
0000. AE, D, DC, MC, V. Moderate.*

Lyceum. The Lyceum's great claim to fame is that Alexander Graham Bell made his first public phone call from this building in 1877.
The decor connotes the '40s, with paneled ceilings, a wood bar, fans,
and old photographs. Entrées include chicken cutlets with lemon-
cucumber sauce, swordfish steak, and black angus sirloin. *43
Church St., tel. 508/745–7665. Reservations advised. AE, D, MC,
V. Moderate.*

Maharani Fine Indian Cuisine. The decor is, of course, Indian, and
the spicy menu includes a large variety of lamb, chicken, beef,
shrimp, and vegetarian dishes. *6 Hawthorne Blvd. (Rte. 1A), tel.
508/744–6570. MC, V. Inexpensive.*

Dining and　**Hawthorne's Hotel.** The imposing redbrick structure is the only full-
Lodging　service hotel in Salem—conveniently situated on the green just a
short walk from the commercial center and most attractions. Guest
rooms in brown and beige are appointed with reproduction antiques,
armchairs, and desks—business clients are numerous. The formal
restaurant, Nathaniel's, is hung with chandeliers and serves lobster, swordfish in mustard cream, prime rib, and poached sole on
spinach with champagne cream sauce. *On-the-Common, 01970, tel.
508/744–4080. 83 rooms, 6 suites. Facilities: restaurant, lounge,
tavern, exercise room, meeting rooms, ballroom. AE, D, DC, MC,
V. Expensive.*

Lodging　**The Inn at Seven Winter St.** Built in 1870, this conveniently located
inn has been accurately restored to re-create the Victorian era.
Rooms, although a little dark, are spacious and well furnished, with
heavy mahogany and walnut antiques, working marble fireplaces,
and Oriental rugs on polished hardwood floors. Two large, three-
room suites are perfect for families, with fully equipped eat-in kitchens and a sitting room. *7 Winter St., 01970, tel. 508/745–9520. 7
rooms with bath, 2 suites, 1 studio. Facilities: parlor, deck. Continental breakfast included. MC, V. Expensive.*

Amelia Payson Guest House. This Greek Revival house built in 1845
has been tastefully converted into a bright, airy bed-and-breakfast
inn near the common and all of Salem's historic attractions. Pretty
rooms are decorated with floral-print wallpaper, brass and canopy
beds, nonworking marble fireplaces, and white wicker furnishings.
The downstairs parlor has a grand piano, and a reading room upstairs is filled with tourist information. *16 Winter St., 01970, tel.
508/744–8304. 3 rooms with bath, 1 studio. Facilities: 2 parlors.
Continental breakfast included. AE, MC, V. Moderate–Expensive.*

The Arts

Music　**Castle Hill** (Argilla Rd., Ipswich, tel. 508/356–7774) holds an annual
festival, July 4 through mid-August, of pop, folk, and classical music, plus a jazz ball. The magnificent organ at the **Hammond Castle
Museum** (80 Hesperus Ave., Gloucester, tel. 508/283–2080) is used
for organ concerts year-round, and in summer pops concerts are
added to the schedule.

Theater　The **North Shore Music Theatre** (62 Dunham Rd., Beverly, tel. 508/
922–8500) is a professional company that, from May through December, performs popular and modern musicals as well as children's the-

ater. On Cape Ann the **Gloucester Stage Company** (267 E. Main St., Gloucester, tel. 508/281–4099) is a nonprofit professional group staging new plays and revivals May–September. If you like your meal spiced with intrigue, the **Mystery Cafe** (225 Newbury St., Danvers, tel. 617/524–2233 or tel. 800/697–2583; Sat. only), a six-year-old Boston dinner show, recently began playing at the Village Green restaurant in Danvers. Costumed actors double as waiters, playing out a mystery that evolves around your table.

Nightlife

A selection of popular local spots includes: **The Grog** (13 Middle St., Newburyport, tel. 508/465–8008), which hosts live entertainment downstairs Thursday–Sunday nights and features a wide variety of blues and rock bands; downstairs at **Roosevelt's** restaurant (300 Derby St., Salem, tel. 508/745–9608), where local rock bands play Wednesday–Saturday nights; and the **Blue Star Lounge** (Rtes. 1/99, Saugus, tel. 617/233–8027), a rockabilly roadhouse on a busy strip, playing country music Wednesday–Sunday evenings.

The Pioneer Valley

The Pioneer Valley, a string of historic settlements along the Connecticut River from Springfield in the south up to the Vermont border, formed the western frontier of New England from the early 1600s until the late 18th century. The fertile banks of the river (called Quinnitukut, or "long tidal river," by Native Americans) first attracted farmers and traders; later it became a source of power and transport for the earliest industrial cities in America.

Today, the northern regions of the Pioneer Valley remain rural and tranquil, supporting farms and small towns with typical New England architecture. Farther south, the cities of Holyoke and Springfield are more industrial.

Educational pioneers came to this region as well—to form America's first college for women and four other major colleges, as well as several well-known prep schools.

Important Addresses and Numbers

Visitor Information The **Amherst Area Chamber of Commerce** (11 Spring St., tel. 413/253–0700) and the **Greater Northampton Chamber of Commerce** (62 State St., tel. 413/584–1900), open weekdays 9–5, supply information on these two towns and the surrounding area. The **Greater Springfield Convention and Visitors Bureau** (34 Boland Way, Springfield, 01103, tel. 413/787–1548) provides information about the entire Pioneer Valley area.

Emergencies **Cooley Dickenson Hospital** (30 Locust St., Northampton, tel. 413/582–2000 or TDD 413/586–8866) has 24-hour service for the Northampton area; **Holyoke Hospital** (575 Beech St., Holyoke, tel. 413/534–2500) and **Baystate Medical Center** (759 Chestnut St., Springfield, tel. 413/784–0000) serve the lower valley.

Weather Call 413/499–2629.

Getting Around the Pioneer Valley

By Car Interstate 91 runs north–south the entire valley, from Greenfield to Springfield; I–90 links Springfield to Boston; and Route 2 connects Boston with Greenfield in the north.

By Train **Amtrak** (tel. 800/872–7245) serves Springfield from New York City, stopping in New Haven and Hartford, Connecticut, along the way; Amtrak's *Montrealer* stops in Amherst on its way from Washington, D.C., to Canada. The *Lake Shore Limited* between Boston and Chicago calls at Springfield once daily in each direction, and three more trains run between Boston and Springfield every day.

By Bus **Peter Pan Bus Lines** (tel. 413/781–2900 or 800/237–8747) serves the Pioneer Valley from Boston and links Springfield, Holyoke, Northampton, Amherst, and South Hadley. Local bus companies with regular service are the **Pioneer Valley Transit Authority** (tel. 413/781–7882) and **Greenfield Montague Transportation Area** (tel. 413/773–9478).

Guided Tours

Sightseeing tours of the Pioneer Valley, along a 12-mile stretch of the Connecticut River between Northfield and Gill, are available on the *Quinnetukut II* riverboat. Excursions last 1½ hours, and commentary covers geographical, natural, and historical features of the region. *Northfield Mountain Recreation Center, RR 2, Box 117, Northfield 01360, tel. 413/659–3714. Cost: $7 adults, $6 senior citizens, $3 children under 14. Operates June 1–early Oct., Wed.–Sun.*

Exploring the Pioneer Valley

Numbers in the margin correspond to points of interest on the Pioneer Valley map.

Off scenic Route 2 (the Mohawk Trail; *see* Exploring the Berkshires, *below*) the village of **Shelburne Falls,** a nearly perfect example of small-town Americana, straddles the Deerfield River. The **Bridge of Flowers** (tel. 413/625–2544) is an arched, 40-foot abandoned trolley bridge transformed by the Shelburne Women's Club into a unique gardened promenade bursting with colors. In the riverbed just downstream are 50 immense **glacial potholes** ground out of the granite during the last ice age. A sprinkling of antiques shops and the excellent Flower Bridge restaurant overlook the river, making the village a good place to spend the morning.

After lunch head 10 miles south on Route 5 to the area's most impressive attraction, **Historic Deerfield.** Settled by Native Americans 8,000 years ago, Deerfield was originally a Pocumtuck village—deserted after deadly epidemics brought by the English and a disastrous war with the Mohawks all but wiped out the Pocumtuck tribe. Pioneers eagerly settled in this frontier outpost surrounded by rich farmlands in 1660s and 1670s, but two bloody massacres at the hands of the Indians and the French caused the village to be abandoned until 1707, when construction began on the buildings that remain today.

Historic Deerfield, a preserved village within the town, now basks in a far more genteel aura as the site of the prestigious Deerfield Academy preparatory school; parts of the village are protected and maintained as a museum site. "The Street," a tree-lined avenue with 50 grand 18th- and 19th-century houses standing at attention salut-

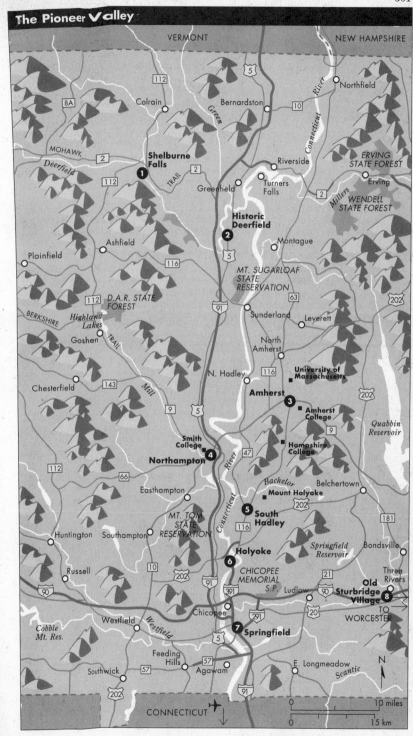

The Pioneer Valley

VERMONT   NEW HAMPSHIRE

112

8A

Colrain

Bernardston

5

10

Northfield

MOHAWK

Deerfield

2

Shelburne Falls

①

112

TRAIL

2

Green

Greenfield

Riverside

Turners Falls

Connecticut River

ERVING STATE FOREST

Erving

2

Millers

WENDELL STATE FOREST

Historic Deerfield

②

Montague

Ashfield

Plainfield

116

5

MT. SUGARLOAF STATE RESERVATION

112

D.A.R. STATE FOREST

63

202

BERKSHIRE

Highland Lakes

91

Sunderland

Leverett

Goshen

TRAIL

North Amherst

Chesterfield

143

Mill

N. Hadley

116

University of Massachusetts

202

9

5

Amherst

③

Amherst College

Quabbin Reservoir

Smith College

Northampton

④

River

47

Hampshire College

112

66

Easthampton

Connecticut

Bachelor

Mount Holyoke

Belchertown

South Hadley

⑤

202

181

Huntington

Southampton

MT. TOM STATE RESERVATION

116

Holyoke

⑥

CHICOPEE MEMORIAL S.P.

Springfield Reservoir

Bondsville

Russell

10

202

91

21

Ludlow

90

Three Rivers

90

391

20

Old Sturbridge Village

⑧

TO WORCESTER

Cobble Mt. Res.

Westfield

Westfield

Chicopee

291

Springfield

⑦

5

Feeding Hills

57

E. Longmeadow

Scantic

N

Southwick

57

Agawam

91

202

CONNECTICUT

0   10 miles

0   15 km

ing each other, is the village highlight. There are also 14 museums within the village, each open for tours year-round. Some, as period homes, contain antique furnishings and decorative arts; others exhibit collections of textiles, silver, pewter, or ceramics. The **Barnard Tavern** has a ballroom with a fiddlers' gallery and several hands-on displays. The whole village is an impressive reflection on 18th- and 19th-century American life. *The Street, tel. 413/774–5581. Two-day admission: $10 adults, $5 children 6–17. Open daily 9:30–4:30.*

3 Head south of Deerfield on Route 5, then southeast along Route 116, to come upon the college town of **Amherst.** Three of the valley's five major colleges—the University of Massachusetts (UMass), Amherst College, and Hampshire College—are in this small but lively country town with its large "village green." Not surprisingly, the area has a youthful bias, reflected in its numerous bookstores, bars, and cafés.

Time Out Stop into **Café Mediterranean** (1 E. Pleasant St., tel. 413/549–7122) for an afternoon nosh on the fresh, innovative light lunch fare, or try one of their delicious pastries and coffee.

The poet Emily Dickinson was born and spent most of her life here; the **Emily Dickinson Homestead** (280 Main St., tel. 413/542–8161; admission: $3), now owned by Amherst College, offers afternoon guided tours by appointment.

The **Strong House** (67 Amity St., tel. 413/256–0678), built in the mid-1700s, has an extensive collection of furniture, china, and clothing that reflects the changing styles of interior decoration. Take the free tour, Wednesdays and Saturdays, spring through fall, to get a sense of local history or just to get a chance to amble around this creaky old house.

4 Another college town, **Northampton,** lies 8 miles west of Amherst on Route 9, which is lined with strip malls and is extremely unappealing, but unfortunately it's the only road connecting the two towns. **Smith College,** founded in 1871, is the nation's largest liberal arts college for women. Stroll through the redbrick quadrangles; they're strongly reminiscent of the women's colleges at Cambridge University, England, which were built around the same period. Worth visiting are the **Lyman Plant House,** the **botanic gardens,** and the **College Art Museum** (Rte. 9, tel. 413/584–2700), which has more than 18,000 paintings and is open afternoons, Tuesday through Sunday.

The history of this small city, settled in 1654 and listed on the National Register of Historic Places, can be traced at **Historic Northampton,** an organization that maintains three houses that represent its cultural heritage: Parsons House (1730), Shepherd House (1798), and Damon House (1813). *46 Bridge Rd., tel. 413/584–6011. Admission: $3 adults. Tours Mar.–Dec., Wed.–Sun. noon–4.*

If you've had enough history, the folks who brought us the infamous Teenage Mutant Ninja Turtles are headquartered here and have opened the **Words and Pictures Museum,** a repository of sequential art where you can sample the latest comic books and graphic novels and even create your own. *244 Main St., tel. 413/586–8545. Admission free. Open Tues.–Sun. noon–5.*

Northampton was also the Massachusetts home of the 30th U.S. president, Calvin Coolidge. He practiced law here and served as mayor from 1910 to 1911. The **Coolidge Room** at the Forbes Library

(20 West St., tel. 413/584–6037) contains a collection of papers and memorabilia.

⑤ Smith's cohort in the higher education of women, **Mount Holyoke** dominates the small village of **South Hadley.** Founded in 1837, Mount Holyoke was the first women's college in the United States. Among its famous alumnae is Emily Dickinson. The handsome wooded campus was landscaped by Frederick Law Olmsted. The **College Art Museum** (tel. 413/538–2245) has exhibits of Asian, Egyptian, and classical art.

Time Out **Woodbridge's** (tel. 413/536–7341), on the common at South Hadley, was the village meetinghouse between 1733 and 1764. Now it is a restaurant that serves sandwiches and burgers.

---

⑥ The southern end of the Pioneer valley is more blue-collar than collegiate: **Holyoke,** just a few miles south of South Hadley, is a somewhat downtrodden town of crumbling redbrick factories and murky canals. The **Heritage State Park** tells the story of this papermaking center, the nation's first planned industrial city, which has been hard hit by a recent recession. The park is in a pleasantly restored part of town and is the starting point for the **Heritage Park Railroad** and its antique steam train. Unfortunately, due to tough economics, no one knows yet whether the train, designed to take visitors on a two-hour ride through the valley, will be operating this year. *Heritage State Park, 221 Appleton St., tel. 413/534–1723. Admission free. Open Wed., Thurs., Sun. noon–4:30.*

Right beside Heritage Park is the **Children's Museum,** housed in a converted mill by the canal. Packed with hands-on games and educational toys, the museum features a TV station, water guns, and a sand pendulum. *444 Dwight St., tel. 413/536–5437. Admission: $3. Open Tues.–Sat. 10–4:30, Sun. noon–5.*

In the same building, the **Volleyball Hall of Fame** is a one-room tribute to the sport and to William Morgan, who invented it here in 1895. *444 Dwight St., tel. 413/536–0926. Admission free. Open Tues.–Fri. 10–5, weekends noon–5.*

⑦ South of Holyoke is **Springfield,** the largest city in the Pioneer Valley—an industrial town where modern skyscrapers rise between grand historic buildings. Although few people would stop here to see the city itself, it does has some unusual museums. The city owed much of its early development to the establishment in 1779 of the **Springfield Armory,** the country's first arsenal, which made small arms for the U.S. military until it closed in 1968. It still holds one of the most extensive firearms collections in the world. *1 Armory Sq. (off State St.), tel. 413/734–8551. Admission free. Open daily 9–5.*

Perhaps the city's greatest claim to fame, however, is that Dr. James Naismith invented basketball here in 1891. The **Naismith Memorial Basketball Hall of Fame** features a cinema, basketball fountain, and a moving walkway from which visitors can shoot baskets. *W. Columbus Ave. at Union St., tel. 413/781–6500. Admission: $6 adults, $4 children 7–15 and senior citizens. Open daily 9–5 (until 6 July–Labor Day).*

Four more conventional museums are situated at the museum quadrangle near downtown. The **Connecticut Valley Historical Museum** (tel. 413/732–3080) commemorates the history of the Pioneer Valley. The **George Walter Vincent Smith Art Museum** (tel. 413/733–4214) contains a private collection of Japanese armor, ceramics, and textiles. The **Museum of Fine Arts** (tel. 413/732–6092) has paintings by

Gauguin, Renoir, Degas, and Monet. The **Springfield Science Museum** (tel. 413/733–1194) contains an "Exploration Center" of touchable displays, a planetarium, and dinosaur exhibits. *Admission (valid for all museums): $4 adults, $1 children 6–18. Open Thurs.–Sun. 12–4.*

Take the Massachusetts Turnpike 30 miles east out of Springfield and you'll reach the star attraction of central Massachusetts—**Old Sturbridge Village,** one of the country's finest period restorations. The village is a living, working model of an early 1800s New England town with more than 40 buildings on a 200-acre site. Working exhibits include a 200-year-old newspaper printing press and a blacksmith and forge. A wool carding mill and a sawmill beside the duck pond are both powered by water wheels, and down the lane—you can travel there in a horse-drawn carriage or cart—is a pioneer farm complete with cattle and sheep. Some of the village houses are furnished in style, with canopy beds and elaborate decoration; in the simpler, single-story cottages interpreters wearing period costume demonstrate such home-based crafts as spinning, weaving, shoemaking, and cooking. Local schoolchildren often take field-trip lessons in the old schoolroom, and the village store contains an amazing variety of goods necessary for everyday life in the 19th century. *1 Old Sturbridge Village Rd., 01566, tel. 508/347–3362. Admission (valid for two consecutive days): $15 adults, $7.50 children 6–15. Open late Apr.–late Oct., daily 9–5; off-season, Tues.–Sun. 10–4.*

Almost due north of Sturbridge, the **Quabbin Reservoir** provides drinking water for the whole of the greater Boston area. It was created in 1939 by flooding the Swift River valley, along with five towns, which had officially ceased to exist on April 28, 1938, when their buildings were razed to the ground. Even the bodies in the churchyards were exhumed and reburied elsewhere. The only traces of the settlements are a few cellar holes and overgrown lanes that disappear eerily beneath the water. Today the Quabbin is a quiet spot of beauty, with facilities for fishing, cycling, hiking, and picnicking. The two great dams that hold back 400 billion gallons of water can be viewed at the south end, near the visitor's center, which contains pictures of the drowned villages. *Quabbin Park Visitor's Center, 485 Ware Rd. (off Rte. 9), Belchertown, tel. 413/323–7561. Admission free. Open weekdays 8:30–5, weekends 10–5.*

What to See and Do with Children

Forest Park, Springfield (tel. 413/733–2251) has many recreational facilities, including a children's zoo.
Look Memorial Park (300 N. Main St., Florence, tel. 413/584–5457) maintains a small zoo, wading and swimming pools, and children's playgrounds.
Old Sturbridge Village, Sturbridge
Riverside Park, the largest amusement park in New England, features a giant roller coaster and many other rides; there are picnic facilities as well. *1623 Main St., Agawam, tel. 413/786–9300 or 800/992–7488. Admission: $18.95 adults, $9.95 children under 54" tall, $9 senior citizens. Open weekends Apr. 3–Memorial Day and Labor Day–Oct. 31; daily Memorial Day–Labor Day.*

Off the Beaten Track

The reopening of the Connecticut River to salmon and shad began with the construction of the **Robert Barrett Fishway** at the Holyoke Dam (tel. 413/536–5520) in 1955. Two elevators lift more than a million migrating fish over the dam each year, and the operation can be seen through viewing windows mid-April to the end of June.

The **Hitchcock Center for the Environment** is a nonprofit organization situated in the Larch Hill Conservation area in Amherst that maintains self-guided nature trails, has a resource library that focuses on environmental issues, and offers natural history programs and workshops for adults and children. *525 Pleasant St., tel. 413/256-6006. Open Tues.-Fri. 9-5, Sat. 11-3.*

Mattoon Street in Springfield consists of picturesque redbrick Victorian rowhouses that call to mind the Brahmin-built Back Bay neighborhood of Boston. Gaslight-style street lamps add atmosphere, and a two-day arts festival takes place here each September.

Almost 50 miles east of Springfield on the Massachusetts Turnpike is **Worcester,** the second-largest town in New England. This busy commercial and cultural center has little to attract the tourist, except for the **Worcester Art Museum,** which contains paintings from Egypt, ancient Greece and Rome, and many works by well-known artists such as Monet, Renoir, Rembrandt, and Warhol. *55 Salisbury St., tel. 508/799-4406. Admission: $4 adults, $2.50 students and senior citizens, under 18 free. Open Tues.-Fri. 11-4, Thurs. 11-8, Sat. 10-5 (free admission), Sun. 1-5.*

Although few people have heard of Dr. Sylvester Graham, a onetime Northampton resident, most Americans are familiar with the graham cracker, which was named after him. Graham believed in eating natural foods and exercising, unpopular ideas in the 1830s: Emerson called him "the poet of bran bread and pumpkins." His home at 111 Pleasant Street is now **Sylvester's Restaurant** (tel. 413/586-5343), offering homemade breads and healthy soups.

Shopping

Shopping Malls
Thorne's Marketplace (150 Main St., Northampton, tel. 413/584-5582) is an old department store converted into a funky indoor mall with lots of shops that fill four floors. Try the **Mall at Center Square** in downtown Springfield, with Steiger's department store, or the **Holyoke Mall,** at Ingleside (Exit 15 off I-91), with 150 stores including JCPenney, Sears, and Steiger's.

Outlet Stores
Factory stores and mill shops are concentrated in Holyoke. The **Becker Jean Factory** (323 Main St., tel. 413/532-5797) carries Becker as well as Lee and Levi jeans for men, women, and children. Of course, paper products and furniture are widely available: The **City Paper Co.** (390-394 Main St., tel. 413/532-1352) offers wholesale and retail paper and plastic disposables; **Deerfield Woodworking** (420 Dwight St., tel. 413/532-2377) and **Riverbends Woodworks** (110 Lyman St., tel. 413/532-3227) sell firsts and seconds of wood furnishings.

Farm Stands
The **Amherst** and **Northampton farmers markets** (in the town centers of each) operate each Saturday morning from spring through autumn; local farmers, craftspeople, and area artisans offer their wares at these bustling outdoor marketplaces. The area around Shelburne Falls is rich with maple-syrup operations; for a complete list, write to the **Massachusetts Maple Producers Association** (Box 377, Ashfield 01330). For lists of pick-your-own orchards, contact the **Department of Agriculture** (Attn. Jane Christenson, 100 Cambridge St., Boston MA 02202, tel. 617/727-3018, ext. 173).

Specialty
Stores
Antiques

For a list of members of the **Pioneer Valley Antique Dealers Associa-**
tion, which guarantees the honest representation of merchandise,
write to Maggie Herbert, Secretary, 201 N. Elm St., Northampton
01060. The **Antique Center of Northampton** (9½ Market St., tel. 413/
584–3600) covers 8,000 square feet and houses 60 dealers; the
Hadley Antique Center (Rte. 9, tel. 413/586–4093) contains more
than 70 different stores.

Books

The college towns of the Pioneer Valley are brimming with excellent
bookstores. In Amherst, try the **Atticus/Albion Bookshop** (Main St.)
or the nearby **Jeffery Amherst Bookshop** (55 South Pleasant St.);
Food for Thought (106 N. Pleasant St.) has a huge selection of political, environmental, and social-commentary works. The **Odyssey**
Bookstore (29 College St., South Hadley) serves Mount Holyoke students, and **Beyond Words** (189 Main St.) is Northampton's largest
bookstore.

Crafts

Among the larger, permanent crafts stores are the **Leverette Crafts**
and Arts Center (Montague Rd., Leverett, tel. 413/548–9070), housing 15 resident artists in jewelry, ceramics, glass and fibers; the
Salmon Falls Artisans Showroom (Ashfield St., tel. 413/625–9833),
with art, sculpture, pottery, and more by 175 local artisans, at
Shelburne Falls; and the **Ferrin Gallery at Pinch Pottery** (179 Main
St., Northampton, tel. 413/586–4509), with exhibits of contemporary ceramics, jewelry, glass, and wood.

Food

Atkins Farms and Fruit Bowl (Rte. 116, South Amherst, tel. 413/
253–9528), surrounded by a sea of apple orchards and gorgeous
views of the Holyoke Ridge, is an institution in the Pioneer Valley.
Sample from their many varieties of apples and other fresh produce,
and don't miss the famous cider doughnuts!

Sports and Outdoor Activities

Biking

The **Norwottuck Rail Trail,** a paved 8½-mile path that links Northampton and Amherst, runs along the old Boston & Maine Railroad
bed and is great for pedaling, blading, jogging, and cross-country
skiing. **Valley Bicycles** (319 Main St., tel. 413/256–0880) in Amherst
is a source of advice and rentals.

Boating and
Canoeing

The Connecticut River is navigable by all types of craft between the
Turners Falls Dam, just north of Greenfield, and the Holyoke Dam.
Canoes can also travel north of Turners Falls beyond the Vermont
border. The large dams control the water level daily, so you will notice a tidal effect; those with larger craft should beware of sand-
banks.

Canoes can be rented during summer and early fall from **Sports-**
man's Marina (Rte. 9, Hadley, tel. 413/584–7141). From Memorial
Day through Labor Day, **Northfield Mountain Recreation Center**
(*see* Guided Tours, *above*) rents out canoes and rowboats at Barton
Cove, from where you can paddle to the Munn's Ferry campground,
accessible only by canoe.

Farther south at the wide place in the river known as the Oxbow, the
Massachusetts Audubon Society's **Arcadia Wildlife Sanctuary** (Fort
Hill Rd., Easthampton, tel. 413/584–3009) is open Tuesday–Saturday 9–3 and organizes canoe trips and maintains hiking and nature
trails.

Camping

A list of private campgrounds throughout Massachusetts can be obtained free from the **Commonwealth of Massachusetts Office of**
Tourism (100 Cambridge St., Boston 02202, tel. 617/727–3201). The

following regional parks also have camping facilities: **Chicopee Memorial State Park, D.A.R. State Forest, Erving State Forest, Granville State Forest,** and **Mohawk Trail State Forest** (*see* State Parks, *below*).

Fishing A massive cleanup program of the Connecticut River has resulted in the return of shad and even salmon to the purer waters, and in fact the river now supports 63 species of fish.

The privately owned **Red-Wing Meadow Farm** raises trout; for a fee visitors may fish in the ponds, paying for fish they catch. *500 Sunderland Rd., Amherst, 01002, tel. 413/549–4118. Admission: $2, $5 family.*

Hiking The abundance of state parks and forests in this region makes for a bounty of well-maintained hiking trails. At the **Mount Tom State Reservation** (*see* State Parks, *below*), a 3.3-mile round-trip hike will take you to the summit with its impressive sheer basalt cliffs, formed by volcanic activity 200 million years ago. From the top there are excellent views over the Pioneer Valley and the Berkshires. An easy 2-mile hike through the Audubon Society's **Arcadia Wildlife Sanctuary** at the Oxbow in the Connecticut River encompasses nature trails with plenty of birds and wildlife, and farther north, **Northfield Mountain Recreation Center** (*see* Guided Tours, *above*) has 29 miles of varied hiking trails. Stop into **Eastern Mountain Sports** (Rte. 9, Hadley, tel. 413/253–9504) for hiking gear, maps, books, and other information.

State Parks

Of the 29 state parks and forests in the Pioneer Valley, the following have a wide variety of facilities for outdoor recreation: **Chicopee Memorial State Park** (Burnett Rd., Chicopee), **D.A.R. State Forest** (Rte. 9, Goshen), **Erving State Forest** (Rte. 2A, Erving), **Granville State Forest** (S. Hartland Rd., Granby), **Hampton Ponds State Park** (Rte. 202, Westfield), **Mohawk Trail State Forest** (Rte. 2, Charlemont), **Mount Sugarloaf State Reservation** (Deerfield), **Mount Tom State Reservation** (Rte. 5, Holyoke), and **Wendell State Forest** (Wendell Rd., Wendell).

Dining and Lodging

Berkshire Bed-and-Breakfast Service (Box 211, Williamsburg, tel. 413/268–7244) provides information and makes reservations at a wide range of area accommodations. Additional accommodations selections will be found in the Berkshire East and Mt. Tom sections of the Skiing New England chapter. Dress is casual unless otherwise noted.

Amherst **Judie's.** A glassed-in porch where students crowd around small ta-
Dining bles creates the atmosphere of a cheerful street café. Cuisine is Continental and imaginative American; specialties are salads, sandwiches, popovers, and a selection of gourmet chocolate cakes. Judie's sells cookery books as well as apple butter and bottles of house dressing. *51 N. Pleasant St., tel. 413/253–3491. No reservations. AE, D, MC, V. Moderate.*

Dining and **Lord Jeffery Inn.** This gabled brick inn with green shutters sits
Lodging right on the green between the town center and the Amherst Col-
★ lege campus. Recently purchased and renovated by friendly new management, the light floral decor remains in many bedrooms; the newly decorated rooms are less formal, with simple cream walls and

pastel-painted woodwork. The large, elegant dining room has an open fireplace, antique reproduction chandeliers, heavy drapes, and white-painted wood beams. The menu offers a wide variety of dishes, including Hawaiian spicy chicken with peanuts and pineapple, pork schnitzel, and Cajun grilled rib-eye steak. Boltwood's Tavern wraps around the main dining room and offers sandwiches, salads, pizza, and other light dishes. *30 Boltwood Ave., 01002, tel. 413/253–2576. 44 rooms, 6 suites. Facilities: restaurant (reservations advised), lounge, tavern, garden courtyard. AE, DC, MC, V. Expensive.*

Lodging
★
The Allen House. This inn, opened in 1991 and honored with a Historic Preservation Award from the Amherst Historical Commission, is a rare find: Restored with historic precision and attention to every last detail, it's a glorious reproduction of the Aesthetic period of the Victorian era. Antiques include a burled walnut bedhead and dresser set, wicker "steamship" chairs, pedestal sinks, screens, carved golden oak or brass beds, goose down comforters, painted wooden floors, and clawfoot tubs. It's a short walk from the center of Amherst, and rates are reasonable. *599 Main St., 01002, tel. 413/253–5000. 5 rooms with bath. Full breakfast and afternoon tea included. No credit cards. Moderate.*

Campus Center Hotel. Literally atop the UMass campus, the spacious rooms of this modern hotel have large windows with excellent views over campus and countryside. The decor is exposed cinderblock, with simple, convenient furnishings. Guests can use university exercise facilities with prior reservation, and the campus status means no tax is charged for accommodations. *Murray D. Lincoln Tower, Univ. of Mass., 01003, tel. 413/549–6000. 116 rooms, 6 suites. Facilities: 2 indoor pools, 3 tennis courts, gym. AE, MC, V. Moderate.*

Buckland
Lodging
1797 House. Built almost 200 years ago, this white clapboard house stands on the green in tiny, quiet Buckland Village. Guest rooms are furnished with antiques, and the beds—one brass, one iron, and one four-poster—have quilts. In summer, breakfast is served on the large screened porch overlooking the woods; in winter it's in the dining room with an open fireplace. *Charlemont Rd., 01338, tel. 413/625–2975. 3 rooms with bath. No credit cards. Full breakfast included. Moderate.*

Deerfield
Dining and Lodging
★
Deerfield Inn. This inn is perfectly located in the center of Historic Deerfield and is superbly run by friendly, helpful owner-managers. Guest rooms have recently been redecorated with period wallpapers designed for the inn, which was built in 1884. It was substantially modernized after a fire in 1981, and a new wing was added. Rooms have antiques and replicas, sofas and bureaus; some have four-poster or canopy beds. One bed is so high that a ladder is provided! The large, sunny dining room is elegantly decorated; specialties include venison and rack of lamb with Dijon mustard and garlic. *The Street, 01342, tel. 413/774–5587. 23 rooms. Facilities: restaurant (reservations, jacket and tie advised), lounge, coffee shop. AE, DC, MC, V. Full breakfast included. Inn: Very Expensive. Restaurant: Expensive.*

The Whately Inn. Guest rooms with sloping old wood floors are furnished simply with antiques and four-poster beds. Two are located over the restaurant, which can be noisy. The dining room has exposed beams, tables on a raised stage at one end, and some booths. The room is dimly lighted, with candles on the tables. Roast duck, baked lobster with shrimp stuffing, and rack of lamb all come with salad, appetizer, and dessert. The restaurant is very busy on weekends. *Chestnut Plain Rd., Whately Center 01093, tel. 413/665–3044 or 800/942–8359. 4 rooms. Facilities: restaurant (reservations advised; no lunch except Sun.). MC, V. Moderate.*

Lodging **Sunnyside Farm Bed and Breakfast.** Country-style guest rooms of varying sizes are appointed with maple antiques and family heirlooms. All rooms, which are hung with fine art reproductions, have views across the fields, and some overlook the large strawberry farm next door. Guests share a small library. Breakfast is served family-style in the dining room, which has a wood-burning stove. The farm is about 8 miles south of Deerfield. *11 River Rd., Whately (Box 486, S. Deerfield 01373), tel. 413/665–3113. 5 rooms share 2 baths. Facilities: outdoor pool. No credit cards. Full breakfast included. Moderate.*

Greenfield **Brickers.** Right beside I–91, this restaurant is set in a converted ice-
Dining cream factory. Decor is country style, in a large room with exposed brick walls and a high ceiling supported by metal beams and pillars. The sunny porch at one end is a pleasant place to eat lunch. Entrées include Cajun chicken, pan-fried sole, and pasta dishes; burgers and sandwiches are also available. *Shelburne Rd., tel. 413/774–2857. AE, D, MC, V. Moderate.*

Holyoke **Yankee Pedlar Inn.** This attractive, sprawling inn stands at a busy
Dining and crossroads near I–91. A recent renovation and redecoration has in-
Lodging dividual rooms superbly furnished with antiques and four-poster or
★ canopy beds. Victorian guest rooms are elaborate and heavily curtained, with lots of lace, while the carriage house has beams and rustic furnishings, with simple canopy beds. The dining room has exposed beams and antique wood paneling; candle chandeliers provide the lighting. Try lobster Savannah (lobster in Newburg sauce with mushrooms and green peppers), beef Wellington, New England boiled dinner, and Cornish game hen. *1866 Northampton St., 01040, tel. 413/532–9494. 30 rooms, 12 suites. Facilities: restaurant (reservations advised), meeting rooms, oyster bar, live entertainment. Continental breakfast included. AE, D, DC, MC, V. Moderate–Expensive.*

Northampton **Eastside Grill.** The airy dining room is laced with pastels, evoking
Dining more tropical venues, and a place at one of the stools lined up before the busy bar is a coveted commodity. The menu changes seasonally but always includes a blackened fish of day and, when available, fresh oysters on the half shell. *19 Strong Ave., tel. 413/586–3347. Reservations advised. AE, D, MC, V. Moderate–Expensive.*

Paul and Elizabeth's. This classy natural-foods restaurant serves such seasonal specials as butternut-squash soup, home-baked corn muffins, and Indian pudding, as well as Japanese tempura and innovative fish entrées. Rooms are airy with lots of plants and trelliswork, and fans hang from the high ceiling. *150 Main St., tel. 413/584–4832. Reservations advised. MC, V. Moderate.*

La Cazuela. This well-established Mexican restaurant, perched above South Street, is a local favorite. The large square dining room is decorated with plates, Mexican artifacts, and many cacti. On the menu are enchiladas, chimichangas, burritos, and many other typical Mexican and Tex-Mex dishes. *7 Old South St., tel. 413/586–0400. AE, D, MC, V. No lunch Mon.–Fri. Inexpensive.*

Northampton Brewery. At the Pioneer Valley's own microbrewery and restaurant, quality pub food—on the order of burgers, fish-and-chips, and baskets of onion rings piled sky-high—and outdoor seating in the warmer months, complement the popularity of recent brew concoctions on tap. *11 Brewster Ct., tel. 413/584–4176. Reservations accepted. AE, D, MC, V. Inexpensive.*

Dining and **Hotel Northampton.** In the town center, the hotel was built in 1927.
Lodging Antique and reproduction furnishings combine with open fires in the parlor, lounge, and dining rooms to give the atmosphere of a cozy inn. The porch has a piano and wicker chairs. Guest rooms are appointed with Colonial reproductions, heavy curtains, and some four-poster beds. Some rooms come with balconies that overlook a busy street. The Wiggins Tavern specializes in such New England dishes as Yankee cider pot roast, chicken potpie, and Boston scrod; Indian pudding, rice pudding, and apple pie follow. Open fires burn in three dimly lighted, "old world" dining rooms, where heavy exposed beams support low ceilings and antique kitchen appliances decorate every available space. *36 King St., 01060, tel. 413/584–3100. 73 rooms, 5 suites. Facilities: restaurant (reservations advised; no lunch; closed Mon., Tues.), café, bar, lounge, ballroom. AE, D, DC, MC, V. Inn: Very Expensive. Restaurant: Expensive.*

Lodging **The Knoll Bed and Breakfast.** A spacious private home, this B&B sits well away from the busy road and backs onto steep woodlands. There's a sweeping staircase and Oriental rugs on polished woodfloors; guest rooms are furnished with a mixture of antiques and hand-me-downs, and some have high four-poster beds. *230 N. Main St., Florence 01060, tel. 413/584–8164. 5 rooms share 2 baths. Facilities: lounge, library. Full breakfast included. No credit cards. Moderate.*

Twin Maples Bed and Breakfast. Seven miles northwest of Northampton near the village of Williamsburg, this 200-year-old, fully restored farmhouse is surrounded by fields and woods. Inside are exposed beams, wide brick fireplaces, and wood stoves. Colonial-style antique and reproduction furnishings decorate the rather small guest rooms, which have restored brass beds and quilts. *106 South St., Williamsburg 01096, tel. 413/268–7925. 3 rooms share one bath. Full breakfast included. No credit cards. Moderate.*

Northfield **Northfield Country House.** Truly remote, this big English manor
Lodging house is set amid thick woodlands on a small hill that overlooks
★ Northfield's Main Street. A wide staircase leads to the bedrooms, some of which have working fireplaces. The smallest rooms are in the former servants' quarters; larger rooms are furnished with antiques, and several have brass beds. The present owner has considerably renovated this 100-year-old house, and has planted hundreds of tulip and daffodil bulbs in the gardens. *School St., RR 1, Box 617, 01360, tel. 413/498–2692. 7 rooms share 4 baths. Facilities: lounge, outdoor pool. Full breakfast included. MC, V. Moderate.*

Shelburne **Flower Bridge.** This high-quality and unusual Chinese restaurant is
Falls perched between the Bridge of Flowers, which it overlooks, and
Dining Shelburne Falls's main street. Long tables, square tables, benches, chairs, and customers are crammed into a small, bright room, and food is served buffet style at the counter. The young woman who works as chef is from northern China and dishes up many of her local specialties, including eggplant in garlic sauce with new potatoes, and chicken stewed with mushrooms and green beans. More conventional Chinese dishes like sweet and sour chicken are also available. *4 State St., tel. 413/625–2570. No reservations. No credit cards. Closed Mon. Moderate.*

Springfield **Johann's.** This stylish, well-established Dutch restaurant is in the
Dining Marketplace shopping area in the heart of Springfield. Blue-and-white Dutch plates and reproduction Dutch masters decorate the walls, and brass chandeliers hang from the ceilings. The menu features Dutch, French, and Indonesian entrées, such as hot gouda bread, *hachee* (Dutch beef goulash), chateaubriand, and *djahe*

oedgang (gingery shrimp with ginger brandy), and of course Dutch beer. *73 Market St., tel. 413/737–7979. Reservations advised. AE, D, DC, MC, V. Closed Sun. Expensive.*

Theodores'. There's saloon-style dining at booths near the bar or in a small adjacent dining room. The 1930s are re-created with period furniture and framed advertisements for such curious products as foot soap. Brass lights date from 1897. Theodores' serves burgers, sandwiches, some Mexican dishes, chicken, and seafood. Thursday through Sunday there is live entertainment in the evenings. *201 Worthington St., tel. 413/736–6000. AE, DC, MC, V. Moderate.*

Tilly's Restaurant. Tilly's is a cheerful spot for such lighter meals as salads, burgers, and sandwiches, but the restaurant also serves full dinner entrées Wednesday through Saturday nights. The interiors feature carved ceilings, lots of pine woodwork and exposed brick, and seating is at wood booths. *1390 Main St., tel. 413/732–3613. No reservations. AE, MC, V. No Sun. dinner. Inexpensive.*

Lodging **Marriott Hotel.** Conveniently located in the middle of downtown, this recently renovated hotel opens onto the large Baystate West shopping mall. The lobby features green marble, brass chandeliers, and Oriental rugs. Rooms at the front overlook the river, and all are comfortably decorated with oak furniture, Impressionist prints, and mauve or sea-foam-green color schemes. *1500 Main St., 01115, tel. 413/781–7111 or 800/228–9290. 264 rooms, 1 suite. Facilities: restaurant, lounge, bar, indoor pool, 2 saunas, whirlpool, fitness center, meeting rooms. AE, D, DC, MC, V. Very Expensive.*

Sheraton Tara. This hotel, in the middle of downtown, was built in 1987. Guest rooms have reproduction antiques and are plush, with heavy drapes and thick carpets; they surround an impressive 14-story atrium. Hotel staff wear the distinctive red-and-gold Beefeater costume. *1 Monarch Place, 01144, tel. 413/781–1010 or 800/325–3535. 303 rooms, 7 suites. Facilities: 2 restaurants, lounge, health club, exercise room, racquetball, 2 saunas, steam room, whirlpool, indoor pool, conference rooms, ballroom. AE, D, DC, MC, V. Very Expensive.*

Cityspace. The Springfield YMCA offers high-quality, motel accommodations with attractive pastel tones, gray cinderblock walls, modern paintings, large lamps, and large windows. Each has a private bath. The big advantage over other budget motels is that visitors can use all the sports and fitness facilities at the Y for free. Cityspace is close to I–91, near downtown, and a five-minute walk from the Amtrak station. *275 Chestnut St., 01104, tel. 413/739–6951. 124 rooms. Facilities: restaurant, indoor pool, racquetball, squash, fitness center, whirlpool, steam room, sauna, massage. MC, V. Inexpensive.*

Sturbridge **The Whistling Swan.** There are two separate eating areas here; the
Dining Ugly Duckling Loft upstairs serves lighter meals than the main dining room. The ambience in both is fairly formal, with matching floral-print drapes and wallpaper and white linen tablecloths. Specialties include rack of lamb, veal, stuffed rainbow trout, roast chicken, and catch of the day. *502 Main St., tel. 508/347–2321. Reservations advised. AE, DC, MC, V. Closed Mon. Moderate–Expensive.*

Rom's. This has become something of a local institution—after humble beginnings as a sandwich stand, the restaurant was extended to seat about 700 people. The six dining rooms have an Early American decor, with wood paneling and beam ceilings. Now serving Italian and American cuisine ranging from pizza to roast beef, Rom's attracts the crowds with a classic formula: good food at low prices. The veal parmesan is very popular. *Rte. 131, tel. 508/347–3349. AE, MC, V. Inexpensive.*

Dining and Lodging
★

Publick House and Col. Ebenezer Crafts Inn. The Publick House dates to 1771 and is now surrounded by a "complex" of different styles of lodging. Rooms in the Publick House itself are Colonial in design, with uneven wide-board floors; some have canopy beds. The neighboring Chamberlain House consists of larger suites, and the Country Motor Lodge has more modern rooms. The Crafts Inn, just over a mile away, has a library, lounge, and guest rooms with four-poster beds, old desks, and painted wood paneling. The popular restaurant is big, bustling, and very busy on weekends. The high cathedral ceilings in the main dining room are supported by wood beams and hung with enormous period chandeliers. The menu advertises "hearty gourmet meals and hefty desserts," which translates into individually baked lobster pies, double-thick loin lamb chops, followed by Indian pudding, pecan bread pudding, and apple pie. *Rte. 131, On-the-Common, 01566, tel. 508/347–3313. 118 rooms, 12 suites. Facilities: restaurant (reservations advised), bar, outdoor pool, tennis, track, shuffleboard, playground, conference rooms. Continental breakfast included at Crafts Inn. AE, DC, MC, V. Inn: Moderate–Expensive. Restaurant: Expensive.*

Lodging

The Sturbridge Host. Formerly a Sheraton, this inn has now joined the Host group, and the managers have spruced up the place with an updated front lobby and new rugs. It's located just across the street from Old Sturbridge Village on Cedar Lake. Luxuriously appointed bedrooms have Colonial decor and reproduction furnishings, and the lakeside location enhances the recreational offerings. *Rte. 20, 01566, tel. 508/347–7393. 241 rooms, 9 suites. Facilities: 2 dining rooms, lounges, indoor pool, health club, exercise room, minigolf, tennis, racquetball, basketball, sauna, boats, fishing, meeting rooms. AE, D, DC, MC, V. Very Expensive.*

Sturbridge Country Inn. This imposing Greek Revival–facade inn on Sturbridge's busy Main Street was once a farmhouse. With an atmosphere somewhere between an inn and a plush business hotel, it offers lots of extras. Guest rooms—all have working gas fireplaces—are superbly furnished, with reproduction antiques and a Jacuzzi in every room. The best is the top-floor suite, with a cathedral ceiling, a large Jacuzzi in the living room, and big windows. Try to avoid the first-floor rooms—they're comparably priced but small and noisy (with gurgles from the upstairs plumbing!). *530 Main St. (Box 60), 01566, tel. 508/347–5503. 9 rooms, 1 suite. Facilities: lounge, in-room Jacuzzis. Continental breakfast included. AE, D, MC, V. Expensive–Very Expensive.*

The Arts

The **Northampton Center for the Arts** (17 New South St., tel. 413/584–7327) is an innovative performance space for theater, dance, and musical events. The **William D. Mullens Memorial Center** (tel. 413/545–0505), at the University of Massachuetts, opened in 1993, showcases concerts, theatrical productions, and other entertainment.

Dance

The **Berkshire Ballet** performs twice a year at Springfield's American International College—usually in fall and spring. Call the college (tel. 413/737–7000) for details. Other major ballet and modern dance companies appear in season at the **UMass Fine Arts Center** in Amherst (tel. 413/545–2511).

Music A variety of concerts are hosted fall through spring at the **Paramount Performing Arts Center** (1700 Main St., 01103, tel. 413/734–5874) and the **Springfield Civic Center** (127 Main St., 01103, tel. 413/787–6610). The **Springfield Symphony Orchestra** performs October through May at Symphony Hall, and mounts a summer program of concerts in Springfield's parks. *1391 Main St., Suite 1006, 01103, tel. 413/733–2291.*

Theater Springfield is the home of **StageWest** (1 Columbus Ctr., tel. 413/781–2340.) the only resident professional theater company in western Massachusetts. The schedule includes a series of plays and musicals October through May. The **Children's Theatre of Massachusetts** (tel. 413/788–0705), based at the Springfield Symphony Hall, performs a series of family-oriented performances year-round.

Nightlife

The collegiate population ensures a lively club and nightlife scene in the valley. Popular spots include the **Iron Horse** (20 Center St., Northampton, tel. 413/584–0610), with a variety of folk, blues, jazz, Celtic, and alternative music seven nights a week, and **Pearl Street** (tel. 413/584–7771), which presents live music several nights a week and is the area's largest dance club. **The Vertex** (Rte. 9, Hadley, tel. 413/586–4463) specializes in rock and blues bands seven nights a week; **Sheehan's Café** (24 Pleasant St., Northampton, tel. 413/586–4258) features rock and blues six nights a week; and **Theodores'** (201 Worthington St., Springfield, tel. 413/736–6000) has live blues and rock bands Thursday through Sunday evenings.

The Berkshires

More than a century ago, wealthy families from New York and Boston built "summer cottages" in western Massachusetts's Berkshire hills—great country estates that earned Berkshire County the nickname "inland Newport." Although most of those grand houses have since been converted into schools or hotels, the region is still popular, for obvious reasons. Occupying the entire far western end of the state, the area is only about a 2½-hour drive directly west from Boston or north from New York City, yet it lives up to the storybook image of rural New England, with its wooded hills, narrow winding roads, and compact charming villages. Summer offers an astonishing variety of cultural events, not the least of which is the Tanglewood festival in Lenox; fall brings a blaze of brilliant foliage; in winter, it's a popular ski area; and springtime visitors can enjoy maple-sugaring. Keep in mind, however, that the Berkshire's popularity often goes hand-in-hand with high prices and crowds, especially on weekends.

Important Addresses and Numbers

Visitor **Berkshire Visitor's Bureau** (Berkshire Common, Pittsfield 01201,
Information tel. 413/443–9186 or 800/237–5747; open weekdays 8:30–4:30). The **Great Barrington Chamber of Commerce** (362 Main St., tel. 413/528–1510; open weekdays 9:30–12:30 and 1:30–4:30, weekends noon–3). **Lenox Chamber of Commerce** (Lenox Academy Building, 75 Main St., 01240, tel. 413/637–3646; open June–Sept., Mon.–Thurs. 10–4, Fri. and Sat. 10–6, Sun. 10–2; Oct.–May, Mon. 10–noon and 1–3, Tues.–Sat. 9:30–4:30).

For further information, write to the **Mohawk Trail Association** (Box 722, Charlemont 01339, tel. 413/664–6256).

Emergencies **Fairview Hospital** (29 Lewis Ave., Great Barrington, tel. 413/528–0790); **Hillcrest Hospital** (165 Tor Ct., Pittsfield, tel. 413/443–4761); **North Adams Regional Hospital** (Hospital Ave., North Adams, tel. 413/663–3701).

Weather Call 413/499–2629.

Getting Around the Berkshires

By Car The Massachusetts Turnpike (I–90) connects Boston with Lee and Stockbridge, and continues into New York, where it becomes the New York State Thruway. To reach the Berkshires from New York City, take either I–87 or the Taconic State Parkway.

Within the Berkshires the main north–south road is Route 7. The scenic Mohawk Trail (Rte. 2) runs from the northern Berkshires to Greenfield at the head of the Pioneer Valley, and continues across Massachusetts into Boston.

By Bus **Peter Pan Bus Lines** (tel. 413/442–4451) serves Lee and Pittsfield from Boston, New York City, and Albany. **Bonanza Bus Lines** (tel. 800/556–3815) connects points throughout the Berkshires with Albany, New York City, and Providence.

By Train **Amtrak** (tel. 800/872–7245) runs the *Lake Shore Limited*, which stops at Pittsfield once daily in each direction on its route between Boston and Chicago.

Guided Tours

Balloon tours over the Berkshires are offered twice daily throughout the summer, on weekends during the off-season (weather permitting) by **American Balloon Works, Inc.** (East Nassau, NY 12062, tel. 518/766–5111).

Berkshire Hiking Holidays offers a variety of guided hiking tours: Less ambitious walkers can combine easy hikes with visits to Tanglewood and Berkshire towns; the more experienced trekker can tackle mountain trails. "Hike, bike, and canoe" combines three alternative ways to experience the Berkshires. Overnight accommodation is provided in Berkshire inns. *Box 2231, Lenox, 01240, tel. 413/499–9648.*

New England Hiking Holidays organizes guided hiking vacations through the Berkshires, with overnight stays at a country inn. Hikes vary from 5 to 9 miles per day. *Box 1648, North Conway, NH 03860, tel. 603/356–9696.*

Exploring the Berkshires

Numbers in the margin correspond to points of interest on the Berkshires map.

Many visitors will approach the Berkshires along Route 2 from Boston and the east coast. The **Mohawk Trail**, a 67-mile stretch, follows the former Native American path that ran along the Deerfield River through the Connecticut Valley to the Berkshire hills. Just beyond the town of Charlemont stands **Hail to the Sunrise**, a 900-pound bronze statue of an Indian facing east, with arms uplifted, dedicated to the five Native American nations who lived along the Mohawk Trail. A handful of somewhat tacky "Indian trading posts" on the highway carry out the Mohawk theme. Also along the road are many antiques stores and flea markets.

Bypassing the entrance to the **Hoosac railway tunnel** (which took 24 years to build and, at 4.7 miles, was the longest in the nation when it was completed in 1875), the road begins a steep ascent to Whitcomb Summit, the highest point on the trail, then continues to the spectacular Western Summit, with excellent views, before dropping through a series of hairpin turns into **North Adams.**

Once a railroad boomtown and a thriving industrial city, North Adams is still industrial but no longer thriving—the dilapidated mills and row houses are reminiscent of northern industrial England. It's not really worth stopping here unless you're intrigued by the ghosts of the Industrial Revolution or a railway buff, in which case visit the **Western Gateway Heritage State Park,** housed in the restored freight-yard district. It tells the story of the town's past successes, including the construction of the Hoosac Tunnel. The freight-yard district also contains a number of specialty stores and restaurants. *Tel. 413/663–6312. Admission free. Open Memorial Day–Oct., daily 10–4:30; Nov.–Memorial Day, Thur.–Mon. 10–4:30.*

The only natural bridge in North America caused by water erosion is the marble arch at **Natural Bridge State Park.** It stands above a narrow 500-foot chasm with numerous potholes, faults, and fractures lining the walls. *Rte. 8 N, North Adams, tel. 413/663–6392. Admission: $3 per car. Open May–Oct., Mon.–Fri. 10–6, weekends 10–8.*

A little farther west along Route 2, **Williamstown** is entirely different in character from North Adams. When Col. Ephraim Williams left money to found a free school in what was then known as West Hoosuck, he stipulated that the name be changed to Williamstown. Williams College opened in 1793, and even today the town revolves around it. Gracious campus buildings line the wide main street and are open to visitors. Highlights include the **Gothic cathedral,** built in 1904, and the **Williams College Museum of Art,** with works emphasizing American, modern, and contemporary art. *Main St., tel. 413/597–2429. Admission free. Open Tues.–Sat. 10–5, Sun. 1–5.*

Formerly a private collection, the **Sterling and Francine Clark Art Institute** is now one of the nation's outstanding small art museums. Its famous works include more than 30 paintings by Renoir, as well as works by Monet, Pissarro, and Degas. *225 South St., tel. 413/458–9545. Admission free. Open Tues.–Sun. 10–5.*

Leaving Williamstown and heading south along Route 7 takes travelers into the heart of the Berkshires. After the lakeside village of Lanesborough, signs will direct you to the top of **Mt. Greylock,** at 3,491 feet the highest point in Massachusetts. The 10,327-acre **Mt. Greylock State Reservation** (*see* National and State Parks, *below*) provides facilities for cycling, fishing, hiking, horseback riding, hunting, and snowmobiling.

Continuing south on Route 7 will bring you to the built-up town of **Pittsfield,** county seat and geographic center of the region. Though not particularly attractive, the town has a lively small-town atmosphere. The **Berkshire Museum** especially appeals to children, with its aquarium, animal exhibits, and glowing rocks. A local repository with a "bit of everything," the museum also contains works of art and historical relics. *39 South St., tel. 413/443–7171. Admission: $3 adults, $2 senior citizens and students, $1 children 12–18. Open Tues.–Sat. 10–5, Sun. 1–5.*

The Berkshires

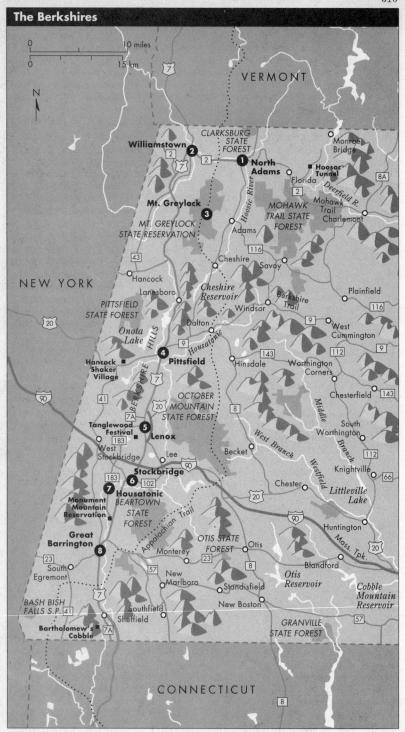

VERMONT

10 miles

15 km

N

7

CLARKSBURG
STATE
FOREST

Monroe
Bridge

Williamstown
2

2

① North
Adams

Hoosac
Tunnel

8A

Florida

Deerfield R.

Mt. Greylock
③

2

Mohawk
Trail

MOHAWK
TRAIL STATE
FOREST

Charlemont

MT. GREYLOCK
STATE RESERVATION

Adams

NEW YORK

43

Hancock

Cheshire

116

Savoy

Plainfield

Lanesboro

Cheshire
Reservoir

Berkshire
Trail

116

PITTSFIELD
STATE FOREST

Windsor

9

West
Cummington

20

Onota
Lake

Dalton

Housatonic

143

112

9

9

④ Pittsfield

Hinsdale

Worthington
Corners

Chesterfield

143

Hancock
Shaker
Village

41

7

OCTOBER
MOUNTAIN
STATE FOREST

8

South
Worthington

112

Tanglewood
Festival

7A

⑤ Lenox

West
Branch

Knightville

66

183

Lee

West
Stockbridge

90

Becket

Westfield

Littleville
Lake

⑥ Stockbridge

102

Chester

Huntington

20

183

⑦

Housatonic

20

Monument
Mountain
Reservation

BEARTOWN
STATE
FOREST

90

Mass. Tpk.

20

Great
Barrington

⑧

Appalachian Trail

OTIS STATE
FOREST

Otis

Blandford

Cobble
Mountain
Reservoir

23

South
Egremont

Monterey

23

8

Otis
Reservoir

57

7

New
Marlboro

Standisfield

New Boston

GRANVILLE
STATE FOREST

57

BASH BISH
FALLS S.P.

41

Southfield

Sheffield

Bartholomew's
Cobble

7A

CONNECTICUT

8

At the **Berkshire Athenaeum** (Berkshire Public Library, 1 Wendell Ave.), the **Herman Melville Memorial Room** (tel. 413/499–9486) houses a collection of books, letters, and memorabilia of the author of *Moby-Dick*. **Arrowhead,** the house Melville purchased in 1850, is just outside Pittsfield; the somewhat underwhelming tours include the study in which *Moby-Dick* was written. *780 Holmes Rd., tel. 413/442–1793. Admission: $4 adults, $2.50 children 6–16, $3.50 senior citizens. Open Memorial Day–Labor Day, Mon.–Sat. 10–4:15, Sun. 11–3:15; Labor Day–late-Oct., Thurs.–Mon. 10–4:15, Sun. 11–3.*

Take Route 20 west out of the center of Pittsfield to discover the town's star attraction—**Hancock Shaker Village.** Founded in the 1790s, Hancock was the third Shaker community in America. At its peak in the 1840s, the village had almost 300 inhabitants, who made their living from farming, selling seeds and herbs, making medicines, and producing crafts. The religious community officially closed in 1960, its 170-year life span a small miracle considering its vows of celibacy—they took in orphans to maintain their constituency. In 1961 the site opened as a museum. Many examples of the famous Shaker ingenuity are visible at Hancock today: The **Round Stone Barn** with its labor-saving devices and the **Laundry and Machine Shop** with its water-powered instruments are two of the most interesting buildings. *Rte. 20, 5 mi west of Pittsfield, tel. 413/443–0188. Admission: $9 adults, $8 senior citizens and students, $4.50 children 6–12. Open May–Oct., daily 9:30–5; Apr.–Nov., daily 10–3. Guided tours only.*

❺ Five miles south of Pittsfield on Route 7, the village of **Lenox** epitomizes the Berkshires for many visitors. In the thick of the "summer cottage" region, it's rich with old inns and majestic buildings. One of the most interesting to visit is **The Mount,** former summer home of novelist Edith Wharton. The house and grounds were designed and built under Wharton's direction in 1902. An expert in the field of design, Wharton used the principles set forth in her book *The Decoration of Houses* (1897) to plan The Mount for a calm, well-ordered lifestyle. *Plunkett St., tel. 413/637–1899. Admission: $4.50 adults, $3 children 13–18, $4 senior citizens. Open late May–Aug., Tues.–Sun. 10–5; Sept.–late Oct., weekends 10–5.*

Lenox is the nearest Berkshire village to **Tanglewood,** summer home of the Boston Symphony. The 200-acre estate attracts thousands every summer to hear concerts featuring world-famous performers. One of the most popular ways to experience Tanglewood is to take a blanket and picnic on the grounds while listening to the performance from the lawn. (*See* The Arts, *below,* for information.)

Time Out   **The Garden Gourmet** (8 Franklin St., Lenox, tel. 413/637-4156), a deli and restaurant (open daily, May–Oct.), offers a variety of vegetarian dishes for those who wish to eat in. But it is a particular bonus for Tanglewood goers, as the bakery makes picnic meals to go. The excellent sandwiches come with dessert, drink, fruit, and all necessary utensils for a relaxing visit to the Tanglewood lawns.

Just west of Tanglewood, turn left onto Hawthorne Road. Sitting atop Propect Hill, 3 miles south, is **Naumkeag,** a Berkshire cottage that provides an informative perspective on the gracious living of the "gilded era" of the Berkshires. The 26-room gabled mansion, designed by Stanford White, is decorated with furniture and art that spans three centuries, including an outstanding collection of Chinese export porcelain. The meticulously kept formal gardens are worth a visit in themselves. *Prospect Hill, Stockbridge, tel. 413/ 298–3239. Admission: $7. Open Memorial Day–Labor Day, Tues.– Sun. and holidays 10–4:15; Labor Day–Columbus Day, weekends and holidays 10–4:15.*

At the bottom of Prospect Hill lies the archetypal New England

6 small town of **Stockbridge,** with its history of literary and artistic inhabitants. The painter Norman Rockwell, the sculptor Daniel Chester French, and the writers Norman Mailer and Robert Sherwood lived here. The **Norman Rockwell Museum,** formerly in the center of town, has a new home 2 miles out of Stockbridge on Route 183. Covering 27,000 square feet, the new site has triple the exhibition space of the former museum, and 150 paintings are displayed. The museum owns the largest collection of Rockwell originals in the world; Rockwell lived in Stockbridge from 1953 until his death in 1978. *Rte. 183, tel. 413/298–4100. Admission: $8 adults, $2 children 6–18. Open May 1–Oct. 31, daily 10–5; Nov. 1–Apr. 30, weekdays 11–4, weekends 10–5.*

The **Berkshire Botanical Gardens,** at the intersection of Routes 102 and 183, blanket 15 acres of land laced with pretty landscapes; historic perennial, rose, and herb gardens; greenhouses, ponds, and nature trails. Picnicking is encouraged and tours are available. *Tel. 413/298–3926. Admission: Memorial Day–late Oct. $5; off-season free. Open Memorial Day–late Oct. 10–5; call for hours off-season.*

Nearby **Chesterwood** was for 33 years the summer home of Daniel Chester French, who is best known for his statues of the Minute Man in Concord and of Abraham Lincoln at the Lincoln Memorial in Washington, D.C. *Williamsville Rd. (off Rte. 183), tel. 413/298– 3579. Admission: $5.50 adults, $3 children 6–12. Open May 1–Oct. 31, daily 10–5.*

Route 183 continues south along the Housatonic River and into the

7 town of **Housatonic.** Once bustling with the Industrial Revolution, the town's abandoned mills now provide inexpensive gallery and studio space to a growing community of artists and craftspeople.

8 Heading south on Route 7 will bring you to **Great Barrington.** The southern Berkshires's largest town, Great Barrington is noted as the site of the last attempt by the British to hold court in the country, as well as the freeing of the first slaves under due process of law. It was also the birth place of W. E. B. Du Bois, the civil rights leader, author, and educator. Today, the town is a mecca for antiques hunters, as are the nearby villages of **South Egremont** and **Sheffield.**

Time Out   Drop into **Martin's** (49 Railroad St., Great Barrington, tel. 413/528– 5455), but bring a healthy appetite: They serve hearty, wholesome breakfasts all day, as well as salads, sandwiches, and delectable baked goods.

The **Albert Schweitzer Center** is a museum and educational center dedicated to the Nobel Prize–winning medical doctor and philanthropist. A path behind the center leads to a children's garden, the Philosopher's Walk (a nature trail), and a wildlife sanctuary. The center also sponsors lectures, concerts, film series, and a summer children's program. It's a delightful place for tranquil walks in the woods and picnicking beneath the trees. *50 Hurlbert Rd., Great Barrington, tel. 413/528–3124. Donation suggested. Open Tues.– Sat. 10–4, Sun. noon–4.*

Those in search of more nature may want to make two excursions into the southernmost reaches of the Berkshire countryside from

Great Barrington. **Bartholomew's Cobble** (Rte. 7A, tel. 413/229–8600), near Sheffield, is a natural rock garden beside the Housatonic River. The 277-acre reservation is filled with trees, ferns, wildflowers, and hiking trails.

At **Bash Bish Falls** (Rte. 23, tel. 413/528–0330), 16 miles southwest of Great Barrington on the New York State border, Bash Bish Brook flows through a gorge and over a 50-foot waterfall into a clear natural pool.

What to See and Do with Children

Hancock Shaker Village. Besides its inherent attractions, the village organizes special programs for children.

Jiminy Peak (tel. 413/738–5500). The ski resort at Hancock offers an alpine slide, putting course, tennis, swimming, and trout fishing in summer.

The Railway Museum, in the center of Lenox, is a restoration of the 1902 Lenox station, containing period exhibits and a large working model railway. It's also the starting point for the **Berkshire Scenic Railway,** which operates vintage railroad cars over a portion of the historic New Haven Railway's Housatonic Valley Line. *Willow Creek Rd., tel. 413/637–2210. Fares vary according to destination. Open June–late Oct., weekends and holidays.*

The Robbins-Zust Family Marionettes have been performing puppet shows for children and families in Pittsfield, Lenox, and Great Barrington since 1971. Each year they mount a varied program, which always includes the old favorite—Punch and Judy. *East Rd., Richmond 01254, tel. 413/698–2591. Tickets: $3. Late June–late Aug. Call for performance schedule.*

Off the Beaten Track

The **Chapin Library of Rare Books and Manuscripts** at Williams College contains the Four Founding Documents of the United States, as well as 35,000 other books, manuscripts, and illustrations dating from the 9th to the 20th centuries, including a copy of the Declaration of Independence that had been owned by one of the signers. *Stetson Hall, Main St., Williamstown, tel. 413/597–2462. Admission free. Open Mon.–Fri. 10–noon and 1–5.*

Dalton is the home of paper manufacturers Crane and Co., a business started by Zenas Crane in 1801 and now the major employer in town. The **Crane Museum of Paper Making,** housed in the Old Stone Mill (1844), has been beautifully restored with oak beams, Colonial chandeliers, and wide oak floorboards. Exhibits trace the history of American papermaking from Revolutionary times to the present. *Off Rte. 9, Dalton, tel. 413/684–2600. Admission free. Open June–mid-Oct., Mon.–Fri. 2–5.*

Shopping

Shopping Districts The only enclosed shopping mall in the region is the **Berkshire Mall,** on Route 8 east of Lanesboro. The mall consists of 65 shops and department stores.

Outlet Stores Along Route 7 just north of Lenox are two factory-outlet malls, **Lenox House Country Shops** and **Brushwood Farms.** The **Buggy Whip Factory** (Main St., Rte. 272, Southfield, tel. 413/229–3576) is a restored buggy whip factory housing about 50 outlet stores selling brand-name goods and wares from smaller manufacturers.

Art and Antiques There are hundreds of antiques stores throughout the Berkshires, but the greatest concentration is around Great Barrington, South Egremont, and Sheffield. For a list of storekeepers who belong to the **Berkshire County Antiques Dealers Association,** send a SASE to RD 1, Box 1, Sheffield 01257.

Great Barrington **Coffman's Country Antiques Market** (Rte. 7, Jennifer House Commons, tel. 413/528–9282) houses 50 quality antiques dealers on three floors, selling furniture, quilts, baskets, and silverware from the 16th century to the 1940s. **Corashire Antiques** (Rtes. 23 and 7 at Belcher Square, tel. 413/528–0014), a shop in a red barn, carries American country furniture and accessories, including the occasional rare Shaker piece. **Mullin-Jones Antiquities** (525 S. Main St., Rte. 7, tel. 413/528–4871) has 18th- and 19th-century country French antiques: armoires, buffets, tables, chairs, and gilded mirrors.

Housatonic **Le Petit Museé** (137 Front St., tel. 413/274–3838) is a gallery for small works of art. **Spazi** (3rd Floor, Barbien's Lumber Mill, Rte. 183, tel. 413/274–3805) focuses on contemporary painting, sculpture, and photography.

Lanesboro **Amber Springs Antiques** (29 S. Main St., Rte. 7, tel. 413/442–1237), in a shop behind a fine old white-clapboard house, shows an eclectic assortment of American furnishings from the 19th to mid-20th centuries. Tools, pottery, and country store items are the house specialties.

Lenox **UTE Stebich Gallery** (104 Main St., tel. 413/637–3566) specializes in international folk art and contemporary art. **Artuoso** (67 Church St., tel. 413/637–0668) has a fine collection of Israeli and Judaic art.

Sheffield **Bradford Galleries** (Rte. 7, tel. 413/229–6667) holds monthly auctions of furniture, paintings and prints, china, glass, silver, and Oriental rugs. A tag sale of household items is open daily. **Darr Antiques and Interiors** (S. Main St., Rte. 7, tel. 413/229–7773) displays elegant 18th- and 19th-century American, English, Continental, and Oriental furniture and accessories in impressive, formal room settings in a fine Colonial house. A new, second store houses another 1,600 square feet of antiques. **Dovetail Antiques** (Rte. 7, tel. 413/ 229–2628) shows American clocks, pottery, and country furniture in a small, friendly hop. **Good & Hutchinson Associates** (Rte. 7, tel. 413/229–8832) specializes in American, English, and Continental furniture, paintings, fine pottery, and china "for museums and antiquarians."

South Egremont **Red Barn Antiques** (Rte. 23, tel. 413/528–3230) has a wide selection of antique lamps and 19th-century American furniture, glass, and accessories. **The Splendid Peasant** (Rte. 23 and Old Sheffield Rd., tel. 413/528–5755) concentrates on 18th- and 19th-century American and European country-primitive furnishings, including painted chests, and a gallery of museum-quality American folk art from prehistoric times to the 20th century.

Southfield **Antiques at the Buggy Whip Factory** (Main St., Rte. 272, tel. 413/ 229–3576, provides space for around 50 dealers to show American country antiques including furniture, 19th-century fabrics, and dolls.

West Stockbridge **Sawyer Antiques** (Depot St., tel. 413/232–7062) offers Early American furniture and accessories in a large, spare, clapboard structure that was once a Shaker mill.

Sports and Outdoor Activities

Biking · The gently rolling Berkshire hills make for excellent cycling terrain. Mountain bike trails can be found at the Mt. Greylock State Reservation (tel. 413/499–4262). **Plaine's Cycling Center** (55 W. Housatonic St., Pittsfield, tel. 413/499–0294) and **Main Street Sports and Leisure** (102 Main St., Lenox, tel. 413/637–4407) rent mountain and road bikes, as well as provide maps and route suggestions.

Boating and Canoeing · The **Housatonic River** (the Native American name means "river beyond the mountains") flows south from Pittsfield between the Berkshire hills and the Taconic Range toward Connecticut. Suggested canoe trips in the Berkshires include Dalton–Lenox (19 miles), Lenox–Stockbridge (12 miles), Stockbridge–Great Barrington (13 miles) and, for the experts, Great Barrington–Falls Village (25 miles). Information about these and other trips can be found in *The AMC River Guide to Massachusetts, Rhode Island, and Connecticut* (AMC, 5 Joy St., Boston, 02198). Canoes, rowboats, and small motorboats can be rented from the **Onota Boat Livery** (455 Pecks Rd., Pittsfield, tel. 413/442–1724), which also provides dock space on Onota Lake, and **Quirk's Marine** (1249 North St., Rte. 7, Pittsfield, tel. 413/447–7512).

Fishing · The rivers, lakes, and streams of Berkshire County abound with fish—bass, pike, and perch, to name but a few. Stocked trout waters include the Hoosic River (south branch) near Cheshire; Green River, Great Barrington; Notch Brook and Hoosic River (north branch), North Adams; Goose Pond and Hop Brook, Lee; and Williams River, West Stockbridge. **Points North Outfitters** (Rte. 8, Adams, tel. 413/743–4030) organizes fly-fishing schools May through September at Jiminy Peak, which include instruction in knot tying, fly casting, and fishing in a trout pond. **Onota Boat Livery** (455 Pecks Rd., Pittsfield, tel. 413/442–1724) sells fishing tackle and live bait.

Golf · The following Berkshires golf clubs welcome guests: **Pontoosuc Lake Country Club** (18 holes; Kirkwood Dr., Pittsfield, tel. 413/445–4217), **Waconah Country Club** (18 holes; Orchard Rd., Dalton, tel. 413/684–1333), and **Waubeeka Golf Links** (18 holes; Rte. 7, Williamstown, tel. 413/458–5869).

Hiking · The **Appalachian Trail** goes right through Berkshire County and attracts many walkers. Hiking is encouraged in most state parks; **Mt. Greylock State Reservation** (*see* National and State Parks, *below*) has trail maps available for a wide variety of hikes at higher elevations, including a stretch of the Appalachian Trail. Many treks start from the parking lot at the summit of Mt. Greylock, where there's also accommodation May through October. Farther south, 3 miles north of Great Barrington, you can leave your car in a parking lot beside Route 7 and climb Squaw Peak on **Monument Mountain**. The 2.7-mile circular hike (a trail map is displayed in the parking lot) takes you up 900 feet, past glistening white quartzite cliffs, from where Native Americans are said to have leapt to their deaths to placate the gods. From the top there are excellent views of the surrounding mountains. For more information on trails and hiking, contact **Berkshire Region Headquarters** (740 South St., Pittsfield, 01202, tel. 413/442–8928).

Rafting · Rafting takes place at just one location in the Berkshires—along the Deerfield River at Charlemont, on the Mohawk Trail. One-day raft tours over 10 miles of class II–III rapids take place daily April through October. *Zoar Outdoor, Mohawk Trail, Charlemont 01339, tel. 413/339–4010.*

National and State Parks

There are 19 state parks and forests in the Berkshires. Those with camping include **Beartown State Forest** (Blue Hill Rd., Monterey, tel. 413/528–0904), **Clarksburg State Forest** (Middle Rd., Clarksburg, tel. 413/664–8345), **Mt. Greylock State Reservation** (Rockwell Rd., Lanesboro, tel. 413/499–4262/3), **October Mountain State Forest** (Woodland Rd., Lee, tel. 413/243–1778), **Otis State Forest** (Rte. 23, Otis, tel. 413/528–0904), **Pittsfield State Forest** (Cascade St., Pittsfield, tel. 413/442–8992), **Sandisfield State Forest** (West St., Sandisfield, tel. 413/258–4774), **Savoy Mountain State Forest** (Rte. 2, Florida; Rte. 116, Savoy, tel. 413/663–8469), **Tolland State Forest** (Rte. 8, Otis, tel. 413/269–6002), and **Windsor State Forest** (Windsor, tel. 413/442–8928).

Dining and Lodging

The **Lenox Chamber of Commerce** (tel. 413/637–3646 or 800/25–LENOX) and the **Great Barrington Chamber of Commerce** (tel. 413/528–4006) have lodging referral services. Additional accommodations selections will be found in the Bousquet, Brodie, Butternut, and Jiminy Peak sections of the Skiing New England chapter. Dress is casual and reservations are not needed unless otherwise noted.

Dalton
Lodging

Dalton House. This bed-and-breakfast has expanded over the years to include a sunny breakfast room with pine chairs and tables at the front of the 170-year-old house, and deluxe rooms in the carriage house. Guests share a split-level sitting room; the average-size bedrooms in the main house are cheerful, with floral-print drapes and wallpaper and white wicker chairs. The spacious carriage house rooms are more impressive, with exposed beams, period furnishings, and quilts. Ski packages including dinner are offered in season. *955 Main St., 01226, tel. 413/684–3854. 9 rooms, 2 suites, all with bath. Facilities: outdoor pool, lounge. Breakfast included. AE, MC, V. Moderate–Expensive.*

Great Barrington
Dining
★

Boiler Room Café. In a turn-of-the-century clapboard house, three comfortable dining rooms are painted in warm colors accented by arches with white moldings and whimsical wood sculptures. Owner Michèle Miller serves an eclectic, sophisticated menu that may include delicious, light New England seafood stew, mouthwatering grilled baby back ribs, or osso bucco Piedmontese. For starters there are outstanding fresh salads, tapas, and chèvre soufflè. *405 Stockbridge Rd., tel. 413/528–4280. Reservations advised. D, MC, V. No lunch. Closed Mon. and Tues. Expensive.*

20 Railroad St. The exposed brick and subdued lighting lend atmosphere to this bustling restaurant, which features a 28-foot mahogany bar taken from the Commodore Hotel in New York City in 1919. Small wood tables are packed together in the long, narrow room. Specialties include sausage pie, beef stew, burgers, and sandwiches. *20 Railroad St., tel. 413/528–9345. MC, V. Inexpensive.*

Lodging

Windflower Inn. A comfortable, casual atmosphere prevails at the family-run Windflower. Everything is homemade, and many vegetables and herbs come from the inn garden. The dining room is sunny, and in summer food is served on the screened porch. Bedrooms of varying sizes—mostly spacious—have four-poster beds and are filled with antiques. Several rooms contain working fireplaces: The most impressive has a stone surround that covers most of the wall. *Rte. 23 (Egremont Star Rte., Box 25), 01230, tel. 413/528–2720 or*

800/992–1993. 13 rooms with bath. Facilities: restaurant, outdoor pool, gardens. Full breakfast included; MAP available. No credit cards. Very Expensive.

Hancock
Dining

Drummond's Restaurant. At the Jiminy Peak ski resort, this restaurant is designed like a ski lodge, with cathedral ceilings, lots of wood, and a stone chimney with wood-burning stove. Tables at the back overlook the slopes, which are lit for night skiing in season. Entrées include fresh salmon, roast duck, and pasta primavera. *Corey Rd., tel. 413/738–5500. Reservations advised. AE, D, DC, MC, V. Moderate.*

The Springs. This restaurant sits in the shadow of Brodie Mountain and its ski resort. A fireplace in the lobby, exposed-brick walls, and wood ceiling (from which hangs the biggest chandelier in the Berkshires) make for a country-lodge atmosphere. The menu offers lobster blended with mushrooms in cream sauce, duckling flambé in cherry sauce, steak Diane, and veal dishes. *Rte. 7, New Ashford, tel. 413/458–3465. AE, D, DC, MC, V. Moderate.*

Lee
Dining

Cork 'n Hearth. A large stone fireplace separates the long dining room into two: On one side, wood beams show off all kinds of brassware; on the other, they are hung with bundles of dried herbs. Picture windows look onto Laurel Lake, which practically laps against the side of the building. The menu is traditional, offering steak, seafood, chicken Kiev, and veal cordon bleu. *Rte. 20, tel. 413/243–0535. Reservations advised. AE, MC, V. No lunch. Closed Mon. Expensive.*

Lodging

The Pilgrim Motel. This motel is well furnished with gleaming reproduction antiques and color-coordinated drapes, but the rates are very high during the Tanglewood season. The location in the very center of Lee is busy but convenient. *127 Housatonic St., 01238, tel. 413/243–1328. 24 rooms with bath. Facilities: outdoor pool, laundry, Jacuzzi. AE, DC, MC, V. Moderate (Very Expensive in Tanglewood season).*

Oak n' Spruce Resort. Rooms in the main lodge are like high-quality motel rooms; large rooms in the building next door have modern furniture, kitchen units, and sliding doors onto the spacious grounds surrounding this former farm. The lodge lounge is a converted cow barn built around the original brick silo. *Meadow St. (Box 237), South Lee 01260, tel. 413/243–3500 or 800/424–3003. 17 rooms, 26 suites, 107 condos. Facilities: restaurant, lounge, live entertainment, indoor and outdoor pool, Jacuzzi, sauna, health club, cross-country ski trails, shuffleboard, basketball, tennis, badminton, horseshoes, volleyball, hiking trails. AE, MC, V. Inexpensive–Moderate.*

The Morgan House. Most guest rooms in this inn, which dates to 1817, are small, but the rates reflect that. Some are so narrow they resemble servants' quarters, with their scrubbed boards and brightly painted wood furniture; others have four-poster beds, stenciled walls, and well-worn antiques. The lobby is papered with the pages from old guest registers; among the signatures are those of George Bernard Shaw and Ulysses S. Grant. Mrs. Nat King Cole owned the inn until 1981. *31 Main St., 01238, tel. 413/243–0181. 14 rooms, 2 with bath. Facilities: 3 dining rooms, bar. Continental breakfast included. AE, D, DC, MC, V. Inexpensive (Moderate–Expensive in Tanglewood season).*

Lenox
Dining

Church St. Cafe. A well-established, popular Lenox restaurant, the stylish café serves excellent food at reasonable prices. The walls are covered with original art, tables are surrounded by ficus trees, and classical music plays in the background. Specialties include roast duck with thyme and Madeira sauce, rack of pork with wild mush-rooms, and crab cakes. *69 Church St., tel. 413/637–2745. MC, V. Closed Nov.–Apr. and Sun.–Mon. Moderate.*

Sophia's Restaurant and Pizza. This unpretentious establishment serves up pizza, generous Greek salads, pasta dishes, and grinders (the Massachusetts equivalent of a submarine sandwich). Seating is in booths with imitation-leather seats. *Rtes. 7/20, tel. 413/499–1101. AE, MC, V. Closed Mon. Inexpensive.*

Dining and Lodging **Gateways Inn.** This formal and elegant mansion was built as a sum-mer home in 1912 by Harley Proctor of Proctor and Gamble. From the large entrance hall, a grand open staircase lit by a skylight leads to the second-floor guest rooms. The huge Fiedler Suite (Tangle-wood conductor Arthur Fiedler stayed here and gave his name to it) has two working fireplaces and a dressing room. All rooms have light, period wallpapers, antiques, and Oriental rugs. Four dining rooms are hung with chandeliers and tapestries; working fireplaces soften the otherwise formal tone. The Rockwell Room is small and sunny. Continental and American cuisine includes veal, pheasant, salmon, and rack of lamb. *71 Walker St., 01240, tel. 413/637–2532. 8 rooms. Facilities: restaurant (reservations advised; closed Sun., Nov.–May). Continental breakfast included. AE, D, DC, MC, V. Very Expensive.*

Lodging **Blantyre.** The competition in Lenox is tough, but Blantyre has to be
★ the best inn in town. If its unique, castlelike Tudor architecture, the sheer size of its public rooms, and its 85 acres of beautifully main-tained grounds are not impressive enough, guest rooms in the main house are also fabulous: huge and lavishly decorated, with hand-carved four-poster beds, overstuffed chaise longues, chintz chairs, boudoirs, walk-in closets, and Victorian bathrooms. Although rooms in the carriage house and the cottages are well appointed, they can't compete with the formal grandeur of the main house. The stylishly prepared, five-course evening meal is superb. *Off Rte. 7, 01240, tel. 413/637–3556 or 413/298–3806. 13 rooms with bath, 10 suites. Facilities: restaurant, lounge, outdoor pool, Jacuzzi, sauna, tennis, croquet, working fireplaces. Continental breakfast in-cluded. AE, DC, MC, V. Very Expensive.*

Wheatleigh. One of the most expensive Berkshire inns, Wheatleigh was constructed in 1893 as a wedding present for a New York heiress who married a Spanish count. Based on a 16th-century Florentine palace, it's an awe-inspiring place, with a breathtaking entrance hall and guest rooms that range from medium-size to enormous. They have elegant furnishings, high ceilings, and some working fire-places with grand marble surrounds. The inn has an excellent, ex-pensive restaurant. *Hawthorne Rd., 02140, tel. 413/637–0610 or 800/321–0610, fax 413/637–4507. 17 rooms with bath. Facilities: 2 dining rooms, lounge, 9 rooms with fireplaces, outdoor pool, tennis, meeting rooms. AE, D, DC, MC, V. Very Expensive.*

Rookwood Inn. This "painted lady" was built in 1885 as a summer cottage for a wealthy New York family. Guest rooms are generally roomy and some have working fireplaces; the Victorian era is per-fectly re-created with period wallpapers, matching linen, and En-glish and American antiques. Some rooms have balconies. The elegant lounge has reading material, an open fire, and a screened porch with wicker furniture. The hosts are rather reserved and breakfast a bit meager, but the inn is on a quiet street, two minutes' walk from the center of Lenox. *19 Old Stockbridge Rd. (Box 1717), 01240, tel. 413/637–9750. 18 rooms. Facilities: breakfast room, lounge. Buffet breakfast and afternoon tea included. AE. Ex-pensive–Very Expensive.*

★ **Whistler's Inn.** The antiques decorating the parlor of this English Tudor mansion are ornate with a touch of the exotic—some are in the Louis XVI style, others the innkeepers brought back from various travels abroad. Bedrooms are decorated with designer drapes and bedspreads. Some rooms have working fireplaces, and most have great views across the valley. *5 Greenwood St., 01240, tel. 413/637-0975. 12 rooms with bath. Facilities: lounge, library, badminton, croquet, 7 acres of gardens. Full breakfast included. AE, MC, V. Expensive–Very Expensive.*

Apple Tree Inn. Perched on a hillside across the street from Tanglewood's main gate, the Apple Tree Inn is perfect for summer concertgoers. You don't even need a ticket—the music wafts right across the front lawn! The parlor contains a grand piano, velvet couches, hanging plants, and German nutcracker decorations. Guest rooms have four-poster or brass beds, Victorian washstands, and lots of wicker; some rooms have working fireplaces. Avoid Room No. 5 because it's hot, noisy, and over the kitchen. The 20 rooms in the lodge next door have more modern, motel-style furnishings. *224 West St., 01240, tel. 413/637-1477. 29 rooms, 27 with bath; 2 suites. Facilities: restaurant, bar, outdoor pool, gardens, fireplaces. AE, D, DC, MC, V. Closed Jan.–Apr. Expensive.*

The Candlelight Inn. Attractive, spacious bedrooms have floral-print wallpapers and antiques; those on the top floor are especially charming, with sloping ceilings and skylights. This elegant inn is right in the middle of Lenox village and has a popular Continental restaurant. *53 Walker St., 01240, tel. 413/637-1555. 8 rooms. Facilities: 4 dining rooms, bar. Continental breakfast included. AE, MC, V. Expensive (Very Expensive in Tanglewood season).*

The Garden Gables. Set on 5 acres of wooded grounds and just a two-minute walk from the center of Lenox, this 250-year-old "summer cottage" has been an inn since 1947. The inn's 14 rooms come in a wide variety of shapes, sizes, and colors; some have brass beds, others have pencil four-posters. There are sloping ceilings, working fireplaces, whirlpool baths, and woodland views; one room has a deck and its own entrance close to the 72-foot outdoor swimming pool. Breakfast is served buffet-style in the big, airy dining room with wide-board floors, and guests have access to the kitchen, fridge, and microwave oven. The long, narrow living room has a piano, antique writing desks, and painted wooden beams. *141 Main St., Box 52, 01240, tel. 413/637-0193. 14 rooms. Facilities: dining room, pool. Full breakfast included. D, MC, V. Moderate–Expensive (Very Expensive in Tanglewood season).*

Eastover. An antidote to the posh atmosphere prevailing in most of Lenox, this resort was opened by an ex–circus roustabout, and the tradition of noisy fun and informality continues with gusto. Guest rooms are functional and vary from dormitory to motel-style; although the period wallpapers are stylish, some rooms with four or more beds resemble hospital wards with their metal rails and white bedspreads. Dining rooms are vast and very noisy, but period decor and furnishings temper the absolute informality to some extent. The grounds are huge, and wandered by buffalo; facilities are extensive. *East St. (off Rte. 7), Box 2160, 01240, tel. 413/637-0625. 195 rooms, 120 with bath. Facilities: tennis, indoor and outdoor pools, golf range, volleyball, cross-country and downhill skiing, exercise room, sauna, badminton, horseback riding. Rates are all inclusive. AE, D, DC, MC, V. Closed weekdays, Labor Day–July. Moderate.*

Pittsfield
Dining

Dakota. Moose and elk heads watch over diners at this large restaurant decorated like a rustic hunting lodge. A canoe swings overhead, and Native American artifacts hang on the walls. A broiler stocked with Texan mesquite wood is used for specialties, which include swordfish steaks, shrimp, sirloin, and grilled chicken. *Rtes. 7 and 20, tel. 413/499–7900. AE, DC, MC, V. No lunch Mon.–Sat. Moderate.*

Dining and Lodging
Berkshire Hilton Inn. This is a typically comfortable, sophisticated Hilton with a spacious hall featuring wingback chairs, glass, and brass. Guest rooms have new reproductions and floral-print drapes, and upgraded rooms on the two top floors have the best views over the town and mountains. The large swimming pool, beneath a glass dome, is surrounded by two tiers of rooms, which are a great option for families. The small, classy restaurant on the second floor is decorated in low-key greens and browns, with seating at semicircular booths. The menu offers steak, chicken, and seafood dishes, with a delicious white-chocolate chimichanga for dessert. *Berkshire Common, South St., 01201, tel. 413/499–2000 or 800/445–8667. 175 rooms. Facilities: restaurant (reservations advised), lounge, bar, live entertainment, indoor pool, sauna, Jacuzzi, meeting rooms. AE, DC, MC, V. Hotel: Moderate–Expensive. Restaurant: Expensive.*

Sheffield Dining
Stagecoach Hill Inn. Constructed in the early 1800s as a stagecoach stop, the restaurant offers a character inspired by England—there are numerous pictures of the British royal family and several hunting scenes, as well as steak and kidney pie and British ale on tap. Other menu items include pasta dishes, steak au poivre, and chicken al forno. *Rte. 41, tel. 413/229–8585. AE, DC, MC, V. Closed Tues., Wed., and Nov.–May. Expensive.*

Lodging
Ivanhoe Country House. The Appalachian Trail runs right across the property of this bed-and-breakfast. The house was originally built in 1780, but various wings were added later. The antiques-furnished guest rooms are generally spacious; several have private porches or balconies, and all have excellent country views. The large sitting room has antique desks, a piano, and comfortable couches. *Undermountain Rd., Rte. 41, 01257, tel. 413/229–2143. 9 rooms, 1 suite with kitchen. Facilities: lounge, outdoor pool, refrigerators. Continental breakfast included. No credit cards. Expensive.*

South Egremont Dining and Lodging
The Egremont Inn. The public rooms in this 1780 inn are enormous—the main lounge, with its vast open fireplace and coffee table made from an old door, is worth a visit in itself. New renovations include a wraparound porch with white wicker chairs and upgraded bedrooms with new linens, some new carpets, and climate control heaters. Although the bedrooms are now more comfortable, they're still on the small side and furnishings are plain. Some have four-poster beds and clawfoot baths. There are three dining rooms; the largest has windows around two sides, uneven, polished pine floors, and a huge brick fireplace. Specialties include chicken breast stuffed with crabmeat in lemon-thyme yogurt cream sauce, and salmon with fennel seed and Pernod butter. *Old Sheffield Rd. (Box 418), 01258, tel. 413/528–2111. 22 rooms with bath. Facilities: restaurant (reservations required weekends in season), bar, outdoor pool, tennis. Continental breakfast included. AE, MC, V. Inn: Expensive. Restaurant: Moderate–Expensive.*

Stockbridge Dining
Hoplands. Located about a mile north of Stockbridge center, this restaurant was bought in late 1992 by a friendly family from Great Barrington. Diners can eat downstairs around the bar or upstairs in a simply furnished room with polished wood chairs and tables and thick carpeting. The menu features scallops, roast chicken, and pork

chops. *Rte. 102, tel. 413/243-4414. AE, MC, V. Closed Mon. and, Oct.-May., Tues. Moderate.*

Dining and Lodging **The Red Lion Inn.** An inn since 1773, and rebuilt after a fire in 1896, the Red Lion is now a massive place, with guest rooms situated both in the main building and in several annexes on the property. It's a well-known landmark and gets plenty of tour-bus traffic—it *is* old, and many of the guest rooms are small. In general, the annex houses are more appealing. Rooms are individually decorated with floral-print wallpapers and country curtains (from the mail-order store Country Curtains, owned by the innkeepers and operated out of the inn). All are furnished with antiques and hung with Rockwell prints; some have Oriental rugs. The dining rooms at this distinguished inn are filled with antiques, and tables are set with pewter plates. New England specialties include oyster pie; broiled scallops prepared with sherry, lemon, and paprika; and steamed or stuffed lobster. *Main St., 02162, tel. 413/298-5545. 108 rooms, 75 with bath, 10 suites. Facilities: restaurant (reservations advised; jacket and tie required), bar, outdoor pool, exercise room, massage, meeting rooms. AE, D, DC, MC, V. Expensive (Very Expensive in Tanglewood season).*

Lodging **The Golden Goose.** This friendly, informal place 5 miles south of Lee is cluttered with antiques, bric-a-brac, and dozens of geese in various shapes and sizes (many were donated by guests). Bedrooms are Victorian in style; with quilts and stenciled walls. Guests' names are chalked up on the little welcome board on each door. *Main Rd. (Box 336), Tyringham 01264, tel. 413/243-3008. 6 rooms, 4 with bath. Facilities: dining room, 2 sitting rooms. Continental breakfast included. AE, D, MC, V. Moderate-Expensive.*

★ **Merrell Tavern Inn.** This is a genuine old New England inn, built as a stagecoach stopover around 1792. Despite its age, it has some good-size bedrooms, several with working fireplaces. In 1992 innkeepers Charles and Faith Reynolds upgraded this already excellent inn, which has polished wide-board floors, painted plaster walls, and wood antiques. They added new rugs, new linens, and vanities, as well as curtains and country-style framed prints, but thankfully they retained the authentic, unfussy style that makes this inn stand out among its peers. The breakfast room has an open fireplace and contains the only complete "birdcage" Colonial bar in America. *Rte. 102, South Lee 01260, tel. 413/243-1794 or 800/243-1794. 10 rooms with bath. Facilities: breakfast room, parlor, gardens. Full breakfast included. AE, MC, V. Moderate-Expensive.*

West Stockbridge Dining **Shaker Mill Tavern.** The only concession to Shakers here is a row of Shaker pegs on the wall, but the restaurant is located just down the street from the Shaker mill, hence its name. In summer dining can be outside on the "deck café"; otherwise it's in the large modern dining room with wood floors and ceilings and lots of plants. American dishes include burgers, fried chicken, buffalo wings, pizza, and pasta dishes. *Rte. 102, tel. 413/232-8565. AE, MC, V. Inexpensive-Moderate.*

Dining and Lodging **The Williamsville Inn.** A couple of miles south of West Stockbridge, this inn—bought by a mother-and-daughter team in 1990—re-creates the late 1700s, when it was built. Guest rooms have wide-board floors, embroidered chairs, and four-poster or canopy beds; several have contemporary furnishings and working fireplaces, and four rooms in the converted barn have wood-burning stoves. The main dining room is decorated with gray Colonial-style wallpaper and has a fireplace of unpolished, locally hewn marble. Lamps burn on the table in the evening, and the windows look onto the surrounding woodlands. Entrées include veal Normandy, salmon in puff pastry, and rack of lamb. *Rte. 41, Williamsville 01266, tel. 413/274-6118. 12 rooms with bath, 1 suite, 2 cottages. Facilities: restaurant (reservations advised), bar, croquet, outdoor pool, tennis, horseshoes, badminton, volleyball. Continental breakfast included. MC, V. Very Expensive.*

Williamstown
Dining

Le Jardin. Set on a hillock above the road just west of Williamstown, this French restaurant has the feel of an inn (there are guest rooms on the upper floor). The two dining rooms are paneled and candlelit, and a fire burns in the hall in season. The menu offers snails in garlic butter, oysters baked with spinach and Pernod, sole florentine, filet mignon, and rack of lamb. *777 Cold Spring Rd. (Rte. 7), tel. 413/ 458-8032. Reservations advised. MC, V. Closed Tues. Expensive.*

Four Acres. On the commercial strip of Route 2 just east of Williamstown, this pleasant restaurant has two dining rooms: One is casual, decorated with street signs, paneling, and mirrors; the other is more formal, with collegiate insignia and modern paintings on the walls. American and Continental cuisine includes sautéed calf's liver glazed in applejack; veal cutlet sautéed in butter and topped with a Newburg of lobster and asparagus; and pork tenderloin with cognac and walnut sauce. *Rte. 2, tel. 413/458-5436. Reservations advised. AE, MC, V. Closed Sun. Moderate.*

Savories. Convenient to the center of Williamstown, this restaurant has several dining rooms in a large old house with exposed beams, fireplaces, painted plaster walls, and vaulted ceilings. The menu includes grilled Norwegian salmon, smoked breast of duck, pasta, and beef mignon. *123 Water St., tel. 413/458-2175. Reservations advised. AE, MC, V. Closed Mon. Moderate.*

Lodging

The Orchards. After seeing the pale-orange stucco exterior, and perhaps wondering about the location on a commercial strip of Route 2 east of town, it's a pleasant surprise to enter the quiet, tasteful interior of this small luxury hotel built in 1985. Church pews and a heavy pulpit adorn the corridors, the cozy lounge has wall cases of silverware and an open fireplace, and most guest rooms are furnished with elegant four-poster beds, antiques, and reproductions. Ask for a room with a view of the hills or the small modern courtyard and its lily pond. *Main St. (Rte. 2), 01267, tel. 413/458-9611. 49 rooms. Facilities: restaurant, lounge, tavern, outdoor pool, sauna, Jacuzzi. AE, DC, MC, V. Very Expensive.*

Williams Inn. The spacious guest rooms in this new inn have good-quality, modern furnishings, with floral-print drapes and bedspreads. The lounge has an open fireplace and is comfortable—the atmosphere is collegiate. The inn allows pets for a $5 fee; children under 14 stay free in their parents' room. *On-the-Green at Williams College, 01267, tel. 413/458-9371. 103 rooms. Facilities: dining room, lounge, coffee shop, live entertainment (Fri. and Sat. nights), indoor pool, sauna, Jacuzzi. AE, D, DC, MC, V. Very Expensive.*

Berkshire Hills Motel. This excellent motel is housed in a two-story brick-and-clapboard building about 3 miles south of Williamstown. All guest rooms are furnished in Colonial style—each with a rocking chair and reproduction furniture. The lounge, complete with a teddy-bear collection, has an open fireplace and a piano. Outside, the pool is located across a brook amid 2½ acres of woodland and landscaped garden. *Rte. 7, 01267, tel. 413/458-3950. 20 rooms with bath. Facilities: lounge, outdoor pool. Continental breakfast included. AE, MC, V. Moderate.*

River Bend Farm. Listed on the National Historic Register, the farm, constructed in 1770 by one of the founders of Williamstown,

WATCH WHERE YOU'RE GOING!

Get in gear and explore the wild world of sports adventure. Fodor's® *Interactive Sports and Adventure Vacations*™ is a jam-packed multimedia CD-ROM devoted solely to adventure sports, travel and leisure.

There's mountain biking, kayaking, skiing, 4-wheel drive tours, cattle drives, sports fantasy camps - the kinds of vacations families and solo adventurists will remember forever. *Action footage, interactive maps, photos, information,* and *direct contacts* are included, plus a *travel planner* that recommends trips based on your personal preferences.

For a far-from-ordinary vacation, grab the phone and call
1-800-262-7668.

A Multimedia CD-ROM product from

CREATIVE MULTIMEDIA

Fodor's

All the Best Trips Start with Fodor's

COMPASS AMERICAN GUIDES

Titles in the series: Arizona, Canada, Chicago, Colorado, Hawai'i, Hollywood, Las Vegas, Maine, Manhattan, New Mexico, New Orleans, Oregon, San Francisco, South Carolina, South Dakota, Utah, Virginia, Wisconsin, Wyoming.

"A literary, historical, and near-sensory excursion."—*Denver Post*

"Tackles the 'why' of travel...as well as the nitty-gritty details."—*Travel Weekly*

FODOR'S BED & BREAKFASTS AND COUNTRY INN GUIDES

Titles in the series: California, Canada, England & Wales, Mid-Atlantic, New England, The Pacific Northwest, The South, The Upper Great Lakes Region.

"In addition to information on each establishment, the books add notes on things to see and do in the vicinity."
— *San Diego Union-Tribune*

THE BERKELEY GUIDES

Titles in the series: California, Central America, Eastern Europe, Europe, France, Germany, Great Britain & Ireland, Italy, London, Mexico, The Pacific Northwest & Alaska, Paris, San Francisco.

The best choice for budget travelers, from the Associated Students at the University of California at Berkeley.

"Berkeley's scribes put the funk back in travel." — *Time*

"Fresh, funny and funky as well as useful." — *The Boston Globe*

EXPLORING GUIDES

Titles in the series: Australia, Britain, California, Caribbean, Florida, France, Germany, Ireland, Italy, London, New York City, Paris, Rome, Singapore & Malaysia, Spain, Thailand.

"Authoritatively written and superbly presented, they make worthy reading before, during or after a trip."
— *The Philadelphia Inquirer*

"A handsome new series of guides, complete with lots of color photos, geared to the independent traveler."
— *The Boston Globe*

Visit your local bookstore, or call 24 hours a day 1-800-533-6478
Fodor's The name that means smart travel.

has been restored with complete authenticity by old house–enthusiasts David and Judy Loomis. Guests enter through a kitchen with an open range stove and bake oven hung with dried herbs. Upstairs some bedrooms have wide-plank walls, curtains of unbleached muslin, and four-poster beds with canopies or rope beds with feather mattresses. Some rooms have nonworking brick fireplaces, and all are sprinkled with antique pieces—chamberpots, washstands, wingback chairs, and spinning wheels. For visitors in search of another era, River Bend Farm is the perfect spot. *643 Simonds Rd., 01267, tel. 413/458–5504. 5 rooms without bath. Facilities: kitchen, lounge. Continental breakfast included. No credit cards. Closed Nov.–Apr. Moderate.*

The Arts

Tickets should be purchased in advance through individual offices, especially for weekend performances.

Listings are published weekly in the *Williamstown Advocate;* major concert listings are published Thursday in the *Boston Globe.* The quarterly *Berkshire Magazine* contains "The Berkshire Guide," a comprehensive listing of local events ranging from theater to sports.

Dance The **Berkshire Ballet** (Koussevitzky Arts Center, Berkshire Community College, West St., Pittsfield, tel. 413/445–5382) performs classical and contemporary works year-round. **Jacob's Pillow Dance Festival,** the oldest in the nation, mounts a 10-week summer program every year. Performers vary from well-known classical ballet companies to Native American dance groups and contemporary choreographers. Before the main events, free showings of works-in-progress are staged outdoors. Visitors can picnic on the grounds or eat at the Pillow Café. *Rte. 20, Becket (mailing address: Box 287, Lee, 01238), tel. 413/243–0745. Open June–Sept.*

Music The best-known music festival in New England is the **Tanglewood** concert series near Lenox from June through September. The main shed seats 6,000; the Chamber Music Hall holds 300 for smaller concerts. *Lenox, tel. 617/266–1492 Sept.–May; 413/637–1940 June–Aug. Tickets $10–$50.*

The **Berkshire Performing Arts Center** (40 Kemble St., Lenox, tel. 413/637–4088), the newest arts center in the county, attracts top-name artists in jazz, folk, rock, and blues.

Opera The **Berkshire Opera Company** (17 Main St., Box 598, Lee, tel. 413/243–1343) performs two operas in English from the Baroque repertoire during July and August at the Cranwell Opera House in Lenox.

Theater The **Berkshire Theatre Festival** stages nightly performances in summer at the century-old theater in Stockbridge. A series of children's plays, usually written by local schoolchildren, are performed weekends during the day. *Box 797 (Rte. 102), Stockbridge, tel. 413/298–5576 or 413/298–5536.*

The **Williamstown Theatre Festival** presents well-known theatrical works on the Main Stage, and contemporary works on the Other Stage. *Adams Memorial Theatre, Williams College Campus, tel. 413/597–3400. July–Aug.*

Shakespeare and Company (Plunkett St., Lenox, tel. 413/637–3353) performs Shakespeare and Edith Wharton's works throughout the summer at The Mount. **Berkshire Public Theatre** (30 Union St.,

Pittsfield, tel. 413/445–4634), the county's only year-round repertory company, performs a variety of modern and traditional pieces.

Nightlife

The emphasis in the Berkshires is definitely on classical entertainment. However, the most popular local nightspot is **The Lion's Den**
(tel. 413/298–5545) downstairs at the Red Lion Inn in Stockbridge,
with nightly folk music and some contemporary local bands every
evening throughout the year. **Coasters** (Rte. 8, Cheshire Rd.,
Lanesboro, tel. 413/499–3993) offers dancing Friday and Saturday
nights, and **Jay's** (1220 North St., Pittsfield, tel. 413/442–0767) has
live bands on Saturday and Sunday, and DJs Tuesday through Friday.

6 Vermont

by Mary H. Frakes, with an introduction by William G. Scheller

Updated by Tara Hamilton

Everywhere you look around Vermont, the evidence is clear: This is not the state it was 25 years ago.

That may be true for the rest of New England as well, but the contrasts between the present and recent past seem all the more sharply drawn in the Green Mountain State, if only because an aura of timelessness has always been at the heart of the Vermont image. Vermont was where all the quirks and virtues outsiders associate with up-country New England were supposed to reside. It was where the Yankees were Yankee-est and where there were more cows than people.

Not that you should be alarmed, if you haven't been here in a while; Vermont hasn't become southern California, or even, for that matter, southern New Hampshire. This is still the most rural state in the Union (meaning that it has the smallest percentage of citizens living in statistically defined metropolitan areas), even if there are, finally, more people than cows. It's still a place where cars occasionally have to stop while a dairyman walks his cows across a secondary road; and up in Essex County, in what George Aiken dubbed the Northeast Kingdom, there are townships with zero population. And the kind of scrupulous, straightforward, plainspoken politics practiced by Governor (later Senator) Aiken for 50 years has not become outmoded in a state that still turns out on town-meeting day.

How has Vermont changed? In strictly physical terms, the most obvious transformations have taken place in and around the two major cities, Burlington and Rutland, and near the larger ski resorts, such as Stowe, Killington, Stratton, and Mt. Snow. Burlington's Church Street, once a paradigm of all the sleepy redbrick shopping thoroughfares in northern New England, is now a pedestrian mall complete with chic bistros; outside the city, suburban development has supplanted dairy farms in towns where someone's trip to Burlington might once have been an item in a weekly newspaper. As for the ski areas, it's no longer enough simply to boast the latest in chairlift technology. Stratton has an entire "Austrian Village" of restaurants and shops, while a hillside adjacent to Bromley's slopes has sprouted instant replica Victorians for the second-home market. The town of Manchester, convenient to both resorts, is awash in designer-fashion discount outlets.

But the real metamorphosis in the Green Mountains has to do more with style, with the personality of the place, than with the mere substance of development. The past couple of decades have seen a tremendous influx of outsiders—not just skiers and "leaf peekers," but people who've come to stay year-round—and many of them are determined either to freshen the local scene with their own idiosyncrasies or to make Vermont even more like Vermont than they found it. On the one hand, this translates into the fact that one of the biggest draws to the tiny town of Glover each summer is an outdoor pageant that promotes leftist political and social causes; on the other, it means that sheep farming has been reintroduced into the state, largely to provide a high-quality product for the hand-weaving industry.

This ties in with another local phenomenon, one best described as Made in Vermont. Once upon a time, maple syrup and sharp cheddar cheese were the products that carried Vermont's name to the world. The market niche that they created has since been widened by Vermonters—a great many of them refugees from more hectic arenas of commerce in places like Massachusetts and New York—offering a dizzying variety of goods with the ineffable cachet of Vermont man-

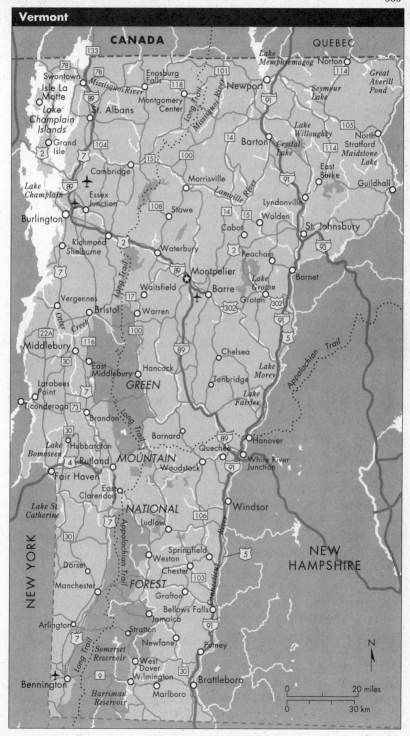

Vermont

ufacture. There are Vermont wood toys, Vermont apple wines, Vermont chocolates, even Vermont gin. All of it is marketed with the tacit suggestion that it was made by Yankee elves in a shed out back on a bright autumn morning.

The most successful Made in Vermont product is the renowned Ben & Jerry's ice cream. Neither Ben nor Jerry comes from old Green Mountain stock, but their product has benefited immensely from the magical reputation of the place where it is made. Along the way, the company (which started in Burlington under the most modest circumstances more than 15 years ago) has become the largest single purchaser of Vermont's still considerable dairy output. Proof that the modern and the traditional—wearing a red-plaid cap and a Johnson Woolen Mills hunting jacket—can still get along very nicely in Vermont.

Essential Information

Visitor Information

Vermont Travel Division (134 State St., Montpelier 05602, tel. 802/828–3236; open weekdays 7:45–4:30). **Vermont Chamber of Commerce** (Box 37, Montpelier 05601, tel. 802/223–3443; open weekdays 9–5).

Information centers are on the Massachusetts border at I–91, the New Hampshire border at I–89, the New York border at Route 4A, and the Canadian border at I–89.

Emergencies Vermont's **Medical Health Care Information Center** (tel. 802/864–0454) and **Telecommunications Device for the Deaf** (TDD) (802/253–0191) have 24-hour hotlines.

Weather Call 802/862–2475.

Tour Groups

General-Interest Tours **New England Vacation Tours** (Box 560, Rte. 100, West Dover 05356, tel. 802/464–2076 or 800/742–7669) specializes in air/motorcoach packages that take in Boston and the New England countryside.

Special-Interest Tours
Biking Vermont is great bicycle-touring country, and a number of companies offer weekend tours and weeklong trips that range throughout the state. Most chambers of commerce have brochures highlighting good cycling routes in their area, and many bookstores sell *25 Bicycle Tours in Vermont* by John Freidin, the founder of **Vermont Bicycle Touring** (Box 711, Bristol 05443, tel. 802/453–4811), the first bike tour operator in the United States and one of the most respected. It operates numerous tours throughout the state.

Canoeing **Umiak Outdoor Outfitters** (Gale Farm Center, 1880 Mountain Rd., Stowe 05672, tel. 802/253–2317) has shuttles to nearby rivers for day excursions as well as customized overnight trips. **Vermont Canoe Trippers/Battenkill Canoe, Ltd.** (Box 65, Arlington 05250, tel. 802/362–2800) organizes canoe tours.

Country Inns **Country Inns Along the Trail** (Churchill House Inn, RD 3, Box VTG, Brandon 05733, tel. 802/247–3300) organizes self-guided skiing, cycling, and inn-to-inn hiking tours, as well as guided treks.

Educational **Vermont Off Beat** (Box 4366, South Burlington 05406, tel. 802/863–2535) has an extraordinary lineup of special-interest workshops. These weekend-long getaways can be on anything from fly-fishing (in Waitsfield) to bird-watching (in Shoreham) to gathering Vermont mushrooms (in Waitsfield).

Hiking **North Wind Touring** (Box 46, Waitsfield 05673, tel. 802/496–5771) offers guided walking tours through Vermont's countryside. **Vermont Hiking Holidays** (Box 750, Bristol 05443, tel. 802/453–4816) leads guided walks from May through October, with lodging in country inns.

Horseback **Kedron Valley Stables** (Box 368, South Woodstock 05071, tel. 802/
Riding 457–1480) has one- to six-day riding tours with lodging in country inns.

Arriving and Departing

By Plane **Burlington International Airport** (tel. 802/863–2874) has scheduled daily flights on Continental, Delta, Northwest, United, and USAir. West of Bennington and convenient to southern Vermont, **Albany–Schenectady County Airport** in New York State is served by 10 major U.S. carriers.

By Car Interstate–91, which stretches from Connecticut and Massachusetts in the south to Québec (Hwy. 55) in the north, reaches most points along Vermont's eastern border. I–89, from New Hampshire to the east and Québec (Hwy. 133) to the north, crosses central Vermont from White River Junction to Burlington. Southwestern Vermont can be reached by Route 7 from Massachusetts and Route 4 from New York.

By Train Amtrak's (tel. 800/872–7245) *Montrealer* links Washington D.C., New York City, and Montréal, stopping at Brattleboro, Bellows Falls, Claremont, White River Junction, Montpelier, Waterbury, Essex Junction, and St. Albans. The *Adirondack*, which runs from New York City to Montréal, serves Albany, Ft. Edward (near Glens Falls), Ft. Ticonderoga, and Plattsburgh, allowing relatively convenient access to western Vermont.

By Bus **Vermont Transit** (tel. 802/864–6811, 800/451–3292, or, in VT, 800/642–3133) connects Bennington, Brattleboro, Burlington, Rutland, and other Vermont cities and towns with Boston, Springfield, Albany, New York, Montréal, and cities in New Hampshire. **Bonanza** (tel. 800/556–3815) connects New York City with Bennington.

Getting Around Vermont

By Plane Aircraft charters are available at Burlington International Airport from **Montair** (tel. 802/862–2246), **Mansfield Heliflight** (tel. 802/864–3954), **Northern Airways** (tel. 802/658–2204), and **Valley Air Services** (tel. 802/863–3626).

Southern Vermont Helicopter (West Brattleboro, tel. 802/257–4354) provides helicopter transportation throughout New England.

By Car The official speed limit in Vermont is 50 mph, unless otherwise posted; on most highways it's 65 mph. You can get a state map, which has mileage charts and enlarged maps of major downtown areas, free from the Vermont Travel Division. *The Vermont Atlas and Gazetteer*, sold in many bookstores, shows nearly every road in the state and is great for driving on the back roads.

Dining

Vermont restaurants have not escaped common efforts in the northeast to adapt traditional New England fare to the ways of nouvelle cuisine. The New England Culinary Institute, based in Montpelier, has trained a number of Vermont chefs who have now turned their attention to such native New England foods as fiddlehead ferns (available only for a short time in the spring); maple syrup (Vermont is the largest U.S. producer); dairy products, especially cheese; native fruits and berries that are often transformed into jams and jellies; "new Vermont" products such as salsa and salad dressings; and venison, quail, pheasant, and other game.

Your chances of finding a table for dinner vary dramatically with the season: Many restaurants have lengthy waits during peak seasons (when it's always a good idea to reserve ahead) and then shut down during the slow months of April and November. Some of the best dining is found in country inns. Casual dress is the rule unless otherwise noted; the formal dining rooms of a few upscale country inns are the dressiest places, but even there you'll rarely need a tie—though you'll often find wearing a jacket useful on nippy Vermont evenings.

Highly recommended restaurants are indicated by a star ★.

Category	Cost*
Very Expensive	over $35
Expensive	$25–$35
Moderate	$15–$25
Inexpensive	under $15

average cost of a three-course dinner, per person, excluding drinks, service, and 5% sales tax

Lodging

Vermont's largest hotels are in Burlington and near the major ski resorts. Elsewhere you'll find a variety of inns, bed-and-breakfasts, and small motels. Rates are highest during foliage season, from late September to mid-October, and lowest in late spring and November, when many properties close. Many of the larger hotels offer package rates. Some antiques-filled inns discourage bringing children.

Bed-and-breakfast referral services include **American Country Collection of Bed and Breakfast** (984 Gloucester Pl., Schenectady, NY 12309, tel. 518/370–4948) and **American–Vermont Bed and Breakfast Reservation Service** (Box 1, E. Fairfield 05448, tel. 802/827–3827). You can also try calling the chambers of commerce in many ski areas.

The **Vermont Chamber of Commerce** (*see* Visitor Information, *above*) publishes the *Vermont Travelers' Guidebook*, which is an extensive list of lodgings, and additional guides to country inns and vacation rentals. The **Vermont Travel Division** (*see* Visitor Information, *above*) has a brochure that lists lodgings at working farms.

Highly recommended lodgings are indicated by a star ★.

Category	Cost*
Very Expensive	over $150
Expensive	$100–$150
Moderate	$60–$100
Inexpensive	under $60

All prices are for a standard double room during peak season, with no meals unless noted, and excluding service charge.

Southern Vermont

The Vermont tradition of independence and rebellion began in southern Vermont. Many towns founded in the early 18th century as frontier outposts or fortifications were later important as trading centers. In the western region the Green Mountain Boys fought off both the British and the claims of land-hungry New Yorkers—some say their descendants are still fighting. In the 19th century, as many towns turned to manufacturing, the eastern part of the state preserved much of its rich farming and orchard areas.

Important Addresses and Numbers

Visitor Information
Bennington Area Chamber of Commerce (Veterans Memorial Dr., Bennington 05201, tel. 802/447–3311; open weekdays 9–5). **Brattleboro Chamber of Commerce** (180 Main St., Brattleboro 05301, tel. 802/254–4565; open weekdays 8–5). **Chamber of Commerce, Manchester and the Mountains** (Adams Park Green, Box 928, Manchester 05255, tel. 802/362–2100; open weekdays 9–5, Sat. 10–4). **Mt. Snow/Haystack Region Chamber of Commerce** (E. Main St., Box 3, Wilmington 05363, tel. 802/464–8092; open weekdays 9–noon and 1–4:45). **Windsor Area Chamber of Commerce** (Box 5, Windsor 05089, tel. 802/672–5910; open weekdays 9–5).

Emergencies
Brattleboro Memorial Hospital (9 Belmont Ave., tel. 802/257–0341).

Getting Around Southern Vermont

By Car
In the south the principal east–west highway is Route 9, the Molly Stark Trail, from Brattleboro to Bennington. The most important north–south roads are Route 7, the more scenic Route 7A to the west, and I–91 and Route 5 to the east. Route 100, which runs north–south through the state's center, and Route 30 from Brattleboro to Manchester are scenic drives. All routes are heavily traveled during peak tourist seasons.

By Bus
Vermont Transit (tel. 802/864–6811, 800/451–3292, or, in VT, 800/642–3133) links Bennington, Manchester, Brattleboro, and Bellows Falls.

Guided Tours

Back Road Country Tours (tel. 802/442–3876) offers Jeep tours on the back roads of Bennington County during September and October—a great way to experience the fall foliage.

Exploring Southern Vermont

Numbers in the margin correspond to points of interest on the Southern Vermont map.

Here in southern Vermont you'll see endless acres of verdant farm-land, sprawling ski resorts, freshly starched New England towns, well-traveled highways, and quiet back roads. We begin in the east, south of the junction of I–91 and Route 9.

❶ At the confluence of the West and Connecticut rivers, **Brattleboro,** a town of about 13,000, originated as a frontier scouting post and became a thriving industrial center and resort town in the 1800s. More recently, such organizations as the Experiment in International Living (which trains Peace Corps volunteers) have helped build the area's reputation as a haven for left-leaning political activists and aging hippies. Its downtown, bustling with activity, is the center of commerce for southeastern Vermont.

A former railroad station, the **Brattleboro Museum and Art Center** has replaced locomotives with art and historical exhibits as well as an Estey organ from the days when the city was home to one of the world's largest organ companies. *Canal and Bridge Sts., tel. 802/257–0124. Admission: $2 adults, $1 senior citizens. Open May–Oct., Tues.–Sun. noon–6.*

Larkin G. Mead, Jr., a Brattleboro resident, stirred 19th-century America's imagination with an 8-foot snow angel he built at the intersection of Routes 30 and 5. **Brooks Memorial Library** has a replica of the angel as well as rotating art exhibits. *224 Main St., tel. 802/254–5290. Open Mon.–Thurs. 9–9, Fri. 9–6, Sat. 9–5.*

Time Out | Hamelmann's Bakery (Elliot St.) creates crusty country breads in hand-shaped loaves, as well as thick napoleons and delicate fruit and almond tarts.

From Brattleboro head north along the eastern edge of the state to Putney, where **Harlow's Sugar House** (Rte. 5, 2 mi north of Putney, tel. 802/387–5852) has horse-drawn sleigh or wagon rides into the sugar bush to watch the maple sugaring in spring, berry picking in summer, and apple picking in autumn. You can buy the fruits of these labors in the gift shop.

❷ Nearly 10 miles west of Brattleboro on Route 9 is **Marlboro,** a tiny town that draws musicians and audiences from around the world each summer to the Marlboro Music Festival, founded by Rudolf Serkin and led for many years by Pablo Casals. Perched high on a hill just off Route 9, **Marlboro College** is the center of musical activity. The demure white-frame buildings have an outstanding view of the valley below, and the campus is studded with apple trees.

The **Luman Nelson New England Wildlife Museum** (tel. 802/464–5494), housed in a gift shop on Route 9 opposite the Skyline Restaurant, is taxidermy heaven. The display of large animals includes majestic deer heads, a bobcat eyeing a couple of concerned-looking squirrels, and a wild boar who seems surprised to be there. The large room downstairs is filled with stuffed bird species in cages with hand-lettered signs.

❸ **Wilmington,** the shopping and dining center for the Mt. Snow ski area to the north, lies 8 miles west of Marlboro on Route 9. Here you can begin one of Vermont's most scenic (though well-trodden) drives, a 35-mile circular tour that affords panoramic views of the

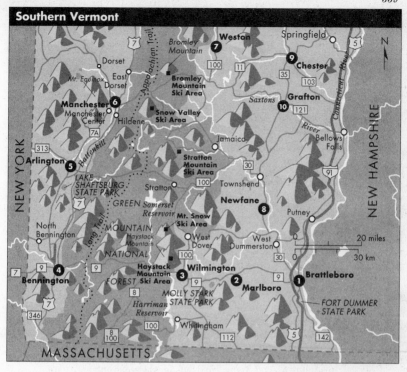

Southern Vermont

region's mountains, farmland, and abundant cow population. Drive west on Route 9 to the intersection with Route 8, turn south and continue to the junction with Route 100, follow Route 100 through Whitingham (the birthplace of the Mormon prophet Brigham Young), and stay with the road as it turns north again and takes you back to Route 9. On this last leg you can visit the **North River Winery,** which occupies a converted farmhouse and barn on Route 112 and produces such fruit wines as Green Mountain Apple. *Rte. 112, 6 mi south of Wilmington, tel. 802/368–7557. Admission free. Open late Apr.–Dec., daily 10–5; Jan.–late Apr., Fri.–Sun. 11–5.*

Take Route 9 west through the Green Mountain National Forest to see **Bennington,** now the state's third-largest city and the commercial focus of Vermont's southwest corner. It's retained much of the industrial character it developed in the 19th century, when paper mills, grist mills, and potteries formed the city's economic base. It was in Bennington, at the Catamount Tavern, that Ethan Allen organized the Green Mountain Boys, who helped capture Ft. Ticonderoga in 1775. Here also, in 1777, American general John Stark urged his militia to attack the Hessians across the New York border: "There are the Redcoats; they will be ours or tonight Molly Stark sleeps a widow!"

Two self-guided walking tours described in a chamber of commerce brochure will familiarize you with the town. The more interesting tour is of **Old Bennington,** a National Register Historic District just west of downtown, where impressive white-column Greek Revival and sturdy brick Federal homes stand around the village green. In the graveyard of the **Old First Church,** at the corner of Church

Street and Monument Avenue, the tombstone of the poet Robert Frost proclaims, "I had a lover's quarrel with the world."

The **Bennington Battle Monument,** a 306-foot stone obelisk with an elevator to the top, commemorates General Stark's victory over the British, who attempted to capture Bennington's stockpile of supplies. The battle, which took place near Walloomsac Heights in New York State, helped bring about the surrender two months later of the British commander, "Gentleman Johnny" Burgoyne. *15 Monument Ave., tel. 802/447–0550. Admission: $1 adults, 50¢ children 6– 11. Open mid-Apr.–late Oct., daily 9–5.*

The **Bennington Museum**'s rich collections of early Americana include vestiges of rural life, a good percentage of which are packed into towering glass cases. The decorative arts are well represented; one room is devoted to early Bennington pottery, then known as Norton pottery, the product of one of the first ceramic makers in the country. Another room covers the history of American glass and contains fine Tiffany specimens. Devotees of folk art will want to see the largest public collection of the work of Grandma Moses, who lived and painted in the area. Among the 30 paintings and assorted memorabilia is her only self-portrait and the famous painted caboose window. *W. Main St. (Rte. 9), tel. 802/447–1571. Admission: $5 adults, $4 senior citizens, children under 12 free, $12 family. Open daily 9–5.*

Contemporary stone sculpture and white-frame neo-Colonial dorms, framed by acres of cornfields, punctuate the green meadows of **Bennington College**'s placid campus. The small coeducational liberal arts college, one of the most expensive in the country, is noted for its progressive program in the arts. To reach the campus, take Route 67A off Route 7 and look for the stone entrance gate.

The **Park-McCullough House,** a 35-room restored mansion in North Bennington, shows what the forty-niners did with the money they made in the California gold rush. The elaborately carved Second Empire mahogany furnishings, massive oak staircase, and etched glass doors are original. Guided tours begin on the hour. *Rte. 67A, North Bennington, tel. 802/442–5441. Admission: $4 adults, $3.50 senior citizens, $2.50 children 12–17. Open May–Oct., weekdays 9–4.*

❺ Don't be surprised to see familiar-looking faces among the roughly 2,200 people of **Arlington,** about 15 miles north of Bennington on Route 7A. The illustrator Norman Rockwell lived here for 14 years, and many of the models for his portraits of small-town life were his neighbors. Settled first in 1763, Arlington was called Tory Hollow for its Loyalist sympathies—even though a number of the Green Mountain Boys lived here, too. Smaller than Bennington and more down-to-earth than upper-crust Manchester to the north, Arlington displays a certain Rockwellian folksiness. It's also known as the home of Dorothy Canfield Fisher, a novelist popular in the 1930s and 1940s.

Don't expect to find original paintings at the **Norman Rockwell Exhibition;** it has none. Instead, the exhibition rooms are crammed with reproductions, arranged in every way conceivable: chronologically, by subject matter, and juxtaposed with photos of the models, some of whom work at the exhibition. The gift shop in the white church (ca. 1875) that houses the exhibit sells yet more reproductions. *Rte. 7A, Arlington, tel. 802/375–6423. Admission: $1, children under 6 free. Open May–Oct., daily 9–5; Nov.–Apr., daily 10–4.*

⑥ **Manchester,** where Ira Allen proposed financing Vermont's participation in the American Revolution by confiscating Tory estates, has been a popular summer retreat since the mid-19th century. Manchester Village's tree-shaded marble sidewalks and stately old homes reflect the luxurious resort lifestyle of a century ago, while Manchester Center's upscale factory outlets appeal to the affluent 20th-century ski crowd drawn by nearby Bromley and Stratton mountains.

Time Out At the **Gourmet Deli** (Factory Point Square, Rte. 7A) you'll find homemade soups, sandwiches, and baked goods that can be eaten at outdoor tables with umbrellas in summer.

Hildene, the summer home of Abraham Lincoln's son Robert, is a 412-acre estate that the former chairman of the board of the Pullman Company built for his family and their descendants; Mary Lincoln Beckwith, Robert's granddaughter, lived here as recently as 1975. With its Georgian Revival symmetry, gracious central hallway, and grand curved staircase, the 24-room mansion is unusual in that its rooms are not roped off. When "The Ride of the Valkyries" is played on the 1,000-pipe Aeolian organ, the music emanates from the mansion's very bones. Tours include a short film on the owner's life and a walk through the elaborate formal gardens. *Rte. 7A, Manchester, tel. 802/362–1788. Admission: $7 adults, $4 children 6–15. Open mid-May–Oct., daily 9:30–4.*

If you're a fly-fishing devotee, stop by the **American Museum of Fly Fishing,** which displays more than 1,500 rods, 800 reels, 30,000 flies, and the tackle of such celebrities as Bing Crosby, Daniel Webster, and Winslow Homer. Its 2,500 books on angling comprise the largest public library devoted to fishing. Only the fish are missing here (though the Battenkill River is only a back cast away!). *Rte. 7A, Manchester, tel. 802/362–3300. Admission: $2 adults, children under 12 free. Open May–Oct., daily 10–4; Nov.–Apr., weekdays 10–4.*

The **Southern Vermont Art Center's** 10 rooms are set on 375 acres dotted with contemporary sculpture. A popular retreat for local patrons of the arts, the center has a permanent collection, changing exhibits, and a serene botany trail that passes by a 300-year-old maple tree. The graceful Georgian mansion is also the frequent site of concerts, dramatic performances, and films (call for current programs). *West Rd., Box 617, Manchester, tel. 802/362–1405. Admission: $3 adults, 50¢ students. Open Memorial Day–Oct. 15, Tues.–Sat. 10–5, Sun. noon–5, and for occasional winter concerts.*

Time Out **Mother Myrick's** (Rte. 7A) offers sugar in all its forms: ice-cream sundaes, cakes, cookies, handmade chocolates, and fudge. The waiting lines even in winter attest to its popularity.

You may want to keep your eye on the temperature gauge of your car as you drive the 5.2 miles to the top of 3,825-foot **Mt. Equinox.** Remember to look out the window periodically for views of the Battenkill trout stream and the surrounding Vermont countryside. Picnic tables line the drive, and there's an outstanding view down both sides of the mountain from a notch known as "the Saddle." *Rte. 7A, Manchester, tel. 802/362–1114. Admission: $4.50 car. Open May–Oct., daily 8 AM–10 PM.*

⑦ Head east on Route 11 and then north on Route 100 to reach **Weston,** perhaps best known for the Vermont Country Store (Rte. 100, tel.

802/362–4667), which may be more a way of life than a shop. For years the retail store and its mail-order catalogue have carried such nearly forgotten items as Lilac Vegetal aftershave, Monkey Brand black tooth powder, Flexible Flyer sleds, pickles in a barrel, and tiny wax bottles of colored syrup. Nostalgia-laden implements dangle from the store's walls and ceiling.

Weston Priory, a Benedictine monastery just north of the junction of Routes 100 and 155, is a tranquil spot in an already fairly serene state. Guests are welcome to join in services (evening vespers is the most impressive), walk by the pond, picnic under the trees, and visit the gift shop, which has records of the well-known monastery choir. *¹⁄₁₀ mi north of junction of Rtes. 100 and 155.*

From Weston you might head south on Route 100 through Jamaica and then down Route 30 through Townshend and Newfane, pretty hamlets typical of small-town Vermont. **Newfane** is especially attractive for its crisp white buildings surrounding the village green. Just south of Townshend, near the Townshend Dam on Route 30, is the state's longest single-span bridge, which is now closed to traffic.

Another option from Weston is to travel east to Route 11, which will take you to **Chester.** There, on North Street, look for Stone Village, two rows of buildings constructed from quarried stone, all built by two brothers and said to have been used during the Civil War as stations on the Underground Railroad.

To examine the oldest one-room schoolhouse in the state, take Route 11 east almost to I–91. Completed in 1790, the **Eureka Schoolhouse** has a collection of 19th-century primers and other education materials. It'll make you think about our current state of education and wonder how far we have or haven't come. *Rte. 11, off I–91, tel. 802/828–3226. Admission free. Open Memorial Day–mid-Oct., Wed.–Sun. 9–4.*

It's 8 miles south on Route 35 from Chester to **Grafton,** the picturesque village that got a second lease on life when the Windham Foundation provided funds for the restoration of most of the town, now one of the best-kept in the state. The Grafton Historical Society documents the change and has other exhibits. *Townshend Rd., tel. 802/843–2255. Admission free. Open Memorial Day–Columbus Day, Sat. 2:30–4:40; July–Aug., Sun. 2:30–4:40.*

What to See and Do with Children

Battle Monument and Museum, Bennington
Harlow's Sugar House, Putney
Luman Nelson New England Wildlife Museum, Marlboro
Mt. Equinox, Manchester

Off the Beaten Track

In Bellows Falls, on the Connecticut River at the eastern edge of the state, about 12 miles east of Grafton, you can board the *Green Mountain Flyer* for a 26-mile two-hour round-trip to Chester's restored 1872 train station in superbly restored cars that date from the golden age of railroading. The journey takes you through scenic countryside past covered bridges and along the Brockway Mills gorge. A six-hour tour is also offered, in fall only. *Island St. off Bridge St. (Rte. 12), tel. 802/463–3069. Fare for 2-hr. trip: $10 adults, $6 children 3–12. Fare for 6-hr. trip: $23 adults, $14 children 3–12. Open mid-June–mid-Oct., daily 11–2.*

Native American petroglyphs can be found on the banks of the Connecticut River in Bellows Falls, but you'll have to scramble down the side of the riverbank to examine the carvings. The Bellows Falls Chamber of Commerce (tel. 802/463–4280) has a brochure about the site; follow the small sign off Bridge Street near the river.

Shopping

Shopping
Districts
Candle Mill Village's (Old Mill Rd., off Rte. 7A, East Arlington, tel. 802/375–6068) shops specialize in community cookbooks from around the country, bears in all forms, music boxes, and, of course, candles. The nearby waterfall makes a pleasant backdrop for a picnic. **Manchester Commons** (Rtes. 7 and 11/30, tel. 802/362–3736), the largest and spiffiest of three large factory-direct minimalls, has such big-city names as Joan and David, Coach, Boston Trader, Ralph Lauren, Hickey-Freeman, and Cole-Haan. Not far off are **Factory Point Square** (Rte. 7) and **Battenkill Place** (Rte. 11). **Wilmington Flea Market** (Rtes. 9 and 100 S, tel. 802/464–3345; open weekends Memorial Day–mid-Oct.) is a cornucopia of leftovers and never-solds.

Food and
Drink
Allen Bros. (Rte. 5 south of Bellows Falls, tel. 802/722–3395) bakes apple pies, cider doughnuts, and an array of Vermont foods. **Equinox Nursery** (Rte. 7A, between Arlington and Manchester, tel. 802/362–2610) carries a wide selection of produce and local foods, including ice cream. **H & M Orchard** (Dummerston Center, tel. 802/254–8100) lets you watch sugaring and pick your own fruit seasonally. **Vermont Country Store** (Rte. 100, Weston, tel. 802/824–3184) sets aside one room of its old-fashioned emporium for Vermont Common Crackers and bins of fudge and other candy.

Specialty
Stores
*Art and
Antiques*
Carriage Trade (tel. 802/362–1125) and **1812 House** (tel. 802/362–1189), just north of Manchester Center on Route 7, contain room after room of Early American antiques; Carriage Trade has especially fine collections of clocks and ceramics. **Danby Antiques Center** (⅛ mi off Rte. 7, 13 mi north of Manchester, tel. 802/293–9984) has 11 rooms and a barn filled with furniture and accessories, folk art, textiles, and stoneware. **Four Corners East** (307 North St., Bennington, tel. 802/442–2612) has Early American antiques. **Gallery North Star** (Townshend Rd., Grafton, tel. 802/843–2465) focuses on oils, watercolors, and lithographs by Vermont artists, as well as sculpture. **Newfane Antiques Center** (Rte. 30, south of Newfane, tel. 802/365–4482) displays antiques from 20 dealers on three floors.

Books
The Book Cellar (120 Main St., Brattleboro, tel. 802/254–6026), with three floors of books, is strong on Vermont and New England volumes. **Johnny Appleseed** (next to The Equinox hotel, Manchester Village, tel. 802/362–2458) specializes in Vermont lore and the hard-to-find. **Northshire Bookstore** (Main St., Manchester, tel. 802/362–2200) has a large inventory of travel and children's books.

Crafts
Basketville (Rte. 5, Putney, tel. 802/387–5509) is, appropriately, an immense space filled with baskets from around the world. **Bennington Potters Yard** (324 County St., tel. 802/447–7531) has seconds from the famed Bennington Potters. Prepare to get dusty digging through the bad stuff to find an almost-perfect piece at a modest discount. The complex of buildings also houses a glass factory outlet and John McLeod woodenware. **Green Mountain Spinnery** (Exit 4, I-91, Putney, tel. 802/387–4528; tour is $1 adults, 50¢ children) offers yarns, knit items, and tours of its yarn factory at 1:30 on the first and third Tuesday of each month. **Handworks on the Green** (Rte. 7, Manchester, tel. 802/362–5033) deals in contemporary

crafts—ceramics, jewelry, glass—with an emphasis on sophisticated, brightly colored decorative work. **Newfane Country Store** (Rte. 30, Newfane, tel. 802/365–7916) has an immense selection of quilts—they can be custom ordered as well—and homemade fudge. **Vermont Artisan Design** (115 Main St., Brattleboro, tel. 802/257–7044), one of the state's best crafts shops, displays contemporary ceramics, glass, wood, and clothing. **Weston Bowl Mill** (Rte. 100, Weston, tel. 802/824–6219) has finely crafted wood products at mill prices.

Men's Clothing **Orvis Retail Store** (Rte. 7A, Manchester, tel. 802/362–3750) carries the outdoorsman's clothing and home furnishings featured in its popular mail-order catalog. A nearby outlet (Union St., tel. 802/362–3881), housed in what was Orvis's shop in the 1800s, has relatively good bargains.

Women's **Anne Klein, Liz Claiborne, Donna Karan, Esprit, Giorgio Armani,**
Clothing **Jones New York,** and **Coach** are among the shops on Routes 11/30 and 7 South in Manchester—a center for women's designer factory stores.

Sports and Outdoor Activities

Biking The 20-mile Dorset–Manchester trail runs from Manchester Village north on West Street to Route 30, turns west at the Dorset village green onto West Road, and heads back south to Manchester. **Battenkill Sports** (Rte. 7, at Rte. 11/30, tel. 802/362–2634) and **Pedal Pushers** (Rte. 11/30, ½ mi east of Rte. 7A, tel. 802/362–5200) in Manchester rent bikes.

A 26-mile loop out of Chester follows the Williams River along Route 103 to Pleasant Valley Road north of Bellows Falls. At Saxtons River, turn west onto Route 121 and follow along the river to connect with Route 35. When the two routes separate, follow Route 35 north back to Chester. **Neal's Wheels** (Rte. 11, tel. 802/875–3627) has rentals.

In Bennington **Mountain Bike Peddlers** (954 E. Main St., tel. 802/447–7968) and **Up and Downhill** (160 Benmont Ave., tel. 802/442–8664) offer rentals and repairs.

Canoeing The Connecticut River between Bellows Falls and the Massachusetts border, interrupted by one dam at Vernon, is relatively easy. A good resource is *The Complete Boating Guide to the Connecticut River,* available from **CRWC Headquarters** (125 Combs Rd., Easthampton, MA 01027, tel. 413/584–0057). **Connecticut River Safari** (Rte. 5, Brattleboro, tel. 802/257–5008) has guided and self-guided tours as well as canoe rentals. **Battenkill Canoe** (River Rd., Arlington, tel. 802/375–9559) offers day trips and rentals on the Battenkill and can arrange custom inn-to-inn tours.

Fishing **The Orvis Co.** (Manchester Center, tel. 802/362–3900) hosts a nationally known fly-fishing school on the Battenkill, the state's most famous trout stream, with three-day courses given weekly, April–October. The Connecticut River contains small-mouth bass, walleye, and perch; shad are beginning to return via the fish ladders at Vernon and Bellows Falls. Harriman and Somerset reservoirs in the central part of the state offer both warm- and cold-water species; Harriman has a greater variety.

Strictly Trout (tel. 802/869–3116) will arrange a fly-fishing trip on any Vermont stream or river.

Hiking   One of the most popular segments of the Long Trail starts at Route 11/30 west of Peru Notch and goes to the top of Bromley Mountain (four hours). About 4 miles east of Bennington, the Long Trail crosses Route 9 and runs south to the summit of Harmon Hill (two–three hours). On Route 30 about 1 mile south of Townshend is Townshend State Park; from here the hiking trail runs to the top of Bald Mountain, passing an alder swamp, a brook, and a hemlock forest (two hours).

The **Mountain Goat** (Rte. 7A just south of Rte. 11/30, Manchester, tel. 802/362–5159) sells hiking, backpacking, and climbing equipment; it also offers climbing clinics. The **Green Mountain Club** (Rte. 100, Box 650, Waterbury Center 05677, tel. 802/244–7037) publishes a number of helpful hiking maps and guides.

Water Sports   **Lake Front Restaurant** (Harriman Reservoir, tel. 802/464–5838) rents sailboats, canoes, and rowboats by the hour or day. **West River Canoe** (Rte. 100, off Rte. 30, Townshend, tel. 802/896–6209) has sailboard rentals and lessons.

National and State Parks

The 275,000 acres of Green Mountain National Forest extend down the center of the state, providing scenic drives, picnic areas, 95 campsites, lakes, and hiking and cross-country ski trails. Contact the **Forest Supervisor, Green Mountain National Forest** (151 West St., Box 519, Rutland 05701, tel. 802/773–0300).

The waterfalls at the Lye Brook Wilderness Area are popular. Contact the **U.S. Forest Service** (Rte. 11/30, east of Manchester, tel. 802/362–2307; open weekdays 8–4:30).

The following state parks have camping sites and facilities as well as picnic tables. **Emerald Lake State Park** (Rte. 7, 9 mi north of Manchester, tel. 802/362–1655; 430 acres) has a marked nature trail, an on-site naturalist, boat and canoe rentals, and a snack bar. The hiking trails at **Fort Dummer State Park** (S. Main St., 2 mi south of Brattleboro, tel. 802/254–2610; 217 acres) afford views of the Connecticut River Valley. **Lake Shaftsbury State Park** (Rte. 7A, 10½ mi north of Bennington, tel. 802/375–9978; 101 acres) is one of a few parks in Vermont with group camping; it has a swimming beach, self-guided nature trails, and boat and canoe rentals. **Molly Stark State Park** (Rte. 9, east of Wilmington, tel. 802/464–5460; 158 acres) has a hiking trail to a vista from a fire tower on Mt. Olga. **Townshend State Park** (3 mi north of Rte. 30, between Newfane and Townshend, tel. 802/365–7500; 856 acres), the largest in southern Vermont, is popular for the swimming at Townshend Dam and the stiff hiking trail to the top of Bald Mountain. **Woodford State Park** (Rte. 9, east of Bennington, tel. 802/447–4169; 400 acres) has an activities center on Adams Reservoir, a playground, boat and canoe rentals, and marked nature trails.

Dining and Lodging

Manchester, which has a lodging referral service (tel. 802/824–6915), and Bennington have a number of rambling, luxurious inns. For additional accommodations selections, see the Bromley, Mt. Snow, and Stratton sections of the Skiing in New England chapter. In the region's restaurants, dress is casual and reservations are unnecessary except where noted.

Arlington
Dining and
Lodging
★

West Mountain Inn. A llama ranch on the property, African violets and llama-shape chocolates in the rooms, quilted bedspreads, and a front lawn with a spectacular view of the countryside were factors in Michael J. Fox's decision to be married here. This former farmhouse of the 1840s, restored over the last several years, sits on 150 acres and seems to be a world apart. Rooms 2, 3, and 4 in the front of the house overlook the front lawn; the three small nooks of room 11 resemble railroad sleeper berths and are perfect for kids. A low-beamed, paneled, candlelit dining room is the setting for six-course prix fixe dinners featuring such specialties as veal chops topped with sun-dried tomatoes and Asiago cheese. Aunt Min's Swedish rye and other toothsome breads, as well as desserts, are all made on the premises. Tables by the windows allow a glorious view of the mountains. *Rte. 313, 05250, tel. 802/375–6516, fax 802/375–6553. 13 rooms with bath, 3 suites. Facilities: restaurant (reservations advised), bar, walking and ski trails, accessible by people with disabilities. AE, MC, V. Rates are MAP (full breakfast). Inn: Expensive. Restaurant: Moderate.*

★ **Arlington Inn.** The Greek Revival columns at the entrance to this railroad magnate's home of 1848 give it an imposing presence, yet the inn is more welcoming than forbidding. The cozy charm is created by linens that coordinate with the Victorian-style wallpaper, clawfoot tubs in some bathrooms, and the house's original moldings and wainscoting. The carriage house, built at the turn of the century and renovated in 1985, has country French and Queen Anne furnishings. Having changed hands twice in as many years, the restaurant struggles to retain its reputation as one of the most respected in the state. The new owner still uses local products from Vermont farms whenever possible; her contemporary and classic Continental menu, which changes seasonally, might include penne pasta with grilled chicken and escarole smothered in garlic alongside salmon potato cakes. Polished hardwood floors, green tablecloths and rose walls, and soft candlelight complement the food; so might a bottle of wine from the extensive collection. *Rte. 7A, 05250, tel. 802/375–6532. 13 rooms with bath. Facilities: restaurant (reservations advised), bar, tennis. AE, MC, V. Rates are MAP (Continental breakfast). Inn: Moderate. Restaurant: Expensive.*

Lodging

Hill Farm Inn. This homey inn still has the feel of the country farmhouse it used to be: The mix of sturdy antiques and hand-me-downs, the spinning wheel in a corner of the hallway, the paintings by a family member, the buffalo that roam the 50 acres—all convey a relaxed, friendly atmosphere. Room 7 has a beamed cathedral ceiling and porch views of Mt. Equinox; the rooms in the 1790 guest house are very private; the cabins are rustic and fun. *Rte. 7, Box 2015, 05250, tel. 802/375–2269 or 800/882–2545. 11 rooms, 6 with bath; 2 suites; 4 cabins in summer. Facilities: restaurant. AE, D, MC, V. Full breakfast included. Inexpensive–Moderate.*

Bennington
Dining

Main Street Café. Since it opened in 1989, this small storefront with polished hardwood floors, candlelit tables, and fresh flowers has drawn raves, its Northern Italian cuisine judged well worth the few minutes' drive from downtown Bennington. Favorites include the rigatoni tossed with Romano, Parmesan, broccoli, and sausage in a cream sauce and the chicken stuffed with ham, provolone, and fresh spinach and served in a Marsala-onion sauce. The look is casual chic, like that of a Manhattan loft transplanted to a small town. *Rte. 67A, North Bennington, tel. 802/442–3210. Reservations advised. AE, DC, MC, V. No lunch. Closed Mon. and Tues. Expensive.*

Alldays and Onions. It may look like a deli—it *is* a deli during the day—yet its dinner menus, which change weekly, feature such creative fare as sautéed scallops and fettuccine in a jalapeño-ginger sauce, and rack of lamb with a honey-thyme sauce. Desserts are baked on the premises. *519 E. Main St., tel. 802/447–0043. MC, V. Closed Sun. Moderate.*

The Brasserie. The Brasserie's fare is some of the city's most creative. A mozzarella loaf swirls cheese through bread topped with anchovy-herb butter, and the soups are filling enough for a meal. The decor is as clean-lined and contemporary as the Bennington pottery that is for sale in the same complex of buildings. *324 County St., tel. 802/447–7922. MC, V. Closed Tues. Moderate.*

★ **Blue Benn Diner.** Breakfast is served all day in this authentic diner, and the eats are as down-home as turkey hash and as off-the-wall as tabbouleh or breakfast burritos that wrap scrambled eggs, sausage, and chiles in a tortilla. There can be a long wait. *Rte. 7 N, tel. 802/442–8977. No credit cards. No dinner Sun.–Tues. Inexpensive.*

Lodging **South Shire Inn.** Canopy beds in lushly carpeted rooms, ornate plaster moldings, and a dark mahogany fireplace in the library create turn-of-the-century grandeur. Furnishings are antique except for the reproduction beds that provide contemporary comfort. The inn is in a quiet residential neighborhood within walking distance of the bus depot and downtown stores. Breakfast is served in the peach-and-white wedding cake of a dining room. *124 Elm St., 05201, tel. 802/447–3839. 9 rooms with bath. Facilities: fireplaces in 7 rooms, whirlpool baths in 4 rooms. AE, MC, V. Full breakfast included. Moderate–Expensive.*

★ **Molly Stark Inn.** This gem of a B&B always gives the feeling that you're staying with old friends. Tidy blue plaid wallpaper, gleaming hardwood floors, antique furnishings, and a wood-burning stove in a brick alcove of the sitting room add country charm to this 1860 Queen Anne Victorian. Molly's Room, at the back of the building, gets less noise from Route 9; the attic suite is most spacious. The innkeeper's genuine hospitality and quirky charisma delight guests, as does the full country breakfast that's been known to feature cinnamon-apple cheddar cheese quiche. *1067 E. Main St., 05201, tel. 802/442–9631. 6 rooms, 2 with bath. MC, V. Full breakfast included. Inexpensive–Moderate.*

Brattleboro **Walker's Restaurant.** Brass railings, oak Windsor chairs, and a long
Dining bar give this family-style restaurant a turn-of-the-century feel. The food is unassuming, with such standards as fish-and-chips, charbroiled steak, burgers, and cream pies for dessert. *132 Main St., tel. 801/254–6046. AE, MC, V. Moderate.*

Common Ground. The political posters and concert fliers that line the staircase make you conscious of Vermont's strong progressive element. Owned cooperatively by the staff, this vegetarian restaurant serves the likes of cashew burgers, veggie stir-fries, and the "humble bowl of brown rice." A chocolate cake with peanut butter frosting and other desserts (sans white sugar, of course) will lure confirmed meat-eaters. *25 Elliot St., tel. 802/257–0855. No credit cards. Closed Tues. Inexpensive–Moderate.*

Mole's Eye Cafe. Built in the 1930s as the tavern for the long gone old Brooks Hotel, this neighborhood gathering place is pretty much an institution. The appeal of this cozy basement establishment is its neighborly hospitality—not to mention the home-baked turkey, cheesey sandwich melts, Mexican munchies, and homemade soups and desserts. *High St., tel. 802/257–0771. MC, V. No reservations. Inexpensive.*

Dining and **Latchis Hotel.** Restoration of the downtown landmark's Art Deco
Lodging grandeur was completed in 1989, and everything old is new again:

black-and-white-check bathroom tiles, painted geometric borders along the ceiling, multicolored patterns of terrazzo on the lobby floor. All deluxe rooms have refrigerator, complimentary Continental breakfast, movie passes, and shopping discounts at Brattleboro stores. Odd-numbered rooms offer a view of the Connecticut River and Main Street. The Latchis Grille is home to the Windham Brewery and serves rich ales and lagers, as well as an eclectic array of pub grub—grilled chicken and fish sandwiches, fried calamari, burgers, salads, and the like. *50 Main St., 05301, tel. 802/254–6300. 35 rooms with bath. Continental breakfast included. Facilities: restaurant. AE, MC, V. Hotel: Inexpensive–Moderate. Restaurant: Moderate.*

Chester
Lodging

Inn at Long Last. An army of toy soldiers fills a glass case beside the enormous fieldstone fireplace in the pine-floor lobby of this Victorian inn, where guests like to gather for after-dinner drinks before the fire. Bookshelves in the large wood-panel library hold volumes in literature, science, biography, music, history, and labor economics; one entire shelf is devoted to George Orwell. Individual rooms are named after people, places, and things important to innkeeper Jock Coleman, former president of Haverford College in Pennsylvania, and are decorated simply with personal memorabilia. The Dickens Room, with a high carved headboard, is the most spacious; the Audubon and Tiffany rooms have porch access. Some bathrooms are fairly small. The quietest section of the house is at the back. *Main St., Box 589, 05143, tel. 802/875–2444. 30 rooms, 1 with bath in hall. Facilities: restaurant, tennis. MC, V. Full breakfast included. Expensive.*

Grafton
Dining and Lodging

The Old Tavern at Grafton. The white-column porches on both stories of the main building wrap around a carefully restored structure that dates to 1788 and has hosted Daniel Webster and Nathaniel Hawthorne. The inn has 14 rooms in the main building and 21 rooms in two structures across the street. Individually decorated, all rooms have private bath; rooms in the older part of the inn are furnished in antiques, and some have crocheted canopies or four-poster beds. Two dining rooms, one with formal Georgian furniture and oil portraits, the other with rustic paneling and low beams, serve such hearty traditional New England dishes as venison stew or grilled quail; some offerings feature cheeses made just down the road. *Rte. 35, 05146, tel. 802/843–2231, fax 802/843–2245. 35 rooms with bath. Facilities: restaurant, lounge, swimming pond, tennis, indoor platform tennis, game room. AE, MC, V. Closed Apr. Inn: Moderate–Expensive. Restaurant: Expensive.*

Lodging
★

Eaglebrook of Grafton. A mix of well-preserved antiques and abstract art give this small country inn an air of city sophistication. The cathedral-ceilinged sun room, built overlooking the Saxtons River, the seven fireplaces with soapstone mantels, and the watercolor stencils in the hallways warrant this elegant retreat being featured in a glossy interior-design magazine. Blue-checked fabric gives one of the three rooms a French provincial air; another leans toward American country; the third has a Victorian flavor. Outside, the landscaped stone terrace is a perfect place to sit with a bottle of wine on a summer evening. Although the inn is small, the lush furnishings and care extended by the innkeepers toward their guests assures an indulgent stay. *Main St., 05146, tel. 802/843–2564. 1 room with bath, 2 rooms share 1 bath. Continental breakfast included. No credit cards. Moderate.*

Manchester
Dining

Chantecleer. Five miles north of Manchester, intimate dining rooms have been created in a converted dairy barn with a large fieldstone fireplace. The menu reflects the chef's Swiss background: The appetizers include *Bündnerfleisch* (air-dried Swiss beef) and frogs' legs in garlic butter; chateaubriand and Wiener schnitzel are typical entrées. *Rte. 7, East Dorset, tel. 802/362–1616. Reservations required. DC, MC, V. No lunch. Closed Mon., Tues. Expensive–Very Expensive.*

Garden Cafe. This sunny room with hanging plants has a terrific view of the spacious Southern Vermont Art Center grounds and an outdoor terrace; the menu includes such fare as sautéed trout with almonds; ragout of mushrooms in puff pastry; and home-baked fruit tart. *West Rd., tel. 802/362–4220. No credit cards. Closed mid-Oct.–Memorial Day. Moderate.*

Laney's. Boisterous and informal, the open kitchen with a wood-burning brick oven and popular bar lend character to this restaurant's good-time feel. Fresh-baked breads and pizza are house favorites. *Rte. 11/30, tel. 802/362–4456. AE, MC, V. Inexpensive–Moderate.*

Quality Restaurant. Gentrification has reached the down-home neighborhood place that was the model for Norman Rockwell's *War News* painting. The Quality now has Provençal wallpaper and polished wood booths, and the sturdy New England standbys of grilled meat loaf and hot roast beef or turkey sandwiches have been joined by tortellini Alfredo with shrimp and smoked salmon. Breakfast is always popular. *Main St., tel. 802/362–9839. AE, MC, V. Inexpensive–Moderate.*

Dining and Lodging **Reluctant Panther.** The spacious rooms each have goose-down duvets and a complimentary half-bottle of wine. The decor features soft, elegant grays and peaches, while the furnishings are an eclectic mix of antique, country, and contemporary. Ten rooms have fireplaces—the Mary Porter suite has two—and all suites have whirlpools. The best views are from rooms B and D. In Wildflowers, the restaurant long known for its sophisticated cuisine, a huge fieldstone fireplace dominates the larger of the two dining rooms; the other is a small greenhouse with five tables. Glasses and silver sparkle in the candlelight, the service is impeccable, and the menu, which changes daily, might include boneless stuffed chicken with spinach, Gruyère, and Chardonnay-thyme sauce, or fricassee of lobster with Nantucket Bay scallops and Gulf shrimp. *West Rd., Box 678, 05254, tel. 802/362–2568 or 800/822–2331, fax 802/362–2586. 16 rooms with bath, 4 suites. Facilities: restaurant (reservations required; closed Tues., Wed.), lounge, conference room. AE, MC, V. Rates are MAP (full breakfast). Inn: Expensive–Very Expensive. Restaurant: Expensive.*

Lodging **The Equinox.** This white-column resort was a fixture even before Abe Lincoln's family began summering here. A complete overhaul in 1992 restored the rooms and public spaces, as well as the Marsh Tavern restaurant and the golf course. Rooms and public areas are furnished in the casually elegant Vermont country-grand style. Unusual for a Vermont inn are the relaxing programs in the hotel's spa, which have medical supervision and are tailored to the needs of the individual. The resort is often the site of large conferences. *Rte. 7A, Manchester Village 05254, tel. 802/362–4700 or 800/362–4747, fax 802/362–4861. 119 rooms with bath, 18 suites, 9 3-bedroom town houses. Facilities: restaurant, tavern, tennis, golf, health club, sauna, steam room, indoor and outdoor pools. AE, D, DC, MC, V. Very Expensive.*

★ **1811 House.** The atmosphere of an elegant English country home can be enjoyed without crossing the Atlantic. A pub-style bar that serves 26 kinds of single-malt scotches and is decorated with horse brasses; the Waterford crystal in the dining room; equestrian paintings; and the English floral landscaping of three acres of lawn all contribute to make this an inn worthy of royalty. The rooms contain period antiques; six have fireplaces, and many have four-poster beds. Bathrooms are old-fashioned but serviceable, particularly the Robinson Room's marble-enclosed tub. *Rte. 7A, 05254, tel. 802/362–1811 or 800/432–1811. 14 rooms with bath. Facilities: lounge. AE, MC, V. Full breakfast included. Expensive.*

Wilburton Inn. The stone-wall Tudor estate sits atop 20 acres of manicured grounds enhanced with sculpture, and the dining room and outdoor terrace overlook the Battenkill Valley. Rooms are spacious, especially those on the second floor, but the chenille-covered beds in some rooms detract from an otherwise elegant inn. The public areas—with an ornately carved mantel on the first floor, mahogany paneling and stained-glass door in one of the small dining rooms, and a sweeping stone staircase to the lawn—are as elaborate as a railroad magnate's fortune could make them. *River Rd., 05254, tel. 802/362–2500 or 800/648–4944, fax 802/362–1107. 34 rooms with bath. Facilities: restaurant, lounge, outdoor pool, tennis. AE, MC, V. Full breakfast and afternoon tea included. Expensive.*

Marble West Inn. On a rambling back road just outside of town, the serenity of the grounds—rambling gardens and ponds, rockers on a porch facing meadows and mountains—matches the hospitality and warmth emanating from within. A baby grand piano, fireplaces in both sitting rooms, and afternoon tea greet guests seeking repose, as do rooms highlighted with delicate stenciling, hardwood floors, and well-appointed antiques. *Dorset West Rd., Dorset 05251, tel. 802/867–4155. 8 rooms with bath. Facilities: 2 fireplaces in common areas. AE, MC, V. Inexpensive–Moderate.*

Marlboro
Lodging

Whetstone Inn. A favorite of visitors to the Marlboro Music Festival, the 200-year-old inn mixes authentic Colonial architecture and furnishings with pottery lamps, stenciled curtains, Scandinavian-style wall hangings, and a library filled with the works of Thoreau, Tolstoy, and Proust. Three rooms have kitchenettes, and two can be joined to form a suite. During the music festival, mid-July through mid-August, a one-week minimum stay is required. *South Rd., 05344, tel. 802/254–2500. 12 rooms, 8 with bath. Facilities: restaurant, skating pond. No credit cards. Inexpensive–Moderate.*

Newfane
Dining and Lodging

The Four Columns. Erected 150 years ago for a homesick Southern bride, the majestic white columns of the Greek Revival mansion are more intimidating than the Colonial-style rooms inside. Room 1 in the older section has an enclosed porch overlooking the town common; three rooms and a suite were added in an annex eight years ago. All rooms have antiques, brass beds, and quilts; some have fireplaces. The third-floor room in the old section is the most private. In the restaurant, chef Greg Parks has introduced such nouvelle American dishes as mixed grilled game sausages, jumbo shrimp with poblano butter and tapenade toast, and grilled marinated quail with pesto couscous. The classy dining room is decorated with antique tools and copper pots, and the tables sport such coverings as Towle place settings and Limoges china. *West St., Box 278, 05345, tel. 802/365–7713. 17 rooms with bath. Facilities: restaurant (reservations and jacket and tie advised; closed Tues.; weekdays Apr.; early Dec.), hiking trails. AE, MC, V. Rates are MAP in foliage season (full breakfast). Inn: Very Expensive. Restaurant: Expensive–Very Expensive.*

Weston
Dining

The Inn at Weston. The food served in the large candlelit room—such entrées as lamb sautéed with mushrooms and Dijon mustard sauce and grilled chicken breast marinated in olive oil and lemon and served with raspberry sauce—has been praised by gourmet magazines. Breads and desserts are made on the premises. *Main St., tel. 802/824–5804. Reservations advised. No credit cards. No lunch. Closed Wed. in winter, Mon. in summer. Moderate–Expensive.*

Lodging **Darling Family Inn.** The rooms in this renovated farmhouse of 1830 have baskets of apples and hand-stenciling by Joan Darling, and some rooms have folk art or an antique silver pitcher. Two cottages in back are less meticulously furnished, with twin beds, refrigerator, and shower stall. *Rte. 100, 05161, tel. 802/824–3223. 5 rooms with bath, 2 cottages. Facilities: outdoor pool. No credit cards. Full breakfast included. Moderate.*

Wilmington **The Hermitage.** Staying in this 19th-century inn is a bit like visiting *Dining and* an English country manor in hunting season. English setters prance *Lodging* about the grounds amid various collections of decoys, while game ★ birds roam the fields near a duck pond—don't get too attached to the birds, however; you'll probably have one for dinner during your stay. Rooms are in four buildings, the most formal of which is the Federal main inn. Furnishings are simple turn-of-the-century New England: muslin curtains, white shutters; beds are four poster or have towering oak headboards. The restaurant features a traditional Continental menu that shows off home-raised game birds and venison—try a vintage from the 2,000 label wine list. *Coldbrook Rd., Box 457, 05363, tel. 802/464–3511. 25 rooms with bath, 4 share 2 baths. Facilities: restaurant (reservations advised), fireplaces or Franklin stoves in common areas and 11 rooms, sauna, outdoor pool, tennis, cross-country ski center and trails, skeet shooting. Rates are MAP. AE, DC, MC, V. Inn: Moderate–Expensive. Restaurant: Expensive.*

The Arts

Music **Marlboro Music Festival** (Marlboro Music Center, tel. 802/257–4333) presents a broad range of classical and contemporary music in weekend concerts in July and August. **New England Bach Festival** (Brattleboro Music Center, tel. 802/257–4523), with a chorus under the direction of Blanche Moyse, is held in fall. **Vermont Symphony Orchestra** (tel. 802/864–5741) performs in Bennington and Arlington in winter, in Manchester and Brattleboro in summer.

Opera **Brattleboro Opera Theatre** (tel. 802/254–6649) stages a complete opera once a year and holds an opera workshop.

Theater **Dorset Playhouse** (north of Manchester, tel. 802/867–5777) hosts a community group in winter and a resident professional troupe in summer. **Oldcastle Theatre Co.** (Southern Vermont College, Bennington, tel. 802/447–0564) performs from April to October. **Whetstone Theatre** (River Valley Playhouse, Putney, tel. 802/387–5678) stages six productions from April to December.

Nightlife

Much of southern Vermont nightlife centers on Wilmington and the Mt. Snow ski area and Manchester near the Stratton and Bromley ski areas. In ski season you'll find live entertainment most nights; in summer it will be limited to weekends—or nonexistent. Check local newspapers for listings.

Bars and **Avalanche** (Rte. 11/30, Manchester, tel. 802/362–2622) features a lit-
Lounges tle of everything—country, blues, soft rock. **Marsh Tavern** (Rte. 7A,

Manchester, tel. 802/362–4700), the lounge in The Equinox hotel, hosts individual performers Tuesday to Saturday in summer. **Mole's Eye Cafe** (High St., Brattleboro, tel. 802/257–0771; cover charge, Fri.–Sat.) has Mexican food, burgers, and live bands: perhaps acoustic or folk on Wednesday, danceable R&B, blues, or reggae weekends. At **Poncho's Wreck** (S. Main St., south of Rte. 9, Wilmington, tel. 802/464–9320), acoustic jazz or mellow rock is the standard lineup.

Nightclubs **Colors** (20 Elliot St., Brattleboro, tel. 802/254–8646; cover charge) has a DJ Thursday–Saturday; Thursday is ladies' night, Friday belongs to the guys. **Flat Street Night Club** (17 Flat St., Brattleboro, tel. 802/254–8257; cover charge) has a DJ on the weekend, an oldies band Thursday, and a huge video screen.

Central Vermont

Manufacturing has dwindled in central Vermont even as strip development and the creation of service jobs in tourism and recreation have increased. Some manufacturing is still found, particularly in the west around Rutland, the state's second-largest city. Yet the southern tip of Lake Champlain and several major ski resorts make the area an economically diverse section of the state. Freshwater lakes are here, as are the state's famed marble industry and large dairy herds. But the heart of the area is the Green Mountains, running up the state's spine, and the surrounding wilderness of the Green Mountain National Forest, which offers countless opportunities for outdoor recreation and soulful pondering of the region's intense natural beauty—even for those inclined not to venture beyond the confines of their vehicle.

Important Addresses and Numbers

Visitor Information The following offices are open weekdays 9–5. **Addison County Chamber of Commerce** (2 Court St., Middlebury 05753, tel. 802/388–7951). **Quechee Chamber of Commerce** (Box 106, Quechee 05059, tel. 802/295–7900). **Rutland Region Chamber of Commerce** (7 Court Sq., Box 67, Rutland 05701, tel. 802/773–2747). **Sugarbush Chamber of Commerce** (Rte. 100, Box 173, Waitsfield 05673, tel. 802/496–3409). **Windsor Area Chamber of Commerce** (Main St., Box 5, Windsor 05089, tel. 802/674–5910). **Woodstock Area Chamber of Commerce** (4 Central St., Woodstock 05091, tel. 802/457–3555).

Emergencies **Rutland Medical Center** (160 Allen St., Rutland, tel. 802/775–7111). **Porter Medical Center** (South St., Middlebury, tel. 802/388–7901).

Getting Around Central Vermont

By Car The major east–west road is Route 4, which stretches from White River Junction in the east to Fair Haven in the west. Route 125 connects Middlebury on Route 7 with Hancock on Route 100; Route 100 splits the region in half along the eastern edge of the Green Mountains. Route 17 travels east–west from Waitsfield over the Appalachian Gap through Bristol and down to the shores of Lake Champlain. I–91 and the parallel Route 5 follow the eastern border; Routes 7 and 30 are the north–south highways in the west. I–89 links White River Junction with Montpelier to the north.

By Bus **Vermont Transit** (tel. 802/864–6811, 800/451–3292, or, in VT, 800/642–3133) links Rutland, White River Junction, Burlington, and many smaller towns.

Guided Tours

The Icelandic Horse Farm (Common Rd., Waitsfield, tel. 802/496–6707) offers year-round guided riding expeditions on easy-to-ride Icelandic horses. Full-day and half-day rides, weekend tours, and inn-to-inn treks are available. **Land o' Goshen Farm** (Rte. 73, Brandon, tel. 802/247–6015; open mid-May–mid-Oct.) raises llamas for sale and offers guided day or overnight trips in which llamas carry the luggage. Day trips cost $75 per person (two-person minimum), overnight trips $210–$250 (six-person minimum).

Exploring Central Vermont

Numbers in the margin correspond to points of interest on the Central Vermont map.

Our tour begins in Windsor, on Route 5 near I–91, at the eastern edge of the state.

❶ **Windsor** was the delivery room for the birth of Vermont. The **Old Constitution House,** where, in 1777, grant holders declared Vermont an independent republic, was moved to its present site, where it contains 18th- and 19th-century furnishings, American paintings and prints, and Vermont-made tools, toys, and kitchenware. *Rte. 5, tel. 802/674–6628. Admission: $1. Open late May–mid-Oct., Wed.–Sun. 10–4.*

The firm of Robbins & Lawrence became famous for applying the "American system"—the use of interchangeable parts—to the manufacture of rifles. Although the company no longer exists, the **American Precision Museum,** in the restored 1840 Windsor House, extols the Yankee ingenuity that created a major machine-tool industry here in the 19th century. The Windsor House also houses the **Vermont State Crafts Center** (tel. 802/674–6729), a gallery of juried, skillfully made Vermont crafts. *Main St., tel. 802/674–5781. Admission: $2 adults, 75¢ children 6–12. Open mid-May–Nov. 1, weekdays 9–5, weekends and holidays 10–4.*

The **covered bridge** just off Route 5 that spans the Connecticut River between Windsor and Cornish, New Hampshire, is—at 460 feet—the longest in the state.

❷ **White River Junction,** on the Connecticut River 14 miles north of Windsor, is the home of the **Catamount Brewery,** one of the state's several microbreweries. Still relatively new, Catamount's popularity is growing with its golden ale, a British-style amber, a dark porter, and such seasonal specialties as a hearty Christmas ale. Samples are available at the tour's conclusion, and there's a company store. *58 S. Main St., tel. 802/296–2248. Open Mon.–Sat. 9–5, Sun. 1–5. 3 tours Mon.–Sat., 2 tours Sun.*

❸ **Quechee,** 6 miles west of White River Junction, is perched astride the Ottauquechee River. Nearby, the impressive, though tourist-hounded, 165-foot-deep **Quechee Gorge** bears visiting. You can see the mile-long gorge, carved by a glacier, from Route 4, but many visitors picnic nearby or scramble down one of several descents for a closer look. More than a decade ago **Simon Pearce** set up a glassblowing factory in an old mill by the bank of a waterfall here, using the water power to drive his furnace. The glass studio produces exquisite wares and houses a pottery workshop, a shop, and a restaurant; visitors can watch craftspeople at work. *Main St., tel. 802/295–2711. Workshops open weekdays 10–5, store open daily 9–9.*

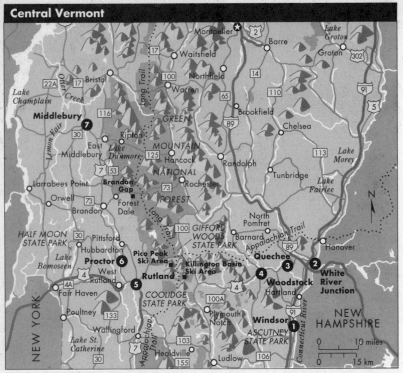

Central Vermont

4 Four miles east of Quechee on Route 4, **Woodstock** realizes virtually every expectation of a quaint New England town (except for the crowds). Perfectly preserved Federal houses surround the tree-lined village green, and streams flow around the town center, which is anchored by a covered bridge. The town owes much of its pristine appearance to the Rockefeller family's keen interest in historic preservation and land conservation.

Other town shapers include the 19th-century forerunner to modern environmentalism, George Perkins Marsh, who is credited largely with the creation of Washington D.C.'s Smithsonian Institute, and Frederick Billings, for whom the **Billings Farm and Museum** is named. Exhibits in the reconstructed Queen Anne farmhouse, school, general store, workshop, and former Marsh homestead demonstrate the lives and skills of early Vermont settlers. Splitting logs doesn't seem nearly so quaint when you've watched the effort that goes into it! *Rte. 12, ½ mi north of Woodstock, tel. 802/457–2355. Admission: $6 adults, $3.50 children 6–12. Open early May–late Oct., daily 10–5.*

Period furnishings of the Woodstock Historical Society fill the rooms of the white clapboard **Dana House** (ca. 1807). Exhibits include the town charter, furniture, maps, and locally minted silver. The elaborate sleigh once owned by Frederick Billings, displayed in the barn, conjures up visions of romantic rides through the snow. *26 Elm St., tel. 802/457–1822. Admission: $3.50 adults, $2.50 senior citizens, $1 children 12–18. Open May–late Oct., Mon.–Sat. 10–5, Sun. 2–5.*

Near Woodstock, the **Raptor Center** of the **Vermont Institute of Natural Science** houses 26 species of birds of prey, among them a bald eagle, a peregrine falcon, and the 3-ounce saw-whet owl. All the caged birds have been found injured and unable to survive in the wild. This nonprofit, environmental research and education center is on a 77-acre nature preserve with self-guided walking trails. *Church Hill Rd., tel. 802/457–2779. Admission: $5 adults, $1 children 5–15. May–Oct., open daily 10–4; Nov.–Apr., closed Sun.*

Time Out | Relax at one of the outdoor tables at the **Dunham Hill Bakery** (Central St.) and enjoy a light lunch or pastry and cappuccino.

Former U.S. President Calvin Coolidge was born and buried in **Plymouth Notch,** a town that shares his character: low-key and quiet. South of Route 4 on Route 100A, the small cluster of state-owned buildings looks more like a large farm than a town; in addition to the homestead there's the general store once run by Coolidge's father, a visitor center, an operating cheese factory, a one-room schoolhouse, and the summer White House. Coolidge's grave is in the cemetery across Route 100A. *Rte. 100A, 6 mi south of Rte. 4, east of Rte. 100, tel. 802/672–3773. Admission: $3.50 adults, children under 12 free. Open Memorial Day–mid-Oct., daily 9:30–5:30.*

The intersection of Routes 4 and 100 is at the heart of central Vermont's ski country, with the Killington, Pico, and Okemo resorts nearby. For a side trip into the area's principal city, **Rutland,** continue west 10 miles on Route 4.

⑤ In **Rutland** the homes of blue-collar workers vastly outnumber the mansions of the marble magnates who made the town famous, as do strips of shopping centers and a seemingly endless row of traffic lights. Rutland's traditional economic ties to railroading and marble, the latter an industry that supplied stone to such illustrious dwellings as the central research building of the New York Public Library in New York City, have been rapidly eclipsed by the growth of the Pico and Killington ski areas to the east.

⑥ At the **Vermont Marble Exhibit,** 4 miles north of Rutland in **Proctor,** visitors can watch the sculptor-in-residence transform stone into finished works of art. The gallery illustrates various industrial applications of marble—note the hall of presidents and the replica of Leonardo da Vinci's *Last Supper*—as well as depicting the industry's history via exhibits and slide shows. You can buy factory seconds and both foreign and domestic marble items here, too. *Follow signs off Rte. 3. Tel. 802/459–3311. Admission: $3.50 adults, $1.50 children 6–12. Open Memorial Day–Oct. 31, daily 9–5:30; Nov.–Memorial Day, Mon.–Sat. 9–4.*

Wilson Castle, a reminder of the area's 19th-century wealth and America's infatuation with European culture, is a 32-room Romanesque mansion complete with turrets, a stone portico, fresco ceilings, and a potpourri of Oriental and European furniture and objets d'art. Quite an anomaly in rural Vermont, it represents the Gilded Age at its most indulgent. *W. Proctor Rd., Proctor, tel. 802/773–3284. Admission: $6 adults, $5.50 senior citizens and children 6–12. Open late May–Oct., daily 9–6.*

Just what goes into producing all those jugs of maple syrup? The **New England Maple Museum** in Pittsford gives the historical perspective (the process originated with Native Americans, who cooked the sap over an open fire) and shows antique sugaring implements, folk murals, and a film. *Rte. 7, Pittsford, tel. 802/483–9414. Admission: $1.50 adults, 50¢ children 6–12. Open late May–late*

Oct., daily 8:30–5:30; late Oct.–Dec. and Apr.–late May, daily 10–4.

Head north on Route 100 for a scenic drive into the heart of the Green Mountains. The intersection of Routes 100 and 125 in Hancock offers options for two of Vermont's most inspiring mountain drives. The shorter one runs west on Route 125, passing nature trails and the picnic spot at Texas Falls Recreation Area. It then traverses a moderately steep mountain pass before reaching Middlebury. This is Robert Frost country; Vermont's late poet laureate spent 23 summers at a farm just east of Ripton. Three miles east of Ripton are the mustard-color buildings of Middlebury College's Breadloaf Campus, home of the renowned writer's conference begun by Frost; back track a mile to hike the easy ¾-mile **Robert Frost Interpretive Trail,** which winds through quiet woodland. Plaques along the way bear quotations from Frost's poems. There's a picnic area across the road from the trailhead.

The longer option continues on Route 100 and, after snaking through the Granville Gulf Nature Reserve, enters the rolling **Mad River Valley,** home to the Sugarbush and Mad River Glen ski areas. Although in close proximity to these popular resorts, the valley towns of **Warren** and **Waitsfield** have maintained a decidedly low-key atmosphere. The gently carved ridges cradling the valley and expansive pastures and fields lining the river seem to keep further notions of ski-resort sprawl at bay. Pick up a map from the Sugarbush Chamber of Commerce (*see* Important Addresses and Numbers, *above*) and investigate the back roads that spur off Route 100 for some exhilarating valley views.

Time Out The gourmet deli and bakery in the **Warren Store** (Main St.) has innovative sandwich, salad, and pastry offerings that you can savor on an outdoor deck overlooking a cascading brook.

Route 17 West winds up and over the Appalachian Gap, one of Vermont's most panoramic mountain passes: The views from the top and on the way down the other side toward charming but (thankfully) ungentrified Bristol are a just reward for the challenging drive.

❼ In the late 1800s **Middlebury** was the largest Vermont community west of the Green Mountains: an industrial center of river-powered wool, grain, and marble mills. Otter Creek, the state's longest river, traverses the town center. Still a cultural and economic hub amid the Champlain Valley's serene pastoral patchwork, the town and countryside beckon a day of exploration.

Smack in the middle of town, **Middlebury College,** founded in 1800, was conceived as an accessible alternative to the more worldly University of Vermont—although the two schools have since traded reputations. The provocative contrast of early-19th-century stone buildings against the postmodern architecture of the Fine Arts Building and sports center make for an opinion-provoking campus stroll. The **Johnson Memorial Art Gallery** has a permanent collection of paintings and sculpture that includes work by Rodin and Hiram Powers. *Fine Arts Bldg., tel. 802/388–3711, ext. 5235. Admission free. Open Tues.–Fri. 10–5, weekends noon–5.*

The **Vermont Folklife Center** is in the basement of the restored 1801 home of Gamaliel Painter, the founder of Middlebury College. The rotating exhibits explore all facets of Vermont life using means as diverse as contemporary photography, antiques, paintings by folk artists, and manuscripts. *2 Court St., tel. 802/388–4964. Donations accepted. Open weekdays 9–5 and, May–Oct., Sat. noon–4.*

Take the guided tour at the **Sheldon Museum,** an 1829 marble-merchant's house whose period rooms contain furniture, toys, clothes, kitchen tools, and paintings that span from colonial times to the early 20th century. *1 Park St., tel. 802/388–2117. Admission: $3.50 adults, $3 senior citizens and students, 50¢ children under 12. Open June–Oct., Mon.–Sat. 10–5; Nov.–May, weekdays 10–5.*

Time Out Calvi's (Merchants Row, Middlebury) has an old-fashioned marble-counter soda fountain and an extensive menu of ice-cream dishes.

More than a crafts store, the **Vermont State Craft Center at Frog Hollow** is a juried display of the work of more than 250 Vermont artisans. The center sponsors classes with some of those artists. *Mill St., tel. 802/388–3177. Open Mon.–Sat. 9:30–5 and, June–Dec., Sun. noon–5.*

The Morgan horse—the official state animal—is known for its even temper and stamina even though its legs are a bit truncated in proportion to its body. The University of Vermont's **Morgan Horse Farm,** about 2½ miles from Middlebury, is a breeding and training farm where, in summer, you can tour the stables and paddocks. *Rte. 23, tel. 802/388–2011. Admission: $3.50 adults, $1 children 13–19. Open May–Oct., daily 9–4:30; Nov.–Apr., weekdays 9–4:30, Sat. 9–noon.*

What to See and Do with Children

Billings Farm and Museum, Woodstock
Morgan Horse Farm, Middlebury
New England Maple Museum, Pittsford
Raptor Center, Woodstock

Off the Beaten Track

At the **Crowley Cheese Factory**'s converted barn, you can watch workers turn milk into cheese by hand, as they did in centuries past, rather than by machine. Turn south from Route 103 about 5 miles west of Ludlow (at the sign for Healdville) and continue 1 mile. *Tel. 802/259–2340. Open Mon.–Sat. 10–5, Sun. 11–5.*

Crossing the **floating bridge at Brookfield** feels like driving on water. The bridge, supported by almost 400 barrels, sits at water level and is the scene of the annual ice harvest festival in January (the bridge is closed in winter). Take Route 65 off I–89 to Brookfield and follow the signs.

The **Green Mountain Audubon Nature Center** (Huntington-Richmond Rd., Richmond, tel. 802/434–3068) bursts with great things to do, see, and learn; this is a wonderful place to orient yourself to Vermont's outdoor wonders. The center's 230 acres of diverse habitats are a sanctuary for all things wild, and the 5 miles of trails beg you to explore and understand the workings of differing natural communities. The center offers such events as dusk walks, wildflower and birding rambles, nature workshops, and educational activities for both kids and adults.

Shopping

Shopping Districts Historic Marble Works (Middlebury, tel. 802/388–3701), a renovated marble manufacturing facility, is a collection of unique shops set amid quarrying equipment and factory buildings. **The Marketplace at Bridgewater Mills** (Rte. 4, west of Woodstock, tel. 802/672–3332), set in a three-story converted woolen mill, houses such crafts boutiques as Vermont Clock Craft and Vermont Marble, as well as The Mountain Brewers, producers of Long Trail Ale, where tours and tastings are available. **Timber Rail Village** (Rte. 4, Quechee, tel. 802/295–1550) bills itself as an antiques mall and stocks inventory from 225 dealers in its immense reconstructed barn. A small-scale working railroad will take the kids for a ride while Mom and Dad browse.

Food and Drink Bristol Market (28 North St., Bristol, tel. 802/453–2448), open since the early 1900s, proffers gourmet health foods and local products. **The Village Butcher** (Elm St., Woodstock, tel. 802/457–2756) is an emporium of Vermont comestibles.

Specialty Stores
Art and Antiques The **Antiques Center at Hartland** (Rte. 5, Hartland, tel. 802/436–2441), one of the best known in Vermont, displays, in two 18th-century houses, inventory from 50 dealers. The **Chaffee Art Gallery** (16 S. Main St., tel. 802/775–0356) exhibits and sells the work of more than 250 Vermont artists who work in a variety of media. **Luminosity** (Rte. 100, Waitsfield, tel. 802/496–2231) is in a converted church and, fittingly, specializes in stained glass, among other wares. **Minerva** (61 Central St., Woodstock, tel. 802/457–1940) is a cooperative of eight artisans whose work includes stoneware, porcelain, and jewelry, as well as handwoven clothing, rugs, and blankets. **North Wind Artisans' Gallery** (81 Central St., Woodstock, tel. 802/457–4587) has contemporary, mostly Vermont-made, artwork with sleek, jazzy designs. **Windsor Antiques Market** (53 N. Main St., Windsor, tel. 802/674–9336) occupies a Gothic Revival church and sells Oriental, Native American, and military items in addition to American furniture, folk art, and accessories.

Books **Charles E. Tuttle** (28 S. Main St., Rutland, tel. 802/773–8930) is a major publisher of books on Asia, particularly Asian art. In addition to its own publications, Tuttle has rare and out-of-print books, genealogies, and local histories.

Clothing **Scotland by the Yard** (Rte. 4, Quechee, tel. 802/295–5351) has authentic Scottish kilts, kilt pins in imaginative designs, and jewelry bearing traditional Scottish emblems and symbols. **Who Is Sylvia?** (26 Central St., Woodstock, tel. 802/457–1110) stocks vintage clothing and antique linens and jewelry.

Crafts **All Things Bright and Beautiful** (Bridge St., Waitsfield, tel. 802/496–3997) is a 12-room Victorian house jammed to the rafters with stuffed animals of all shapes, sizes, and colors. **East Meets West** (Rte. 7 at Sangamon Rd., north of Rutland, tel. 802/443–2242) shows carvings, masks, statues, textiles, pottery, and baskets from the Third World, the American Southwest, the Pacific Northwest, and the Arctic. **Folkheart** (18 Main St., Bristol, tel. 802/453–4101; 71 Main St., Middlebury, tel. 802/388–0367) carries an unusual selection of jewelry, toys, and crafts from around the world. **Holy Cow** (52 Seymour St., Middlebury, tel. 802/388–6737) is where Woody Jackson creates and sells his infamous Holstein cattle-inspired T-shirts and memorabilia. **Log Cabin Quilts** (9 Central St., Woodstock, tel. 802/457–2725) has an outstanding collection of quilts in traditional designs and supplies. **Three Bags Full** (at the Black Sheep Farm, Rte.

100, Waitsfield, tel. 802/496–4298) features everything wool, including handmade sweaters, blankets, sheep pelts, and yarn. **Warren Village Pottery** (Main St., Warren, tel. 802/496–4162) sells unique, handcrafted wares from its home-based retail shop.

Sports and Outdoor Activities

Biking The popular 14-mile Waitsfield–Warren loop begins when you cross the covered bridge in Waitsfield. Keep right on East Warren Road to the four-way intersection in East Warren; continue straight, then bear right, riding down Brook Road to the village of Warren; return by turning right (north) on Route 100 back toward Waitsfield. **Mad River Bike Shop** (Rte. 100, Waitsfield, tel. 802/496–9500) offers rentals, mountain bike tours, and maps.

A more challenging, 32-mile ride starts in Bristol: Take North Street from the traffic light in town and continue north to Monkton Ridge and on to Hinesburg; to return, follow Route 116 south through Starksboro and back to Bristol. The **Bike and Ski Touring Center** (74 Main St., Middlebury, tel. 802/388–6666) offers rentals.

A bike trail runs alongside Route 106 south of Woodstock. Visit **Cyclery Plus** (36 Rte. 4 W, West Woodstock, tel. 802/457–3377) to rent equipment and get help planning an extended trip in the area.

Canoeing **Otter Falls Outfitters** (Marble Works, Middlebury, tel. 802/388–4406) has maps, guides, and gear. **North Star Canoes** (Balloch's Crossing, tel. 603/542–5802) in Cornish, New Hampshire, rents canoes for half-day, full-day, and overnight trips on the Connecticut River.

Fishing Central Vermont is the heart of the state's warm-water lake and pond fishing. **Lake Dunmore** produced the state-record rainbow trout; **Lakes Bomoseen** and **St. Catherine** are good for rainbows and largemouth bass. In the east, **Lakes Fairlee** and **Morey** feature bass, perch, and chain pickerel, while the lower part of the **Connecticut River** has bass, pickerel, walleye, and perch. **The Vermont Fly Fishing School** (Quechee Inn, Clubhouse Rd., Quechee 05059, tel. 802/295–7620) provides workshops, and **Yankee Charters** (20 S. Pleasant St., Middlebury 05753, tel. 802/388–7365) sets up trips on Lake Champlain; both rent gear.

Golf Spectacular views and challenging play are the trademarks of the Robert Trent Jones–designed 18-hole course at **Sugarbush Resort** (Golf Course Rd., Warren, tel. 802/583–2722). Jones also designed the 18-hole course at **Woodstock Country Club** (South St., Woodstock, tel. 802/457–2112), run by the Woodstock Inn.

Hiking Several day hikes in the vicinity of Middlebury take in the Green Mountains. About 8 miles east of Brandon on Route 73, one trail starts at Brandon Gap and climbs steeply up **Mt. Horrid** (1 hour). On Route 116, about 5½ miles north of East Middlebury, a U.S. Forest Service sign marks a dirt road that forks to the right and leads to the start of the hike to **Abbey Pond,** which has a view of Robert Frost Mountain (two–three hours).

About 5½ miles north of Forest Dale on Route 53, a large turnout marks a trail to the **Falls of Lana** (two hours). Three other trails—two short ones of less than a mile each and one of 2½ miles—lead to the old abandoned fortifications at **Mt. Independence;** to reach them, take Route 22A west of Orwell for 3½ miles and continue on the right fork almost 2 miles to a parking area.

Horseback Riding	**Kedron Valley Stables** (Rte. 106, South Woodstock, tel. 802/457–2734) has lessons and guided trail rides.
Polo	**Quechee Polo Club** (Dewey's Mill Rd., ½ mi off Route 4, Quechee, tel. 802/295–7152) draws several hundred spectators on summer Saturdays to its matches near the Quechee Gorge. Admission is $2 adults, $1 children, or $5 per car.
Water Sports	Rent boats from **Chipman Point Marina** (Rte. 73A, Middlebury, tel. 802/948–2288), where there is dockage for 60 boats.

State Parks

The following state parks have camping and picnicking facilities: **Ascutney State Park** (Rte. 5, 2 mi north of I–91 [Exit 8], tel. 802/674–2060; 1,984 acres) has a scenic mountain toll road and snowmobile trails. **Coolidge State Park** (Rte. 100A, 2 mi north of Rte. 100, tel. 802/672–3612; 500 acres), in Calvin Coolidge National Forest, includes the village where Calvin Coolidge was born and is great for snowmobiling. **Gifford Woods State Park**'s Kent Pond (Rte. 100, ½ mi north of Rte. 4, tel. 802/775–5354; 114 acres) is a terrific fishing hole. **Half Moon State Park**'s principal attraction is Half Moon Pond (Town Rd., 3½ mi off Rte. 30 west of Hubbardton, tel. 802/273–2848; 50 acres). The park has approach trails, nature trails, and a naturalist, as well as boat and canoe rentals.

Dining and Lodging

Country inns and bed-and-breakfasts abound in Woodstock and near Killington and Sugarbush, though accommodations are usually found in even the smallest towns as well. The **Woodstock Area Chamber of Commerce** (tel. 802/457–2389) and **Sugarbush Reservations** (tel. 800/537–8427) provide lodging referral services. For additional accommodations selections, see the Ascutney, Killington, Okemo, Pico, and Sugarbush sections of the Skiing in New England chapter. In the restaurants, dress is casual and reservations are unnecessary except where noted.

Bristol *Dining* ★	**Mary's.** Walking off the unassuming streets of Bristol and into this little storefront restaurant is like finding a precious antique in a dusty attic. Mary's is one of the most inspired eateries in the state. Seasonal offerings include Vermont rack of lamb with a rosemary mustard sauce, Norwegian salmon Szechuan style, and venison au poivre. For dessert try the Bailey's white-chocolate-chip cheesecake. *11 Main St., tel. 802/453–2432. Reservations advised. AE, MC, V. Moderate–Expensive.*
Middlebury *Dining* ★	**Woody's.** The peach walls with diner-deco fixtures, the abstract paintings, and the cool jazz create a setting where assistant professors celebrate special occasions. Of the three levels, the lowest has the best view of Otter Creek. The nightly specials might include a homemade soup of roast pheasant broth with barley; a dinner entrée could be charbroiled strip steak with smoked-cheddar nachos and salsa butter; and there's usually a Vermont lamb offering. *5 Bakery La., tel. 802/388–4182. Reservations advised. DC, MC, V. Moderate–Expensive.*
Dining and Lodging	**Middlebury Inn.** Queen Anne furniture, white fluted columns, a baby grand piano, and a black marble fireplace in the lobby reflect the heritage of Middlebury's foremost lodging since 1827. The Otis elevator dates from 1926. Rooms in the main building mix the formal with country antiques: Reproduction mahogany cabinets house tele-

vision sets. The 20 motel rooms have newer plumbing, sofa beds for a third person, quilt hangings, and floor-to-ceiling windows. At lunchtime the big bay window of the blue-and-white Colonial dining room lets in lots of light, and in the evening the candles above the fireplace give the pristine white columns, curtains, and lace table-cloths a romantic glow. Entrées include such dishes as veal Madeira, bourbon shrimp, and chicken teriyaki; the specialty of the house is hot popovers. *Court House Sq., 05753, tel. 802/388-4961 or 800/842-4666. 75 rooms with bath. Facilities: restaurant (reservations advised), lounge. AE, MC, V. Afternoon tea included. Inn: Moderate-Expensive. Restaurant: Expensive.*

Lodging
★ **Swift House Inn.** The white-panel wainscoting, elaborately carved mahogany and marble fireplaces, and cherry paneling in the dining room give this Georgian home of a 19th-century governor and his philanthropist daughter a formal elegance. Rooms, each with Oriental rugs and nine of them with fireplaces, are decorated with such antique reproductions as canopy beds, swag curtains, and clawfoot tubs. Some bathrooms have double whirlpool tubs. *25 Stewart La., 05753, tel. 802/388-9925, fax 802/388-9927. 21 rooms with bath. Facilities: restaurant, lounge, sauna and steam room, accessible for people with disabilities. Full breakfast included. AE, D, MC, V. Moderate-Expensive.*

Waybury Inn. The Waybury Inn may look familiar; it appeared as the "Stratford Inn" on television's *Newhart*. Guest rooms, some of which have the awkward configuration that can result from the conversion of a building of the early 1800s, have quilted pillows, antique furnishings, and middle-aged plumbing. Comfortable sofas around the fireplace create a homey living room, and the pub—which serves more than 100 different kinds of beer—is a favorite local gathering spot. *Rte. 125, 05740, tel. 802/388-4015 or 800/348-1810. 14 rooms with bath. Facilities: restaurant, lounge. AE, MC, V. Moderate-Expensive.*

Quechee
Dining
Simon Pearce. Candlelight and fresh flowers, sparkling glassware from the studio downstairs, contemporary dinnerware, and large windows that overlook the banks of the Ottauquechee River all contribute to a romantic setting. Beef and Guinness stew (which reflects the owner's Irish background) and roast duck with mango chutney sauce are specialties of the house. *Main St., tel. 802/295-1470. Reservations advised. AE, MC, V. Moderate-Expensive.*

Dining and
Lodging
Parker House. The spacious peach-and-blue rooms of this renovated 1857 Victorian mansion are named for former residents. Emily boasts a marble fireplace and an iron-and-brass bed. The armoire and dressing table in Rebecca have delicate faux inlays. Walter is the smallest room. Joseph has a spectacular view of the Ottauquechee River. The new rooms on the third floor are air-conditioned. The formal dining room of Isabelle's, the restaurant, was redone in 1990, resulting in a lighter, more contemporary feel. Lace window panels, high-back chairs, and traditional period stenciling on peach walls give Isabelle's an elegant atmosphere. The menu features such entrées as roasted local rabbit with homemade plum chutney as well as lighter bistro fare. In warm weather check out the terrace with its spectacular river view. *Main St., Box 0780, 05059, tel. 802/295-6077. 7 rooms with bath. Facilities: restaurant (no lunch; closed Mon. and Tues. except summer). AE, MC, V. Closed mid-Apr., early Nov. Expensive.*

Lodging
Quechee Inn at Marshland Farm. The home of Vermont's first lieutenant governor, this 1793 building has Queen Anne furniture and wide-plank pine floors. The sitting room flaunts an enormous fire-

place; a piano stands in one corner and a 5-foot teddy bear looks comfy sitting at a table in another. *Clubhouse Rd., 05059, tel. 802/ 295–3133, fax 802/295–6587. 24 rooms with bath. Facilities: restaurant, lounge, conference rooms, ski center, fly-fishing school, bike and canoe rentals. AE, DC, MC, V. Rates are MAP. Expensive– Very Expensive.*

★ **Quechee Bed and Breakfast.** Dried herbs hang from the beams in the living room, where a wood settee sits before a floor-to-ceiling fireplace that dates to the original structure of 1795. In the guest rooms, handwoven throws cover the beds and soft pastels coordinate linens and decor. Jessica's Room is the smallest; the Bird Room, with its exposed beams, is one of four that overlook the Ottauquechee River. Rooms at the back are farther from busy Route 4. The wide front porch is adorned with seasonal decorations such as luminarias and cornstalks, and the inn is within walking distance of Quechee Gorge. *Rte. 4, 05059, tel. 802/295–1776. 8 rooms with bath. MC, V. Full breakfast included. Moderate–Expensive.*

Rutland **Ernie's Hearthside.** Known also as Royal's Hearthside, Royal's Grill
Dining and Bar, and Ernie's Grill and Bar, this Rutland institution features an open hearth with hand-painted tiles, behind which the staff prepares mesquite-grilled chicken with basil, tomato, and mushrooms; roast prime rib; and lamb chops grilled with ginger and rosemary. *37 N. Main St., tel. 802/775–0856. Reservations advised. AE, DC, MC, V. Moderate.*

★ **Back Home Cafe.** Wood booths, black-and-white linoleum tile, and exposed brick give this second-story café the air of a hole-in-the-wall in New York City—where the owners come from. Dinner might be baked stuffed fillet of sole with spinach, mushrooms, feta cheese, and tarragon sauce, or any of a number of Italian specialties. Daily lunch specials offer soup, entrée, and dessert for less than $5. *21 Center St., tel. 802/775–2104. MC, V. Inexpensive–Moderate.*

Dining and **Vermont Marble Inn.** The innkeepers are the sort of people who beg
Lodging you to put on your coat so you don't catch cold; they also present an
★ elaborate afternoon tea on a sterling silver service. Two ornate Carrara marble living room fireplaces look and feel as though they were carved from solid cream. Guest rooms are named for authors (Byron, Elizabeth Barrett Browning), whose works are placed beside the bed. The antique furnishings may include a canopy bed, a working fireplace, an antique trunk; the bathrooms are large enough to have accommodated the full, flowing dresses of 1867, when the inn was built as a private home. Eight baths have shower stall only. The dining room, with 16 tables, is intimate enough to lead to new friendships. Anything less than the classical music, crystal chandelier, and candlelight would scarcely do justice to a meal that might include veal loin sautéed in saffron oil with sweet peppers and olives in a chive pesto, or braised duckling in port and raspberry sauce with wild rice. A vegetarian plate may offer lentil-and-vegetable-stuffed zucchini and grilled polenta, and there's a selection of home-baked desserts. *Fair Haven, 05743, tel. 802/265–8383. 13 rooms with bath. Facilities: restaurant, lounge. Rates are MAP. AE, MC, V. Inn: Very Expensive. Restaurant: Moderate–Expensive.*

Lodging **The Inn at Rutland.** Mary and Michael Clark gave Rutland an alternative to motel and hotel chain accommodations when they renovated a Victorian mansion in 1988. The ornate oak staircase lined with heavy embossed metallic paper wainscoting leads to rooms that blend modern bathrooms with turn-of-the-century touches: botanical prints, elaborate ceiling moldings, frosted glass, pictures of ladies in long white dresses. Second-floor rooms are larger than

those on the third (once the servants' quarters). *70 N. Main St.,
05701, tel. 802/773–0575, fax 802/775–3506. 12 rooms with bath. AE,
D, MC, V. Continental breakfast included. Moderate.*

Comfort Inn. This hotel just in back of the Trolley Barn shops may
look as though it's intended for business travelers, but it also has a
large tourist clientele. Guest room decor is a cut above the hotel
chain standard, though the bathrooms are a bit small. Rooms with
even numbers face away from the parking lot. *170 S. Main St.,
05701, tel. 802/775–2200 or 800/432–6788, fax 802/775–2694. 103
rooms with bath. Facilities: restaurant, lounge, indoor pool, racquetball, tennis, sauna, whirlpool, exercise equipment. Continental breakfast included. AE, D, DC, MC, V. Inexpensive–Moderate.*

Waitsfield
Dining

Chez Henri. Tucked in the shadows of Sugarbush Mountain, this bistro has garnered a year-round following with traditional French
dishes such as grilled swordfish with a coulis, rabbit in red wine
sauce, and fillet of beef peppercorn. After dinner, ease your diges-
tion with dancing in the "Back Room." *Sugarbush Village, tel. 802/
583–2600. AE, MC, V. Moderate–Expensive.*

Richard's Special Vermont Pizza (RSVP). Walk through the door,
and you're immediately transported through time (to the 1950s) and
space (to anywhere but Vermont). The pizza—legendary around
these parts with its paper-thin crust and toppings like cilantro
pesto, cob-smoked bacon, pineapple, and sautéed spinach—has become known for transport as well: Richard will Federal Express a
frozen pie almost anywhere in the world overnight. And there are
plenty of takers. Salads and sandwiches are also available. *Bridge
St., tel. 802/496–RSVP. MC, V. Inexpensive.*

Lodging

The Inn at the Round Barn Farm. Art exhibits have replaced cows in
the big round barn here, but the Shaker-style building still dominates the farm's 85 countryside acres. One of the 12 remaining round
barns in the state, it's used for summer concerts, weddings, and parties. The inn's 10 rooms are in the 1806 farmhouse, where books line
the walls of the cream-color library and breakfast is served in a
cheerful solarium that overlooks a small landscaped pond and rolling
acreage. The rooms are elegance country-style, with eyelet-
trimmed sheets, new quilts on four-poster beds, and brass wall
lamps for easy bedtime reading. You could relax here until the cows
come home. *E. Warren Rd., RR 1, Box 247, 05673, tel. 802/496–
2276. 10 rooms with bath. Facilities: whirlpools, swimming pool.
Full breakfast included. AE, MC, V. Moderate–Expensive.*

Windsor
Dining

Windsor Station. This converted main-line railroad station serves
such main-line entrées as chicken Kiev or filet mignon (prime rib on
Saturday night). The booths with their curtained brass railings
were created from the high-back railroad benches in the depot. *Depot Ave., tel. 802/674–2052. AE, MC, V. Closed early Nov. Moderate.*

*Dining and
Lodging*

Juniper Hill Inn. An expanse of green lawn with Adirondack chairs
and a garden of perennials sweeps up to the portico of this Greek Revival mansion, built at the turn of the century and now on the National Historic Register. The central living room with its hardwood
floors, oak paneling, Oriental carpets, and thickly upholstered wing
chairs and sofas has a stately feel. The spacious rooms are furnished
with antiques, and some have fireplaces. The four-course dinners
served in the candlelit dining room may include roast pork glazed
with mustard and brandy sauce. The inn is just 7 miles from Mt.
Ascutney and is thus popular with skiers from Ascutney's resort.
Juniper Hill Rd., Box 79, 05089, tel. 802/674–5273 or 800/359–2541,

fax 802/674–5273. 16 rooms with bath. Facilities: restaurant, pool,
walking trails. MC, V. Full breakfast included. Moderate.

Woodstock **The Prince and the Pauper.** Here is a romantically candlelit Colonial
Dining setting, a prix fixe menu, and nouvelle French fare with a Vermont
★ accent. The roast duckling might be served with a black cherry or
Cointreau glaze; escalopes de veau could have a Madeira demiglace
or creamed onions with tarragon vinegar. Homemade lamb and pork
sausage in puff pastry with a honey-mustard sauce is another possi-
bility. *24 Elm St., tel. 802/457–1818. Reservations advised. D, MC,*
V. No lunch. Closed Sun.–Mon. some seasons. Expensive.

Bentleys. In addition to the standards—burgers, chili, homemade
soups, omelets, croissants with various fillings—entrées at this informal and often busy restaurant include duck in raspberry purée,
almonds, and Chambord, and tournedos with red zinfandel sauce.
Remy rum-raisin ice cream is one of the tempting desserts. You'll
find jazz or blues here on weekends. *3 Elm St., tel. 802/457–3232.*
AE, MC, V. Moderate.

Dining and **Kedron Valley Inn.** The inn is imbued with the personalities of its
Lodging owners, Max and Merrily Comins; in 1985 they began the renovation
★ of what in the 1840s had been the National Hotel, one of the state's
oldest. Many rooms have either a fireplace or a Franklin stove, and
each is decorated with a quilt. Two rooms have private decks, another has a private veranda, and a fourth has a private terrace overlooking the stream that runs through the inn's 15 acres. The exposed-log
walls in the motel units in back are more rustic than the rooms in the
main inn, but they're decorated in similar fashion. The classically
trained chef creates such French masterpieces as fillet of Norwegian
salmon stuffed with herb seafood mousse in puff pastry, and shrimp,
scallops, and lobster with wild mushrooms sautéed in shallots and
white wine and served with a Fra Angelico cream sauce. The decor,
too, is striking; a terrace looking onto the grounds is open in summer. *Rte. 106, 05071, tel. 802/457–1473, fax 802/457–4469. 28 rooms*
with bath. Facilities: restaurant, lounge, 1½-acre pond with sand
beach, riding center. D, MC, V. Closed Apr. Full breakfast in-
cluded. Inn: Expensive–Very Expensive. Restaurant: Expensive.

Woodstock Inn and Resort. The hotel's floor-to-ceiling fieldstone
fireplace in the lobby with its massive wood-beam mantel embody
the spirit of New England, and it comes as no surprise to learn that
the resort is owned by the Rockefeller family. The rooms' modern
ash furnishings are high-quality institutional, enlivened by patchwork quilts on the beds; the inoffensive decor is designed to please
the large clientele of corporate conference attendees. Some of the
newer rooms, constructed in 1990, have fireplaces. The dinner fare
is nouvelle New England; the menu changes seasonally and may include such entrées as salmon steak with avocado beurre blanc;
Maine lobster and scallops with fresh vegetable mélange; and such
standbys as beef Wellington and prime rib. The wall of windows affords diners a view over the inn's putting green. *Rte. 4, 05091, tel.*
802/457–1100 or 800/448–7900, fax 802/457–6699. 146 rooms with
bath. Facilities: restaurant (reservations advised; jacket requested
after 6 PM), conference rooms, indoor and outdoor pools, indoor and
outdoor tennis, sports center, squash and racquetball, whirlpool, sau-
nas, ski center, putting green, golf, croquet, lounge. AE, MC, V. Ex-
pensive–Very Expensive.

Lodging **Twin Farms.** At the center of this exclusive 235-acre resort stands
the 1795 farmhouse where Sinclair Lewis and Dorothy Thompson
lived. In recent years the stone-and-pine house has been fully renovated and four stone cottages have been added. Rooms and cottages

are decorated with such luxurious touches as original watercolors, ample bookshelves, fireplaces, needlepoint rugs, and wood-and-stone furniture. The exception is one avant-garde studio with huge arch windows, a cathedral-ceiling living room done in spare classical furnishings, and a king-size bed covered in woven raffia in a loft overhead. Chef Neil Wigglesworth prepares a prix fixe menu of rich contemporary cuisine that draws occasionally on local recipes. *Rte. 12, 8 mi north of Woodstock (Box 115, Barnard, VT 05031), tel. 802/ 234–9999 or 800/894–6327, fax 802/234–9990. 4 rooms with bath, 4 cottages. Facilities: dining room, 2 bars, lounge, conference room, games room, fitness center, free use of skis, bikes, and boats. AE, MC, V. Very Expensive.*

Village Inn at Woodstock. This renovated Victorian mansion features oak wainscoting, ornate pressed-tin ceilings, and a front porch perfect for studying the passersby on the sidewalks of Main Street; it's also convenient to downtown. Rooms are decorated simply with country antiques, quilts or chenille bedspreads, and dried flowers. *Rte. 4, 05091, tel. 802/457–1255. 8 rooms, 6 with bath. Facilities: restaurant, lounge. Full breakfast included. MC, V. Closed early Nov. Moderate.*

★ **Pond Ridge Motel.** The strip of rooms was renovated in 1989, so the furnishings are simple but fresh and tidy. Unlike many motels, it's set far enough back from Route 4 to mute the noise of the traffic. The big surprise here is the spacious back lawn that runs down to the Ottauquechee River. Many visitors choose one of the two-bedroom apartments with refrigerator, table, and stove. *Rte. 4, 05091, tel. 802/457–1667. 21 rooms with bath. AE, MC, V. Inexpensive–Moderate.*

The Arts

Green Mountain Cultural Center (Inn at the Round Barn, E. Warren Rd., Waitsfield, tel. 802/496–7722), a nonprofit organization, brings concerts and art exhibits, as well as educational workshops, to the Mad River Valley. **Middlebury College** (tel. 802/388–3711) sponsors music, theater, and dance performances throughout the year at Wright Memorial Theatre. The **Pentangle Council on the Arts** (tel. 802/457–3981) in Woodstock organizes performances of music, theater, and dance at the Town Hall Theater. In Rutland, the **Crossroads Arts Council** (tel. 802/775–5413) presents music, opera, dance, jazz, and theater events.

Music **Vermont Symphony Orchestra** (tel. 802/864–5741) performs in Rutland and, during the summer, in Woodstock.

Opera **Opera North** (Norwich, tel. 802/649–1060) does three opera productions annually at locations throughout the state.

Theater **The Valley Players** (Rte. 100, Waitsfield, tel. 802/496–3485) presents a year-round mix of musicals, dramas, follies, and holiday shows. **Vermont Ensemble Theater** (tel. 802/388–2676 or 802/388–3001) has a three-week summer season in a tent on the Middlebury College campus.

Nightlife

Most nighttime activity takes place around the ski resorts of Killington, Pico, and Sugarbush.

Bars and **Giorgio's Café** (Tucker Hill Lodge, Rte. 17, Waitsfield, tel. 802/496–
Lounges 3983) is a cozy spot to warm by the fire to the sounds of soft folk and jazz. **Inn at the Long Trail** (Rte. 4, Killington, tel. 802/775–7181) has

a comfortable lounge that hosts Irish music on weekends. **The Back Room at Chez Henri** (Sugarbush Village, tel. 802/583–2600) is popular with the après-ski and late-night dance crowd. **Bentleys** (3 Elm St., Woodstock, tel. 802/457–3232), a popular restaurant, also offers live jazz and blues on weekends. **Gallaghers** (Rtes. 100 and 17, Waitsfield, tel. 802/496–8800) is a popular spot, with danceable local bands. **The Pickle Barrel** (Killington Rd., Killington, tel. 802/422–3035), a favorite with the après-ski crowd, presents up-and-coming acts.

Northern Vermont

Northern Vermont, where much of the state's logging and dairying takes place, is a land of contrasts: It has the state's largest city—which is also the nation's smallest state capital—some of New England's most rural areas, and an abundance of wildlife. With Montréal only an hour from the border, the Canadian influence is strong and Canadian accents and currency common.

Important Addresses and Numbers

Visitor Information
The following offices are open weekdays 9–5. **Central Vermont Chamber of Commerce** (Box 336, Barre 05641, tel. 802/229–5711). **Greater Newport Area Chamber of Commerce** (The Causeway, Newport 05855, tel. 802/334–7782). **Lake Champlain Regional Chamber of Commerce** (209 Battery St., Box 453, Burlington 05402, tel. 802/863–3489). **St. Johnsbury Chamber of Commerce** (30 Western Ave., St. Johnsbury 05819, tel. 802/748–3678). **Smugglers' Notch Area Chamber of Commerce** (Box 3264, Jeffersonville 05464, tel. 802/644–2239). **Stowe Area Association** (Main St., Box 1320, Stowe 05672, tel. 802/253–7321 or 800/247–8693; open Apr.–Oct., weekdays 9–5; Nov.–Mar., weekdays 9–9, Sat. 10–6, Sun. 10–4).

Emergencies
Medical Center Hospital of Vermont (Colchester Ave., Burlington, tel. 802/656–2345) in Burlington is the most comprehensive medical facility in the region.

Getting Around Northern Vermont

By Car
In north-central Vermont, I-89 heads west from Montpelier to Burlington and continues north to Canada. Interstate-91 is the principal north–south route in the east, and Route 100 runs north–south through the center of Vermont. North of I-89, Routes 15 and 104 provide a major east–west transverse.

By Bus
Vermont Transit (tel. 802/864–6811, 800/451–3292, or, in VT, 800/642–3133) links Burlington, Stowe, Montpelier, Barre, St. Johnsbury, and Newport.

Guided Tours

The **Lamoille Valley Railroad,** a working line, augments its income by carrying passengers on one- to two-hour excursions along the Lamoille River, where the green and gold cars crisscross the water and pass through one of the rare covered railroad bridges in the country. *Stafford Ave., Morrisville, tel. 802/888–4255. Fare: $10 adults, $5 children 5–12. July–early Sept., Fri. and Sat. 10, 12:45, and 2; mid-Sept.–mid-Oct, Mon.–Sat. 10, 12:45, and 2.*

Exploring Northern Vermont

Numbers in the margin correspond to points of interest on the Northern Vermont map.

You'll find plenty to do in the busy ski area at Stowe; in the region's cities, Burlington, Montpelier, St. Johnsbury, and Barre; and in rural and even remote areas in the Lake Champlain islands and the Northeast Kingdom.

❶ The Vermont legislature anointed **Montpelier** as the state capital in 1805. Today, with fewer than 10,000 residents, the city is the country's least populous seat of government. Built in 1859, following its predecessor's destruction by fire, the current **Vermont State House**—with its gold dome and granite columns 6 feet in diameter—has an impressive scale. Inside, the small House chamber, and even smaller Senate chamber, reflect the intimacy of the state's citizen legislature. Tour the building on your own or with a guide; tours are offered on the half hour. *State St., tel. 802/828–2228. Admission free. Open weekdays 8–4.*

Are you wondering what the last panther shot in Vermont looked like? Why New England bridges are covered? What a niddy-noddy is? Or what Christmas was like for a Bethel boy in 1879? ("I skated on my new skates. In the morning Papa and I set up a stove for Gramper.") The **Vermont Museum,** on the ground floor of the Vermont Historical Society offices in Montpelier, has the answers. *109 State St., tel. 802/828–2291. Admission: $3 adults, $2 senior citizens. Open Tues.–Fri., 9–4:30, Sat. 9–4, Sun. noon–4.*

The intersection of State and Main streets is the city hub, bustling with the activity of state and city workers. Turn onto Main and follow the signs to Vermont College's **T. W. Wood Art Gallery,** named for a Montpelier artist and a prominent painter of the Academy school of realism, who endowed this facility with his collection of his own art and that of his peers. Changing exhibits feature contemporary work. *Vermont College Arts Center, E. State St., tel. 802/828–8743. Admission: $2. Open Tues.–Sun. noon–4.*

Northwest of Montpelier, in Waterbury, one of Vermont's best-loved attractions is **Ben and Jerry's Ice Cream Factory,** a mecca, nirvana, and Valhalla for ice-cream lovers. Ben and Jerry, who began selling ice cream from a renovated gas station in the 1970s, have created a business that has grown to become one of the most influential voices in community-based activism in the country. Their action-oriented social and environmental consciousness—which initiated such projects as the "1 Percent for Peace" program—have made the company a model of corporate responsibility. Fifty percent of tour proceeds go to Vermont community groups. The plant tour is a bit too self-congratulatory—a flaw forgiven when the out-of-this-world free samples are offered. *Rte. 100, 1 mi north of I–89, tel. 802/244–5641. Tour: $1, children under 12 free. Open Mon.–Sat. 9–5. Tour every ½ hour.*

❷ For more than a century the history of **Stowe**—northwest of Montpelier on Route 100, 10 miles north of I–89—has been determined by the town's proximity to Mt. Mansfield, the highest elevation in the state. As early as 1858, visitors were trooping to the area to view the mountain whose shape suggests the profile of the face of a man lying on his back. In summer, you can take the 4½-mile **toll road** to the top for a short scenic walk and a magnificent view. *Mountain Rd., 7 mi from Rte. 100, tel. 802/253–3000. Admission: $9 car, $6 motorcycle. Open late May–early Oct., daily 10–5.*

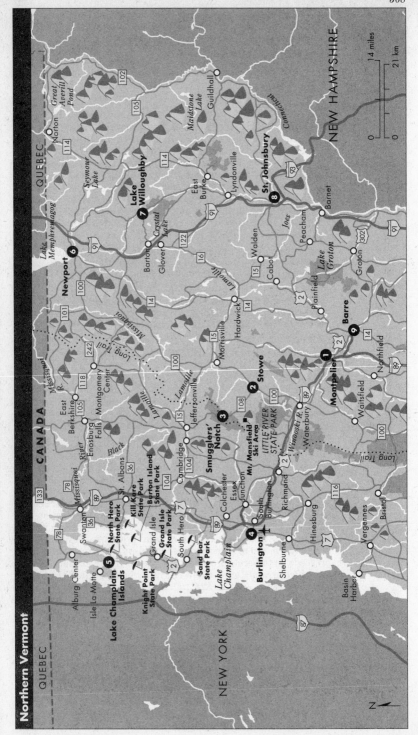

Northern Vermont

QUEBEC

CANADA

QUEBEC

NEW YORK

NEW HAMPSHIRE

0   4 miles

0   21 km

N

Lake Champlain Islands ⑤

Alburg Center

Isle La Motte

Swanton

St. Albans

Kill Kare State Park

North Hero State Park

Grand Isle

Grand Isle State Park

Knight Point State Park

South Hero

Sand Bar State Park

Lake Champlain

Shelburne

Basin Harbor

Vergennes

Bristol

Hinesburg

Richmond

Burlington ④

South Burlington

Essex Junction

Colchester

Cambridge

Smugglers' Notch

③

Mt. Mansfield Ski Area

LITTLE RIVER STATE PARK

Long Trail

Waitsfield

Waterbury

Montpelier ①

Barre ⑨

Northfield

Stowe ②

Morrisville

Hardwick

Cabot

Plainfield

Groton

Lake Groton

Peacham

Barnet

Ioes

St. Johnsbury ⑧

Lyndonville

East Burke

Lake Willoughby ⑦

Crystal Lake

Glover

Barton

Seymour Lake

Norton

Great Averill Pond

Newport ⑥

Lake Memphremagog

Walden

Montgomery Center

East Berkshire

Enosburg Falls

Black River

Missisquoi

Missisquoi River

Missisquoi R.

Long Trail

Lamoille

Lamoille River

Jeffersonville

Winooski R.

Connecticut

Guildhall

Maidstone Lake

Waterbury

An alternative means of reaching the Mt. Mansfield summit is the eight-seat **gondola** that shuttles continuously up 4,393 feet to the area of "the Chin," which has a small restaurant (dinner reservations required). *Mountain Rd., 7 mi from Rte. 100, tel. 802/253–3000 or 800/253–4754. Admission: $10 adults, $5 children 6–12. Open June–early Oct., daily 10–5; Dec.–Apr., daily 8:30–4; Oct.–Nov. and May, weekends 10–5.*

The Mount Mansfield Co. also operates a 2,300-foot **Alpine slide** on Spruce Peak. *Spruce Peak Lodge, Mountain Rd. Cost of ride $6 adults, $4 children 6–12; unlimited rides $18 adults, $14 children 6–12. Open June–early Sept., daily 10–5; early Sept.–early Oct., weekends 10–5.*

Time Out   The **Blue Moon Café** serves hearty bistro fare in a renovated landmark building on Stowe's School Street.

To many, Stowe rings a bell as the place the von Trapp family, of *Sound of Music* fame, chose to settle after fleeing Austria. The views from the **Trapp Family Lodge** (Luce Hill Rd., tel. 802/253–8511) are worth the long drive up. Set amid acres of pastures that fall away dramatically and allow for wide-angle panoramas of the mountains beyond, the resort is the site of a popular outdoor music series in summer and an extensive cross-country ski trail network in winter.

❸ Northwest of Stowe lies a scenic but indirect route to Burlington: **Smugglers' Notch,** the narrow pass over Mt. Mansfield that is said to have sheltered 18th-century outlaws in its rugged, bouldered terrain. You can park and picnic at roadside and, as you begin the descent on the western side of the mountain, you'll notice a spectacular waterfall on your left, though you may have to look over your shoulder to see it. The notch road is closed in winter. Follow Route 108 to Route 15, which turns west and south at Jeffersonville.

❹ Vermont's largest population center, **Burlington** was founded in 1763 and had a long history as a trade center following the growth of shipping on Lake Champlain in the 18th century. More recently, energized by the roughly 20,000 students from the area's five colleges, including the University of Vermont, and an abundance of culture-hungry, transplanted urban dwellers, Burlington draws an eclectic element. It was for years the only city in America with a socialist mayor—now the nation's sole socialist congressman. The **Church Street Marketplace**—a pedestrian mall of down-to-earth shops, chic boutiques, and an appealing menagerie of sidewalk cafés, food and craft vendors, and street performers—is an animated downtown focal point. Burlington's festive town center is where most people in central and northern Vermont are drawn at least occasionally to do errands or see a show.

Crouched on the shores of Lake Champlain, which shimmers in the shadows of the Adirondacks to the west, Burlington's recently revitalized **waterfront** teems with outdoor enthusiasts in summer who stroll along its recreation path and ply the waters in sailboats and motorcraft. A replica of an old Champlain paddlewheeler, *The Spirit of Ethan Allen,* hosts narrated cruises on the lake and, in the evening, dinner and moonlight dance sailings that drift by the Adirondacks and the Green Mountains. *Perkins Pier, tel. 802/862–9685. $8 adults, $4 children 5–11. Cruises June–mid-Oct., daily 10–9.*

Time Out   Need a pick-me-up? Stop by **Speeder & Earl's Espresso Bar** (104 Church St.) for a quick cup o' joe or sit down, stay a while, and learn about coffees from all over the world.

After emerging from the built-up strip heading south out of Burlington, Route 7 gives way to the fertile farmland of the Champlain Valley, affording chin-dropping views of the rugged Adirondacks across the lake. Five miles from the city, one could trace all New England history simply by wandering the 45 acres of the **Shelburne Museum,** whose 37 buildings seem a collection of individual museums. The large collection of Americana contains 18th- and 19th-century period homes and furniture, fine and folk art, farm tools, more than 200 carriages and sleighs, Audubon prints, even a private railroad car from the days of steam. And an old-fashioned jail. And an assortment of duck decoys. And an old stone cottage. And a display of early toys. And the *Ticonderoga,* an old sidewheel steamship, curiously misplaced amid lawn and trees. *Rte. 7, 5 mi south of Burlington, tel. 802/985–3346. Admission (good for 2 consecutive days): $16 adults, $7 children 6–14. Open mid-May–mid-Oct., daily 10–5; limited winter hours, call ahead.*

Nearby **Shelburne Farms** has a history of improving the farmer's lot by developing new agricultural methods. Founded in the 1880s as the private estate of a gentleman farmer, the 1,000-acre property is now an educational and cultural resource center. Here you can see a working dairy farm, listen to nature lectures, or simply stroll the immaculate grounds on a scenic stretch of Lake Champlain waterfront. The original landscaping, designed by Frederick Law Olmsted, the creator of Central Park and Boston's Emerald Necklace, gently channels the eye to expansive vistas and aesthetically satisfying views of such buildings as the five-story, 2-acre Farm Barn. *East of Rte. 7, 6 mi south of Burlington, tel. 802/985–8686. Admission: $5.50 adults, $5 senior citizens, $2.50 children 6–15. Guided tour $2.50. Visitor center and shop open daily 9:30–5, last tour at 3:30; tours given Memorial Day–mid-Oct.*

At the 6-acre **Vermont Wildflower Farm,** the display along the flowering pathways changes constantly: violets in the spring, daisies and black-eyed Susans for summer, and fall colors that rival the foliage. The farm is the largest wildflower seed center in the eastern part of the country, and you can buy crafts and books here, too. *Rte. 7, 5 mi south of the Shelburne Museum, tel. 802/425–3500. Admission: $3 adults, $1.50 senior citizens. Open mid-May–Oct., daily 10–5.*

On your way back up north, visit the **Vermont Teddy Bear Company** (2301 Shelburne Rd., 1 mi north of Shelburne Museum, tel. 802/ 985–3001; open Mon.–Sat. 9–6, Sun. 11–5) to catch the increasing popularity of another of the state's progressive entrepreneurial companies, whose goals include employee empowerment and environmental sensitivity. The free factory tour lets you in on how the handcrafted bears are born.

Retrace Route 7 back through Burlington and head north, where more of the state's history is revealed. Ethan Allen, Vermont's famous early settler, is a figure of some mystery. The visitor center at his **homestead** by the Winooski River both raises and answers questions about his flamboyant life. The house, about 70% original, has such frontier hallmarks as nails pointing through the roof on the top floor, rough saw-cut boards, and an open hearth for cooking. *North Ave., off Rte. 127, north of Burlington, tel. 802/865–4556. Admission: $3.50 adults, $3 senior citizens, $2 children 6–12, $10 family.*

Open mid-May-mid-June, Tues.-Sun. 1-5; mid-June-Labor Day, Mon.-Sat 10-5, Sun. 1-5; Labor Day-late Oct., daily 1-5.

The **Discovery Museum,** northeast of Burlington in Essex Junction, is a cornucopia of hands-on natural science, art, and history, with changing exhibits. *51 Park St., Essex Junction, tel. 802/878-8687. Admission: $3 adults, $2 children. Open Tues.-Sat. 10-5, Sun. 1-5.*

Samuel de Champlain's claim on the islands dotting the northern expanses of Lake Champlain is represented on Isle La Motte by a granite statue that looks south toward the site of the first French settlement and its shrine to St. Anne. Today the **Lake Champlain Islands** are a center of water recreation in summer, ice fishing in winter. North of Burlington, the scenic drive through the islands on Route 2 begins at I-89 and travels north through South Hero, Grand Isle, and Isle La Motte to Alburg Center, 5 miles from the Canadian border. Here Route 78 will take you east to the mainland.

To cross northern Vermont, take Route 78 east through the **Missisquoi National Wildlife Refuge** (tel. 802/868-4781), 5,800 acres of federally protected wetlands, meadows, and woods, to Route 105. Continue to Route 118 in East Berkshire, and follow that to Route 242 and the Jay Peak area. From the top of the mountain pass there are vast views of Canada to the north, and to the east of Vermont's rugged **Northeast Kingdom.**

The descent from Jay Peak on Route 101 leads to Route 100, which takes you east to the city of **Newport** on Lake Memphremagog (accent on *gog*). The waterfront is the dominant view of the city, which is built on a peninsula. The grand hotels of the last century are gone, yet the buildings still drape dramatically along the lake's edge and climb the hills behind.

The drive south from Newport on I-91 encounters some of the most unspoiled areas in all Vermont. This is the Northeast Kingdom, named for the remoteness and stalwart independence that has helped to preserve its rural nature; some of the towns here still have no people living in them. From the northern shore of **Lake Willoughby,** 7 miles northwest of Barton off I-91, the cliffs of surrounding Mts. Pisgah and Hor dropping to water's edge give this glacially carved, 500-foot-deep lake a striking resemblance to a Norwegian fjord. The lake is popular for both summer and winter recreation, and the trails to the top of Mt. Pisgah reward hikers with glorious views.

The southern gateway to this section of the state is the city of **St. Johnsbury,** directly off I-91. Though chartered in 1786, St. Johnsbury's identity was not firmly established until 1830, when Thaddeus Fairbanks invented the platform scale, a device that revolutionized weighing methods that had been in use since the beginning of recorded history. The impact of his company on the city is still pervasive: a distinctly 19th-century industrial feel onto which a strong cultural and architectural imprint has been superimposed, the result of the Fairbanks family's philanthropic bent. The **Fairbanks Museum and Planetarium** attests to the family inquisitiveness about all things scientific. The redbrick building in the squat Romanesque architectural style of H. H. Richardson houses collections of Vermont plants and animals, other Vermont items, and an intimate 50-seat planetarium. *Main and Prospect Sts., tel. 802/748-2372. Admission: $3 adults, $2.50 children, $7.50 family; planetarium $1.50. Open July-Aug., Mon.-Sat. 10-6, Sun. 1-5; Sept.-*

*June, Mon.–Sat. 10–4, Sun. 1–5. Planetarium shows: July–Aug.,
daily at 11, 1:30; Sept.–June, weekends at 1:30.*

The **St. Johnsbury Athenaeum,** with its dark rich paneling, polished
Victorian woodwork, and ornate circular staircases that rise to the
gallery around the perimeter, is a tiny gem. The gallery at the back
of the building has the overwhelming *Domes of Yosemite* by Albert
Bierstadt and a lot of sentimental 19th-century material. *30 Main
St., tel. 802/748–8291. Admission free. Open Mon., Wed. 10–8;
Tues., Thurs., Fri. 10–5:30; Sat. 9:30–4.*

Heading east from St. Johnsbury along Route 2, an 8-mile detour to
the south leads to the village of **Peacham.** This tiny hamlet's almost-
too-picturesque scenery and 18th-century charm have made it a favorite for urban refugees and artists seeking solitude and inspiration, as well as movie directors looking for the quintessential New
England village: The critically acclaimed *Ethan Frome* was filmed
here.

Time Out Stop into the **Peacham Store** (Rte. 2) for a quirky combination of
Yankee Vermont sensibility and Hungarian eccentricity. Transylva-
nian goulash, stuffed peppers, and lamb-and-barley soup are among
the take-out specialties.

❾ **Barre** has been famous as the source of Vermont granite ever since
two men began working the quarries in the early 1800s, and the
large number of immigrant laborers attracted to the industry made
the city prominent in the early years of the American labor movement.

The attractions of the **Rock of Ages granite quarry** (I–89 [Exit 6]; follow Rte. 63) range from the awe-inspiring—the quarry resembles a
man-made miniature of the Grand Canyon—to the absurd: The company invites you to consult a directory of tombstone dealers
throughout the United States. At the craftsman center, which you
pass on the drive to the visitor center, the view seems to take in a
scene out of Dante's *Inferno:* A dusty, smoky haze hangs above the
acres of men at work, with machines screaming as they bite into the
rock. The process that transfers designs to the smooth stone and
etches them into it is fascinating. *Rte. 63, tel. 802/476–3115. Quarry
and visitor center open May–mid-Oct., daily 8:30–5. Quarry shuttle bus tour weekdays 9:30–3:30; admission: $2 adults, $1 children
5–12. Craftsman center open weekdays 8–3:30.*

What to See and Do with Children

Ben and Jerry's Ice Cream Factory, Waterbury
The Discovery Museum, Essex Junction
Lamoille Valley Railroad, Morrisville
The Spirit of Ethan Allen, Burlington
The Vermont Teddy Bear Company, Shelburne

Off the Beaten Track

The **Lake Champlain Maritime Museum** commemorates the days
when steamships sailed along the coast of northern Vermont carrying logs, livestock, and merchandise bound for New York City. The
exhibits housed here in a one-room stone schoolhouse 25 miles south
of Burlington include historic maps, nautical prints, and a collection
of small craft. *Basin Harbor Rd., 5 mi west of Vergennes, tel. 802/*

475–2317. Admission: $3 adults. Open Memorial Day–mid-Oct., daily 10–5.

South of I–91 (Exit 25), in the town of Glover, is the **Bread and Puppet Museum,** an unassuming, ramshackle barn that houses a surrealistic collection of props used in past performances by the world-renowned Bread and Puppet Theater. The troupe, whose members live communally on the surrounding farm, have been performing social and political commentary with the towering (they're supported by people on stilts), eerily expressive puppets for almost 30 years. *Rte. 122, Glover, 1 mi east of Rte. 16, tel. 802/525–3031. Admission free. Call for hours.*

North of Route 2, midway between Barre and St. Johnsbury, the biggest cheese producer in the state, the **Cabot Creamery,** has a visitor center with an audiovisual presentation about the state's dairy and cheese industry, tours of the plant, and—best of all—samples. *Cabot, 3 mi north of Rte. 2, tel. 802/563–2231. Admission: $1. Open Mon.–Sat. 8–4:30.*

Shopping

Shopping Districts **Church Street Marketplace** (Main St.–Pearl St., Burlington, tel. 802/863–1648), a pedestrian thoroughfare, is lined with boutiques, cafés, and street vendors. **Burlington Square Mall,** off Church Street, has Porteous (the city's major department store) and some 50 shops. **The Champlain Mill** (Rte. 2/7, northeast of Burlington, tel. 802/655–9477), a former woolen mill on the banks of the Winooski River, has three floors of stores. The **Mountain Road** in Stowe is lined with shops from town up toward the ski area.

Food and Drink **Cabot Creamery Annex** (Rte. 100, 2½ mi north of I–89, Waterbury, tel. 802/244–6334) is the new retail store for Vermont's king of cheese (*see* Off the Beaten Track, *above*). **Cold Hollow Cider Mill** (Rte. 100, Waterbury Center, tel. 802/244–8771) offers cider, baked goods, Vermont produce, and free samples at the pressing machine. **Green Mountain Chocolate Co.** (Rte. 100, Waterbury Center, tel. 802/244–1139) greets you with cases and cases of hand-rolled truffles, extravagant pastries, umpteen-zillion types of candy, and free samples. **Harrington's** (Rte. 7 opposite Shelburne Museum, south of Burlington, tel. 802/985–2000) cob-smoked hams, bacon, turkey, and summer sausage will generate thoughts of lunch at any hour. The store also stocks cheese, syrup, and other New England specialties. **Morse Farm** (County Rd., 2 mi north of Montpelier, tel. 802/223–2740) has been producing maple syrup for three generations. The sugarhouse is open for viewing in spring when the syrup is being made; the shop is open year-round.

Specialty Stores
Antiques **Architectural Salvage Warehouse** (212 Battery St., Burlington, tel. 802/658–5011) has clawfoot tubs, stained-glass windows, mantels, andirons, and the like. **Barton & Boardman Interiors** (184 Battery St., Burlington, tel. 802/865–4406) is a beautiful store filled to the rafters with fine collectibles and gifts. **Great American Salvage** (3 Main St., Montpelier, tel. 802/223–7711) supplies architectural detailing: moldings, brackets, stained-glass and leaded windows, doors, and trim retrieved from old homes. **Sarah Bustle Antiques** (Mountain Rd., Stowe, tel. 802/253–2552) fills its store with delicate glass and porcelain objects, jewelry, and lamps. **Sign of the Dial Clock Shop** (63 Eastern Ave., St. Johnsbury, tel. 802/748–5044) specializes in antique-clock sales, repairs, and restorations. **Tailor's Antiques** (68 Pearl St., Burlington, tel. 802/862–8156) carries small primitive paintings as well as glass and china for collectors.

Books Both locations of **Bear Pond Book** (77 Main St., Montpelier, tel. 802/
229–0774; Main St., Stowe, tel. 802/253–8236) are inviting stores
with comfy browsing areas and comprehensive selections. **Chass-
man & Bem Booksellers** (1 Church St., Burlington, tel. 802/862–
4332), probably the best bookstore in Vermont, has more than
40,000 titles, with a discriminating selection of children's books and
a large magazine rack.

Clothing **Handblock** (97 Church St., Burlington, tel. 802/962–8211) carries a
fun collection of casual yet indulgent women's clothing; it also specializes in rich, hand-dyed linens and colorful stoneware. **Moriarty
Hat and Sweater Shop** (Mountain Rd., Stowe, tel. 802/253–4052) is
the home of the original ski hat with the funny peak on top; the assortment is mind-boggling, and you can order a custom knit. **Vermont Trading Company** (2 State St., Montpelier, tel. 802/223–2142;
151 N. Main St., Barre, tel. 802/476–6865) has natural-fiber clothing
and funky accessories.

Crafts **Bennington Potters North** (127 College St., Burlington, tel. 802/
863–2221) has glassware, baskets, small household items, and a seconds outlet downstairs. **Ducktrap Bat Trading Co.** (84 Church St.,
Burlington, tel. 802/865–0036), one of the only wildlife and marine
art galleries in New England, specializes in exquisite hand-carved
decorative decoys. **Vermont State Craft Center** (85 Church St., Burlington, tel. 802/863–6458) is an elegant gallery displaying contemporary and traditional crafts by more than 200 Vermont artisans.

Sports and Outdoor Activities

Biking In Burlington a recreational path runs 9 miles along the waterfront.
South of Burlington, a moderately easy 18½-mile trail begins at the
blinker on Rte. 7, Shelburne, and follows Mt. Philo Road, Hinesburg
Road, Route 116, and Irish Hill Road. **Earl's** (135 Main St., tel. 802/
862–4203) and **North Star Cyclery** (100 Main St., tel. 802/863–3832)
rent equipment and provide maps.

Stowe's recreational trail begins behind the Community Church on
Main Street and meanders for 5.3 miles behind the shops that line
Mountain Road. The junction of Routes 100 and 108 is the start of a
21-mile tour with scenic views of Mt. Mansfield; the route takes you
along Route 100 to Stagecoach Road, to Morristown, over to
Morrisville, and south on Randolph Road. **Mountain Bike** (Mountain
Rd., tel. 802/253–7919) supplies equipment.

Canoeing **Sailworks** (176 Battery St., Burlington, tel. 802/864–0111) rents canoes and gives lessons at Sand Bar State Park in summer. **Umiak
Outdoor Outfitters** (Gale Farm Center, 1880 Mountain Rd., Stowe,
tel. 802/253–2317) specializes in canoes and rents them for day trips;
they also lead guided overnight excursions. The **Village Sport Shop**
(Lyndonville, tel. 802/626–8448) rents canoes near the Connecticut
River.

Fishing Rainbow trout inhabit the Missisquoi, Lamoille, Winooski, and Willoughby rivers, and there's warm-water fishing at many smaller
lakes and ponds. Lakes Seymour, Willoughby, and Memphremagog
and Great Averill Pond in the Northeast Kingdom are good for salmon and lake trout. The **Fly Rod Shop** (Rte. 100, 3 mi south of Stowe,
tel. 802/253–7346) rents and sells equipment.

Lake Champlain, stocked annually with salmon and lake trout, has
become the state's ice-fishing capital; walleye, bass, pike, channel
catfish are also taken. Ice fishing is also popular on Lake Memphremagog.

Marina services are available north and south of Burlington. **Malletts Bay Marina** (228 Lakeshore Dr., Colchester, tel. 802/862–4077) and **Point Bay Marina** (Thompson's Point, Charlotte, tel. 802/425–2431) both provide full service and repairs.

Groton Pond (Rte. 302, off I–91, 20 mi south of St. Johnsbury, tel. 802/584–3829) is popular for trout fishing; boat rentals are available.

Health and Fitness Club The **Fitness Advantage** (137 Iroquois Ave., Essex Junction, tel. 802/878–6568) has spa and fitness equipment, a licensed day-care center, and massage therapy.

Hiking Stop into the headquarters of the **Green Mountain Club,** 1 mile north of Waterbury Center (Rte. 100, RR 1, Box 650, Waterbury Center 05677, tel. 802/244–7037), which maintains the Long Trail—the north–south border-to-border footpath that runs the length of the spine of the Green Mountains—as well as other trails nearby. They sell a number of maps and guides.

Mount Mansfield State Forest and **Little River State Park** (Rte. 2, 1½ mi west of Waterbury) provide an extensive trail system, including one that reaches the site of the Civilian Conservation Corps unit that was here in the 1930s.

For the climb to Stowe Pinnacle, go 1½ miles south of Stowe on Route 100 and turn east on Gold Brook Road opposite the Nichols Farm Lodge; bear left at the first fork, continue through an intersection at a covered bridge, turn right after 1.8 miles, and travel 2.3 miles to a parking lot on the left. The trail crosses an abandoned pasture and takes a short, steep climb to views of the Green Mountains and Stowe Valley (two hours).

Tennis The **Stowe Area Association** (tel. 802/253–7321), which hosts a grand prix tennis tournament in early August, can recommend nearby public courts.

Water Sports **Burlington Community Boathouse** (foot of College St., Burlington Harbor, tel. 802/865–3377) has sailboard and boat rentals (some captained) and lessons. **Chiott Marine** (67 Main St. Burlington, tel. 802/862–8383) caters to all realms of water sports with two floors of hardware, apparel, and accessories. The yacht *Intrepid,* an America's Cup winner, can be chartered from **International Yacht Sales** (Colchester, tel. 802/864–6800).

Beaches

Some of the most scenic Lake Champlain beaches are on the Champlain islands. **North Hero State Park** (tel. 802/372–8727) has a children's play area nearby; **Knight Point State Park** (tel. 802/372–8389) is the reputed home of "Champ," Lake Champlain's answer to the Loch Ness monster; and **Sand Bar State Park** (tel. 802/372–8240) is near a waterfowl preserve. Arrive early to beat summer crowds. *Admission: $1 adults, 50¢ children. Open mid-May–Oct.*

The **North Beaches** are on the northern edge of Burlington: North Beach Park (North Ave., tel. 802/864–0123), Bayside Beach (Rte. 127 near Malletts Bay), and Leddy Beach, which is popular for sailboarding.

State Parks

The following have camping and picnicking facilities: **Burton Island State Park** (Rte. 105, 2 mi east of Island Pond, then south on marked local road, tel. 802/524–6353; 253 acres) is accessible only by ferry or boat; at the nature center a naturalist discusses the island habitat. There's a 100-slip marina with hookups and 20 moorings, and a snack bar. **Grand Isle State Park** (Rte. 2, 1 mi south of Grand Isle, tel. 802/ 372–4300; 226 acres) has a fitness trail and a naturalist. **Kill Kare State Park** (Rte. 36, 4½ mi west of St. Albans Bay, then south on town road 3½ mi, tel. 802/524–6021; 17.7 acres) is popular for sailboarding, and it provides ferry access to Burton Island. **Little River State Park** (Little River Rd., 3½ mi north of Rte. 2, 2 mi east of Rte. 100, tel. 802/244–7103; 12,000 acres) has marked nature trails for hiking on Mt. Mansfield and Camel's Hump, boat rentals, and a ramp. **Smugglers' Notch State Park** (Rte. 108, 10 mi north of Mt. Mansfield, tel. 802/253–4014; 25 acres) is good for picnicking and hiking on wild terrain among large boulders.

Dining and Lodging

There's an odd dearth of inns and B&Bs in Burlington, although a bounty of chain hotels provides dependable accommodations. The rest of the region offers inns, B&Bs, and small motels. For additional accommodations selections, see the Bolton Valley, Burke Mountain, Jay Peak, Smugglers' Notch, and Stowe sections of the Skiing in New England chapter. The Stowe area has a **lodging referral service** (tel. 800/247–8693). In the restaurants, dress is casual; reservations may be helpful in the peak season.

Barton **Fox Hall Inn.** Throughout this 1890 Cottage Revival, listed on the
Lodging National Register of Historic Places, furnishings and rooms are embellished by moose miscellany—a response to northern Vermont's passionate interest in these once-scarce creatures. The generous wraparound veranda overlooking Lake Willoughby is well appointed with swinging seats and comfortable chairs, perfect for a summer evening spent listening to the loons. Although the two corner turret rooms are the most distinctive and spacious and have the lake views, the other rooms are also bright and furnished with wicker and quilts. *Rte. 16, 05822, tel. 802/525–6930. 9 rooms, 4 with bath. Facilities: hiking and cross-country ski trails, canoes. MC, V. Full breakfast and afternoon snacks included; MAP available. Inexpensive–Moderate.*

Burlington **The Daily Planet.** Contemporary plaid oilcloth, an old jukebox play-
Dining ing Aretha Franklin, a solarium, and a turn-of-the-century bar add
★ up to one of Burlington's hippest restaurants. This is Marco Polo cuisine—basically Mediterranean with Oriental influences: lobster risotto with peas; braised lamb loin with polenta and chutney; various stir-fries. *15 Center St., tel. 802/862–9647. Reservations advised. AE, DC, MC, V. Moderate.*

Déjà Vu. High Gothic booths made from ornately carved church pews, fringed silk lampshades, and brass accents that gleam in the candlelight create a lushly romantic yet informal dining room. Dinner entrées might be smoked duck breast and confit leg with a Concord grape demiglace, or Vermont pheasant stuffed with apples, cranberries, and pecans. Sandwiches and crepes are available, too. *185 Pearl St., tel. 802/864–7917. AE, DC, MC, V. Moderate.*

★ **Isabel's.** Located in part of an old lumber mill, the high ceilings, exposed-brick walls, and knockout views that look west from its Lake Champlain frontage provide an ideal setting for this eclectic, inspired American cuisine restaurant notable for its artful presentation. The menu changes weekly and has included salmon stuffed with spinach and feta wrapped in a phyllo pastry with béchamel sauce, and New Zealand lamb with walnut pesto. Lunch and Sunday brunch are quite popular; outdoor patio dining beckons on warm days. *112 Lake St., tel. 802/865–2522. Reservations advised. No lunch weekends; no dinner Mon.–Wed. AE, DC, MC, V. Moderate.*

Bourbon Street Grill. With a 1–10 heat scale where three is "everyone else's medium," you know this place doesn't lack any moxie—even if the chef is a Yankee and the guests wear ski parkas instead of Mardi Gras beads. If New England's cold has you yearning for spicy food, try the jambalaya or Cajun grilled flank steak. The menu offers a bunch of grill entrées, Jamaican jerk chicken, and shrimp popcorn—most can be spiced according to the number of taste buds you have left. Try the Black and Voodoo lager to cool things off. *213 College St., tel. 802/865–2800. Reservations advised. AE, DC, MC, V. Inexpensive–Moderate.*

★ **Five Spice Cafe.** This tiny spot has only a dozen tables set against whitewashed barn-board walls enlivened with framed sheet music or perhaps a drawing of Laurel and Hardy. The chef experiments with Asian cuisines to create such specialties as the searing Thai fire shrimp and a more traditional Kung Pao chicken. The menu has an extensive selection of vegetarian dishes, and there's a dim sum brunch on Saturday and Sunday. *175 Church St., tel. 802/864–4045. AE, DC, MC, V. Inexpensive–Moderate.*

★ **Sweet Tomatoes.** The wood-fired oven of this bright and boisterous trattoria sends off a mouth watering aroma. With hand-painted ceramic pitchers, bottles of dark olive oil perched against a backdrop of exposed brick, and crusty, bull-headed bread that comes with a bowl of oil and garlic for dunking, this soulful eatery beckons you to Italy's countyside. The selections on the extensive, exclusively Italian wine list have been thoroughly tested—vineside—by the owners. The menu includes *caponata* (roasted eggplant with onions, capers, olives, parsley, celery, and tomatoes), *cavatappi* (pasta with roasted chicken and sautéed mushrooms, peas, and walnuts in a pecorino-romano-carbonara sauce), and an extensive selection of pizzas. *83 Church St., tel. 802/660–9533. Reservations accepted for large parties. MC, V. Inexpensive–Moderate.*

Dining and Lodging **The Inn at Shelburne Farms.** This is storybook land: Built at the turn of the century as the home of William Seward and Lila Vanderbilt Webb, the Tudor-style inn perches on Saxton's Point overlooking Lake Champlain, the distant Adirondacks, and the sea of pastures that make up this 1,000-acre working farm. Each guest room is different, from the wallpaper to the period antiques, but all have such nice accents as a washing bowl and pitcher, bookcases, and sterling views. The two dining rooms define elegance. A seasonal menu features home-grown products that might include loin of pork with an apple cider–sundried-cranberry chutney, or rack of lamb with spinach-and-roasted-garlic pesto. The inn's profits help support the farm's environmental education programs at local schools. *Harbor Rd., Shelburne 05482, tel. 802/985–8498. 24 rooms, 17 with bath. Facilities: restaurant (reservations advised), tennis, game rooms, canoes, walking trails, lake fishing and swimming. AE, DC, MC, V. Closed mid-Oct.–mid-May. Moderate–Very Expensive.*

★ **Inn at Essex.** This Georgian-style hotel that sits back aways from the suburban sprawl encircling Burlington—about 10 miles from downtown—is a state-of-the-art conference center dressed in country-inn clothing. Attentive staff, individually decorated rooms with flowered wallpaper, working fireplaces in some rooms, and library books on the reproduction desks lend character. The two restaurants—the refined Butler's and the more casual Birchtree Cafe—are run by the New England Culinary Institute. Students are coached by an executive chef and rotate through each position, from sous-chef to waitstaff—these are great chefs in the making. The updated New England style shows off sweet dumpling squash with ginger-garlic basmati rice, and lobster in yellow corn sauce with spinach pasta at Butler's; chicken potpie and seafood stew with saffron risotto in the café. *70 Essex Way, off Rte. 15, Essex Junction 05452, tel. 802/878–1100 or 800/288–7613, fax 802/878–0063. 97 rooms with bath. Facilities: restaurant (reservations advised), pool, library, fireplaces in 30 rooms. AE, D, DC, MC, V. Moderate–Expensive.*

Lodging **Radisson Hotel–Burlington.** This sleek corporate giant is the hotel closest to downtown shopping, and it faces the lakefront. Odd-numbered rooms have the view; rooms whose number end in 1 look onto both lake and city. *60 Battery St., 05401, tel. 802/658–6500 or 800/333–3333, fax 802/658–4659. 256 rooms with bath. Facilities: restaurant, lounge, indoor pool, whirlpool, garage, complimentary airport shuttle. AE, D, DC, MC, V. Moderate–Expensive.*

Sheraton-Burlington. The biggest hotel in the city (90% of the rooms and the health club were added in 1989) and the closest to the airport, the Sheraton accommodates large groups as well as individuals. Upholstered wing chairs and dust ruffles give a New England look to the upscale mauve and burgundy decor of the rooms. On the concierge level are a cocktail bar, complimentary hors d'oeuvres, and Continental breakfast. *870 Williston Rd., 05403, tel. 802/862–6576 or 800/325–3535, fax 802/865–6670. 309 rooms with bath, 30 rooms equipped for people with disabilities. Facilities: restaurant, conference center, health club, pool with retractable roof, complimentary airport shuttle, in-room modems, corporate business center with clerical services. AE, D, DC, MC, V. Moderate–Expensive.*

Marriott Fairfield Inn. Clean, convenient, and entirely adequate, this hotel-cum-motel fills the niche for travelers in search of no-frills, yet dependable, accommodations. The spacious rooms, free local calls, and complimentary breakfast indicate a willingness to please, much more so than the average motel. *15 South Park Dr., Colchester 05446, tel. or fax 802/655–1400. 117 rooms with bath. Facilities: pool. Continental breakfast included. AE, D, DC, MC, V. Inexpensive.*

Montpelier **Tubb's.** Nearly everyone working here is student at the New En-
Dining gland Culinary Institute, and this is their training ground, yet the quality and inventiveness are anything but beginner's luck. The menu changes daily, and the cuisine and atmosphere are somewhat more formal than that of the Elm Street Cafe, the sister operation down the block. *24 Elm St., tel. 802/229–9202. Reservations advised. MC, V. Closed Sun. Moderate–Expensive.*

Horn of the Moon. Bowls of honey, mismatched wooden chairs and tables, and the bulletin board of political notices at the entrance hint at Vermont's prominent progressive contingent. This vegetarian restaurant has attracted a following for an inventive cuisine that includes a little Mexican, a little Thai, a lot of flavor, and not too much tofu. *8 Langdon St., tel. 802/223–2895. No credit cards. No dinner Sun., Mon. Inexpensive–Moderate.*

Lodging **The Inn at Montpelier.** This spacious home built in the early 1800s
★ was renovated in 1988 with the business traveler in mind, yet the architectural detailing, antique four-poster beds, Windsor chairs, stately upholstered wing chairs, and the classical guitar on the stereo attract casual visitors as well. Maureen's Room has a private sundeck, and the wide wraparound Colonial Revival porch is conducive to relaxing. The rooms in the annex across the street are equally elegant. *147 Main St., 05602, tel. 802/223–2727, fax 802/223–0722. 19 rooms with bath, 2 suites. Facilities: meeting rooms. AE, MC, V. Continental breakfast included. Moderate–Expensive.*

Newport
Dining

East Side Restaurant and Lounge. The green napkins match the green padded booths, which match the green lampshades, which match the plants. This is the sort of family restaurant that will comply with customers' pleas to keep the fried chicken livers on the menu along with burgers, sandwiches, soups, and bar food. *E. Main St., tel. 802/334-2340. Closed Mon. MC, V. Inexpensive-Moderate.*

Lodging

Top of the Hills Motel. The motel rooms are attached to a small inn whose Victorian architectural detailing is meticulous and well-cared for. One of the five rooms in the inn has a kitchenette, three have private baths. *Rtes. 5 and 105, 05855, tel. 802/334-6748 or 800/258-6748. 11 rooms, 9 with bath; 2 cottages. Facilities: picnic area, grill, snowmobile trail. AE, D, MC, V. Full breakfast included. Closed mid-Nov.-Apr. Inexpensive.*

St. Johnsbury
Dining

Tucci's Bistro. Veal topped with crisp fried eggplant, mozzarella, and ham, and beef scallopini sautéed with capers and anchovies go beyond the standard red-sauce recipes. The whitewashed barnboard trim and kelly green tablecloths complete the simple but tasteful decor. *41 Eastern Ave., tel. 802/748-4778. AE, MC, V. Moderate.*

Dining and Lodging
★

Rabbit Hill Inn. Guests are welcomed into a warmth that melts away even the most stressful of journeys. In the formal, Federal parlor, mulled cider is served from the fireplace crane on chilly afternoons. The low wooden beams of the Irish-style pub next door offer a casual contrast to the rest of the inn. Rooms are each as stylistically different as they are consistently indulgent: The Loft, with its 8-foot Palladian window, king canopy bed, double Jacuzzi, and corner fireplace, is one of the most requested. Rooms toward the front of the inn get views of the Connecticut River and New Hampshire's White Mountains. The low-ceiling dining room offers eclectic, regional cuisine—perhaps grilled sausage of Vermont pheasant with pistachios or smoked chicken and red lentil dumplings nestled in red pepper linguine. Meat and fish are smoked on the premises, and the herbs and vegetables often come from gardens out back. *Rte. 18, Lower Waterford 05848, tel. 802/748-5168 or 800/762-8669. 6 double rooms with baths, 7 suites. Facilities: restaurant (reservations advised), pub, whirlpools in some rooms, fireplaces in many rooms, walking/cross-country ski trails, canoes. MC, V. Rates are MAP. Closed Apr. and first 3 weeks in Nov. Moderate-Expensive.*

Lodging

Fairbanks Motor Inn. A location convenient to I-91, a putting green, a view that makes visitors want to sit for hours on the balcony, and a honeymoon suite with whirlpool and wet bar make this more than the average Holiday Inn clone. *Rte. 2 E, 05819, tel. 802/748-5666. 44 rooms with bath. Facilities: pool. AE, MC, V. Moderate.*

Stowe
Dining

Foxfire Inn. A restored Colonial building might seem an unusual place in which to find such superb Italian delicacies as veal rollantine, steak saltimbocca, and *tartufo* (vanilla and chocolate gelato in a chocolate cup with a raspberry center). However, this old farmhouse a couple of miles north of Stowe proper blends the two well, and its popularity with locals proves it's worth the short drive. *Rte. 100, Stowe, tel. 802/253-4887. MC, V. Moderate-Expensive.*

Number One Main Street. The low-ceiling Colonial dining room livens cuisine basics with a hint of creativity: broiled swordfish with garlic butter and Pernod in a cream sauce, roast pork with red currant and crème de cassis sauce. *1 Main St., tel. 802/253-7301. Reservations advised. AE, MC, V. Moderate-Expensive.*

Stubb's. Jim Dinan is one of those New England chefs who are rethinking such traditional dishes as calf's liver—he prepares it with a balsamic vinegar–shallot sauce—and Vermont ham, which he combines with veal ribs, sage, and apples. The marbleized walls and pink-on-burgundy linens add a sophisticated note to the rustic beams and fireplaces at either end of the two rooms. *Mountain Rd., tel. 802/253–7110. Reservations advised. AE, DC, MC, V. Moderate–Expensive.*

★ **Villa Tragara.** A converted farmhouse has been carved into intimate dining nooks where romance reigns over such specialties as ravioli filled with four cheeses and served with a half-tomato, half-cream sauce. The tasting menu is a five-course dinner for $35 (plus $15 for coordinating wines). *Rte. 100, south of Stowe, tel. 802/244–5288. Reservations advised. AE, MC, V. Moderate–Expensive.*

Lodging **10 Acres Lodge.** The 10 rooms in the main inn are cozier and more innlike than those in the new building high on the hill, which have a definite condominium feel to them. Contemporary pottery or low-key abstract art complement the antique horse brasses over the fireplace in the living room. This is truly in the country; the cows are just across the road. *Luce Hill Rd., Box 3220, 05672, tel. 802/253–7638 or 800/327–7357, fax 802/253–4036. 18 rooms, 16 with bath; 2 cottages. Facilities: restaurant, lounge, outdoor pool, tennis. Full breakfast included. AE, MC, V. Moderate–Very Expensive.*

★ **The Inn at the Brass Lantern.** Home-baked cookies in the afternoon, a basket of logs by your fireplace, and stenciled hearts along the wainscoting reflect the care taken in turning this 18th-century farmhouse into a place of welcome. All rooms have quilts and country antiques; most are oversize. The honeymoon room has a brass and iron bed with a heart-shape headboard; the breakfast room (like some guest rooms) has a terrific view of Mt. Mansfield. *Rte. 100, ½ mi north of Stowe, 05672, tel. 802/253–2229 or 800/729–2980. 9 rooms with bath. Facilities: some fireplaces in rooms. Full breakfast included. AE, MC, V. Moderate.*

The Arts

Barre Opera House (City Hall, Main St., Barre, tel. 802/476–8188) hosts music, opera, theater, and dance performances. **Catamount Arts** (60 Eastern Ave., St. Johnsbury, tel. 802/748–2600) brings avant-garde theater and dance performances to the Northeast Kingdom, as well as classical music and nightly film screenings.

Flynn Theatre for the Performing Arts, a grandiose old structure, is the cultural heart of Burlington; it schedules the Vermont Symphony Orchestra, theater, dance, and lectures. The box office also has tickets for other performances and festivals in the area. *153 Main St., Burlington, tel. 802/864–8778 for what's on; 802/863–5966 for tickets.*

Music **Stowe Performing Arts** (tel. 802/253–7321) sponsors a series of classical and jazz concerts during July and August in a meadow high above the village, next to the Trapp Family Lodge. **Vermont Symphony Orchestra** (tel. 802/864–5741) performs at the Flynn Theatre in Burlington in winter and outdoors at Shelburne Farms in summer.

Theater **Champlain Shakespeare Festival** performs each summer at the Royall Tyler Theater (tel. 802/656–0090) at the University of Vermont. **Stowe Stage Co.** (Stowe Playhouse, Mountain Rd., Stowe, tel. 802/253–7944) does musical comedy, July to early October. **Vermont Repertory Theater** (tel. 802/655–9620) mounts five productions in a season that runs from September through May.

Nightlife

Nighttime activities are centered in Burlington, with its business travelers and college students, and in the ski areas. Many resort hotels have après-ski entertainment.

Vermont Pub and Brewery (College and St. Paul Sts., Burlington, tel. 802/865–0500) makes its own beer and fruit seltzers and is arguably the most popular spot in town. It also serves a full lunch and dinner menu and late-night snacks. Folk musicians play here regularly. **The Butter Tub** at Topnotch (Mountain Rd., Stowe, tel. 802/253–8585) has live entertainment most nights in ski season. **Sha-na-na's** (101 Main St., Burlington, tel. 802/865–2596) plays music from the 1950s and 1960s. **Last Elm Cafe** (N. Winooski Ave., Burlington, no tel.), a good old-fashioned coffeehouse, is a good bet for folk music. **Papa's Blues Cellar** (101 Main St., below Sha-na-na's, Burlington, tel. 802/865–2596), a comfortable spot with dark, cozy corners, is the place to go for jazz and blues; it also serves dinner. **Club Metronome** (188 Main St., Burlington, tel. 802/865–4563) stages an eclectic musical mix that ranges from the newest in cutting edge to funk, blues, reggae, and the occasional big name. **Club Toast** (167 Church St., Burlington, tel. 802/860–1226) offers local musicians in addition to danceable bar bands. **Nectar's** (188 Main St., Burlington, tel. 802/658–4771) never charges a cover and is always jumping to the sounds of local bands. **Comedy Zone** (Radisson Hotel, 60 Battery St., Burlington, tel. 802/658–6500) provides the laughs in town Friday and Saturday nights.

7 New Hampshire

By Michelle Seaton, with an introduction by William G. Scheller

Michelle Seaton, a resident of New Hampshire for three years, is the food editor of Yankee magazine, where she also edits a column on New England history.

When General John Stark coined the expression Live Free or Die, he knew what he was talking about. Stark had been through the Revolutionary War battles of Bunker Hill and Bennington—where he was victorious—and was clearly entitled to state the choice as he saw it. It was, after all, a choice he was willing to make. But Stark could never have imagined that hundreds of thousands of his fellow New Hampshire men and women would one day display the same fierce sentiment as they traveled the streets and roads of the state: Live Free or Die is the legend of the New Hampshire license plate, the only state license plate in the Union to adopt a sociopolitical ultimatum instead of a tribute to scenic beauty or native produce.

The citizens of New Hampshire are a diverse lot who cannot be tucked neatly into any pigeonhole. To be sure, a white-collar worker in one of the high-tech industries that have sprung up around Nashua or Manchester is no mountaineer defending his homestead with a muzzle-loader, no matter what it says on his license plate.

Yet there is a strong civic tradition in New Hampshire that has variously been described as individualistic, mistrustful of government, even libertarian. This tradition manifests itself most prominently in the state's long-standing aversion to any form of broad-based tax: There is no New Hampshire earned-income tax, nor is there a retail sales tax. Instead, the government relies for its revenue on property taxes, sales of liquor and lottery tickets, and levies on restaurant meals and lodgings—the same measures that other states use to varying degrees. Nor are candidates for state office likely to be successful unless they declare themselves opposed to sales and income taxes.

Another aspect of New Hampshire's suspiciousness of government is its limitation of the gubernatorial term of service to two years: With the running of the reelection gauntlet ever imminent, no incumbent is likely to take the risk of being identified as a proponent of an income or a sales tax—or any other similarly unpopular measure.

And then there's the New Hampshire House of Representatives. With no fewer than 400 members, it is the most populous state assembly in the nation and one of the largest deliberative bodies in the world. Each town with sufficient population sends at least one representative to the House, and he or she had better be able to give straight answers on being greeted—on a first-name basis—at the town hardware store on Saturday.

Yankee individualism, a regional cliché, may or may not be the appropriate description here, but New Hampshire does carry on with a quirky, flinty interpretation of the Jeffersonian credo that the government governs best that governs least. Meanwhile, visitors to New Hampshire see all those license plates and wonder whether they're being told that they've betrayed General Stark's maxim by paying an income tax or a deposit on soda bottles—still another indignity the folks in the Granite State have spared themselves.

Essential Information

Visitor Information

New Hampshire Office of Travel and Tourism Development (Box 1856, Concord 03302, tel. 603/271–2343). **Events, foliage, and ski conditions** (tel. 800/258–3608 or 800/262–6660). **New Hampshire**

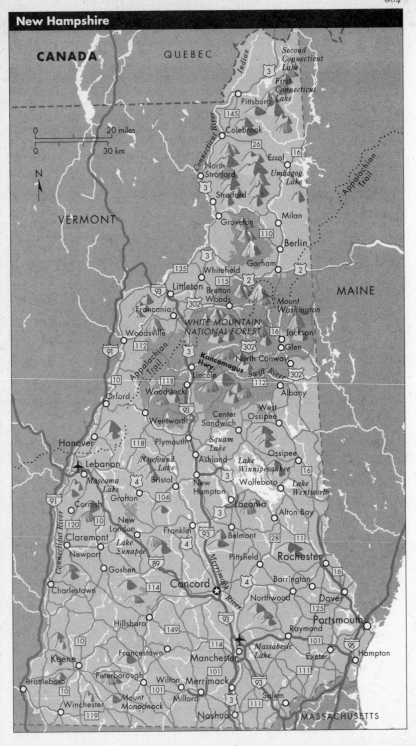

New Hampshire

CANADA

QUEBEC

Second
Connecticut
Lake

First
Connecticut
Lake

Pittsburg

145

Colebrook

26

North
Stratford

16

Errol

Stratford

Umbagog
Lake

Connecticut River

Milan

Groveton

110

Berlin

VERMONT

3

Gorham

2

135

Whitefield

115

2

Littleton

93

Bretton
Woods

302

Mount
Washington

MAINE

Franconia

WHITE MOUNTAIN
NATIONAL FOREST

16

Jackson

Woodsville

112

302

Glen

91

Appalachian Trail

3

Kancamagus
Hwy.

North Conway

302

Lincoln

Swift River

118

Woodstock

112

Albany

10

Orford

93

Center
Sandwich

West
Ossipee

Wentworth

Hanover

118

Plymouth

Squam
Lake

Ossipee

Newfound
Lake

Ashland

16

Lebanon

3

Lake
Winnipesaukee

Mascoma
Lake

4

Bristol

New
Hampton

Wolfeboro

Lake
Wentworth

91

Cornish

104

Laconia

Grafton

Alton Bay

120

10

New
London

Franklin

93

Belmont

28

11

Claremont

Lake
Sunapee

4

Newport

89

Pittsfield

Rochester

Goshen

Merrimack River

16

Charlestown

114

Concord

Barrington

Dover

Northwood

4

125

Hillsboro

149

93

Portsmouth

Raymond

101

95

10

114

Massabesic
Lake

Exeter

111

Hampton

Keene

Francestown

Manchester

101

Peterborough

101

Merrimack

111

Brattleboro

Wilton

Mount
Monadnock

Milford

93

3

Salem

10

Winchester

119

Nashua

MASSACHUSETTS

Appalachian Trail

Indian

0   20 miles
0   30 km

N

State Council on the Arts (40 N. Main St., Concord 03301, tel. 603/271–2789).

New Hampshire Campground Owners Association (Box 320, Twin Mountain 03595, tel. 800/822–6764) will send you a list of all private, state, and national-forest campgrounds.

Bicycle Tours

Bike & Hike New Hampshire's Lakes (tel. 603/968–3775), **Bike the Whites** (tel. 800/933–3902), **Great Outdoors Hiking & Biking Tours** (tel. 603/356–3271 or 800/525–9100), **Monadnock Bicycle Touring** (Box 19, Harrisville 03450, tel. 603/827–3925), **New England Hiking Holidays** (tel. 603/356–9696 or 800/869–0949), and **Sunapee Inns Hike & Bike Tours** (tel. 800/662–6005) organize bike tours.

Arriving and Departing

By Plane   **Manchester Airport** (tel. 603/624–6556), the state's largest, has scheduled flights by USAir, Delta, Continental, Northwest Airlink, United, and TWA. **Keene Airport's** (tel. 603/357–9835) Colgan Air offers flights to Rutland, Vermont, and Newark, New Jersey. **Lebanon Municipal Airport** (tel. 603/298–8878), near Dartmouth College, is served by Northwest, Delta and USAir. **Pease International Tradeport** (tel. 603/433–6088), near Portsmouth, is served by Delta.

By Car   Interstate–93 is the principal north–south route through Manchester, Concord, and central New Hampshire. To the west, I–91 traces the Vermont–New Hampshire border. To the east, I–95, which is a toll road, passes through the coastal area of southern New Hampshire on its way from Massachusetts to Maine. I–89 travels from Concord to Montpelier and Burlington, Vermont.

By Train   **Amtrak's** (tel. 800/872–7245) *Montrealer* stops daily at Claremont (4:30 AM) on its Washington, D.C.–Montreal runs.

By Bus   **Greyhound** (tel. 800/231–2222) and its subsidiary **Vermont Transit** (tel. 603/228–3300 or 800/451–3292) link the cities of New Hampshire with major cities in the eastern United States.

Getting Around New Hampshire

By Plane   Small local airports that handle charters and private planes are **Berlin Airport** (tel. 603/449–7383) in Milan, **Concord Airport** (tel. 603/224–4033), **Jaffrey Municipal Airport** (tel. 603/532–7763), **Laconia Airport** (tel. 603/524–5003), **Nashua Municipal Airport** (tel. 603/882–0661) and **Sky Haven Airport** (tel. 603/332–0005) in Rochester.

By Car   The official state map, available free from the Office of Travel and Tourism Development (*see* Visitor Information, *above*), has directories for each of the tourist areas and is useful for navigating the state's major roads.

By Bus   **Coast** (Durham, tel. 603/862–2328), **C&J** (tel. 603/742–5111), **Concord Trailways** (tel. 800/639–3317), **Peter Pan Bus Lines** (tel. 603/889–2121), and **Vermont Transit** (tel. 603/228–3300 or 800/451–3292) provide bus service among the state's cities and towns.

Dining

New Hampshire's visitors need not live on boiled dinners alone. The state is home to some of the best seafood in the country, and not just lobster, but everything from salmon pie to steamed mussels, fried clams to seared tuna steak. Each region has its share of country French dining rooms and nouvelle American kitchens, but the best advice is to eat where the locals do. That can be anywhere from a local greasy-spoon diner to an out-of-the-way inn whose chef builds everything—including the home-churned butter—from scratch. And while it's still in vogue to stop by country stores for fudge and penny candy, roadside farmstands and small gourmet groceries— stocking the likes of cranberry chutnies and hot pepper jellies—are growing in popularity.

Highly recommended restaurants are indicated by a star ★.

Category	Cost*
Very Expensive	over $35
Expensive	$25–$35
Moderate	$15–$25
Inexpensive	under $15

per person for a three-course meal, excluding drinks, service, and 8% meals tax.

Lodging

New Hampshire has long been a mecca for summer vacationers. In the mid-19th century, wealthy Bostonians would pack up and move to their grand summer homes in the countryside for two- or three-month stretches. Today many of these homes have been restored and converted into country inns, offering the truest local experience. An occupational hazard of innkeepers is that they invariably know, and feel compelled to tell you, where to find the best off-the-beaten track restaurant, secluded hiking trail, and heretofore undiscovered antiques shop. Inns vary greatly in size and feel. The smallest have only a couple of rooms; typically, they're done in period style. The largest let more than 30 rooms and offer private baths, fireplaces, even Jacuzzis. A few of the grand old resorts still stand, with their world-class cooking staffs and their tradition of top-notch service. And for those who prefer cable TV to precious antiques, the hotel chains are well represented in the larger cities and along major highways.

Highly recommended lodgings are indicated by a star ★.

Category	Cost*
Very Expensive	over $150
Expensive	$100–$150
Moderate	$60–$100
Inexpensive	under $60

All prices are for a standard double room during peak season, with no meals unless noted, and excluding service charge and 8% occupancy tax.

The Coast

The first VIP to vacation on the New Hampshire coast was George Washington in 1789. By all accounts he had a pretty good time, although a bizarre fishing accident left him with a nasty black eye. President Washington couldn't have had nearly as much fun as today's traveler. Accompanied as he was by 14 generals (all in full-dress uniform), he couldn't walk barefoot along the sandy beaches, or picnic at Odiorne Point overlooking the ocean. He probably did get a nice look at the of the homes of John Paul Jones and John Langdon, however, both of which still stand.

Today's visitor will find swimming, boating, fishing, and water sports amid the beaches and state parks of New Hampshire's 18-mile coastline. Hampton Beach features a 1940s-style boardwalk, complete with arcade and nightly entertainment. Portsmouth has it all: the shopping, the restaurants, the music, the theater, and one of the best historic districts in the nation. In Exeter, New Hampshire's enclave of Revolutionary War history, visitors can take a walking tour that explores the 18th- and early-19th-century homes clustered around Phillips Exeter Academy. If President Washington could do it all again, he would probably leave the generals at home and enjoy a leisurely dinner at a quiet seaside inn.

Important Addresses and Numbers

Visitor Information
Hours are generally Monday through Friday, 9–5. **Exeter Area Chamber of Commerce** (120 Water St., Exeter 03833, tel. 603/772–2411). **Greater Dover Chamber of Commerce** (229 Central Ave., Dover 03820, tel. 603/742–2218). **Greater Portsmouth Chamber of Commerce** (500 Market St., Portsmouth 03801, tel. 603/436–1118). **Hampton Beach Area Chamber of Commerce** (836 Lafayette Rd., Hampton 03842, tel. 603/926–8717). **Seacoast Council on Tourism** (235 West Rd., Suite 10, Portsmouth 03801, tel. 603/436–7678 or, outside NH, 800/221–5623).

Emergencies
New Hampshire State Police (tel. 800/852–3411). **Portsmouth Regional Hospital** (333 Borthwick Ave., tel. 603/435–5110 or 433–4042). **Exeter Hospital** (10 Buzzell Ave., tel. 603/778–7311).

Late-Night Pharmacy
Kingston Rexall (Kingston Plaza, Main St., Kingston, tel. 603/642–3323).

Getting Around the New Hampshire Coast

By Car
For coastal scenery, follow Route 1A, which shows off the water, the beaches, and some breathtaking summer estates. For convenience, follow Route 1, which wends slightly inland. Route 1B tours the island of Newcastle, and Route 4 connects Portsmouth with Dover, Durham, and Rochester.

Guided Tours
Audubon Society of New Hampshire (3 Silk Farm Rd., Concord 03301, tel. 603/224–9909) schedules monthly field trips throughout the state and a special fall bird-watching tour to Star Island and the Isles of Shoals.

Insight Tours (tel. 603/436–4223 or 800/745-4213) gives one- to three-hour bus tours focusing on the history and architecture of Portsmouth.

New Hampshire Seacoast Cruises (tel. 603/964–5545) offers narrated tours of the Isles of Shoals and whale-watching expeditions from June to Labor Day out of Rye Harbor Marina.

Portsmouth Harbor Cruises (tel. 603/436-8084) takes passengers on a historic tour of the 14 islands of Portsmouth harbor. Ask about the inland tour of the Great bay and about sunset and foliage cruises.

Portsmouth Livery Company (tel. 603/427–0044) provides narrated horse-and-carriage tours of Colonial Portsmouth and Strawbery Banke.

Exploring the New Hampshire Coast

Numbers in the margin correspond to points of interest on the New Hampshire Coast map.

New Hampshire shares a mere 18 miles of its border with the ocean, yet a tour of the coast can take as long as a Sunday afternoon or last for several days. On Route 1, about 2 miles north of the Massachusetts border, is the old town of **Seabrook,** which is the site of the controversial nuclear power plant of the same name. Adjacent is the **Seabrook Nature & Science Center** (Lafayette Rd., tel. 800/338–7482; open Mon.–Sat. 10–4), where you can see control-room operators in training and tour an extensive exhibit on the science of power. Here you can pedal a bike to create electricity and use interactive computer games to learn about nuclear power. On the nature side, the center maintains a ¾-mile nature trail, a touch pool for kids, and several large aquariums of local sea life.

Two miles farther north, in **Hampton Falls,** where Route 1 meets Route 88, is the **Applecrest Farm Orchards,** a pick-your-own apple grove and berry patch and bakery where you can buy fresh fruit pies and cookies. In winter you can follow a cross-country ski trail through the orchard. *Rte. 88, Hampton Falls, tel. 603/926–3721. Open daily 10–dusk.*

If you prefer raspberries, try the **Raspberry Farm** (Rte. 84, Hampton Falls, tel. 603/926–6604), 3 miles inland on Route 84. The farm offers eight varieties of pick-your-own berries, including blackberries and black raspberries. They also sell fresh berry tarts, jams, vinegars, and sauces.

Return to Route 1, where, at the junction of Route 101, the coastal Route 1A veers east and passes near **Hampton Beach,** the liveliest on the coast. An estimated 150,000 people visit on the 4th of July alone. If you like fried dough, loud music, arcade games, palm readers, parasailing, and tens of thousands of bronze bodies, don't miss it. The 3-mile boardwalk looks like it was snatched out of the 1940s. Here kids can play games and see how saltwater taffy is made. Free outdoor concerts are held many evenings along with a once-a-week fireworks display. There are talent shows and karaoke performances in the Seashell Stage—right on the beach. Big names perform in the club of the seven-acre, multiple-arcade **Hampton Beach Casino and Ballroom** (tel. 603/926–4541). Each summer locals crown a Miss Hampton Beach, hold a children's festival, and celebrate the end of the season with a huge seafood feast the weekend after Labor Day. For a quieter time, stop by for a sunrise stroll, when only seagulls and the odd jogger interrupt the serenity.

From here you can take Route 101 a few miles inland to the quiet town of **Exeter.** In 1638, the town's first settlers built their homes around the falls where the fresh-water Exeter river meets the salty

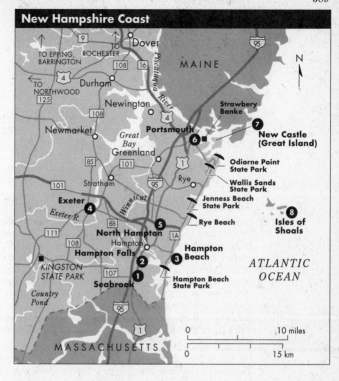

New Hampshire Coast

Squamscot. During the Revolutionary War, Exeter was the state capitol, and it was here that the first state constitution and the first declaration of independence from Great Britain were put to paper. The **Phillips Exeter Academy** opened its doors in 1783 and is still one of the nation's most esteemed prep schools. The **American Independence Museum,** in the Ladd-Gilman House (adjacent to the campus), celebrates the birth of our nation. Built by Nathaniel Ladd and the first brick house in town, it was eventually converted into a governor's mansion for John Taylor Gilman. The story of the revolution unfolds during each guided tour, which shows off drafts of the U.S. Constitution and the first Purple Heart. *1 Governor's La., Exeter, tel. 603/772–2622. Admission: $4 adults, $3 senior citizens, $2 children 6–12. Open May 1–Oct. 31, Wed.–Sun. noon–5.*

Time Out   **Masseno's, The Cook's Choice** (33 Water St., Exeter, tel. 603/778–7585) serves up such gourmet picnic items as roast beef–and–Boursin sandwiches or curried chicken with apples and walnuts. You can also have a seat in the bright café for some coffee and pastries.

⑤ Route 101 takes you back to Route 1A north and a scenic drive to **North Hampton** and Rye Beach. Just north of Hampton Beach sits a group of immodest mansions known as Millionaires' Row. Because of the way the road curves, the drive south along this route is even more breathtaking than the drive north. The **Fuller Gardens** bloom all summer long with 1,500 rosebushes of every shade and type, a Hosta display garden, and a serenity-inspiring groomed Japanese garden. *10 Willow Ave., North Hampton, tel. 603/964–5414. Admis-*

sion: $4 adults, $3.50 senior citizens. Open early May–mid-Oct., daily 10–6.

Jenness Beach and **Wallis Sands State Park,** north of Rye Beach, are swimmer's beaches with bright white sand and ample parking. Further north you'll find the **Odiorne Point State Park** and the Seacoast Science Center. In 1623, the first European settlers landed here, making Odiorne Point the birthplace of New Hampshire. Today the park encompasses 230 acres of protected land. You can pick up an interpretive brochure on any one of the nature trails or simply stroll and enjoy the beautiful vistas of the nearby Isles of Shoals. The tidal pools here are considered the best in New England and show off crabs, periwinkles, and sea anemones. The Science Center houses a small museum, which organizes lectures, guided bird-walks, and interpretive programs. Exhibits include a two-pool touch tank and historical displays that trace Odiorne point to the Ice Ages. *Rte. 1A, Rye, tel. 603/436–8043. Parking: $2.50. Open Tues.–Sun. 10–5.*

❻ Routes 1, 1A, and 1B, and I–95 all converge on **Portsmouth,** the largest city and the cultural epicenter of the coast. Here you will find restaurants of every stripe and in every price range, plus theater, music, art galleries, and an excellent historic district. Originally settled in 1623 as Strawbery Banke, it became a prosperous port until the Revolutionary War. Many of the homes built prior to the war still stand as part of the Portsmouth Historic District, which includes the **Portsmouth Trail** and a section of town still called Strawbery Banke. Pick up a map from the information kiosk on Market Square or from any of the marked historic houses, which are all within walking distance of one another.

On Little Harbor Road at the South Street Cemetery stands the **Wentworth-Coolidge Mansion** (tel. 603/436–6607), originally the residence of Benning Wentworth, New Hampshire's first Royal Governor. Notable among the period furnishings is the carved pine mantelpiece in the council chamber; also notice the Wentworth's own imported lilac trees, which bloom each May.

The **Portsmouth Historical Society,** in the **John Paul Jones House** (Middle and State Sts., tel. 603/436–8420), contains costumes, glass, guns, portraits, and documents of the late 18th century. It's now one of six houses on the Portsmouth Trail, a historic walking tour that opens on the third Friday in August and lasts through October 15. Tickets cost $4 per house and may be purchased at any of the houses.

Time Out Gourmet coffee shops abound in Portsmouth. **Breaking New Grounds** (16 Market St.) serves cappuccino, espresso, and all the hybrids along with cheesecake and cookies. The **Ceres Street Bakery** (51 Penhallow St.) offers elaborate tarts and tortes, as well as soups and light lunches.

Bring a picnic lunch to historic **Prescott Park,** on the waterfront between Strawbery Banke and the Piscataqua river. The large formal garden and its fountains are the perfect place to while away an afternoon. The park also contains the Point of Graves, Portsmouth's oldest burial ground, and two historic warehouses that date from the early 17th century. One of them, the Sheafe Warehouse, was where John Paul Jones outfitted the USS *Ranger,* one of the U.S. Navy's earliest ships. *Prescott Park, Marcy St., tel. 603/431–8748. Admission free. Open Memorial Day–Labor Day, Wed.–Sun. 8–4.*

The **Port of Portsmouth Maritime Museum,** in Albacore Park, is home of the USS *Albacore,* which was built here in 1953 as a prototype submarine—a floating laboratory assigned to test a new hull design, dive brakes, and sonar systems for the Navy. A documentary prior to the tour shows visitors how the 55-man crew lived and worked. The nearby Memorial Garden and its reflecting pool have been dedicated as a memorial to the crews and officers lost in submarine service. *500 Market St., tel. 603/436–3680. Admission: $4 adults, $3 senior citizens, $2 children 7–12, $10 families. Open May–Columbus Day, daily 9:30–5:30; call for winter hours.*

Time Out For light lunch, gourmet ice cream, or coffee, try **Annabelle's** (Ceres St.). The health conscious might like **Izzy's Frozen Yogurt** (corner Bow and Ceres Sts.), which has such frozen delights as low-fat sundaes and an amazing sugar- and fat-free hot fudge sauce.

The first English settlers named this area for the abundant wild strawberries they found along the shore of the Piscataqua River. Today **Strawbery Banke** is a 10-acre outdoor museum with period gardens and more than 40 buildings that date from 1695 to 1820. The district was slated for urban renewal in the late 1950s, but a group of concerned residents successfully fought to preserve it. The museum is now a study in the evolution of a neighborhood, with nine furnished homes representing several different time periods. For example, the Drisco House, built in 1795, was first used as a dry-goods store, and one room still depicts this history; the living room, on the other hand, is decorated just as it was in the 1950s. The boyhood home of Thomas Bailey Aldrich (author of *The Story of a Bad Boy*) is still called **Nutter House,** the name he gave it in that novel—it's been restored just as it was when he wrote about it, right down to the wallpaper and hanging bookshelves. In the **Wheelwright House** you can see daily demonstrations of 18th-century cooking. Continental breakfast, lunch, and Sunday brunch are served at the **Washington Street Eatery** (61 Washington St., tel. 603/430–9442). *Marcy St., tel. 603/433–1100 or 603/433–1106. Admission: $10 adults, $9 senior citizens, $7 children under 17, $25 families. Tickets good for 2 consecutive days. Open May–Oct., daily 10–5; first 2 weekends in Dec., 3:30–8:30.*

7 The small island of **New Castle,** just east of Portsmouth, was once known as Great Island, although it's made up of a single square-mile of land. To get here, follow Route 1B (New Castle Ave.). The narrow roads lined with pre-Revolutionary houses make the island perfect for walking. On the way here you'll pass the old **Wentworth By The Sea,** the last of the great seaside resorts. It sits empty today and overlooks a golf course; it was the site of the signing of the Russo-Japanese Treaty in 1905, a fact that attracts many Japanese tourists. **Ft. Constitution** was originally Ft. William and Mary, a British stronghold overlooking Portsmouth Harbor. The fort was raided by rebel patriots in 1774 in one of the first overt acts of defiance against the King of England. The rebels later used the stolen munitions against the British at the Battle of Bunker Hill. Interpretive panels throughout the park further explain its history. *Ft. Constitution, Great Island. Open mid-June–Labor Day, daily 9–5; Labor Day–mid-June, weekends 9–5.*

Island Excursions **8** Ten miles off the coast lie nine small islands (eight at high tide): the **Isles of Shoals.** Many, like Hog Island, Smuttynose, and Star Island, retain the earthy names given them by the transient fishermen who first visited in the early 17th century. A colorful history of piracy, murder, and ghosts surrounds the archipelago, long populated by an independent lot who, according to one writer, hadn't the sense to winter on the mainland (there remains a small summer population). Not all of the islands lie within the New Hampshire border: After an ownership dispute between Maine and New Hampshire, they were divvied up between the two states (5 went to Maine, 4 to New Hampshire).

Celia Thaxter, a native islander, romanticized these islands with her poetry in *Among the Isles of Shoals*, published in 1873. In her time, **Appledore Island** became an offshore retreat for her coterie of writers, musicians, and artists. The island is now used by the Marine Laboratory of Cornell University, but Thaxter's lovely garden still blooms each summer, tended by volunteers.

Star Island houses a nondenominational conference center. In summer, scheduled cruises take visitors to Star in the morning for a picnic and a narrated walking tour (only conference attendees may stay overnight).

The Isles of Shoals Steamship Company runs island cruises and whale-watching expeditions. Captain Bob Whittaker hosts these voyages aboard the MV *Thomas Laighton*, a replica of a Victorian steamship, on which he regales passengers with tall tales. Breakfast, lunch, and light snacks are available on board, or you can bring your own. Some trips include a stopover and historic walking tour on Star Island. *Barker Wharf, 315 Market St., Portsmouth, tel. 603/431–5500 or 800/441-4620. Reservations advised. Tour cruises mid-June–Labor Day, Oct. Whale-watching cruises May–Oct.*

What to See and Do with Children

The Children's Museum of Portsmouth. Hands-on exhibits explain such subjects as lobstering, geography, computers, recycling, and outer space. Some programs require advance reservations. *280 Marcy St., tel. 603/436–3853. Admission: $3.50 adults and children over 1, $3 senior citizens. Open Tues.–Sat. 10–5, Sun. 1–5. Also open Mon. 10–5 in summer and during school vacations.*
Hampton Playhouse, Hampton (*see* Theater, *below*)
Port of Portsmouth Maritime Museum and Albacore Park, Portsmouth

Off the Beaten Track

Birdwatchers will love the **Great Bay Estuary,** 4 miles west of Portsmouth. Here, among the 4,471 acres of tidal waters, mud flats, and about 48 miles of inland shoreline, visitors can see the Great Blue Heron, Osprey, and the Snowy Egret, especially conspicuous during the spring and fall migrations. The area is most famous, however, for having New Hampshire's largest concentration of winter eagles. Hikers will find trails at Adam's Point and at Sandy Point, and canoeists can put in at Chapman's Landing (Rte. 108) on the Squamscot River. Access to the Great Bay is a bit tricky and parking limited, but the Fish and Game Department's **Sandy Point Discovery Center** (Depot Rd. off Rte. 101, Greenland, tel 603/868–1095) distributes maps and information, and has displays about the estuary.

Shopping

Shopping Districts Portsmouth's Market Square has gift and clothing boutiques, card shops, and exquisite crafts stores. Portsmouth has two shopping malls and an outlet center, although the serious outlet shoppers head to Maine.

Antiques Antiques shops line Route 1 in **Hampton Falls,** including **Antiques New Hampshire** (tel. 603/926–9603), **Antiques One** (tel. 603/926–5332), **Antiques at Hampton Falls** (tel. 603/926–1971), and the **Barn at Hampton Falls** (tel. 603/926–9003). **Northwood,** along Route 4, also has dozens of antiquaries. **Portsmouth** has several funky consignment shops and antiquarian book stores near the town square. Sunday flea markets are held in the **Star Center** (25 Fox Run Rd., Newington, tel. 603/431–9403).

In addition to the **Applecrest** and **Raspberry** farms in Hampton Falls (see Exploring the New Hampshire Coast, *above*), country and farm products, such as homemade jams and pickles, are available at **Emery Farm** (Rte. 4, Durham, tel. 603/742–8495), **Tuttle's Farm** (Dover Point Rd., Dover, tel. 603/742–4313), and **Calef's Country Store** (Rte. 9, Barrington, tel. 603/664–2231).

Factory Outlets For shoppers who don't care to drive north to Kittery, the **North Hampton Factory Outlet Center** (Lafayette Rd. [Rte. 1], North Hampton, tel. 603/964–9050) offers tax-free goods and discounts on such brand names as Van Heusen, Famous Footwear, and American Tourister. The center has a diverse group of stores including the Leather Outpost, the Ribbon Outlet, and the Sports Outpost. Bass and Timberland have their own factory outlets here.

Galleries and Crafts Shops **Alie Jewelers** (1 Market St., Portsmouth, tel. 603/436–0531) carries gold, silver, and gemstone jewelry designed by New England craftsmen. **Country Curtains** (2299 Woodbury Ave., Newington, tel. 603/431-2315), on the Old Beane Farm, sells curtains, bedding, furniture, and folk art. **Exeter League of New Hampshire Craftsmen** (61 Water St., Exeter, tel. 603/778–8282) showcases original jewelry, woodworking, and pottery produced by select, juried members. **The Museum Shop at the Dunaway Store** (Marcy St., Portsmouth, tel. 603/433–1114) stocks reproduction and contemporary furniture, quilts, crafts, candy, gifts, postcards, and books about the history of the area. **N.W. Barrett** (53 Market St., Portsmouth, tel. 603/431–4262) specializes in fine art and crafts from both local and nationally acclaimed artists. The second floor showcases furniture in every price range from affordable steam-bent oak to one-of-a-kind lamps and rocking chairs. On the first floor you can browse the leather, jewelry, pottery, and fiber displays. **Pierce Gallery** (105 Market St., tel. 603/436-1988) sells reasonably priced prints and paintings of both the Maine and New Hampshire coast. **A Picture's Worth a Thousand Words** (65 Water St., Exeter, tel. 603/778–1991) sells antique and contemporary prints and frames them in-house. You can also choose from a wonderful collection of old maps, town histories, and rare books. **Salmon Falls Stoneware** (Oak Street Engine House, Dover, tel. 603/749–1467 or 800/621–2030) produces handmade, salt-glaze stoneware, using a method that was popular among early American potters. Potters are on hand if you want to place a special order or just watch them work. **Tulips** (19 Market St., Portsmouth, tel. 603/431–9445) was Portsmouth's first crafts gallery and still specializes in wood crafts and quilts.

Malls **Fox Run Mall** (Fox Run Rd., Newington, tel. 603/431–5911) is huge and generic, as a mall should be. This one houses Filene's, Jordan Marsh, JC Penney, Sears, and 100 other stores. **Newington Mall** (45 Gosling Rd., Newington, tel. 603/431-4104) has Bradlees, Montgomery Ward, Porteuos, and 40 more stores—as well as Friendly's and Papa Ginos.

Sports and Outdoor Activities

Bicycling   The volume of traffic along Route 1 and the major highways on the Seacoast makes cycling difficult and dangerous for people unfamiliar with the area. The safest route is the bike path along Route 1A, for which you can park at Odiorne point and follow the road 14 miles south to Seabrook. Avoid Route 1, Route 4, and Route 101. Some bikers begin at Prescott Park and take Route 1B into Newmarket, but beware of the traffic. Another pretty route begins at the Newington Town Hall and heads out to the Great Bay Estuary.

Boating   Between April and October, deep-sea fishermen head out for cod, mackerel, and bluefish. There are rentals and charters aplenty, offering half- and full-day cruises, as well as some night fishing at Hampton, Portsmouth, Rye, and Seabrook piers. Try **Eastman Fishing & Marine** (Seabrook, tel. 603/474–3461), **Atlantic Fishing Fleet** (Rye Harbor, tel. 603/964–5220), **Al Gauron Deep Sea Fishing** (Hampton Beach, tel. 603/926–2469), and **Smith & Gilmore** (Hampton Beach, tel. 603/926–3503).

Camping   **Exeter Elms Family Campground** (188 Court St., Exeter 03833, tel. 603/778-7631) has riverfront sites. **Pine Acres Family Campground** (55 Prescott Rd., Raymond 03077, tel. 603/895–2519) has a giant water slide. There is also **Tidewater Campground** (160 Lafayette Rd., Hampton 03842, tel. 603/926–5474) and **Tuxbury Pond Camping Area** (W. Whitehall Rd., South Hampton 03842, tel. 603/394–7660).

Hiking   An excellent 1-mile trail climbs to the summit of **Blue Job Mountain** (Crown Point Rd. off Rte. 202A, 1 mi from Rochester), where there is a firetower with a good view. The **Urban Forestry Center** (45 Elwyn Road, Portsmouth, tel. 603/431–6774), the **Great Bay Estuary,** and the **Odiorne Point State Park** also have several marked trails. The **New Hampshire Division of Parks and Recreation** (tel. 603/271–3254) has just opened the Rockingham Recreation Trail, which wends 27 miles from Epping to Manchester and is open to hikers, bikers, snowmobiles, and cross-country skiers.

Beaches   The beaches tend to be crowded on weekends and more comfortable midweek, with the sun worshipers arriving in droves around 10. Changing rooms and showers are available at the southern end of **Hampton Beach State Park.** You'll usually find the beaches in **Jenness, Rye,** and **Wallis Sands** less congested than in Hampton, but you can view them and take your pick as you cruise Route 1A; they're all within 18 miles of each other. For freshwater swimming, try **Kingston State Park** (tel. 603/642–5471) at Kingston on Great Pond (not to be confused with Great Bay). Coastal beaches outside the state park system include **Foss Beach, Rye,** and **New Castle Common, New Castle.** The state maintains some metered parking spaces near Hampton Beach, but these tend to be scarce. Private lots charge around $5 a day along the coast.

Dining and Lodging

With 84 restaurants, 54 in the downtown area alone, Portsmouth is considered by many to be the restaurant capital of New England. And yet every other small town in the region has its own favorite restaurant that will leave a unique culinary taste in your mouth. Inns and hotels are most crowded from mid-June to mid-October, so reserve well ahead. Restaurants, too, appreciate reservations on summer weekends and throughout October, or until the last leaf falls. Dress is casual unless otherwise noted.

Dover
Dining

Newick's Lobster House. Rumor has it that Newick's serves the best lobster roll on the New England coast, but regulars cherish the onion rings, too. This casual lobster shack serves seafood and atmosphere in heaping portions. Picture windows allow terrific views over Great Bay. *431 Dover Point Rd., tel. 603/742–3205. Reservations not accepted. AE, D, MC, V. Moderate.*

Durham
Lodging

New England Center Hotel. Set in a lush wooded area on the campus of the University of New Hampshire, this hotel is large enough to be a full-service conference center, but quiet enough to feel like a retreat. You'll find larger rooms in the new wing, each with two queen-size beds. Decor is typical of most chain hotels. *15 Strafford Ave., 03824, tel. 603/862–2800, fax 603/862–4351. 115 rooms with bath. Facilities: 2 restaurants, lounge, exercise room. AE, MC, V. Moderate–Expensive.*

Exeter
Dining

The Loaf and Ladle. This understated café serves hearty chowders, soups, stews, and huge sandwiches on homemade bread—all cafeteria-style. Check the blackboard for the ever-changing rotation of stews, breads, and desserts. Overlooking the river, the café is handy to the shops, galleries, and historic houses along Water Street. *9 Water St., tel. 603/778–8955. No reservations. AE, D, DC. Inexpensive.*

Dining and
Lodging

Exeter Inn. This three-story brick, Georgian-style inn, set on the campus of Phillips Exeter Academy, is furnished lavishly with antique and reproduction pieces but possesses every modern amenity. It's been the choice of visiting Phillips Exeter parents for the past half-century. The dining room's house specialty is the chateaubriand served on an oaken plank with duchess potatoes and a béarnaise sauce, although the chef also boasts of a show-stopping veal culinaire, the preparation of which changes daily. On Sundays, the line forms early for a brunch of more than 60 delicious options. Sit in the big, bright sun porch and admire the fig tree growing in the center of the room. *90 Front St., 03833, tel. 603/772–5901 or 800/782–8444, fax 603/778–8757. 50 rooms with bath. Facilities: restaurant (reservations advised; not accepted for Sun. brunch), fitness room. AE, D, DC, MC, V. Inn: Moderate. Restaurant: Expensive.*

Hampton
Dining

Ron's Beach House. Here you'll discover not one but seven fresh fish dishes of the day. Order any one of them prepared in any way you can imagine: baked, steamed, blackened, pan-seared. Start with the *cioppino* (Italian seafood stew). Ingredients are from the sea: Even the mariner's chicken is stuffed with seafood. The restaurant occupies a renovated summer cottage in the Plaice Cove section of Hampton, 3 miles north of the main beach. *965 Ocean Blvd., tel. 603/926–1870. Reservations advised. AE, D, DC, MC, V. Moderate–Expensive.*

Lodging

The Victoria Inn. Built as a carriage house in 1875, this romantic bed-and-breakfast is done in the style Victorians loved best: wicker, chandeliers, and lace. One room is done all in lilac; the honeymoon suite has white eyelet coverlets and a private sunroom. Though innkeepers Linda and Leo LeBlank have named one room in honor of a former U.S. president—Franklin Pierce, who for years summered in the home next door—they've created a breakfast that's better fit for a king. No one leaves hungry after Saturday's Logger's Breakfast: a sausage bake with baked beans, fruit, and muffins. *430 High St. (½ mi from Hampton Beach), 03842, tel. 603/929–1437. 6 rooms, 3 with bath. Full breakfast included. MC, V. Moderate.*

Hampton Beach *Lodging*	**Ashworth by the Sea.** This hotel was built across the street from Hampton Beach in 1912; most rooms have private decks, and the furnishings vary from period to contemporary. The beachside rooms offer a breathtaking ocean view, while the others look out onto the pool or the quiet street, offering solitude from the noisy beach. *295 Ocean Blvd., 03842, tel. 603/926–6762 or 800/345–6736, fax 603/926–2002. 105 rooms with bath. Facilities: 3 restaurants, pool, hair salon. AE, D, DC, MC, V. Moderate–Expensive.*

Newmarket
Lodging

Moody Parsonage Bed and Breakfast. The first things guests notice about this red-clapboard Colonial are the original paneling, beautiful old staircases, and wide pine floors. With a fire crackling on chilly evenings and a spinning wheel in the living-room corner, some think they've stepped back in time. The house was built in 1730 for John Moody, the first minister of Newmarket, and if he came back today, he'd recognize it inside and out. One bedroom and bath are on the first floor. The three rooms upstairs share a bath. Innkeeper Debbie Reed serves summer breakfasts on the front porch, which looks out over a nearby golf course. Located 2 miles south of Newmarket center, the inn is just across the street from the Rockingham Ballroom. *15 Ash Swamp Rd., 03857, tel. 603/659–6675. 4 rooms, 1 with bath. Facilities: 1 room with fireplace. Continental breakfast included. No credit cards. Inexpensive.*

Portsmouth
Dining

The Blue Strawberry Restaurant. This restaurant was opened 20 years ago by a chef who never used recipes but cooked by inspiration alone. Though he's long gone, the restaurant retains his inventive spirit. The menu changes daily according to the freshest available ingredients. *29 Ceres St., tel. 603/431–6420. Reservations required. No credit cards. No lunch. Closed Mon.–Wed. Oct. 15–July 3. Very Expensive.*

Guido's Trattoria. This second-story dining room overlooking the harbor serves traditional Tuscan cuisine. Because the cooking is light and healthful, it's possible to polish off four generous courses and not feel stuffed. Appetizers include grilled bread that you can rub with fresh garlic; calamari simmered in white wine with red peppers, porcini mushrooms, and garlic; and *tortelli alla Bolognese* (cheese-stuffed pasta topped with ground veal, tomatoes, herbs, and wine). Entrées include wild boar, grilled breast of duck, and moist halibut garnished with capers and leeks. Guido offers a fine selection of Italian vintages, but even the house Chiantis are choice. Save room for poached pears or tiramisu for dessert. *67 Bow St., 2nd floor, tel. 603/431–2989. Reservations advised. AE, MC, V. Closed Sun., Mon. Moderate–Expensive.*

The Library at the Rockingham House. This Portsmouth landmark was once a luxury hotel and the site of the press signing of the Russo-Japanese Treaty in 1905. Most of the building has been converted to condominiums, but the restaurant retains the original atmosphere, with hand-carved Spanish mahogany-paneling and bookcases on every wall. Here even the dividers between booths are stacked with old tomes, and the waitresses present each bill in the pages of a vintage bestseller. The food, too, seems to belong in a social club of another century. Don't miss the roasted Long Island duckling with a maple-bourbon glaze, or the roasted, brine-cured pork loin chop stuffed with apples, sage, and walnuts. *401 State St., tel. 603/431–5202. Reservations advised on weekends. AE, DC, MC, V. Moderate–Expensive.*

The Oar House and Deck. With a deck beside the Heritage Cruise dock—perfect for romantic dinners or nightcaps—the Oar House is a hub of Portsmouth summer nightlife. Try the bouillabaisse, the rack of lamb, or the veal *Barbara* (with avocado, crab, cheese, and mushroom topping). *55 Ceres St., tel. 603/436–4025. Reservations advised. AE, MC, V. Moderate–Expensive.*

B.G.'s Boathouse Restaurant. Another local favorite, this place looks like an old fisherman's shack but serves the best seafood in town and plenty of it. Many customers arrive by boat. *Rte. 1B, tel. 603/431–1074. No reservations. AE, D, MC, V. Inexpensive–Moderate.*

The Brewery. You can watch the brewing process of 15 different kinds of ale through the interior windows of this in-house brewery. The pub-style fare includes spicy shrimp, stir-fry combinations, burritos, fresh tuna steak au poivre, and fish-and-chips. Live entertainment is offered Wednesday through Saturday. *56 Market St., tel. 603/431–1115. AE, D, MC, V. Inexpensive–Moderate.*

Karen's. Pass through the purple door and into the restaurant that locals would like to keep secret. Karen's specializes in light, simple seafood dishes prepared to perfection. The dinner menu changes completely every few days, according to the chef's whims. The lunch menu features a lot of sautés, stir-fries, such sandwiches as open-face blackened swordfish, and a few pasta choices. For Sunday brunch look for the eggs Sardou or the eggnog French toast, but even on an ordinary morning you can design your own omelet and enjoy homemade cornbeef hash. *105 Daniel St., tel. 603/431–1948. No reservations. No smoking. No lunch Sun.–Wed. AE, D. Inexpensive–Moderate.*

Lodging **Sheraton Portsmouth Hotel.** Portsmouth's only luxury hotel, this five-story redbrick building offers a nice harbor view and a central location. The hotel houses the area's main conference center, making it a perfect choice for business travelers. Suites have full kitchens and living rooms. *250 Market St., 03801, tel. 603/431–2300 or 800/325–3535, fax 603/431–7805. 148 rooms with bath, 29 suites. Facilities: restaurant, lounge, nightclub, health spa, indoor pool. AE, D, DC, MC, V. Expensive.*

Sise Inn. If you can't decide between a hotel and a small inn with period decor, this Queen Anne town house in Portsmouth's historic district captures the best of both worlds. Each room is individually decorated with silks, rubbed woods, and antique reproductions but has cable TV and whirlpool baths as well. Victorian style meets postmodern convenience, and Continental breakfast is thrown in. The inn is close to the Market area and within walking distance of the theater district and several nice restaurants. *40 Court St., 03801, tel. or fax (ext. 505) 603/433–1200 or 800/267–0525. 34 rooms with bath. Facilities: VCRs, some rooms have whirlpool tubs. Continental breakfast included. AE, DC, MC, V. Expensive.*

The Bow Street Inn. This 10-room inn for nonsmokers is on the second floor of a converted late-19th-century brick brewery. On the Piscataqua River, guests have only a short walk to both the downtown shopping area and the Strawbery Banke Historic District. Rooms are contemporary, with wall-to-wall carpeting, TVs, and telephones. *121 Bow St., 03801, tel. 603/431–7760, fax 603/433–1680. 10 rooms with bath. Continental breakfast included. MC, V. Moderate–Expensive.*

Governor's House B&B. This 1917 Georgian mansion was for more than 30 years the home to New Hampshire's Governor, Charles Dale. Innkeepers Nancy and John Grossman reopened it 1992 as a bed-and-breakfast and have fully restored the four rooms with period antiques, right down to the canopy beds. A look at Nancy's hand-painted mosaic tiles in the bathrooms justifies at least a visit. Guests enjoy a gourmet, low-fat breakfast each morning. *32 Miller Ave., 03801, tel. 603/431–6546, fax 603/427–0803. 4 rooms with bath. Fa-*

cilities: tennis, ceiling fans, off-street parking. Full breakfast included. MC, V. Moderate.

Leighton Inn. Built in 1809 by cabinetmaker Samuel Wyatt, this Colonial inn features a three-story suspended staircase and a fireplace in every room. In summer, you'll find breakfast waiting for you on the sunporch overlooking the herb garden and afternoon tea in the parlor. The rooms vary in decor: two have the usual Victorian frill and lace; two, thankfully, do not. *69 Richards Ave., 03801, tel. 603/ 433–2188. 4 rooms. Facilities: off-street parking. Full breakfast included. MC, V. Moderate.*

Rochester **The Governor's Inn.** Enjoy a quiet, candlelit dinner on the weekends
Dining and or a lively theme-oriented dinner mid-week, which could involve a
Lodging murder mystery, a cabaret, or a performance by the singing waitstaff. The prix fixe menu, by reservation only, changes weekly but may include appetizers of black sturgeon caviar or summer-squash bisque, grilled beef tenderloin stuffed with Danish blue cheese, and a light dessert of lemon meringue. The new á la carte lunch is served weekdays and offers a very popular seafood lasagna. *78 Wakefield St., 03867, tel. 603/332–0107. AE, MC, V. Moderate.*

Rye **Rock Ledge Manor.** Built out on a point and offering a 270° ocean
Lodging view from a full wraparound porch, this mid-19th-century mansion was once part of a resort colony and just predates the houses along Millionaire's Row. It is the only area inn directly on the ocean, and all rooms have water views. The owners speak French and English and serve a huge breakfast each morning in the sunny dining room overlooking the Atlantic. *1413 Ocean Blvd. (Rte. 1A), 03870, tel. 603/431–1413. 4 rooms, 2 with bath. Full breakfast included. No credit cards. Moderate.*

The Arts

Music **Music in Market Square** (tel. 603/436–9109) is a summer series of free concerts given on Fridays at noon. Classical musicians, both vocal and instrumental, perform just outside the North Church in Market Square. **Prescott Park Arts Festival** (Marcy St., Portsmouth, tel. 603/436–2848), kicks off with the Independence Day pops concert and then continues for eight weeks featuring the art of more than 100 regional artists, as well as music, dance, and one outdoor production four nights weekly. Don't miss the Chowder Festival or the jazz picnics on Sundays. Free admission.

Theater **Hampton Playhouse** (357 Winnacunnet Rd., Rte. 101E, Hampton, tel. 603/926–3073) brings familiar Hollywood and New York theater faces to the Seacoast with its summer theater July through September. Matinees are Wednesdays and Fridays at 2:30; children's shows are Saturdays at 11 and 2. Schedules and tickets are available at the box office or at the Chamber of Commerce Sea Shell (Ocean Blvd., tel. 603/926–8717). **The Music Hall** (28 Chestnut St., Portsmouth, tel. 603/436–2400) is the 14th oldest operating theater in the country (ca. 1878), and its mission is to bring the best touring events to the Seacoast—from classical and pop to dance and theater. The hall also hosts an ongoing art-house film series. **The Seacoast Repertory Theatre** (125 Bow St., Portsmouth, tel. 603/433–4472 or 800/639–7650) is one of the top regional theaters in the country and the coast's only year-round professional live theater. The Portsmouth Academy of Performing Arts, the Bow Street Theater, and the Portsmouth Youth Theatre combine to fill its calendar with musicals, classic dramas, and new works by upcoming playwrights.

Nightlife

The **Hampton Beach Casino Ballroom** (Ocean Beach Blvd., Hampton Beach, tel. 603/926–4541; open Apr.–Oct.) has been bringing name entertainment to the Hampton Beach area for more than 30 years. Tina Turner, the Monkees, Jay Leno, and Loretta Lynn have all played here. Expect a crowd of as many as 2,500 people. The **Portsmouth Gaslight Co.** (64 Market St., Portsmouth, tel. 603/430–8582; courtyard opens at 5; the band starts at 7) is a popular brick-oven pizzeria and restaurant by day. But on summer nights, this place transforms itself into a party. That's when the management opens up the back courtyard, brings in live local rock bands, and serves a special punch in plastic sandpails. By midnight, not only is the courtyard full, but the three-story parking garage next door has become a makeshift auditorium. People come from as far away as Boston and Portland to hang out at **The Press Room** (77 Daniel St., Portsmouth, tel. 603/431–5186; name entertainment weekends; open gig Tues.–Sat.), in an old three-story brick building, for folk, jazz, blues, and bluegrass performances. Tuesday night features an open mike; On Sundays the jazz starts at 7. UNH students tend toward Portsmouth and the several bars along Durham's Main Street.

Lakes Region

Lake Winnipesaukee, a Native American name for "Smiling Water," is the largest of the dozens of lakes scattered across the eastern half of central New Hampshire. In fact, with 283 miles of shoreline, it's the largest in the state. Dotted as it is with so many islands, some claim Winnipesaukee has an island for every day of the year. In truth, there are 274 of them, which fails this speculation by about three months.

Unlike Winnipesaukee, which hums with activity all summer long, the more secluded Squam Lake, with a dearth of public-access points, seems to shun visitors. Perhaps it was this tranquility that attracted producers of the 1981 film *On Golden Pond*, several of whose scenes were shot here. Nearby Lake Wentworth is named for the first Royal Governor of the state, who, in building his country manor here, established North America's first summer resort.

The land is rich with historic landmarks and some well-preserved Colonial and 19th-century villages nearby. And eating and recreation opportunities abound, too: There are dozens of good restaurants, several golf courses, hiking trails, and good antiquing along the way. But to experience the Lakes Region to its fullest, you'll really want to enjoy some form of water play, whether it be swimming, fishing, sailing, or just sitting on an old dock dangling your toes in any of these icy lakes.

Important Addresses and Numbers

Visitor Information
Hours are generally Monday–Friday, 10–5. **Lakes Region Association** (Box 589, Center Harbor 03226, tel. 603/253–8516). **Lakes Region Chamber of Commerce** (11 Veterans Square, Laconia 03246, tel. 603/524–5531 or 800/531–2347). **Wolfeboro Chamber of Commerce** (Railroad Ave., Wolfeboro 03894, tel. 603/569–2200).

Emergencies
Lakes Region General Hospital (Highland St., Laconia, tel. 603/524–3211 or 800/852–3311).

Pharmacy   **The Laconia Clinic** (724 Main St., Laconia, tel. 603/524–5151) has a
pharmacy open daily until 6.

Getting Around the Lakes Region

By Car   On the western side of the region, I–93 is the principal north–south
artery. Exit 20 leads to Route 11 and the southwestern side of Lake
Winnipesaukee. Take Exit 23 to Route 104 to Route 25 and the
northwestern corner of the region. From the coast, Route 16
stretches to the White Mountains, with roads leading to the lakeside
towns.

By Bus   **Concord Trailways** (tel. 800/639–3317) has daily stops in Tilton, Laconia, Meredith, Center Harbor, Moultonborough, and Conway.

By Plane   **Moultonborough Airport Charter** (Rte. 25, Moultonborough, tel.
603/476–8801) offers chartered flights and tours.

Guided Tours

Cruising Golden Pond visits filming sites of the movie *On Golden
Pond* aboard the *Lady of the Manor*, a 28-foot pontoon craft. *Manor
Resort, Holderness, tel. 603/968–3348 or 800/545–2141. Fare: $10
adults, $5 children. Runs Memorial Day–late Oct.*

Squam Lake Tours takes up to 20 passengers on a two-hour pontoon
tour of "Golden Pond," with a visit to Church Island. The boat can
also be chartered for guided fishing trips and wedding or anniversa-
ry parties, as well as for lake excursions. *Box 185, Holderness
03245, tel. 603/968–7577. Open late May–Oct.*

The **M/S *Mount Washington*** (Box 5367, Weirs Beach 03247, tel. 603/
366–2628 or 603/366–5531) is a 230-foot craft that makes three-hour
cruises of Lake Winnipesaukee. Departures are May through October, daily from Weirs Beach and Wolfeboro, three times weekly from
Center Harbor, and four times weekly from Alton Bay. Ask about
the moonlight dinner-and-dance cruises.

The **MV *Sophie C.*** (Weirs Beach, tel. 603/366–2628) has been the area's floating post office for more than a century. It even has its own
cancellation stamp. The boat departs Weirs Beach with the mail and
passengers.

The historic cars of the **Winnipesaukee Railroad** carry passengers
along the lakeshore on an hour-long ride; boarding is at Weirs Beach
or Meredith. *Box 9, Lincoln 03251, tel. 603/279–3196. Fare: $7
adults, $4.50 children. Runs weekends Memorial Day–late June,
late Sept.–mid-Oct.*

You can also see the area by air. **Sky Bright** (Laconia Airport, tel.
603/528–6818) offers airplane and helicopter tours of the area and instruction on aerial photography. **Seaplane Services** (tel. 603/524–
0446) takes off right from the Paugus Bay dock for custom, guided
tours of the area.

Exploring the Lakes Region

*Numbers in the margin correspond to points of interest on the New
Hampshire Lakes map.*

This tour begins at Lake Winnipesaukee's southernmost tip, and
moves clockwise through the lakeside towns, starting on Route 11.
Neither quiet nor secluded, the lake's southern shore is alive with

tourists from the moment the first flower blooms until the last maple has shed its leaves.

Two mountain ridges hold 7 miles of Winnipesaukee in Alton Bay. **1** At the southern extremity of the lake you'll find the town of **Alton Bay.** Aside from the lake's cruise boats, which dock here, there are a dance pavilion, minigolf, a public beach, and a Victorian-style bandstand for summer concerts.

A few miles east on Route 11A is the **Gunstock Recreation Area** (tel. 603/293–4341), a sprawling park with an Olympic-size pool, a children's playground, hiking trails, horses, paddleboats, and a campground with 300 tent and trailer sites. A major downhill-skiing center, it once claimed the longest tow rope in the country—an advantage that helped local downhill skier and Olympic silver medalist Penny Pitou perfect her craft.

One of the larger public beaches is at the resort community of **2** **Gilford.** When incorporated in 1812, the town decided to ask its oldest resident to name it. A veteran of the Battle of the Guilford Courthouse, in North Carolina, he borrowed that town's name—though apparently he didn't know how to spell it. The town today is as quiet and peaceful as it must have been then. Commercial development has been shunned here; you couldn't buy a T-shirt or piece of pottery if you tried.

3 North of Gilford on Route 11A, **Weirs Beach**—dubbed New Hampshire's Coney Island—forms the lake's center for arcade activity. Anyone who loves souvenir shops, fireworks, bumper cars, and hordes of children will be right at home. Several cruise ships (*see* Guided Tours, *above*) depart from this dock, and the **Winnipesaukee Railroad** (tel. 603/279–3196) picks up passengers here for an hour-long tour of the shore. You'll find water slides in town at **Surf Coaster** (tel. 603/366–4991) and **Water Slide** (tel. 603/366–5161), or you can spend all night working your way through the minigolf course, 20 lanes of bowling, and more than 500 games at **Funspot** (tel. 603/366–4377).

Time Out **Kellerhaus** (Daniel Webster Hwy., tel. 603/366–4466), just north of Weirs Beach and overlooking the lake, is an alpine-style building that has been selling homemade chocolates, hard candy, and ice cream since 1906. Kids love the ice-cream smorgasbord, which has a great variety of toppings. Fortunately, the price is based not on the number of scoops but on the size of the dish.

4 **Meredith,** on Route 3 at the western extremity of Winnipesaukee, is known primarily as the home of **Annalee's Doll Museum** (tel. 603/279–4144). Visitors can view a vast collection of the famous felt dolls and learn about the woman behind their creation. The town has a fine collection of crafts shops and art galleries. An information center is across from the Town Docks.

5 The town of **Center Harbor,** set on the middle of three bays at the northern end of Winnipesaukee, also borders Lakes Squam, Waukewan, and Winona. On rainy days you can visit the **Center Harbor Children's Museum,** where kids can make bubbles and play instruments, among other activities. *Senter's Market, Center Harbor, tel. 603/253–8697. Admission: $5. Open Tues.–Sat. 9:30–5, Sun. 11–5.*

At this point you can detour around Squam Lake. Route 25B will take you to Route 25, which leads to the town of Holderness. At the junction of Routes 113 and 25, on the shores of the lake, is the 200-

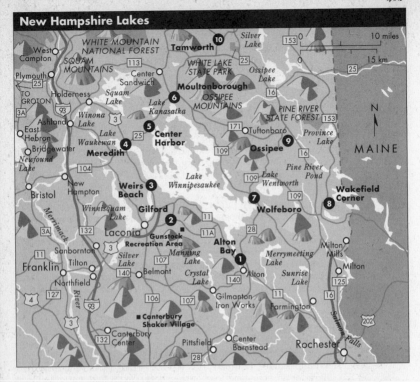

New Hampshire Lakes

acre wildlife preserve, the **Science Center of New Hampshire** (tel.
603/968–7194). The center maintains a ¾-mile nature trail that features such wildlife as black bears, bobcats, otters, and snowy owls.
It also sponsors educational events, including a daily "Up Close to
Animals" series in which visitors get a closer look at such species as
the Red Shouldered Hawk. *Admission: $6 adults, $3 children 5–15
(admission is slightly higher July–Aug.). Open May–Oct., daily 9–
4:30.*

From here you can take Route 113 east up and around Squam Lake,
through the beautiful village of Center Sandwich. Its **Historical Society Museum** (Maple St., tel. 603/284–6269; open June–Sept.,
Mon.–Sat. 11–5) traces the history of the town largely through the
faces of its inhabitants. Mid-19th-century portraitist and town son
Albert Gallatin Hoit has eight works here; they are hung alongside a
local photographer's exhibit portraying the town's mothers and
daughters.

6 From here, take Route 109 south to **Moultonborough,** which claims
6½ miles of shoreline on Lake Kanasatka, as well as a piece of
Squam. Although people love to browse in the **Old Country Store**
(Moultonborough Corner, tel. 603/476–5750) and its museum of antique farming and forging tools. (admission free), the best-known
attraction is the **Castle in the Clouds.** Construction began in 1911 on
this odd, elaborate mansion and went on for three years; owner
Thomas Gustave Plant pumped $7 million into this dwelling, which,
amazingly, was built without nails. It has 16 rooms, 8 bathrooms,
and doors made of lead. Unfortunately, Plant spent the bulk of his
huge fortune on this project and died penniless in 1946. *Rte. 171,*

Moultonboro, tel. 603/476–2352 or 800/729–2468. Open mid-June–mid-Oct., daily 10–4; mid-May–mid-June, weekends 10–4.

7 **Wolfeboro,** 15 miles southeast of Moultonbourough, has been a resort since John Wentworth built his summer home on the shores of Lake Wentworth in 1763. The original Wentworth house burned in 1820, but some of his belongings were salvaged, and you can see them at the **Libby Museum** (Rte. 109, Wolfeboro, tel. 603/569–1035; open Memorial Day–Labor Day, Tues.–Sun. 10–4), along with an unusual natural history collection. **The Clark House Historical Exhibit and Museum** (S. Main St., tel. 603/569–4997; open July–Aug., Mon.–Sat. 10–4) takes a more conventional look at the town's history; one exhibit re-creates a late-19th-century fire station, complete with a red fire engine. The downtown area is right on Winnipesaukee, attracting droves of tourists summer-long: The chamber of commerce estimates that the population increases tenfold each June.

Wolfeboro is also headquarters to the **Hampshire Pewter Company** (tel. 603/569–4944), where craftsmen still use 17th-century techniques to make pewter hollowware and accessories. Shop tours begin on the hour, weekdays in summer, less often off-season. A few miles north on Route 109 is the trailhead to **Abenaki Tower.** A short (¼-mile) hike to the 100-foot post-and-beam tower, followed by a more rigorous climb to the top, rewards you with a vast view of Winnipesaukee and the Ossipee mountain range.

8 East of Winnipesaukee lie several villages that, thankfully, lack the lakeside towns' bustle of tourism. **Wakefield Corner,** on the Maine border, is a registered historic district, with a church, houses, and an inn looking just as they did in the 18th century. The nearby town of Wakefield encompasses 10 lakes. Here you'll find the charming **Museum of Childhood,** where exhibits include a one-room schoolhouse from 1890, model trains, a collection of antique children's sleds, and 3,000 dolls. *Off Rte. 16 in Wakefield Corner, tel. 603/522–8073. Admission: $3 adults, $1.25 children. Open Memorial Day–Columbus Day, Mon., Wed.–Sat. 11–4, Sun. 1–4.*

9 From here, Route 16N leads to the three **Ossipee** villages. Or you can take Route 153, the slower road among the scenic lakes on Maine's border. Between Ossipee and West Ossipee, Route 16N passes sparkling Lake Ossipee, known for fine fishing and swimming. Among these hamlets you'll also find several antiques shops and galleries.

10 **Tamworth,** northwest of Ossipee on Route 113, also has a clutch of villages within its borders. The view through the birches of Chocorua Lake has been so often photographed that you may get a sense of having been here before.

What to See and Do with Children

Annalee's Doll Museum, Meredith
Center Harbor Children's Museum, Center Harbor
Funspot, Surf Coaster, and **Water Slide,** Weirs Beach
Museum of Childhood, Wakefield
New Hampshire Farm Museum. It's not just a collection of farm implements and tools, but a living museum with weekend events demonstrating farm-related crafts. *Rte. 125, Milton, tel. 603/652–7840. Admission: $4 adults, $1.50 children under 13. Open mid-June–Columbus Day, Tues.–Sat. 10–4, Sun. noon–4.*
Science Center of New Hampshire, Holderness
Winnipesaukee Railroad, Meredith and Weirs beaches

Off the Beaten Track

Expert tour guides at the **Canterbury Shaker Village** kindly welcome visitors to this historic village with a detailed 90-minute tour
of the grounds. Guides will answer questions about the history and
philosophy of the Shakers. Established in 1792, this religious community flourished in the 1800s. It was the sixth of nine self-contained Shaker villages that practiced equality of the sexes and races,
common ownership, celibacy, and pacifism. Shakers were known for
the perfection of their workmanship and for the simplicity and integ-
rity of their design, especially in household furniture. Because they
believed in efficient work, they became prolific inventors of indis-
pensable time-savers, such as the clothespin and the flat broom.
This outdoor museum has crafts demonstrations and a large shop of
books and fine Shaker reproductions. The Creamery Restaurant
brings to life Shaker recipes for Sunday brunch, lunch daily, and
candlelight dinners before the 7 PM tour on Friday and Saturday
nights. Most visitors spend the better part of a day here. *7 mi from
Exit 18 off I-93. 288 Shaker Rd., Canterbury, tel. 603/783-9511.
Admission: $7 adults, $3.50 children. Open May-Oct., Mon.-Sat.
10-5, Sun. noon-5; Apr., Nov.-Dec., Fri.-Sat. 10-5, Sun.
noon-5.*

Shopping

The area's crafts shops, galleries, and boutiques are all geared to
the summer influx of tourists. Many close in the off-season (late
Oct.-mid-Apr.), and the wares tend toward T-shirts and somewhat
tacky trinkets. You'll find most antiques shops along the eastern
side of Winnipesaukee near Wolfeboro and around Ossipee.

Specialty **Dow's Corner Shop** (Rte. 171, Tuftonboro Corner, tel. 603/539-4790)
Shops has not one but two of everything. So crowded with historic memo-
Art and rabilia, this antiques shop could pass as a museum. At **The Old Print**
Antiques **Barn** (Meredith, tel. 603/279-6479), choose from 1,000 rare prints
from around the world in this huge barn. This is the largest print
gallery in northern New England. From Route 104 in Meredith follow Winona Road and look for "Lane" on the mailbox.

Crafts **Keepsake Quilting & Country Pleasures** (Senter's Marketplace on
Rte. 25, Center Harbor, tel. 603/253-4026) calls itself America's
largest quilt shop and proves it with 5,000 bolts of fabric, hundreds
of quilting books, and countless supplies, plus a wide selection of
yarn and needlework kits. The **Meredith League of New Hampshire
Craftsmen** (Rte. 3, ½ mi north of jct. Rtes. 3 and 104, Meredith, tel.
603/279-7920) sells the juried work of area craftspersons. **The Old
Country Store and Museum** (Moultonborough Corner, tel. 603/476-
5750) has been selling everything from handmade soaps to antiques,
maple products, aged cheeses, and penny candy since 1781. **Sandwich Home Industries** (Rte. 109, Center Sandwich, tel. 603/284-
6831), the 65-year-old grandparent of the League of New Hampshire Craftsmen, was formed to foster cottage crafts. There are
crafts demonstrations in July and August and sales of home furnishings and accessories mid-May-October.

Crystal **Pepi Hermann Crystal** (3 Waterford Pl., Gilford, tel. 603/528-1020)
sells hand-cut crystal chandeliers and stemware; you can also take a
tour and watch the artists at work.

Shopping **Mill Falls Marketplace** (tel. 603/279-7006), on the bay in Meredith,
Malls contains nearly two dozen shops, as well as restaurants and an inn.

Belknap Mall (tel. 603/524–5651), on Route 3 in Laconia, has boutiques, crafts stores, and a New Hampshire state liquor store.

Sports and Outdoor Activities

Boating The **Lakes Region Association** (Box 1545, Center Harbor 03226, tel. 603/253–8555) can give boating advice. Power boats can be rented in Meredith from **Meredith Marina and Boating Center** (tel. 603/279–7921). You'll find pontoon boats, power boats, and personal watercraft at **Thurston's Marina** (tel. 603/366–4811) in Weirs Beach.

Camping **Gunstock** (Rte. 11A, Gilford, tel. 603/293–4344) is a protected woodland in which you can ski, hike, bike, swim, and take guided horseback tours. **Meredith Woods** (New Hampton 03256, tel. 603/279–5449 or 800/848–0328) offers year-round camping and RV facilities, as well as an indoor heated pool. **Yogi Bear's Jellystone Park** (Ashland 03217, tel. 603/968–3654) is especially good for families. **Clearwater Campground** (Meredith 03253, tel. 603/279–7761) is a wooded, tent and RV campground on Lake Pemigewasset. **Squam Lakeside Camp Resort and Marina** (Rte. 3, Holderness 03245, tel. 603/968–7227) is open year-round and has full hookups and cable TV. **White Lake State Park** (Tamworth 03886, tel. 603/323–7350), between Tamworth and Ossipee, has two camping areas with 200 tent sites and a camp store, a shaded picnic area, swimming, and canoe rentals.

Fishing You'll find lake trout and salmon in Winnipesaukee, trout and bass in the smaller lakes, and trout in various streams all around the area. Alton Bay has an "Ice Out" salmon derby in spring. In winter, on all the lakes, intrepid ice fishers fish from huts known as "ice bobs." For up-to-date fishing information, call the **New Hampshire Fish and Game** office (tel. 603/744–5470).

Golf The area's one 18-hole golf course is **White Mountain Country Club** (N. Ashland Rd., Ashland, tel. 603/536–2227).

Hiking The region is full of beautiful trails. Contact the **Alexandria headquarters of the Appalachian Mountain Club** (tel. 603/744–8011) or the **Laconia Office of the U.S. Forest Service** (tel. 603/528–8721) for advice and information. **Red Hill,** on Bean Road off Route 25, northeast of Center Harbor, really does turn red in autumn. The reward at the end of the trail in any season is a beautiful view of Squam Lake and the mountains; try also **Mt. Major** in Alton, **Squam Range** in Holderness, and **Pine River State Forest,** east of Route 16.

Water Sports The lake is teeming with boats in summer. Look for waterskiing regulations at every marina. Scuba divers can explore a 130-foot-long cruise ship that sunk in 30 feet of water off Glendale in 1895. **Dive Winnipesaukee Corp.** (4 N. Main St., Wolfeboro, tel. 603/569–2120) runs charters out to this and other wrecks and offers instruction, rentals, repairs, and scuba sales. They also give lessons in water-skiing and windsurfing.

State Parks

White Lake State Park (Rte. 16, Tamworth) has a 72-acre stand of native pitch pine, which is a National Natural Landmark. The park also has hiking trails, a sandy beach, trout fishing, canoe rentals, and two separate camping areas. Both the **Plummer Ledge Natural Area** (Town Rd., Wentworth) and the **Sculptured Rocks Natural Area** (between Rte. 3A and 118, Groton) show off striking glacial potholes that vary in size from 2 feet to more than 10 feet across.

Beaches

Ellacoya State Beach (Rte. 11, Gilford) consists of 600 feet along the southwestern shore of Lake Winnipesaukee and offers views of the Ossipee and Sandwich mountain ranges. **Wentworth State Beach** (Rte. 109, Wolfeboro) has good swimming and picnicking areas, as well as a bath house. One of the most beautiful area beaches is the **Wellington State Beach** (off Rte 3A, Bristol), on the western shore of Newfound Lake. You can swim or picnic along the ½-mile sandy beach or take the scenic walking trail. Among the free beaches are **Bartlett Beach** (Winnisquam Ave., Laconia), **Opechee Park** (N. Main St., Laconia), and the **Alton Bay Beach** (Alton Bay).

Dining and Lodging

Because restaurants around the lakes serve throngs of visitors in summer, be sure to call for reservations. In peak season, everything is booked. Off-season, whole communities seem to close for the winter. For additonal accommodations selections, see the Gunstock section of the Skiing in New England chapter.

Belmont
Dining and Lodging

Hickory Stick Farm. The specialty is roast duckling with country herb stuffing and orange-sherry sauce, which you order by portion—the quarter, half, or whole duck. Dinner includes salad, orange rolls, a vegetable, and potato. Consider also seafood, beef tenderloin, rack of lamb, or a vegetarian casserole. The 200-year-old Cape-style inn has two large, old-fashioned upstairs bed-and-breakfast rooms with cannonball beds, stenciled wallpaper, lace curtains, and full bathrooms. Breakfast is on the sun porch and offers such goodies as peach–and–cream cheese stuffed French toast. It's 4 miles from Laconia. *60 Bean Hill Rd., 03246, tel. 603/524–3333. 2 rooms with bath. Facilities: restaurant (reservations accepted; no lunch). Full breakfast included. AE, D, MC, V. Closed Mon.–Wed., mid-Oct.–late Apr. Inexpensive–Moderate.*

Bridgewater
Dining and Lodging

Pasquaney Inn on Newfound Lake. Just across the road from Newfound Lake, only the sunset can distract diners from the French–Belgian cuisine. Start with smoked salmon with endive and mustard-truffle dressing, followed by veal sweetbreads with mushrooms and Madeira wine, or monkfish with tomato coulis. The mousse, made with real Belgian chocolate, makes a perfect finale. The restaurant's vegetables, herbs, and flowers are grown in the backyard gardens. Owner-chef Bud Edrick also gives lessons in French cooking during the off-season. The antiques-filled bedrooms in this 1840s house tempt you to stay the night after you've worked your way through the menu. *Rte. 3A, 03222, tel. 603/744–9111. 30 rooms, 19 with bath. Facilities: restaurant (reservations advised), pub, cruises in summer, private beach. AE, D, DC, MC, V. Moderate–Expensive.*

Center Barnstead
Dining

The Crystal Quail. The namesake quail dish is only available in-season, but this tiny restaurant, in an 18th-century farmhouse, is worth the drive in any season. The prix fixe menu is presented verbally with a couple of choices for appetizer, main dish, and dessert. Those choices may include saffron-garlic soup, a house pâté, quenelle-stuffed sole, or duck in crisp potato shreds, but they don't serve wine or beer, so bring your own. Seating just 12 patrons, this is the most intimate dining experience in New Hampshire. If you like your dinner (and you will), stop by the kitchen and say so to chef and owners Cynthia and Harold Huckaby. *Pitman Rd., tel. 603/269–4151.*

Reservations required. No credit cards. BYOB. No lunch. Closed Mon., Tues. Expensive.

Center Harbor
Dining and Lodging

Red Hill Inn. Chef Elmer Davis loves dessert. On any given night, the waitstaff must recite close to a dozen choices, including his famous vinegar pie (which is sweeter than it sounds), his windswept chocolate torte, and his Kentucky high pie. But before you get that far, try one of his special appetizers, maybe the baked brie wrapped in phyllo, or any one of two dozen entrées featuring seafood, lamb, and duck. The inn was once the entire campus of Belknap College. Before that, it was a rambling summer mansion with a history of interesting past owners, including an artist who painted nursery-rhyme characters on the walls of one of the rooms. The current owners have carefully renovated the house and grounds. The large bay window in the common room overlooks "Golden Pond." Furnished with Victorian pieces and country furniture, many of the rooms have fireplaces, and some have whirlpool baths. The popular Runabout Lounge is an antique speedboat halved to form a pub. *RD 1, Box 99M (Rte. 25B), 03226, tel. 603/279–7001, fax 603/279–7003. 21 rooms with bath. Facilities: restaurant (reservations advised). Full breakfast included. AE, D, DC, MC, V. Moderate–Expensive.*

Center Sandwich
Dining and Lodging

The Corner House Inn. This quaint Victorian inn serves home-cooked meals in a converted barn. Before you get to the white chocolate cheesecake with key lime filling, you may want to try the chef's lobster-and-mushroom bisque, or the mouth-watering crab cakes. The room's mood mixes exposed beams with candlelight and a whimsical decor of local arts and crafts. Come by on Thursday to hear storytellers perform in the glow of the wood stove. The four comfortable, old-fashioned rooms upstairs (one with private bath) display the original paintings and quilted wall-hangings of local artists. *Jct. Rtes. 109 and 113, 03277, tel. 603/284–6219 or 800/832–7829, fax 603/284–6220. 4 rooms, 1 with bath. Facilities: restaurant (reservations advised). Full breakfast included. AE, MC, V. Closed Mon. and Tues. Nov.–mid-June. Inexpensive–Moderate.*

East Hebron
Lodging

Six Chimneys. It does, in fact, have six chimneys. More impressive, though, is its setting atop a hill overlooking Newfound Lake, midway between Bristol and Plymouth, which makes it equally convenient to the lakes and the White Mountains. Two common rooms have cable TV and VCRs; more than 200 tapes are stored in an English monk's bench. An upstairs sitting room with Oriental rugs and pine and cherry furniture sits under a pitched roof. The old wide-board floors in this house tilt a bit, and there are gun-stock corner posts and pine wainscoting in some bedrooms. Bountiful country breakfasts (fruit compote, French toast, sausage, and raspberry muffins, for example) are cooked on a 125-year-old wood-burning range, then served in a dining room with exposed beams and pegs and rush-seat chairs. *Star Rte. 114, 03232, tel. 603/744–2029. 6 rooms, 2 with bath. Facilities: lake beach. MC, V. Closed late Mar.–early Apr. Inexpensive.*

Holderness
Lodging

The Inn on Golden Pond. This informal country home, built in 1879 and set on 50 wooded acres, is just across the road from Squam Lake. Visitors have lake access and can stroll among the property's many nature trails. The rooms have a traditional country decor of hardwood floors, braided rugs, easy chairs, and calico-print bedspreads and curtains. The quietest rooms are in the rear on the third floor. Breakfast includes homemade rhubarb jam, from rhubarb grown on the property. *Rte. 3, Box 680, 03245, tel. 603/968–7269. 9 rooms with bath. Full breakfast included. AE, MC, V. Moderate–Expensive.*

The Manor on Golden Pond. Built in 1913 as a private retreat for Mr. Isaac Van Horn, it thankfully retains a dignified air with well-groomed grounds, clay tennis courts, a swimming pool, a private dock with canoes, paddle boats, and a boathouse. Guests feast on a five-course prix-fixe dinner with such specialties as rack of lamb, filet mignon, shrimp Aegean, and nonpareil apple pie. Guests can stay in the main inn, the carriage-house suites, or one of the four housekeeping cottages. *Rte. 3, 03245, tel. 603/968–3348 or 800/545–2141, fax 603/968–2116. 27 rooms with bath. Facilities: restaurant, pub. AE, MC, V. Moderate–Expensive.*

Meredith
Lodging

The Nutmeg Inn. The white Cape-style house with black shutters was built in 1763 by a sea captain who obtained the dwelling's timber by dismantling his ship. He paneled the dining room with extra-wide "king's boards," which were supposed to be reserved for royal construction. An 18th-century ox yoke is bolted to the wall over a walk-in-size fireplace, and the wide-board floors are also original. All the rooms are named after spices and decorated accordingly. The inn is on a rural side-street off Route 104, the main link between I–93 and Lake Winnipesaukee. *Pease Rd., RFD 2, 03253, tel. 603/279–8811. 7 rooms with bath; 1 suite. Facilities: working fireplaces in some rooms; swimming pool, meeting facilities. Full breakfast included. D, MC, V. Moderate.*

Moulton-borough
Dining

Sweetwater Inn. Chef and owner Mike Love makes dishes from scratch, right down to the home-churned blackberry-honey butter. The breads, the demiglaces, the salad dressings, the desserts are all prepared here. He makes the pasta daily for the lobster ravioli (with a pepper-vodka sauce) and the fettuccine jambalaya (sautéed chicken, scallops, and andouille sausage with garlic, sherry, peppers, and Cajun spices). Although he calls the cuisine traditional French, he does offer some Spanish and nouvelle Italian dishes—paellas and *pollo con gambas* (chicken breast and shrimp sautéed with brandy). He uses only herbs and spices as seasonings; no salt. The decor is as eclectic as the menu. The formality of linen tablecloths and effusive service is cut by the wood stoves and proliferation of local art. *Rte. 25, tel. 603/476–5079. Reservations advised. AE, DC, MC, V. Moderate.*

The Woodshed. This 1860s barn and farmhouse looks like a woodshed, with farm implements and antiques hanging on the walls. You'll get hearty meals here, beef (including prime rib), lamb, and seafood—all cooked to order. Eat from the raw bar or try the New England section of the menu, which lists clam chowder, scrod, and Indian pudding; guests love the Denver chocolate pudding, a dense pudding-cake served warm with vanilla ice cream. *Lee's Mill Rd., tel. 603/476–2311. Reservations advised. AE, D, DC, MC, V. Moderate.*

Tamworth
Dining and Lodging

Tamworth Inn. The barn out back used to be home to the Barnstormer Theater, which has now moved to a bigger and more respectable stage across the street. The actors, though, still rehearse here. Summer guests never miss a theater performance, unless they're out hiking one of the trails in the nearby Nemenway State Forest. Every room is done in 19th-century American pieces and handmade quilts. In the dining room, the most popular appetizer among the pretheater set is the provolone-and-pesto terrine. Among entrées, try the pork tenderloin with apple-walnut cornbread stuffing and an apple-cider sauce, or the beef Stroganoff. If you order the profiterole Tamworth (with the chef's own hot fudge sauce), your waiter should give warning: It *is* big enough for two. The pub offers lighter fare and a look at an antique sled collection. Sunday brunch is ever popular. *Main St., Box 189, 03886, tel. 603/323-7721 or 800/ 642-7352. 15 rooms with bath. Facilities: restaurant (reservations advised; closed Sun. and Mon. in summer and Mon. and Tues. in winter), pub, pool, video library with VCR. Full breakfast included; MAP available. MC, V. Moderate-Expensive.*

Tilton
Dining

Le Chalet Rouge. On the west side of Tilton, this yellow house, with a modestly decorated dining room, is not unlike the country bistros of France. Neither the decor nor the menu is flashy, which most diners find refreshing. Choose from among a wonderful house pâté, escargots, or steamed mussels as a starter. Steak au poivre is one of the better entrées, but don't miss the duckling prepared with seasonal sauces: rhubarb in spring, raspberry in summer, orange in fall, creamy mustard in winter. *321 W. Main St., tel. 603/286-4035. Reservations advised. AE. Closed first 2 weeks in Nov. Moderate-Expensive.*

Wakefield
Lodging

Wakefield Inn. The restoration of this 1804 stage-coach inn, in Wakefield's historic district, has been handled with an eye for detail. The dining room windows retain the original panes and Indian shutters. But the centerpiece of the building is the free-standing spiral staircase that rises three stories. Rooms are named for famous guests (such as John Greenleaf Whittier) or honor past owners. The large guest rooms have wide pine floors, big sofas, and handmade quilts. But guests can make their own quilt in one weekend with the Quilting Package course offered in late fall and early spring. *RR 1, Box 2185, Mountain Laurel Rd., 03872, tel. 603/522-8272 or 800/ 245-0841. 7 rooms with bath. Facilities: restaurant (open to guests only, by reservation). Full breakfast included. MC, V. Moderate.*

Wolfeboro
Dining

The Bittersweet. This converted barn has been decorated with an eclectic display of old quilts, pottery, sheet music, china, and other odd implements, all of which are for sale. Although it may feel like a cozy crafts shop, it's really a restaurant that locals love for the lamb-and-cider pie, duck with raspberry sauce, wiener schnitzel, and spinach salad. *Rte. 28, tel. 603/569-3636. Reservations accepted. MC, V. Moderate.*

Dining and Lodging

The Wolfeboro Inn. This white-clapboard house on Main Street was built nearly 200 years ago but has 19th- and 20th-century additions, which extend to the waterfront of Wolfeboro Bay. The rooms have polished cherry and pine furnishings, and armoires (to hide the TVs), along with stenciled borders and country quilts. Wolfe's Tavern serves food cooked in a bake-oven fireplace, plus more than 45 brands of beer. Try the veal Wolfeboro, with its unlikely but delicious combination of veal, lobster, and shrimp sautéed and served with a cream sauce. The main dining room offers a very popular twin-lobster special. *44 N. Main St., 03894, tel. 603/569-3016 or 800/451-2389, fax 603/569-5375. 38 rooms with bath, 5 suites. Facilities: 2 restaurants, tavern, private lake beach, excursion boat, canoes, bicycles, golf and tennis nearby. Continental breakfast included. AE, D, MC, V. Moderate-Very Expensive.*

The Arts

The Belknap Mill Society (Mill Plaza, Laconia, tel. 603/524-8813) is a year-round cultural center housed in a 19th-century textile mill. The society sponsors concerts, exhibits, a lecture series, and workshops in arts and crafts and on history.

Music

Arts Council of Tamworth (tel. 603/323-7793) produces concerts—soloists, string quartets, revues, children's programs—from September through June, followed by a summer arts show the last weekend in July. **New Hampshire Music Festival** (88 Belknap Mountain Rd., Gilford, tel. 603/524–1000) brings award-winning professional orchestras to the Lakes Region each summer from early July through mid-August.

Theater **Barnstormers** (Main St., Tamworth, tel. 603/323–8500), New Hampshire's oldest professional theater, performs Equity summer theater in July and August. At **Lakes Region Theatre** (Interlakes Auditorium, Rte. 25, Meredith, tel. 603/279–9933), summer-stock actors perform Broadway musicals six nights a week.

Nightlife

Funspot (Weirs Beach, tel. 603/366–4377) is open 24 hours, July to Labor Day. You can bowl, snack, and play minigolf or any of the 500 arcade games all night long.

M/S *Mount Washington* (tel. 603/366–2628) has moonlight dinner-and-dance cruises Tuesday–Saturday evenings with a different menu each night and two bands.

The White Mountains

Sailors approaching East Coast harbors frequently recognize the White Mountains—the highest range in the northeastern United States—towering in the distance, often mistaking these pale peaks for clouds. It was 1642 when explorer Darby Field could no longer contain his curiosity about one mountain in particular. He set off from his Exeter homestead and became the first man to climb what would eventually be called Mt. Washington, king of the Presidential range. More than a mile high, Mt. Washington must have presented Field with a slew of formidable obstacles—its peak claims the harshest winds and lowest temperatures ever recorded.

A few hundred years after Field's climb, curiosity about the mountains has not abated. People come here by the tens of thousands to hike and climb in spring and summer, to photograph the dramatic vistas and the vibrant sea of foliage in autumn, and to ski in winter. In this four-season vacation hub, many year-round resorts (some of which have been in business since the mid-1800s) are destinations in themselves, with golf, tennis, swimming, hiking and cross-country skiing, and renowned restaurants.

Important Addresses and Numbers

Visitor Information Hours are generally Monday through Friday, 9–5. **Mt. Washington Valley Visitors Bureau** (Box 2300, North Conway 03860, tel. 603/356–5701 or 800/367–3364). **White Mountain Attractions Association** (Box 10, North Woodstock 03262, tel. 603/745–8720).

Emergencies **Memorial Hospital** (Intervale Rd., North Conway, tel. 603/356–5461).

Getting Around the White Mountains

By Plane **Berlin Airport** (Milan, tel. 603/449–7383) and the **Eastern Slope Regional Airport** (Fryeburg, ME, tel. 207/935–288) both take charters and private planes.

By Car Interstate–93 and Route 3 bisect the White Mountain National Forest, running north from Massachusetts to Quebec. To the east,

Route 16 brings visitors north from the New Hampshire coast. The Kancamagus Highway (Rte. 112), the east–west thoroughfare through the White Mountain National Forest, is a scenic drive but is often impassable in winter. Route 302, a longer, more leisurely east–west path, connects Lincoln to North Conway.

By Bus **Concord Trailways** (tel. 800/639–3317) stops in Chocorua, Conway, and Jackson.

Exploring the White Mountains

Numbers in the margin correspond to points of interest on the White Mountains map.

Although traveling at Mach One along I–93 is the fastest way to the White Mountains, it's hardly the most scenic. Try instead hopping off the interstate at Exit 32 in Lincoln and latching onto the **Kancamagus Highway** (aka "the Kank"), which allows classic White Mountains vistas. One caveat: This 34-mile trek erupts into fiery color each fall; photo-snapping drivers can really slow things down at this time. Prepare yourself for a leisurely pace, and enjoy the four scenic overlooks and picnic areas (all well marked).

A couple of short hiking trails off the Kank offer great rewards for relatively little effort. About 20 miles east of Exit 32, the parking and picnic area for **Sabbaday Falls** is the trailhead for an easy ½-mile trail to the falls, a multilevel cascade that plunges through two potholes and a flume. Travel another two miles east on the Kank for the **Russel Colbath Historic House** (ca. 1831), the only 19th-century homestead in the area and today a U.S. Forest Service information center. This marks the beginning of the **Rail 'N River Forest Trail,** a gentle ½-mile self-guided tour of White Mountains logging and geological history. It's wheelchair- and stroller-accessible.

1 Continue on the Kank to Route 16 and **North Conway,** a shopper's paradise, with more than 150 outlet stores ranging from Anne Klein to Wallet Works to Joan & David. Most of them lie along Route 16.

Nonshoppers may wish to spend an hour on the **Conway Scenic Railroad,** which makes an 11-mile round-trip in vintage open-air trains pulled either by steam or diesel engines. Lunch is available in the dining car. The Victorian train station has displays of railroad artifacts, lanterns, and old tickets and timetables. *Main St., tel. 603/ 356–5251 or 800/232–5251. Admission: $7.50 adults, $5 children 4– 12. Operates May–Oct. daily 9–6, Apr. and Nov.–late Dec. weekends 9–6. Reserve early during foliage season.*

You needn't be a rock climber to glimpse views from the 1,000-foot **White Horse** and **Cathedral** ledges. Two stoplights north of the Scenic Railroad's station, turn left onto River Road and then right onto West Side Road; then follow signs to the ledges. You can also drive up from **Echo Lake State Park** (North Conway, tel. 603/356–2672). From the top you'll see the entire valley in which Echo Lake shines like a diamond. Continue another ⁷⁄₁₀-mile on West Side Road to the unmarked trailhead to **Diana's Baths,** a spectacular series of waterfalls.

Time Out The **Thompson House Eatery** (Rte. 16, tel. 603/383–9341), just south of Jackson, serves inventive fare that includes a ham-and-cheddar sandwich laced with apples and maple Dijon and the Currier & Ives salad of chicken, toasted almonds, tomatoes, and raisins over greens with a light curry dressing.

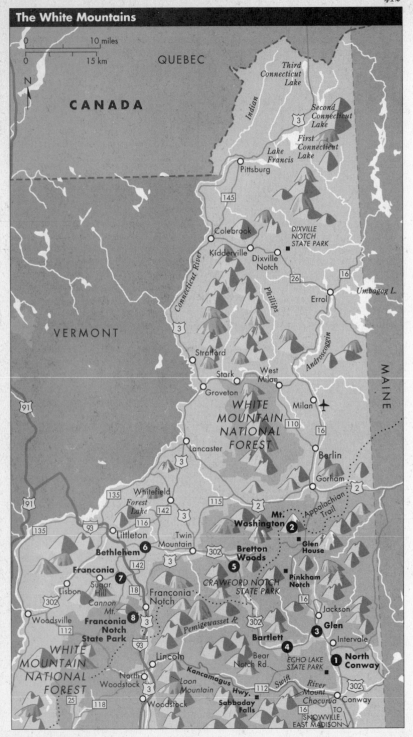

The White Mountains

0   10 miles
0   15 km

N

QUEBEC

CANADA

Third
Connecticut
Lake

Indian

Second
Connecticut
Lake

First
Connecticut
Lake

Lake
Francis

Pittsburg

3

145

Colebrook

Kidderville

Dixville
Notch

DIXVILLE
NOTCH
STATE PARK

VERMONT

Connecticut River

Phillips

26

16

Errol

Umbagog L.

Stratford

Stark

West
Milan

Androscoggin

Groveton

Milan

91

WHITE
MOUNTAIN
NATIONAL
FOREST

110

16

Lancaster

Berlin

3

Gorham

2

Whitefield

Forest
Lake

135

142

3

115

2

Mt.
Washington

Appalachian
Trail

91

116

Littleton

Twin
Mountain

302

Bretton
Woods

2

Glen
House

93

Bethlehem

6

142

3

Franconia

7

Sugar
Hill

18

Franconia
Notch

CRAWFORD NOTCH
STATE PARK

5

Pinkham
Notch

Lisbon

Cannon
Mt.

Franconia
Notch
State Park

8

3

Pemigewasset R.

16

302

Jackson

Glen

3

Woodsville

302

93

Lincoln

Bartlett

4

Intervale

1   North
Conway

112

WHITE
MOUNTAIN
NATIONAL
FOREST

North
Woodstock

3

Kancamagus

Loon
Mountain

Hwy.

Bear
Notch Rd.

ECHO LAKE
STATE PARK

302

25

118

Woodstock

Sabbaday
Falls

112

Swift

River

Mount
Chocorua

Conway

16

TO
SNOWVILLE,
EAST MADISON

MAINE

When the snow flies, the village of Jackson, just north of Glen on Route 16, becomes the state's cross-country skiing capital. **Jackson X-C** (Rte. 16A, Jackson, tel. 603/383–9355 or 800/927–6697) offers a network of 64 trails of varying levels.

② Yes, you can drive to the top of **Mt. Washington,** the highest mountain (6,288 feet) in the northeastern United States and the spot where weather observers have recorded 231-mile-per-hour winds (the strongest in the world), but you'll have to endure the **Mt. Washington Auto Road** to get here. This toll road opened in 1861 and is said to be the nation's first man-made tourist attraction. The road, which is closed in inclement weather, begins at Glen House, a gift shop and rest stop 15 miles north of Glen. Allow two hours roundtrip and check your brakes first. Cars with automatic transmissions that can't shift down into first gear aren't allowed on the road at all. A better option is to hop into one of the vans at Glen House for a 1½-hour guided tour. Up top, visit the **Sherman Adams Summit Building,** which contains a museum of memorabilia from each of the three hotels that have stood on this spot. There's also a nice display of native plant life and alpine flowers, as well as a glassed-in viewing area where you can hear the roar of that record-breaking wind. *Tel. 603/ 466–3988. Toll: $14 car and driver, $5 adult passengers, $3 children 5–12. Van fare: $17 adults, $10 children 5–12. Open daily mid-May–late Oct.*

③ That cluster of fluorescent buildings on Route 16 in **Glen** is **Storyland,** a theme park with life-size storybook and nursery-rhyme characters, a flume ride, Cinderella's castle, a Victorian-theme river-raft ride, a farm-family variety show, and a simulated voyage to the moon. The kids will want to stay all day. *Rte. 16, Glen, tel. 603/ 383–4293. Admission: $13 (free under 4). Open Father's Day–Labor Day, daily 9–6; Labor Day–Columbus Day, weekends 10–5.*

Next door, a trip to **Heritage New Hampshire** is as close as you may ever come to experiencing time travel. Theatrical sets, sound effects, and animation usher you aboard the *Reliance* and carry you from a village in 1634 England over tossing seas to the New World. You will saunter along Portsmouth's streets in the late 1700s, applaud a speech by George Washington, and explore Portsmouth during the Industrial Revolution. Other exhibits include New England's largest historic mural. *Rte. 16, Glen, tel. 603/383–9776. Admission: $7 adults, $4.50 children 4–12. Open mid-May–mid-Oct., daily 9–5.*

④ From Glen, Route 302 follows the Saco River to **Bartlett** and the **Attitash Ski Area** (Rte. 302, tel. 603/374–2368), which has a dry Alpine Slide, a water slide, a driving range, and a chair lift to the White Mountain Observation Tower, offering 270° views of the Whites. Also in Bartlett, Bear Notch Road has the only midpoint access to the Kank (closed winter).

Route 302 passes through **Crawford Notch State Park** (tel. 603/374–2272), where you can stop for a picnic and a short hike to Arethusa Falls or the Silver and Flume cascades. Or you can just drive **⑤** straight through to **Bretton Woods,** home of the Mount Washington, one of the nation's few remaining grand hotels. Early in this century, as many as 50 private trains a day brought the rich and famous from New York and Philadelphia to the hotel. In July 1944 the World Monetary Fund Conference convened here and established the American dollar as the basic unit of international exchange.

From Bretton Woods, take the marked road 6 miles northeast from Route 302 to the **Mt. Washington Cog Railway.** In 1858, when Reverend Thompson asked the state legislature for permission to build a steam railway up Mt. Washington, one legislator responded that he'd have better luck building a railroad to the moon. In spite of such skeptic views, the railway opened in 1869 and has since been giving tourists a thrilling alternative to driving or climbing to the top. Allow three hours round-trip. *Rte. 302, Bretton Woods, tel. 603/846–5404 or, outside NH, 800/922–8825, ext. 7. Round-trip: $32. Reservations advised. Open May, weekends 8:30–4:30; June–Oct., daily 8:30–4:30, weather permitting.*

6 In the 1920s the quiet town of **Bethlehem,** 25 miles west of Bretton Woods on Route 302, was known for only one thing: hay fever relief. The crisp air at this elevation (1,462 feet) boasts a blissfully low pollen count. In the days before antihistamines, hay fever sufferers arrived by the busload. The town also became home to a group of Hasidic Jews who established a kosher resort in the Arlington and Alpine hotels.

7 Take Route 142 south to Route 18 to reach **Franconia,** where Route 116 leads south (follow the signs) to **The Frost Place,** Robert Frost's home from 1915 to 1920. It was here that he wrote his most remembered poem, "Stopping by Woods on a Snowy Evening." To be sure, the mountain views from this house would inspire any writer. Two rooms contain memorabilia and a few signed editions of his books. Outside, you can follow a short trail marked with lines of Frost's poetry. The house is still lived in by poets-in-residence and is the sight of occasional poetry readings. *Ridge Rd., tel. 603/823–5510. Admission: $3 adults, $2 senior citizens, $1.25 children 6–15. Open Memorial Day–June, weekends 1–5; July–Columbus Day, Wed.–Mon. 1–5.*

Time Out A short drive along Route 117, west of Franconia, to Sugar Hill leads to **Polly's Pancake Parlor** (tel. 603/823–5575), where you can sample whole wheat, buckwheat, cornmeal, and oatmeal-buttermilk pancakes with real maple syrup or a light lunch of baked beans and cob-smoked ham.

8 Just south of Franconia on I–93 is **Franconia Notch State Park,** which contains a few of New Hampshire's best-loved attractions. The **Cannon Mountain Aerial Tramway** will lift you 2,022 feet for one more sweeping mountain vista. It's a five-minute ride to the top, where marked hiking trails lead from the observation platform. *Cannon Mountain Ski Area, tel. 603/823–5563. Admission: $7. Open Memorial Day–3rd weekend in Oct., daily 9–4.*

Just north of Cannon Mountain at the foot of the tramway, the **New England Ski Museum** has old trophies, skis and bindings, boots, and ski apparel dating from the late 1800s, as well as a collection of photos. *Tel. 603/823–7177. Admission: $1. Open late Dec.–late Mar. 11–4, late May–mid-Oct. 11–5.*

No one should leave the White Mountains without seeing the granite profile of the **Old Man of the Mountains,** the icon of New Hampshire, located in the Franconia Notch State Park. Nathaniel Hawthorne wrote about it; New Hampshire resident Daniel Webster bragged about it; P. T. Barnum wanted to buy it. The two best places to view the giant, stone face are the highway parking area on Route 3 or along the shores of Profile Lake.

The Flume is an 800-foot-long natural chasm discovered at about the same time as the Old Man by a local woman en route to her favorite fishing hole. Today the route through the flume has been built up with a series of boardwalks and stairways. The narrow walls give the gorge's running water a deeply eerie echo. *Exit 1 off I–93, tel. 603/745–8391. Admission: $6 adults, $3 children under 18. Open May–Oct., daily 9–4.*

What to See and Do with Children

Attitash Alpine Slide, Bartlett
Conway Scenic Railroad, North Conway
Mt. Washington Cog Railway, Bretton Woods
Storyland, Glen

Off the Beaten Track

Pittsburg lies just north of the White Mountains and contains the four Connecticut Lakes and the springs that form the Connecticut River. In fact, the entire northern tip of the state—a chunk of about 250 square miles—lies within its town borders, the result of a border dispute between the United States and Canada in the early 19th century. The international border not yet fixed, the inhabitants of this region declared themselves independent of both countries in 1832 and wrote a constitution providing for an assembly, council, courts, and militia. They named their nation the Indian Stream Republic, after the river that passes through the territory—the capital of which was Pittsburg. In 1835 the feisty, 40-man Indian Stream militia invaded Canada—with only limited success. The Indian Stream war ended more by common consent than surrender, and in 1842 the Webster-Ashburton Treaty fixed the international boundary. Indian Stream was incorporated as Pittsburg, making it the largest township in New Hampshire. Favorite uses of the land today are canoeing and photography; the pristine wilderness brims with moose. Contact the **Colebrook-Pittsburg Chamber of Commerce** (Colebrook 03576, tel. 603/237–8939) for information about the region.

Dixville Notch. Located just 12 miles from the Canadian border, this tiny community is known for only two things. It's the home of the Balsams Grand Resort Hotel, one of the oldest and most esteemed resorts still in existence (if also the most remote). Perhaps more important, Dixville Notch is also the first election district in the nation to vote in the presidential elections. Long before the sun rises on election day, the 34 or so voters gather in the little meeting room beside the hotel bar to cast their ballots and make national news.

Shopping

Some say that in the White Mountains, skiing is only the second-most popular sport, shopping being the hands-down favorite. Among the more than 200 area retail stores, you'll find custom-made hiking boots, sportswear (especially ski-related), one-of-a-kind boutiques, import shops, and outlets galore.

Specialty Shops
Antiques

Antiques & Collectibles Barn (Rte. 16/302, North Conway, tel. 603/356–7118), 1½ miles north of the village, is a 35-dealer colony with everything from furniture and jewelry to coins and other collectibles. **North Country Fair Jewelers** (Main and Seavy Sts., North Conway, tel. 603/356–5819) carries diamonds, antique and estate jewelry, silver, watches, coins, and accessories. **Richard M. Plusch Fine Antiques** (Rte. 16/302, North Conway, tel. 603/356–3333) deals in period furniture and accessories including glass, sterling silver, Oriental porcelains, rugs, and paintings. **Sleigh Mill An-**

tiques (Snowville, off Rte. 153, tel. 603/447–6791), an old sleigh and carriage mill 6 miles south of Conway, has become a shop specializing in 19th-century oil lighting and early gas and electric lamps.

Crafts The **Basket & Handcrafters Outlet** (Kearsarge St., North Conway, tel. 603/356–5332) bills itself as the shop your husband doesn't want you to find. It's perfect for those looking for gift baskets, dried-flower arrangements, and country furniture. **Handcrafters Barn** (Rte. 16, North Conway, tel. 603/356–8996), a one-stop shopping emporium, features the work of 350 area artists and craftsmen, and has a shipping area for you to send your purchases home. **League of New Hampshire Craftsmen** (Main St., North Conway, tel. 603/356–2441) features the area's best juried artisans.

Sportswear You'll wait about a year for made-to-order **Limmer Boots** (Intervale, tel. 603/356–5378) and pay more than $200 (plus shipping), but believers say they're worth the price.

Popular stores for skiwear include **Chuck Roast** (Rte. 16, North Conway, tel. 603/356–5589), the **Jack Frost Shop** (Main St., Jackson Village, tel. 603/383–4391), **Joe Jones** (tel. 603/356–9411), and **Tuckerman's Outfitters** (Norcross Circle, North Conway, tel. 603/356–3121).

Factory Most of the area's more than 150 factory outlets huddle around **Outlets** Route 16 and North Conway, where you'll find the likes of Timberland, Pfaltzgraff, London Fog, Anne Klein, and Reebok; you can call the **Mount Washington Valley Visitors Bureau** (Box 2300, North Conway 03860, tel. 603/356–5701) for further information.

Lincoln Square Outlet Stores (Rte. 112, Lincoln, tel. 603/745–3883) stock predominantly factory seconds including London Fog, Van Heusen, and Bass—as well as a few restaurants. Take Exit 32 off I–93 and head 1½ miles east.

Malls **Millfront Marketplace, Mill at Loon Mountain** (jct. I–93 and the Kancamagus Hwy., Lincoln, tel. 603/745–6261), a former paper factory, has become a full-service shopping center and inn, with restaurants, boutiques, a bookstore, a pharmacy, and a post office.

Sports and Outdoor Activities

In addition to the skiing, hiking, camping, and canoeing popular throughout the area, **Nestlenook Farm** (Dinsmore Rd., Jackson Village, tel. 603/383–0845) offers romantic sleigh rides and, in winter, maintains an outdoor ice skating rink complete with music and a bonfire. You can rent skates here or get yours sharpened.

Biking Not surprisingly, the best way to cycle in the Whites is on a mountain bike. You'll find excellent routes detailed in the mountain bike guide map "20 Off Road and Back Road Routes in Mt. Washington Valley," sold at area sports shops. There's also a bike path in Franconia Notch State Park, at the Lafayette Campground.

Camping **White Mountain National Forest** (Box 638, Laconia 03247, tel. 603/528–8721) has 20 roadside campgrounds on a first-come first-served and 14-day-limit basis.

The **Appalachian Mountain Club** headquarters at Pinkham Notch was built in 1920 and now offers lectures, workshops, slide shows, and movies June–October. In addition to the 100-bunk main lodge and eight rustic cabins here, accommodations are also available through their other programs, which include AMC–The Friendly Huts and the AMC Backcountry Host Program. *Box 298, Gorham*

03581, tel. 603/466–2721. Trail information: tel. 603/466–2725; for reservations or for the free AMC guide to the huts and lodges, tel. 603/466–2727.

The **Lafayette Campground** (Franconia Notch State Park, 03580, tel. 603/823–9513) has hiking and biking trails, 97 tent sites, showers, a camp store, and easy access to the Appalachian Trail. Other state parks have camping facilities, too. Reservations are not accepted.

Canoeing River outfitter **Saco Bound & Downeast** (Box 119, Center Conway 03813, tel. 603/447–2177 or 603/447–3801) offers gentle canoeing expeditions, guided kayak trips, whitewater rafting on seven rivers, lessons, equipment and a full transportation service.

Fishing The **North Country Angler** (N. Main St., North Conway, tel. 603/356–6000) schedules intensive guided fly-fishing weekends and programs.

For trout and salmon fishing, try the Connecticut Lakes, though any clear stream in the White Mountains will do. Many are stocked, and there are 650 miles of them in the national forest alone. **Conway Lake** (Conway) is the largest of the area's 45 lakes and ponds; it's noted for smallmouth bass and, early and late in the season, good salmon fishing. The **New Hampshire Fish and Game office** (tel. 603/788–3164) has up-to-date information.

Hiking With 86 major mountains in the area, the hiking possibilities seem endless. Innkeepers can usually start you toward the better nearby trails; some inns schedule guided daytrips for their guests. On a larger scale, **New England Hiking Holidays** (Box 1648, North Conway 03860, tel. 603/356–9696 or 800/869–0949) offers inn-to-inn, guided hiking tours that include two, three, or five nights in country inns.

Some good hikes other than those mentioned throughout Exploring the New Hampshire Coast (*above*) include the **Doublehead Ski Trail** (off Dundee Rd., Rte. 16B) in Jackson; **Artist's Bluff,** (off Rte. 18), **Lonesome Lake,** (Lafayette Pl.), and **Basin-Cascades Trails,** (off Rte. 3) in Franconia Notch State Park; **Boulder Loop** and **Greeley Ponds** off the Kancamagus Highway; and **Sanguinari Ridge Trail** in Dixville Notch. The trail up **Mt. Chocorua** begins just north of Chocorua Lake, which is north of the Piper Trail building off Route 16.

Appalachian Mountain Club (Box 298, Pinkham Notch, Gorham 03581, tel. 603/466–2727) has free information on hiking trails, hiking safety, and area wildlife.

The **AMC Hut System**'s (Box 298, Gorham 03581, tel. 603/466–2721) eight huts provide reasonably priced meals and dorm-style lodging on several different trails throughout the Whites.

White Mountain National Forest (U.S. Forest Service, Box 638, Laconia 03247, tel. 603/528–8721 or 800/283–2267).

Llama Trekking **Snowvillage Inn** (Snowville 03849, tel. 603/447–2818 or 800/447–4345) conducts a guided trip up Foss Mountain. Your elegant picnic will include gourmet food from the inn's kitchen along with champagne. Luckily you don't have to carry the food, the fine china, or the silverware—llamas do that for you. *Reservations required.*

White Mountain Llamas at the Stag Hollow Inn (Jefferson 03583, tel. 603/586–4598) will introduce you to llama trekking, with one- to four-day hikes on beautiful, secluded trails. The hiking trips do include picnic foods, but the primary focus is on the surrounding nature.

Recreation
Areas

Bretzfelder Park (Bethlehem), a 77-acre nature and wildlife park, has a picnic shelter. At **Lost River Reservation** (North Woodstock, tel. 603/745–8031; open May–Oct.) you can tour the gorge and view such geological wonders as the Guillotine Rock and the Lemon Squeezer. **Loon Mountain Park** (Lincoln, tel. 603/745–8111), on the western end of the Kancamagus Highway, is a winter ski area with 41 trails and 9 lifts. In summer it becomes a park with aerial rides, hiking, horseback riding, picnicking, and tennis. It also has a pool, a hotel, and a restaurant. **Waterville Valley Recreation Area** (Waterville Valley, tel. 603/726–3804 or 800/468–2553) is a complex of hotels and restaurants, with skiing in winter and golfing, hiking, swimming, tennis, and a summer music festival off-season.

State Parks

Crawford Notch State Park (Rte. 302, Harts Location), 6 miles of unspoiled mountain pass, has scenic waterfalls perfect for picnicking, hiking, and photography. The Dry River Campground has 30 tent sites and is a popular base for hiking the White Mountain National Forest. **Dixville Notch State Park** (Rte. 26, Dixville, tel. 603/788–3155), the northernmost notch, has a waterfall, picnic areas, and a hiking trail to Table Rock. **Echo Lake State Park** (Conway), the mountain lake beneath White Horse Ledge, has swimming, picnicking, and a scenic road to the 700-foot Cathedral Ledge for a heart-stopping view of the White Mountains. **Franconia Notch State Park** (Franconia and Lincoln) is a 6,440-acre valley between the Franconia and Kinsman mountain ranges. Here you can swim, camp, picnic, bike, and hike on a 27-mile network of Appalachian-system trails, or view the Old Man of the Mountains, a 40-foot granite profile that's the official symbol of New Hampshire. The park also contains the Flume, Echo Lake, Liberty Gorge, the Cascades, the Basin, and the New England Ski Museum.

Dining and Lodging

The **Mt. Washington Valley Visitors Bureau** (tel. 603/356–3171 or 800/367–3364), **Country Inns in the White Mountains** (tel. 603/356–9460 or 800/562–1300), and the **Jackson Resort Association** (tel. 800/866–3334) are reservation services. For additonal accommodations selections, see the Attitash, Black Mountain, Bretton Woods, Cannon Mountain, Loon Mountain, Mt. Cranmore, Waterville Valley, and Wildcat Mountain sections of the Skiing New England Chapter. In restaurants, dress is casual unless otherwise noted.

Bethlehem
Lodging

Adair. In 1922 attorney Frank Hogan built this three-story Georgian Revival home as a wedding present for his daughter Dorothy Adair. Each of the guest rooms has a mountain view and is elegantly decorated in antique reproductions. Play pool downstairs in the tap room, or roam about the 200-acre estate. *Old Littleton Rd., 03574, tel. 603/444–2600, fax 603/444–4823. 8 rooms with bath, 1 suite. Facilities: restaurant, tennis. Full breakfast included. AE, MC, V. Expensive.*

Bretton
Woods
Lodging

Mount Washington Hotel. The 1902 construction of this leviathan-esque hotel was one of the most ambitious projects of its day. It quickly became one of the nation's favorite grand resorts, most notable for its 900-foot-long veranda, which offers a full view of the Presidential range. With its stately public rooms and its large, Victorian-style bedrooms and suites, the atmosphere still courts a turn-of-the-century formality; jacket and tie are expected in the dining room at dinner and in the lobby after 6. This 2,600-acre property has an extensive recreation center. *Rte. 302, 03575, tel. 603/278-1000 or 800/258-0330, fax 603/278-3457. 280 rooms with bath. Facilities: 5 restaurants, golf, indoor and outdoor pools, sauna, tennis, children's programs. Rates are MAP. AE, MC, V. Closed mid-Oct.–mid-May. Very Expensive.*

Conway
Dining and Lodging

Darby Field Inn. After a day of cross-country skiing, snowshoeing, or hiking in the White Mountain National Forest (which borders the property), you can warm yourself before the living room's fieldstone fireplace or by the woodstove in the bar. Built in 1826, this converted farmhouse retains an unpretentious feel. Most of the rooms have mountain views; the one with the queen-size mahogany sleigh bed is most popular. In the restaurant, the prix fixe menu usually features the inn's signature dish, chicken *marquis* (a sautéed breast of chicken with mushrooms, scallions, tomatoes, and white wine), or roast Wisconsin duckling glazed with Chambord or Grand Marnier. Don't leave without trying the dark chocolate pâté with white-chocolate sauce or the famous Darby cream pie. *Bald Hill, 03818, tel. 603/447-2181 or 800/426-4147, fax 603/447-5726. 15 rooms, 14 with bath, and 1 suite. Facilities: restaurant (reservations advised), cross-country ski trails, pool. Closed Apr. Rates are MAP from Jan. to Mar. AE, MC, V. Expensive.*

Dixville Notch
Dining and Lodging

The Balsams Grand Resort Hotel. This 230-room resort began as the Dix farm, where, in 1861, a family could get a room and dinner for $2. Repeat guests of this famed compound find a personalized bottle of maple syrup in their rooms. The full slate of activities keeps families on the go—choose from among magic shows, aerobics, cooking demonstrations, dancing, skiing (lessons, too), and late-night games of broomball. The Tower Suite, with its 20-foot conical ceiling, is in a Victorian-style turret and offers 360° views. Standard rooms have views of the 15,000-acre estate and the mountains beyond as well as overstuffed chairs and soft queen-size beds, which is exactly what you'll need after running around all day. In summer the buffet lunch is heaped upon a 100-foot-long table. Given this awesome amount of food, it's amazing that anyone has room left for the stunning dinners—but they do. A starter might be chilled strawberry soup spiked with Grand Marnier, followed by poached fillet of salmon with golden caviar sauce, and ending with chocolate hazelnut cake. *Dixville Notch 03576, tel. 603/255-3400 or 800/255-0600, fax 603/255-4221. 232 rooms with bath. Facilities: restaurant (reservations, jacket and tie required), biking, boating, children's programs, golf, pool, tennis, downhill and cross-country skiing. Rates are AP in summer, MAP in winter, and include sports and entertainment. AE, D, MC, V. Closed Apr. 1–May 15, Oct. 15–Dec. 15. Very Expensive.*

East Madison
Lodging

Purity Spring Resort. In the late 1800s, Purity Spring was a farm and sawmill. Set on a private lake, since 1944 it's been a four-season resort with swimming, fishing, hiking, tennis, and lawn games. The compound consists of two colonial inns, a series of lakeside cottages, and a ski lodge. In winter families take advantage of the King Pine Ski Area, located on the property. You have a choice between hotel-style rooms in the ski area or inn-style rooms in the main lodge. *Rte. 153, 03849, tel. 603/367-8896 or 800/367-8897, fax 603/367-8664. 48 rooms, 38 with bath. Facilities: restaurant, lake, tennis, volleyball, indoor pool, and Jacuzzi. Rates are MAP or AP. D, MC, V. Inexpensive–Moderate.*

Franconia
Dining and Lodging

Franconia Inn. This country resort has every manner of recreation. Choose from croquet in summer and both skiing and skating in winter. You can golf next door at Sunset Hill's nine-hole course. Movies are shown evenings in the lounge. You can play tennis, ride horse-back, swim in the pool or sit in the hot tub, order your lunch-to-go for a day of hiking—even try soaring from the inn's own airstrip. The rooms have designer chintzes and canopied beds and country furnishings; some have whirlpool baths or fireplaces. The owners refer to the food here as French gourmet with an American twist, but its real focus is the family. The children choose from a separate menu, which includes "The Young Epicurean Cheeseburger" and a "Petite Breast of Chicken." Adults stick to such specialties as medallions of veal with apple-mustard sauce, or filet mignon with sun-dried tomatoes. *Easton Rd., 03580, tel. 603/823–5542. 34 rooms with bath. Facilities: restaurant (reservations advised), pool, bicycles, croquet, hot tub, soaring center, horseback riding, tennis, ice skating in winter. Full breakfast included; MAP available. Closed Apr.–mid-May. AE, MC, V. Moderate–Expensive.*

Glen
Dining

Margaritaville. The taste of this authentic Mexican food is only enhanced by the tart, locally renowned drinks for which this restaurant is named. Guests enjoy outdoor dining on the patio in summer and the exceptional service of this family-run establishment. *Rte. 302, tel. 603/383–6556. Reservations accepted. No credit cards. Inexpensive.*

Dining and
Lodging

The Bernerhof. This Old World hotel is right at home in its Alpine setting. Rooms eschew the lace-and-doily decor of many Victorian inns, opting instead for such understated touches as hardwood floors with hooked rugs, antique reproductions, and large, plain windows. The fanciest four rooms have brass beds and spa-size bathtubs. One suite, on the third floor, even has a Finnish sauna. Stay three days, and you'll be served a champagne breakfast in bed. The chef describes his cuisine as a cross between Central European and New American. One side of the menu features such Swiss specialties as fondue, wiener schnitzel, and *delices de gruyère* (a blend of Swiss cheeses breaded and sautéed and served with a savory tomato sauce). The other side of the menu is a changing variety of classic French and New American dishes. The wine list favors French and Austrian labels. Ask about the Taste of the Mountains, a hands-on cooking school hosted by some of the region's top chefs. *Rte. 302, 03838, tel. 603/383–4414 or 800/548–8007, fax 603/383–0809. 9 rooms with bath. Facilities: restaurant (reservations advised), pub, playground. Full breakfast included. AE, MC, V. Moderate–Expensive.*

Jackson
Dining and
Lodging

Inn at Thorn Hill. This Victorian house, designed in 1895 by Stanford White, has frilly decor with polished dark woods, rose-motif papers, and plenty of lace, fringe, and knick-knacks. Guests are just a few steps away from beautiful cross-country trails and the village itself. The specialty at dinner may be lobster pie with a brandy Newburg sauce, but that's not the only special thing on the menu. The four-course prix-fixe menu changes frequently and may include the *duck á deux* (a sautéed breast of duck with blackberry sauce and confit of duck leg) or a pounded tenderloin with apples, Calvados, cream, and Stilton cheese. Recent desserts included cappuccino crème caramel, dark-chocolate torte, and saffron-poached pears with raspberry coulis. The owners, from California, maintain an extensive wine list. *Thorn Hill Rd., 03846, tel. 603/383–4242 or 800/ 289–8990, fax 603/383–8062. 20 rooms with bath. Facilities: restaurant (reservations required), pub, pool. Closed Sun.–Thurs. in Apr. Rates are MAP. AE, DC, MC, V. Inn: Expensive. Restaurant: Moderate–Expensive.*

Christmas Farm Inn. Despite its winter-inspired name, this 200-

year-old village inn is an all-season retreat. Rooms in the main inn and the saltbox next door are all done with Laura Ashley prints. In the cottages, log cabin, and dairy barn, suites have beam-ceilings and fireplaces and more rustic Colonial furnishings. These rooms are better suited to families. The restaurant's menu is mixed and varies with the seasons, but some standbys include vegetable-stuffed chicken, shrimp scampi, grilled salmon, and New York sirloin; the list of homemade soups and desserts varies nightly. The menu also includes "heart-healthy" options approved by the American Heart Association. *Box CC, Rte. 16B, 03846, tel. 603/383-4313 or 800/443-5837, fax 603/383-6495. 38 rooms with bath, 5 with Jacuzzi. Facilities: restaurant (reservations advised), pub, children's play area, game rooms, pool, putting green, sauna, volleyball. Rates are MAP. AE, MC, V. Moderate–Expensive.*

The Wentworth. This resort was built in 1869 as a wedding gift to General Marshall C. Wentworth from his future father-in-law. It still retains a Victorian look, although the new owner has added such European touches as French provincial antiques. All rooms have TVs and telephones; some have working fireplaces and Jacuzzis, too. Although the dining room food is innovative—guests rave about the sautéed shrimp with a tequila lime sauce—take at least one snack in the lounge, where you can order *raclette* (melted cheese served with boiled potatoes, cornichons, pickles, pearl onions, and dark bread), and Swiss or chocolate fondue. *Rte. 16A, 03846, tel. 603/383-9700 or 800/637-0013, fax 603/383-4265. 60 rooms with bath in summer, 40 in winter. Facilities: restaurant (reservations accepted), lounge, cross-country ski trails, sleigh rides, ice skating, tennis, outdoor pool, golf. AE, D, DC, MC, V. Moderate.*

Lodging **The Inn at Jackson.** This Victorian inn, built in 1902 from a design by Stanford White, has spacious rooms with oversize windows and an open, airy feel. Other than an imposing grand staircase in the front foyer, the house is unpretentious: The hardwood floors, braided rugs, smattering of antiques, and beautiful mountain views are sure to make you feel at home. The hearty breakfast, with homemade breads, coffeecakes, and an egg casserole or quiche, will fill you up for the entire day. *Thornhill Rd., 03846, tel. 603/383-4321 or 800/289-8600. 9 rooms with bath. Facilities: cross-country ski trails, hot tub, Jacuzzi, fireplaces in 2 rooms. AE, D, DC, MC, V. Moderate–Expensive.*

North Conway **The Scottish Lion.** This restaurant and pub serves more than Scotch,
Dining although you can choose from 50 varieties. The tartan-carpeted dining rooms serve scones and Devonshire cream for breakfast, game and steak-and-mushroom pies for lunch and dinner. The "rumpldethump" potatoes (mashed potatoes mixed with cabbage and chives; then baked au gratin) are deservedly famous in the region, and hot oatcakes come with your meal. *Rte. 16, tel. 603/356-6381. Reservations advised. AE, D, DC, MC, V. Moderate.*

Lodging **Hale's White Mountain Hotel and Resort.** Just in front of the White Horse ledges, this is one of the area's newest resorts. The decor and room furnishings have a Victorian flair. Alone in a meadow, the resort has rooms that offer spectacular mountain views. The proximity to the White Mountain National Forest and Echo Lake State Park makes guests feel farther away from civilization (and the nearby outlet malls) than they actually are. And the presence of a serene nine-hole golf course and 17 miles (30 kilometers) of cross-country ski trails help, too. *Box 1828, West Side Rd., 03860, tel. or fax 603/356-7100 or tel. 800/533-6301. 80 rooms with bath, 11 suites. Facilities: restaurant, tavern, golf, tennis, health club, hiking and cross-*

country ski trails, heated outdoor pool, Jacuzzi. AE, D, MC, V. Moderate–Very Expensive.

Red Jacket Mountain View Inn. This motor inn–cum–resort has some of the amenities of a fine hotel: spacious bedrooms, indoor and outdoor pools, a games room, and tennis courts. The cozy public rooms have deep chairs and plants, and the grounds are neatly landscaped. The manager, with 30 years experience, runs quite a tight ship. *Rte. 16, Box 2000, 03860, tel. 603/356–5411 or 800/752–2538, fax 603/356–3842. 152 rooms with bath, 12 condo units. Facilities: restaurant, indoor and outdoor pools, saunas, whirlpool, tennis, children's activities in summer, playground, game room. AE, DC, MC, V. Expensive.*

Cranmore Inn. At the foot of Mt. Cranmore, this is an authentic country inn, not a converted summer home or farmhouse. It opened in 1863, and the decor reflects this history with furnishings that date back to the mid-1800s. In summer local high school students serve the meals. *Kearsarge St., 03860, tel. 603/356–5502 or 800/526–5502, fax 603/356–6052. 18 rooms with bath. Facilities: restaurant, pool, privileges to nearby health club. Full breakfast included. AE, MC, V. Inexpensive–Moderate.*

Pittsburg
Lodging

The Glen. This rustic lodge, with lots of stick furniture, fieldstone, and pine, is on the First Connecticut Lake, surrounded by log cabins, seven of which are right on the water. The cabins are best for families and come equipped with efficiency kitchens and minirefrigerators—not that you'll need either: The rates include meals in the lodge restaurant. *Box 77, Rte. 3, 03592, tel. 603/538-6500 or 800/445–4536. 8 rooms, 10 cabins, all with bath. Facilities: restaurant, dock. Rates are AP. No credit cards. Closed mid-Oct.–mid-May. Moderate.*

Snowville
Dining and Lodging

Snowvillage Inn. The main gambrel-roof house began as a personal retreat built in 1916 by journalist Frank Simonds. The current owners, who bought the inn in 1986, appreciated the tome-jammed bookshelves and decided to keep the theme intact, naming the guest rooms after the likes of Faulkner, Hemingway, and Twain. Of course, the nicest of the rooms is a tribute to native son Robert Frost. Each of the two additional buildings—the carriage house and the chimney house—has a library, too. The innkeepers take guests on gourmet-picnic hikes up the mountains. The Austrian chef brings a touch of home to the cuisine here, as evidenced by the walnut beer bread and the Viennese beef tenderloin—mainstays of this five-course prix fixe menu. Her assistant, however, is French, setting the stage for a little culinary dueling; for instance, dessert might force you to choose between apple strudel and French silk pie. *Box 176, Stuart Rd., 03849, tel. 603/447–4414 or 800/447–4345. 18 rooms with bath. Facilities: restaurant (reservations required), cross-country trails, sauna, tennis. Full breakfast included; MAP available. AE, D, DC, MC, V. Closed Apr. Moderate–Expensive.*

Sugar Hill
Dining and Lodging

Hilltop Inn. Guests declare staying with innkeepers Mike and Meri Hern is just like staying at Grandma's house. The rooms are done in a quirky mix of antiques: handmade quilts, Victorian ceiling fans, piles of pillows, and big, fluffy towels. The library, upstairs, has books on every subject, and the TV room, downstairs, has hundreds of movies on tape. When the weather is nice, guests take morning coffee on one of the big porches and watch the sunset during dinner on the deck out back. Meri's cooking is so locally loved that she's opened the Hilltop dining room to the public. The eclectic menu changes weekly, the only constant being duck glazed with a dazzling array of sauces such as poached pear, raspberry port, and curried

apple-and-Vidalia-onion sauce. There are some nice vegetarian options, such as eggplant with artichoke-olive pesto. Reserve early—
there are just seven tables. *Rte. 117, Main St., 03585, tel. 603/823–
5695, fax 603/823–5518. 5 rooms with bath, 1 suite. Facilities: restaurant (reservations required; no lunch; closed Sun.–Tues. and,
in winter and spring, Wed.–Thurs.), bar. Full breakfast included.
D, MC, V. Inn: Moderate. Restaurant: Expensive.*

Lodging **Sugar Hill Inn.** The old carriage on the lawn and wicker chairs on the
wraparound porch contribute to the Colonial charm of this converted 1789 farmhouse. Many rooms have hand-stenciled walls and
contain antiques bought from nearby farms, then restored and re-
finished by the owners. Because the building has begun to tilt and
sag over the years, not a single room is square or level, and many
have rippled antique windows. Climb out of your four-poster, canopy, or brass bed, and set foot on braided rugs strategically placed to
show off the pumpkin pine and northern-maple floorboards, some of
which are as wide as 25 inches. Most rooms have a view of Franconia
Notch. Afternoon tea includes scones and tea breads. The restaurant serves hearty New England fare that includes lamb and beef
dishes, homemade chowders and soups (try the mushroom-dill
soup), and delicious desserts. There are 10 rooms in the inn and six
in three country cottages. *Rte. 117, 03585, tel. 603/823–5621 or 800/
548–4748, fax 603/823–5904. 16 rooms with bath. Facilities: restaurant. Full breakfast included; MAP available. MC, V. Closed Apr.,
Christmas week. Cottages closed Nov.–May. Moderate–Expensive.*

The Arts

Mt. Washington Valley Theater Company (Eastern Slope Playhouse,
North Conway, tel. 603/356–5776) has musicals and summer theater
from July through September, as well as a local group called the Resort Players, who give pre- and post-season performances. **North
Country Center for the Arts** (Mill at Loon Mountain, Lincoln, tel.
603/745–2141) presents concerts, children's theater, and art exhibitions from July through October. At **Waterville Valley Music Festival**
(Waterville Valley, tel. 603/236–8371 or 800/468–2553), performers
of every ilk of music, from folk to country to blues, play on the Concert Pavilion in the Town Square Saturday nights from July through
Labor Day.

Nightlife

On Tuesdays the tavern in the **New England Inn** (Intervale, tel. 603/
356-5541) hosts a high-quality open-mike session that the locals call
"hoot night." **Red Parka Pub** (Glen, tel. 603/383–4344) is a hangout
for barbecue lovers. The crowd swells to capacity on the weekends.
Thunderbird Lounge (Indian Head Resort, North Lincoln, tel. 603/
745–8000) has nightly entertainment year-round. **The Shannon
Door Pub** (Rte. 16, Jackson) is the place to enjoy a Greek salad,
Guinness on draft, and the area's best British and Scottish musicians. **Wildcat Inn & Tavern** (Jackson, tel. 603/383–4245) also offers
live music.

Western and Central New Hampshire

Here is the unspoiled heart of New Hampshire. While the beaches to the east attract sun worshipers, and the resort towns to the north keep the skiers and hikers beating a well-worn path up I–93, Western and Central New Hampshire has managed to keep the water-slides and the outlet malls at bay. In the center of New Hampshire you'll see the pristine town green 50 times over. Here each village has its own historical society, a tiny museum filled with odd bits of historical memorabilia: a cup from which George Washington took tea, a piano that belonged to the Alcotts. The town of Fitzwilliam remembers Amos J. Parker. He was not a famous man, but a 19th-century lawyer whose belongings and papers survived him. His home has become a museum and a window into his era.

Beyond the museums and picture-perfect greens, this area offers the shining waters of Lake Sunapee and the looming presence of Mt. Monadnock, the second-most climbed mountain in the world. When you're done climbing and swimming and visiting the past, look for the wares and small studios of area artists. The region has long been an informal artists' colony where people come to write, paint, and weave in solitude.

Important Addresses and Numbers

Visitor Information
Hours are generally Monday to Friday, 9 to 5. **Concord Chamber of Commerce** (244 N. Main St., Concord 03301, tel. 603/224–2508). **Hanover Chamber of Commerce** (Box A–105, Hanover 03755, tel. 603/643–3115). **Lake Sunapee Business Association** (Box 400, Sunapee 03782, tel. 603/763–2495 or, in New England, 800/258–3530). **Manchester Chamber of Commerce** (889 Elm St., Manchester 03101, tel. 603/666–6600). **Monadnock Travel Council** (8 Central Sq., Keene 03431, tel. 603/352–1303). **Peterborough Chamber of Commerce** (Box 401, Peterborough 03458, tel. 603/924–7234). **Southern New Hampshire Visitor & Convention Bureau** (Box 115, Windham 03087, tel. 800/932–4282).

Emergencies
Dartmouth Hitchcock Medical Center (Hanover, tel. 603/646–5000). **Cheshire Medical Center** (580 Court St., Keene, tel. 603/352–4111). **Monadnock Community Hospital** (452 Old Street Rd., Peterborough, tel. 603/924–7191). **Elliot Hospital** (955 Auburn St., Manchester, tel. 603/669–5300 or 800/235–5468). **Concord Hospital** (250 Pleasant St., Concord, tel. 603/225–2711). **Nashua Memorial Hospital** (8 Prospect St., Nashua, tel. 603/883–5521).

Monadnock Mutual Aid (tel. 603/352–1100) responds to any emergency, from a medical problem to a car fire.

Getting Around Western and Central New Hampshire

By Car
Most people who travel up from Massachusetts do so on I–93, which passes through Manchester and Concord before cutting a path through the White Mountains. Interstate–89 connects Concord to the Merrimack Valley and continues on to Vermont. Interstate–91 follows the Vermont border and the Connecticut River. On the New Hampshire side, Routes 12 and 12A are picturesque but slower back roads. Route 4 crosses the region, winding between Lebanon and

the seacoast. Further south, Route 101 connects Keene and Manchester, then continues to the seacoast.

By Bus **Concord Trailways** (tel. 800/639–3317) runs from Concord to Berlin and from Littleton to Boston. **Advance Transit** (tel. 603/448–2815) services towns in the upper valley.

Exploring Western and Central New Hampshire

Numbers in the margin correspond to points of interest on the Dartmouth–Lake Sunapee map.

From Concord, the journey to the Dartmouth–Lake Sunapee region can be an efficient 25-mile run on I–89 to the New London Exit, or a more leisurely drive along scenic Route 4. Assuming the latter,

① you'll want to stop in the small town of **Andover,** about 20 miles northwest of Concord, if only to visit the **Andover Historical Society Museum** (Potter Pl., tel. 603/735–5950; open Sat. 10–3, Sun. 1–3), housed in a beautiful and ornamental mid-19th-century railway station. Museum exhibits include an original Western Union Telegraph office, a dugout canoe, and—on the tracks outside—an old caboose.

② Follow Route 11 to Route 114 north and into **New London,** the home of Colby-Sawyer College (1837). The **Norsk Cross Country Ski Center** (Rte. 11, tel. 603/526–4685) maintains several scenic cross-country ski trails, which are perfect for hiking in the warmer months. Be sure to visit the 10,000-year-old **Cricenti's Bog,** just off Business Route 11. A short trail, maintained by the local conservation commission, shows off the shaggy mosses and fragile ecosystem of this ancient pond.

③ In the distance you can see the sparkle of **Lake Sunapee.** Beyond it, Mt. Sunapee rises to an elevation of nearly 3,000 feet. Together they have become the region's outdoor recreation center. **Mt. Sunapee State Park** (Rte. 103, Newbury, tel. 603/763–2356) offers 130 acres of hiking and picnic areas along with a beach and bathhouse. You can rent canoes at the beach or take a narrated cruise on either the MV *Mt. Sunapee II* (tel. 603/763–4030) or the MV *Kearsarge* (tel. 603/763–5477). The park also operates a chair lift to the summit and hosts a barbecue picnic at the top. In winter the mountain becomes a downhill ski area and host to national ski competitions. In summer the park holds the League of New Hampshire Craftsmen's Fair, a Fourth of July flea market, the Antique and Classic Boat Parade, and the Gem and Mineral Festival. The **Lake Sunapee Association** (Box 400, Sunapee 03782, tel. 603/763–2495) has information on local events.

④ Take the Lebanon exit from I–89 north to visit **Hanover** and the Dartmouth College campus. Eleazer Wheelock founded **Dartmouth** in 1769 to educate Native American youth. Daniel Webster graduated in 1801. Robert Frost spent part of a brooding freshman semester on this campus before giving up on college altogether. Today Dartmouth is the northernmost Ivy League school and the cultural center of the region. The buildings that cluster around the green include the Baker Memorial Library, which houses a number of literary treasures, including a collection of 17th-century editions of Shakespeare. If the towering arcade at the entrance to the **Hopkins Center** (tel. 603/646–2422) appears familiar, it's probably because it resembles the project that architect Wallace K. Harrison completed just after designing it: New York City's famed Metropolitan Opera House at Lincoln Center. In addition to the exhibits on African, Asian, European, and American art, the **Hood Museum of Art** owns

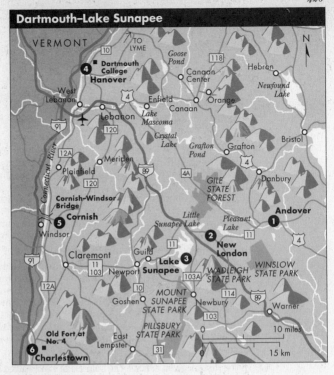

Dartmouth–Lake Sunapee

Picasso's Vollard etchings, Paul Revere's silver, and paintings by Winslow Homer. Rivaling the collection's force is the museum's architecture: a series of a austere redbrick buildings with copper roofs arranged around a small courtyard. Free guided tours are given on weekend afternoons. *Wheelock St., tel. 603/646–2808. Admission free. Open Tues.–Sat. 10–5, Sun. 9:30–5.*

5 About 15 miles south on Route 12A you'll find the village of **Cornish,** best known today for its four covered bridges, one of which is the longest in the United States: The **Cornish-Windsor Bridge** was built in 1866 and rebuttressed in 1988–89. It spans the Connecticut River, connecting New Hampshire with Vermont. At the turn of the century Cornish was known primarily as the home of Winston Churchill, then the country's most popular novelist. His novel *Richard Carvell* sold more than a million copies. Churchill was such a celebrity that he hosted Teddy Roosevelt during the president's 1902 visit. At that time the town was an enclave of artistic talent. Painter Maxfield Parrish lived and worked here, and sculptor Augustus Saint-Gaudens (1848–1907) set up his studio and created the heroic bronzes for which he is known. Today the site of the **Saint-Gaudens National Historic Site,** Saint-Gaudens's house, studio, gallery, and 150 acres of gardens can now be toured. Scattered throughout are full-size replicas of the sculptor's work, as well as sketches and casting molds. Sunday afternoons at 2, you can sit on the lawn and enjoy chamber music. *Off Rte. 12A, Cornish, tel. 603/675–2175. Admission: $1 adults 17–62, free to all others. Open mid-May–Oct., daily 8:30–4:30; grounds open until dusk.*

6 Follow Route 12A south until it merges with Routes 12/11, about 20 miles, to find **Charlestown,** which boasts the state's largest historic district. Sixty-three homes of Federal, Greek Revival, and Gothic Revival architecture are clustered about the center of town; ten of them predate 1800. Several merchants on Main Street distribute brochures that outline an interesting walking tour of the district. Just 1½ miles north of town, you'll find the **Fort at No. 4,** which in 1747 was an outpost on the lonely periphery of Colonial civilization. That year it withstood a massive attack of 400 French soldiers, which changed the course of New England history. Today it is the only living history museum from the era of the French and Indian War. Costumed interpreters cook dinner over an open hearth and demonstrate weaving, gardening, and candlemaking. In one building a blacksmith forges tools as he talks about the past. Each year the museum holds full reenactments of militia musters and battles from the French and Indian War–era. *Rte. 11W, Springfield Rd., Charlestown, tel. 603/826–5700. Admission: $6 adults, $4 children. Open late May–Oct., Wed.–Mon. 10–4.*

On a bright, breezy day you may want to detour to the **Morningside Flight Park** (Rte. 12/11, Charlestown, tel. 603/542–4416), not necessarily to take hang-gliding lessons, although you could. Safer to watch the bright colors of the gliders as they swoop over the school's 450-foot peak.

Numbers in the margin correspond to points of interest on the Monadnock Region and Central New Hampshire map.

❼ Continue south along the Connecticut River on Route 12 to **Walpole** and yet another perfect town green. This one is surrounded by homes built about 1790, when the town constructed a canal around the Great Falls of the Connecticut River and brought commerce and wealth to the area. The town now boasts 3,200 inhabitants, more than a dozen of whom are millionaires. James Michener visited and wrote here, as did Louisa May Alcott, author of *Little Women.* The **Old Academy Museum** (Main St., tel. 603/756–3449; open Sun. 2–4) contains the original piano mentioned in that novel; it had been a gift to the Alcott sisters.

❽ Route 12 continues on to **Keene,** the largest city in the southwest corner, and the proud owner of the widest main street in America. On that tree-lined avenue is Keene State College, hub of the local arts community. Its **Arts Center on Brickyard Pond** (tel. 603/358–2168) has three theaters and eight art studios. The Thorne-Sagendorph Art Gallery houses George Ridci's *Landscape,* alongside traveling exhibits from museums around the country. Indoor and outdoor concerts are given here by nationally known rock and folk stars as well as local musicians and chamber groups. The **Putnam Art Lecture Hall** (tel. 603/352–1909) offers a continuing art and international film series.

Time Out   **Timoleans** (25–27 Main St.) is a classic diner. You won't get a seat any time during the rush between noon and 1, but it's perfect for early and late lunches or the best pie in town.

From Keene, Route 101 leads east to Marlborough. At the junction of Route 124 you'll find the best used bookstore in the region, the **Homestead Bookshop** (tel. 603/876–4213), which carries an extraordinary collection of town histories, biographies, and cookbooks.

❾ Turn north off Route 101 for **Harrisville.** Founded in 1774 by Abel Twitchell, it's now a perfectly preserved mill town (Historic Harrisville, Inc., Church Hill, Harrisville 03450, tel. 603/827–3722)—the Harris Mill, an old woolen mill, still stands in the heart of

Monadnock Region and Central New Hampshire

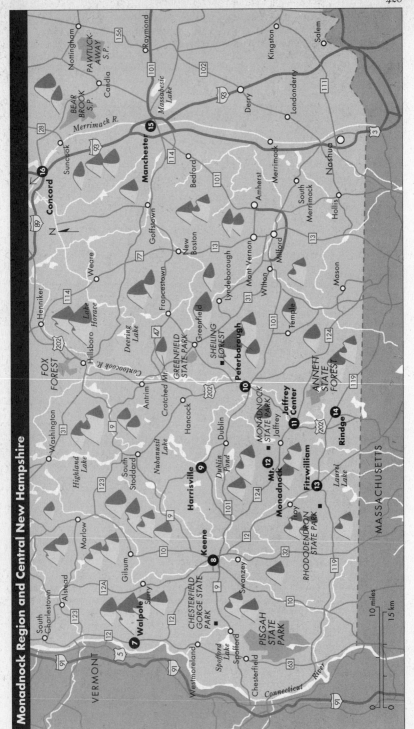

VERMONT

MASSACHUSETTS

Connecticut River

Salem
Kingston
Nottingham
Raymond
156
Candia
PAWTUCK-AWAY S.P.
101
102
111
BEAR BROOK S.P.
Massabesic Lake
98
Derry
Londonderry
28
Merrimack R.
Suncook
98
15 Manchester
Bedford
Merrimack
South Merrimack
Nashua
3
16 Concord
114
101
Amherst
Hollis
89
N
Goffstown
New Boston
13
Mont Vernon
Milford
13
Weare
77
Francestown
Lyndeborough
Wilton
Mason
Henniker
114
Lake Horace
Deering Lake
47
31
Temple
101
124
Hillsboro
202
Contoocook R.
Crotched Mt.
GREENFIELD STATE PARK
Greenfield
SHEILING FOREST
10 Peterborough
101
ANNETT STATE FOREST
119
FOX FOREST
Antrim
202
Hancock
Jaffrey Center
11 Jaffrey
202
14 Rindge
Washington
31
Nubanusit Lake
Dublin
MONADNOCK STATE PARK
Jaffrey
Highland Lake
South Stoddard
123
9
9 Harrisville
Dublin Pond
101
124
12 Mt. Monadnock
Fitzwilliam
13
Laurel Lake
Marlow
9
12
RHODODENDRON STATE PARK
Gilsum
10
Keene
8
12
Troy
32
119
12A
Surry
9
Swanzey
10
Alstead
123
CHESTERFIELD GORGE STATE PARK
South Charlestown
12
Spofford Lake
Spofford
PISGAH STATE PARK
7 Walpole
Westmoreland
Chesterfield
63
5
91
91
91

10 miles
15 km
0

town. The combination of redbrick and blue sky reflecting off Harrisville Pond is worth at least one picture. **Harrisville Designs** (tel. 603/827–3996) operates out of a historic building and sells handspun and hand-dyed yarn sheared from local sheep, as well as looms for the serious weaver. The shop also teaches classes in knitting and weaving.

Beyond Harrisville is the town of Dublin, the highest town in the state, at an elevation of 1,493 feet. It is also the longtime home of *Yankee* magazine and the *Old Farmer's Almanac*.

⑩ Farther east, in **Peterborough,** you'll find the nation's first free public library, which opened here in 1833, and the Historical Society's **Museum of Americana** (19 Grove St., tel. 603/924–3235; open Mon.–Fri. 9–5), which houses an 1840 millworker's house, a country store, and a Colonial kitchen. The **MacDowell Colony** (100 High St., tel. 603/924–3886 or 212/966–4860) was founded by the composer Edward MacDowell in 1907 as an artists' retreat. Willa Cather wrote part of *Death Comes for the Archbishop* here. Thornton Wilder was in residence when he wrote *Our Town;* Peterborough's resemblance to fictitious Grover's Corners is no coincidence. Artists reside here in solitude, so only a small portion of the colony is open to visitors.

Time Out At **Twelve Pine** (1 Summer St., Peterborough, tel. 603/924–6140), you can stock your picnic basket with chicken burritos—famous throughout the region—or one of the special pasta salads. They even sell leftovers out of the fridge for a reduced price. Don't expect to linger: There are no tables in this tiny place, just room enough for the line to form.

---

⑪ From Peterborough, drive south on Route 202 to Jaffrey and turn right onto Route 124 into the historic village of **Jaffrey Center.** Novelist Willa Cather came to town in 1919 and stayed in the Shattuck Inn, which now stands empty on Old Meeting House Road. She pitched a tent not far from here in which she wrote several chapters of her signature work, *My Antonia.* She returned to Jaffrey nearly every summer thereafter until her death, and now she is buried here in the Old Burying Ground according to her last wishes. Nearby, the **Amos Fortune Forum** (tel. 603/532–1303) brings nationally known speakers to the 1773 meeting house on summer evenings.

⑫ The oft quoted statistic about **Mt. Monadnock** is that it's the most climbed mountain in America—second in the world to Japan's Mt. Fuji. Whether this is true or not, locals agree that it's never lonely at the top. Some days more than 400 people crowd its bald peak. Monadnock rises to 3,165 feet, and on a clear day the hazy Boston skyline is visible from its summit. Five trailheads branch into more than two dozen trails of varying difficulty that wend their way to the top. Some are considerably shorter than others, but you should allow between three and four hours for any round-trip hike. A visitor center contains a small museum documenting the mountain's history with photos and memorabilia. **Monadnock State Park** (4 mi north of Jaffrey, off Rte. 124, tel. 603/532–8862) maintains picnic grounds and some tent campsites and sells a trail map for $2.

⑬ A well-preserved historic district of Colonial and Federal houses has made the town of **Fitzwilliam,** on Route 119, the subject of thousands of picture postcards—particularly views of its landscape in winter, when a fine white snow settles on the oval common. Town business is still conducted in the 1817 meeting house. The Historical Society maintains a museum and country store in the **Amos J. Blake**

House (tel. 603/585–3134; open late May–mid-Oct., Sat. 10–4, Sun. 1–4.). Blake's law office looks much as it did when he used it. The rest of the museum displays period antiques and artifacts.

Two and a half miles northwest of the common is the **Rhododendron State Park** (off Rte. 12), where more than 16 acres of wild rhododendrons burst into bloom in mid-July. This is the largest concentration of *Rhododendron maximum* north of the Alleghenies. Bring a picnic lunch and sit in a nearby pine grove or just follow the marked footpaths through the flowers.

⑭ In the village of **Rindge,** 8 miles east of Fitzwilliam on Route 119, you can spend a quiet moment at the **Cathedral of the Pines,** an outdoor church and a memorial to the American women, both civilian and military, who sacrificed their lives in service to their country. The church offers an inspiring view of Mt. Monadnock and Mt. Kearsarge from its Altar of the Nation, which was composed of rock from every U.S. state and territory. All faiths hold services here, with organ meditations at midday, Monday through Thursday. The Memorial Bell Tower, with its carillon of international bells, is built of native stone; Norman Rockwell designed the bronze tablets over the four arches. Flower gardens, an indoor chapel, and a museum of military memorabilia share the hilltop. *Off Rte. 119, Rindge, tel. 603/899–3300. Open May–Oct., dawn–sunset.*

Route 202 leads back to Peterborough, where you can continue east on Route 101. You'll pass Temple Mountain, a wintertime cross-country and downhill ski area that's perfect for beginners, and **Miller State Park,** with an auto road that takes you almost 2,300 feet up Mt. Pack Monadnock. Further east on Route 101 (past Milford), Amherst is known for both its town green and the dawn-to-dusk flea market held Sundays on the western outskirts of town. It operates April through October and attracts dealers and decorators from all over New England.

⑮ Farther along Route 101 is **Manchester,** New Hampshire's largest city, with just over 100,000 residents. The town grew around the power of the Amoskeag Falls on the Merrimack River, which fueled several small textile mills through the 1700s. By 1828, a group of investors from Boston had bought the rights to the river's water power and built on its eastern bank the **Amoskeag Textile Mills.** At its peak in 1906, the mills employed 17,000 people and churned out more than 4 million yards of cloth per week. They formed the entire economic base of Manchester, and when they closed in 1936, the town was devastated. As part of an economic recovery plan, the mill buildings have been converted into warehouses, classrooms, restaurants, and office space. You can wander among these huge blood-red buildings; contact the **Manchester Historic Association** (129 Amherst St., tel. 603/622–7531) for a map.

The **Currier Gallery of Art,** in the Beaux Arts building downtown, has a permanent collection of paintings, sculpture, and decorative arts from the 13th through the 20th centuries. Don't miss the Zimmerman House, designed by Frank Lloyd Wright in 1950. A response to the Depression, Wright called this sparse, utterly functional living space "Usonian." It's one of only five Wright houses in the northeast and New England's only Wright-designed residence open to the public. *192 Orange St., Manchester 03101, tel. 603/669–6144. Open Tues., Wed., Fri., Sat. 10–4; Thur. 10–9, Sun. 1–5. Gallery admission: $4 adults, $3 senior citizens and children. Zimmerman House admission: $6 adults, $4 senior citizens; reservations required.*

Thirty miles north of Manchester is New Hampshire's capital, **Concord.** This quiet, conservative town (population 38,000) tends to the state's business but little else. The residents joke that the sidewalks roll up promptly at 6. Aside from shopping in the boutiques on Main Street, you may want to follow the **Coach and Eagle** walking trail through Concord's historic district. The tour includes the Greek Revival home that was the residence of Franklin Pierce (14 Penacook St., no tel.; open mid-June–Labor Day, weekdays 11–3; admission $2) until he moved to Washington to become our nation's 14th president. You can also walk through the gilt-dome **State House** (107 N. Main St., 603/271–1110; open weekdays 8–4:30), the oldest state house in which a legislature still meets. Get trail maps from the Chamber of Commerce (244 N. Main Street) or from stores along the marked trail. Visit the **New Hampshire Historical Society Museum** (30 Park St., tel. 603/225–3381) to see an original Concord Coach. During the 19th century, when more than 3,000 of them were built in Concord, this was about as technologically perfect a vehicle as you could find—many say it's the coach that won the West.

The **Christa McAuliffe Planetarium,** one of the world's most advanced, was named for the teacher who was killed in the *Challenger* space-shuttle explosion in 1986. Shows on the solar system, constellations, and space exploration combine state-of-the-art computer graphics and sound equipment with views through the 40-foot dome telescope. Children especially love seeing the tornado tubes, magnetic marbles, and other hands-on exhibits. *3 Institute Dr., New Hampshire Technical Institute, tel. 603/271–STAR. Exhibit admission free. Show admission: $5 adults, $3 senior citizens and children 3–12. Reservations advised for shows. Open Tues.–Thurs. 9–4, Fri. 9–7, Sat. noon–5, Sun. noon–4. Call for show times.*

What to See and Do with Children

Christa McAuliffe Planetarium, Concord
Maple sugarhouse (*see* Off the Beaten Track, *below*)
Old Fort at No. 4, Charlestown

Off the Beaten Track

If you take I–89 from Concord to the Lake Sunapee region, a short detour is in order to **Rollins State Park** (off Rte. 103, Warner). Here a scenic auto road snakes nearly 3,000 feet up the southern slope of Mt. Kearsarge, where you can then tackle on foot the ½-mile trail to the summit. Along the way is the **Mount Kearsage Indian Museum,** a moving monument to Native American culture. You'll find incomparable artistry, including moose-hair embroidery, a tepee, quillwork, and basketry, and you'll learn of the bond between the region's Native American population and nature. Self-guided walks lead through gardens of vegetables and through "medicine woods" of herbs and healing plants. *Kearsage Mountain Rd., Warner, tel. 603/456–2600. Admission: $5 adults, $3 children 6–12. Open May 1–mid-Dec., Mon.–Sat. 10–5, Sun. 1–5.*

Sugaring-Off Around here, maple-sugar season is the first harbinger of spring, occurring about the first week in March. The days now are a bit warmer but the nights are still frigid; this is when a drive along maple-lined backroads reveals thousands of taps and buckets catching the fresh but labored flow of unrefined sap. Plumes of smoke rise from nearby sugarhouses—the residue of furiously boiling down this precious liquid. Many sugarhouses open to the public; after a short tour and demonstration, you can sample the syrup with tradi-

tional unsweetened doughnuts and maybe a pickle—or taste hot
syrup over fresh snow, a favorite confection. Open to the public are
Bacon's Sugar House (Dublin Rd., Jaffrey Center, tel. 603/532–
8836); **Bascom's** (Mt. Kingsbury, Rte. 123A, Alstead, tel. 603/835–
2230), which serves maple pecan pie and maple milkshakes; **Clark's
Sugar House** (off Rte. 123A, Alstead, tel. 603/835–6863); **Old Brick
Sugar House** (Summit Rd., Keene, tel. 603/352–6812); **Parker's Maple Barn** (Brookline Rd., Mason, tel. 603/878–2308), where a restaurant serves a whole grain–pancake breakfast any time of day along
with less maply items; and **Stuart & John's Sugar House & Pancake
Restaurant** (jct. Rtes. 12 and 63, Westmoreland, tel. 603/399–4486),
which offers a tour and pancake breakfast. Always call ahead for
hours and to see that the sap is running.

Shopping

You can lose yourself in the huge malls of Manchester and Concord or
in the strip malls along Nashua's Route 3, but there's more colorful
shopping in the downtown retail areas of Concord, Keene, Peterborough, and Hanover. Better yet, wander into one of the dozens of galleries and open studios marked along the roads by blue New
Hampshire state signs. Summertime fairs, such as the **League of
New Hampshire Craftsmen**'s, at Mt. Sunapee State Park, and **Hospital Day,** in New London, showcase some of the area's best juried arts
and crafts.

**Specialty
Stores**
Antiques
People sometimes joke that New Hampshire's two cash crops are
fudge and antiques. Particularly in the Monadnock region, dealers
abound in barns and home stores that are strung along back roads
and "open by chance or by appointment"; don't ignore the flea markets and yard sales rampant during the short summer—deals are
just waiting to happen. Best antiquing concentrations are along
Route 119, from Fitzwilliam to Hinsdale; Route 101, from Marlborough to Wilton; and the towns of Hopkinton, Hollis, and Amherst. A
few good shops include **The Antique Shops** (Rte. 12, Westmoreland,
tel. 603/399–7039), where 40 dealers sell a little bit of everything,
Bell Hill Antiques (Rte. 101 at Bell Hill Rd., Bedford, tel. 603/472–
5580), **Fitzwilliam Antique Center** (jct. Rtes. 12 and 119,
Fitzwilliam, tel. 603/585–9092), **The New Hampshire Antiquarian
Society** (Main St., Hopkinton, tel. 603/746–3825), and **Peterborough
Antiques** (76 Grove St., Peterborough, tel. 603/924–7297).

Crafts
Artisan's Workshop (Edgewood Inn, Main St., New London, tel. 603/
526–4227) carries jewelry, hand-blown glass, and other local
handcrafts. **Dorr Mill Store** (Rte. 11/103, Guild, tel. 603/863–1197),
the yarn and fabric center of the Sunapee area, draws droves of rug
hookers, knitters, and quilters to browse the huge collection of fiber. **The Fiber Studio** (9 Foster Hill Road, Henniker, tel. 603/428–
830) sells beads, hand-spun natural-fiber yarns, spinning equipment, and looms. The **League of New Hampshire Craftsmen** (36 N.
Main St., tel. 603/228–8171) offers a vast array of juried crafts in
many media. The owners of the **Mouse Menagerie of Fine Crafts**
(West Lebanon, tel. 603/542–9691) have created a collector's series
of toy mice in every profession and sport, but they also sell furniture, wind chimes, and hundreds of other gifts.

Galleries
North Gallery at Tewksbury's (Rte. 101 E, Peterborough, tel. 603/
924-3224) has a wide selection of thrown pots, sconces and candle-
stick holders, and woodworkings. **Partridge Replications** (83 Grove
St., Peterborough, tel. 603/924–3002; 53 S. Main, Hanover, tel. 603/
643–1660) specializes in reproductions of Colonial furniture and dec-

orative accessories, including sconces, chandeliers, ironware, mirrors, and trivets. **Sharon Arts Center** (Rte. 123, Sharon, tel. 603/924–7256) is not just a gallery of local pottery, fabric, and woodwork, but a learning center with classes on everything from photography to paper marbling.

Jewelry Goldsmith Paul Gross, of **Designer Gold** (3 Lebanon St., Hanover, tel. 603/643–3864), designs settings for color gemstones and opals—all one-of-a-kind or limited-edition. He also carries some silver jewelry by other American craftsmen. **Mark Knipe Goldsmiths** (2 Capitol Plaza, Main St., Concord, tel. 603/224–2920) will set your antique stones into rings, earrings, and pendants of Knipe's design.

Sporting and The corporate headquarters and retail outlet of **Eastern Mountain**
Outdoors **Sports** (Vose Farm Rd., Peterborough, tel. 603/924–7231) not only
Equipment sells everything from tents to skis to hiking boots, but also offers hiking and camping classes and gives kayaking and canoeing demonstrations.

Malls **Colony Mill Marketplace** (222 West St., Keene, tel. 603/357–1240) was an old mill building but has been converted into a shopping center of specialty stores and boutiques, including **Autumn Woods** (tel. 603/352–5023), which sells fine Shaker-style furniture and Colonial reproductions in birch, maple, and pine; **Country Artisans** (tel. 603/352–6980), which showcases the stoneware, textiles, prints, and glassware of regional artists; the **Toadstool Bookshop** (tel. 603/352–8815), which has a huge selection of children's books, and also carries good reading material on regional travel and history; and **Ye Goodie Shoppe** (tel. 603/352–0326), dating from 1931 and specializing in handmade chocolates and confections.

The Powerhouse (Rte. 12A, 1 mi north of Exit 20 off I–89, West Lebanon, tel. 603/448–1010), a onetime power station, comprises these three adjacent buildings of specialty stores, boutiques, and restaurants decorated with free-standing sculpture and picture-window views of the Mascoma River.

Steeplegate Mall (270 Loudon Road, Concord, tel. 603/224–1523), has more than 70 stores, including chain department stores and some smaller crafts shops.

The enormous **Mall of New Hampshire** (South Willow Street, Exit 1, tel. 603/669-0433) has every conceivable store and is anchored by Sears, Filene's, and Lechmere.

Sports and Outdoor Activities

Bicycling **Eastern Mountain Sports** (*see* Shopping, *above*) and the **Greater Keene Chamber of Commerce** (8 Central Sq., Keene 03431, tel. 603/352–1303) have maps and information on local bike routes. For information on organized bike rides in southern New Hampshire contact the **Granite State Wheelmen** (16 Clinton St., Salem, no tel.). **Monadnock Bicycle Touring** (Box 19, Keene Rd., Harrisville 03450, tel. 603/827–3925) has inn-hopping tours of the region.

Camping The following grounds have sites and are open mid-May–mid-October, unless otherwise noted. **Crow's Nest Campground** (Rte. 10, Newport 03773, tel. 603/863–6170; open year-round), **Greenfield State Park** (Forest Rd. off Rte. 136, Greenfield 03047, tel. 603/547–3497), **Monadnock State Park** (Rte. 124, Jaffrey 03452, tel. 603/532–8862; open year-round), **Northstar Campground** (278 Coonbrook Rd., Newport 03773, tel. 603/863–4001), **Otter Lake Camping Area** (Otterville Rd., New London 03257, tel. 603/763-5600), **Rand's Pond**

Campground (Brook Rd., Goshen 03752, tel. 603/863-3350) and **Surry Mt. Dam** (271 Rte. 12A, Surry 03431, tel. 603/352-9770).

Canoeing The Connecticut River is generally considered safe after June 15, but canoeists should always use caution. This river is not for beginners.

Hannah's Paddles, Inc. (RFD 11, Box 260A-32, Concord 03301, tel. 603/753-6695; open daily July–Aug., weekends spring and fall) rents canoes for use on the Merrimack and Contoocook rivers. **Northstar Canoe Livery** (Rte. 12A, Balloch's Crossing, Cornish, tel. 603/542-5802) rents canoes for half- or full-day trips on the Connecticut River. **Ledyard Canoe Club of Dartmouth** (Hanover 03755, tel. 603/643-6709), on the Connecticut River, offers rentals and classes.

Fishing **Lake Sunapee** has brook and lake trout, salmon, smallmouth bass, and pickerel. Nearby **Pleasant Lake,** in Elkins, has salmon, brook trout, and bass. In **Lake Mascoma** you can fish for rainbow trout, pickerel, and horned pout.

In the Monadnock region there are more than 200 lakes and ponds, most of which offer good fishing. **Dublin Pond** (Dublin), **Gilmore Pond** (Jaffrey) **Nubanusit Lake** (Nelson), and **Granite Lake** (Stoddard) have several types of trout. You'll find rainbow trout, smallmouth and largemouth bass, and some northern pike in **Spoffard Lake** (Chesterfield). **Goose Pond** (West Canaan) has smallmouth bass and white perch. You can find rainbow and golden trout, pickerel, and horned pout in **Laurel Lake** (Fitzwilliam); and there are rainbow and brown trout in the **Ashuelot River.** For word on what's biting where, contact the **Department of Fish and Game** in Keene (tel. 603/352-9669).

Hiking The region is rife with opportunity. Try the mile-long trail to the summit of **Mt. Kearsage** in Winslow State Park; three trails wend to the summit of **Mt. Sunapee; Pillsbury State Park,** a pristine wilderness area in Washington, has a number of trails and rugged camping areas. You'll find a good beginner route, the Westridge Trail, on **Mt. Cardigan** (Orange), from which you can see Mt. Washington on a clear day. **Drummer Hill Preserve** (Keene), **Fox State Forest** (Hillsboro), **Horatio Colony Trust** (Keene), **Sheiling Forest** (Peterborough), and **Wapack Reservation** (Greenfield) all have trails. The **Harris Center for Conservation Education** (Hancock, tel. 603/525-3394) sponsors guided walks.

State Parks **Mt. Sunapee State Park** in Newbury has a tram up the mountain and is the site of a summer-long series of special events including the annual August Craftsmen's Fair. **Bear Den Geological Park** (Gilsum) is a 19th-century mining town surrounded by more than 50 abandoned mines; in **Curtiss Dogwood State Reservation** (Lyndeborough, off Rte. 31), namesake blossoms are out in early May; bring hiking boots, a mountain bike, a fishing pole, or skis to enjoy the 13,000 acres of **Pisgah State Park** (off Rte. 63 or Rte. 119), the largest wilderness area in the state.

Dining and Lodging

Chain hotels and motels dominate the lodging scene in Manchester and Concord and along major highways. But in the Monadnock region, dozens of colorful inns are tucked away in small towns and on back roads. There's a **lodging reservation service** in the Sunapee region (tel. 603/763-2495 or 800/258-3530). For additional accommodations selections, see the King Ridge, Mt. Sunapee, and Pats Peak sections of the Skiing in New England chapter. Dress in all restaurants is casual unless noted.

Andover
Lodging

English House Bed & Breakfast. Afternoon tea is a must at this Edwardian inn. The British owners have furnished the large, sunny bedrooms with English and American antiques and watercolors by innkeeper Gillian Smith's mother and uncle, both well known in Britain. Smith offers occasional classes in quilting and jewelry making. The full English breakfast includes homemade yogurt. *Main St., 03216, tel. 603/735–5987. 7 rooms with bath. Facilities: cross-country ski trails. Full breakfast and afternoon tea included. MC, V. Moderate.*

Bedford
Dining and Lodging

Bedford Village Inn. This luxury Federal-style inn, just minutes from Manchester, was once a working farm and still shows horse-nuzzle marks on its old beams; gone, however, are the hayloft and the old milking room, which have been converted into lavish suites, complete with king-size beds, imported marble in the whirlpool baths, and three telephones. The other 12 rooms are equally sumptuous. The tavern has seven intimate dining rooms, each with the original wide pine floors and huge fireplaces. The menu features such New England favorites as lobster and a cedar-planked Atlantic salmon with a chardonnay beurre blanc, but it changes every two weeks. *2 Old Bedford Rd., 03110, tel. 603/472–2602 or 800/852–1166. 12 suites and 2 apartments. Facilities: restaurant (reservations advised), meeting facilities. AE, DC, MC, V. Expensive–Very Expensive.*

Concord
Dining

Hermanos Cocina Mexicana. On the weekends the line to get in forms at 5 sharp; if you're not in it, don't bother. This restaurant's popularity has spawned a gift shop next door. The food is standard Mexican, raised to a higher level by fresh ingredients and the cook's ability to resist gloppy sauces. *6 Pleasant St. Ext., tel. 603/224–5669. No reservations. MC, V. Moderate.*

Vercelli's. If you can resist the homemade bread and olive butter (good luck), you might have room for one of the generous Italian entrées on this extensive menu. The many veal specialties are stellar, although the seafood is exceptional, too. *11 Depot St., tel. 603/228–3313. Reservations advised. MC, V. Moderate–Expensive.*

Cornish
Lodging

Chase House Bed & Breakfast. This is the birthplace of Salmon P. Chase, who was Abraham Lincoln's secretary of the treasury, a chief justice of the United States, and the founder of the Republican Party. A few years ago it was restored to 19th-century elegance with Colonial furnishings and Waverly fabrics throughout. Ask for a room with a canopied bed or one with a view of the Connecticut River. The innkeepers will give you the history of the house and can point out all of the area's historical landmarks. Breakfast often includes pancakes made from an Amish friendship bread starter. *Rte. 12A (1.4 mi south of the Cornish-Windsor covered bridge), RR 2, Box 909, 03745, tel. 603/675–5391. 7 rooms with bath. Facilities: canoes. Full breakfast included. MC, V. Moderate.*

Fitzwilliam
Dining and Lodging

Fitzwilliam Inn. Vermont Transit buses from Boston's Logan Airport stop at the door, just as the stagecoach once did. Indoors, too, much remains as it was in 1796. Upstairs in the rooms the furniture is a hodgepodge of early and late hand-me-downs. The imperfections suggest that this is how inns really were in bygone times. Locals dally in the tavern, and the restaurant serves standard Yankee cooking spiced up with such innovations as pork medallions with a mustard cream sauce and jalapeño chutney chicken. *The Green, 03447, tel. 603/585–9000, fax 603/585–3495. 28 rooms, 15 with bath. Facilities:*

restaurant (reservations advised), bar, pool, cross-country ski trail. AE, MC, V. Inexpensive.

Lodging **Hannah Davis House.** This 1820 Federal house has, despite a full refurbishment and conversion into a B&B, lost none of its original elegance. The view of a nearby bog is marred only by the natural flaws in the antique windows. The original beehive oven still sits in the kitchen, and one suite has two Count Rumford fireplaces. The inn is just two buildings off the village green, and your host has the scoop on area antiquing. There's cable TV and a VCR in the common area. *186 Depot Rd., 03447, tel. 603/585–3344. 5 rooms with bath. Full breakfast included. No credit cards. Moderate–Expensive.*

Amos Parker House. The garden of this old Colonial B&B is the most spectacular in town, complete with lily ponds, Oriental stone benches, and Dutch waterstones. Two rooms offer garden views, although any guest is welcome to sit on the deck and listen to the birds. Avid gardeners will want to visit, even if staying elsewhere. *Rte. 119, Box 202, 03447, tel. 603/585–6540. 4 rooms with baths. Full breakfast included. No credit cards. Inexpensive–Moderate.*

Francestown **Inn at Crotched Mountain.** This 1823 Colonial inn has nine fire-
Dining and places, four of which are in private rooms. The other five spread
Lodging cheer among several common areas, which makes this a particularly romantic place to stay when the snow is falling on Crotched Mountain. Rooms are done with early Colonial reproductions. The chef splits the menu between such Eastern specialties as Indonesian charbroiled swordfish with a sauce of ginger, green pepper, onion, and lemon and more regional dishes such as cranberry-port pot roast. *Mountain Rd., 03043, tel. 603/588–6840. 13 rooms, 8 with bath. Facilities: restaurant (reservations accepted), bar, pool, cross-country ski trails, tennis. Full breakfast included; MAP required weekends. No credit cards. Moderate–Expensive.*

Hancock **John Hancock Inn.** This Federal inn dates from 1789 and is the pride
Lodging of its historically preserved town. Common areas possess the warmth of a tavern, with fireplaces, big wing chairs, couches, dark-wood paneling, and murals. Rooms are done in the traditional Colonial style with high four-poster antique beds. One room features a pastoral mural painted by Rufus Porter in 1810; the work paid for a night's stay! The dining room serves unspectacular Yankee fare by candlelight; the rubbed natural woodwork gives an intimate feel. *Main St., 03447, tel. 603/525–3318, fax 603/525–9301. 11 rooms with bath. Facilities: restaurant, lounge. AE, D, MC, V. Moderate.*

Hanover **Hanover Inn.** Owned and operated by Dartmouth College, this Geor-
Dining and gian brick house rises four white-trimmed stories and is the oldest
Lodging continuously operating business in New Hampshire. The building was converted to a tavern in 1780 and has been open ever since. A recent renovation created 16 rooms—done in Colonial reproductions, pastels, and Audubon prints—with large sitting areas. The highly acclaimed and very formal Daniel Webster Room serves such regional American dishes as soy-seared tuna steak with shrimp dumplings. The contemporary Ivy Grill offers a lighter menu. *The Green, Box 151, 03755, tel. 603/643–4300 or 800/443–7024, fax 603/646–3744. 92 rooms with bath. Facilities: 2 restaurants (reservations advised). AE, D, DC, MC, V. Inn: Expensive–Very Expensive. Restaurant: Moderate–Expensive.*

Henniker **The Colby Hill Inn.** The cookie jar is always full in this Federal Colo-
Lodging nial farmhouse with a charming tavern for its guests, who are greeted warmly by a pair of Great Danes. There is no shortage of relaxing activities: Guests can curl up with a book by the parlor fire-

place, stroll through the gardens and 5 acres of meadow, ice-skate out back in winter or play badminton in summer. Rooms in the main house contain Colonial reproductions and such frills as lace curtains and Laura Ashley prints. Carriage-house rooms are more austere, with white walls, exposed beams, and plain country furnishings. The innovative breakfast might include scrambled eggs and Boursin on a puff pastry or raspberry-stuffed French toast. The dining room, which is only open to guests, is excellent; try the chicken *Colby Hill* (breast of chicken stuffed with lobster, leeks, and Boursin cheese), the autumn venison, or the New England seafood pie. *The Oaks, 03242, tel. 603/428–3281 or 800/531–0330, fax 603/ 428–9218. 16 rooms with bath. Facilities: dining room (closed Mon., Tues.), tavern, some rooms with working fireplaces, games room, skating rink, outdoor pool. Full breakfast included. AE, D, DC, MC, V. Moderate–Expensive.*

Henniker House. This vintage Victorian inn has fine views of the tumbling Contoocook River and serves lavish breakfasts: soufflé roulade with béchamel sauce and toasted pine nuts; cottage-cheese crepes with fresh strawberries and pecans; and a sumptuous sausage-and-apple bake. *Box 191, 2 Ramsdell Rd., 03242, tel. 603/428– 3198. 4 rooms, 3 with bath. Facilities: Jacuzzi. Full breakfast included. MC, V. Moderate.*

Keene **Henry David's.** The ambience is that of a greenhouse, especially up-
Dining stairs, with hundreds of plants hanging from and perched upon the exposed beams of this airy restaurant that was once a private home. Start with the crab bisque or tomato cheddar soup. The house sandwiches, though named for area towns and villages, are thinly veiled versions of such popular standbys as Reubens and turkey clubs. A nice light lunch or dinner can be made of the sweet pea spinach salad served with a variety of breads. *81 Main St., tel. 603/352–0608. Reservations accepted for 5 or more. DC, MC, V. Inexpensive–Moderate.*

One Seventy Six Main. Similar in quality to Henry David's, this restaurant distinguishes itself with a pub serving a vast selection of international beers. The menu features seafood, burgers, pasta, and a delightfully spicy summer gazpacho. *176 Main St., tel. 603/357– 3100. Reservations accepted. AE, D, MC, V. Inexpensive–Moderate.*

Lodging **Carriage Barn Guest House.** The Main Street location across from Keene State College puts major sights within walking distance. The house is furnished with antiques and quilts, most of which were made locally; the nightstands, for example, are fashioned out of antique desks from a local school. In the warmer months, breakfast is served in a summerhouse out under a willow tree. *358 Main St., 03431, tel. 603/357–3812. 4 rooms with bath. Continental breakfast included. No credit cards. Moderate.*

Lyme **D'Artagnan.** The four-course prix-fixe menu might begin with juli-
Dining enne of shrimp on a mousse of avocado and watercress, followed by pan-roasted Vermont venison with gratin of potato. For dessert, look for terrine of dark chocolate with mocha sauce, a fresh pear-and-almond-cream tartelette, or, at the height of season, native strawberry galette with strawberry coulis. Each night two desserts feature Cool Moose–brand ice cream, with flavors created here by the chef and owner. Try the milk-chocolate orange blossom and true Maine blueberry. *13 Dartmouth College Hwy. (Rte. 10), tel. 603/ 795–2137. Reservations advised. AE, DC, MC, V. No lunch except Sun. Closed Mon., Tues. Expensive.*

Milford
Dining

Colonel Shepard House. This Colonial house dates to 1757. Its four dining rooms evoke romance and intimacy, with dark-wood wainscoting, Oriental rugs, and candlelight flickering off the gilt-frame prints. The meat-intensive menu features filet mignon, veal, and rack of lamb, complemented by nightly seafood specials and an extensive wine list. Attentive service is only enhanced by the French chef who makes pan sauces to order for each entrée. *29 Mt. Vernon St., tel. 603/672–2527. Reservations required. AE, D, MC, V. No lunch. Closed Mon. Expensive–Very Expensive.*

New London
Dining and Lodging

New London Inn. This rambling 1792 country inn in the center of town has two porches, with rocking chairs, overlooking Main Street. Rooms are individually decorated with mostly Victorian pieces; those in the front of the house overlook the pretty campus of Colby-Sawyer College. The owners' son runs the kitchen, and his nouvelle-inspired menu is likely to start with such specials as homemade pierogies filled with apples, smoked duck, and Gorgonzola, served on a bed of carmelized onions with crème fraîche, and such entrées as sautéed medallion of monkfish in a sauce of fennel, black olives, ginger, and vermouth. He also offers a wide selection of wines by the glass. *140 Main St., 03257, tel. 603/526–2791 or 800/526–2791, fax 603/526–2749. 29 rooms with bath. Facilities: restaurant (reservations advised; no lunch; closed Sun.–Mon.). Full breakfast included. AE, MC, V. Moderate–Expensive.*

Peterborough
Dining

The Boilerhouse Restaurant. A mid-19th-century woolen mill has been converted into offices, shops, a café, and this upscale restaurant, which manages a diverse menu that includes everything from venison to pasta. Dinner entrées include gravlax of Norwegian salmon (cured on the premises with salt, sugar, dill, and vodka, then served with Bermuda onions, capers, and caviar) or veal with forest mushrooms in a brandy-Madeira cream sauce. Popular lunch entrées are tricolor tortellini with red pepper, and the lemon chicken with pine nuts and capers. A dish of homemade ice cream tops things off nicely. *Rte. 202 S, tel. 603/924–9486. Reservations advised. D, MC, V. Moderate–Expensive.*

Latacarta. Put a New Age restaurant in an old movie theater and you get the essence of Peterborough. The low-fat, low-cholesterol menu features foods from a variety of cultures, and the menu changes daily. Salt-free and reduced-calorie dishes are available on request. You won't believe that the incredible desserts—Indian pudding, pear crisp—are all sugar-free. *6 School St., tel. 603/924–6878. Reservations advised. AE, MC, V. Closed Mon. Inexpensive–Moderate.*

Plainfield
Lodging

Home Hill Country Inn. A restored 1800 mansion set back from the river on 25 acres of meadow and woods, this is a tranquil place. The chef-owner, from Brittany, has given the inn a French influence with 19th-century patrician antiques and collectibles. A suite in the guest house is a romantic hideaway. The dining room serves classic and nouvelle French cuisine. *River Rd., 03781, tel. 603/675–6165. 7 rooms with bath, 2 suites. Facilities: pool, tennis, cross-country ski trails. Continental breakfast included. AE, MC, V. Closed early Nov. Moderate–Expensive.*

Temple
Dining and Lodging

Birchwood Inn. Thoreau slept here, probably on his way to climb Monadnock or to visit Jaffrey or Peterborough. In 1825 Rufus Porter painted the mural in the dining room. Country furniture and handmade quilts outfit the bedrooms, as they did in 1775 when the house was new and no one dreamed it would someday be listed in the National Register of Historic Places. In the dining room, she-crab soup and roast duckling are two Saturday-night specials, and if you're really lucky you might find cream-cheese pecan pie or one of the fresh fruit cobblers on the blackboard dessert menu. Everything is cooked to order, so allow time for lingering. *Rte. 45, 03084, tel. 603/ 878–3285. 7 rooms, 5 with bath. Facilities: restaurant (reservations required; BYOB; no lunch, closed Sun.–Mon. spring–fall, Sun.– Thurs. winter), piano. Full breakfast included. No credit cards. Moderate.*

Troy
Lodging

Inn at East Hill Farm. At this 1830 farmhouse inn, children are not only allowed, they are expected. In fact, if you don't have kids, you may be happier elsewhere. Children collect the eggs for the next day's breakfast—they milk the cows and feed the animals, too. Later they participate in the likes of arts and crafts, storytelling, hiking, and games. Three meals are included in the room rate, all served family-style. The innkeepers schedule weekly sleigh rides or hay rides, and can whip up a picnic lunch for families who want to spend the day away. Almost anything you want in an easygoing family vacation is available here, including babysitting. *Monadnock St., 03465, tel. 603/242–6495 or 800/242–6495, fax 603/242–7709. 42 rooms with bath. Facilities: restaurant, boating, fishing, indoor pool, 2 outdoor pools, sauna, indoor and outdoor whirlpools, tennis, waterskiing. AP required. MC, V. Moderate.*

West Chesterfield
Dining and Lodging

Chesterfield Inn. The inn sits on a rise above Route 9, the main Brattleboro–Keene road, surrounded by gardens. The rooms, which are quite spacious, are tastefully decorated with armoires, fine antiques, and period-style fabrics, but they also smack of luxury with air-conditioning, whirlpool baths, refrigerators, and telephones in the bathroom. The dining room entrance leads through the kitchen, allowing a sneak preview of what's to come. Favorites include the country pâté and the duck with mango chutney. *Rte. 9, 03466, tel. 603/256–3211 or 800/365–5515, fax 603/256–6131. 11 rooms with bath, 2 suites. Facilities: restaurant (reservations advised; closed Sun., Mon.), some rooms with whirlpool baths. Full breakfast included. AE, DC, MC, V. Inn: Expensive. Restaurant: Moderate–Expensive.*

Wilton
Dining

The Ram in the Thicket. The first course of this inviting prix-fixe menu might be artichoke hearts and mushrooms in brie served warm over French bread or perhaps a kalamata-olive paste on polenta—the choices change monthly but are always delicious. Do try the filet mignon—which is prepared to order—the rack of lamb, or the pork tenderloin. The late-19th-century house has a screened-in porch that's perfect for summer dining. *Off Rte. 101, ½ mi from Wilton, tel. 603/654–6440. Reservations advised. Closed Mon., Tues. No lunch. AE. Moderate.*

The Arts

The Arts Center at Brickyard Pond (Keene, tel. 603/358–2168) offers year-round performances in music, theater and dance. **Claremont Opera House** (Claremont, tel. 603/542–4433) is a beautifully restored 19th-century opera house with plays and musicals from September through May. **Hopkins Center** (Dartmouth College, Hanover, tel. 603/646–2422) has a 900-seat theater for film and music, a 400-seat theater for plays, and a black-box theater for new plays and the Dartmouth Symphony Orchestra. Each summer, the Big Apple Circus comes to the Hopkins Center.

Music

Monadnock Music (Peterborough, tel. 603/924–7610) produces a summer series of concerts from mid-July to late August, with solo recitals, chamber music, and orchestra and opera performances by renowned musicians. Concerts usually take place evenings at 8 and Sundays at 4; many are free. The **Temple Town Band** (tel. 603/878–2829), founded in 1799 and believed to be the oldest band in the nation, and the **Apple Hill Chamber Players** (E. Sullivan, tel. 603/847–3371) also produce summer concert series.

Theater **American Stage Festival** (Rte. 13 N, Milford, tel. 603/673–4005) is the state's largest professional theater. The season runs from early June through Labor Day and includes five Broadway plays and one new work, as well as a children's theater series. The **New London Barn Playhouse** (tel. 603/526–6570), a converted barn on Main Street, has been putting on nonequity Broadway-style and children's plays every summer since 1933. The **Palace Theatre** (80 Hanover St., Manchester, tel. 603/668–5588) is the state's performing arts center—home to the state symphony and opera and the New Hampshire Philharmonic. It also hosts national tours and musical acts. **The Peterborough Players** (Stearns Farm, Middle Hancock Rd., Peterborough, tel. 603/924–7585) have been taking summer stock theater to a new level for more than 60 seasons. The plays are held in a converted barn (now fully air-conditioned) and recently featured Thornton Wilder's *Our Town*, which was modeled after Peterborough's small-town life.

Nightlife

The **Colonial Theater** (95 Main St., Keene, tel. 603/352–2033) opened in 1924 as a vaudeville stage. It still hosts some folk and jazz concerts and has the largest movie screen in town **Del Rossi's Trattoria** (jct. Rtes. 137 and 101, Dublin, tel. 603/563–7195) brings big names in jazz, bluegrass, and blues to the Monadnock region Friday and Saturday nights. Come early and dine on homemade pasta in this unpretentious Italian restaurant (reservations advised). **The Folkway** (85 Grove St., Peterborough, tel. 603/924–7484), a restaurant and coffeehouse, has become a New England institution, with such artists as the Story, Greg Brown, Trout Fishing in America, and dozens of local musicians. The best seats are saved for those who have dinner, too (reservations advised). The crafts shop, upstairs, has a great selection of folk tapes and CDs, as well as the work of local artisans and weavers. **Rynborn** (Main St., Antrim, tel. 603/588–6162) has Chicago blues on Saturday nights, although the room is too small for dancing. The restaurant upstairs offers good food before the show. **Peter Christian's Tavern** (39 S. Main St., Hanover, tel. 603/643–2345) has live folk and jazz performances Tuesday and Thursday evenings. **The Moving Company Dance Center** (76 Railroad, Keene, tel. 603/357–2100) holds theme dances on Friday and Saturday nights, which range from swing to line dancing to Latin ballroom.

8 Maine

By David
Laskin with
an
introduction
by William
G. Scheller

Updated by
Kathleen M.
Brandes and
Suki
Casanave

If any two individuals can be associated directly with the disparate images evoked by the very mention of the state of Maine, they are George Bush and Carolyn Chute.

Former president George Bush is the most famous summer resident of Kennebunkport, where he and his family vacation in his grandfather's rambling seaside mansion. Having so recently had a summer White House on the Maine coast reminds Americans that this craggy, wildly irregular stretch of shoreline has long enjoyed an aristocratic cachet: Here Nelson Rockefeller was born in the millionaires' enclave at Bar Harbor; here the Brahmin historian Samuel Eliot Morison sailed the cold waters of Frenchman Bay. In those times, anyone living on the coast of Maine who wasn't rich, famous, or powerful was almost certainly an old-stock yeoman, probably someone with a lobster boat.

Carolyn Chute is the novelist who wrote *The Beans of Egypt, Maine*. Chute's fictional Egypt and its inhabitants are a reminder that Appalachia stretches far to the north of the Cumberland Gap and that not far inland from the famous rockbound coast there are places where rusting house trailers are far more common than white Federalist sea captains' mansions.

In fact, neither stereotype (and both have strong foundations in fact) makes a serious dent in the task of defining or explaining Maine. Reality in most of the state resembles neither a cross between a Ralph Lauren ad and a Winslow Homer painting nor a milieu in which modern history dates from the day they began renting videos at the gas station.

Maine is by far the largest state in New England. At its extremes it measures 300 miles north to south and 200 miles across; all five other New England states could fit within its perimeters. There is an expansiveness to Maine, a sense of real distance between places that hardly exists elsewhere in the region, and along with the sheer size and spread of the place there is a tremendous variety of terrain. One speaks of "coastal" Maine and "inland" Maine, as though the state could be summed up under the twin emblems of lobsters and pine trees. Yet the state's topography and character are a good deal more complicated.

Even the coast is several places in one. South of the rapidly gentrifying city of Portland, such resort towns as Ogunquit, Kennebunkport, and Old Orchard Beach (sometimes called the Québec Riviera because of its popularity with French Canadians) predominate along a reasonably smooth shoreline. Development has been considerable; north of Portland and Casco Bay, secondary roads turn south off Route 1 onto so many oddly chiseled peninsulas that it's possible to drive for days without retracing your route and to conclude that motels, discount outlets, and fried-clam stands are taking over the domain of presidents and lobstermen. Freeport is an entity unto itself, a place where a bewildering assortment of off-price, name-brand outlets has sprung up around the famous outfitter L. L. Bean (no relation to the Egypt clan).

Inland Maine likewise defies characterization. For one thing, a good part of it is virtually uninhabited. This is the land Henry David Thoreau wrote about in *The Maine Woods* nearly 150 years ago; aside from having been logged over several times, much of it hasn't changed since Thoreau and his Native American guides passed through. Ownership of vast portions of northern Maine by forest-products corporations has kept out subdivision and development; many of the roads here are private, open to travel only by permit.

The north woods' day of reckoning may be coming, however, for the paper companies plan to sell off millions of acres in a forested belt that reaches all the way to the Adirondacks in New York State. In the 1990s state governments and environmental organizations are working to preserve as much as possible of the great silent expanses of pine.

Logging the north created the culture of the mill towns, the Rumfords, Skowhegans, Millinockets, and Bangors that lay at the end of the old river drives. The logs arrive by truck today, but Maine's harvested wilderness still feeds the mills and the nation's hunger for paper.

Our hunger for potatoes has given rise to an entirely different Maine culture, in one of the most isolated agricultural regions of the country. Northeastern Aroostook County is where the Maine potatoes come from, and this place, too, is changing. In what was once called the Potato Empire, farmers are as pressed between high costs and low prices as any of their counterparts in the Midwest; add to the bleak economic picture a growing national preference for Idaho baking potatoes rather than the traditional small, round Maine boiling potatoes, and Aroostook's troubles are compounded.

The visitor seeking an untouched fishing village with locals gathered around a pot-bellied stove in the general store may be sadly disappointed; that innocent age has passed in all but the most remote of villages. Tourism has supplanted fishing, logging, and potato farming as Maine's number one industry, and most areas are well equipped to receive the annual onslaught of visitors. But whether you are stepping outside a motel room for an evening walk or watching a boat rock at its anchor, you can sense the infinity of the natural world. Wilderness is always nearby, growing to the edges of the most urbanized spots.

Essential Information

Visitor Information

Maine Publicity Bureau (325B Water St., Box 2300, Hallowell 04347, tel. 207/623–0363 or, outside ME, 800/533–9595; fax 207/623–0388). **Maine Innkeepers Association** (305 Commercial St., Portland 04101, tel. 207/773–7670) publishes a statewide lodging and dining guide.

Tour Groups

Golden Age Festival (5501 New Jersey Ave., Wildwood Crest, NJ 08260, tel. 609/522–6316 or 800/257–8920) offers a four-night bus tour geared to senior citizens, with shopping at Kittery outlets and L. L. Bean, a Boothbay Harbor boat cruise, and stops at Kennebunkport, Mount Battie in Camden, and Acadia National Park. Tours operate May to mid-October.

Arriving and Departing

By Plane Maine's major airports are **Portland International Jetport** (tel. 207/774–7301) and **Bangor International Airport** (tel. 207/947–0384); each has scheduled daily flights by major U.S. carriers.

Hancock County Airport (tel. 207/667–7329), in Trenton, 8 miles northwest of Bar Harbor, is served by Colgan Air (tel. 207/667–7171 or 800/272–5488). **Knox County Regional Airport** (tel. 207/594–

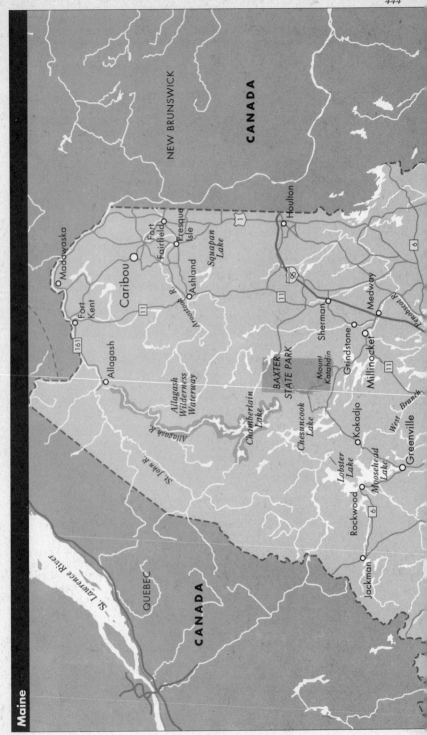

Maine

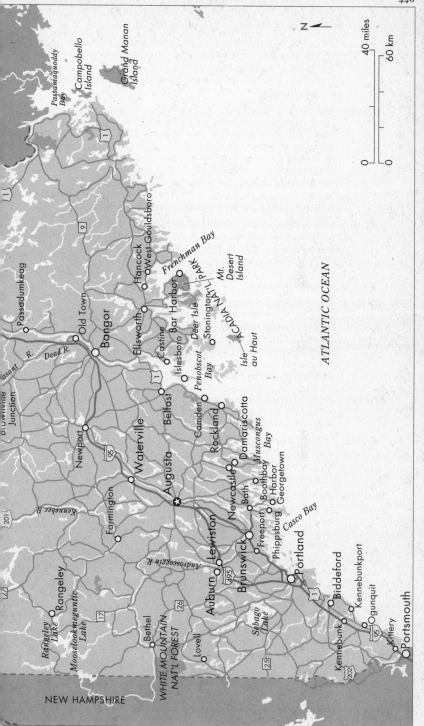

4131), in Owls Head, 3 miles south of Rockland, has flights to Boston on Colgan Air (tel. 207/596–7604 or 800/272–5488).

By Car Interstate 95 is the fastest route to and through the state from coastal New Hampshire and points south, turning inland at Brunswick and going on to Bangor and the Canadian border. Route 1, more leisurely and scenic, is the principal coastal highway from New Hampshire to Canada.

By Train **Amtrak** (tel. 800/872–7245) is expected to have added service between Boston and Portland by January 1995. Plans are for three round-trip runs daily with four stops in Maine and three in New Hampshire; round-trip fare will be about $30. Canada's **VIA Rail** (Box 8116, 2 Place Ville-Marie, Montréal, Québec, tel. 800/361–3677) provides northern Maine's only passenger rail service. The run between Montréal and Halifax crosses the center of the state three times a week, stopping at Jackman, Greenville, Brownville Junction, Mattawamkeag, Danforth, and Vanceboro.

By Bus **Vermont Transit** (tel. 207/772–6587), a subsidiary of **Greyhound**, connects towns in southwestern Maine with cities in New England and throughout the United States. **Concord Trailways** (tel. 800/639–3317) has daily year-round service between Boston and Bangor (via Portland), with a coastal route connecting towns between Brunswick and Searsport.

By Boat **Marine Atlantic** (tel. 207/288–3395 or 800/341–7981) operates a carferry service year-round between Yarmouth (Nova Scotia) and Bar Harbor; **Prince of Fundy Cruises** (tel. 800/341–7540 or, in ME, 800/482–0955) operates a car ferry between Yarmouth and Portland (May–Oct.).

Getting Around Maine

By Plane Regional flying services, operating from regional and municipal airports (*see above*), provide access to remote lakes and wilderness areas as well as to Penobscot Bay islands.

By Car In many areas a car is the only practical means of travel. The *Maine Map and Travel Guide*, available for a small fee from offices of the Maine Publicity Bureau, is useful for driving throughout the state; it has directories, mileage charts, and enlarged maps of city areas.

By Train During the ski season, **Sunday River Ski Resort** operates the *Sunday River Silver Bullet Ski Express* (tel. 207/824–7245) through scenic terrain between Portland and Bethel. No reservations are necessary for the once-a-day run; lift tickets can be purchased aboard the train.

By Boat **Casco Bay Lines** (tel. 207/774–7871) provides ferry service from Portland to the islands of Casco Bay, and **Maine State Ferry Service** (tel. 207/596–2202 or 800/491–4883) provides ferry service from Rockland, Lincolnville, and Bass Harbor to islands in Penobscot and Blue Hill bays.

Dining

For most visitors, Maine means lobster. As a general rule, the closer you are to a working harbor, the fresher your lobster will be. Aficionados eschew ordering lobster in restaurants, preferring to eat them "in the rough" at classic lobster pounds, where you select your lobster swimming in a pool and enjoy it at a waterside picnic table. Shrimp, scallops, clams, mussels, and crab are also caught in the cold waters off Maine, and the better restaurants in Portland and the coastal resort towns prepare the shellfish in creative combinations with lobster, haddock, salmon, and swordfish. Blueberries are grown commercially in Maine, and Maine cooks use them generously in pancakes, muffins, jams, pies, and cobblers. Full country breakfasts of fruit, eggs, breakfast meats, pancakes, and muffins are commonly served at inns and bed-and-breakfasts.

Highly recommended restaurants are indicated by a star ★.

Category	Cost*
Very Expensive	over $35
Expensive	$25–$35
Moderate	$15–$25
Inexpensive	under $15

*average cost of a three-course dinner, per person, excluding drinks, service, and 7% restaurant sales tax

Lodging

Bed-and-breakfasts and Victorian inns furnished with lace, chintz, and mahogany have joined the family-oriented motels of Ogunquit, Boothbay Harbor, Bar Harbor, and the Camden-Rockport region. Two world-class resorts with good health club and sports facilities are on the coast near Portland and on Penobscot Bay near Rockland. Although accommodations tend to be less luxurious away from the coast, Bethel, Center Lovell, and Rangeley offer sophisticated hotels and inns. In the far north the best alternative to camping is to stay in a rustic wilderness camp, most of which serve hearty meals. For a list of camps, write to the **Maine Sporting Camp Association** (Box 89, Jay 04239).

At many of Maine's larger hotels and inns with restaurants, Modified American Plan (includes breakfast and dinner) is either an option or required during the peak summer season.

Highly recommended lodgings are indicated by a star ★.

Category	Cost*
Very Expensive	over $100
Expensive	$80–$100
Moderate	$60–$80
Inexpensive	under $60

*Prices are for a standard double room during peak season, excluding 7% lodging sales tax.

North from Kittery

Maine's southernmost coastal towns won't give you the rugged, windbitten "downeast" experience, but they offer all the amenities, they are easily reached from the south, and most have the sand beaches that all but vanish beyond Portland.

Kittery, which lacks a large sand beach, hosts a complex of factory outlets. North of Kittery the Maine coast has long stretches of hard-packed white-sand beach, closely crowded by nearly unbroken ranks of beach cottages, motels, and oceanfront restaurants. The summer colonies of York Beach, Ogunquit, and Wells Beach have the crowds and the ticky-tacky shorefront overdevelopment. Farther inland, York's historic district is on the National Register.

More than any other region south of Portland, the Kennebunks—and especially Kennebunkport—offer the complete Maine coast experience: classic townscapes where perfectly proportioned white-clapboard houses rise from manicured lawns and gardens; rocky shorelines punctuated by sandy beaches, beach motels, and cottages; quaint downtown districts packed with gift shops, ice-cream stands, and tourists; harbors where lobster boats bob alongside yachts; lobster pounds and well-appointed dining rooms. The range of accommodations includes rambling Victorian-era hotels, beachside family motels, and inns.

Important Addresses and Numbers

Visitor Information Off-season, most chambers are open weekdays 9–5; the hours below are for summer only.

Kennebunk-Kennebunkport Chamber of Commerce (Cooper's Corner, Rtes. 9 and 35, tel. 207/967–0857; open Mon.–Sat. 8:30–8, Sun. noon–4). **Kittery-Eliot Chamber of Commerce** (191 State Rd., Kittery, tel. 207/439–7545; open weekdays 9–5). **Maine Publicity Bureau** (Rte. 1 and I–95, tel. 207/439–1319; open daily 9–5; extended hours in summer). **Ogunquit Chamber of Commerce** (Box 2289, Ogunquit, tel. 207/646–2939 or 207/646–5533, mid-May–mid-October; open daily 9–5, later Fri. and Sat.). **Wells Chamber of Commerce** (Box 356, Wells 04090, tel. 207/646–2451; open daily 9–5, Fri. until 8). **The Yorks Chamber of Commerce** (Box 417, York, tel. 207/363–4422; open daily 9–6; extended hours on weekends).

Emergencies **Maine State Police** (Gray, tel. 207/793–4500 or 800/482–0730). **Kennebunk Walk-in Clinic** (Rte. 1 N, tel. 207/985–6027). **Southern Maine Medical Center** (1 Medical Center Dr., Biddeford, tel. 207/283–7000; emergency room: 207/283–7100).

Getting Around North from Kittery

By Car Route 1 from Kittery is the shopper's route north, while other roads hug the coastline. Interstate–95 should be faster for travelers headed for specific towns. The exit numbers can be confusing: As you go north from Portsmouth, Exits 1–3 lead to Kittery and Exit 4 leads to the Yorks. After the tollbooth in York, the Maine Turnpike begins, and the numbers start over again, with Exit 2 for Wells and Ogunquit and Exit 3 (and Rte. 35) for Kennebunk and Kennebunkport. Route 9 goes from Kennebunkport to Cape Porpoise and Goose Rocks.

By Trolley A trolley circulates among the Yorks from June to Labor Day. Eight trolleys serve the major tourist areas and beaches of Ogunquit, including four that connect with Wells from mid-May through mid-October. The trolley from Dock Square in Kennebunkport to Kennebunk Beach runs from late June to Labor Day. *Fare: $1–$3 depending on destination; $1 children 5–12.*

Exploring North from Kittery

Numbers in the margin correspond to points of interest on the Southern Maine Coast map.

① Begin at **Kittery,** just across the New Hampshire border, off I–95 on Route 1. Kittery will be of most interest to shoppers headed for its factory outlet stores—all 115 of them. Here along a several-mile stretch of Route 1 you can find just about anything you want, from hardware to underwear. And when you've had it with shopping (or if you want to skip the shopping all together, for that matter), head east on Haley Road, at the northern end of "outlet row," straight for the water. At the end of Haley Road, along Route 103, lies the hidden Kittery most tourists miss. This winding stretch includes some history: **Ft. Foster** (1872), an active military installation until 1949, and **Ft. McClary** (1690), manned during five wars. Along the way there are also hiking and biking trails, and, best of all, great views of the water.

② Beyond Kittery, Route 1 heads north to **the Yorks,** and a right onto Route 1A (York Street) leads to the **York Village Historic District,** where a number of 18th- and 19th-century buildings have been restored and maintained by the Old York Historical Society. Most of the buildings are clustered along York Street and Lindsay Road, and you can buy an admission ticket for all the buildings at the **Jefferds Tavern** (Rte. 1A and Lindsay Rd.), a restored late-18th-century inn. Other historic buildings open to the public include the **Old York Gaol** (1720), once the King's Prison for the Province of Maine, which has dungeons, cells, and jailer's quarters; and the **Elizabeth Perkins House** (1731), with Victorian-era furniture that reflects the style of its last occupants, the prominent Perkins family. The historical society offers tours with guides in period costumes, crafts workshops, and special programs in summer. *Tel. 207/363–4974. Admission: $6 adults, $2.50 children 6–16, $16 family. Open mid-June–Sept., Tues.–Sat. 10–5, Sun. 1–5.*

Complete your tour of the Yorks by driving down Nubble Road (turn right off Rte. 1A) to the end of Cape Neddick, where you can park and gaze out at the **Nubble Light** (1879), which sits on a tiny island just offshore. The keeper's house is a tidy Victorian cottage with pretty gingerbread woodwork and a red roof.

Shore Road to Ogunquit passes the 100-foot Bald Head Cliff, which allows a view up and down the coast; on a stormy day the surf can be
③ quite wild here. Shore Road will take you right into **Ogunquit,** a coastal village that became a resort in the 1880s and gained fame as an artists' colony. Today visitors enjoy exploring the town's art galleries, including the Ogunquit Art Association Gallery on Route 1 and the Barn Gallery on Bourne Lane, where the works of many local and regional artists are displayed.

On Shore Road, the **Ogunquit Museum of Art,** a low-lying concrete building overlooking the ocean and set amid a 3-acre sculpture garden, shows works by Henry Strater, Marsden Hartley, William Bailey, Gaston Lachaise, Walt Kuhn, and Reginald Marsh. The huge windows of the sculpture court command a view of cliffs and ocean. *Shore Rd., tel. 207/646–4909. Admission free. Open July–mid-Sept., Mon.–Sat. 10:30–5, Sun. 2–5.*

Perkins Cove, a neck of land connected to the mainland by Oarweed Road and a pedestrian drawbridge, is ½ mile from the art museum. "Quaint" is the only word for this jumble of sea-beaten fish houses transformed by the tide of tourism to shops and restaurants. When

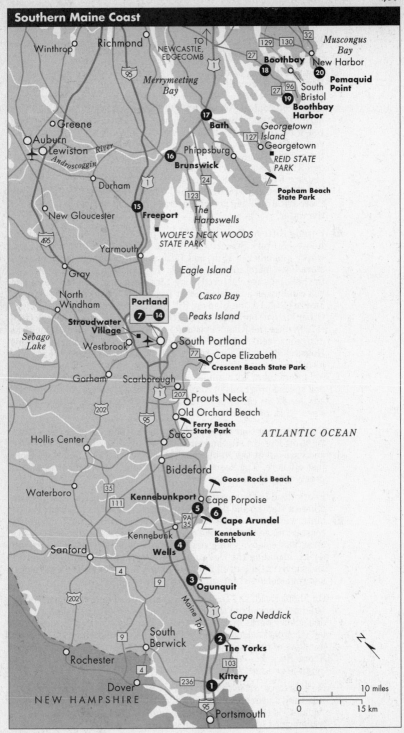

Southern Maine Coast

450

Winthrop
Richmond
TO
NEWCASTLE,
EDGECOMB
129 130   32   *Muscongus*
Bay
27
Boothbay   New Harbor
18
Pemaquid
Point
Merrymeeting
Bay
27 96
South
Bristol
19
Boothbay
Harbor
95
Greene
Georgetown
Island
Auburn
17
Lewiston   *River*
Bath
127
Georgetown
Androscoggin
REID STATE
PARK
Phippsburg
Durham
16
1
Brunswick
24
Popham Beach
State Park
123
New Gloucester
15
Freeport
The
Harpswells
495
Yarmouth
WOLFE'S NECK WOODS
STATE PARK
Gray
Eagle Island
North
Windham
Casco Bay
Portland
7 — 14
Peaks Island
Stroudwater
Village
Sebago
Lake
Westbrook
South Portland
Gorham   Scarborough
77
Cape Elizabeth
Crescent Beach State Park
1 207
Prouts Neck
202
95
Old Orchard Beach
Hollis Center
Saco
Ferry Beach
State Park
ATLANTIC OCEAN

Waterboro
Biddeford
Goose Rocks Beach
35
Kennebunkport   Cape Porpoise
111
5
9A
35
6   **Cape Arundel**
Kennebunk
Kennebunk
Beach
Sanford
4
Wells
9
3
Ogunquit
Cape Neddick
202
Maine Tpk.
1
South
9
Berwick
2
The Yorks
Rochester
103
4
Kittery
236
Dover
95
NEW HAMPSHIRE
Portsmouth

0   10 miles
0   15 km

you've had your fill of browsing and jostling the crowds at Perkins Cove, stroll out along the Marginal Way, a mile-long footpath that hugs the shore of a rocky promontory known as Israel's Head.

❹ Follow Route 1 north to **Wells,** a family-oriented beach community consisting of several densely populated summer communities along 7 miles of shore. The 1,600-acre Wells Reserve at Laudholm Farm consists of meadows, orchards, fields, salt marshes, and an extensive trail network, as well as two estuaries and 9 miles of seashore. The Visitor Center features an introductory slide show and five rooms of exhibits. *Laudholm Farm Rd., tel. 207/646–1555. Admission free. Grounds open daily 8–5; Visitor Center open May–Oct., Mon.–Sat. 10–4, Sun. noon–4; Nov.–Apr., weekdays only.*

Five miles north of Wells, Route 1 becomes Main Street in Kennebunk. For a sense of the area's history and architecture, begin here at the **Brick Store Museum.** The cornerstone of this block-long preservation of early-19th-century commercial buildings is William Lord's Brick Store, built as a dry-goods store in 1825 in the Federal style, with an open-work balustrade across the roof line, granite lintels over the windows, and paired chimneys. Walking tours of Kennebunk's National Historic Register District depart from the museum on Friday at 1 and on Wednesday at 10, June through October. *117 Main St., tel. 207/985–4802. Admission: $3 adults, $1 children 6–16. Open Tues.–Sat. 10–4:30. Closed Sat. in winter.*

❺ While heading for **Kennebunkport** on Summer Street (Rte. 35), keep an eye out for the **Wedding Cake House** about a mile along on the left. The legend behind this confection in fancy wood fretwork is that its sea-captain builder was forced to set sail in the middle of his wedding, and the house was his bride's consolation for the lack of a wedding cake. The home, built in 1826, is not open to the public but there is a gallery and studio in the attached carriage house.

Route 35 merges with Route 9 and takes you right into Kennebunkport's **Dock Square,** the busy town center, which is lined with shops and galleries and draws crowds in the summer. Parking is tight in Kennebunkport in peak season. Possibilities include the municipal lot next to the Congregational Church ($2/hour, May–Oct.), the Consolidated School on School Street (free, June 25–Labor Day), and, except on Sunday mornings, St. Martha's Church (free year-round) on North Street.

When you stroll the square, walk onto the drawbridge to admire the tidal Kennebunk River. Then turn around and head up Spring Street two blocks to Maine Street and the very grand **Nott House,** known also as White Columns, an imposing Greek Revival mansion with Doric columns that rise the height of the house. The Nott House is the gathering place for village walking tours on Wednesdays and Fridays in July and August. *Maine St., tel. 207/967–2751. Admission free. Open June–late Oct., Wed.–Fri. 1–4.*

Return to your car for a leisurely drive on Ocean Avenue, which follows the Kennebunk River to the sea and then winds around the peninsula of **Cape Arundel.** Parson's Way, a small and tranquil stretch of rocky shoreline, is open to all. As you round Cape Arundel, look to the right for the entrance to George Bush's summer home at Walker's Point.

❻

The **Seashore Trolley Museum,** on Log Cabin Road about 3 miles from Dock Square, shows a century of streetcars (1872–1972) and includes trolleys from major metropolitan areas and world capitals—Boston to Budapest, New York to Nagasaki, and San Francisco to Sydney, Australia—all beautifully restored. Best of all, you can take a trolley ride for nearly four miles over the tracks of the former Atlantic Shoreline trolley line, with a stop along the way at the museum restoration shop, where trolleys are transformed from junk into gems. *Log Cabin Rd., tel. 207/967–2800. Admission: $6 adults, $5 senior citizens, $4 children 6–16. Open May–mid-Oct., daily 10–5:30; reduced hours in spring and fall.*

What to See and Do with Children

Maine Aquarium. Live sharks, seals, penguins, a petting zoo, a tidal pool, snack bar, and gift shop make a busy stop on a rainy day. *Rte. 1, Saco, tel. 207/284–4511. Admission: $6.50 adults, $5.50 senior citizens, $4.50 children 5–12, $2.50 children 2–4. Open June–mid-Sept., daily 9–9; mid-Sept.–May, daily 9–4.*
Wells Auto Museum. A must for motor fanatics as well as youngsters, the museum has 70 vintage cars, antique coin games, and a restored Model T you can ride in. *Rte. 1, tel. 207/646–9064. Admission: $3.50 adults, $2 children 6–12. Open mid-June–mid-Sept., daily 10–5; Memorial Day–Columbus Day, weekends 10–5 .*

Off the Beaten Track

Old Orchard Beach, a 3-mile strip of sand beach with an amusement park reminiscent of Coney Island, is only a few miles north of Biddeford on Route 9. Despite the summertime crowds and fried-food odors, the carnival atmosphere can be infectious. **Palace Playland** (tel. 207/934–2001) on Old Orchard Street has an array of rides and booths, including a 1906 carousel and a Ferris wheel with dizzying ocean views. There is no free parking anywhere in town. *Open June–Labor Day.*

Shopping

Several factory outlet stores along Route 1 in Kittery and Wells offer clothing, shoes, glassware, and other products from top-of-the-line manufacturers. As an outgrowth of its long-established art community, Ogunquit has numerous galleries, many on Shore Road. Perkins Cove in Ogunquit and Dock Square in Kennebunkport have seasonal gift shops, boutiques, and galleries.

Antiques **J. J. Keating** (Rte. 1, Kennebunk, tel. 207/985–2097) deals in antiques, reproductions, and auctions. **Kenneth & Ida Manko** (Seabreeze Dr., Wells, tel. 207/646–2595) shows folk art, rustic furniture, paintings, and a large selection of 19th-century weather vanes. (From Rte. 1, head east on Eldridge Rd. for ½ mile, turn left on Seabreeze Dr.) **Old Fort Inn and Antiques** (Old Fort Ave., Kennebunkport, tel. 207/967–5353) stocks a small but choice selection of primitives, china, and country furniture in a converted barn adjoining an inn. **R. Jorgensen** (Rte. 1, Wells, tel. 207/646–9444) features an eclectic selection of 18th- and 19th-century formal and country period antiques from the British Isles, Europe, and the United States.

Books **Douglas N. Harding Rare Books** (Rte. 1, Wells, tel. 207/646–8785) has a huge stock of old books, maps, and prints. **Kennebunk Book Port** (10 Dock Sq., Kennebunkport, tel. 207/967–3815), housed in a rum warehouse built in 1775, has a wide selection of titles and specializes in local and maritime subjects.

Crafts **Marlows Artisans Gallery** (109 Lafayette Center, Kennebunk, tel. 207/985–2931) features wood, glass, weaving, and pottery crafts. **The Wedding Cake Studio** (104 Summer St., Kennebunkport, tel. 207/985–2818) offers faux finishes, trompe l'oeil, decorative painting, hand-painted clothing, and original artwork.

Women's **Chadwick's** (10 Main St., Kennebunk, tel. 207/985–7042) carries a
Clothing selection of women's casual clothing. **The Shoe String** (Rte. 1, Ogunquit, tel. 207/646–3533) has a range of shoes and handbags, from the sporty (including athletic wear) to the dressy.

Sports and Outdoor Activities

Biking **Cape-Able Bike Shop** (Townhouse Corners, Kennebunkport, tel. 207/967–4382) has bicycles for rent and free maps of the area; rates are $8–$25.

Bird-Watching **Biddeford Pool East Sanctuary** (Rte. 9, Biddeford) is a nature preserve where shorebirds congregate. **Rachel Carson National Wildlife Refuge** (Rte. 9, Wells) is a mile-long loop through a salt marsh bordering the Little River and a white-pine forest.

Boat Trips **Finestkind** (Perkins Cove, Ogunquit, tel. 207/646–5227) has cruises to Nubble Lighthouse, cocktail cruises, lobstering trips, and sailing cruises. **Chick's Marina** (Ocean Ave., Kennebunkport, tel. 207/967–2782) offers sightseeing and whale-watching cruises for up to six people.

Canoeing The **Maine Audubon Society** (tel. 207/781–2330 or 207/883–5100 June–Labor Day) offers daily guided canoe trips in **Scarborough Marsh** (Rte. 9, Scarborough), the largest salt marsh in Maine. Programs at Maine Audubon's Falmouth headquarters include nature walks and a discovery room for children. Call ahead for information.

Deep-Sea **Cape Arundel Cruises** (Performance Marine, Rte. 9, Kenne-
Fishing bunkport, tel. 207/967–5595) has half-day and full-day trips on its deepwater fishing boat. *Elizabeth II* (Performance Marine, Kennebunkport, tel. 207/967–5595) carries passengers on 1½-hour narrated cruises down the Kennebunk River and out to Cape Porpoise. The *Nautilus,* run by the same outfit, goes on whale-watching cruises from May through October daily at 10 AM. *Ugly Anne* (Perkins Cove, tel. 207/646–7202) offers half- and full-day trips.

Whale- *Indian* (Ocean Ave., Kennebunkport, tel. 207/967–5912) offers half-
Watching day trips.

Beaches

Maine's sand beaches tend to be rather hard-packed and built up with beach cottages and motels. Yet the water is clean (and cold), the surf usually gentle, and the crowds manageable except on the hottest summer weekends.

Kennebunk Beach. Gooch's Beach, Middle Beach, and Kennebunk Beach (also called Mother's Beach) are the three areas of Kennebunk Beach. Beach Road with its cottages and old Victorian boarding-houses runs right behind them. For parking permits (fee charged), go to the Kennebunk Town Office (1 Summer St., tel. 207/985–3675 or 985–2102 in summer). Gooch's and Middle beaches attract lots of teenagers; Mother's Beach, which has a small playground and tidal puddles for splashing, is popular with moms and kids.

Kennebunkport. Goose Rocks, a few minutes' drive north of town, is the largest beach in the Kennebunk area and the favorite of families with small children. For a parking permit (fee charged), go to the Kennebunkport Town Office (Elm St., tel. 207/967–4244; open weekdays 8–4:30) or the police department on Route 9 (open 24 hrs.).

Ogunquit. The 3 miles of sand beach have snack bars, boardwalk, rest rooms, and changing areas at the Beach Street entrance. The less crowded section to the north is accessible by footbridge and has rest rooms, all-day paid parking, and trolley service. The ocean beach is backed by the Ogunquit River, which is ideal for children because it is sheltered and waveless. There is a parking fee.

York. York's Long Sands Beach has free parking and Route 1A running right behind it; the smaller Short Sands beach has meter parking. Both beaches have commercial development.

Dining and Lodging

Dress is casual unless otherwise noted.

Kennebunkport
Dining

White Barn Inn. The rustic but elegant dining room of this inn serves regional New England cuisine. The menu changes weekly and may include steamed Maine lobster nestled on fresh fettuccine with carrots and ginger in a Thai-inspired honey and sherry vinegar sauce or grilled veal chop with baby carrots, wild rice cakes, sorrel, and lemon grass scented with curry sauce; or roasted breast of free-range chicken with aromatic vegetables Brunoise, fried herbs, olive oil, mashed potatoes, and a thyme-infused consommé. *Beach St., tel. 207/967–2321. Reservations advised. Jacket required, tie advised. AE, D, MC, V. Expensive–Very Expensive.*

Windows on the Water. This restaurant overlooks Dock Square and the working harbor of Kennebunkport. Try the California lobster ravioli or the gorgonzola-stuffed mignon. The "A Night on the Town" special, a five-course dinner for two, including wine, tax, and gratuity, for $69, is a good value if you have a healthy appetite; reservations are required. *Chase Hill Rd., tel. 207/967–3313. Reservations advised. AE, D, DC, MC, V. Expensive–Very Expensive.*

Olde Grist Mill. The bar and lounge occupy a restored grist mill, with original equipment and fixtures intact; the dining room is a spare, modern space with rose-colored linen, china, and picture windows on the Kennebunk River. The Continental menu features sole in papillote with seafood stuffing, sirloin steak au poivre, and a classic shore dinner. The baked Indian pudding is a local legend. *8 Mill La., tel. 207/967–4781 or 800/274–7478. Reservations accepted. AE, D, DC, MC, V. No lunch. Closed Mon. mid-Apr.–July 4 and Labor Day–Oct. Expensive.*

Dining and Lodging
★

Cape Arundel Inn. Were it not for the rocky shore beyond the picture windows, the pillared porch with wicker chairs, and the cozy parlor (with fireplace and backgammon boards) that you pass through en route to the dining room, you might well think you were dining at a major Boston restaurant. The lobster bisque is creamy, with just a bit of cognac. Entrées include marlin with sorrel butter; coho salmon with mushrooms, white wine, and lemon; rack of lamb; and pecan chicken with peaches and crème fraîche. The inn has 14 guest rooms, seven in the Victorian-era converted summer "cottage" and six in a motel facility adjoining. There's also a carriage-house apartment. *Ocean Ave., 04046, tel. 207/967–2125. Facilities: restaurant (reservations advised; no lunch). AE, MC, V. Closed mid-Oct.–mid-May. Expensive–Very Expensive.*

Lodging

The Captain Lord Mansion. A long and distinguished history, a three-story elliptical staircase, and a cupola with widow's walk make this something more than the standard bed-and-breakfast. The rooms, named for clipper ships, are mostly large and stately—11 have a fireplace—though the style relaxes as one ascends from the ground-floor rooms (damask and mahogany) to the country-style third-floor accommodations (pine furniture and leafy views). *Corner of Pleasant and Green Sts., Box 800, 04046, tel. 207/967–3141. 16 rooms with bath. D, MC, V. Very Expensive.*

Inn at Harbor Head. The 100-year-old shingled farmhouse on the harbor at Cape Porpoise has become a tiny bed-and-breakfast full of antiques, paintings, and heirlooms. The Harbor Suite upstairs has murals and a fireplace; the Greenery downstairs boasts a whirlpool tub and a garden view. The Summer suite and the Garden room have the best water views. The grounds are bright with flower beds. *41 Pier Rd., 04046, tel. 207/967–5564. 4 rooms with bath, 1 suite. Facilities: private dock. MC, V. Very Expensive.*

★ **Old Fort Inn.** This inn at the crest of a hill on a quiet road off Ocean Avenue has a secluded, countryish feel and the welcome sense of being just a touch above the Kennebunkport action. The front half of the former barn is an antiques shop (specializing in Early American pieces); the rest of the barn is the reception area and parlor decorated with grandfather clocks, antique tools, and funny old canes. Guest rooms are in a long, low fieldstone-and-stucco carriage house. Rooms are not large, but the decor is witty and creative: There are quilts on the four-poster beds; wreaths, primitive portraits, and framed antique bodices hang on the walls; the loveseats are richly upholstered. Nos. 2 and 12 have choice corner locations. *Old Fort Ave., Box M, 04046, tel. 207/967–5353. 16 double rooms with bath, 2 suites. Facilities: wet bars in rooms, laundry, pool, tennis, bikes for rent. Buffet breakfast included. AE, D, MC, V. Closed mid-Dec.–mid-Apr. Very Expensive.*

Breakwater Inn. Kennebunkport has few accommodations that are elegantly old-fashioned in decor, on the water, and well suited to families with young children—this inn is all three. Overlooking Kennebunk Beach from the breakwater, rooms have stained-pine four-poster beds and hand stenciling or wallpaper. The Riverside building next door offers spacious, airy rooms, some with sliding glass doors facing the water. *Box 1160, Ocean Ave., 04046, tel. 207/ 967–3118. 20 rooms with bath, 2 suites. Facilities: dining room. AE, MC, V. Closed Nov.–Mar. Expensive–Very Expensive.*

Bufflehead Cove. Situated on the Kennebunk River at the end of a winding dirt road, the friendly gray-shingle bed-and-breakfast affords the quiet of country fields and apple trees only five minutes from Dock Square. The guest rooms are dollhouse-pretty, with white wicker and flowers painted on the walls. *Gornitz La., Box 499, 04046, tel. 207/967–3879. 6 rooms with bath, 1 suite. Facilities: private dock, 1 room with fireplace and Jacuzzi. AE, MC, V. Closed Jan.–Feb. Expensive–Very Expensive.*

Captain Jefferds Inn. The three-story white-clapboard sea captain's mansion with black shutters, built in 1804, has been restored and filled with the innkeeper's collections of majolica, American art pottery, and Sienese pottery. Most rooms are done in Laura Ashley fabrics and wallpapers, and many have been furnished with a wide variety of antiques and collections from all over the world. A hearty breakfast is included. *Pearl St., Box 691, 04046, tel. 207/967–2311. 13 rooms with bath; 4 suites in the carriage house. Facilities: croquet. MC, V. Closed mid-Dec.–Mar. Expensive–Very Expensive.*

The Seaside. The modern motel units, all with sliding glass doors opening onto private decks or patios, half of them with ocean views, are appropriate for families; so are the cottages, which have from one to four bedrooms. The four bedrooms in the inn, furnished with antiques, are more suitable for adults. *Gooch's Beach, 04046, tel. 207/967–4461 or 207/967–4282. 26 rooms with bath, 10 cottages. Continental breakfast included. Facilities: private beach, laundry, playground. Continental breakfast included. MC, V. Inn rooms closed Labor Day–June; cottages closed Nov.–Apr. Expensive–Very Expensive.*

Kittery **Warren's Lobster House.** A local institution, this waterfront restau-
Dining rant offers reasonably priced boiled lobster, first-rate scrod, a raw bar, and a huge salad bar. *Rte. 1, tel. 207/439–1630. Reservations advised. AE, MC, V. Inexpensive–Moderate.*

Lodging **Deep Water Landing.** This comfortable, turn-of-the-century New Englander welcomes guests to the three rooms on its third floor. Fruit trees and flower beds border the lawns, and the breakfast room offers water views. *92 Whipple Rd., 03904, tel. 207/439–0824. 3 rooms with shared bath. Full breakfast included. No credit cards. Inexpensive–Moderate.*

Ogunquit **Arrows.** Elegant simplicity is the hallmark of this 18th-century
Dining farmhouse, 2 miles up a back road. The menu changes frequently,
★ offering such entrées as fillet of beef glistening in red and yellow sauces, grilled salmon and radicchio with marinated fennel and baked polenta, and Chinese-style duck glazed with molasses. Appetizers (Maine crabmeat mousse or lobster risotto) and desserts (strawberry shortcake with Chantilly cream or steamed chocolate pudding) are also beautifully executed and presented. *Berwick Rd., tel. 207/361–1100. Reservations advised. Jacket and tie advised. Closed Mon.–Wed. and Thanksgiving–May. MC, V. Expensive–Very Expensive.*

★ **Hurricane.** Don't let its weather-beaten exterior deter you—this small, comfortable seafood bar-and-grill offers first-rate cooking and spectacular views of the crashing surf. Start with lobster chowder, napoleon of smoked salmon, crab Rangoon, or the house salad (assorted greens with pistachio nuts and roasted shallots). Entrées include Cuervo and lime–glazed swordfish with three sauces, veal braised with wild mushrooms, and shrimp scampi served over fresh pasta. Be sure to save room for the classic crème brûlée. *Perkins Cove, tel. 207/646–6348. AE, D, DC, MC, V. Moderate–Expensive.*
Ogunquit Lobster Pound. Select your lobster live, then dine under the trees or in the rustic dining room of the log cabin. The menu includes steamed clams, steak, and chicken; and there is a special children's menu. *Rte. 1, tel. 207/646–2516. No reservations. AE, MC, V. Closed late Oct.–mid-May. Moderate.*

Lodging **The Colonial: A Resort by the Sea.** This complex of accommodations in the middle of Ogunquit includes a large white Victorian inn, modern motel units, and efficiency apartments. Inn rooms have flowered wallpaper, Colonial reproduction furniture, and white ruffle curtains. Efficiencies are popular with families. One-third of the rooms have water views. *Shore Rd., Box 895, 03907, tel. 207/646–5191. 80 units, 44 with bath; 36 suites. Facilities: restaurant, heated outdoor pool, laundry, grills, Jacuzzi, playground, shuffleboard. AE, D, MC, V. Closed Nov.–Apr. Moderate–Very Expensive.*
Seafair Inn. A century-old white-clapboard house set back behind shrubs and lawn in the center of town, the Seafair has a homey atmosphere and proximity to the beach. Rooms are furnished with odds and ends of country furniture; breakfast is served on an enclosed sun porch. *14 Shore Rd., Box 1221, 03907, tel. 207/646–2181. 18 units, 14 with bath; 4 efficiency suites. Continental breakfast included. MC, V. Closed Nov.–Mar. Moderate–Expensive.*

Prouts Neck
Lodging
★

Black Point Inn. At the neck of the peninsula that juts into the ocean at Prouts Neck, 12 miles south of Portland, stands one of the great old-time resorts of Maine. The sun porch has wicker and plants, the music room—in the English country-house style—has wing chairs, silk flowers, Chinese prints, and a grand piano. In the guest rooms are rock maple bedsteads, Martha Washington bedspreads, and white-ruffle Priscilla curtains. Older guests prefer the main inn; families choose from the four cottages. The extensive grounds offer beaches, hiking, a bird sanctuary, and sports. The dining room, done in beautiful floral-pattern wallpaper and water-stained pine paneling, has a menu strong in seafood. *510 Black Point Rd., Scarborough 04074, tel. 207/883–4126 or 800/258–0003; fax 207/883–9976. 80 rooms with bath, 6 suites. Facilities: restaurant, bar, entertainment, tennis, golf, outdoor and indoor pools, Jacuzzi, volleyball, croquet, bicycles, sailboats, fishing boats. AE, MC, V. Closed Dec.–Apr. Very Expensive.*

Wells
Dining

The Grey Gull. This charming Victorian inn offers views of the open sea and rocks on which seals like to sun themselves. In the evening, try any of the excellent seafood dishes, chicken breast rolled in walnuts and baked with maple syrup, Yankee pot roast, or soft-shell crabs almondine. Breakfast is popular here in the summer: Blueberry pancakes, ham-and-cheese strata, or eggs McGull served on crabcakes with hollandaise sauce are good choices. *321 Webhannet Dr., at Moody Point, tel. 207/646–7501. Reservations advised. AE, MC, V. Moderate–Expensive.*

Billy's Chowder House. As the crowded parking lot suggests, this simple restaurant in a salt marsh is popular with locals and tourists alike. For a generous lobster roll or haddock sandwich (not to mention chowders), Billy's is hard to beat. *Mile Rd., tel. 207/646–7558. MC, V. Closed 1 month in winter. Moderate.*

The Yorks
Dining

Cape Neddick Inn. This restaurant and art gallery has an airy ambience, with tables set well apart, lots of windows, and art everywhere. The New American menu has offered lobster macadamia tart (shelled lobster sautéed with shallots, macadamia nuts, sherry, and cream and served in pastry), breaded pork tenderloin, and such appetizers as spicy sesame chicken dumplings and gravlax with Russian pepper vodka. Duckling flamed in brandy is always on the menu. *Rte. 1, Cape Neddick, tel. 207/363–2899. Reservations advised. AE, MC, V. No lunch. Closed Mon. and Tues. Columbus Day–May 31. Moderate–Expensive.*

★

York Harbor Inn. The dining room of this inn has country charm and great ocean views. In the past, Frank Jones, king of New England alemakers, patronized the inn; nowadays you might spot local resident and poet May Sarton enjoying a meal here. For dinner, start with escargot and brie in a puff pastry, the special Mediterranean salad, or a creamy seafood chowder, and then try the veal-and-shrimp Niçoise or the beef tenderloin garnished with fresh asparagus and crabmeat. Just save room for the black-bottom cheesecake or any of the other wonderful desserts. *Rte. 1A (Box 573), York Harbor 03911, tel. 207/363–5119 or 800/343–3869. Reservations advised. AE, DC, MC, V. No lunch off-season. Moderate–Expensive.*

Dining and Lodging

Dockside Guest Quarters and Restaurant. On an 8-acre private island in the middle of York Harbor, the Dockside promises water views, seclusion, and quiet. Rooms in the Maine House, the oldest structure on the site, are furnished with Early American antiques, marine artifacts, and nautical paintings and prints. Four modern cottages tucked among the trees have less character but bigger windows on the water, and many have kitchenettes. Entrées in the esteemed dining room may include scallop-stuffed shrimp Casino, broiled salmon, steak au poivre with brandied mushroom sauce, and roast stuffed duckling. There's also a children's menu. *York Harbor off Rte. 103, Box 205, York 03909, tel. 207/363–2868. 22 rooms, 20 with bath; 5 suites. Facilities: restaurant (tel. 207/363–2722; reservations advised on weekends; closed Mon.), private dock, motorboat, croquet, badminton, bicycles. MC, V. Closed late Oct.–Apr. Inn: Moderate–Very Expensive. Restaurant: Moderate.*

The Arts

Music **Hamilton House** (Vaughan's La., South Berwick, tel. 603/436–3205), the Georgian home featured in Sarah Orne Jewett's *The Tory Lover*, presents "Sundays in the Garden," a series of free summer concerts in July and August. Concerts begin at 3; the grounds are open noon until 5 for picnicking.

Theater **Ogunquit Playhouse** (Rte. 1, tel. 207/646–5511), one of America's oldest summer theaters, mounts plays and musicals from late June to Labor Day.

Portland to Pemaquid Point

Maine's largest city, yet small enough to be seen with ease in a day or two, Portland is undergoing a cultural and economic renaissance. New hotels and a bright new performing arts center have joined the neighborhoods of historic homes; the Old Port Exchange, perhaps the finest urban renovation project on the East Coast, balances modern commercial enterprise with a salty waterfront character in an area bustling with restaurants, shops, and galleries. The piers of Commercial Street abound with opportunities for water tours of the harbor and excursions to the Calendar Islands.

Freeport, north of Portland, is a town made famous by the L. L. Bean store, whose success led to the opening of scores of other clothing stores and outlets. Brunswick is best known for Bowdoin College. Bath has been a shipbuilding center since 1607, and the Maine Maritime Museum preserves its history.

The Boothbays—the coastal areas of Boothbay Harbor, East Boothbay, Linekin Neck, Southport Island, and the inland town of Boothbay—attract hordes of vacationing families and flotillas of pleasure craft. The Pemaquid peninsula juts into the Atlantic south of Damariscotta and just east of the Boothbays, and near Pemaquid Beach one can view the objects unearthed at the Colonial Pemaquid Restoration.

Important Addresses and Numbers

Visitor Information Off-season, most information offices are open weekdays 9–5; the hours below are for summer only.

Bath Area Chamber of Commerce (45 Front St., Bath, tel. 207/443–9751; open weekdays 8:30–5). **Boothbay Harbor Region Chamber of Commerce** (Box 356, Boothbay Harbor, tel. 207/633–2353; open weekdays 9–6, Sat. 11–4, Sun. 12–4). **Brunswick Area Chamber of Commerce** (59 Pleasant St., Brunswick, tel. 207/725–8797; open weekdays 8:30–5). **Convention and Visitors Bureau of Greater Portland** (305 Commercial St., tel. 207/772–5800; open weekdays 9–5). **Freeport Merchants Association** (Box 452, Freeport, tel. 207/865–1212; open weekdays 9–5). **Greater Portland Chamber of Commerce**

(145 Middle St., Portland, tel. 207/772–2811; open weekdays 8–5). **Maine Publicity Bureau, the Maine Information Center** (Rte. 1 [Exit 17 off I–95], Yarmouth, tel. 207/846–0833).

Emergencies **Maine Medical Center** (22 Bramhall St., Portland, tel. 207/871–0111).**Mid Coast Hospital** (1356 Washington St., Bath, tel. 207/443–5524; 58 Baribeau Dr., Brunswick, tel. 207/729–0181). **St. Andrews Hospital** (3 St. Andrews Ln., Boothbay Harbor, tel. 207/633–2121).

Getting Around Portland to Pemaquid Point

By Car The Congress Street exit from I–295 takes you into the heart of Portland. Numerous city parking lots have hourly rates of 50¢ to 85¢; the Gateway Garage on High Street, off Congress, is a convenient place to leave your car while exploring downtown. North of Portland, I–95 takes you to Exit 20 and Route 1, Freeport's Main Street, which continues on to Brunswick and Bath. East of Wiscasset you can take Route 27 south to the Boothbays, where Route 96 is a good choice for further exploration.

By Bus Greater Portland's **Metro** (tel. 207/774–0351) runs seven bus routes in Portland, South Portland, and Westbrook. The fare is $1 for adults and 50¢ for senior citizens, people with disabilities, and children (under 5 free); exact change ($1 bills accepted) is required. Buses run from 5:30 AM to 11:45 PM.

Exploring Portland

Numbers in the margin correspond to points of interest on the Southern Maine Coast and Portland maps.

❼ Congress Street, **Portland**'s main street, runs the length of the peninsular city from the Western Promenade in the southwest to the Eastern Promenade in the northeast, passing through the small downtown area. A few blocks southeast of downtown, the bustling Old Port Exchange sprawls along the waterfront.

❽ One of the notable homes on Congress Street is the **Neal Dow Memorial,** a brick mansion built in 1829 in the late Federal style by General Neal Dow, a zealous abolitionist and prohibitionist. The library has fine ornamental ironwork, and the furnishings include the family china, silver, and portraits. Don't miss the grandfather clocks and the original deed granted by James II. *714 Congress St., tel. 207/ 773–7773. Admission free. Open for tours weekdays 11–4.*

❾ On Congress Square, the distinguished **Portland Museum of Art** has a strong collection of seascapes and landscapes by such masters as Winslow Homer, John Marin, Andrew Wyeth, and Marsden Hartley. Homer's *Pulling the Dory* and *Weatherbeaten,* two quintessential Maine coast images, are here. The Joan Whitney Payson Collection includes works by Monet, Picasso, and Renoir. The strikingly modern Charles Shipman Payson building was designed by Harry N. Cobb, an associate of I. M. Pei, in 1983. *7 Congress Sq., tel. 207/775–6148 or 207/773–2787. Admission: $6 adults, $5 senior citizens, $1 children 6–18, free Sat. 10–noon. Tues.–Sat. 10–5 (Thurs. until 9), Sun. noon–5. Call for winter hours.*

❿ Walk east on Congress Street to the **Wadsworth Longfellow House** of 1785, the boyhood home of the poet and the first brick house in Portland. The late-Colonial-style structure sits well back from the street and has a small portico over its entrance and four chimneys surmounting the hip roof. Most of the furnishings are original to the house. *485 Congress St., tel. 207/772–1807 or 207/774–1822. Admis-*

460

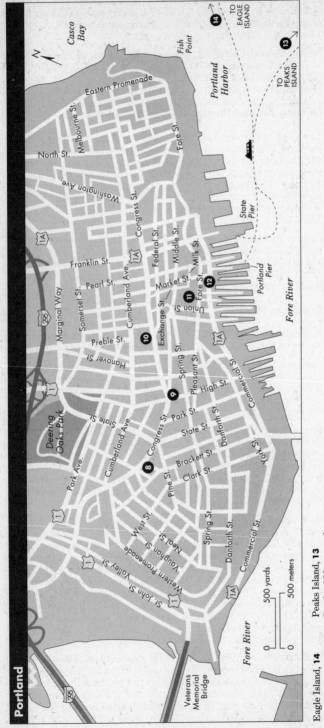

Portland

Eagle Island, **14**
Mariner's Church, **12**
Neal Dow Memorial, **8**
Old Port Exchange, **11**

Peaks Island, **13**
Portland Museum of
Art, **9**
Wadsworth Longfellow
House, **10**

sion: $4 adults, $1 children under 12. Open June–Oct., Tues.–Sun. 10–4. Garden open daily 9–5.

⑪ You can walk from downtown to the **Old Port Exchange,** or you can drive and park your car either at the city garage on Fore Street (between Exchange and Union streets) or opposite the U.S. Customs House at the corner of Fore and Pearl streets. Like the Customs House, the brick buildings and warehouses of the Old Port Exchange were built following the Great Fire of 1866 and were intended to last for ages. When the city's economy slumped in the middle of the present century, however, the Old Port declined and seemed slated for demolition. Then artists and craftspeople began opening shops here in the late 1960s, and in time restaurants, chic boutiques, bookstores, and gift shops followed.

The Old Port is best explored on foot. Allow a couple of hours to wander at leisure on Market, Exchange, Middle, and Fore streets. The
⑫ **Mariner's Church** (376 Fore St.) has a fine facade of granite columns, and the Elias Thomas Block on Commercial Street demonstrates the graceful use of bricks in commercial architecture. Inevitably the salty smell of the sea will draw you to one of the wharves off Commercial Street; Custom House Wharf retains some of the older, rougher waterfront atmosphere.

Island The brightly painted ferries of **Casco Bay Lines** (tel. 207/774–7871)
Excursions are the lifeline to the Calendar Islands of Casco Bay, which number about 136, depending on the tides and how one defines an island.

⑬ **Peaks Island,** nearest Portland, is the most developed, and some residents commute to work in Portland. Yet you can still commune with the wind and the sea on Peaks, explore an old fort, and ramble along the alternately rocky and sandy shore.

⑭ The 17-acre **Eagle Island,** owned by the State of Maine and open to the public for day trips in summer, was the home of Admiral Robert E. Peary, the American explorer of the North Pole. Peary built a stone-and-wood house on the island as a summer retreat in 1904, then made it his permanent residence. The house remains as it was when Peary was here with his stuffed Arctic birds and the quartz he brought home and set into the fieldstone fireplace. The *Kristy K.,* departing from Long Wharf, makes a four-hour narrated tour. *Long Wharf, tel. 207/774–6498. Excursion tour: $15 adults, $12 senior citizens, $9 children 5–12. Departures mid-June–Labor Day, daily 10 AM.*

Exploring North of Portland

⑮ **Freeport,** on Route 1, 15 miles northeast of Portland, has charming back streets lined with old clapboard houses and even a small harbor on the Harraseeket River, but the overwhelming majority of visitors come to shop, and L. L. Bean is the store that put Freeport on the map. Founded in 1912 as a small mail-order merchandiser of products for hunters, guides, and fisherfolk, L. L. Bean now attracts some 3.5 million shoppers a year to its giant store in the heart of Freeport's shopping district on Route 1. Here you can still find the original hunting boots, along with cotton, wool, and silk sweaters; camping and ski equipment; comforters; and hundreds of other items for the home, car, boat, or campsite. Across the street from the main store, a Bean factory outlet has seconds and discontinued merchandise at discount prices. *Rte. 1, Freeport, tel. 800/341–4341. Open 24 hrs.*

All around L. L. Bean, like seedlings under a mighty spruce, some 70 outlets have sprouted, offering designer clothes, shoes, housewares, and toys at discount prices (*see* Shopping, *below*).

16 It's 9 miles northeast on Route 1 from Freeport to **Brunswick.** Follow the signs to the Brunswick business district, Pleasant Street, and—at the end of Pleasant Street—Maine Street, which claims to be the widest (198 feet across) in the state. Friday from May through October sees a fine farmer's market on the town mall, between Maine Street and Park Row.

Maine Street takes you to the 110-acre campus of **Bowdoin College,** an enclave of distinguished architecture, gardens, and grassy quadrangles in the middle of town. Campus tours (tel. 207/725–3000) depart every day but Sunday from Chamberlain Hall, the admissions office. Among the historic buildings are Massachusetts Hall, a stout, sober, hip-roofed brick structure that dates from 1802 and that once housed the entire college. Hubbard Hall, an imposing 1902 neoGothic building is home to Maine's only gargoyle. In addition, it houses the **Peary-MacMillan Arctic Museum.** The museum contains photographs, navigational instruments, and artifacts from the first successful expedition to the North Pole, in 1909, by two of Bowdoin's most famous alumni, Admiral Robert E. Peary and Donald B. MacMillan. *Tel. 207/725–3416. Admission free. Open Tues.–Sat. 10–5, Sun. 2–5.*

Don't miss the **Bowdoin College Museum of Art,** a splendid limestone, brick, and granite structure in a Renaissance Revival style, with three galleries upstairs, and four more downstairs, radiating from a rotunda. Designed in 1894 by Charles F. McKim, the building stands on a rise, its facade adorned with classical statues and the entrance set off by a triumphal arch. The collections encompass Assyrian and Classical art and that of the Dutch, Italian, French, and Flemish old masters; a superb gathering of Colonial and Federal paintings, notably the Gilbert Stuart portraits of Madison and Jefferson; and a Winslow Homer Gallery of engravings, etchings, and memorabilia (open summer only). The museum's collection also includes 19th- and 20th-century American painting and sculpture, with works by Mary Cassatt, Andrew Wyeth, John Sloan, Rockwell Kent, Jim Dine, and Robert Rauschenberg. *Walker Art Bldg., tel. 207/725–3275. Admission free. Open Tues.–Sat. 10–5, Sun. 2–5.*

Before going on to Bath, drive down Route 123 or Route 24 to the peninsulas and islands known collectively as the **Harpswells.** The numerous small coves along Harpswell Neck shelter the boats of local lobstermen, and summer cottages are tucked away amid the birch and spruce trees.

17 **Bath,** 7 miles east of Brunswick on Route 1, has been a shipbuilding center since 1607. Today the Bath Iron Works turns out guided-missile frigates for the U.S. Navy and merchant container ships.

The **Maine Maritime Museum and Shipyard** in Bath (take the Bath Business District exit from Route 1, turn right on Washington Street, and follow the signs) has ship models, journals, photographs, and other artifacts to stir the nautical dreams of old salts and young. The 142-foot Grand Banks fishing schooner *Sherman Zwicker,* one of the last of its kind, is on display when in port. You can watch apprentice boatbuilders wield their tools on classic Maine boats at the restored Percy & Small Shipyard and Apprentice Shop. The outdoor shipyard is open May–November; during these months visitors may take scenic tours of the Kennebec River on the *Hardy II.* During off-season, the Maritime History Building has indoor exhibits, videos, and activities. *243 Washington St., tel. 207/443–1316. Admission: $6 adults, $5.40 senior citizens, $2.50 children 6–15. Open daily 9:30–5.*

From Bath it's 10 miles northeast on Route 1 to Wiscasset, where the huge rotting hulls of the schooners *Hester* and *Luther Little* rest, testaments to the town's once-busy harbor. Those who appreciate both music and antiques will enjoy a visit to the **Musical Wonder House** to see and hear the vast collection of antique music boxes from around the world. *18 High St., tel. 207/882–7163. 1-hr presentation on main floor: $10 adults, $6 children under 12 and senior citizens; 3-hr tour of entire house: $25. Open May 15–Oct. 15, daily 10–6. Tours are usually until 4 PM; call ahead for 3-hr tours.*

(18) Across the river, drive south on Route 27 to reach the **Boothbay Railway Village,** about a mile north of **Boothbay,** where you can ride 1½ miles on a narrow-gauge steam train through a re-creation of a turn-of-the-century New England village. Among the 24 village buildings is a museum with more than 50 antique automobiles and trucks. *Rte. 27, Boothbay, tel. 207/633–4727. Admission: $5 adults, $2 children 2–12. Open mid-June–mid-Oct., daily 9:30–5.*

(19) Continue south on Route 27 into Boothbay Harbor, bear right on Oak Street, and follow it to the waterfront parking lots. **Boothbay Harbor** is a town to wander through: Commercial Street, Wharf Street, the By-Way, and Townsend Avenue are lined with shops, galleries, and ice-cream parlors. Excursion boats (*see* Sports and Outdoor Activities, *below*) leave from the piers off Commercial Street.

Time Out The **P&P Pastry Shoppe** (6 McKown St., tel. 207/633–6511) is a welcome stop for a sandwich or a pastry.

Having explored Boothbay Harbor, return to Route 27 and head north again to Route 1. Proceed north to Business Route 1, and follow it through Damariscotta, an appealing shipbuilding town on the Damariscotta River. Bear right on the Bristol Road (Rte. 129/130), and when the highway splits, stay on Route 130, which leads to Bris-
(20) tol and terminates at **Pemaquid Point.**

About 5 miles south of Bristol you'll come to New Harbor, where a right turn will take you to Pemaquid Beach and the **Colonial Pemaquid Restoration.** Here, on a small peninsula jutting into the Pemaquid River, English mariners established a fishing and trading settlement in the early 17th century. The excavations at **Ft. William Henry,** begun in the mid-1960s, have turned up thousands of artifacts from the Colonial settlement, including the remains of an old customs house, tavern, jail, forge, and homes, and from even earlier Native American settlements. The State of Maine operates a museum displaying many of the artifacts. *Rte. 130, Pemaquid Point, tel. 207/677–2423. Admission: $1.50 adults, 50¢ children 6–12. Open Memorial Day–Labor Day, daily 9:30–5.*

Route 130 terminates at the **Pemaquid Point Light,** which looks as though it sprouted from the ragged, tilted chunk of granite that it commands. The former lighthouse-keeper's cottage is now the **Fishermen's Museum,** with photographs, models, and artifacts that explore commercial fishing in Maine. Here, too, is the Pemaquid Art Gallery, which mounts changing exhibitions from July 1 through Labor Day. *Rte. 130, tel. 207/677–2494. Museum admission by contribution. Open Memorial Day–Columbus Day, Mon.–Sat. 10–5, Sun. 11–5.*

What to See and Do with Children

Boothbay Railway Village, Boothbay
Children's Museum of Maine. Touching is okay at this museum where little ones can pretend they are lobstermen, shopkeepers, or computer experts. *142 Free St., Portland, tel. 207/828–1234. Admission: $3.75 adults, $2 senior citizens and children over 1. Open Mon., Wed., Thur. 10–5, Fri. 10–8, Tues. and Sun. 12–5.*

Off the Beaten Track

Stroudwater Village, 3 miles west of Portland, was spared the devastation of the fire of 1866 and thus contains some of the best examples of 18th- and early-19th-century architecture in the region. Here are the remains of mills, canals, and historic homes, including the Tate House, built in 1755 with paneling from England. It overlooks the old mast yard where George Tate, Mast Agent to the King, prepared tall pines for the ships of the Royal Navy. The furnishings date to the late 18th century. *Tate House, 1270 Westbrook St., tel. 207/774–9781. Admission: $3 adults, $1 children. Open July–Sept. 15, Tues.–Sat. 10–4, Sun. 1–4.*

Shopping

The best shopping in Portland is at the Old Port Exchange, where many shops are concentrated along Fore and Exchange streets. Freeport's name is almost synonymous with shopping, and shopping in Freeport means **L. L. Bean** and the 70 factory outlets that opened during the 1980s. Outlet stores are located in the Fashion Outlet Mall (2 Depot St.) and the Freeport Crossing (200 Lower Main St.), and many others crowd Main Street and Bow Street. The *Freeport Visitors Guide* (Freeport Merchants Association, Box 452, Freeport 04032, tel. 207/865–1212) has a complete listing. Boothbay Harbor, and Commercial Street in particular, is chockablock with gift shops, T-shirt shops, and other seasonal emporia catering to visitors.

Antiques **F. O. Bailey Antiquarians** (141 Middle St., Portland, tel. 207/774–1479), Portland's largest retail showroom, features antique and reproduction furniture and jewelry, paintings, rugs, and china. **Harrington House Gallery Store** (45 Main St., Freeport, tel. 207/865–0477) is a restored 19th-century merchant's home owned by the Freeport Historical Society; all the period reproductions that furnish the rooms are for sale. In addition, you can buy wallpaper, crafts, Shaker items, toys, and kitchen utensils. **Maine Trading Post** (80 Commercial St., Boothbay Harbor, tel. 207/633–2760) sells antiques and fine reproductions that include rolltop desks able to accommodate personal computers, as well as gifts and decorative accessories. **Mary Alice Reilley Antiques** (83 India St., Portland, tel. 207/773–8815) carries china, glass, tins, primitives, and a large selection of English and Irish country pine furniture.

Books and Maps **Carlson and Turner** (241 Congress St., Portland, tel. 207/773–4200) is an antiquarian book dealer with an estimated 40,000 titles. **DeLorme's Map Store** (Rte. 1, Freeport, tel. 207/865–4171) carries an exceptional selection of maps and atlases of Maine, New England, and the rest of the world; nautical charts; and travel books. **Raffles Cafe Bookstore** (555 Congress St., Portland, tel. 207/761–3930) presents an impressive selection of fiction and nonfiction, plus the best selection of periodicals north of Boston. Coffee and a light lunch are served, and there are frequent readings and literary gatherings.

Clothing **A. H. Benoit and Co.** (188 Middle St., Portland, tel. 207/773–6421) sells quality men's clothing from sportswear to evening attire. **House of Logan** (Townsend Ave., Boothbay Harbor, tel. 207/633–2293) has specialty clothing for men and women, plus children's clothes next door at the Village Store. **Joseph's** (410 Fore St., tel. 207/773–1274) has elegant tailored designer clothing for men and women.

Crafts **Edgecomb Potters** (Rte. 27, Edgecomb, tel. 207/882–6802) sells glazed porcelain pottery and other crafts. **Sheepscot River Pottery** (Rte. 1, Edgecomb, tel. 207/882–9410) has original hand-painted pottery as well as a large collection of American-made crafts including jewelry, kitchenware, furniture, and home accessories.

Galleries **Abacus** (44 Exchange St., Portland, tel. 207/772–4880) has unusual gift items in glass, wood, and textiles, plus fine modern jewelry. **The Pine Tree Shop & Bayview Gallery** (75 Market St., Portland, tel. 207/773–3007 or 800/244–3007) has original art and prints by prominent Maine painters. **Stein Glass Gallery** (20 Milk St., Portland, tel. 207/772–9072) specializes in contemporary glass, both decorative and utilitarian.

Sports and Outdoor Activities

Boat Trips *Appledore* (tel. 207/633–6598), a 66-foot windjammer, departs from
Boothbay Pier 6 at 9:30, noon, 3, and 6 for voyages to the outer islands. **Argo**
Harbor **Cruises** (tel. 207/633–2500) runs the *Islander* for morning cruises, Bath Hellgate cruises, whale watching, and the popular Cabbage Island Clambake; the *Islander II* for 1½-hour trips to Seal Rocks; the *Miss Boothbay*, a licensed lobster boat, for lobster-trap hauling trips. Biweekly evening cruises feature R&B or reggae. Departures are from Pier 6. **Balmy Day Cruises** (tel. 207/633–2284 or 800/298–2284) has day trips to Monhegan Island and tours of the harbor and nearby lighthouses. *Bay Lady* (tel. 207/633–6990), a 31-foot Friendship sloop, offers sailing trips of under 2 hours from Fisherman's Wharf. **Cap'n Fish's Boat Trips** (tel. 207/633–3244) offers sightseeing cruises throughout the region, including puffin cruises, lobster-hauling and whale-watching rides, trips to Damariscove Harbor, Pemaquid Point, and up the Kennebec River to Bath, departing from Pier 1. *Eastward* (tel. 207/633–4780) is a Friendship sloop with six-passenger capacity that departs from Ocean Point Road in East Boothbay for full- or half-day sailing trips. Itineraries vary with passengers' desires and the weather.

Portland For tours of the harbor, Casco Bay, and the nearby islands, try **Bay View Cruises** (Fisherman's Wharf, tel. 207/761–0496), **The Buccaneer** (Long Wharf, tel. 207/799–8188), **Casco Bay Lines** (Maine State Pier, tel. 207/774–7871), **Eagle Tours** (Long Wharf, tel. 207/774–6498), or **Old Port Mariner Fleet** (Long Wharf, tel. 207/775–0727).

Deep-Sea Half- and full-day fishing charter boats operating out of Portland in-
Fishing clude *Anjin-San* (tel. 207/772–7168) and *Devils Den* (DeMillo's Marina, tel. 207/761–4466). Operating out of Boothbay Harbor, **Cap'n Fish's Deep Sea Fishing** (tel. 207/633–3244) schedules full- and half-day trips, departing from Pier 1, and **Lucky Star Charters** (tel. 207/633–4624) runs full- and half-day private charters for up to six people, with departures from Pier 8.

Nature Walks **Wolfe's Neck Woods State Park** has self-guided trails along Casco Bay, the Harraseeket River, and a fringe salt marsh, as well as walks led by naturalists. Picnic tables and grills are available, but there's no camping. Follow Bow Street opposite L. L. Bean off

Route 1. *Wolfe's Neck Rd., tel. 207/865–4465. Admission Memorial Day–Labor Day: $2 adults ($1 off-season), 50¢ children 5–11.*

Beaches

Crescent Beach State Park (Rte. 77, Cape Elizabeth, tel. 207/767–3625; admission late Apr.–mid-Oct.: $2.50 adults [$1 off-season], 50¢ children 5–11), about 8 miles from Portland, has a sand beach, picnic tables, seasonal snack bar, and bathhouse. **Ferry Beach State Park** (follow signs off Rte. 9 in Saco, tel. 207/283–0067; admission late Apr.–mid-Oct.: $2 adults [$1 off-season], 50¢ children 5–11), near Old Orchard Beach, has picnic facilities with grills and extensive nature trails. **Popham Beach State Park** (Phippsburg, tel. 207/389–1335; admission late Apr.–mid-Oct.: $2 adults [$1 off-season], 50¢ children 5–11), at the end of Route 209, south of Bath, has a good sand beach, a marsh area, and picnic tables. **Reid State Park** (tel. 207/371–2303; admission late Apr.–mid-Oct.: [$1 off-season], $2.50 adults, 50¢ children 5–11), on Georgetown Island, off Route 127, has 1½ miles of sand on three beaches. Facilities include bathhouses, picnic tables, fireplaces, and snack bar. Parking lots fill by 11 AM on summer Sundays and holidays.

Dining and Lodging

Many of Portland's best restaurants are in the Old Port Exchange district. Dress is casual unless otherwise noted.

Bath
Dining

Kristina's Restaurant & Bakery. This frame house–turned–restaurant, with a front deck built around a huge maple tree, turns out some of the finest pies, pastries, and cakes on the coast. A satisfying dinner menu features new American cuisine, including fresh seafood and grilled meats. All meals can be packed to go. *160 Centre St., tel. 207/442–8577. Reservations accepted. D, MC, V. No dinner Sun. Call ahead in winter. Inexpensive–Moderate.*

Lodging

Fairhaven Inn. This cedar-shingle house built in 1790 is set on 27 acres of pine woods and meadows sloping down to the Kennebec River. Guest rooms are furnished with handmade quilts and mahogany pineapple four-poster beds. The home-cooked breakfast offers such treats as peach soup, blintzes, and apple upside-down French toast. *RR 2, Box 85, N. Bath, 04530, tel. 207/443–4391. 8 rooms, 6 with bath. Facilities: hiking and cross-country ski trails. Full breakfast included. AE, MC, V. Moderate.*

Boothbay
Lodging

Kenniston Hill Inn. The oldest inn in Boothbay (ca. 1786), this classic center-chimney colonial with its white clapboards and columned porch offers comfortably old-fashioned accommodations on 4 acres of land only minutes from Boothbay Harbor. Four guest rooms have fireplaces, some have four-poster beds, rocking chairs, and gilt mirrors. *Rte. 27, Box 125, 04537, tel. 207/633–2159. 10 rooms with bath. Full breakfast included. MC, V. Moderate–Expensive.*

Boothbay Harbor
Dining

Black Orchid. The classic Italian fare includes fettuccine Alfredo with fresh lobster and mushrooms, and *petit filet à la diabolo* (fillets of Angus steak with marsala sauce). The upstairs and downstairs dining rooms sport a Roman-trattoria ambience, with frilly leaves and fruit hanging from the rafters and little else in the way of decor. In the summer there is a raw bar outdoors. *5 By-Way, tel. 207/633–6659. AE, MC, V. No lunch. Closed Nov.–Apr. Moderate–Expensive.*

Andrew's Harborside. The seafood menu is typical of the area—lobster, fried clams and oysters, haddock with seafood stuffing—but the harbor view makes it memorable. Lunch features lobster and crab rolls; children's and seniors' menus are available. You can dine outdoors on a harborside deck during the summer. *8 Bridge St., tel. 207/633–4074. Dinner reservations accepted for 5 or more. MC, V. Closed mid-Oct.–mid-May. Moderate.*

Lodging   **Fisherman's Wharf Inn.** All rooms overlook the water at this Colonial-style motel built 200 feet out over the harbor. The large dining room has floor-to-ceiling windows, and several day-trip cruises leave from this location. *42 Commercial St., 04538, tel. 207/633–5090 or 800/628–6872. 54 rooms with bath. Facilities: restaurant. AE, D, DC, MC, V. Closed late Oct.–late May. Expensive–Very Expensive.*

Anchor Watch. This country Colonial on the water overlooks the outer harbor and lies within easy walking distance of town. Guest rooms are decorated with quilts and stenciling and are named for the Monhegan ferries that ran in the 1920s. Breakfast includes apple puff pancake, muffins, fruit, omelets, blueberry blintzes, and more. *3 Eames Rd., 04538, tel. 207/633–7565. 4 rooms with bath. Facilities: pier. Full breakfast included. MC, V. Closed Jan. Expensive.*

The Pines. Families seeking a secluded setting with lots of room for little ones to run will be interested in this motel on a hillside a mile from town. Rooms have sliding glass doors opening onto private decks, two double beds, and small refrigerators. *Sunset Rd., Box 693, 04538, tel. 207/633–4555. 29 rooms with bath. Facilities: tennis, pool, playground. D, MC, V. Closed mid-Oct.–early May. Moderate.*

Brunswick   **The Great Impasta.** This small, storefront restaurant is a great spot *Dining*   for lunch, tea, or dinner. Try the seafood lasagna, or match your favorite pasta and sauce to create your own dish. *42 Maine St., tel. 207/729–5858. No reservations. AE, D, DC, MC, V. Inexpensive–Moderate.*

Lodging   **Captain Daniel Stone Inn.** This Federal inn overlooks the Androscoggin River. While no two rooms are furnished identically, all offer executive-style comforts and many have whirlpool baths and pullout sofas in addition to queen-size beds. A guest parlor, 24-hour breakfast room, and excellent service in the Narcissa Stone Restaurant make this an upscale escape from college-town funk. *10 Water St., 04011, tel. 207/725–9898. Continental breakfast included. AE, DC, MC, V. Expensive–Very Expensive.*

Freeport   **Harraseeket Lunch & Lobster Co.** This no-frills, bare-bones, genu-*Dining*   ine lobster pound and fried-seafood place is located beside the town landing in South Freeport. Seafood baskets and lobster dinners are what it's all about; there are picnic tables outside and a dining room inside. *Main St., South Freeport, tel. 207/865–4888. No reservations. No credit cards. Inexpensive.*

Dining and   **Harraseeket Inn.** This gracious Greek Revival home of 1850, just two *Lodging*   blocks from the biggest retailing explosion ever to hit Maine, includes a three-story addition that looks like an old New England inn—white clapboard with green shutters—but is in fact a steel and concrete structure with elevators, Jacuzzis, and modern fireplaces throughout. Despite these modern appointments, the Harraseeket gives its visitors a country-inn experience, with afternoon tea served in the mahogany drawing room. Guest rooms (vintage 1989) have reproductions of Federal canopy beds and bright, coordinated fabrics. The formal, no-smoking dining room upstairs is a simply decorated, light and airy space with picture windows facing the inn's garden courtyard. The New England–influenced Continental cuisine emphasizes fresh, local ingredients. Downstairs, the Broad Arrow Tavern appears to have been furnished by L. L. Bean, with fly rods, snowshoes, moose heads, and other hunting-lodge trappings. The fare is hearty, with less formal lunches and snacks, and dinners of charbroiled skewered shrimp and scallops, ribs, burgers, pasta, or lobster. *162 Main St., 04032, tel. 207/865–9377 or 800/342–6423. 54 rooms with bath, including 6 suites. Facilities: restaurant (reservations advised; collar shirt at dinner), tavern, croquet, working fireplace in some rooms. AE, D, DC, MC, V. Inn: Very Expensive. Restaurant: Expensive–Very Expensive.*

Georgetown
Dining

The Osprey. Located in a marina on the way to Reid State Park, this gourmet restaurant may be reached both by land and sea. The appetizers alone are worth the stop: homemade garlic and Sicilian sausages; artichoke strudel with three cheeses; and warm braised duck salad with Oriental vegetables in rice paper. Entrées might include such classics as saltimbocca or such originals as salmon en papillote with julienne leeks, carrots, and fresh herbs. The wine list is excellent. The glassed-in porch offers water views and breezes. *6 mi down Rte. 127, turn left at restaurant sign on Robinhood Rd., tel. 207/371–2530. Reservations advised. MC, V. Call ahead for off-season hours. Moderate–Expensive.*

Newcastle
Lodging
★

Newcastle Inn. The white-clapboard house, vintage mid-19th century, has a romantic living room with a fireplace, loveseat, plenty of books, and river views. It also has a sun porch with white wicker furniture and ice-cream parlor chairs. The "Stencil Room," a favorite common room, has a hand-decorated hardwood floor. Guest rooms have been carefully appointed with unique beds—an old spool bed, wrought-iron beds, a brass-pewter bed, a sleigh bed, and several canopy beds—and rabbits are everywhere: stuffed, wooden, ceramic. Breakfast is a gourmet affair that might include scrambled eggs with caviar in puff pastry, ricotta cheese pie, or frittata. The five-course, single-entrée dinner served nightly brings people back again and again. *River Rd., 04553, tel. 207/563–5685 or 800/832–8669. 15 rooms with bath. Facilities: 2 dining rooms. Full breakfast included; MAP available. MC, V. Expensive–Very Expensive.*

Peaks Island
Lodging

Keller's B&B. This turn-of-the-century home offers rustic accommodations with deck views of Casco Bay and the Portland skyline. The beach is only steps away from your room. Belgian waffles are served as part of the delicious breakfast. *20 Island Ave., tel. 207/766–2441. 4 rooms with bath. Full breakfast included. No credit cards. Moderate.*

**Pemaquid
Point**
*Dining and
Lodging*

The Bradley Inn. Within walking distance of the Pemaquid Point lighthouse, beach, and fort, the 1900 Bradley Inn began as a rooming house for summer rusticators and alternated between abandonment and operation as a B&B until its complete renovation in the early 1990s. Rooms are comfortable and uncluttered; ask for one of the cathedral-ceilinged, waterside rooms on the third floor, which offer breathtaking views of the sun setting over the water. The Ship's Restaurant offers a frequently rotating menu, including a variety of fresh seafood dishes; there's light entertainment in the pub on weekends. *Rte. 130, HC 61, Box 361, New Harbor 04554, tel. 207/677–2105. 12 rooms with bath, 1 cottage, carriage house. Facilities: restaurant, pub, croquet, bicycles, light entertainment on weekends. Continental breakfast included. Closed Jan.–Mar. AE, MC, V. Expensive–Very Expensive.*

Portland
Dining
★

The Back Bay Grill. Mellow jazz, a 28-foot mural of Portland, an impressive wine list, and good food make this simple, elegant restaurant a popular spot. Appetizers such as black-pepper raviolis of red swiss chard, pancetta, and Fontina cheese in chicken broth are followed by grilled chicken, halibut, oysters, salmon, trout, veal chops, or steak. Don't miss the desserts—the crème brûlée is legendary. *65 Portland St., tel. 207/772-8833. Reservations advised. Jacket advised. AE, D, DC, MC, V. Closed Sun. Expensive–Very Expensive.*

Alberta's. Small, bright, casual, and friendly, Alberta's specializes in what one waiter described as "electric American" cuisine: dishes like London broil spiced with garlic, cumin, and lime; pan-blackened rib-eye steak with sour cream and scallions; and Atlantic salmon fillet with orange-ginger sauce, grilled red cabbage, and apple salad. The two-tier dining room has photos mounted on salmon-hued walls, and the music ranges from country to classical. *21 Pleasant St., tel. 207/774-0016. Reservations accepted. AE, D, DC, MC, V. Beer and wine only. No lunch weekends. Moderate–Expensive.*

★ **Cafe Always.** White linen tablecloths, candles, and Victorian-style murals by local artists set the mood for innovative cuisine. Begin with Pemaquid Point oysters seasoned with pink peppercorns and champagne, or chicken and wild rice in a nori roll, before choosing from vegetarian dishes, pasta, or more substantial entrées, such as grilled tuna with a fiery Japanese sauce or leg of lamb with goat cheese and sweet peppers. *47 Middle St., tel. 207/774-9399. Reservations advised. MC, V. Closed Sun., Mon. Moderate–Expensive.*

Seamen's Club. Built just after Portland's Great Fire of 1866, and an actual sailors' club in the 1940s, this restaurant has become an Old Port Exchange landmark, with its Gothic windows and carved medallions. Seafood is an understandable favorite—moist, blackened tuna, salmon, and swordfish prepared differently each day and lobster fettuccini are among the highlights. *375 Fore St., tel. 207/772-7311. Reservations advised. AE, DC, MC, V. Moderate–Expensive.*

★ **Street and Co.** If the secret of a restaurant's success can be "keep it simple," Street and Co., the best seafood restaurant in Maine, goes one step further—"keep it small." You enter through the kitchen, with all its wonderful aromas, and dine amid dried herbs and shelves of staples on one of a dozen copper-topped tables (so your waiter can place a skillet of steaming seafood directly in front of you). Begin with lobster bisque or grilled eggplant—vegetarian dishes are the only alternatives to fish. Choose from an array of superb entrées, ranging from calamari, clams, or shrimp served over linguine, to blackened, broiled, pan-seared, or grilled seafood. The desserts are top-notch. *33 Wharf St., tel. 207/775-0887. Reservations advised. AE, MC, V. No lunch. Moderate–Expensive.*

Katahdin. Somehow, the painted tables, flea-market decor, mismatched dinnerware, and faux-stone bar work together here. The cuisine, large portions of home-cooked New England fare, is equally unpretentious and fun: Try the chicken potpie, fried trout, crab cakes, or the nightly Blue Plate special—and save room for a fruit cobbler for dessert. *106 High St., tel. 207/774-1740. No reservations. MC, V. Moderate.*

Lodging **Pomegranate Inn.** Clever touches such as faux marbling on the moldings and mustard-colored rag-rolling in the hallways give this bed-and-breakfast a bright, postmodern air. Most guest rooms are spacious and bright, accented with original paintings on floral and tropical motifs; the location on a quiet street in the city's Victorian Western Promenade district ensures serenity. Telephones and televisions, rare in an inn, make this a good choice for businesspeople. *49 Neal St., 04102, tel. 207/772-1006 or 800/356-0408. 7 rooms with* *bath, 1 suite. Full breakfast included. AE, D, MC, V. Expensive–Very Expensive.*

★ **Portland Regency Hotel.** The only major hotel in the center of the Old Port Exchange, the Regency building was Portland's armory in the late 19th century and is now the city's most luxurious, most distinctive hotel. The bright, plush, airy rooms have four-poster beds, tall standing mirrors, floral curtains, and loveseats. The health club, the best in the city, offers massage and has an aerobics studio, free weights, Nautilus equipment, a large Jacuzzi, sauna, and steam room. *20 Milk St., 04101, tel. 207/774–4200 or 800/727–3436. 95 rooms with bath, 8 suites. Facilities: restaurant, health club, nightclub, banquet and convention rooms. AE, D, DC, MC, V. Expensive.*

Sonesta Hotel. Across the street from the art museum and in the heart of the downtown business district, the 12-story brick building, vintage 1927, looks a bit dowdy today. Rooms in the tower section (added in 1961) have floor-to-ceiling windows, and the higher floors have harbor views. The small health club offers Universal gym equipment, rowing machines, stationary bikes, and a sauna. *157 High St., 04101, tel. 207/775–5411 or 800/777–6246. 202 rooms with bath. Facilities: 2 restaurants, 2 bars, health club, banquet and convention rooms. AE, D, DC, MC, V. Moderate–Expensive.*

The Arts

The Chocolate Church Arts Center (804 Washington St., tel. 207/442–8455) offers changing exhibits by Maine artists in a variety of mediums, including textiles, photography, painting and sculpture. The Center also hosts folk, jazz, and classical concerts; theater productions; and performances for children, including puppet shows and Portland Symphony Orchestra Kinderkonzerts. Sign up for classes and workshops in visual and performing arts. **Portland Performing Arts Center** (25A Forest Ave., Portland, tel. 207/761–0591) hosts music, dance, and theater performances.

Dance **Ram Island Dance Company** (25A Forest Ave., Portland, tel. 207/773–2562), the city's resident modern dance troupe, appears at the Portland Performing Arts Center.

Music **Bowdoin Summer Music Festival** (Bowdoin College, Brunswick, tel. 207/725–3322 for information or tel. 207/725-3895 for tickets) is a six-week concert series featuring performances by students, faculty, and prestigious guest artists. **Carousel Music Theater** ("The Meadows," Boothbay Harbor, tel. 207/633–5297) mounts musical revues from Memorial Day to Columbus Day. **Cumberland County Civic Center** (1 Civic Center Sq., Portland, tel. 207/775–3458) hosts concerts, sporting events, and family shows in a 9,000-seat auditorium. **Portland Symphony Orchestra** (30 Myrtle St., Portland, tel. 207/773–8191) gives concerts October through August.

Theater **Mad Horse Theatre Company** (955 Forest Ave., Portland, tel. 207/797–3338) performs contemporary and original works. **Maine State Music Theater** (Pickard Theater, Bowdoin College, Brunswick, tel. 207/725–8769) stages musicals from mid-June through August. **Portland Stage Company** (25A Forest Ave., Portland, tel. 207/774–0465), a producer of national reputation, mounts six productions, from November through April, at the Portland Performing Arts Center. **Theater Project of Brunswick** (14 School St., Brunswick, tel. 207/729–8584) performs from late June through August.

Nightlife

Gritty McDuff's—Portland's Original Brew Pub (396 Fore St., Portland, tel. 207/772–2739) has been serving its fine ales—brewed on the premises—to Portland and its visitors for more than five years. British pub fare, including steak-and-kidney pie and fish-and-chips, is served along with local seafood dishes. **Three Dollar Dewey's** (446 Fore St., Portland, tel. 207/772–3310), long a popular Portland night spot, is an English-style ale house. **Top of the East** (Sonesta Hotel, 157 High St., Portland, tel. 207/775–5411) has a view of the city and live entertainment—jazz, piano, and comedy.

McSeagull's Gulf Dock (Boothbay Harbor, tel. 207/633–4041) draws young singles with live music and a loud bar scene. **Raoul's Roadside Attraction** (865 Forest Ave., tel. 207/775–2494), southern Maine's hippest nightclub/restaurant, books both local and name bands, especially R&B, folk, and reggae groups.

Penobscot Bay

Purists hold that the Maine coast begins at Penobscot Bay, where the vistas over the water are wider and bluer, the shore a jumble of broken granite boulders, cobblestones, and gravel punctuated by small sand beaches, and the water numbingly cold. Port Clyde in the southwest and Stonington in the southeast are the outer limits of Maine's largest bay, 35 miles apart across the bay waters but separated by a drive of almost 100 miles on scenic but slow two-lane highways.

Rockland, the largest town on the bay, is Maine's major lobster distribution center and the port of departure for several bay islands. The Camden Hills, looming green over Camden's fashionable waterfront, turn bluer and fainter as one moves on to Castine, the elegant small town across the bay. Deer Isle is connected to the mainland by a slender, high-arching bridge, but Isle au Haut, accessible from Deer Isle's fishing town of Stonington, can be reached by passenger ferry only: More than half of this steep, wooded island is wilderness, the most remote section of Acadia National Park.

Important Addresses and Numbers

Visitor Information
Belfast Area Chamber of Commerce (Box 58, Belfast 04915, tel. 207/338–5900; Information booth: 31 Front St., open daily 10–6, May–Oct.). **Blue Hill Chamber of Commerce** (Box 520, Blue Hill 04614, no tel.). **Castine Town Office** (Emerson Hall, Court Street, Castine 04421, tel. 207/326–4502). **Deer Isle–Stonington Chamber of Commerce** (Box 459, Stonington 04681, tel. 207/348–6124). **Rockland–Thomaston Area Chamber of Commerce** (Harbor Park, Box 508, Rockland 04841, tel. 207/596–0376; open daily 8–5 in summer, weekdays 9–4 in winter). **Rockport-Camden-Lincolnville Chamber of Commerce** (Public Landing, Box 919, Camden 04843, tel. 207/236–4404; open weekdays 9–5, Sat. 10–5, Sun. 12–4 in summer; weekdays 9–5, Sat. 10–4 in winter). **Searsport Chamber of Commerce** (East Main St., Searsport 04974, tel. 207/548–6510).

Emergencies
Blue Hill Memorial Hospital (Water St., Blue Hill, tel. 207/374–2836). **Island Medical Center** (Airport Rd., Stonington, tel. 207/367–2311). **Penobscot Bay Medical Center** (Rte. 1, Rockport, tel. 207/596–8000). **Waldo County General Hospital** (56 Northport Ave., Belfast, tel. 207/338–2500).

Getting Around Penobscot Bay

By Car   Route 1 follows the west coast of Penobscot Bay, linking Rockland, Rockport, Camden, Belfast, and Searsport. On the east side of the bay, Route 175 (south from Rte. 1) takes you to Route 166A (for Castine) and Route 15 (for Blue Hill, Deer Isle, and Stonington). A car is essential for exploring the bay area.

Exploring Penobscot Bay

Numbers in the margin correspond to points of interest on the Penobscot Bay map.

From Pemaquid Point at the western extremity of Muscongus Bay to Port Clyde at its eastern extent, it's less than 15 miles across the water, but it's 50 miles for the motorist, who must return north to Route 1 to reach the far shore.

Travelers on Route 1 can make an easy detour south through Tenants Harbor and Port Clyde before reaching Rockland. Turn onto Route 131S at Thomaston, 5 miles west of Rockland, and follow the winding road past waterside fields, spruce woods, ramshackle barns, and trim houses. **Tenants Harbor,** 7 miles from Thomaston, is a quintessential Maine fishing town, its harbor dominated by squat, serviceable lobster boats, its shores rocky and slippery, its center a scattering of clapboard houses, a church, a general store. The fictional Dunnet Landing of Sarah Orne Jewett's classic sketches of Maine coastal life, *The Country of the Pointed Firs,* is based on this region.

Route 131 ends at Port Clyde, a fishing village that is the point of departure for the *Laura B.* (tel. 207/372–8848 for schedules), the mailboat that serves Monhegan Island. Tiny, remote **Monhegan Island,** with its high cliffs, fronting the open sea was known to Basque, Portuguese, and Breton fishermen well before Columbus "discovered" America. About a century ago Monhegan was discovered again by some of America's finest painters, including Rockwell Kent, Robert Henri, and Edward Hopper, who sailed out to paint the savage cliffs, the meadows, the wild ocean views, and the shacks of fisherfolk. Tourists followed, and today Monhegan is overrun with visitors in summer.

Returning north to Route 1, you have less than 5 miles to go to **Rockland** on Penobscot Bay. This large fishing port is the commercial hub of the coast, with working boats moored alongside a growing flotilla of cruise schooners. Although a number of boutiques and restaurants have emerged in recent years, the town has retained its working-class flavor—you are more likely to find rusting hardware than ice-cream shops at the water's edge.

The outer harbor is bisected by a nearly mile-long granite breakwater, which begins on Samoset Road and ends with a lighthouse that was built in 1888. Next to the breakwater, on the Rockland–Rockport town line, is the **Samoset Resort** (Warrenton St., Rockport, tel. 207/594–2511 or, outside ME, 800/341–1650), a sprawling oceanside resort featuring an 18-hole golf course, indoor and outdoor swimming pools, tennis, racquetball, restaurant, and fitness center.

In downtown Rockland is the **William A. Farnsworth Library and Art Museum.** Here are oil and watercolor landscapes of the coastal areas you have just seen, among them Andrew Wyeth's *Eight Bells* and N.C. Wyeth's *Her Room.* Jamie Wyeth is also represented in the col-

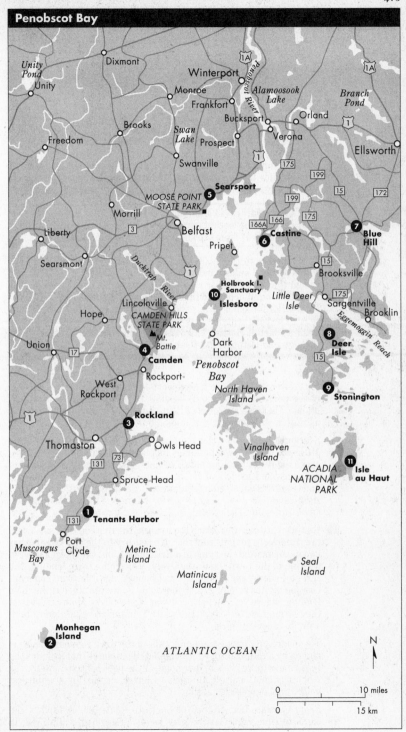

Penobscot Bay

Unity Pond
Unity
Dixmont
Winterport
1A
1A
Monroe
Alamoosook Lake
Branch Pond
Frankfort
Bucksport
Orland
Freedom
Brooks
Swan Lake
Prospect
Verona
1
Prospect
Swanville
175
199
Ellsworth
Searsport 5
MOOSE POINT STATE PARK
199
15
172
Morrill
Belfast
166A 166
175
Castine 6
Blue Hill 7
Liberty
3
Pripet
15
Searsmont
Ducktrap River
1
Brooksville
Holbrook I. Sanctuary
Little Deer Isle
Sargentville
Brooklin
Lincolnville
Islesboro 10
175
Hope
CAMDEN HILLS STATE PARK
Eggemoggin Reach
Union
Mt. Battie
Dark Harbor
Deer Isle 8
17
4 **Camden**
Penobscot Bay
15
West Rockport
Rockport
North Haven Island
Stonington 9
1
Rockland 3
Thomaston
Owls Head
Vinalhaven Island
131
73
ACADIA NATIONAL PARK
Isle au Haut 11
Spruce Head
1 **Tenants Harbor**
131
Port Clyde
Metinic Island
Seal Island
Muscongus Bay
Matinicus Island
2 **Monhegan Island**
ATLANTIC OCEAN
N

0   10 miles
0   15 km

lections, as are Winslow Homer, Rockwell Kent, and the sculptor Louise Nevelson. Next door, and part of the museum's holdings, is the Farnsworth Homestead, a handsome Greek Revival dwelling furnished in the Victorian style. *19 Elm St., tel. 207/596–6457. Admission (museum and homestead): $5 adults, $2 senior citizens, $1 children 8–18. Open Mon.–Sat. 10–5, Sun. 1–5. Museum closed Mon. Oct.–May; homestead closed Oct.–May.*

❹ From Rockland it's 8 miles north on Route 1 to **Camden,** "Where the mountains meet the sea"—an apt description, as you will discover when you step out of your car and look up from the harbor. Camden is famous not only for geography but for the nation's largest fleet of windjammers—relics and replicas from the age of sail. At just about any hour during the warmer months you're likely to see at least one windjammer tied up in the harbor, and windjammer cruises are a superb way to explore the ports and islands of Penobscot Bay.

Time Out | **Ayer's Fish Market** (43 Main St.) has the best fish chowder in town; take a cup to the pleasant park at the head of the harbor when you're ready for a break from the shops on Bay View and Main streets.

The entrance to the 5,500-acre **Camden Hills State Park** (tel. 207/ 236–3109) is 2 miles north of Camden on Route 1. If you're accustomed to the Rockies or the Alps, you may not be impressed with heights of not much more than 1,000 feet, yet the Camden Hills are landmarks for miles along the low, rolling reaches of the Maine coast. The park contains 20 miles of trails, including the easy Nature Trail up Mount Battie. The 112-site camping area, open mid-May through mid-October, has flush toilets and hot showers. *Admission to trails and auto road up Mount Battie: $2 adults, 50¢ children 5–11.*

❺ Farther north on Route 1, **Searsport**—Maine's second-largest deepwater port (after Portland)—claims to be the antiques capital of Maine. The town's stretch of Route 1 hosts a seasonal weekend flea market in addition to its antiques shops.

Searsport preserves a rich nautical history at the **Penobscot Marine Museum,** whose seven buildings display photos of 284 sea captains, artifacts of the whaling industry (lots of scrimshaw), hundreds of paintings and models of famous ships, navigational instruments, and treasures collected by seafarers. *Church St., tel. 207/548–2529. Admission: $5 adults, $3.50 senior citizens, $1.50 children 7–15. Open June–mid-Oct., Mon.–Sat. 9:30–5, Sun. 1–5.*

❻ Historic **Castine,** over which the French, the British, the Dutch, and the Americans fought from the 17th century to the War of 1812, has two museums and the ruins of a British fort, but the finest aspect of Castine is the town itself: the lively, welcoming town landing, the serene Federal and Greek Revival houses, and the town common. Castine invites strolling, and you would do well to start at the town landing, where you can park your car, and walk up Main Street past the two inns and on toward the white Trinitarian Federated Church with its tapering spire.

Turn right on Court Street and walk to the town common, which is ringed by a collection of white-clapboard buildings that includes the Ives House (once the summer home of the poet Robert Lowell), the Abbott School, and the Unitarian Church, capped by a whimsical belfry that suggests a gazebo.

From Castine, take Route 166 north to Route 199 and follow the ❼ signs to **Blue Hill.** Castine may have the edge over Blue Hill in

charm, for its Main Street is not a major thoroughfare and it claims a
more dramatic perch over its harbor, yet Blue Hill is certainly appealing and boasts a better selection of shops and galleries. Blue Hill
is renowned for its pottery, and two good shops are right in town.

The scenic Route 15 south from Blue Hill passes through Brooksville
and on to the graceful suspension bridge that crosses Eggemoggin
❽ Reach to **Deer Isle.** The turnout and picnic area at Caterpillar Hill, 1
mile south of the junction of Routes 15 and 175, commands a fabulous
view of Penobscot Bay, the hundreds of dark green islands, and the
Camden Hills across the bay, which from this perspective look like a
range of mountains dwarfed and faded by an immense distance—yet
they are less than 25 miles away.

Route 15 continues the length of Deer Isle—a sparsely settled landscape of thick woods opening to tidal coves, shingled houses with
lobster traps stacked in the yards, and dirt roads that lead to sum-
❾ mer cottages—to **Stonington,** an emphatically ungentrified community that tolerates summer visitors but makes no effort to cater to
them. Main Street has gift shops and galleries, but this is a working
port town, and the principal activity is at the waterfront, where
fishing boats arrive with the day's catch. The high, sloped island
that rises beyond the archipelago of Merchants Row is Isle au Haut
(accessible by mailboat from Stonington), which contains sections of
Acadia National Park.

Island **Islesboro,** reached by car-and-passenger ferry from Lincolnville
Excursions Beach (Maine State Ferry Service, tel. 207/789–5611 or 800/491–
❿ 4883), on Route 1 north of Camden, has been a retreat of wealthy,
very private families for more than a century. The long, narrow,
mostly wooded island has no real town to speak of; there are scatter-
ings of mansions as well as humbler homes at Dark Harbor and at
Pripet near the north end. Since the amenities on Islesboro are
quite spread out, you don't want to come on foot. If you plan to spend
the night on Islesboro, you should make a reservation well in advance (*see* Islesboro in Dining and Lodging, *below*).

Time Out **Dark Harbor Shop** (Main Rd., tel. 207/734–8878; open Memorial
Day–Labor Day) on Islesboro is an old-fashioned ice cream parlor
where tourists, locals, and summer folk gather for sandwiches,
newspapers, gossip, and gifts.

⓫ **Isle au Haut** thrusts its steeply ridged back out of the sea 7 miles
south of Stonington. Accessible only by passenger mailboat (tel.
207/367–5193), the island is worth visiting for the ferry ride alone, a
half-hour cruise amid the tiny, pink-shore islands of Merchants
Row, where you may see terns, guillemots, and harbor seals. More
than half the island is part of Acadia National Park; 17½ miles of
trails extend through quiet spruce and birch woods, along cobble
beaches and seaside cliffs, and over the spine of the central mountain
ridge. From late June to mid-September, the mailboat docks at
Duck Harbor within the park. The small campground here, with five
Adirondack-type lean-tos (open mid-May–mid-Oct.), fills up quickly; reservations are essential, and they can be made only after April
1 by writing to Acadia National Park (Box 177, Bar Harbor 04609).

What to See and Do with Children

Owls Head Transportation Museum, 2 miles south of Rockland on
Route 73, displays antique aircraft, cars, and engines and stages
weekend air shows. *Rte. 73, Owls Head, tel. 207/594–4418. Admis-*

sion: $4 adults, $3.50 senior citizens, $2.50 children 6–18. Open May–Oct., daily 10–5; Nov.–Apr., weekdays 10–4, weekends 10–3.

Off the Beaten Track

The Haystack Mountain School of Crafts, on Deer Isle, attracts internationally renowned glassblowers, potters, sculptors, jewelers, blacksmiths, printmakers, and weavers to its summer institute. You can attend evening lectures or visit the studios of artisans at work (by appointment only). *South of Deer Isle Village on Rte. 15, turn left at Gulf gas station and follow signs for 6 mi, tel. 207/348–2306. Admission free. Open June–Sept.*

Shopping

The most promising shopping areas are Main and Bay View streets in Camden, Main Street in Blue Hill, and Main Street in Stonington. Antiques shops are clustered in Searsport and scattered around the outskirts of villages, in farmhouses and barns; yard sales abound in summertime.

Antiques **Old Cove Antiques** (Rte. 15, Sargentville, tel. 207/359–2031) has folk art, quilts, hooked rugs, and folk carvings. **Old Deer Isle Parish House Antiques** (Rte. 15, Deer Isle Village, tel. 207/348–9964) is a place for poking around in the jumbles of old kitchenware, glassware, books, and linen. Billing itself the antiques capital of Maine, **Searsport** hosts a massive weekend flea market on Route 1 during the summer months. Indoor shops, most of them in old houses and barns, are also on Route 1, in Lincolnville Beach as well as in Searsport. Shops are open daily during the summer months, by chance or by appointment from mid-October through the end of May.

Art Galleries **Blue Heron Gallery & Studio** (Church St., Deer Isle Village, tel. 207/348–6051) features the work of the Haystack Mountain School of Crafts faculty. **Deer Isle Artists Association** (Rte. 15, Deer Isle Village, no tel.) has group exhibits of prints, drawings, and sculpture from mid-June through Labor Day. **Gallery 68** (68 Main St., Belfast, tel. 207/338–1558) carries contemporary art in all media. **Leighton Gallery** (Parker Point Rd., Blue Hill, tel. 207/374–5001) shows oil paintings, lithographs, watercolors, and other contemporary art in the gallery, and sculpture in its garden. **Maine's Massachusetts House Galleries** (Rte. 1, Lincolnville, tel. 207/789–5705) offers a broad selection of regional art, including bronzes, carvings, sculptures, and landscapes and seascapes in pencil, oil, and watercolor. The **Pine Tree Shop & Bayview Gallery** (33 Bay View St., Camden, tel. 207/236–4534) specializes in original art, prints, and posters—almost all with Maine themes.

Books **The Owl and Turtle Bookshop** (8 Bay View St., Camden, tel. 207/236–4769) sells a thoughtfully chosen selection of books, CDs, cassettes, and cards, including Maine-published works. The two-story shop has special rooms devoted to marine books and children's books. **Reading Corner** (408 Main St., Rockland, tel. 207/596–6651) carries an extensive inventory of cookbooks, children's books, Maine titles, best-sellers, and one of the area's best newspaper and magazine selections.

Crafts and Pottery **Chris Murray Waterfowl Carver** (Upper Main St., Castine, tel. 207/326–9033) sells award-winning wildfowl carvings and offers carving instruction. **Handworks Gallery** (Main St., Blue Hill, tel. 207/374–5613) carries unusual crafts, jewelry, and clothing. **North Country**

Textiles (Main St., Blue Hill, tel. 207/374–2715) specializes in fine woven shawls, placemats, throws, baby blankets, and pillows in subtle patterns and color schemes. **Rackliffe Pottery** (Rte. 172, Blue Hill, tel. 207/374–2297) is famous for its vivid blue pottery, including plates, tea and coffee sets, pitchers, casseroles, and canisters. **Rowantrees Pottery** (Union St., Blue Hill, tel. 207/374–5535) has an extensive selection of styles and patterns in dinnerware, tea sets, vases, and decorative items.

Furniture **The Windsor Chairmakers** (Rte. 1, Lincolnville, tel. 207/789–5188) sells custom-made, handcrafted beds, chests, china cabinets, dining tables, highboys—and, of course, chairs.

Gourmet **The Good Table** (72 Main St., Belfast, tel. 207/338–4880) carries an
Supplies imaginative array of gifts and gourmet items. **Heather Harland** (37 Bay View St., Camden, tel. 207/236–9661) is a two-story cornucopia of cookbooks, imported pottery and cookware, designer linens, and unusual condiments. **The Store** (435 Main St., Rockland, tel. 207/594–9246) features top-of-the-line cookware, table accessories, and an outstanding card selection.

Sports and Outdoor Activities

Boat Trips Windjammers create a stir whenever they sail into Camden harbor, and a voyage around the bay on one of them, whether for an afternoon or a week, is unforgettable. The season for the excursions is June through September. Excursion boats, too, provide a great opportunity for getting afloat on the waters of Penobscot Bay.

Camden *Angelique* (Yankee Packet Co., Box 736, tel. 207/236–8873 or 800/282–9989) makes three- and six-day trips. *Appledore* (0 Lily Pond Dr., tel. 207/236–8353 or 800/233–7437) has two-hour day sails as well as private charters. *Betselma* (35 Pearl St., tel. 207/236–4446) offers two two-hour excursions and eight one-hour trips from Camden's Public Landing every day between June and October. No reservations needed. **Maine Windjammer Cruises** (Box 617, tel. 207/236–2938 or 800/736–7981) has three two-masted schooners making three- and six-day trips along the coast and to the islands. *Roseway* (Box 696, tel. 207/236–4449 or 800/255–4449) takes three-, six-, and eight-day cruises.

Rockland **North End Shipyard Schooners** (Box 482, tel. 800/648–4544) operates three- and six-day cruises on the schooners *American Eagle, Isaac H. Evans*, and *Heritage*. The **Vessels of Windjammer Wharf** (Box 1050, tel. 207/236–3520 or 800/999–7352) organizes three- and six-day cruises on the *Pauline*, a 12-passenger motoryacht, and the *Stephen Taber*, a windjammer.

Rockport *Timberwind* (Box 247, tel. 207/236–0801 or 800/759–9250) is a 100-foot windjammer that sails out of Rockport harbor.

Stonington *Palmer Day IV* (tel. 207/367–2207) departs Stonington Harbor each day at 2 between July 1 and Labor Day for a two-hour excursion. Each Thursday morning, a special four-hour cruise stops at North Haven and Vinalhaven Islands.

Biking **Maine Sport** (Rte. 1, Rockport, tel. 207/236–8797) rents bikes, camping and fishing gear, canoes, kayaks, sailboards, ice skates, and skis.

Deep-Sea The 42-foot *Henrietta* (tel. 207/594–5411) departs the Rockland
Fishing Landings Marina (end of Sea St.) at 7:30 daily, returning at 5, from late May to September, weather permitting. Bait and tackle are provided, alcohol is prohibited, reservations are essential.

Water Sports Eggemoggin Reach is a famous cruising ground for yachts, as are the coves and inlets around Deer Isle and the Penobscot Bay waters between Castine and Camden. **Bay Island Yacht Charters** (Box 639, Camden, tel. 207/236–2776 or 800/421–2492) offers bareboat and crewed charters, daysailer rentals, and sailing lessons. **Maine Sport** (Rte. 1, Rockport, tel. 207/236–8797), the best sports outfitter north of Freeport, rents sailboards and organizes whitewater-rafting and sea-kayaking expeditions, starting at the store.

State Parks

Holbrook Island Sanctuary (on Penobscot Bay in Brooksville, tel. 207/326–4012) has a gravelly beach with a splendid view; hiking trails through meadow and forest; no camping facilities. **Moose Point State Park** (Rte. 1, between Belfast and Searsport, tel. 207/548–2882) is ideal for hikes and picnics overlooking Penobscot Bay; no camping facilities.

Dining and Lodging

The Camden-Rockport area has the greatest variety of restaurants, bed-and-breakfasts, and inns in the region. Dress is casual unless otherwise noted.

Blue Hill **The Firepond.** Reopened in 1994 after a two-year hiatus, the
Dining Firepond attracts customers from all over the region. The upstairs
★ dining room has the air of an English country gentleman's library, with built-in bookshelves, antiques, and Oriental carpets; a new street-level dining area increases the seating capacity to 120. The menu features favorites from the previous incarnation (lobster Firepond, with three cheeses, served over pasta) as well as new veal, pork, and scallop specialties. *Main St., tel. 207/374–9970. Reservations advised. AE, MC, V. Closed Jan.–Apr. Moderate.*

Jonathan's. The recently renovated downstairs room has captain's chairs, linen tablecloths, and local art; in the post-and-beam upstairs, there's wood everywhere, plus candles with hurricane globes and high-back chairs. The menu may include chicken breast in a fennel sauce with peppers, garlic, rosemary, and shallots; shrimp *scorpio* (served on linguine with a touch of ouzo and feta cheese); pan-seared medallions of venison with sweet-potato pancakes; and several fresh-fish entrées. The wine list has 200 selections from French and California vineyards as well as from the Bartlett Maine Estate Winery in Gouldshore. *Main St., tel. 207/374–5226. Reservations advised in summer. MC, V. Moderate.*

Lodging **The John Peters Inn.** The John Peters is unsurpassed for the privacy
★ of its location and the good taste in the decor of its guest rooms. The living room has two fireplaces, books and games, a baby grand piano, and Empire furniture. Oriental rugs are everywhere. Huge breakfasts in the light and airy dining rooms include the famous lobster omelet, served complete with lobster-claw shells as decoration. The Surry Room, one of the best rooms (all are nice), has a king-size bed, a fireplace, curly-maple chest, gilt mirror, and six windows. The large rooms in the carriage house, a stone's throw down the hill from the inn, have dining areas, cherry floors and woodwork, wicker and brass accents, and a modern feel. *Peters Point, Box 916, 04614, tel. 207/374–2116. 7 rooms with bath, 1 suite in inn; 6 rooms with bath in carriage house. Facilities: fireplaces in 9 bedrooms; pool, canoe, rowboats, sailboat, pond, 2 moorings. Full breakfast included. MC, V. Closed Nov.–Apr. Very Expensive.*

Camden **The Waterfront Restaurant.** A ringside seat on Camden Harbor can
Dining be had here; the best view is from the outdoor deck, open in warm
weather. The fare is primarily seafood: boiled lobster, scallops,
bouillabaisse, steamed mussels, Cajun barbecued shrimp. Lunchtime features include some Tex-Mex dishes, as well as lobster salad,
crabmeat salad, lobster and crab rolls, tuna niçoise, turkey melt,
and burgers. *Bay View St., tel. 207/236–3747. No reservations. AE,
MC, V. Moderate.*

Cappy's Chowder House. Lobster traps, a moose head, and a barbershop pole decorate the bar this lively but cozy eatery; the Crow's
Nest dining room upstairs is quieter and has a harbor view. Simple
fare is the rule here: burgers, sandwiches, seafood, and, of course,
chowder. A bakery downstairs sells breads, cookies, and filled croissants to go. *1 Main St., tel. 207/236–2254. No reservations. MC, V.
Inexpensive–Moderate.*

Dining and **Whitehall Inn.** Camden's best-known inn, just north of town on
Lodging Route 1, boasts a central white-clapboard, wide-porch ship-cap-
★ tain's home of 1843 connected to a turn-of-the-century wing. Just off
the comfortable main lobby with its faded Oriental rugs, the Millay
Room preserves memorabilia of the poet Edna St. Vincent Millay,
who grew up in the area. Rooms are sparsely furnished, with dark-
wood bedsteads, white bedspreads, and clawfoot bathtubs. Some
rooms have ocean views. The dining room is open to the public, offering traditional and creative American cuisine. Dinner entrées include Eastern salmon in puff pastry, swordfish grilled with roast
red pepper sauce, and lamb tenderloin. *52 High St. (Rte. 1), Box
558, 04843, tel. 207/236–3391 or 800/789–6565, fax 207/236–4427. 50
rooms with bath. Facilities: restaurant (reservations advised; no
lunch), tennis, shuffleboard, golf privileges. Rates are MAP. AE,
MC, V. Closed mid-Oct.–late May. Very Expensive.*

The Belmont. On a quiet side street three blocks from downtown and
a block off Route 1, this attractive inn has five cozy rooms and a
suite—all recently refurbished with antiques. The restaurant, open
to the public, has round tables well spaced in a setting of smoke-col-
ored walls and soft classical music or jazz. Chef Jerry Clare has been
featured on PBS; his changing menu of New American cuisine might
include lobster pad Thai, grilled pheasant with cranberries, chicken
with a tomato-coconut curry, or braised lamb shanks. *6 Belmont
Ave., 04843, tel. 207/236–8053. 5 rooms with bath, 1 suite. Facilities:
restaurant (reservations advised; no lunch). Full breakfast included. MC, V. Closed Dec.–May. Inn: Expensive–Very Expensive. Restaurant: Expensive.*

Lodging **Norumbega.** The stone castle amid Camden's elegant clapboard
★ houses, built in 1886 by Joseph B. Stearns, the inventor of duplex
telegraphy, was obviously the fulfillment of a fantasy. The public
rooms boast gleaming parquet floors, oak and mahogany paneling,
richly carved wood mantels over four fireplaces on the first floor
alone, gilt mirrors, and Empire furnishings. At the back of the
house, several decks and balconies overlook the garden, the gazebo,
and the bay. The view improves as you ascend; the penthouse suite
features a small deck, private bar, and a skylight in the bedroom. On
arrival, guests are welcomed with a complimentary apéritif and
wine. *61 High St., 04843, tel. 207/236–4646, fax 207/236–0824. 12
rooms with bath. Full breakfast included. AE, MC, V. Very Expensive.*

Windward House. A choice bed-and-breakfast, this Greek Revival
house of 1854, at the edge of downtown, features rooms furnished
with fishnet lace canopy beds, cherry highboys, curly-maple bedsteads, and clawfoot mahogany dressers. Guests are welcome to use

any of three sitting rooms, including the Wicker Room with its glass-top white wicker table where morning coffee is served. Breakfasts may include quiche, apple puff pancakes, peaches-and-cream French toast, or soufflés. A pleasant, private deck in back overlooks extensive English cutting gardens. *6 High St., 04843, tel. 207/236-9656. 6 rooms with bath, 1 suite. Full breakfast included. AE, MC, V. Expensive–Very Expensive.*

Castine
Dining and Lodging

The Pentagoet. The rambling, pale-yellow Pentagoet, a block from Castine's waterfront, has been a favorite stopping place for more than a century. The porch wraps around three sides of the inn and has two charming "courting swings." Decor in guest rooms includes hooked rugs, a mix of Victorian antiques, and floral wallpapers. Dinner in the deep-rose-and-cream formal dining room is an elaborate affair; entrées always include lobster creatively prepared, plus two other selections, such as grilled salmon with Dijon sauce, or pork loin braised in apple cider. Complimentary hors d'oeuvres are served evenings in the library-cum-music room, where there is often live chamber music. Inn guests can choose from a hearty breakfast or a lighter breakfast buffet. *Main St., 04421, tel. 207/326-8616. 16 rooms with bath. Facilities: restaurant (reservations required; jacket and tie advised; no lunch). Rates are MAP. MC, V. Closed Nov.–late May. Very Expensive.*

★ **The Castine Inn.** Light, airy rooms, upholstered easy chairs, and fine prints and paintings are typical of the guest-room furnishings here. One room has a pineapple four-poster bed. The third floor has the best views: the harbor over the handsome formal gardens on one side, Main Street on the other. The dining room, decorated with a wraparound mural of Castine and its harbor, is open to the public for breakfast and dinner; the menu features traditional New England fare—Maine lobster, crabmeat cakes with mustard sauce, roast leg of lamb, and chicken-and-leek potpie—plus such creative entrées as sweetbreads with hazelnut butter and roast duck with peach chutney. In the snug, English-style pub off the lobby are small tables, a fireplace, and antique spirit jars over the mantel. *Main St., Box 41, 04421, tel. 207/326-4365, fax 207/326-4570. 20 rooms with bath, 3 suites. Facilities: restaurant, pub. Full breakfast included. MC, V. Closed Nov.–mid-Apr. Moderate–Expensive.*

Deer Isle
Dining and Lodging
★

Pilgrim's Inn. The bright red, four-story, gambrel-roof house dating from about 1793 overlooks a mill pond and harbor in Deer Isle Village. The library has wing chairs and Oriental rugs; a downstairs taproom has a huge brick fireplace, pine furniture, braided rugs, and parson's benches. A generous array of hors d'oeuvres is served in the taproom and common room before dinner each evening. Guest rooms, each with its own character, sport English fabrics and select antiques. The dining room is in the attached barn, an open space both rustic and elegant, with farm implements, French oil lamps, and tiny windows. The five-course, single-entrée menu changes nightly; it might include rack of lamb or fresh local seafood, scallop bisque, asparagus and smoked salmon, and poached pear tart for dessert. *Rte. 15A, Deer Isle 04627, tel. 207/348-6615. 13 rooms, 8 with bath, 1 seaside cottage. Facilities: restaurant (reservations required; jacket advised; no lunch), bicycles. Full breatfast included; MAP available. No credit cards. Closed mid-Oct.–mid-May. Expensive.*

Goose Cove Lodge. The heavily wooded property at the end of a back road has 2,500 feet of ocean frontage, two sandy beaches, a long sandbar that leads to the Barred Island nature preserve, and nature trails. Some cottages and suites are in secluded woodlands, some on the shore, some attached, some with a single large room, others with one or two bedrooms. All but two units have fireplaces. In July and August the minimum stay is one week. The restaurant's prix-fixe four-course repast (always superb and always including at least one vegetarian entrée) is preceded by complimentary hors d'oeuvres. Friday nights, there's a lobster feast on the inn's private beach. *Box 40, Sunset 04683, tel. 207/348–2508, fax 207/348–2624. 11 cottages, 10 suites. Facilities: restaurant (reservations required; no lunch), sea kayaks, rowboat, canoe, volleyball. MC, V. Rates are MAP. Closed mid-Oct.–mid-May. Moderate–Expensive.*

Lodging **The Captain's Quarters Inn & Motel.** Accommodations, as plain and unadorned as Stonington itself, are in the middle of town, a two-minute walk from the Isle au Haut mailboat. You have your choice of motel-type rooms and suites or efficiencies, and you can take your breakfast muffins and coffee to the sunny deck overlooking the water. *Main St., Box 83, Stonington 04681, tel. 207/367–2420 or 800/942-2420. 13 units, 11 with bath. AE, D, MC, V. Inexpensive–Moderate.*

Isle au Haut **The Keeper's House.** This converted lighthouse-keeper's house, set
Lodging on a rock ledge surrounded by thick spruce forest, has its own special flavor. There is no electricity, but every guest receives a flashlight at registration; guests dine by candlelight on seafood or chicken and read in the evening by kerosene lantern. Trails link the historic inn with Acadia National Park's Isle au Haut trail network, and you can walk to the village—a collection of simple houses, a church, a tiny school, and a general store. The innkeepers are happy to pack lunches for anyone who wants to spend the day exploring the island. The five guest rooms are spacious, airy, and simply decorated with painted wood furniture and local crafts. A separate cottage, the Oil House, has no indoor plumbing. Access to the island is via the daily (except Sunday and holidays) mailboat from Stonington—a scenic, 40-minute trip. *Box 26, 04645, tel. 207/367–2261. 5 rooms with shared bath, 1 cottage. Facilities: dock, bicycle rentals. Three meals included, BYOB. No credit cards. No Sun. or holiday check-in. Closed Nov.–Apr. Expensive–Very Expensive.*

Islesboro **Dark Harbor House.** The yellow-clapboard, neo-Georgian summer
Lodging "cottage" of 1896 has a stately portico and a dramatic hilltop setting on the island of Islesboro. An elegant double staircase curves from the ground floor to the bedrooms, which are spacious, some with balconies, four with fireplaces, two with four-poster beds. The dining room, open to the public for dinner by reservation, features seafood specialties. *Main Rd., Box 185, 04848, tel. 207/734–6669. 10 rooms with bath. Facilities: restaurant. MC, V. Closed mid-Oct.–mid-May. Very Expensive.*

Lincolnville **Chez Michel.** This unassuming restaurant, serving up a fine rabbit
Beach pâté, mussels marinière, steak au poivre, and poached salmon,
Dining might easily be on the Riviera instead of Lincolnville Beach. Chef Michel Hetuin creates bouillabaisse as deftly as he whips up New England fisherman chowder, and he welcomes special requests. *Rte. 1, tel. 207/789–5600. Reservations accepted for 6 or more. D, MC, V. Closed Nov.–mid-Apr. Inexpensive–Moderate.*

North **The Lookout.** The stately white-clapboard building stands in a wide
Brooklin field at the tip of Flye Point, with a superb view of the water and the
Dining and mountains of Mount Desert Island. Although the floors slope and a
Lodging century of damp has left a certain mustiness, the rustic rooms are nicely furnished with country antiques original to the house and newer matching pieces. The larger, south-facing rooms command the view. Six cottages have one to four bedrooms each. With the din-

ing room expanded onto the porch, seven tables enjoy a view of the outdoors. Entrées could include filet mignon, grilled salmon, and shrimp and scallops Provençale; Thursday night is the lobster cookout. *HC 64, Box 4025, Brooklin 04616, tel. 207/359–2188. 6 rooms with shared bath, 6 cottages. Facilities: restaurant (reservations advised). MC, V. Full breakfast included. Closed mid-Oct.–mid-Apr (some cottages open off-season). Moderate.*

Rockland
Dining
★

Jessica's. Perched on a hill at the extreme southern end of Rockland, Jessica's occupies four cozy dining rooms in a tastefully renovated Victorian home. Billed as a European bistro, this restaurant lives up to its Continental label with creative entrées that include veal Zurich, paella, and pork Portofino; other specialties of the Swiss chef are focaccia with a selection of toppings and a half-dozen pasta and risotto offerings. *2 S. Main St. (Rte. 73), tel. 207/596–0770. Reservations advised. D, MC, V. Closed Tues. in winter. Moderate.*

Spruce Head
Dining and
Lodging

The Craignair Inn. Built in the 1930s as a boardinghouse for stonecutters and converted to an inn a decade later, the Craignair commands a dramatic view of rocky shore and lobster boats. Inside the three-story gambrel-roof house you'll find country clutter, books, and cut glass in the parlor; braided rugs, brass beds, and dowdy dressers in the guest rooms. In 1986 the owners converted a church dating from the 1890s into another accommodation with six rooms—each with bath—that have a more modern feel. Popular with birdwatchers, the Craignair has access to miles of hiking trails on adjacent Clark Island. The waterside dining room, decorated with Delft and Staffordshire plates, serves such fare as bouillabaisse, lemonpepper seafood kebab, and those New England standards: shore dinner, prime rib, and scampi. Lobster is on the menu every day. Homemade pies, bourbon pecan tart, and crème brûlée are the dessert headliners. *Clark Island Rd., HC 33, Box 533, 04859, tel. 207/594–7644 or 800/760–7644, fax 207/596–7124. 23 rooms, 8 with bath. Facilities: restaurant (reservations required; no lunch, closed mid-Oct.–mid-May), canoe, hiking trails. Full breakfast included. AE, MC, V. Closed Feb. Moderate–Expensive.*

Tenants
Harbor
Dining and
Lodging

East Wind Inn & Meeting House. On Route 131, 10 miles off Route 1, and set on a knob of land overlooking the harbor and the islands, the East Wind offers simple hospitality, a wraparound porch, and unadorned but comfortable guest rooms, each furnished with an iron bedstead, flowered wallpaper, and heritage bedspread. The dinner menu features seafood supreme, prime rib, boiled lobster, and baked stuffed haddock. *Rte. 131, Box 149, 04860, tel. 207/372–6366, fax 207/372–6320. 23 rooms, 12 with bath; 3 suites with bath. Facilities: restaurant (reservations advised; no lunch). Full breakfast included. AE, MC, V. Closed Feb. Moderate–Expensive.*

The Arts

Music
Bay Chamber Concerts (Rockport Opera House, Rockport, tel. 207/236–2823) offers chamber music every Thursday night and some Friday nights during July and August; concerts are given once a month September through May. **Kneisel Hall Chamber Music Festival** (Kneisel Hall, Rte. 15, Blue Hill, tel. 207/374–2811) has concerts Sunday and Friday in summer.

Theater
Camden Civic Theatre (Camden Opera House, tel. 207/236–7595), a community theater, specializes in musicals June through August. **Cold Comfort Productions** (Box 259, Castine 04421, no tel.), a community theater, mounts plays in July and August.

Nightlife

Dennett's Wharf (Sea St., Castine, tel. 207/326–9045) draws a crowd every lunchtime for a terrific view, and every evening for drinking and dancing. It's open from May to October. **Left Bank Bakery and Cafe** (Rte. 172, Blue Hill, tel. 207/374–2201) rates a gold star for bringing top-notch musical talent from all over the country to sleepy Blue Hill. **Peter Ott's Tavern** (16 Bay View St., Camden, tel. 207/236–4032) is a steakhouse with a lively bar scene. **Sea Dog Tavern & Brewery** (43 Mechanic St., Camden, tel. 207/236–6863) is a popular brew pub offering locally made lagers and ales in a retrofitted woolen mill.

Acadia

East of Penobscot Bay, Acadia is the informal name for the area that includes Mount Desert Island (pronounced dessert) and its surroundings: Blue Hill Bay; Frenchman Bay; and Ellsworth, Hancock, and other mainland towns. Mount Desert, 13 miles across, is Maine's largest island, and it harbors most of Acadia National Park, Maine's principal tourist attraction with more than 4 million visitors a year. The 40,000 acres of woods and mountains, lake and shore, footpaths, carriage roads, and hiking trails that make up the park extend as well to other islands and some of the mainland. Outside the park, on Mount Desert's east shore, an upper-class resort town of the 19th century has become a busy tourist town of the 20th century in Bar Harbor, which services the park with a variety of inns, motels, and restaurants.

Important Addresses and Numbers

Visitor Information **Acadia National Park** (Box 177, Bar Harbor 04609, tel. 207/288–3338; the Hulls Cove Visitor Center, off Rte. 3, at start of Park Loop Rd., is open daily 8–4:30, May–June and Sept.–Oct.; until 6 PM July–Aug.). **Bar Harbor Chamber of Commerce** (93 Cottage St., Box 158, Bar Harbor 04609, tel. 207/288–3393, 207/288–5103, or 800/288–5103; open weekdays 8–5 in summer, weekdays 8–4:30 in winter). There's also an information office in **Bluenose Ferry Terminal** (Rte. 3, Eden St.; open daily 8 AM–11 PM July–early Oct.; daily 9–5 mid-May–July and early Oct.–mid-Oct.).

Emergencies **Mount Desert Island Hospital** (10 Wayman La., Bar Harbor, tel. 207/288–5081). **Maine Coast Memorial Hospital** (50 Union St., Ellsworth, tel. 207/667–5311). **Southwest Harbor Medical Center** (Herrick Rd., Southwest Harbor, tel. 207/244–5513).

Getting Around Acadia

By Car North of Bar Harbor, the scenic 27-mile Park Loop Road takes leave of Route 3 to circle the eastern quarter of Mount Desert Island, with one-way traffic from Sieur de Monts Spring to Seal Harbor and two-way traffic between Seal Harbor and Hulls Cove. Route 102, which serves the western half of Mount Desert, is reached from Route 3 just after it crosses onto the island or from Route 233 west from Bar Harbor. All of these island roads pass in, out, and through the precincts of Acadia National Park.

Guided Tours

Acadia Taxi and Tours (tel. 207/288–4020) conducts half-day historic and scenic tours of the area.

National Park Tours (tel. 207/288–3327) operates a 2½-hour bus tour of Acadia National Park, narrated by a local naturalist. The bus departs twice daily, May–October, across from Testa's Restaurant at Bayside Landing on Main Street in Bar Harbor.

Acadia Air (tel. 207/667–5534), on Route 3 in Trenton, between Ellsworth and Bar Harbor at Hancock County Airport, offers aircraft rentals and seven different aerial sightseeing itineraries, from spring through fall.

Exploring Acadia

Numbers in the margin correspond to points of interest on the Acadia map.

Coastal Route 1 passes through Ellsworth, where Route 3 turns south to Mount Desert Island and takes you into the busy town of ❶ **Bar Harbor.** Most of Bar Harbor's grand mansions were destroyed in a mammoth fire that devastated the island in 1947, but many of the surviving estates have been converted to attractive inns and restaurants. Motels abound, yet the town retains the beauty of a commanding location on Frenchman Bay. Shops, restaurants, and hotels are clustered along Main, Mt. Desert, and Cottage streets.

Bar Harbor Historical Society Museum, on the lower level of the Jesup Memorial Library, displays photographs of Bar Harbor from the days when it catered to the very rich. Other exhibits document the great fire of 1947. *34 Mt. Desert St., tel. 207/288–4245. Admission free. Open mid-June–Oct., Mon.–Sat. 1–4 or by appointment.*

❷ The **Hulls Cove** approach to Acadia National Park is four miles northwest of Bar Harbor on Route 3. Even though it is often clogged with traffic in summer, the Park Loop Road provides the best introduction to Acadia National Park. At the start of the loop at Hulls Cove, the visitor center shows a free 15-minute orientation film. Also available at the center are books, maps of the hiking trails and carriage roads in the park, the schedule for naturalist-led tours, and cassettes for drive-it-yourself park tours.

Follow the road to the small ticket booth, where you pay the $5-per-❸ vehicle entrance fee. Take the next left to the parking area for **Sand Beach,** a small stretch of pink sand backed by the mountains of Acadia and the odd lump of rock known as The Beehive. The **Ocean Trail,** which parallels the Park Loop Road from Sand Beach to the Otter Point parking area, is a popular and easily accessible walk with some of the most spectacular scenery in Maine: huge slabs of pink granite heaped at the ocean's edge, ocean views unobstructed to the horizon, and **Thunder Hole,** a natural seaside cave into which the ocean rushes and roars.

Those who want a mountaintop experience without the effort of hik-❹ ing can drive to the summit of **Cadillac Mountain,** at 1,532 feet the highest point along the eastern seaboard. From the smooth, bald summit you have a 360-degree view of the ocean, islands, jagged coastline, and the woods and lakes of Acadia and its surroundings.

On completing the 27-mile Park Loop Road, you can continue your auto tour of the island by heading west on Route 233 for the villages on Somes Sound, a true fjord—the only one on the East Coast—

Acadia

5 which almost bisects Mount Desert Island. **Somesville,** the oldest settlement on the island (1621), is a carefully preserved New England village of white-clapboard houses and churches, neat green lawns, and bits of blue water visible behind them.

6 Route 102 south from Somesville takes you to **Southwest Harbor,** which combines the rough, salty character of a working port with the refinements of a summer resort community. From the town's Main Street (Rte. 102), turn left onto Clark Point Road to reach the harbor.

Time Out At the end of Clark Point Road in Southwest Harbor, **Beal's Lobster Pier** serves lobsters, clams, and crab rolls in season at dockside picnic tables.

7 Those who want to tour more of the island can continue south on Route 102, following Route 102A where the road forks, and passing through the communities of Manset and Seawall. The Bass Harbor Head lighthouse, which clings to a cliff at the eastern entrance to Blue Hill Bay, was built in 1858. The tiny lobstering village of **Bass Harbor** has cottages for rent, inns, a restaurant, a gift shop, and the Maine State Ferry Service's car-and-passenger ferry to Swans Island. *Tel. 207/244–3254, 5 daily runs June–Nov., fewer trips rest of year.*

Island Excursions Situated off the southeast shore of Mount Desert Island at the entrance to Somes Sound, the five **Cranberry Isles**—Great Cranberry, Islesford (or Little Cranberry), Baker Island, Sutton Island, and Bear Island—escape the hubbub that engulfs Acadia National Park in summer. Great Cranberry and Islesford are served by the **Beal &**

Bunker passenger ferry (tel. 207/244–3575) from Northeast Harbor, and by **Cranberry Cove Boating Company** (tel. 207/244–5882) from Southwest Harbor. Baker Island is reached by the summer cruise boats of the **Islesford Ferry Company** (tel. 207/276–3717) from Northeast Harbor; Sutton and Bear islands are privately owned.

❽ **Islesford** comes closest to having a village: a collection of houses, a church, a fishermen's co-op, a market, and a post office near the ferry dock. The **Islesford Historical Museum,** run by Acadia National Park, has displays of tools, documents relating to the island's history, and books and manuscripts of the writer Rachel Field (1894–1942), who summered on Sutton Island. The simple **Islesford Dock Restaurant** (tel. 207/244–7446), overlooking the island's harbor, serves lunch and dinner mid-June to mid-September. *Islesford Historical Museum, tel. 207/288–3338. Admission free. Open mid-June–Labor Day, Tues.–Sat. 10:30–noon, 12:30–4:30.*

❾ The 123-acre **Baker Island,** the most remote of the group, looks almost black from a distance because of its thick spruce forest. The Islesford Ferry cruise boat from Northeast Harbor offers a 4½-hour narrated tour, during which you are likely to see ospreys nesting on a sea stack off Sutton Island, harbor seals basking on ledges, and cormorants flying low over the water. Because Baker Island has no natural harbor, the tour boat ties up off-shore, and you take a fishing dory to get to shore.

What to See and Do with Children

Acadia Zoo has 30 acres of pastures, streams, and woods that shelter about 40 species of wild and domestic animals, including reindeer, wolves, monkeys, and a moose. A barn has been converted to a rainforest habitat for monkeys, birds, reptiles, and other Amazon creatures. *Rte. 3, Trenton, tel. 207/667–3244. Admission: $5 adults, $4 senior citizens and children 3–12. Open May–Nov., daily 9:30–5 (slightly later hours in midsummer).*

Mount Desert Oceanarium has exhibits in three locations on the fishing and sea life of the Gulf of Maine, as well as hands-on "touch tanks." *Clark Point Rd., Southwest Harbor, tel. 207/244–7330; Rte. 3, Thomas Bay, Bar Harbor, tel. 207/288–5005; Lobster Hatchery at 1 Harbor Pl., Bar Harbor, tel. 207/288–2344. Call for admission fees (combination tickets available for all 3 sites). Open mid-May–mid-Oct., Mon.–Sat. 9–5; hatchery open evenings July–Aug.*

Off the Beaten Track

Bartlett Maine Estate Winery offers tours, tastings, and gift packs. Wines are produced from locally grown apples, pears, blueberries, and other fruit. *Rte. 1, Gouldsboro, north of Bar Harbor (via Ellsworth), tel. 207/546–2408. Open June–mid-Oct., Tues.–Sat. 10–5, Sun. 12–5.*

Jackson Laboratory, a center for research in mammalian genetics, studies cancer, diabetes, heart disease, AIDS, muscular dystrophy, and other diseases. *Rte. 3, 3½ mi south of Bar Harbor, tel. 207/288–3371. Free audiovisual presentations mid-June–mid-Sept., Tues. and Thurs. at 3.*

Shopping

Bar Harbor in summer is prime territory for browsing for gifts, T-shirts, and novelty items; for bargains, head for the outlets that line

Route 3 in Ellsworth, which have good discounts on shoes, sportswear, cookware, and more.

Antiques   **E. and L. Higgins** (Bernard Rd., Bernard, tel. 207/244–3983) has a good stock of wicker, along with pine and oak country furniture. **Marianne Clark Fine Antiques** (Main St., Southwest Harbor, tel. 207/244–9247) has an eclectic array of formal and country furniture, American paintings, and accessories from the 18th and 19th centuries.

Books   **Port in a Storm Bookstore** (Main St., Somesville, tel. 207/244–4114) is a book lover's nirvana on a rainy day (or even a sunny one) on Mount Desert Island.

Crafts   **Acadia Shops** (5 branches: inside the park at Cadillac Mountain summit; Thunder Hole on Ocean Dr.; Jordan Pond House on Park Loop Rd.; and 45 and 85 Main St., Bar Harbor) sell crafts and Maine foods and books. **Island Artisans** (99 Main St., Bar Harbor, tel. 207/288–4214) is a crafts cooperative. **The Lone Moose–Fine Crafts** (78 West St., Bar Harbor, tel. 207/288–4229) has ship models, art glass, and works in clay, pottery, wood, and fiberglass. The **Nestegg Gallery** (12 Mt. Desert St., Bar Harbor, tel. 207/288–9048) carries upscale, handcrafted baubles.

Sports and Outdoor Activities

Biking, Jogging, Cross-Country Skiing   The network of carriage roads that wind through the woods and fields of Acadia National Park is ideal for biking and jogging when the ground is dry and for cross-country skiing in winter. The Hulls Cove Visitor Center has a carriage-road map.

Bikes can be rented at **Acadia Bike & Canoe** (48 Cottage St., Bar Harbor, tel. 207/288–9605); **Bar Harbor Bicycle Shop** (141 Cottage St., tel. 207/288–3886); and **Southwest Cycle** (Main St., Southwest Harbor, tel. 207/244–5856).

Boat Trips   ***Acadian Whale Watcher*** (Golden Anchor Pier, West St., tel. 207/
Bar Harbor   288–9794 or 800/421–3307) runs 3½-hour whale-watching cruises June–mid-October. ***Chippewa*** (Bar Harbor Inn Pier, tel. 207/288–4585 or 207/288–2373) is a 65-foot classic motor vessel that cruises past islands and lighthouses three times a day (including sunset) in summer. **Frenchman Bay Company** (Harbor Place, tel. 207/288–3322 or 800/508–1499) operates the windjammer *Bay Lady*, the nature/sightseeing cruise vessel *Acadian*, and the 300-passenger *Whale Watcher* in summer. ***Natalie Todd*** (Bar Harbor Inn Pier, tel. 207/288–4585 or 207/288–2373) offers two-hour cruises on a three-masted windjammer mid-May–mid-October.

Bass Harbor   **Bass Harbor Cruises** (Bass Harbor Ferry Dock, tel. 207/244–5365) operates two-hour nature cruises (with an Acadia naturalist) twice daily in summer.

Northeast   ***Blackjack*** (Town Dock, tel. 207/276–5043 or 207/288–3056), a 33-
Harbor   foot Friendship sloop, makes four trips daily, mid-June–mid-October.

Camping   The two campgrounds in Acadia National Park—**Blackwoods** (Rte. 3, tel. 800/365–2267), open year-round, and **Seawall** (Rte. 102A, tel. 207/244–3600), open late May to late September—fill up quickly during the summer season, even though they have a total of 530 campsites. Space at Seawall is allocated on a first-come, first-served basis, starting at 8 AM. Between mid-May and mid-October, reserve a Blackwoods site within eight weeks of a scheduled visit. No reservations are required off-season. Off Mount Desert Island, but convenient to it, the campground at **Lamoine State Park** (Rte. 84, Lamoine, tel. 207/667–4778) is open mid-May–mid-October; the 55-acre park has a splendid front-row seat on Frenchman Bay.

Canoeing and Sea Kayaking For canoe rentals and guided kayak tours, try **Acadia Bike & Canoe,** above, or **National Park Canoe Rentals** (137 Cottage St., Bar Harbor, tel. 207/288–0342, or Pretty Marsh Rd., Somesville, at the head of Long Pond, tel. 207/244–5854).

Carriage Rides **Wildwood Stables** (Park Loop Rd., near Jordan Pond House, tel. 207/276–3622) offers romantic tours in traditional horse-drawn carriages on the 51-mile network of carriage roads designed and built by philanthropist John D. Rockefeller. There are three two-hour trips and three one-hour trips daily, including a "tea-and-popover ride" that stops at Jordan Pond House (*see* Dining and Lodging, *below*) and a sunset ride to the summit of Day Mountain.

Hiking Acadia National Park maintains nearly 200 miles of foot and carriage paths, ranging from easy strolls along flatlands to rigorous climbs that involve ladders and handholds on rock faces. Among the more rewarding hikes are the Precipice Trail to Champlain Mountain, the Great Head Loop, the Gorham Mountain Trail, and the path around Eagle Lake. The Hulls Cove Visitor Center has trail guides and maps.

Sailing and Boating **Harbor Boat Rentals** (Harbor Pl., 1 West St., tel. 207/288–3757) has 13- and 17-foot Boston whalers and other powerboats. **Manset Yacht Service** (Shore Rd., tel. 207/244–4040) rents sailboats.

Dining and Lodging

Bar Harbor has the greatest concentration of accommodations on Mount Desert Island. Much of this lodging has been converted from elaborate 19th-century summer cottages. A number of fine restaurants are also tucked away in these old homes and inns. Dress is casual unless otherwise noted.

Bar Harbor **Dining** **Porcupine Grill.** Named for a cluster of islets in Frenchman Bay, this two-story restaurant has earned culinary fame for its cornbread-stuffed pork chops, crabmeat terrine made with local goat cheese, salmon with citrus relish, fresh pastas, and a Caesar salad tossed with croutons of fried shrimp. Soft green walls, antique furnishings, and Villeroy & Boch porcelain create an ambience that complements the cuisine. *123 Cottage St., tel. 207/288–3884. Reservations advised in summer. AE, MC, V. No lunch. Closed Mon.–Thurs. Jan.–June. Expensive.*

★ **George's.** Candles, flowers, and linens grace the tables in four small dining rooms in an old house. The menu shows a distinct Mediterranean influence in the phyllo-wrapped lobster; the lamb and wild game entrées are superb. Couples tend to linger in the romantic setting. *7 Stephen's La., tel. 207/288–4505. Reservations advised. AE, D, DC, MC, V. No lunch. Closed late Oct.–mid-June. Moderate–Expensive.*

Jordan Pond House. Oversize popovers (with homemade strawberry jam) and tea are a century-old tradition at this rustic restaurant in the park, where in fine weather you can sit on the terrace or the lawn and admire the views of Jordan Pond and the mountains. Teatime is 2:30 to 5:30. The dinner menu offers lobster stew, seafood thermidor, and fisherman's stew. *Park Loop Rd., tel. 207/276–3316. Reserve a day ahead in summer. AE, D, MC, V. Closed late Oct.–May. Moderate.*

Lodging **Holbrook House.** Built in 1876 as a summer home and originally
known as Ashley Cottage, the lemon-yellow Holbrook House stands
right on Mt. Desert Street, the main access route through Bar Harbor. The downstairs public rooms include a lovely, formal sitting
room with bright, summery chintz on chairs and framing windows
and a Duncan Phyfe sofa upholstered in white silk damask. The
guest rooms and two separate cottages are all furnished with loving-
ly handled family pieces in the same refined taste as the public
rooms. *74 Mt. Desert St., 04609, tel. 207/288–4970 or 800/695–
1120. 10 rooms with bath in inn, 2 cottage suites with private patios
and hammocks. Facilities: croquet, cable TV in library and cottage
suites, off-street parking. Full breakfast and afternoon refreshments included. MC, V. Closed late-Oct.–May. Very Expensive.*

★ **Inn at Canoe Point.** Seclusion and privacy are bywords of this snug,
100-year-old Tudor-style house on the water at Hulls Cove, 2 miles
from Bar Harbor and ¼ mile from Acadia National Park's Hulls Cove
Visitor Center. The Master Suite, a large room with a fireplace, is a
favorite for its size and for its French doors, which open onto a waterside deck. The inn's large living room has huge windows on the
water, a granite fireplace, and a waterfront deck where a full breakfast is served on summer mornings. *Box 216, Rte. 3, 04609, tel. 207/
288–9511. 3 rooms with bath, 2 suites. Full breakfast included. No
credit cards. Very Expensive.*

Cleftstone Manor. Attention, lovers of Victoriana! This inn was
made in high Victorian heaven expressly for you. Ignore the fact
that it is set amid sterile motels just off Route 3, the road along
which traffic roars into Bar Harbor. Do not be put off by the unprom-
ising, rambling, green-shuttered exterior. Inside, a deeply plush
mahogany-and-lace world of Victorian splendor awaits you. The
parlor is cool and richly furnished with red velvet and brocade-trim
sofas with white doilies, grandfather and mantel clocks, and oil
paintings hanging on powder-blue walls. Guest rooms are similarly
ornate, and six rooms have fireplaces. *Rte. 3, Eden St., 04609, tel.
207/288–4951 or 800/962–9762. 14 rooms with bath, 2 suites. Full
breakfast and afternoon and evening refreshments included. D,
MC, V. Closed Nov.–late Apr. Expensive–Very Expensive.*

Mira Monte Inn & Suites. Built as a summer home in 1864, the Mira
Monte bespeaks Victorian leisure, with columned verandas, latticed
bay windows, and 2 acres of landscaped grounds for strolling and
sunning; and the inn is set back far enough from the road to ensure
quiet and seclusion. Guest rooms have brass or four-poster beds,
white wicker, hooked rugs, lace curtains, and oil paintings in gilt
frames. The rear-facing rooms offer sunny garden views. Many
rooms have porches, fireplaces, and separate entrances. Three
suites in a separate building overlook the gardens and offer such
amenities as Jacuzzis, fireplaces, and private decks. *69 Mt. Desert
St., 04609, tel. 207/288–4263 or 800/553–5109, fax 207/288–3115. 12
rooms with bath, 3 deluxe suites. Facilities: croquet, badminton,
horseshoes. Full breakfast included. AE, D, MC, V. Closed Nov.–
May. Expensive–Very Expensive.*

Wonder View Inn. Although the rooms here are standard motel accommodations, with two double beds and nondescript furniture,
this establishment is distinguished by its extensive grounds, an imposing view of Frenchman Bay, and a convenient location opposite
the Bluenose Ferry Terminal. The woods muffle the sounds of traffic
on Route 3. The gazebo-shaped dining room—the Rinehart Dining
Pavilion—has picture windows overlooking the bay and is open to
the public for breakfast and dinner. *Rte. 3, Box 25, 04609, tel. 207/
288–3358 or 800/341–1553. 80 rooms with bath. Facilities: dining*

*room, pool. AE, D, MC, V. Closed late Oct.–mid-May. Moderate–
Expensive.*

Hancock
*Dining and
Lodging*
★

Le Domaine. The seven rooms in the inn are done in French country
style, with chintz and wicker, simple desks, and window seats. Five
of the rooms have balconies or porches over the gardens. The 100-
acre property 9 miles east of Ellsworth offers paths for walking and
badminton on the lawn. The elegant but not intimidating dining
room has polished wood floors, copper pots hanging from the mantel, and silver, crystal, and linen on the tables. A new screened-in
dining area overlooks the gardens in back. Owner Nicole Purslow,
trained at Cordon Bleu in her native France, prepares such specialties as *lapin pruneaux* (rabbit in a rich brown sauce), sweetbreads
with lemon and capers, and coquilles St. Jacques. *Rte. 1, Box 496,
04640, tel. 207/422–3395, 207/422–3916, or 800/554–8498; fax 207/
422–2316. 7 rooms with bath. Facilities: restaurant (reservations
advised; no lunch), nature trails, rowboat, trout pond. AE, MC, V.
Rates are MAP. Closed Nov.–mid-May. Inn: Very Expensive. Restaurant: Expensive.*

**Northeast
Harbor**
*Dining and
Lodging*

Asticou Inn. This grand turn-of-the-century inn at the head of exclusive Northeast Harbor serves a loyal clientele. Guest rooms in the
main building have a country feel, with bright fabrics, white lace
curtains, and white painted furniture. The more modern cottages
scattered around the grounds afford greater privacy; among them,
the decks and picture windows make the Topsider Cottages particularly attractive. Also part of the inn is the Victorian-style Cranberry Lodge, across the street. At night, guests of the inn trade
Topsiders and polo shirts for jackets and ties to dine in the stately
formal dining room, which is open to the public by reservation. A
typical menu might feature swordfish with orange mustard glaze,
lobster, shrimp scampi, and chicken in a lemon cream and mushroom
sauce. *Rte. 3, 04662, tel. 207/276–3344 or 800/258–3373, fax 207/
276–3373. 27 rooms with bath, 23 suites, 6 cottages. Facilities: restaurant (reservations required; jacket and tie advised; no lunch),
tennis, pool. Rates are MAP in summer. MC, V. Inn and restaurant closed mid-Sept.–mid-June; cottages, lodge closed Jan.–Apr.
Inn: Very Expensive (lodge: Moderate–Expensive). Restaurant:
Expensive.*

**Southwest
Harbor**
*Dining and
Lodging*

Claremont Hotel. Built in 1884 and operated continuously as an inn,
the Claremont calls up memories of long, leisurely vacations of days
gone by. The yellow-clapboard structure commands a view of Somes
Sound, croquet is played on the lawn, and cocktails and lunch are
served at the Boat House in midsummer. The highlight of the summer season is the annual Claremont Croquet Classic, held at the hotel the first week in August. Guest rooms are bright, white, and
quite plain; cottages and two guest houses on the grounds are homier and woodsier. The large, airy dining room of the inn, open to the
public for breakfast and dinner, is awash in light streaming through
the picture windows. The atmosphere is elegant, with crystal, silver, and china service. The menu changes weekly and always includes fresh fish and at least one vegetarian entrée. *Off Clark Point
Rd., Box 137, 04679, tel. 207/244–5036, fax 207/244–3512. 24 rooms,
all with bath; 12 cottages, 2 guest houses. Facilities: restaurant (reservations required; jacket required for dinner; no lunch), clay tennis court, croquet, bicycles, rowboats, dock and moorings. Rates
are MAP. No credit cards. Hotel and restaurant closed mid-Oct.–
mid-June. Cottages closed Nov.–late May. Hotel: Expensive–Very
Expensive. Restaurant: Moderate.*

The Arts

Music **Arcady Music Festival** (tel. 207/288–3151) schedules concerts (primarily classical) at a number of locations around Mount Desert Island, as well as at selected off-island sites, from mid-July through August. **Bar Harbor Festival** (59 Cottage St., Bar Harbor, tel. 207/288–5744) programs recitals, jazz, chamber music, string orchestra, and pops concerts by up-and-coming young professionals from mid-July to mid-August. **Pierre Monteux School for Conductors and Orchestra Musicians** (Rte. 1, Hancock, tel. 207/422–3931) presents public concerts by faculty and students during the term (late June–late July). Symphonic concerts are Sundays at 5 and chamber-music concerts are Wednesdays at 8—all held in the Pierre Monteux Memorial Hall.

Theater **Acadia Repertory Company** (Masonic Hall, Rte. 102, Somesville, tel. 207/244–7260) mounts plays in July and August.

Nightlife

Acadia has relatively little nighttime activity. Gaining a wide reputation for its funkiness, the **Beat Puppy Showcase Tap** (119 Main St., Bar Harbor, tel. 207/288–4477) concentrates on blues but also headlines reggae, rock, and other styles. The lively nightspot opens at noon daily during the summer (at 3 in the off-season) and is closed Jan. 1–March 31. The lounge at the **Moorings Restaurant** (Shore Rd. Manset, tel. 207/244–7070), accessible by boat and car, is open until after midnight from mid-May through October, and the company is a lively boating crowd.

Western Lakes and Mountains

Less than 20 miles northwest of Portland and the coast, the lakes and mountains of western Maine begin their stretch north along the New Hampshire border to Québec. In winter this is ski country; in summer the woods and waters draw vacationers to recreation or seclusion in areas less densely populated than much of Maine's coast.

The Sebago–Long Lake region has antiques stores and lake cruises on a 42-mile waterway. Kezar Lake, tucked away in a fold of the White Mountains, has long been a hideaway of the wealthy. Bethel, in the Androscoggin River valley, is a classic New England town, its town common lined with historic homes. The far more rural Rangeley Lake area brings long stretches of pine, beech, spruce, and sky—and stylish inns and bed-and-breakfasts with easy access to golf, boating, fishing, and hiking.

Important Addresses and Numbers

Visitor Information Off-season, most chambers are open weekdays 9–5; the hours below are for summer only.

Bethel Area Chamber of Commerce (Box 439, Bethel, 04217, tel. 207/824–2282; open weekdays 9:30–5). **Bridgton–Lakes Region Chamber of Commerce** (Box 236, Bridgton, 04009, tel. 207/647–3472; open daily 10–4 July and Aug., reduced hours rest of year). **Rangeley Lakes Region Chamber of Commerce** (Box 317, Rangeley, 04970, tel. 207/864–5571; open Mon.–Sat. 9–5).

Emergencies **Bethel Area Health Center** (Railroad St., Bethel, tel. 207/824–2193). **Dr. Anne Hunter** (Main St., Rangeley, tel. 207/864–3303).

Getting Around the Western Lakes and Mountains

By Plane **Mountain Air Service** (Rangeley, tel. 207/864–5307) provides air access to remote areas.

By Car A car is essential to a tour of the western lakes and mountains. Of the variety of routes available, the itinerary that follows takes Route 302 to Route 26 to Route 2 to Route 17 to Route 4/16 to Route 142.

Guided Tours

Naples Flying Service (Naples Causeway, tel. 207/693–6591) offers sightseeing flights over the lakes in summer.

Exploring the Western Lakes and Mountains

Numbers in the margin correspond to points of interest on the Western Maine map.

① A tour of the lakes begins at **Sebago Lake,** west of Route 302, fewer than 20 miles northwest of Portland. At the north end of the lake, the **Songo Lock** (tel. 207/693–6231), which permits the passage of watercraft from Sebago Lake to Long Lake, is the one surviving lock of the Cumberland and Oxford Canal. Built of wood and masonry, the original lock dates from 1830 and was expanded in 1911; today it sees heavy traffic during the summer months.

The 1,300-acre **Sebago Lake State Park** on the north shore of Sebago Lake offers opportunities for swimming, picnicking, camping, boating, and fishing (salmon and togue). *Tel. June 20–Labor Day, 207/693–6613; other times, 207/693–6231.*

Route 302 continues north to Naples, where the Naples Causeway has rental craft for fishing or cruising on Long Lake. You can also see the **Naples Historical Society Museum,** which includes a jailhouse, a bandstand, a Dodge 1938 fire truck, a coach, and information about the Cumberland and Oxford Canal and the Sebago–Long Lake steamboats. *Village Green, Rte. 302, tel. 207/693–6364. Admission free. Open July–Aug.; call for hours.*

Continue on to rather drab Bridgton, near Highland Lake, which has antiques shops in and around the town. You might also visit the **Bridgton Historical Society Museum,** housed in a former fire station built in 1902; it displays artifacts of the area's history and materials on the local narrow-gauge railroad. *Gibbs Ave., tel. 207/647–2765. Admission free. Open June–Aug., Mon.–Sat. 1–4.*

The most scenic route to Bethel, 30 miles to the north, follows Route 302 west from Bridgton, across Moose Pond to Knight's Hill Road, turning north to Lovell and Route 5, which will take you on to Bethel. It's a drive that lets you admire the jagged crests of the White Mountains outlined against the sky to the west and the lush, rolling **②** hills that alternate with brooding forests at roadside. At **Center Lovell** you can barely glimpse the secluded Kezar Lake to the west, the retreat of wealthy and very private people; Sabattus Mountain, which rises behind Center Lovell, has a public hiking trail and stupendous views of the Presidential range from the summit.

③ **Bethel** is pure New England, a town with white-clapboard houses and white-steeple churches and a mountain vista at the end of every

Western Maine

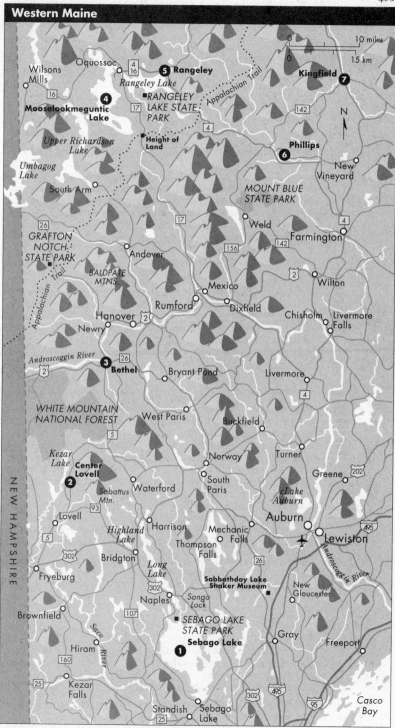

Wilsons Mills

Oquossoc

[4]
[16]

5 Rangeley

Kingfield **7**

Rangeley Lake

■ RANGELEY
LAKE STATE
PARK

[16]

4

**Mooselookmeguntic
Lake**

[17]

[142]

0   10 miles

0   15 km

*Upper Richardson
Lake*

■ *Height of
Land*

[4]

Phillips **6**

N

*Umbagog
Lake*

South Arm

New
Vineyard

[26]

**GRAFTON
NOTCH
STATE PARK**
■

Andover

[17]

MOUNT BLUE
STATE PARK

Weld

[156]

[142]

Farmington

[4]

*BALDPATE
MTNS.*

Appalachian Trail

Mexico

Dixfield

[2]

Wilton

[2]

Rumford

Chisholm

Livermore
Falls

Hanover

Newry

[26]

Androscoggin River

[2]

3 Bethel

Bryant Pond

Livermore

[4]

**WHITE MOUNTAIN
NATIONAL FOREST**

West Paris

Buckfield

[5]

*Kezar
Lake*

**Center
Lovell**

Norway

Turner

2

*Sabattus
Mtn.*

Waterford

South
Paris

*cLake
Auburn*

Greene

[202]

Lovell

[93]

Harrison

Mechanic
Falls

Auburn

[5]

*Highland
Lake*

Thompson
Falls

[26]

Lewiston

[495]

Bridgton

[302]

*Long
Lake*

Sabbathday Lake
Shaker Museum
■

Androscoggin River

Fryeburg

*Songo
Lock*

New
Gloucester

Brownfield

Naples

[107]

*Saco
River*

■ **SEBAGO LAKE
STATE PARK**

Gray

Freeport

Hiram

Sebago Lake **1**

[160]

[26]

[302]

[495]

Kezar
Falls

Standish

Sebago
Lake

[25]

*Casco
Bay*

[95]

N E W   H A M P S H I R E

[25]

street. In the winter this is ski country, and Bethel serves the Sunday River area (*see* Maine Skiing in Chapter 2, Skiing New England). A stroll of Bethel should begin at the **Moses Mason House and Museum,** a Federal home of 1813. On the town common, across from the sprawling Bethel Inn and Country Club, the Mason Museum has nine period rooms and a front hall and stairway wall decorated with murals by Rufus Porter. You can also pick up materials for a walking tour of Bethel Hill Village, most of which is on the National Register of Historic Places. *Broad St., tel. 207/824–2908. Admission: $2 adults, $1 children under 12. Open July–Labor Day, Tues.–Sun. 1–4; day after Labor Day–June, by appointment.*

The **Major Gideon Hastings House** nearby on Broad Street has a columned front portico typical of the Greek Revival style. Around the common, on Church Street, stands the severe white **West Parish Congregational Church** (1847), with its unadorned triangular pediment and steeple supported on open columns. Beyond the church is the campus of **Gould Academy,** a preparatory school chartered in 1835; the dominant style of the school buildings is Georgian, and the tall brick main campus building is surmounted by a white cupola. Main Street will take you from the common past the Town Hall-Cole Block, built in 1891, to the shops.

The routes north from Bethel to the Rangeley district are all scenic, particularly in the autumn when the maples are aflame. On Route 26 it's about 12 miles to **Grafton Notch State Park,** where you can hike to stunning gorges and waterfalls and into the Baldpate Mountains. En route to the park, in the town of Newry, make a short detour to the **Artist's Bridge** (turn off of Rte. 26 onto Sunday River Rd. and drive about 3 mi) the most painted and photographed of Maine's eight covered bridges. Route 26 continues on to Errol, New Hampshire, where Route 16 will return you east around the north shore of Mooselookmeguntic Lake, through Oquossoc, and into Rangeley.

A more direct—if marginally less scenic—tour follows Route 2 north and east from Bethel to the twin towns of Rumford and Mexico, where Route 17 continues north to Oquossoc, about an hour's drive. When you've gone about 20 minutes beyond Rumford, the signs of civilization all but vanish and you pass through what seems like untouched territory; in fact, the lumber companies have long since tackled the virgin forests, and sporting camps and cottages are tucked away here and there. The high point of this route is **Height of Land,** about 30 miles north of Rumford, with its unforgettable views of range after range of mountains and the huge, island-studded blue mass of Mooselookmeguntic Lake directly below. Turnouts on both sides of the highway allow you to pull over for a long look.

❹ Route 4 ends at Haines Landing on **Mooselookmeguntic Lake,** 7 miles west of Rangeley. Here you can stand at 1,400 feet above sea level and face the same magnificent scenery you admired at 2,400 feet from Height of Land on Route 17. Boat and canoe rentals are available at Mooselookmeguntic House.

❺ **Rangeley,** north of Rangeley Lake on Route 4/16, has lured fisherfolk, hunters, and winter-sports enthusiasts for a century to its more than 40 lakes and ponds within a 20-mile radius and 450 square miles of woodlands. Rangeley has a rough, wilderness feel to it—indeed some of its best parts, including the choice lodgings, are tucked away in the woods, around the lake, and along the golf course.

On the south shore of Rangeley Lake, **Rangeley Lake State Park** (tel. 207/864–3858) offers superb lakeside scenery, swimming, picnic tables, a boat ramp, showers, and camping sites set well apart in a spruce and fir grove.

6 In **Phillips,** 20 miles southeast of Rangeley on Route 4, the Sandy River & Rangeley Lakes Railroad, a restored narrow-gauge railroad, has a mile of track through the woods, where you can board a century-old train drawn by a replica of the Sandy River No. 4 locomotive. *Tel. 207/639–3352. Fare: $3 adults, $1.50 children 6–12. Open May–Oct., 1st and 3rd Sun. each month; rides at 11, 1, and 3.*

Just west of Phillips on Route 4, Route 142 takes you northeast to
7 **Kingfield,** prime ski country in the heart of the western mountains. In the shadows of Mt. Abraham and Sugarloaf Mountain, Kingfield has everything a "real" New England town should have: a general store, historic inns, and a white-clapboard church. The **Stanley Museum** houses a collection of original Stanley Steamer cars built by the Stanley twins, Kingfield's most famous natives. *School St., tel. 207/265–2729. Suggested donation: $2 adults, $1 children. Open July 4–Oct., Tues.–Sun. 1–4; Nov.–July 3, call for hours.*

What to See and Do with Children

Songo River Queen II, a 92-foot stern-wheeler, takes passengers on hour-long cruises on Long Lake and longer voyages down the Songo River and through Songo Lock. *Rte. 302, Naples Causeway, tel. 207/693–6861. Admission: Songo River ride, $9 adults, $6 children; Long Lake cruise, $6 adults, $4 children. July–Labor Day, 5 trips daily; June and Sept., weekends.*

Off the Beaten Track

Sabbathday Lake Shaker Museum on Route 26, 20 miles north of Portland, is part of one of the oldest Shaker communities in the United States (established in the late 18th century) and the last one in Maine. Members continue to farm crops and herbs, and visitors are shown the meetinghouse of 1794—a paradigm of Shaker design—and the ministry shop with 14 rooms of Shaker furniture, folk art, tools, farm implements, and crafts of the 18th to early 20th centuries. On Sunday, the Shaker day of prayer, the community is closed to visitors. *Rte. 26, New Gloucester, tel. 207/926–4597. Tour: $4 adults, $2 children 6–12; extended tour, $5.50 adults, $2.75 children. Open Memorial Day–Columbus Day, Mon.–Sat. 10–4:30.*

Shopping

Antiques **The Lyons' Den** (Rte. 2, Hanover, near Bethel, tel. 207/364–8634), a great barn of a place, carries glass, china, tools, prints, rugs, handwrought iron, and some furniture. **Wales & Hamblen Too! Antiques and Gifts** (134 Main St., Bridgton, tel. 207/647–8344) carries quilts, jewelry, country furniture, wicker, and Depression glass.

Crafts **Bonnema Potters** (146 Lower Main St., Bethel, tel. 207/824–2821) features colorful modern designs in plates, lamps, tiles, and vases. **Cry of the Loon Shop Fine Gifts and Crafts Art Gallery** (Rte. 302, South Casco, tel. 207/655–5060) has crafts, gifts, gourmet foods, and two galleries.

Sports and Outdoor Activities

Biking **Sunday River Ski Resort** in Newry operates a mountain bike park (Sunday River Access Rd., tel. 207/824–3000) with lift-accessed trails.

Canoeing The Saco River (near Fryeburg) is a favorite route, with a gentle stretch from Swan's Falls to East Brownfield (19 miles). Another scenic stretch runs from East Brownfield to Hiram (14 miles). Rangeley and Mooselookmeguntic lakes are good for scenic canoeing.

For canoe rentals, try **Canal Bridge Canoes** (Rte. 302, Fryeburg Village, tel. 207/935–2605), **Mooselookmeguntic House** (Haines Landing, Oquossoc, tel. 207/864–2962), **Rangeley Region Sport Shop** (Main St., Rangeley, tel. 207/864–5615), or **Saco River Canoe and Kayak** (Rte. 5, Fryeburg, tel. 207/935–2369).

Camping *See* National and State Parks and Forests, *below*. The Maine Campground Owners Association (655 Main St., Lewiston 04240, tel. 207/782–5874) has a statewide listing of private campgrounds.

Fishing Freshwater fishing for brook trout and salmon is at its best in May, June, and September, and the Rangeley area is especially popular with fly-fishermen. Nonresident freshwater anglers over the age of 12 must have a fishing license. The **Department of Inland Fisheries and Wildlife** (284 State St., Augusta 04333, tel. 207/289–2043) can provide further information.

Guides Try **Clayton (Cy) Eastlack** (Mountain View Cottages, Oquossoc, tel. 207/864–3416), **Grey Ghost Guide Service** (Box 24, Oquossoc, tel. 207/864–5314), and **Kennebago River Guide Service** (523 Maple St., Rumford, tel. 207/364–8786).

Snowmobiling This is a popular mode of winter transportation in the Rangeley, with trails linking lakes and towns to wilderness camps. **Maine Snowmobile Association** (Box 77, Augusta 04330) has information on Maine's nearly 8,000-mile Interconnecting Trail System.

Water Sports Sebago, Long, Rangeley, and Mooselookmeguntic lakes are the most popular areas for sailing and motorboating. For rentals, try **Long Lake Marina** (Rte. 302, Naples, tel. 207/693–3159), **Mountain View Cottages** (Rte. 17, Oquossoc, tel. 207/864–3416), **Naples Marina** (jct. Rtes. 302 and 114, Naples, tel. 207/ 693–6254; motorboats only), or **Sunny Breeze Sports** (Rte. 302, Naples, tel. 207/693–3867).

National and State Parks and Forests

Grafton Notch State Park (tel. 207/824–2912), on Route 26, 14 miles north of Bethel on the New Hampshire border, offers unsurpassed mountain scenery, picnic areas, gorges to explore, swimming holes, and camping. You can take an easy nature walk to Mother Walker Falls or Moose Cave and see the spectacular Screw Auger Falls; or you can hike to the summit of Old Speck Mountain, the state's third-highest peak. If you have the stamina and the equipment, you can pick up the Appalachian Trail here, hike over Saddleback Mountain, and continue on to Katahdin. The **Maine Appalachian Trail Club** (Box 283, Augusta 04330) publishes a map and trail guide.

Rangeley Lake State Park (tel. 207/864–3858) has 50 campsites on the south shore of the lake (*see* Exploring the Western Lakes and Mountains, *above*).

Sebago Lake State Park (tel. June 20–Labor Day, 207/693–6613; other times, 207/693–6231) has 250 campsites on the lake's north shore (*see* Exploring the Western Lakes and Mountains, *above*).

White Mountain National Forest straddles New Hampshire and Maine. Although the highest peaks are on the New Hampshire side, the Maine section includes lots of magnificent rugged terrain, camping and picnic areas, and hiking opportunities from hour-long nature loops to a 5½-hour scramble up Speckled Mountain—with open vistas at the summit. *Evans Notch Ranger District, RR 2, Box 2270, Bethel 04217, tel. 207/824–2134. Open weekdays 8–4:30.*

Dining and Lodging

Bethel has the largest concentration of inns and bed-and-breakfasts, and its Chamber of Commerce (tel. 207/824–3585) has a central lodging reservations service.

Additional accommodations selections will be found under the Saddleback, Shawnee, Sugarloaf, and Sunday River sections of the Skiing in New England chapter.

Bethel
Dining
★

Four Seasons Inn. The three small dining rooms of the region's front-running gourmet restaurant reveal tables draped with linens that brush the hardwood floors, and prim bouquets on the tables. The dinner menu is classic French: escargot, caviar, sautéed mushrooms, or onion soup to start; tournedos, beef Wellington, chateaubriand, veal Oscar, and bouillabaisse for entrées. *63 Upper Main St., tel. 207/824–2755. Reservations advised. AE, MC, V. No lunch except Sun. brunch. Closed Mon. Expensive.*

Mother's Restaurant. This gingerbread house furnished with wood stoves and bookshelves is a cozy place to enjoy the likes of Maine crab cakes, broiled trout, and a variety of pasta offerings. In summer one can dine on the porch. *Upper Main St., tel. 207/824–2589. Reservations accepted for large groups. MC, V. Closed Wed. in summer. Moderate.*

Lodging

Bethel Inn and Country Club. Bethel's grandest accommodation, once a rambling country inn on the town common, is now a full-service resort offering golf, a health club, and conference facilities. Guest rooms in the main inn, sparsely furnished with Colonial reproductions and George Washington bedspreads, are the most desirable, if not very large; the choice rooms have fireplaces and face the mountains over the golf course. The 40 two-bedroom condos on the fairway are clean and a bit sterile, but all units face the mountains. The health club facility is extensive. A formal dining room, done in lemon yellow with pewter accents, serves elaborate dinners of roast duck, prime rib, lobster, scampi, and swordfish. *Village Common, Box 49, 04217, tel. 207/824–2175 or 800/654–0125, fax 207/824–2233. 57 rooms with bath, 40 condo units. Facilities: restaurant, tavern, tennis, golf, health club, heated outdoor pool, cross-country ski trails, conference center. MAP available. AE, D, DC, MC, V. Moderate–Very Expensive.*

Sudbury Inn. The classic white-clapboard inn on Main Street offers good value, basic comfort, and a convenient location. Guest rooms are clean and nicely decorated. The lobby's redbrick fireplace and pressed-tin ceiling are warm and welcoming and the dining room (upholstered booths and square wood tables) has a country charm; the dinner menu runs to prime rib, sirloin au poivre, broiled haddock, and lasagna. The pub, with a large-screen TV, is a popular hangout. A huge country breakfast includes omelets, eggs Benedict, pancakes, and homemade granola. *151 Main St., Box 369,*

*04217, tel. 207/824–2174 or 800/395–7837. 16 rooms with bath, 5
suites, 2 apartments. Facilities: restaurant, pub. Full breakfast included. MC, V. Moderate–Expensive.*

The Hammons House. A sunny two-story conservatory with wicker
furniture and exotic plants is the focal point of this charming, friendly bed-and-breakfast situated in an historic home on the town common. The rooms are furnished with antique spool beds and pine
chests. A large sitting room downstairs has a crackling fire in the
winter and a bookshelf containing, among other things, a well-worn
collection of Nancy Drew and Hardy Boy mysteries. *28 Broad St.,
tel. 207/824–3170. 2 rooms share a bath, 1 suite. MC, V. Moderate.*

Bridgton   **Black Horse Tavern.** The 200-year-old gray Cape contains a country-
Dining   style restaurant with a shiny bar, horse blankets and stirrups for
decor, and an extensive menu of steak and seafood specialties. A
predominantly young crowd dines here on pan-blackened swordfish
or sirloin; scallop pie; and ribs. Starters include nachos, buffalo
wings, and chicken and smoked-sausage gumbo. *8 Portland St., tel.
207/647–5300. No reservations. MC, V. Inexpensive–Moderate.*

Lodging   **Noble House.** Set amid white pines on a hill on a quiet residential
street overlooking Highland Lake and the White Mountains, the
stately bed-and-breakfast with the wide porch dates from the turn
of the century. The parlor is dominated by a grand piano and fireplace; in the dining room beyond, hearty breakfasts (fruit, eggs,
blueberry pancakes, waffles, muffins) are served family-style on
china and linen. The honeymoon suite, a single large room, has a lake
view, a whirlpool bath, and white wicker furniture. *37 Highland
Rd., Box 180, 04009, tel. 207/647–3733. 9 rooms, 6 with bath; 2
suites. Facilities: croquet, canoe, pedal boat, dock, swimming float.
Full breakfast included. AE, MC, V. Closed mid-Oct.–mid-June.
Moderate–Very Expensive.*

Center Lovell   **Westways.** Built in the 1920s as a corporate retreat, it was opened as
Lodging   a sumptuous, secluded hotel in 1975. A stay here today is like a visit
with relatives everyone hopes for—rich, discreet, and very generous. Kezar Lake, the secret of a small set of exclusive summer people, brims at the back door of the gray-shingle main lodge (10
privately owned cottages, rented by the week through the inn, are
tucked away on the densely wooded grounds). The rustic splendor
continues inside in a palatial living room with massive stone fireplace, wood floors, and overstuffed easy chairs. The dining room
(open to the public for dinner by reservation) is a glassed-in porch
facing the lake, where, in summer, hearty meals are served on china
and linen. *Center Lovell 04016, tel. or fax 207/928–2663. 6 rooms, 4
with bath; 10 cottages with 3, 4, or 7 bedrooms. Facilities: restaurant, tennis, lake swimming and boating, canoes, bowling, recreation court. Full breakfast included. AE, MC, V. Closed Nov. and
Mar.–Apr. Expensive–Very Expensive.*

Kingfield   **The Inn on Winter's Hill.** Designed in 1895, this Georgian Revival
Lodging   mansion was the first home in Maine to have central heating. Today
it's an inn with a restaurant renowned for its menu, its seven-course
traditional New England dinners, and its wine tastings. Choose
from, among other things, stuffed pork tenderloin, beef Wellington,
and duck with blueberry-apple sauce. Try the poached pears for
dessert. The mansion's four rooms are eclectically furnished, with
pressed-tin ceilings and picture windows overlooking an apple orchard and the mountains beyond; the renovated barn's 16 rooms are
simply and brightly furnished. *RR 1, Box 1272, 04947, tel. 207/265–
5421 or 800/233–9687. 20 rooms with bath. Facilities: tennis, pool,*

hot tub, cross-country skiing. *AE, D, DC, MC, V. Expensive–Very Expensive.*

Naples **Epicurean Inn.** The rambling pink Victorian building on the edge of
Dining town, originally a stagecoach stop, serves classic French and New American cuisine in its small dining rooms done in muted colors, with wood floors and paisley drapes. Entrées can include cranberry-ginger duck, shrimp curry, tournedos with shrimp, and coho salmon. *Rte. 302, tel. 207/693–3839. Reservations advised. AE, D, DC, MC, V. No lunch. Closed Mon. and, Sept.–June, Tues. Expensive.*

Lodging **Augustus Bove House.** Built as the Hotel Naples in 1850, the brick bed-and-breakfast at the crossroads of Routes 302 and 114 has been restored to show off its gracious charm. Each wallpapered room is done in a different color scheme and furnished with antiques. Open since 1984, the inn offers lake views from the front rooms and convenience to water and shops. *RR 1, Box 501, 04055, tel. 207/693–6365. 11 rooms, 7 with bath. Full breakfast included. D, MC, V. Inexpensive–Expensive.*

Oquossoc **Oquossoc House.** Stuffed bears and bobcats keep you company as
Dining you dine on lobster, prime rib, filet mignon, or pork chops. The lunch menu promises chili, fish chowder, and lobster roll. *Jct. Rtes. 17 and 4, tel. 207/864–3881. Reservations required on summer weekends. No credit cards. Closed weekdays Nov.–mid-May. Inexpensive–Moderate.*

Rangeley **Country Club Inn.** This retreat, built in the 1920s on the Mingo
Lodging Springs Golf Course, enjoys a secluded hilltop location and sweeping lake and mountain views. The inn's baronial living room has a cathedral ceiling, a fieldstone fireplace at each end, and game trophies. Guest rooms downstairs in the main building and in the motel-style wing added in the 1950s are cheerfully if minimally decorated with wood paneling or bright wallpaper. The dining room—open to nonguests by reservation only—is a glassed-in porch where the linen-draped tables are set well apart and the menu features roast duck with cherry sauce and filet mignon. *Box 680, Mingo Loop Rd., 04970, tel. 207/864–3831. 19 rooms with bath. Facilities: restaurant, pool, lounge, golf next door. Rates are MAP. AE, MC, V. Closed Apr.–mid-May, mid-Oct.–Dec. 25. Very Expensive.*

Hunter Cove on Rangeley Lake. These lakeside cabins, which sleep two to six people, offer all the comforts of home in a rustic setting. The interiors are unfinished knotty pine and include fully furnished kitchens, screened porches, full baths, and comfortable, if plain, living rooms. Cabin No. 1 has a fieldstone fireplace and all others have wood-burning stoves for backup winter heat. Cabins No. 5 and No. 8 have hot tubs. Summer guests can take advantage of a sand swimming beach, boat rentals, and a nearby golf course. In winter, snowmobile right to your door or ski nearby (cross-country and downhill). *Mingo Loop Rd., tel. 207/864–3383. 8 cabins with bath. Facilities: some cabins have hot tubs. AE. Expensive–Very Expensive.*

Waterford **The Waterford Inne.** This gold-painted, curry-trimmed house on a
Lodging hilltop provides a good home base for trips to local lakes, ski trails, and antiques shops. The bedrooms, each furnished on a different theme, have lots of nooks and crannies. Nicest are the Nantucket Room, with whale wallpaper and a harpoon, and the Chesapeake Room, with private porch and fireplace. A converted wood shed has five additional rooms, and though they have slightly less character than the inn rooms, four of them have the compensation of sunny decks. *Chadbourne Rd., Box 149, 04088, tel. 207/583–4037. 9 rooms, 6 with bath; 1 suite. Facilities: antiques shop in barn, cross-country*

skiing, ice-skating, badminton. Full breakfast included. AE. Closed Apr. Moderate–Expensive.

The Arts

Rangeley Friends of the Arts (Box 333, Rangeley, tel. 207/864–5364) sponsors musical theater, fiddlers' contests, rock and jazz, pipers, and other summer fare, mostly at Lakeside Park. **Sebago–Long Lake Region Chamber Music Festival** (Deertrees Theatre, Harrison, tel. 207/627–4939) schedules concerts from mid-July to mid-August.

The North Woods

Maine's north woods, a vast area of the north central section of the state, is best experienced by canoe or raft, hiking trail, or on a fishing or hunting trip. The driving tour below takes in the three great theaters for these activities—Moosehead Lake, Baxter State Park, and the Allagash Wilderness Waterway—as well as the summer resort town of Greenville, dramatically situated Rockwood, and the no-frills outposts that connect them.

Important Addresses and Numbers

Visitor Information

Baxter State Park Authority (64 Balsam Dr., Millinocket 04462, tel. 207/723–5140). **Millinocket Chamber of Commerce** (1029 Central St., Millinocket 04462, tel. 207/723–4443; open daily 8–5, Memorial Day–Sept.; weekdays 9–noon Oct.–Memorial Day.) **Moosehead Lake Region Chamber of Commerce** (Main St., Box 581, Greenville 04441, tel. 207/695–2702; open daily Memorial Day–Columbus Day, call for hours). **North Maine Woods** (Box 421, Ashland 04732, tel. 207/435–6213), a private organization, publishes maps, a canoeing guide for the St. John River, and lists of outfitters, camps, and campsites.

Maine Sporting Camp Association (Box 89, Jay 04239, no tel.) publishes a list of its members, with details on the facilities available at each camp.

Emergencies

Charles A. Dean Memorial Hospital (Pritham Ave., Greenville, tel. 207/695–2223). **Mayo Regional Hospital** (75 W. Main St., Dover-Foxcroft, tel. 207/564–8401). **Millinocket Regional Hospital** (200 Somerset St., Millinocket, tel. 207/723–5161).

Getting Around the North Woods

By Plane

Charter flights, usually by seaplane, from Bangor, Greenville, or Millinocket to smaller towns and remote lake and forest areas can be arranged with flying services, which will transport you and your gear and help you find a guide: **Currier's Flying Service** (Greenville Jct., tel. 207/695–2778), **Folsom's Air Service** (Greenville, tel. 207/695–2821), **Jack's Air Service** (Greenville, tel. 207/695–3020), **Katahdin Air Service** (Millinocket, tel. 207/723–8378), **Scotty's Flying Service** (Shin Pond, tel. 207/528–2626).

By Car

A car is essential to negotiating this vast region but may not be useful to someone spending a vacation entirely at a wilderness camp. While public roads are scarce in the north country, lumber companies maintain private roads that are often open to the public (sometimes by permit only). When driving on a logging road, always give lumber company trucks the right of way. Be aware that loggers often take the middle of the road and will neither move over nor slow down for you.

Exploring the North Woods

Numbers in the margin correspond to points of interest on the North Woods map.

① **Moosehead Lake,** Maine's largest, offers more in the way of rustic camps, restaurants, guides, and outfitters than any other northern locale. Its 420 miles of shorefront, three-quarters of which is owned by paper manufacturers, is virtually uninhabited.

② **Rockwood,** on the lake's western shore, is a good starting point for a wilderness trip or a family vacation on the lake. While not offering much in the way of amenities, Rockwood has the most striking location of any town on Moosehead: The dark mass of **Mt. Kineo,** a sheer cliff that rises 760 feet above the lake, looms just across the narrows (you get an excellent view just north of town on Rte. 6/15). Once a thriving summer resort, the original Mount Kineo Hotel (built in 1830 and torn down in the 1940s) was accessed primarily by steamship. An effort to renovate the remaining buildings in the early 1990s failed. Kineo makes a pleasant day trip from Rockwood: Rent a boat or take a shuttle operated by **Rockwood Cottages** (tel. 207/534–7725) or **Old Mill Campground** (tel. 207/534–7333) and hike one of the trails to the summit for a picnic lunch and panoramic views of the region.

From Rockwood, follow Route 6/15 south, with Moosehead Lake on your left. After about 10 miles you'll come to a bridge with a dam to the left; this is the **East Outlet of the Kennebec River,** a popular class II and III whitewater run for canoeists and whitewater rafters that ends at the Harris Station Dam at Indian Pond, headwaters of the Kennebec.

③ Farther south on Route 6/15, **Greenville,** the largest town on the lake, has a smattering of shops, restaurants, and hotels. Turn left at the "T" intersection in town, following signs for Lily Bay State Park and Millinocket (the road is called both Lily Bay Road and Greenville Road). On your left is the **Moosehead Marine Museum** (tel. 207/695–2716), with exhibits on the local logging industry and the steamship era on Moosehead Lake, plus photographs of the Mount Kineo Hotel. The museum also runs cruises on the restored, 110-foot *Katahdin* (fondly called the *Kate*), a steamer (now diesel) built in 1914 that carried passengers to Kineo until 1942 and then was used in the local logging industry until 1975. It's a good idea to get a full tank of gas before leaving town, as it's almost 90 nearly deserted miles to Millinocket, some of it on well-maintained dirt roads.

Eight miles northeast of Greenville is **Lily Bay State Park** (tel. 207/695–2700), with a wooded, 93-site campground, swimming beach, and two boat-launching ramps.

④ Lily Bay Road continues northeast to the outpost of **Kokadjo** on First Roach Pond, population "not many," where one can have a snack or a meal at the **Kokadjo Country Store** (tel. 207/695–2904). Kokadjo is easily recognizable by the sign, "Keep Maine Green. This is God's country. Why set it on fire and make it look like hell?"

As you leave Kokadjo, bear left at the fork in the road and follow signs to Baxter State Park. Five miles along this road (now a dirt road) brings you to the Bowater/Great Northern Paper Company's Sias Hill checkpoint, where June–November you'll need to sign in

The North Woods

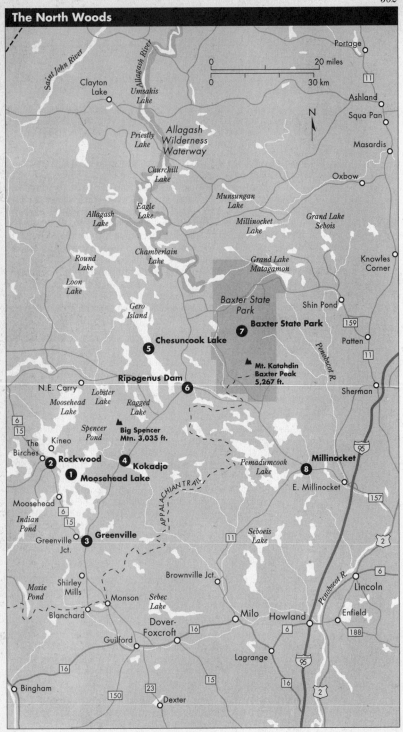

Saint John River

Allagash River

Clayton Lake

Umsakis Lake

Priestly Lake

Allagash Wilderness Waterway

Churchill Lake

Eagle Lake

Allagash Lake

Munsungan Lake

Millinocket Lake

Grand Lake Seboeis

Round Lake

Chamberlain Lake

Loon Lake

Grand Lake Matagamon

Gero Island

Baxter State Park

5 **Chesuncook Lake**

7 **Baxter State Park**

Shin Pond

Ripogenus Dam

6

▲ Mt. Katahdin Baxter Peak 5,267 ft.

N.E. Carry

Lobster Lake

Ragged Lake

Penobscot R.

Sherman

Moosehead Lake

Spencer Pond

▲ **Big Spencer Mtn. 3,035 ft.**

Kineo

The Birches

2 **Rockwood**

1

4 **Kokadjo**

Moosehead Lake

Pemadumcook Lake

Millinocket

8

E. Millinocket

Moosehead

Indian Pond

Greenville Jct.

3 **Greenville**

APPALACHIAN TRAIL

Seboeis Lake

Lincoln

Enfield

Moxie Pond

Shirley Mills

Monson

Sebec Lake

Brownville Jct.

Milo

Howland

Blanchard

Dover-Foxcroft

Guilford

Lagrange

Bingham

Dexter

Portage

Ashland

Squa Pan

Masardis

Oxbow

Knowles Corner

Patten

0   20 miles

0   30 km

N

and pay a user fee ($8 per car for nonresidents, valid for 24 hours) to
travel the next 40 miles of this road. Now you enter the working forest; you're likely to encounter logging trucks (yield right of way),
logging equipment, and work in progress. At the bottom of the hill
after you pass the checkpoint, look to your right—there's a good
chance you'll spot a moose in this boggy area.

❺ At the end of the logging road on your left sits **Chesuncook Lake,**
with **Chesuncook Village** at its far end, accessible only by boat or
seaplane in summer. This tiny wilderness settlement has a church
(open in summer), a few houses, a small store, and a spectacularly
remote setting (it's home to two sporting camps).

East of Chesuncook Lake is Ripogenus Lake. Bear left at the sign
❻ for Pray's Cottages to reach **Ripogenus Dam** and the granite-walled
Ripogenus Gorge, the jumping-off point for the famous 12-mile West
Branch of the Penobscot River whitewater rafting trip and the most
popular jumping-off point for Allagash canoe trips. The **Allagash
Wilderness Waterway** is a 92-mile corridor of lakes and rivers that
cuts across 170,000 acres of wilderness, beginning at the northwest
corner of Baxter and running north to the town of Allagash, 10 miles
from the Canadian border (from the Ripogenus area, take Telos Rd.
north toward Telos Lake). The Penobscot River drops more than 70
feet per mile through the gorge, giving rafters a hold-on-for-your-
life ride.

The best spot to watch the Penobscot rafters is from Pray's Big
Eddy Wilderness Campground, overlooking the rock-choked **Crib
Works rapid** (a class V rapid); be careful not to tread too close to the
edge. To get here, return to the main road, continue northeast, and
head left on Telos Road; the campground is about 10 yards after the
bridge.

Take the main road (here called the Golden Road for the amount of
money it took the Great Northern Paper Company to build it) southeast toward Millinocket. The road soon becomes paved. After you
drive over the one-lane Abol Bridge and pass through the Bowater/
Great Northern Paper Company's Debsconeag checkpoint, bear left
❼ to reach Togue Pond Gatehouse, the southern entrance to **Baxter
State Park** (tel. 207/723–5140). A gift from Governor Percival Baxter, the park is the jewel in the crown of northern Maine, a 201,018-
acre wilderness area that surrounds **Katahdin,** Maine's highest
mountain (5,267 feet at Baxter Peak) and the terminus of the Appalachian Trail. The 50-mile Perimeter Road makes a semicircle
around the western side of the park; maximum speed is 20 mph.

❽ From the Togue Pond Gatehouse it's 24 miles to **Millinocket,** home to
the **Bowater/Great Northern Paper Company mill,** which produces
more than 800,000 tons of paper annually, and the **Ambajejus Boom
House,** listed on the National Register of Historic Places, displays
log drive memorabilia and artifacts. *Accessible by watercraft or
snowmobile. Ambajejus Lake, Millinocket, no tel.*

Off the Beaten Track

For a worthwhile day trip from Millinocket, take Route 11 west to a
trailhead just north of Brownville Junction. Follow the trail to **Katahdin Iron Works,** the site of a once-flourishing mining operation
that employed nearly 200 workers in the mid-1800s; a deteriorated
kiln, a stone furnace, and a charcoal-storage building are all that remain. The trail continues over fairly rugged terrain into **Gulf Hagas,**

the Grand Canyon of the east, with natural chasms, cliffs, a 3-mile gorge, waterfalls, pools, exotic flora, and natural rock formations.

Lumberman's Museum. This museum comprises 10 buildings filled with exhibits depicting the history of logging, including models, dioramas, and equipment. *Shin Pond Rd. (Rte. 159), Patten, tel. 207/ 528–2650. Admission: $2.50 adults, $1 children 6–12. Open Memorial Day–Sept., Tues.–Sat. 9–4, Sun. 11–4.*

Shopping

Crafts **The Corner Shop** (Rte. 6/15, Greenville, tel. 207/695–2142) has a selection of books, gifts, and crafts. **Currier's on Moosehead** (next to Currier's Flying Service, Pritham Ave., Greenville Jct., tel 207/ 695–2921) has wood carvings and other handcrafted items. **Sunbower Pottery** (Scammon Rd., Greenville, tel. 207/695–2870) has local art and pottery, specializing in moose mugs.

Sporting **Indian Hill Trading Post** (Rte. 6/15, Greenville, tel. 207/695–2104)
Goods stocks just about anything you might possibly need for a north woods vacation, including sporting and camping equipment, canoes, casual clothing, shoes, hunting and fishing licenses; there's even an adjacent grocery store.

Sports and Outdoor Activities

Boating **Mt. Kineo Cabins** (Rte. 6/15, Rockwood, tel. 207/534–7744) and **Salmon Run Camps** (Rte. 6/15, Rockwood, tel. 207/534–8880) are only two of the many lodgings that rent boats and canoes on Moosehead Lake for the trip to Kineo.

Moosehead The **Moosehead Marine Museum** (tel. 207/695–2716) offers 2½-hour,
Lake Cruises six-hour, and full-day trips, late May through September, on Moosehead Lake aboard the *Katahdin*, a 1914 steamship (now diesel). **Jolly Roger's Moosehead Cruises** (tel. 207/534–8827 or 207/534– 8817) has scheduled scenic cruises, mid-May through mid-October, aboard the 48-foot *Socatean* from Rockwood. Reservations are advised for the 1½-hour moonlight cruise, which runs only eight evenings in summer. Charters are also available.

Camping Reservations for state park campsites (excluding Baxter State Park) can be made from January until August 15 through the **Bureau of Parks and Recreation** (tel. 207/287–3824 or 800/332–1501 in Maine). Make reservations as far ahead as possible (at least 14 days in advance), because sites go quickly. The camping season in Baxter State Park is May 15 to October 15, and it's important that you reserve in advance by mail if you plan to camp inside the park. Reservations can be made beginning January 1, and some sites are fully booked for midsummer weekends soon after that. Write to Baxter State Park Authority, 64 Balsam Dr., Millinocket 04462; phone reservations are not accepted. Camping is permitted only in authorized locations; when campgrounds are full, you will be turned away. The state also maintains primitive backcountry sites that are available without charge on a first-come, first-served basis.

Camping and Camping and fire permits are required for many areas outside of
Fire Permits state parks. The **Bureau of Parks and Recreation** (State House Sta. 22, Augusta 04333, tel. 207/287–3821) will tell you if you need a camping permit and where to obtain one; the **Maine Forest Service, Department of Conservation** (State House Sta. 22, Augusta 04333, tel. 207/287–2791) will direct you to the nearest ranger station, where you can get a fire permit (Greenville Ranger Station: tel. 207/

695–3721.) **North Maine Woods** (Box 421, Ashland 04732, tel. 207/435–6213) maintains many wilderness campsites on commercial forest land; early reservations are recommended. **Maine Publicity Bureau** (325B Water St., Box 2300, Hallowell 04347, tel. 207/623–0363 or, outside ME, 800/533–9595) publishes a listing of private campsites and cottage rentals. The **Maine Campground Owners Association (MECOA)** (655 Main St., Lewiston 04240, tel. 207/782–5874) publishes a helpful annual directory of its members; a dozen are located in the Katahdin/Moosehead area, and 20 are in the Kennebec and Moose River Valleys.

Canoeing The Allagash rapids are ranked class I and class II (very easy and easy), but that doesn't mean the river is a piece of cake; river conditions vary greatly with the depth and volume of water, and even a class I rapid can hang your canoe up on a rock, capsize you, or spin you around in the wink of an eye. On the lakes, strong winds can halt your progress for days. The Allagash should not be undertaken lightly or without advance planning; the complete 92-mile course requires seven to 10 days. The canoeing season along the Allagash is mid-May through October, although it's wise to remember that the black-fly season ends about July 1. The best bet for a novice is to go with a guide; a good outfitter will help you plan your route and provide your craft and transportation.

The Mount Everest of Maine canoe trips is the 110-mile route on the St. John River from Baker Lake to Allagash Village, with a swift current all the way and two stretches of class III rapids. Best time to canoe the St. John is between mid-May and mid-June, when the river level is high. The **Bureau of Parks and Recreation** (State House Sta. 22, Augusta 04333, tel. 207/287–3821) publishes a list of outfitters that arrange Allagash trips and also provides information on independent Allagash canoeing and camping.

Those with their own canoe who want to go it alone can take Telos Road north from Ripogenus Dam, putting in at Chamberlain Thoroughfare Bridge at the southern tip of Chamberlain Lake, or at Allagash Lake, Churchill Dam, Bissonnette Bridge, or Umsaskis Bridge.

One popular and easy route follows the Upper West Branch of the Penobscot River from Lobster Lake (just east of Moosehead Lake) to Chesuncook Lake. From Chesuncook Village you can paddle to Ripogenus Dam in a day.

The Aroostook River from Little Munsungan Lake to Fort Fairfield (100 mi) is best run in late spring. More challenging routes include the Passadumkeag River from Grand Falls to Passadumkeag (25 mi with class I–III rapids); the East Branch of the Penobscot River from Matagamon Wilderness Campground to Grindstone (38 mi with class I–III rapids); and the West Branch of the Pleasant River from Katahdin Iron Works to Brownville Junction (10 mi with class II–III rapids).

Outfitters Most canoe rental operations will arrange transportation, help you plan your route, and provide a guide when you need one. Transport to wilderness lakes can be arranged through the flying services listed under Getting Around the North Woods by Plane, *above.*

Allagash Canoe Trips (Box 713, Greenville 04441, tel. 207/695–3668) offers guided trips on the Allagash Waterway, plus the Moose, Penobscot, and St. John Rivers. **Allagash Sporting Camps** (Box 169, Allagash 04774, tel. 207/398–3555) rents canoes and camping equipment and arranges trips on the Allagash and the St. John River.

Allagash Wilderness Outfitters/Frost Pond Camps (Box 620, Greenville 04441, tel. 207/695–2821) provides equipment, transportation, and information for canoe trips on the Allagash and the Penobscot River. **North Country Outfitters** (Box 41, Rockwood 04478, tel. 207/534–2242 or 207/534–7305) operates a white-water canoeing and kayaking school, rents equipment, and sponsors guided canoe trips on the Allagash Waterway and the Moose, Penobscot, and St. John rivers. **North Woods Ways** (Box 286, Dover-Foxcroft 04426, tel. 207/564–3032) organizes wilderness canoeing trips on the Allagash, as well as on the Moose, Penobscot, St. Croix, and St. John rivers. **Willard Jalbert Camps** (115 W. Main St., Ft. Kent 04743, tel. 207/834–3448) has been sponsoring guided Allagash trips since the late 1800s.

Fishing   Togue, landlocked salmon, and brook and lake trout lure thousands of fisherfolk to the region from ice-out in mid-May through September; the hardiest return between January 1 and March 30 for the ice fishing. For up-to-date information on water levels, call 800/322–9844.

Guides   Guides are available through most wilderness camps, sporting goods stores, and canoe outfitters. For assistance in finding a guide, contact **Maine Professional Guides Association** (Box 159, Orono, tel. 207/866–0305) or **North Maine Woods** (*see* Visitor Information, *above*).

A few well-established guides are **Gilpatrick's Guide Service** (Box 461, Skowhegan 04976, tel. 207/453–6959), **Maine Guide Fly Shop and Guide Service** (Box 1202, Main St., Greenville 04441, tel. 207/695–2266), **Professional Guide Service** (Box 346, Sheridan 04775, tel. 207/435–8044), and **Taiga Outfitters** (RFD 1, Box 147, Ashland 04732, tel. 207/435–6851).

Hiking   **Katahdin,** in Baxter State Park, draws thousands of hikers every year for the daylong climb to the summit and the stunning views of woods, mountains, and lakes from the hair-raising Knife Edge Trail along its ridge. Roaring Brook Campground, accessible by car, is close to the quickest way up Katahdin, on its east side. Katahdin Stream and Nesowadnehunk field campgrounds, both reached by the park's Perimeter Road, put you on the west side of Katahdin.

Because the crowds at Katahdin can be formidable on clear summer days, those who seek a greater solitude might choose to tackle instead one of the 45 other mountains in the park, all accessible from a 150-mile trail network. South Turner can be climbed in a morning (if you're fit), and it affords a great view of Katahdin across the valley. On the way you'll pass Sandy Stream Pond, where moose are often seen at dusk. The Owl, the Brothers, and Doubletop Mountain are good day hikes.

Pack Trips   **Northern Maine Riding Adventures** (Box 16, Dover-Foxcroft 04426, tel. 207/564–3451 or 207/564–2965), owned by Registered Maine Guides Judy Cross and Bob Strehlke, offers one-day, two-day, and weeklong pack trips (10 people maximum) through various parts of Piscataquis County. A popular two-day trip explores the Whitecap–Barren Mountain Range, near Katahdin Iron Works (*see* Off the Beaten Track, *above*).

Rafting   The Kennebec and Dead rivers, and the West Branch of the Penobscot River, offer thrilling white-water rafting (guides strongly recommended). These rivers are dam-controlled also, so trips run rain or shine daily from May through October (day trips and multi-day trips are offered). Most guided raft trips on the Kennebec and Dead

Rivers leave from The Forks, southwest of Moosehead Lake, on Route 201; Penobscot River trips leave from either Greenville or Millinocket. Many rafting outfitters offer resort facilities in their base towns.

Outfitters The following outfitters are among the more than two dozen that are licensed to lead trips down the Kennebec and Dead rivers and the West Branch of the Penobscot River: **Crab Apple Whitewater** (Crab Apple Acres Inn, The Forks 04985, tel. 207/663–2218), **Eastern River Expeditions** (Box 1173, Greenville 04441, tel. 207/695–2411 or 800/634–7238), **Maine Whitewater, Inc.** (Box 633, Bingham 04920, tel. 207/672–4814 or 800/345–6246), **Northern Outdoors** (Box 100, The Forks 04985, tel. 207/663–4466 or 800/765–7238), **Voyagers Whitewater** (Rte. 201, Box 1, The Forks 04985, tel. 207/663–4423 or 800/289–6307), and **Unicorn Expeditions** (Box T, Brunswick 04011, tel. 207/725–2255 or 800/UNICORN). For additional information, contact the **Raft Maine Association** (tel. 800/359–2106).

Dining and Lodging

Greenville and Rockwood offer the largest selection of restaurants and accommodations in the region. Additional accommodations selections will be found under the Big Squaw Mountain section of the Skiing in New England chapter. Casual dress is the rule.

Greenville **Kelly's Landing.** This casual, family-oriented restaurant on the
Dining Moosehead shorefront has both indoor and outdoor seating, excellent views, and a dock for visiting boaters. The fare includes sandwiches, burgers, lasagna, seafood dinners, and ribs. *Rte. 6/15, Greenville Jct., tel. 207/695–4438. Reservations accepted. MC, V. Inexpensive.*

Dining and **Greenville Inn.** A rambling blue/gray-and-white structure, built
Lodging more than a century ago as the retreat of a wealthy lumbering fami-
★ ly, the inn stands on a rise over Moosehead Lake, a block from town. Indoors, the ornate cherry and mahogany paneling, Oriental rugs, and leaded glass create an aura of masculine ease. Two of the sparsely furnished, sunny bedrooms have fireplaces and two have lake views. Two clapboard cottages with decks overlooking the lake were built in the 1960s. Two dining rooms overlook the lake; a third, with dark-wood paneling, has a subdued, gentlemanly air. The Continental menu, revised daily, reflects the owners' Austrian background: shrimp with mustard dill sauce, fresh salmon marinated in olive oil and basil, veal cutlet with mushroom cream sauce. Fresh seafood is featured in summer. Popovers accompany the meal. *Norris St., Greenville 04441, tel. and fax 207/695–2206. 6 rooms, 4 with bath; 1 suite in carriage house; 2 cottages. Facilities: restaurant (reservations advised; no lunch). D, MC, V. Full breakfast included. Closed Nov. and Apr. Inn: Moderate. Restaurant: Moderate–Expensive.*

Lodging **Chalet Moosehead.** Just 50 yards off Route 6/15, the efficiencies, motel room, and cottages are right on Moosehead Lake and have picture windows to capture the view. The attractive grounds lead to a private beach and dock. *Rte. 6/15, Box 327, Greenville Jct. 04442, tel. 207/695–2950. 8 efficiencies with bath, 1 motel room with bath, 1 cabin with bath. Facilities: cable TV, beach, canoes, dock, horseshoes, boat and mountain-bike rentals. MC, V. Moderate.*
Wilsons on Moosehead Lake. Established in 1867, Wilsons claims to be the oldest continuously operating sporting camp on Moosehead Lake. The log cabins, situated at the headwaters of the Kennebec River, halfway between Greenville and Rockwood, cater to anglers, hunters, and families in summer. Cottages have screened porches,

fully equipped kitchens, and two to five bedrooms. All cottages have furnaces, and some also have fireplaces or woodstoves. Guide service is available. *Rte. 15, HC 37, Box 200, Greenville Jct. 04442, tel. 207/695–2549 or 800/817–2549. 15 cottages with bath. Facilities: launching ramp, private beach, dock, canoes, rental boats, barbecue. MC, V. Inexpensive–Moderate.*

Jackman **Attean Lake Lodge.** Located about an hour west of Rockwood,
Lodging Attean Lake Lodge has been owned and operated by the Holden family since 1900; the 18 log cabins (sleeping two to six) offer a secluded, island environment. Each cabin has hot and cold running water and a full bath; a central lodge—tastefully renovated in 1990—has a library, games, and a public telephone. *Birch Island, Box 457, Jackman 04945, tel. 207/668–3792. 18 cabins with bath. Facilities: beach, boats, and canoes; fishing licenses, supplies, and guides available. Three meals included. AE, MC, V. Closed Oct.– May. Very Expensive.*

Millinocket **Scootic Inn and Penobscot Room.** This informal restaurant and
Dining lounge offers lunches and dinners daily, with a varied menu of steak, seafood, pizza, and sandwiches. A large-screen TV is usually tuned to sports. *70 Penobscot Ave., tel. 207/723–4566. Reservations advised for 5 or more. AE, D, MC, V. Inexpensive–Moderate.*

Lodging **Atrium Inn.** Located off Route 157 next to a shopping center, this motor inn offers facilities that make up for its unappealing location and standard motel furnishings: a large central atrium with an indoor pool, plus a Jacuzzi and health club. *970 Central Ave., Millinocket 04462, tel. and fax 207/723–4555. 60 standard and king rooms, 10 suites, 4 Jacuzzi rooms. Facilities: lounge, Jacuzzi, indoor pool, wading pool and sand box, health club. Continental breakfast included. AE, D, DC, MC, V. Moderate.*

Rockwood **The Birches Resort.** The family-oriented resort offers the full north-
Dining and country experience: Moosehead Lake, birch woods, log cabins, and
Lodging boats for rent. The turn-of-the-century main lodge has four guest rooms, a living room dominated by a fieldstone fireplace, and a dining room overlooking the lake. The dining room is open to the public for breakfast and dinner; the fare is pasta, seafood, and steak. Most guests occupy one of the 17 cottages that have wood-burning stoves or fireplaces and sleep from two to 15 people. *Off Rte. 6/15, on Moosehead Lake, Box 41, Rockwood 04478, tel. 207/534–7305 or 800/ 825–9453, fax 207/534–8835. 4 lodge rooms with shared bath; 17 cottages with bath. Facilities: boats, kayaks, canoes, Sailfish for rent; marina; horseback riding; hot tub and sauna. AE, D, MC, V. Dining room closed Nov.–Apr. Moderate.*

Lodging **Rockwood Cottages.** These eight white cottages with blue trim, on Moosehead Lake off Route 15 and convenient to the center of Rockwood, are ideal for families. The cottages, which have screened porches and fully equipped kitchens, sleep two to seven. There is a one-week minimum stay in July and August. *Rte. 15, Box 176, Rockwood 04478, tel. 207/534–7725. 8 cottages. Facilities: dock, rental craft, barbecue, sauna. D, MC, V. Inexpensive.*

Index

Personal Itinerary

Departure *Date*

Time

Transportation

Arrival *Date*   *Time*

Departure *Date*   *Time*

Transportation

Accommodations

Arrival *Date*   *Time*

Departure *Date*   *Time*

Transportation

Accommodations

Arrival *Date*   *Time*

Departure *Date*   *Time*

Transportation

Accommodations

Personal Itinerary

Arrival *Date*   *Time*

Departure *Date*   *Time*

Transportation

Accommodations

Arrival *Date*   *Time*

Departure *Date*   *Time*

Transportation

Accommodations

Arrival *Date*   *Time*

Departure *Date*   *Time*

Transportation

Accommodations

Arrival *Date*   *Time*

Departure *Date*   *Time*

Transportation

Accommodations

Personal Itinerary

Arrival *Date*   *Time*

Departure *Date*   *Time*

Transportation

Accommodations

Arrival *Date*   *Time*

Departure *Date*   *Time*

Transportation

Accommodations

Arrival *Date*   *Time*

Departure *Date*   *Time*

Transportation

Accommodations

Arrival *Date*   *Time*

Departure *Date*   *Time*

Transportation

Accommodations

Personal Itinerary

Arrival *Date*   *Time*

Departure *Date*   *Time*

Transportation

Accommodations

Arrival *Date*   *Time*

Departure *Date*   *Time*

Transportation

Accommodations

Arrival *Date*   *Time*

Departure *Date*   *Time*

Transportation

Accommodations

Arrival *Date*   *Time*

Departure *Date*   *Time*

Transportation

Accommodations

Personal Itinerary

Arrival	*Date* *Time*
Departure	*Date* *Time*
Transportation	
Accommodations	

Arrival	*Date* *Time*
Departure	*Date* *Time*
Transportation	
Accommodations	

Arrival	*Date* *Time*
Departure	*Date* *Time*
Transportation	
Accommodations	

Arrival	*Date* *Time*
Departure	*Date* *Time*
Transportation	
Accommodations	

Personal Itinerary

Arrival	*Date*	*Time*
Departure	*Date*	*Time*
Transportation		
Accommodations		

Arrival	*Date*	*Time*
Departure	*Date*	*Time*
Transportation		
Accommodations		

Arrival	*Date*	*Time*
Departure	*Date*	*Time*
Transportation		
Accommodations		

Arrival	*Date*	*Time*
Departure	*Date*	*Time*
Transportation		
Accommodations		

Personal Itinerary

Arrival	*Date*	*Time*
Departure	*Date*	*Time*
Transportation		
Accommodations		

Arrival	*Date*	*Time*
Departure	*Date*	*Time*
Transportation		
Accommodations		

Arrival	*Date*	*Time*
Departure	*Date*	*Time*
Transportation		
Accommodations		

Arrival	*Date*	*Time*
Departure	*Date*	*Time*
Transportation		
Accommodations		

Addresses

Name

Address

Telephone

Name

Address

Telephone

Name

Address

Telephone

Name

Address

Telephone

Name

Address

Telephone

Name

Address

Telephone

Name

Address

Telephone

Name

Address

Telephone

Name

Address

Telephone

Name

Address

Telephone

Name

Address

Telephone

Name

Address

Telephone

Name

Address

Telephone

Name

Address

Telephone

Name

Address

Telephone

Name

Address

Telephone

At last — a guide for Americans with disabilities that makes traveling a delight

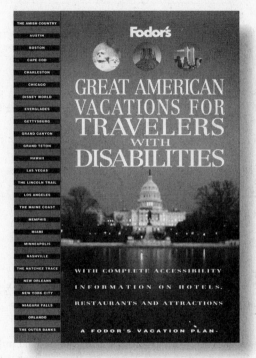

This is the first and only complete guide to great American vacations for the 35 million North Americans with disabilities, as well as for those who care for them or for aging parents and relatives. Provides:

- Essential trip-planning information for travelers with mobility, vision, and hearing impairments
- Specific details on a huge array of facilities, along with solid descriptions of attractions, hotels, restaurants, and other destinations
- Up-to-date information on ISA-designated parking, level entranceways, accessibility to pools, lounges, bathrooms

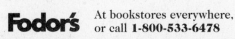

Fodor's

At bookstores everywhere, or call **1-800-533-6478**

The only guide to explore a Disney World you've never seen before:

The one for grown-ups.

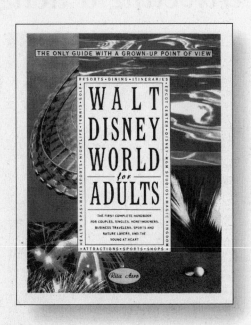

This is the only guide written specifically for the millions of adults who visit Walt Disney World each year <u>without</u> kids. Upscale, sophisticated, packed full of facts and maps, *Walt Disney World for Adults* provides up-to-date information on hotels, restaurants, sports facilities, and health clubs, as well as unique itineraries for adults. With *Walt Disney World for Adults* in hand, you'll get the most out of one of the world's most fascinating, most complex playgrounds.

At bookstores everywhere, or call **1-800-533-6478.**

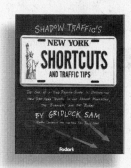

Fodor's Travel Guides

Available at bookstores everywhere, or call 1–800–533–6478, 24 hours a day.

U.S. Guides

Alaska

Arizona

Boston

California

Cape Cod, Martha's Vineyard, Nantucket

The Carolinas & the Georgia Coast

Chicago

Colorado

Florida

Hawaii

Las Vegas, Reno, Tahoe

Los Angeles

Maine, Vermont, New Hampshire

Maui

Miami & the Keys

New England

New Orleans

New York City

Pacific North Coast

Philadelphia & the Pennsylvania Dutch Country

The Rockies

San Diego

San Francisco

Santa Fe, Taos, Albuquerque

Seattle & Vancouver

The South

The U.S. & British Virgin Islands

USA

The Upper Great Lakes Region

Virginia & Maryland

Waikiki

Walt Disney World and the Orlando Area

Washington, D.C.

Foreign Guides

Acapulco, Ixtapa, Zihuatanejo

Australia & New Zealand

Austria

The Bahamas

Baja & Mexico's Pacific Coast Resorts

Barbados

Berlin

Bermuda

Brittany & Normandy

Budapest

Canada

Cancún, Cozumel, Yucatán Peninsula

Caribbean

China

Costa Rica, Belize, Guatemala

The Czech Republic & Slovakia

Eastern Europe

Egypt

Euro Disney

Europe

Florence, Tuscany & Umbria

France

Germany

Great Britain

Greece

Hong Kong

India

Ireland

Israel

Italy

Japan

Kenya & Tanzania

Korea

London

Madrid & Barcelona

Mexico

Montréal & Québec City

Morocco

Moscow & St. Petersburg

The Netherlands, Belgium & Luxembourg

New Zealand

Norway

Nova Scotia, Prince Edward Island & New Brunswick

Paris

Portugal

Provence & the Riviera

Rome

Russia & the Baltic Countries

Scandinavia

Scotland

Singapore

South America

Southeast Asia

Spain

Sweden

Switzerland

Thailand

Tokyo

Toronto

Turkey

Vienna & the Danube Valley

Special Series

Fodor's Affordables

Caribbean

Europe

Florida

France

Germany

Great Britain

Italy

London

Paris

Fodor's Bed & Breakfast and Country Inns Guides

America's Best B&Bs

California

Canada's Great Country Inns

Cottages, B&Bs and Country Inns of England and Wales

Mid-Atlantic Region

New England

The Pacific Northwest

The South

The Southwest

The Upper Great Lakes Region

The Berkeley Guides

California

Central America

Eastern Europe

Europe

France

Germany & Austria

Great Britain & Ireland

Italy

London

Mexico

Pacific Northwest & Alaska

Paris

San Francisco

Fodor's Exploring Guides

Australia

Boston & New England

Britain

California

The Caribbean

Florence & Tuscany

Florida

France

Germany

Ireland

Italy

London

Mexico

New York City

Paris

Prague

Rome

Scotland

Singapore & Malaysia

Spain

Thailand

Turkey

Fodor's Flashmaps

Boston

New York

Washington, D.C.

Fodor's Pocket Guides

Acapulco

Bahamas

Barbados

Jamaica

London

New York City

Paris

Puerto Rico

San Francisco

Washington, D.C.

Fodor's Sports

Cycling

Golf Digest's Best Places to Play

Hiking

The Insider's Guide to the Best Canadian Skiing

Running

Sailing

Skiing in the USA & Canada

USA Today's Complete Four Sports Stadium Guide

Fodor's Three-In-Ones (guidebook, language cassette, and phrase book)

France

Germany

Italy

Mexico

Spain

Fodor's Special-Interest Guides

Complete Guide to America's National Parks

Condé Nast Traveler Caribbean Resort and Cruise Ship Finder

Cruises and Ports of Call

Euro Disney

France by Train

Halliday's New England Food Explorer

Healthy Escapes

Italy by Train

London Companion

Shadow Traffic's New York Shortcuts and Traffic Tips

Sunday in New York

Sunday in San Francisco

Touring Europe

Touring USA: Eastern Edition

Walt Disney World and the Orlando Area

Walt Disney World for Adults

Fodor's Vacation Planners

Great American Learning Vacations

Great American Sports & Adventure Vacations

Great American Vacations

Great American Vacations for Travelers with Disabilities

National Parks and Seashores of the East

National Parks of the West

The Wall Street Journal Guides to Business Travel

Discover New England all over again this year

HALLIDAY'S NEW ENGLAND FOOD EXPLORER
Tours for Food Lovers

Now — a guidebook to New England for food lovers. In 12 tours through 6 states, discover the region's best markets, restaurants, farms, inns, even road-side stands in the literate, opinionated company of veteran food writer Fred Halliday. The best place to start the most delicious vacation of your life.

FODOR'S BED & BREAKFASTS AND COUNTRY INNS — NEW ENGLAND

This meticulously honest and thoroughly up-to-date guide includes critical reviews of more than 280 inns and B&Bs, plus everything you need to know about what to see and do — and where to eat — when you get there. Includes 109 illustrations and 36 pages of maps and charts.

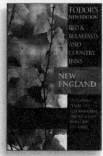

FODOR'S NEW ENGLAND '95
A Four Season Guide with the Best of the B&Bs and Ski Resorts

All the best of New England — its top hotels, resorts, inns, and B&Bs in every category, great restaurants, cafes, and diners, wonderful shops for antiques and crafts, where to stay at 50 ski resorts, festivals and seasonal events, fishing, camping, and other outdoor sports, and 51 pages of maps.

COMPASS MAINE '95
First edition

Discover the captivating beauty and compelling history of Maine in this dramatically illustrated and evocatively written guide to the Down East state.

At bookstores, or call **1-800-533-6478**   **Fodor's**

AT LAST

YOUR OWN PERSONALIZED LIST
OF WHAT'S GOING ON IN THE
CITIES YOU'RE VISITING.

KEYED TO THE DAYS WHEN
YOU'LL BE THERE, CUSTOMIZED
FOR YOUR INTERESTS,
AND SENT TO YOU BEFORE YOU
LEAVE HOME.

GET THE INSIDER'S
PERSPECTIVE. . .

UP-TO-THE-MINUTE
ACCURATE
EASY TO ORDER
DELIVERED WHEN YOU NEED IT

Fodor's WORLDVIEW
TRAVEL UPDATE

Now there is a revolutionary way to get customized, time-sensitive travel information just before your trip.

Now you can obtain detailed information about what's going on in each city you'll be visiting <u>before</u> you leave home—up-to-the-minute, objective information about the events and activities that interest you most.

Travel Updates contain the kind of time-sensitive insider information you can get only from local contacts – or from city magazines and newspapers once you arrive. But now you can have the same information before you leave for your trip.

The choice is yours: current art exhibits, theater, music festivals and special concerts, sporting events, antiques and flower shows, shopping, fitness, and more.

The information comes from hundreds of correspondents and thousands of sources worldwide. Updated continuously, it's like having your own personal concierge or friend in the city.

You specify the cities and when you'll be there. We'll do the rest — personalizing the information for you the way no guidebook can.

It's the perfect extension to your Fodor's guide and the best way to make the most of your valuable travel time.

Use Order Form on back or call 1-800-799-9609

Your Itinerary:
Customized reports available for 160 destinations

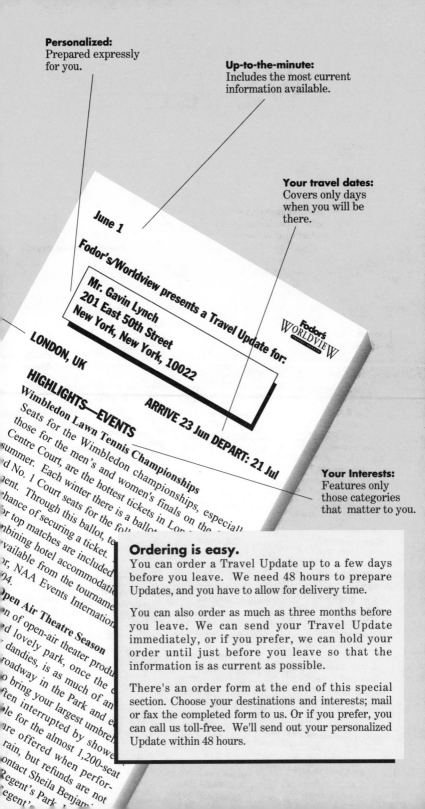

Personalized:
Prepared expressly
for you.

Up-to-the-minute:
Includes the most current
information available.

Your travel dates:
Covers only days
when you will be
there.

June 1

Fodor's/Worldview presents a Travel Update for:

Mr. Gavin Lynch
201 East 50th Street
New York, New York, 10022

Fodor's
WORLDVIEW

LONDON, UK

ARRIVE 23 Jun DEPART: 21 Jul

HIGHLIGHTS—EVENTS

Wimbledon Lawn Tennis Championships

Seats for the Wimbledon championships, especiall
those for the men's and women's finals on the
Centre Court, are the hottest tickets in Lon
summer. Each winter there is a ballot
d No. 1 Court seats for the foll
ent. Through this ballot, te
hance of securing a ticket.
r top matches are included
bining hotel accommodati
vailable from the tourname
r, NAA Events Internation
04.

Open Air Theatre Season
n of open-air theater produ
d lovely park, once the e
dandies, is as much of an
roadway in the Park and e
o bring your largest umbre
ften interrupted by showe
le for the almost 1,200-seat
are offered when perfor-
rain, but refunds are not
ontact Sheila Benjam
egent's Park

Your Interests:
Features only
those categories
that matter to you.

Ordering is easy.
You can order a Travel Update up to a few days
before you leave. We need 48 hours to prepare
Updates, and you have to allow for delivery time.

You can also order as much as three months before
you leave. We can send your Travel Update
immediately, or if you prefer, we can hold your
order until just before you leave so that the
information is as current as possible.

There's an order form at the end of this special
section. Choose your destinations and interests; mail
or fax the completed form to us. Or if you prefer, you
can call us toll-free. We'll send out your personalized
Update within 48 hours.

**Special concerts—
who's performing
what and where**

**One-of-a-kind,
one-time-only events**

**Special interest,
in-depth listings**

Children — Events
Angel Canal Festival
The festivities include a children's funfa
entertainers, a boat rally and displays on t
water. Regent's Canal. Islington. N1. Tub
Angel. Tel: 267 9100. 11:30am-5:30pm. 7/0
Blackheath Summer Kite Festival
Stunt kite displays with parachuting tedd
bears and trade stands. Free admission. SE
BR: Blackheath. 10am. 6/27.
Megabugs
Children will delight in this infestation o
giant robotic insects, including a prayin
mantis 60 times life size. Mon-Sat 10am
6pm; Sun 11am-6pm. Admission 4.5
pounds. Natural History Museum, Cromwel
Road. SW7. Tube: South Kensington. Te
938 9123. Ends 10/01.
Childminders
This establishment employs only women
providing nurses and qualified nannies to

Music — Jazz & Blues
Tito Puente's Golden Men of Latin Jazz
The father of mambo and Cuban rumba king
comes to town. Royal Festival Hall. South Bank.
SE1. Tube: Waterloo. Tel: 928 8800. 8pm. 7/15.
Georgie Fame and The New York Band
Riding a popular tide with his latest album, the
smoky-voiced Fame and his keyboard are on a
tour yet again. The Grand. Clapham Junction.
SW11. BR: Clapham Junction. Tel: 738 9000
7:30pm. 7/07.
Jacques Loussier Play Bach Trio
The French jazz classicist and colleagues.
Kenwood Lakeside. Hampstead Lane.
Kenwood. NW3. Tube: Golders Green, then bus
210. Tel: 413 1443. 7pm. 7/10.
Tony Bennett and Ronnie Scott
Royal Festival Hall. South Bank. SE1. Tube:
Waterloo. Tel: 928 8800. 8pm. 7/11.
Santana
Royal Festival Hall. South Bank. SE1. Tube
Waterloo. Tel: 928 8800. 8pm. 7/12.
Count Basie Orchestra and Nancy Wilson Trio
Royal Festival Hall. South Bank. SE1. Tube
Waterloo. Tel: 928 8800. 8pm. 7/14.
King Pleasure and the Biscuit Boys
Royal Festival Hall. South Bank. SE1. Tube
Waterloo. Tel: 928 8800. 6:30 and 9pm. 7/16.
Al Green and the London Community Gospel Choir
Royal Festival Hall. South Bank. SE1. Tube
Waterloo. Tel: 928 8800. 8pm. 7/13.
BB King and Linda Hopkins
Mother of the blues and successor to Bessi
Smith, Hopkins meets up with "Blues Boy
King Royal Festival Hall. South Bank. SE
6.30 and 9pm

Music — Classical
Marylebone Sinfonia
Kenneth Gowen conducts music by P
and Rossini. Queen Elizabeth Hall.
Bank. SE1. Tube: Waterloo. Tel: 928
7:45pm. 7/16.
London Philharmonic
Franz Welser-Moest and George Be
conduct selections by Alexander (
Messiaen, and some of Benjamin's ow
positions. Queen Elizabeth Hall. South
SE1. Tube: Waterloo. Tel: 928 8800. 8
London Pro Arte Orchestra and Forest
Murray Stewart conducts selecti
Rossini, Haydn and Jonathan Willcoc
Queen Elizabeth Hall. South Ban
Tube: Waterloo. Tel: 928 8800. 7:45p
Kensington Symphony Orchestra
Russell Keable conducts Dvorak's

Here's what you get . . .

Detailed information about what's going on — precisely when you'll be there.

Show openings during your visit

Handy pocket-size booklet

Reviews by local critics

Exhibitions & Shows—Antique & Flower

Westminster Antiques Fair

Over 50 stands with pre-1830 furniture and other Victorian and earlier items. Thu-Fri 11am-8pm; Sat-Sun 11am-6pm. Admission 4 pounds, children free. Old Royal Horticultural Hall. Vincent Square. SW1. Tel: 0444/48 25 14. 6-24 thru 6/27.

Royal Horticultural Society Flower Show

The show includes displays of carnations, summer fruit and vegetables. Tue 11am-7pm; Wed 10am-5pm. Admission Tue 4 pounds, Wed 2 pounds. Royal Horticultural Halls. Greycoat Street and Vincent Square. SW1. Tube: Victoria. 7/20 thru 7/21.

Hampton Court Palace International Flower Show

Major international garden and flower show taking place in conjunction with

Theater — Musical

Sunset Boulevard

In June, the four Andrew Lloyd Webber musicals which dominated London's stages in the 1980s (Cats, Starlight Express, Phantom of the Opera and Aspects of Love) are joined by the composer's latest work, a show rumored to have his best music to date. The 1950 Billy Wilder film about a helpless young writer who is drawn into the world of a possessive, aging silent screen star offers rich opportunities for Webber's evolving style. Soaring, aching melodies, lush technical effects and psychological thrills are all expected. Patti Lupone stars. Mon-Sat at 8pm; matinee Thu-Sat at 3pm. In-person sales only at the box office; credit card bookings, Tel: 344 0055. Admission 15-32.50 pounds. Adelphi Theatre. The Strand. WC2. Tube: Charing Cross. Tel: 836 7611. Starts: 6/21.

Leonardo A Portrait of Love

A new musical about the great Renaissance artist and inventor comes in for a London pre-____ tested by a brief run at Oxford's Old ____. The work explores ____

Spectator Sports — Other Sports

Greyhound Racing: Wembley Stadium

This dog track offers good views of greyhound racing held on Mon, Wed and Fri. No credit cards. Stadium Way. Wembley. HA9. Tube: Wembley Park. Tel: 902 8833.

Benson & Hedges Cricket Cup Final

Lord's Cricket Ground. St. John's Wood Road. NW8. Tube: St. John's Wood. Tel: 289 1611. 11am. 7/10.

Business-Fax & Overnight Mail

Post Office, Trafalgar Square Branch

Offers a network of fax services, the Intelpost system, throughout the country and abroad. Mon-Sat 8am-8pm, Sun 9am-5pm. William IV Street. WC2. Tube: Charing Cross. Tel: 930 9580.

Fodor's WORLDVIEW

TRAVEL UPDATE

London, England
Arriving: June 23
Departing: July 21

Interest Categories

For <u>your</u> personalized Travel Update, choose the categories
you're most interested in from this list. Every Travel Update
automatically provides you with *Event Highlights* - the best of
what's happening during the dates of your trip.

1.	**Business Services**	Fax & Overnight Mail, Computer Rentals, Photocopying, Protocol, Secretarial, Messenger, Translation Services
	Dining	
2.	**All Day Dining**	Breakfast & Brunch, Cafes & Tea Rooms, Late-Night Dining
3.	**Local Cuisine**	In Every Price Range—from Budget Restaurants to the Special Splurge
4.	**European Cuisine**	Continental, French, Italian
5.	**Asian Cuisine**	Chinese, Far Eastern, Japanese, Other
6.	**Americas Cuisine**	American, Mexican & Latin
7.	**Nightlife**	Bars, Dance Clubs, Casinos, Comedy Clubs, Ethnic, Pubs & Beer Halls
8.	**Entertainment**	Theater—Comedy, Drama, English Language, Musicals, Dance, Ticket Agencies
9.	**Music**	Country/Western/Folk, Classical, Traditional & Ethnic, Opera, Jazz & Blues, Pop, Rock
10.	**Children's Activities**	Events, Attractions
11.	**Tours**	Local Tours, Day Trips, Overnight Excursions, Cruises
12.	**Exhibitions, Festivals & Shows**	Antiques & Flower, History & Cultural, Art Exhibitions, Fairs & Craft Shows, Music & Art Festivals
13.	**Shopping**	Districts & Malls, Markets, Regional Specialities
14.	**Fitness**	Bicycling, Health Clubs, Hiking, Jogging
15.	**Recreational Sports**	Boating/Sailing, Fishing, Golf, Ice Skating, Skiing, Snorkeling/Scuba, Swimming, Tennis & Racquet
16.	**Spectator Sports**	Auto Racing, Baseball, Basketball, Boating & Sailing, Football, Golf, Horse Racing, Ice Hockey, Rugby, Soccer, Tennis, Track & Field, Other Sports

Please note that interest category content will vary by season, destination,
and length of stay.

Destinations

The Fodor's/Worldview Travel Update covers more than 160 destinations worldwide. Choose the destinations that match your itinerary from this list. (Choose bulleted destinations only.)

Europe
- Amsterdam
- Athens
- Barcelona
- Berlin
- Brussels
- Budapest
- Copenhagen
- Dublin
- Edinburgh
- Florence
- Frankfurt
- French Riviera
- Geneva
- Glasgow
- Istanbul
- Lausanne
- Lisbon
- London
- Madrid
- Milan
- Moscow
- Munich
- Oslo
- Paris
- Prague
- Provence
- Rome
- Salzburg
* Seville
- St. Petersburg
- Stockholm
- Venice
- Vienna
- Zurich

United States (Mainland)
- Albuquerque
- Atlanta
- Atlantic City
- Baltimore
- Boston
* Branson, MO
* Charleston, SC
- Chicago
- Cincinnati
- Cleveland
- Dallas/Ft. Worth
- Denver
- Detroit
- Houston
* Indianapolis
- Kansas City
- Las Vegas
- Los Angeles
- Memphis

- Miami
- Milwaukee
- Minneapolis/ St. Paul
* Nashville
- New Orleans
- New York City
- Orlando
- Palm Springs
- Philadelphia
- Phoenix
- Pittsburgh
- Portland
* Reno/ Lake Tahoe
- St. Louis
- Salt Lake City
- San Antonio
- San Diego
- San Francisco
* Santa Fe
- Seattle
- Tampa
- Washington, DC

Alaska
- Alaskan Destinations

Hawaii
- Honolulu
- Island of Hawaii
- Kauai
- Maui

Canada
- Quebec City
- Montreal
- Ottawa
- Toronto
- Vancouver

Bahamas
- Abaco
- Eleuthera/ Harbour Island
- Exuma
- Freeport
- Nassau & Paradise Island

Bermuda
- Bermuda Countryside
- Hamilton

British Leeward Islands
- Anguilla

- Antigua & Barbuda
- St. Kitts & Nevis

British Virgin Islands
- Tortola & Virgin Gorda

British Windward Islands
- Barbados
- Dominica
- Grenada
- St. Lucia
- St. Vincent
- Trinidad & Tobago

Cayman Islands
- The Caymans

Dominican Republic
- Santo Domingo

Dutch Leeward Islands
- Aruba
- Bonaire
- Curacao

Dutch Windward Island
- St. Maarten/ St. Martin

French West Indies
- Guadeloupe
- Martinique
- St. Barthelemy

Jamaica
- Kingston
- Montego Bay
- Negril
- Ocho Rios

Puerto Rico
- Ponce
- San Juan

Turks & Caicos
- Grand Turk/ Providenciales

U.S. Virgin Islands
- St. Croix
- St. John
- St. Thomas

Mexico
- Acapulco
- Cancun & Isla Mujeres
- Cozumel
- Guadalajara
- Ixtapa & Zihuatanejo
- Los Cabos
- Mazatlan
- Mexico City
- Monterrey
- Oaxaca
- Puerto Vallarta

South/Central America
* Buenos Aires
* Caracas
* Rio de Janeiro
* San Jose, Costa Rica
* Sao Paulo

Middle East
* Jerusalem

Australia & New Zealand
- Auckland
- Melbourne
* South Island
- Sydney

China
- Beijing
- Guangzhou
- Shanghai

Japan
- Kyoto
- Nagoya
- Osaka
- Tokyo
- Yokohama

Pacific Rim/Other
* Bali
- Bangkok
- Hong Kong & Macau
- Manila
- Seoul
- Singapore
- Taipei

* Destinations available by 1/1/95

Fodor's WORLDVIEW Order Form
TRAVEL UPDATE

THIS TRAVEL UPDATE IS FOR (Please print):

Name

Address

City	State	Country	ZIP

Tel # (   )   -   Fax # (   )   -

Title of this Fodor's guide:

Store and location where guide was purchased:

INDICATE YOUR DESTINATIONS/DATES: You can order up to three (3) destinations from the previous page. Fill in your arrival and departure dates for each destination. <u>**Your Travel Update itinerary (all destinations selected) cannot exceed 30 days from beginning to end.**</u>

		Month	Day		Month	Day
(Sample) LONDON	From:	6	/ 21	To:	6	/ 30
1	From:	/		To:	/	
2	From:	/		To:	/	
3	From:	/		To:	/	

CHOOSE YOUR INTERESTS: Select up to eight (8) categories from the list of interest categories shown on the previous page and circle the numbers below:

1   2   3   4   5   6   7   8   9   10   11   12   13   14   15   16

CHOOSE WHEN YOU WANT YOUR TRAVEL UPDATE DELIVERED (Check one):
❏ Please send my Travel Update immediately.
❏ Please hold my order until a few weeks before my trip to include the most up-to-date information. *Completed orders will be sent within 48 hours. Allow 7-10 days for U.S. mail delivery.*

ADD UP YOUR ORDER HERE. *SPECIAL OFFER FOR FODOR'S PURCHASERS ONLY!*

	Suggested Retail Price	Your Price	This Order
First destination ordered	$ 9.95	$ 7.95	$ 7.95
Second destination (if applicable)	$ 6.95	$ 4.95	+
Third destination (if applicable)	$ 6.95	$ 4.95	+

DELIVERY CHARGE (Check one and enter amount below)

	Within U.S. & Canada	Outside U.S. & Canada
First Class Mail	❏ $2.50	❏ $5.00
FAX	❏ $5.00	❏ $10.00
Priority Delivery	❏ $15.00	❏ $27.00

ENTER DELIVERY CHARGE FROM ABOVE: +

TOTAL: $

METHOD OF PAYMENT IN U.S. FUNDS ONLY (Check one):
❏ AmEx ❏ MC ❏ Visa ❏ Discover ❏ Personal Check (U. S. & Canada only)
❏ Money Order/ International Money Order
  Make check or money order payable to: Fodor's Worldview Travel Update

Credit Card —/—/—/—/—/—/—/—/—/—/—/—/—/—/—/—/ Expiration Date:___/____

Authorized Signature

SEND THIS COMPLETED FORM WITH PAYMENT TO:
Fodor's Worldview Travel Update, 114 Sansome Street, Suite 700, San Francisco, CA 94104

OR CALL OR FAX US 24-HOURS A DAY
Telephone **1-800-799-9609** • Fax **1-800-799-9619** (From within the U.S. & Canada)
(Outside the U.S. & Canada: Telephone 415-616-9988 • Fax 415-616-9989)

(Please have this guide in front of you when you call so we can verify purchase.)
Code: FTG   Offer valid until 12/31/95.